W9-BHF-138

Volume 6

The Broadman Bible Commentary

EDITORIAL BOARD

General Editor
Clifton J. Allen

Old Testament Consulting Editors
John I Durham
Roy L. Honeycutt, Jr.

New Testament Consulting Editors
John William MacGorman
Frank Stagg

Associate Editors
William J. Fallis
Joseph F. Green

Editorial Consultant
Howard P. Colson

BROADMAN PRESS • Nashville, Tennessee

220.7
ALL

238

The Broadman Bible Commentary

Volume 6

Jeremiah - Daniel

Library of
Calvary Baptist Church
Alton, Illinois

© Copyright 1971 · BROADMAN PRESS

All rights reserved

ISBN: 0–8054–1106–2

4211–06

The Bible text in this publication is from the
Revised Standard Version of the Bible, copy-
righted 1946 and 1952 by the Division of
Christian Education of the National Council
of Churches, and is used by permission.

Dewey Decimal Classification: 220.7
Library of Congress catalog card number: 78–93918
Printed in the United States of America

Preface

THE BROADMAN BIBLE COMMENTARY presents current biblical study within the context of strong faith in the authority, adequacy, and reliability of the Bible as the Word of God. It seeks to offer help and guidance to the Christian who is willing to undertake Bible study as a serious, rewarding pursuit. The publisher thus has defined the scope and purpose of the COMMENTARY to produce a work suited to the Bible study needs of both ministers and laymen. The findings of biblical scholarship are presented so that readers without formal theological education can use them in their own Bible study. Footnotes and technical words are limited to essential information.

Writers have been carefully selected for their reverent Christian faith and their knowledge of Bible truth. Keeping in mind the needs of a general readership, the writers present special information about language and history where it helps to clarify the meaning of the text. They face Bible problems—not only in language but in doctrine and ethics—but avoid fine points that have little bearing on how we should understand and apply the Bible. They express their own views and convictions. At the same time, they present alternative views when such are advocated by other serious, well-informed students of the Bible. The views presented, therefore, cannot be regarded as the official position of the publisher.

This COMMENTARY is the result of many years' planning and preparation. Broadman Press began in 1958 to explore needs and possibilities for the present work. In this year and again in 1959, Christian leaders—particularly pastors and seminary professors—were brought together to consider whether a new commentary was needed and what shape it might take. Growing out

of these deliberations in 1961, the board of trustees governing the Press authorized the publication of a multivolume commentary. Further planning led in 1966 to the selection of a general editor and an Advisory Board. This board of pastors, professors, and denominational leaders met in September, 1966, reviewing preliminary plans and making definite recommendations which have been carried out as the COMMENTARY has been developed.

Early in 1967, four consulting editors were selected, two for the Old Testament and two for the New. Under the leadership of the general editor, these men have worked with the Broadman Press personnel to plan the COMMENTARY in detail. They have participated fully in the selection of the writers and the evaluation of manuscripts. They have given generously of time and effort, earning the highest esteem and gratitude of Press employees who have worked with them.

The selection of the Revised Standard Version of the Bible text for the COMMENTARY was made in 1967 also. This grew out of careful consideration of possible alternatives, which were fully discussed in the meeting of the Advisory Board. The adoption of an English version as a standard text was recognized as desirable, meaning that only the King James, American Standard, and Revised Standard Versions were available for consideration.

The King James Version was recognized as holding first place in the hearts of many Christians but as suffering from inaccuracies in translation and obscurities in phrasing. The American Standard was seen as free from these two problems but deficient in an attractive English style and wide current use. The Revised Standard retains the accuracy and clarity of the American Standard and has a pleasing style and a growing use. It thus enjoys a strong advantage over each of the others, making it by far the most desirable choice.

Throughout the COMMENTARY the treatment of the biblical text aims at a balanced combination of exegesis and exposition, admittedly recognizing that the nature of the various books and the space assigned will properly modify the application of this approach.

The general articles appearing in Volumes 1, 8, and 12 are designed to provide background material to enrich one's understanding of the nature of the Bible and the distinctive aspects of each Testament. Those in Volume 12 focus on the implications of biblical teaching in the areas of worship, ethical duty, and the world mission of the church.

The COMMENTARY avoids current theological fads and changing theories. It concerns itself with the deep realities of God's dealings with men, his revelation in Christ, his eternal gospel, and his purpose for the redemption of the world. It seeks to relate the word of God in Scripture and in the living Word to the deep needs of persons and to mankind in God's world.

Through faithful interpretation of God's message in the Scriptures, therefore, the COMMENTARY seeks to reflect the inseparable relation of truth to life, of meaning to experience. Its aim is to breathe the atmosphere of life-relatedness. It seeks to express the dynamic relation between redemptive truth and living persons. May it serve as a means whereby God's children hear with greater clarity what God the Father is saying to them.

Abbreviations

ANET – *Ancient Near Eastern Texts*
ASV – American Standard Version
BA – *Biblical Archaeologist*
BASOR – *Bulletin of the American Schools of Oriental Research*
BBC – *Broadman Bible Commentary*
BDB – Brown, Driver, and Briggs: *Hebrew and English Lexicon*
CBQ – *Catholic Biblical Quarterly*
fn. – footnote
GT – Gesenius-Tregelles: *Hebrew-English Lexicon*
Heb. – Hebrew
IB – *Interpreter's Bible*
ICC – International Critical Commentary
IDB – *The Interpreter's Dictionary of the Bible*
Int. – Introduction

IPH – *Israel's Prophetic Heritage* (bibliography)
JB – Jerusalem Bible
JBC – Jerome Bible Commentary
JBL – *Journal of Biblical Literature*
JNES – *Journal of Near Eastern Studies*
JQR – *Jewish Quarterly Review*
JTS – *Journal of Theological Studies*
KB – Koehler-Baumgartner: *Lexicon in Veteris Testamenti Libros*
KJV – King James Version
LXX – Septuagint
MT – Masoretic Text
NEB – New English Bible
RSV – Revised Standard Version
VT – *Vetus Testamentum*
ZAW – *Zeitschrift für die alttestamentliche Wissenschaft*

Contents

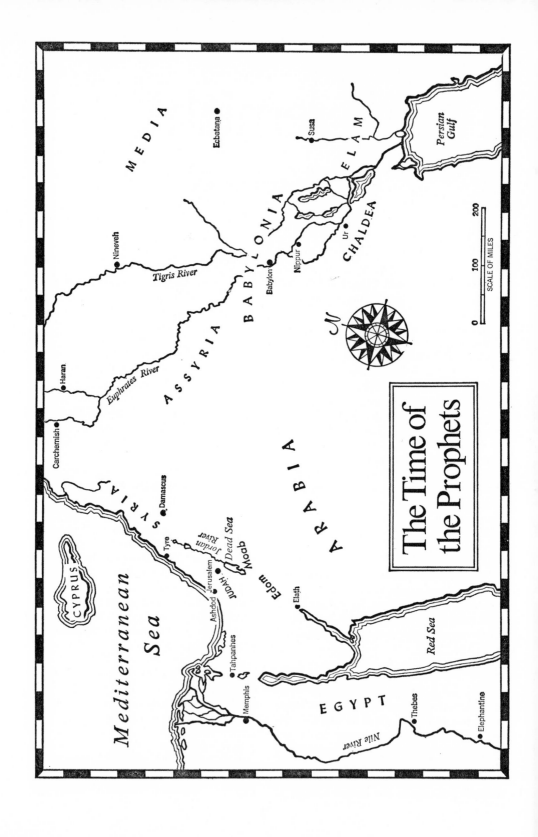

The Time of
the Prophets

Jeremiah

JAMES LEO GREEN

Introduction

"The Lord shoots!" "The Lord hurls!" This is the probable meaning of the word "Jeremiah."

In our study this word will be employed in two ways. It will be used to designate a prophet who labored for the Lord for 40 years in Judah during the most tragic period of her history, a prophet who was "fired," somewhat against his will, like a projectile across the life of the world of his day, a man who was "hurled" by God, so to speak, into the whirling maelstrom of the churning, changing situation of his time.

The term will also be used to denote a canonical book which contains materials from, about, or in some way related to that prophet. It is one of the longest, most difficult, most significant books in the Bible.

I. The Prophet Jeremiah

We know more about Jeremiah than any other prophet, thanks to his unusual frankness and Baruch's utter faithfulness. The rich store of material available enables us to become rather intimately acquainted with him.

1. The Man

As a person, Jeremiah was shy and sensitive, honest and human, somewhat impatient and impulsive, given to times of elation and dejection, courageous and confident, yet torn by a sense of inadequacy and an inner conflict between natural inclination and a sense of divine vocation. In his famous painting in the Sistine Chapel in Rome, Michelangelo portrayed the prophet as a man of great sorrow and gigantic strength, a true proclaimer of ethical judgment, and a tender herald of everlasting hope.

Jeremiah was reared in Anathoth, a tiny town approximately four miles northeast of Jerusalem, in the territory of Benjamin. The name is preserved in modern 'Anata, located a short distance from the site of ancient Anathoth (probably Ras el-Kharrubeh). Like 'Anata, Anathoth was a small settlement of gray stone houses, situated on a slope and surrounded by fig trees, olive groves, and grain fields. To the north one could see the hills of Ephraim; to the south, the mountains of Jerusalem; to the east and southeast, a descending desolation to the Jordan Rift and the Dead Sea—and beyond, the highlands of Gilead and Moab. It was an arid, rocky region.

Perhaps the most unusual thing about Anathoth—never on a major highway and hence seldom seen by the traveler—was that it was the habitation of the descendants of Abiathar, who served as a priest under David and who took the wrong side in the struggle for the throne at the close of David's reign (1 Kings 2:26f.). Thus, Jeremiah was likely of priestly descent. His line probably reached back to Eli and possibly even to the family of Moses (cf. 1 Sam. 14:3; 22:20; Bright, p. lxxxviii).

Jeremiah was probably born toward the end of the reign of Manasseh, i.e., about 650 B.C. Manasseh has been called "the arch villain of Judah." During his long administration an unprecedented wave of paganism and persecution swept over the nation. In 2 Kings 21 he is represented as going the gamut in cruelty and apostasy. It is said that he filled the streets of Jerusalem with the blood of God's servants. Tradition claims that Isaiah was killed during the bloody purge (*The Martyrdom of Isaiah,* 4:10 ff.).

During those dark and dangerous days some children were born who were given the name Jeremiah (35:31; 2 Kings 23:31; 28:18). This may suggest the presence of a hope in the hearts of the faithful that God was going to step in and set the desperate situation straight (Smith, p. 66).

One of those children was the son of "Hilkiah, of the priests who were in Anathoth" (1:1). Hilkiah means "Yahweh is my portion"; Jeremiah means "Yahweh shoots or hurls." [1] These names may be taken as tokens of loyalty to the Lord when many were lapsing into apostasy and idolatry.

It is logical to suppose that Jeremiah was from a priestly family, and it is obvious that he had the best of Hebrew tradition and home training as a part of his heritage. He was steeped in the Mosaic faith and in the preaching of the prophets who preceded him.

This leads us to say that a second primary influence in Jeremiah's early life was that of the prophets. He was profoundly affected by Moses, Amos, Hosea, Isaiah, and Micah. He was especially fond of Hosea's preaching. This is particularly evident in his early ministry.

One wonders how he became so well acquainted with the labors of such men as those mentioned and with both the covenant and the royal Davidic theologies.[2]

Was it through parental instruction, or public worship, or the fellowship of the faithful, or all three (see Anderson and Harrelson, pp. 11–25)?

A third influence on Jeremiah in his youth was life in a small town. Nothing in the personality or preaching of this great prophet can be adequately understood apart from the realization that he grew up in a country village. His messages abound with imagery taken from nature and from everyday life in a rural setting. His whole makeup and ministry were molded in no small measure by his early environment in the little community of Anathoth.

A fourth influence that made quite an impact on Jeremiah was his proximity to Jerusalem. The capital was only an hour's walk away. There must have been fairly frequent trips to the "big city" to make necessary sales and purchases. On these visits he listened to traders and travelers and learned much about what was happening at home and abroad. He may even have met some important people like young Josiah, Zephaniah, and Hilkiah (the high priest), and others.

These are some of the factors and forces that shaped the soul of young Jeremiah as he was growing up. But the thing that really set him forward on his course as a prophet was his call in 627 B.C. We have his own account of that experience in 1:4–19. There he pulls back the curtain briefly and grants us a glimpse into that holy hour when God placed his hand on him and said: "Jeremiah, you are my man now, a conscript for life. I have appointed you a prophet to the nations."

Armed with this strong sense of divine appointment and with some needed insights and assurances, Jeremiah began a long, stormy, and eventful ministry, which was to be "far greater in its range and depth than that of any of his predecessors" (von Rad, p. 206). He would not be privileged to marry, and he would be

---

[1] In preference to "Yahweh exalts or establishes," or "Yahweh loosens" (the womb), KB, GT, BDB, *et al.*

[2] The covenant theology majored on the Mosaic (or Sinaitic) covenant (Ex. 19 ff.) and the mighty acts of God in the early life of Israel. The wilderness period was the ideal period. The royal theology majored on the "sure house," the "sure" throne, and the "sure mercies" of David, the centrality of Jerusalem, etc. (2 Sam. 7:

16,26; 23:5; 1 Kings 11:38; Psalm 132; Isa. 55:3). The Davidic era was "the Golden Age." These theologies were not contradictory but complementary.

denied most of the joys of normal life. Increasingly he would walk the way of a cross, but he would become one of the most colorful, most courageous, and most Christlike characters in Hebrew history.

2. The Ministry

For practical purposes, we shall divide Jeremiah's ministry into four periods: his ministry under Josiah (627–609 B.C.), his ministry under Jehoiakim (609–598), his ministry under Zedekiah (597–587), and his ministry under Gedaliah and in Egypt (587 and beyond).

The nation was affected by and at times caught up in a power struggle which involved the Assyrians, the Babylonians, the Medes, the Scythians, and the Egyptians. Assyria was on the decline. Ashurbanipal, her last strong ruler, died in 627 B.C. Under Nabopolassar (626–605), Babylon was pressing rapidly to the forefront in world affairs. The Medes were becoming more active and aggressive. The Egyptians were experiencing a nationalistic revival under the new 26th dynasty and were looking northward with longing eyes. The Scythians were creating havoc and spreading terror wherever they went.[3] It was a time of international turmoil and tumult.[4]

Because of this turbulence, two of Judah's kings during Jeremiah's career reigned only three months or less. Thus, Jehoahaz and Jehoiachin are not included in the divisions of the prophet's ministry.

God brought four spokesmen on the stage of history in Judah during the four decades of crisis and change (627–587 B.C.). The other three were: Zephaniah, Nahum, and Habakkuk.

(1) Ministry Under Josiah (627–609 B.C.)

Three aspects of Jeremiah's ministry under Josiah stand out rather sharply. The first is the early preaching of the prophet. Insofar as we have a record of that preach-

ing, it is preserved in chapters 2—6 (cf. Skinner, Eissfeldt, von Rad, Weiser, et al.). In the main, the materials in these chapters are to be dated between the prophet's call (627) and the reforms of Josiah (628–622; cf. 2 Kings 23).

A careful, thoughtful reading of these materials reveals a gifted, sensitive, incisive, courageous, God-called young preacher with unusual poetic ability, who was speaking to his people most earnestly about the reality and seriousness of their sin (in the context of God's covenant love), the need and nature of repentance, and the certainty of judgment if they did not return to a right relationship with God. There is much excellent poetry in these early prophecies. This is particularly noticeable in the powerful portrayals of the form the judgment would take (4:5—6:30).

In 622 came one of the epochal events in the life of Judah and one of the pivotal experiences in the ministry of Jeremiah. We call it the Josianic or Deuteronomic reformation. It was sparked by the finding of the lawbook in the Temple during a renovation program, a book surmised by Jerome to be Deuteronomy and now rather commonly identified with that book or some portion thereof. The aim of the reformation was the purification and centralization of worship in Judah. It was the greatest single attempt ever made to bring the life of the nation into conformity to the law of God (cf. 2 Kings 22—23). The major emphases in that effort suggest that the guidebook was Deuteronomy.

One of the thorniest problems in the study of Jeremiah's ministry is that of ascertaining his attitude and action with regard to the reform movement of 622. It is this writer's view that, although the prophet is nowhere mentioned in the historical account of the event, his preaching helped to prepare for the reformation and that he himself was sympathetic with it and gave it his support for a season (cf. 11:1–8). In part, this position is based upon the nature of the movement, Jere-

---

[3] Herodotus I, 104–106; the *Babylonian Chronicle*.
[4] On the history of the period see John Bright, *A History of Israel* (Philadelphia: The Westminster Press, 1959), pp. 288–319.

miah's generous appraisal of Josiah's administration, and the warm friendship of some of the reformers for him in the years that followed.

As Jeremiah saw the movement deteriorating into an empty formalism and arid legalism, he became increasingly cautious and critical (cf. 8:8; 11:15–16). Eventually he broke openly with the movement in the delivery of his famous "temple sermon" in 609 (chs. 7; 26). It is possible that the prophet's advocacy of the reform had much to do with the plot to take his life in his hometown (11:18—12:6).

The years from 622 to 609 have been called "the silent years" in Jeremiah's ministry (cf. Weiser, von Rad). It is true that there is relatively little material in the book which can, with assurance, be assigned to that period. If, as was the case with Isaiah, Jeremiah did withdraw from public activity for a time, there may have been two primary reasons for his action: first, his initial satisfaction over the success of the Josianic reformation, a program which uprooted many entrenched evils against which he had so vigorously preached in his earlier years; and, second, his eventual disillusionment with the movement, together with the praying, wrestling, and evaluating which this involved.

Doubtless this period was a time of much reflection and reorientation. It is possible that the prophet's pictures of judgment in the poems about the foe from the north had caused some loss of face. The judgment had not yet materialized. Also, as suggested, the great "revival" had increasingly degenerated into a perfunctory ritualism, a superstitious trust in the Temple and that which transpired in it. All of this must have caused agonizing thought and prayer.

We are not to assume, however, that Jeremiah was totally inactive. He must have spent time sharing his views with friends, as his communion with God became deeper and more intimate, and as his conceptions of God and religion became more dynamic and more spiritual.

Also, he may have spoken more often in public than the records would suggest.

(2) Ministry Under Jehoiakim (609– 598 b.c.)

In 609 there came a concentration of events which constituted a landmark in the ministry of the prophet: the tragic death of Josiah at the hands of Pharaoh Neco (Necho) at Megiddo, the deportation of Jehoahaz to Egypt, the end of Judean independence, the disillusionment and religious defection of many of the people, and the designation of Jehoiakim by Neco as ruler of Judah (2 Kings 23:29 ff.; 2 Chron. 35:20–25).

Neco marched northward in 609 to lend aid to what was left of the Assyrian army and government, following the fall of Asshur in 614, of Nineveh in 612, and of Haran in 610. This action involved a political "somersault" for him, since Assyria was the former enemy and overlord of Egypt. But Neco did what he did for two reasons: first, to keep Assyria intact as a small buffer state between him and the Medes and Babylonians, and, second, to get for himself a part of the crumbling Assyrian Empire—Palestine and Syria, in particular.

Because he felt that his program of independence for Judah was threatened, and because he apparently decided to "bet" on Babylon rather than risk falling under the control of Egypt, Josiah challenged Neco at Megiddo. He was killed in the ensuing engagement (2 Kings 23: 29 f.).

This was a tragedy of the first order. Josiah was the greatest king Judah had ever had. He had been quite successful in his program of national independence and reunion in reliance upon the covenant God. Now he had been cut down in the prime of life by a pagan ruler. It is no surprise that his untimely death at the age of 39 caused great consternation and lamentation throughout the land (2 Chron. 35:24). The trust in the Temple had failed. The dream of a new Davidic kingdom faded. No one was more deeply affected than Jeremiah (2 Chron. 35:25). He shared the general sorrow and shame. He also sensed what this development would mean for his ministry and for the religious life of the nation.

Shallum was placed on the throne "by the people of the land"—probably full, free citizens of Judah, who at this time were involved in the nationalistic movement (2 Kings 23:30). Eliakim was the heir apparent (2 Kings 23:31,36). Evidently the popular choice was made because of the fact that Shallum's policy was the same as that of his father. Upon his accession, his name was changed to Jehoahaz ("Yahweh has taken hold"). The faith of some, it would seem, was reasserting itself, after recovery from the initial shock.

Jehoahaz was summoned to Riblah in Syria, Neco's headquarters. His policy proved to be unacceptable to the new overlord, and he was sent in chains to Egypt (22:10-12; 2 Kings 23:33).

Neco now made Eliakim, an older son of Josiah, ruler of Judah. He gave him the throne name Jehoiakim (2 Kings 23:34). A puppet of Neco at the start, Jehoiakim reigned for 11 years. He was a petty, bloody, selfish, unscrupulous, ungodly king, whose chief concern was not the will of God or the welfare of the people, but the gratification of his own wishes. He was a typical despot with Solomon as his model (22:13-17), as David had apparently been for his father (2 Chron. 34:3; cf. 22:15-16).

Jeremiah's clash with Jehoiakim is one of the classic encounters of the centuries and catapulted the prophet onto the stage of history as the critic and counselor of kings—a role he would not leave as long as the state stood (cf. 22:1-9,13-19). During the accession year of Jehoiakim, Jeremiah delivered one of the outstanding sermons of the ages. It nearly cost him his life (chs. 7; 26). Along about this time there was a conspiracy against him in Anathoth (11:18—12:6).

His collision with the king had incurred the hatred of his royal highness. His "temple sermon" had aroused a deep-seated opposition on the part of the priests and prophets (26:7 ff.; cf. 18:18; 20:1-6). His preaching had stirred up hostility among the people. His own family members and fellow townsmen had tried to kill him. The situation was becoming almost unbearable.

It is no source of great surprise that a spiritual crisis developed in the life of the prophet, possibly in the first part of Jehoiakim's reign.[5] This crisis is reflected in a group of passages commonly called "Jeremiah's Confessions" (11:18–12:6; 15:10–21; 17:9–10,14–18; 18:18–23; 20:7–18). These intensely personal poems and prayers, possibly originally a separate entity in the prophet's private diary, are somewhat in the style of the psalms of lamentation. They are likely in chronological order (von Rad, p. 203).

The confessions are crucial to an understanding and an interpretation of the ministry of Jeremiah. They reveal a great intimacy in the prophet's relationship with God and a *via dolorosa* opening up for Jeremiah. There is something quite new and very significant in all of this. We get a glimpse of a cross: a cross within (Jeremiah's pain), a cross without (the punishment and pain of the people, and the prophet's involvement in their sin and suffering), and a cross above (the pain of God).

The spiritual crisis experienced by the prophet during Jehoiakim's reign and reflected in the confessions was resolved through complete surrender to the will of God. God's servant moved forward with steady step toward his "calvary."

It seems that Baruch, who appears sev-

---

[5] Some date the crisis between 609 and 605 B.C. Cf. Skinner, pp. 208–215; G. Fohrer, *Introduction to the Old Testament,* trans. David Green (Nashville: Abingdon, 1968), p. 395; others, between 605 and 598; cf. James Muilenburg, "Jeremiah," IDB, 2, p. 827; Sheldon Blank, *Jeremiah, Man and Prophet* (Cincinnati: Hebrew Union College Press, 1961), p. 117. Some scholars reject the idea that there was a crisis.

eral times in the book of Jeremiah (chs. 32; 36; 43; 45), joined the prophet after the latter became a national figure early in the reign of Jehoiakim. The evidence suggests that he was a person of unusual ability and background, a professional scribe who was highly regarded by his peers and who had free access to the cabinet rooms in the palace and in the Temple and could gain a ready hearing for Jeremiah's "roll" among the people and the governmental personnel (ch. 36). He was not only the prophet's scribe but also his constant companion until the end of his ministry. The probability is that he had much to do with the compilation and composition of the materials in the book of Jeremiah.[6]

One of the most important battles of antiquity was fought in 605 B.C. At Carchemish the Babylonians won a decisive victory over the Egyptians. This marked a turning point in the history of the ancient world—the start of the supremacy of Babylon—and in the life of Judah—a shift of allegiance and the beginning of the end.

That event was also a landmark in the ministry of Jeremiah. For some 23 years he had proclaimed the conviction that apart from a radical repentance the nation would experience a divine visitation in the form of a ravaging of the land by a foe from the north. Now it was just a matter of time.

Nebuchadnezzar's triumph over Neco set Jeremiah aflame. A new urgency entered his preaching. He composed two brilliant poem-prophecies about Egypt shortly after hearing the news of the event (ch. 46). He spoke to his people from a soul at white heat (25:1 ff.). He dictated his prophecies for the first time to Baruch to be read in the Temple (from which he was debarred), hoping that the nation might yet repent and receive forgiveness and, hopefully, avert the tragedy (36:

1–8). When Jehoiakim destroyed the scroll during its third reading (604), Jeremiah dictated his prophecies a second time, and many like words were added (36:9–32). Recognizing that his life was in great danger, he was now seeking permanent form for his preaching.

At this time Jeremiah was so preoccupied with the role of Nebuchadnezzar (Nebuchadrezzar) in the purpose of God that he pursued the subject not only as it related to Judah but also as it pertained to other peoples as well. He composed a number of foreign prophecies (see comments on chs. 46—51). In them he came close to the concept of a judgment upon the entire world (von Rad, p. 199).

Certain undated parables come from Jeremiah's ministry under Jehoiakim (13: 1 ff.; 18:1 ff.; 19:1 ff.; 35:1 ff.) All of these symbolic acts are important, but the visit to the potter's house (18:1 ff.) is of unusual significance. It marks the entry into Jeremiah's ministry of a new element, the element of hope for the future of a nation now doomed. By this time (likely *ca.* 604) Jeremiah was convinced that judgment on Judah was certain.

Jehoiakim had to switch loyalty from Egypt to Babylon. For some three years he paid tribute. Then he rebelled (*ca.* 601). Because he could not take care of the situation in person at the moment, Nebuchadnezzar sent against his disloyal vassal contingents of soldiers from neighboring nations (2 Kings 24:1–2). Finally he had to come with his army in December, 598 B.C. (Wiseman). Jehoiakim had died, possibly the victim of a plot (2 Kings 24:10; Bright). Jehoiachin, his young son, was now ruler of Judah. Shortly thereafter Jerusalem capitulated, and the first major Babylonian captivity became a reality. This was in early 597. The leadership of the land, including Jehoiachin, was transported into exile (22: 24–30; 2 Kings 24:10 ff.).[7]

6 See James Muilenburg, "Baruch the Scribe," *Proclamation and Presence*, eds. John I Durham and J. Roy Porter (Richmond: John Knox Press, 1970), pp. 215–238.

7 James B. Pritchard, ed., *Ancient Near Eastern Texts, Relating to the Old Testament* (Princeton: University Press, 1965), p. 308.

(3) Ministry Under Zedekiah (597–587 B.C.)

Another son of Josiah was appointed king of Judah by Nebuchadnezzar (2 Kings 24:17). His name was changed from Mattaniah to Zedekiah ("Yahweh is my righteousness")—probably to bind the new ruler by the name of his covenant God to his oath of allegiance to his overlord. Zedekiah was a weak, vacillating, easily influenced individual.

We reach another turning point in the career of the prophet. Most of his real friends were gone. The leaders who were left were inexperienced and arrogant. The situation was loaded with possibilities for agitation and rebellion. For God's servant, the road would become rougher and his suffering greater.

Jeremiah's chief role as statesman-prophet under Zedekiah was to seek to persuade the government and the people to follow the only path that could lead to any real safety and security: submission to Babylon as God's agent of judgment. He tried—and failed.

There was agitation for revolt in 594–593. Jeremiah's proclamation of the prophetic word through symbolic act may have helped stave off rebellion for a season (ch. 27). But in 589 it broke out. Zedekiah was in the middle of it. The result was the westward march of the Babylonian army, the surrender of "the lesser lights," the defeat of Egypt, the devastation of Judah, and the long siege and final sack of Jerusalem (January, 588—July–August, 587).

During this difficult period there were three major highlights in the ministry of Jeremiah. The first was his release of his message of hope (chs. 24; 29; 32; 33). The second was his clash with his colleagues and his penetrating polemic against the popular religious leadership of the day (chs. 29; 27; 28; 23). The third was his utter fidelity to God in the midst of almost indescribable hardship and suffering during the long terrible siege of Jerusalem (chs. 21; 34; 37–39).

(4) Ministry Under Gedaliah and in Egypt (587 B.C. and Beyond)

After the destruction of Jerusalem, Jeremiah was given a choice: to go back with Nebuchadnezzar to Babylon and spend his final days in ease and honor there, or to remain in the Judean province with the new governor Gedaliah and the poor people left to take care of the fields and the vineyards. He elected to stay with the group in Judah (40:1–6).

Out of this peaceful period, with the pressure of proclaiming judgment removed, he produced some of his greatest work (chs. 30; 31). In the midst of all the wreckage, he envisioned the coming of a new day, with a new community, a new covenant, and a new king.

How long this period lasted is not known. Some feel that it was of some five years' duration (cf. 52:30). The biblical records leave the impression that it was a short time, a matter of months at most. It came to an end. Tragedy struck again. Gedaliah was assassinated. The Judeans were gripped by fear and fled to Egypt. They took with them by force both Jeremiah and his faithful friend Baruch—and this despite the people's request that through prayer Jeremiah discover God's will for them, and his response (after 10 days) that God's will was that they remain in the land (40:7—43:7).

In the last glimpses we get of Jeremiah in Egypt he is still faithfully preaching the word of the Lord, shattering popular illusions and seeking to stab his people awake to reality, in particular, the folly of idolatry (43:8—44:30). After making an appeal to history for vindication, he drops from sight. Tradition claims that he was martyred.

3. The Message

Jeremiah was not a systematic theologian. He was a prophet. Yet the message he proclaimed was set in a theological framework and on a theological foundation. Through his preaching he made a tremendous theological contribution to the life of God's people. For one thing, he greatly helped prepare the Israelites of his day to cope with the theological crisis precipitated by the catastrophe of 587 B.C. Moreover, he cast a long shadow, seen in Ezekiel, Job, the Psalms, Isaiah, the Gospels, Paul, Hebrews, and Revelation. His message is still relevant today.

Some say that there is no theology in the prophets. Actually, there is little else. To systematize that theology is quite another matter. In full recognition of the problems involved, we shall attempt a summation of Jeremiah's message in terms of his major theological concepts.

(1) His Concept of God

Jeremiah believed that there is one God, Yahweh the covenant God of Israel. With merciless scorn, he designated other so-called gods "empty breaths," "things that do not profit," "broken cisterns," "nonentities," "do-nothings," "a work of delusion," "lies," "the work of men's hands," etc. (cf. 2:5,11,13; 10:5; 14:22; 16:19–20). Here we have pure ethical monotheism. The God of Jeremiah is God alone.

He is also God supreme, the sovereign Lord of the universe. He is Lord of nature, its creator and controller (1:11; 3:3; 5:22; 2:7; 10:12 f.; 14:22; 31:35–37; etc.). He is the Lord of the nations. He is not aloof from history, but active in it and in charge of it, directing it toward its divinely appointed goal (cf. 1:10,11–16; 4:1—6:30; 30:1—31:40; 46:1—51:64; etc.). He can use Israel as his elect or Nebuchadnezzar as his "servant." In his sovereignty, he is not bound, but is free to adapt himself to a changed situation in dealing with free men (cf. 18:1 ff.). In his constancy, he continues to address men in history. "History is the whole work of the God who is coming." [8] Its unity, continuity, and finality

are grounded in his sovereignty and his constancy. Its universality stems from his lordship over all reality.

Since God is continually addressing man in history, he is, therefore, a God of deeds, not creeds. He is always doing something or about to do something. He is the living God, who is awake and at work in the realm of nature, of history, and of the human heart (cf. 1:4–19; 2—6; 24:7; 31:33–34; etc.). It is in this third realm that Jeremiah breaks new ground.

His God is everywhere, a majestic spiritual presence who fills the universe, a God both transcendent and immanent, a God afar off who comes very near (23:23–24; etc.). This means that no one can escape encounter with him. Along with this truth goes its corollary: he is a God who can be found anywhere—in Babylon as well as Jerusalem, without Temple personnel or paraphernalia—when sought with the whole heart (29:13).

The God of Jeremiah is a God of righteousness and justice (9:24). He cannot condone sin, but must see that the sinner gets his just recompense (11:20; 17:10; 29:23). Others had applied this truth to the nation. Jeremiah is the first to apply it directly to the individual.

In this connection, it is interesting to observe that the prophet from Anathoth has more to say about the wrath of God than any other prophet (Smith, p. 358). In his view, God's wrath is the reverse side of his love. It is God's basic antagonism to sin and the operation of the principle of retribution in order to save, if possible. It makes necessary judgment upon the rebellious, unrepentant covenant nation Israel, upon foreign peoples living outside the circle of God's will and in opposition to his purpose, and upon the individual who persists in revolt against the Lord of life.

---

[8] H. W. Wolff, "The Understanding of History in the Old Testament Prophets," *Essays on Old Testament Interpretation,* eds. Claus Westermann, English edition, J. L. Mays (London: SCM Press, 1963), p. 332. Jeremiah constantly preserves the polarity between God's action and man's responsibility in the goal-directed

dialogue in history. He also shows particular interest in world history, in the context of salvation-history, "because Israel's unique nature comes to light only in the framework of the history of the nations" (*ibid.,* p. 347).

The God of Jeremiah is also a God of love. It was through an act of love that he elected Israel and entered into covenant with her (cf. 2:2 f.; etc.). In all his dealings with her he has been *chasid*, i.e., one characterized by grace, or steadfast covenant love (3:12). He has treated her as a son (3:19), but she has played him false (3:20). Even though his holy love requires that he discipline her for her persistent breach of the covenant, he still loves his prodigal people "with an everlasting love" and through grace is endeavoring to draw them back into a right relationship with himself (31:3,20). If they truly repent, he stands ever ready to forgive and forget their sin, and to make them into new men with the ability to obey (31:33 f.; 32:39–40; 24:7; etc.).

Jeremiah's God is an intimate friend with whom he has fellowship along life's way. There is little about the glory and majesty of God in Jeremiah (compared to Isaiah, for example), though these elements are not entirely missing. But there is a great deal of stress on God's availability and desire for dialogue with man. In some ways, this is the most distinctive thing in Jeremiah's conception of God (and religion). Man can have a direct, dynamic, life-changing relationship with God as friend with Friend, if man desires it and will meet the conditions.

(2) *His Concept of the Word of God*

Closely related to Jeremiah's conception of God is his conception of the word of God, for God's word is God speaking, God communicating, God making himself known. James Muilenburg observes: "In Jeremiah the theology of the Word reaches its culmination." [9]

The word of God was a living reality to Jeremiah. The account of his call begins with the statement, "Now the word of the Lord came to me" (1:4, lit. became or happened to me). Mowinckel [10] renders

this sentence thus: "The word of the Lord became an active reality with me." Zimmerli [11] speaks of the "word-event." The coming of the word was a happening.

The phrase "the word of the Lord" occurs 241 times in the Old Testament. In 221 of these cases it refers to prophecy. The statement "the word of the Lord came to . . ." appears 123 times. It is found in the earlier prophets, but not often. There is a significant increase in its use in Jeremiah (30 times). This indicates a developing theology of the "word."

For Jeremiah, the reception of the word was an inner event. The word pressed in on him. It burned like a fire in his bones (20:9). It sometimes resulted in powerful emotional excitation, bringing joy or anger or grief (15:16–18; 4:19; 23:9; etc.). The prophet's whole inner being became involved.

He ate the word like a hungry man (15:16; cf. Ezek. 2:8—3:3), and it nourished him. He became dependent upon it for life. This concept of the dependence of man upon the communicating God for life came to the surface emphatically in Jeremiah and became, in a real sense, the foreshadowing of the incarnation of Christ, the Word becoming flesh.

We are told that God communicated the word to Jeremiah (1:9). It was never something which came through mere reflection or speculation, but only through revelation. It was "given" and "received." Often it contravened the prophet's wishes (cf. 28:6–7). It sometimes came after much earnest thought and agonizing prayer (28:11 f.; 42:1–7). There was a price to pay—both in the securing and in the receiving of it.

This was, in part, the basis of Jeremiah's attack upon the false prophets. They had no authentic word of the Lord because they had no vital, personal, exacting relationship with him. They had not stood in his council. [12] Hence they were

9 James Muilenburg, "Jeremiah," IDB, (Nashville: Abingdon Press, 1962), 2, 829.

10 *Erkenntnis Gottes*, p. 19.

11 *Ezechiel*, p. 89.

12 In the Old Testament, God is conceived as a king who presides over a heavenly assembly or coun-

palming off on the people the words of man, spun out of their subconscious or stolen from their colleagues (23:16–32).

Jeremiah understood from the start that it was his primary responsibility to proclaim the word received (1:4 ff.). It was to be a word of judgment and of salvation (1:10). God was watching over it to perform it (1:11–12).

Not only was the word a burning subjective reality, but also, once uttered, it became an objective entity, a dynamic, living, creative thing. It was effective. It could pluck up and pull down. It could build and plant (1:10). It became like wheat, which gives life; like fire, which consumes all that is contrary to God's character and will; and like a hammer, which breaks in bits that which opposes God's purpose (5:14; 23:28–29). It is indestructible (ch. 36). Whether proclaimed in sermon, by symbolic act, or on a scroll, it is the expression of God's purpose and the embodiment of the power to carry it out. It both reveals and helps to make history.

(3) His Concept of Sin

Jeremiah viewed sin in the context of the love of the God who communicates with men. In his outgoing grace, the Lord had brought Israel into being and blessed her as his elect. He had made a covenant with her. Yet she had betrayed his love. She was guilty of filial disloyalty and spiritual adultery. In essence her sin was that of unfaithfulness to God, open rebellion against his sovereign will.

Jeremiah ran the gamut of imagery and emphasis in stressing the nature and

cil (cf. 1 Kings 22; Job 1—2; Isa. 6; 40; etc.). The members of that assembly are his intimate associates and servants. Among these are the prophets. At times the assembly acts as a court. Decisions are made. These are conveyed to the subjects by the royal spokesman, the prophet, appointed a member of the divine council by divine call and commissioned to communicate the divine "word." See H. W. Robinson, "The Council of Yahweh," JTS, 45, 1944, pp. 151 ff.; G. E. Wright, *The Old Testament Against Its Environment* (London: SCM Press, 1950), pp. 30–41; Frank M. Cross, Jr., "The Council of Yahweh in Second Isaiah," JNES, 12, 1953, pp. 274–277.

enormity of Israel's sin as infidelity (e.g., 2:1 ff.). To him, sin was an inner attitude expressing itself in outer acts, a wrong relationship with God resulting in wrong relationships with men. He spoke out vigorously against various manifestations of sin: duplicity, adultery, dishonesty, mendacity, cruelty, idolatry, sensuality or formality in worship. But these were simply expressions of a breach of the covenant.

Jeremiah went beyond his predecessors not only in his assault on sin but also in his search for the ultimate source of sin. He found it in a deceitful, diseased human heart, stubbornly defiant of God's sovereign control (5:23; 7:24; 13:23; 17:9; 23:17). Man chooses at the center of his being (heart) to live at cross-purposes with God. In so doing he becomes a contradiction and is caught in a tragic predicament of frustration, helplessness, and guilt. To the prophet this was shockingly unnatural and almost incredible (2:5–13, 32; 5:23—24; 8:7; etc.). Nothing in nature—and no nation (except Israel)—acts this way!

As Jeremiah saw it, the inevitable consequence of sin is judgment. This is a part of the structure of reality. When man violates the law of his being, there is a penalty wrapped up in the same package with that violation. God had chastened Israel for her waywardness, but she had refused to respond to correction (e.g., 2:30 ff.). Therefore there must be further discipline: the conquest of the country and the Babylonian captivity. But all of this was the people's doing. By their conduct they were bringing retribution upon themselves (2:17,19; 4:18; 6:19; etc.).

However, God does not delight in judgment and stands ever ready to forgive. The condition is real repentance.

(4) His Concept of Repentance

Repentance is a dominant recurring theme in Jeremiah's preaching. He had more to say on the subject than any other prophet, and what he said is central to his message. We find him emphasizing it from the beginning to the end of his ministry (cf. 3:6–18,22; 4:1–4,14; 5:3,6; 8:4–6; 14:7; 15:7,19; 18:8,11; 23:14,22; 24:7; 25:5; 31:18–22; 34:16; 35:15; 36:3; 44:5; etc.). He saw his countrymen in a disaster situation because of their sin. It was an "either-or" affair: either repentance or ruin.

There are two words in the Old Testament for repent: *nacham* and *shub*. The former is used mainly of God and signifies his alteration of his intention or course of action concerning a person or situation. This is in response to a change on man's part and often involves an element of grief (cf. 4:28; 18:8,10; 26:3,13,19). Jeremiah employs *nacham* twice of man's action (8:6; 31:19).

The word so crucial to his concept of repentance is *shub*. It occurs 1059 times in the Old Testament. It has a high frequency of appearance in the prophets and the highest in Jeremiah (111 times). In fact, it is found more in Jeremiah than in any other prophet or Old Testament book. It has "a rich variety of meanings" and "a deliberate, specialized ambiguity." Its central core meaning is "having moved in a particular direction, to move thereupon in the opposite direction, the implication being (unless there is evidence to the contrary) that one will arrive again at the initial point of departure" [13]—hence to return, to come all the way back to the place or person one has left.

In addition to its normal meaning, *shub* has a special covenantal signification. It indicates a change of loyalty on the part of Israel or God (usually Israel), each for the other. Holladay lists 164 cases of covenantal *shub*.[14] They are scattered somewhat unevenly through the Old Testament. The heaviest concentration is in the prophets, and the greatest is in Jeremiah (almost 30% of the total, 48 out of 164). Jeremiah employed and played upon both

the covenantal and noncovenantal meanings of the verb and its derivatives with unusual insight and skill, as he exhorted the people with breaking heart to turn away from evil and to turn all the way back to a right relationship with the covenant God.

According to Jeremiah, repentance is a painful process: a circumcision of the heart, a plowing up of the fallow ground, a complete renunciation of idolatry and a total return to God (4:1–4). This means a radical transformation of life. The only alternative is ruin.

During the earlier years of his preaching the prophet must have entertained considerable hope that the nation might turn and be saved. His exhortations to repent were quite frequent. But as time passed and he saw that the people were increasingly set in their sins, hope began to fade. During this period he had a terrific inner struggle with the mystery and meaning of God's will and ways with men. He became resentful and rebellious. God had to tell him to repent, if he would be a true messenger for him (15:15–21).

In 605, with catastrophe hanging heavy over the head of the nation, Jeremiah made a final desperate effort to get the nation to repent (chs. 36; 25). It failed. It was then, most likely, that he lost all hope as far as the nation was concerned. But at the potter's house he saw that the coming crash and captivity did not mean doom but discipline (18:1 ff.). God was seeking to save. The note of hope came back, not for empirical Israel, but for the new Israel of God. Henceforth his calls to repent sprang "from God's decision to save." [15]

As his ministry came toward a close, Jeremiah saw that real repentance (31: 18–19), coupled with a deep sense of individual ethical responsibility (31:29–30), was that which would make possible "God's new thing," his creation of a new

---

13 W. L. Holladay, *The Root Shubh in the Old Testament* (Leiden: E. J. Brill, 1958), pp. 1, 53.
14 *Ibid.*, pp. 116 ff.

15 H. W. Wolff, "Das Thema 'Umkehr' in der alttestamentlichen Prophetie," *Zeitschrift für Theologie und Kirche* (Tübingen, 1951), 48, p. 142.

man capable of comprehending and obeying the divine will from within (31: 33–34).

(5) His Concept of Religion

As Jeremiah conceived it, real religion roots in redemption. It begins with God's act of saving grace. But it does not stop there. When man comes into a right relationship with God, this reality must express itself in right relationships with his fellowmen.

One does not have to read far into the prophecy of Jeremiah to recognize that there was plenty of bad religion about in the latter part of the seventh century B.C. Among the people there was an unholy coalition of unrighteousness and ritualism, a wedding of wickedness and worship. The Israelites could blatantly break the covenant commands and go to the Temple and say: "We are delivered!" (secure, cf. 7: 9–11).

It is not surprising therefore to find that some of Jeremiah's strongest statements were directed against the cult. This does not mean that Jeremiah opposed the Temple and Temple worship *per se*. The basis of his attack was twofold: first, the infiltration of the cult by pagan ideas and practices; second, the substitution by the people of a proper ritual for right relationships.[16]

In spite of his assault on a cult wrongly oriented and evaluated, Jeremiah stood in close contact with it and took a positive attitude toward it (cf. his preaching in the Temple, his use of cultic forms, his allusion to worship in the new age, as in 31:6, etc.). He believed that ritual has a real place in religion, when it is set in proper perspective and with a right purpose as a divine means of grace for mediating the knowledge of God to man and man's sincere devotion to God.

(6) His Concept of the Future

The eschatology of Jeremiah was simple. He saw that judgment was an absolute moral necessity. But judgment was a step toward the realization of God's salvation. The prophet had great faith in the future of God's purpose and people (cf. 32:9–15). As he gazed out into God's future, he envisioned a new community, redeemed and restored by God and rejoicing in God. Lovely pictures are painted of the joy, prosperity, unity, and security of that community (3:15–18; 30:18–22; 31:2–6,7–14; etc.). The basis of this hope was the strong love of God (31:3,20). That love, working through judgment, would make possible the new community.

The most distinctive feature in Jeremiah's forecast of the future was a new covenant (31:31–34; 32:37 ff.). The new covenant would fulfill the intent of the old. It would be marked by pardon and grace, by firsthand fellowship with God on the part of each "from the least to the greatest," and by a capacity for an inner understanding and obeying of God's will. W. Eichrodt states that this picture of a new man in a new community has "no equal in the Old Testament." [17]

The new community, composed of new men in a new covenant with God, would have a new king. He would be of the line of David. He would rule by reason of his unique relationship to God and in righteousness and peace. His presence among the people would be the pledge of their salvation and security. By the offering of his life as surety he would keep the access to God open. His dominion would be universal (23:5–6; 30:9,21; cf. 31:33 f.; 33:15; etc.).[18]

Jeremiah not only stood in the stream of covenant theology, but he also accepted the concept of the ideal king from the royal Davidic theology (cf. Skinner, von Rad, Weiser, *et al.*). As he spoke about the new age—with a new community, a

---

[16] Clements, pp. 86–102; H. H. Rowley, *From Moses to Qumran* (New York: Association Press, 1963), pp. 67–140.

[17] *Theology of the Old Testament*, trans. J. A. Baker (Philadelphia: The Westminster Press, 1961), I, p. 59.

[18] Artur Weiser remarks: "A forerunner of Deutero-Isaiah, he [Jeremiah] set the crown on his hope for the future by looking forward to the recognition of Yahweh by all nations"; *The Old Testament: Its Formation and Development* (New York: Association Press, 1961), p. 221.

new covenant, and a new king—he set no date on the calendar. It would come in God's time.

When it is all summed up, Jeremiah had a twofold message: judgment and salvation. Judgment was a step toward salvation. Only through repentance could one avert destruction and participate in salvation. The true task of the prophet was to turn men from the way that leads to disaster to the way that leads to deliverance. Properly understood, Jeremiah was ultimately and primarily "a prophet of instructive grace, and not of destructive judgment." [19]

He took the theology of his predecessors and developed it in his own distinctive way, with his penetrating analysis of sin as a betrayal of divine love and a perversion of human life, his emphasis on the urgency of radical repentance, and his portrayal of the glory of the new thing which God in his grace would make possible for man. Curt Kuhl calls him "the greatest preacher of repentance among his people" and says: "In his prophecy of the New Covenant of grace and forgiveness of sins (XXXI, 31 ff.) he surpasses by far the other Old Testament prophets." [20]

II. The Prophecy of Jeremiah

We come now to the book that bears the name of the man. We know more about its origin than we know about the composition of any other prophetical book. But this does not make matters easy, for Jeremiah is at the same time one of the most significant and one of the most difficult books in the Bible.

1. General Characterization

The significance of the book is apparent. For one thing, it records the ministry and message of one of God's most outstanding men. Moreover, its influence has been tremendous on life and literature in bibli-

cal days and since. Further, for the preacher it is a mine of rich homiletical treasures. For the lay Christian it contains a marvelous fund of material for ethical and spiritual edification from and about one of the most dynamically alive, most genuinely human, and most deeply dedicated of all the prophets.

If the significance of the book is obvious, its difficulty is more abundantly clear. Let the reader imagine himself picking it up for the first time. Before he has gone far in the reading of it, he becomes perplexed. The first thing that may strike him (if he is using a modern translation) is that the book is a blend of poetry and prose, and these assume many different forms. He will begin to observe the occurrence of names of obscure places and people and some considerable repetition of thought. But the thing that will impress him the most is that there are sudden shifts in time and types of material, and that the material seems to be in much disarray. It is certainly not easy reading. There is no apparent principle or pattern of arrangement that is followed consistently. One may feel utter confusion and give up on the whole business saying, "This prophecy is a hopeless hodgepodge." At this point, the words of Martin Luther concerning Jeremiah may have some relevance: "We must not trouble ourselves about the order, or allow the want of order to hinder us." The latter part of the statement is especially apropos.

What can we do about the situation? First, we must recognize that Jeremiah is not a book in the ordinary sense. It is more like a library. It is a collection of collections of materials of various kinds. The recognition of this fact is the starting point for the serious student.

Second, it may prove helpful to divide the book into three major sections, with an appendix. Chapters 1—25 have been called "The Words of Jeremiah," and mainly contain prophecies of Jeremiah— mostly in poetry but partly in prose— with some autobiographical and biographical materials interspersed. These chapters have to be read very carefully and prayer-

---

[19] L. Koehler, *Theology of the Old Testament* (London: Lutterworth Press, 1957), p. 223; cf. G. Fohrer, "Remarks on Modern Interpretation of the Prophets," JBL, 80, 1961, p. 319.

[20] *The Old Testament*, trans. C. M. T. Herriott (Richmond: John Knox Press, 1961), p. 192.

fully, even slowly. They are exceptionally rich and rewarding.

Chapters 26—45 sometimes bear the caption "The Biography of Jeremiah." This is a misnomer, in some measure, for there is no complete, chronologically arranged story of the life and work of the prophet to be found here. Instead, we have Baruch's memoirs of Jeremiah's martyrdom, beginning with the "temple sermon" (609 B.C.) and going down to Jeremiah's activity in Egypt (587 and beyond). Still, this section has been termed by a contemporary scholar, Klaus Koch, "the first biography of a prophet" and "the first biography composed in Israel."[21] Interwoven with the Baruch narratives are some prophecies in various forms, and there is one significant insertion, "the book of consolation" (chs. 30—33).

Chapters 46—51 constitute the book of foreign prophecies. Here some of the best poetry in the prophecy is to be found. Partly because they are in poetry, partly because of numerous allusions to unknown or relatively unknown places and people, but primarily because of their tone and thought, these prophecies prove to be rather difficult and forbidding for the average modern reader. Yet a knowledge of them is absolutely essential to a proper understanding of the prophet and his perspective.

The book closes with an appendix (ch. 52), which is an excerpt, with some modification, from 2 Kings 24:18—25:30. It deals with the destruction of Jerusalem, the disposal of rebel leaders and Temple furnishings, the deportations of the Israelites, and the eventual deliverance of Jehoaichin, the Davidic ruler imprisoned for 37 years in Babylon.

Third, the reader should recognize that there are evidences of chronological and topical arrangement in different portions of the prophecy. Quite obviously the arrangement is topical in 22:1—23:8; 23:

9—40; 30—33; 37—44; 46—51; and elsewhere. It is also chronological at points, e.g., in 1—20 (in broad outline), 37—44, etc.

Fourth, an attempt at a reconstruction of the process of the composition of the book should be made, starting with chapter 36. Though one cannot be dogmatic about any reconstruction he makes, any sane and serious effort in this direction will assist tremendously in the study of the book as the inspired record of the life and work of Jeremiah.

Fifth, the reader must realize that there is an unusual abundance and wealth of literary forms and stylistic devices in Jeremiah. If the reader's approach is reverent and balanced, the more he becomes acquainted with these, the more he can appreciate and appropriate the message of the book. "The interpretation of any book is controlled by the type of material it contains."[22]

A word about the language and style of the book is in order. The Hebrew is good —in places, superb. The prose is hortatory and a bit repetitious, sometimes vigorous, sometimes somewhat flat. This does not mean that it was stylistically inferior as prose Hebrew of the period. The poetry is some of the best in the Old Testament. It is marked by vividness, realism, terseness, beauty, and power.[23] There are certain methods fairly frequently employed: wordplays, assonance, use of words based on the same root, chiasmus, irony, abrupt change of speaker and tone, and a heightened vocabulary.

So the prophecy of Jeremiah is an anthology of materials of various kinds from, about, or in some way related to the prophet Jeremiah.

2. The Chief Literary Components

At the turn of the century, Bernard Duhm recognized what he believed to be

---

[21] The Growth of the Biblical Tradition, trans. S. M. Cupitt (New York: Charles Scribner's Sons, 1969), pp. 203 f.

[22] John Bright, "The Book of Jeremiah," Interpretation, 9, 1955, p. 264.

[23] On the poetry, see Bright, Jeremiah, pp. cxxxvi-cxxxviii.

three types of material in Jeremiah: prophecies of Jeremiah, biographical narratives by Baruch, and additions by Deuteronomic editors.[24] Sigmund Mowinckel developed Duhm's thesis, with considerable emphasis on the role of oral tradition in the transmission process. He designated the three types of material A, B, and C.[25]

Type A was composed primarily of Jeremiah's prophecies in poetic form. Included also were his confessions. Type B consisted of stories about Jeremiah in the third person (chs. 19—21; 26—29; 32; 34—45). Type C was made up of prose discourses, characterized by a Deuteronomic style and tone, and scattered throughout chapters 1—35.

The words of Jeremiah were to be found in A. Someone other than Baruch produced B, using authentic Jeremianic materials, but with considerable freedom. A late Deuteronomic school, seeking to capture Jeremiah for their camp and cause, was responsible for C, at times distorting the prophet's views.

With some modifications, Mowinckel's scheme has been accepted by Rudolph and various other Old Testament scholars. However, there has been an increasing recent trend toward dispensing with the sharp distinction between Types B and C, toward regarding Baruch as the biographer, and toward an acceptance of the early date and essential reliability of the material with a Deuteronomic cast in Type C and elsewhere.

In the light of the work done in the field by scholars, past and present, we offer a brief designation and discussion of the principal literary types in the prophecy of Jeremiah. At least three things must be kept in mind in type-analysis. First, because of the limited amount of material available for examination, conclusions reached must of necessity be somewhat subjective and tentative in character. Second, a distinction must be made between form and function. Third, the prophet can and usually does adapt a given type to his purpose—frequently with great effectiveness. If the process is not overpressed and its limitations are not overlooked, type-analysis can serve as a valuable aid to a proper interpretation and appreciation of Jeremiah.

(1) Prophecies

The primary responsibility of the prophet was the proclamation of God's word. This was usually done in public in as striking a manner as possible. Ordinarily the proclamation took one of two basic forms: the prophecy of disaster or the prophecy of deliverance.

The exhortation is regarded by some as a separate type. It occurs fairly frequently in Jeremiah. It normally takes the form of a call to turn from the way of sin to a life of surrender and obedience to God. It is sometimes linked to or interwoven with a prophecy of disaster or a prophecy of deliverance. It is usually present implicitly or explicitly in both.

The prophecy of disaster (called by Westermann "the judgment-speech") could be addressed to an individual (e.g., 22:13-19) or to a group (cf. 23:1-2, 13-15; 6:16-21; 35:13-17; 46:3-12). There are two primary parts to this fundamental pattern,[26] variously referred to as (1) the reproach, diatribe, accusation, statement of the situation, or motivation, and as (2) the threat, prediction, warning, or announcement of judgment. Wolff rightly emphasizes that in the use of this pattern the prophets give evidence of their constant concern to show that future divine retribution is the direct, dynamic

---

24 Das Buch Jeremia (Tübingen: Mohr, 1901), pp. xi-xx.

25 Prophecy and Tradition (Oslo: Dybwad, 1946), pp. 61-65; cf. Zur Komposition des Buches Jeremia (Oslo: Dybwad, 1914).

26 According to Claus Westermann, there are actually four elements in the structure of this basic type: an appeal for attention, the accusation, the messenger formula, and the announcement of judgment. See Basic Forms of Prophetic Speech (Philadelphia: The Westminster Press, 1967), p. 28. According to Koch, there are three: the diatribe or indication of the situation, the threat or prediction of disaster, and a concluding characterization (op. cit., pp. 211 f.).

moral consequence of the present human situation.

Though the reproach and the threat may originally have been separate forms, they have been fused in the prophecy of disaster. This type predominates among the canonical prophets, including Jeremiah. Jeremiah demonstrates time and again that he can use it with tremendous flexibility and force (e.g., 5:1–31). Sometimes he blends a prophecy of disaster to an individual with a prophecy of disaster to a group (e.g., 20:4–6; 28:13–16).

The prophecy of deliverance could also be directed to an individual (e.g., 39: 15–18) or to a group (28:2–4; 30:18–22; 31:2–6,7–14). Its structure usually included the "messenger formula" and/or an appeal for attention. This was followed by an indication of the situation. Next came the promise or prediction of salvation. There might also be a concluding characterization (ordinarily of God, the sender of the messenger).

Prophecies of deliverance are found in various parts of the prophecy of Jeremiah (cf. 3:14–18; 23:3–6; etc.), but primarily in chapters 24,29, and 30—33.

There is no need to be upset by the presence of promises of salvation alongside prophecies of destruction in Jeremiah. This polarity is found throughout the prophetical literature of the Old Testament. It reflects the tensions in the heart of the prophet between his conception of the character of God and his affection for his people and his conviction about their election. Ultimately, it roots back into the being of God himself—the tension between his love and his wrath. The agony of this tension is present in unusual measure in Jeremiah.

(2) Accounts

In Jeremiah there are narratives as well as prophecies. Some of these are recorded in the first person, others in the third.

There is the vision account. As a literary type it precedes the appearance of the canonical prophets by centuries. Especially significant is the inaugural vision, for it marks the call of the prophet to divine service (1:4–10). Other accounts of visionary experiences of various kinds are also present (cf. 1:11–16; 4:23–28; 24:1 ff.). Accounts of symbolic actions are found in chapters 13; 16; 19; 32; 35; 51. There is an account of a letter to the exiles (29:1 ff.) and another of a real estate transaction (32:9–15).

A new form emerges in connection with the recording of the prophet's experiences from 609 to 587 B.C. Found primarily within chapters 26—45, it has been called "the first biography composed in Israel."

(3) Borrowed Forms

The prophets borrowed literary types and rhetorical devices from all realms of life: the cult, the court, the schools of the sages, and the ordinary activities of human existence.

A type found in Jeremiah is the lawsuit pattern (e.g., 2:2—4:4). The principal elements in this form are: a summons to the witnesses (usually, in the Old Testament, the heavens and the earth), the initial statement of the case by the plaintiff and judge, the recital of the gracious acts of the sovereign, the indictment of the accused, and the pronouncement of the sentence.

Although some scholars derive the lawsuit pattern from the cult and others from everyday legal proceedings, it likely goes back in origin to the ancient suzerainty covenants (treaties) made by great powers with vassals from the days of the Hittites (prior to Moses) to the time of the Assyrians (in the days of Isaiah and Hezekiah). These covenants followed a particular form: the preamble, the recital of the acts of suzerain leading to the covenant, the statement of the basic principle or condition underlying the covenant (requiring decision on the part of the vassal), the explication of the terms or stipulations of the covenant, the call to witnesses (usually the gods and the elements in the universe), and the articulation of the blessings (rewards if the covenant was kept) and the curses (the penalties if it was not).

This ancient form influenced the shaping of the covenant form and formulas in Israel. This may be seen in the covenantal lawsuit pattern referred to above: the summons to hear, the call to witnesses, the rehearsal of the gracious deeds of the suzerain (God the King), the indictment of the subject (Israel his people) because of the failure to comply with the stipulations of the covenant (i.e., the holy Law), and the sentence (curse or retribution) because of the breach of the covenant.

Coming out of the background of the suzerainty covenant was the covenant speech or proclamation (message). The basic structure of this type included: a recital of the beneficent acts of the sovereign Lord, a call to obedience, a proclamation of the basic requirements, a conditional sentence, and a closing declaration (cf. Ex. 19:3–6).

Central to this form was the covenant conditional (the protasis-apodosis construction: if . . . , then . . . ; cf. Ex. 19:5–6—the Hittite suzerainty treaties had the same conditional form). The continuation of the covenant was dependent on the compliance of the people with the basic principle of the covenant (the will of the king) in keeping with the covenantal conditions (if . . . , then . . .).

In Jeremiah the protasis-apodosis structure (covenantal conditional) is employed in a new way.[27] He gives it a new emphasis in a setting of proclamation and exhortation (cf. 2:2—4:4; 4:1–2; 7:1–15; etc). The conditional may be seen in 4:1–2; 7:5–7 (7:1–15 is in the form of a covenant speech, lawsuit variety); 26: 4–6; etc. For the exhortation, see 4:3–4; 7:3–4; etc. (also study 2:2 ff.; 11:1–8 with the covenant pattern in mind).

In both Hosea and Jeremiah the proclamation-exhortation emphasis is particularly present. But the covenantal conditional, in

this context, does not appear in Hosea.

In Jeremiah we have a special speech form employed in proclamation: the prose sermon. This literary type makes its appearance in the seventh century. It is not characteristic of the eighth-century prophets. It abounds in Jeremiah (7:1 ff.; 13: 1–14; 16:1 ff.; 17:19–27; 18:1–12; etc.; cf. also Ezekiel). It is often blended with other forms (cf. chs. 13; 16; 18; 19; 25; 35). It may have been borrowed, in part at least, from the Levites. Its prototype may have been the "law sermon": the exposition of the covenant stipulations and the exhortation to keep them. Of course, all of this—the prose sermon, the covenant speech, the covenantal conditional, the lawsuit pattern—became connected with the covenant and cult.

From the cult Jeremiah borrowed the lament—individual (4:19–22; 8:18—9:1; 11:18—12:6; 15:10–21; etc.) and communal (8:14–17; 10:19–23; 14:7–10, 19–22; etc.). The lament was a prayer in a time of stress and strain.

The form of the individual lament often included several of the following: a cry to Yahweh for a hearing, a complaint of distress, a prayer for help, an expression of trust, a protestation of innocence and a cursing of the adversary or a confession of sin and a petition for pardon, various observations, confidence that the prayer would be heard, a vow of thanksgiving for the answer, and, occasionally, a divine oracle in response (an oracle is a divine "word," usually short and poetic in form).

The communal lament was concerned with the needs of the group—congregation, city, or country. Central to its structure were: an impassioned complaint over wrongs experienced, a recalling of God's former favor, an expression of confidence in God's ability to help his people in their extremity, a protestation of innocence, an affirmation (sometimes) of loyalty to the Lord as the cause of the trouble, a vow of thanksgiving for God's response to the plea, and, occasionally, a divine oracle.

From the cult came the liturgy (cf.

[27] James Muilenburg, "Form and Structure of Covenant Stipulations," VT, 9, 1959, 45–365.

3:21—4:4; 14:1—15:4). A liturgy is an arrangement for a dialogue in worship. It includes prescribed rites to be used by leader and congregation. Although there is the possibility that on occasion Jeremiah functioned as cultic prophet, the probability is that he did not and that in his use of the liturgy, as of other cultic forms, he was borrowing, imitating, and adapting. These are not pure cultic forms such as would be employed for liturgical purposes. Instead, they are broken, incomplete, modified to serve the prophet's ends.

Jeremiah shows acquaintance with the ideals and methods of the sages. Evidence of this may be seen in the stylistic form of the accounts of the "visions" in 1:11–16 (cf. 24:1 ff.), in the presence of wisdom sayings (e.g., 17:9,11; 23:23 f.), in the wisdom psalm in 17:5–8, in the stress on the two ways (cf. 21:8–10), etc.

From everyday life came the popular proverb (e.g., 8:20; 31:29), possibly a snatch from a drinking song (13:12), and the dirge (cf. 2:2–3; 22:10; 22:20–23; etc.). The funeral dirge was originally sung at the bier of the deceased by the professional women mourners or by family members and friends to the accompaniment of the flute. It usually dwelt, among other things, on the beauty of the person in life and his bleak appearance in death.

The dirge came to be applied to the "death" of groups (a city, a tribe, a nation). Like the other prophets (e.g., Amos 5:2–3), Jeremiah pressed it into the service of God in portraying the coming destruction of the country, representing the "death" as a reality, though the demise had not yet taken place. The dirge, or funeral song, had a sorrowful tone and a distinctive rhythm familiar to all. When it was used, it had a sobering and sometimes terrifying effect on the people.

We might also mention a few other types which appear in Jeremiah: the monologue (e.g., 3:6–10), the dialogue (e.g., 1:4–16; 5:1–9; 6:9–15; etc.), lyric poetry (e.g., parts of 4:5–31 and elsewhere), prophetic reflection (e.g., 5:1 ff.),

hymn (e.g., 10:6–16), psalm (e.g., 20:13), and possibly satire (e.g., 10:1 ff.).

As one studies the prophecy of Jeremiah, he is made aware that the prophet's strong sense of call and his deep consciousness of a divinely given message did not rob him of his freedom and ability to employ an amazingly rich variety of literary forms from many realms of life in the proclamation of that message. The degree of his adaptation and development of these forms for communication purposes bears eloquent testimony to the strength of his mind, the breadth of his experience, the depth of his dedication, and the reality and vitality of his inspiration.

There is also evidence that Baruch was a gifted, influential, well-trained professional scribe, who was steeped in the covenant faith and who was eminently capable of accurate reporting and excellent editing and composing.[28]

3. Textual, Historical, and Literary Concerns

The prophecy of Jeremiah presents numerous textual, historical, and literary problems. There is no agreement among scholars as to the solutions of these problems. All a commentator can do is to evaluate the evidence to the best of his ability and reach his own conclusion as to the most sensible and tenable position to be taken. This he must do in order to make his commentary meaningful.

(1) Textual

Quite a few textual problems appear in Jeremiah. For a detailed treatment of these the reader is referred to the longer, more technical commentaries (e.g., Bright and Weiser).

There is, however, one particular problem of unusual interest: the differences between the Masoretic Text (MT) and the Septuagint (LXX). They are mainly two. First, the LXX is about one-eighth

---

28 See Muilenburg, "Baruch the Scribe," eds. Durham and Porter, op. cit., pp. 231–238.

shorter than the MT. The most outstanding omissions are: 8:10b–12; 10:6–8,10; 17:1–5a; 29:16–20; 33:14–26; 39:4–13; 52:28–30. Normally the LXX leaves out doublets on their second appearance (a doublet is a passage which appears twice in the book). The reasons for the omissions are not always clear. The second major difference between the LXX and the MT is that the foreign prophecies appear in chapters 46—51 in the MT and after 25:13a in the LXX (and in a different order). There is a sharp difference of opinion as to which was the original position of the prophecies and why the divergence took place.

The preference of many scholars for the LXX arrangement is based primarily on two things. First, the order of the nations corresponds more closely to that in the list in 25:19–26 and to the alleged chronology of the history of those nations. Second, the traditional eschatological scheme is preserved (condemnation of Israel/denunciation and destruction of the pagan nations/salvation of Israel).

Both arguments are somewhat weak and contradictory. If the before/after schema (ethically unconditioned) was the determining principle in compilation, there would scarcely have been great concern about chronology and history. On the other hand, it is highly improbable that the compiler of the materials in Jeremiah would interrupt his composition by injecting so lengthy a unit as chapters 46—51 after 25:13a, or that he would conclude it with Baruch's complaint and God's challenge in 45:1–5. Moreover, Jeremiah's heavy stress on judgment as a moral necessity and as a preparation for the realization of God's salvation offers a tenable reason for the presence of chapters 46—51 at the end of the book. There had to be a tearing down (on the either/or basis of Jeremiah) before there could be a building up.

The arrangement in the LXX is quite arbitrary and can be explained by the desire of the translators to bring this major prophet into line with the pattern in the other two, Isaiah and Ezekiel. So, the MT likely has the original order.

Allowance must be made for the possibility that the LXX translators had an Egyptian recension of the text which was different at points from the Hebrew prototype.

(2) *Historical*

The date of the beginning of Jeremiah's ministry poses a problem for some. They object to the chronological note in 1:2 (cf. 25:3) on two major grounds: the alleged lack of Jeremianic material from the reign of Josiah, and the felt need to synchronize the prophet's predictions with the rapid rise of the Neo-Babylonian Empire. They attempt to solve the problem through emendation or tenuous suggestion and get Jeremiah started about 617 or 612 to 609 B.C.

The emendations and suggestions are without solid support. Along with most scholars, we accept the date given in 1:2 (627) as the time of the beginning of Jeremiah's career.

Another problem of historical nature is that of the identity of the enemy from the north (cf. 4:5—6:30). Several solutions have been proposed. Among these are the Scythian hypothesis, the eschatological interpretation, the Chaldean (Neo-Babylonian) identification, and the revision theory.[29]

The present writer's position is that Jeremiah began his ministry with the conviction that, barring a radical repentance, divine judgment was coming upon Judah in the form of an invasion of the land by a foe from the north (1:13–16). Jeremiah considered the proclamation of this conviction a primary part of his responsibility as a prophet. The conviction was certainly

29 For a discussion of the different views, see A. C. Welch, *Jeremiah His Time and Work* (Oxford: Blackwell, 1951), pp. 97–131; H. H. Rowley, *Men of God* (London: Thomas Nelson & Sons, 1963), pp. 140–153; Guy P. Couturier, "Jeremiah," JBC (Englewood Cliffs: Prentice-Hall, 1968), pp. 309 f.

central to his message throughout his ministry.

At the outset he did not identify the particular agent to be used by God (cf. 1:13–16; 4:5—6:30). He may have had the Neo-Babylonians in mind (von Rad, p. 194). However, it is perhaps better to assume that he had no specific people in mind at first (Lauha, Volz, Rudolph, Leslie, Couturier, Fohrer). In any case, the name of the foe was not Jeremiah's primary concern. He had a deep existential awareness of crisis and imminent catastrophe and was seeking to call his people to repentance.

A careful reading of the poems will reveal not only that he used a great deal of conventional and traditional language in his portrayal of the invader, but also that his chief stress was not on the identity of the enemy but on the moral indictment of the people. The real foe was God. He was going to bring retribution out of the north upon the Israelites because of their persistent rebellion against him. This Jeremiah knew. How much more he knew we do not know.

Later, following the fall of Nineveh (612 B.C.) and constantly after Carchemish (605), he spoke specifically and openly of Babylon as the enemy from the north and of Nebuchadnezzar as God's "servant." He maintained this position with great courage and at tremendous cost until finally the city and the country fell before the armed might of Babylon in 587 (cf. Bright, p. lxxxii; Leslie, p. 51).

A third problem of historical character is that of the relation of Jeremiah to the Josianic reformation. There have been two extreme views on the subject: first, Jeremiah had no sympathy for the movement and gave it no support (Duhm, Hyatt, May); second, he was a legalist and backed the reform from start to finish (Winckler). The truth likely lies between these extremes (Rudolph, Weiser, Eissfeldt, Rowley).[30]

[30] The writer has already stated his position on the matter; for a detailed discussion, see Rowley, *From Moses to Qumran*, pp. 187–208.

(3) Literary

The problem just cited brings up another, the problem of the relationship of the prophet and prophecy to Deuteronomy. There are obvious parallels between Jeremiah and Deuteronomy. These parallels are present in various parts of the book but are most prominent in the prose portions. They are especially noticeable in the "prose sermons" (Mowinckel's Type C).

This intricate problem has been approached in various ways. Some have said that Jeremiah wrote Deuteronomy. Others have suggested that Deuteronomy was composed after Jeremiah and was influenced by it. Neither of these positions has gained much support. Still others have maintained that Jeremiah was edited by Deuteronomists during the exilic or postexilic period, setting it in the context of the Deuteronomic theology and seeking to gain the prophet's support for their principles and program. The result was a serious distortion of Jeremiah's message.

This is probably the most crucial literary problem in the book. Its importance will be realized when one recognizes that the prose sermons include some of the greatest passages in the prophecy (e.g., the "temple sermon" in 7:1 ff. and the epoch-making "new covenant passage" in 31:31–34) and that the position taken will radically affect his understanding and appraisal of Jeremiah.

It is being increasingly recognized today that the so-called "Deuteronomic prose style" was the prose style of the seventh and sixth centuries B.C. It was not confined to the Deuteronomic literature. Jeremiah must have spoken in prose, at least occasionally (Shakespeare and Milton did!). It is reasonable to conclude that when he did he spoke in the prose style of his day.

A further factor should be introduced. Through study and worship Jeremiah was probably trained in and influenced by the Deuteronomic terminology, theology, and expository style—both before and after 622 B.C. When he broke with the Josianic reform, he was not breaking with the Mosaic faith as expounded in Deuteronomy and revived in 622. He was breaking with a distortion of it.

Eissfeldt holds to the Jeremianic origin of the prose sermons and includes many of them in the scroll of 605–604 (pp. 352 f.). Weiser also maintains their genuineness and finds the *Sitz im Leben* of their prose style in liturgical exhortations for the edification of the people. Rudolph posits the existence of a Jeremianic prose preserving the prophet's own words, but assigns the material in written form to the Deuteronomists (his list—somewhat shorter than Mowinckel's—includes: 7:1—8:3; 11:1–14; 16:1–13; 17:19–27; 18:1–12; 21:1–10; 22:1–5; 25:1–14; 34:8–22; 35).

John Bright has made a thorough study of the problem of the prose sermons of Jeremiah. Through a careful analysis of the entire group of passages involved (much larger than that of Rudolph or Mowinckel), and through a close examination of the stylistic characteristics and historical allusions in them and a comparison of them with the rest of the book, he has arrived at certain sound conclusions. First, the style of the prose sermons is homogeneous. Second, the style is not peculiar to Jeremiah or to Deuteronomy but is very similar to the prose style of the day. Third, it is therefore not late. In fact, its greatest affinities are not with later literature but with earlier literature. Fourth, though there are similarities between the prose of Jeremiah and that of Deuteronomy, there are also striking differences. Jeremiah had a prose style in his own right. Fifth, the presence of a strong "eyewitness flavor" indicates the existence of a "Jeremiah" prose tradition during the prophet's lifetime and incorporated in the book by the biographer before or shortly after his death. Sixth, the Jeremiah of the prose passages is not essentially different from the Jeremiah of the poetry.[31]

It may be added that recent study by men like Notscher, Bright, Holladay, and Weiser is showing that some of the "prose" may actually be poetry (e.g., 16:1 ff.) and that there are links in phraseology and ideas between the prose sermons and the poetical and other prose portions of the book. Much remains to be done in this area.

To conclude, the prose sermons of Jeremiah are precisely that. They have been passed on to us, in the providence of God, by a second party (probably Baruch), though some of them are set in an autobiographical framework. They are reliable. Any attempt to recover the *ipsissima verba* of the prophet by removing from the prose sections what one believes to be an addition or expansion or alteration (by the biographer or anyone else) is a highly subjective enterprise, not necessarily sound scholarship. Moreover, it is not necessary. It is a bit like trying to discover the exact words of Jesus in a statement made by him but reported in slightly different phraseology by two or more of the Gospel writers. What we have is God's word, to be received, interpreted, and applied by us to the best of our ability, using all the helps we can get, including the help of the Holy Spirit.

There is a problem of doublets. An unusual number of them appear in Jeremiah.[32] Some of these will be noted in the commentary.

There are two types, the real and the alleged. The real doublets are cases of the actual occurrence of a passage in two places in the book, e.g., 23:19–20 and 30:23–24. The alleged doublets are instances where some scholars think there are duplicate accounts of the same speech or incident, e.g., 2:3–7 and 3:4–11; 37:11–21 and 38:1 ff. Of the latter group, this writer is skeptical. He sees the dissimilarities as well as the similarities, and has no aversion to the notion that the prophet could have had essentially the same experience or spoken on the same

---

31 John Bright, "The Date of the Prose Sermons of Jeremiah," JBL, 70, 1950, pp. 15–35.

32 A list may be found in S. R. Driver's *Introduction to the Literature of the Old Testament* (New York: Charles Scribner's Sons, 1913), p. 277.

subject more than once. The doublets of the first type probably say more about the method of transmission than anything else.

There is one very unusual "doublet." Jacob Alting first set forth the view in 1687 that chapters 7 and 26 deal with the same incident. This is now almost universally accepted. This doublet is in a separate category and sheds much light on a number of things.

There is the problem of the authenticity of certain passages (other than the prose sermons). It would be impossible to present here a list of all the different passages questioned by all the scholars past and present, let alone enter into a discussion of them. Quite a few scholars delete as secondary 3:14*b*–18; 5:18–19; 9:12–16; 10:1–16; 16:10–13; 17:19–27; 18:7–12; 23:5–8,34–40; 25:27–33; varying portions of 30—33; and parts or all of 46—51. Some attention will be given to such passages in the commentary. The dominant view today is to minimize the number of later additions to the prophecy.

4. The Composition of the Book

We are told that Jeremiah dictated his prophecies to Baruch in 605 B.C. (36:1 ff.). The first edition was destroyed and a new one brought out in 604 (36: 9 ff.). It is stated that many words "were added to them," i.e., to the words dictated at first (36:32). These words may have been added then or later or both.

This second scroll represents the first formal stage in the composition of Jeremiah. Unfortunately we do not have a copy of it. In all probability it has been incorporated within chapters 1—25, with chapter 1 as an authentication and introduction and 25:1 ff. as a conclusion. Beyond that it is difficult to go without becoming involved in pure guesswork.

Scholars have made valiant and intelligent efforts to discover the contents of the scroll (cf. Eissfeldt, pp. 350–354). All such efforts, however scholarly and sincere, are necessarily hypothetical, though they may be both interesting and helpful.

The reader may note that the words "everything written in this book, which Jeremiah prophesied against all nations" appear in 25:13 (cf. 36:2). Allusion is made to a "book" in 51:60. Chapters 46—51 contain a collection of oracles concerning foreign countries. Jeremiah may have written out or dictated these prophecies— or parts thereof—in 604 and later. Though it is possible, as some think, that they circulated as a separate collection for a season, they could be among the "many similar words" added to the scroll of 604.

Mention is made in Jeremiah of one other "book" (30:2). It has to do with the prophecies of hope and salvation found in chapters 30—33. These prophecies— insofar as they are Jeremianic—could have been included also, but rather late in the prophet's career.

We come therefore to a second major stage in the story of the formation of the book. It has to do with the work of Baruch. It is this writer's conclusion, shared by many others, that in addition to whatever else he did as scribe and compiler, Baruch was also biographer (cf. Bright, Eissfeldt, Koch, von Rad, Westermann, Muilenburg, Fohrer, Kuhl, Hyatt, et al.). He likely added to the scroll which he took down by dictation in 604 other prophecies of Jeremiah delivered after that time, including parts of chapters 2—25 and the prophecies mentioned above. But he also produced a work of his own, already referred to as "the first biography" of a prophet or anybody else in Israel. Although this cannot be proved, he is the most logical candidate for the task. His story is that of the suffering of the prophet in the service of God, beginning with the Temple episode in 609 (ch. 26) and going down to 587 and beyond (43:3). His narratives are chiefly found in chapters 19; 20; 21; 26—29; 34—45. Interwoven with them are prophecies of various types (cf. chs. 27; 28; 29; 34; 35; etc.).

It is impossible to know how much of the composing and compiling was done by Baruch and how much by Jeremiah, when and where it was done, and on what basis it was done. The position accepted here is that Baruch gave the book its essential present structure.[33] The reasons for making additions at particular places probably varied. Sometimes it was topical, sometimes chronological. At times a key word may have caused the placing of passages in juxtaposition (cf. Bright's imaginary account of how all this may have happened, pp. lxxvii f.).

Apparently there was a third stage during the Exile, a final redaction, at which time there were additions of various types (cf. ch. 52). These were not nearly so numerous or so different as some have supposed. Any additions made do not represent distortion but adaptation.

Our knowledge of the methods of compilation and transmission of the prophetic materials is so limited that it is actually impossible to be very specific or dogmatic about such matters. That the book is a compilation is obvious. No one really knows when, where, and by whom the prophecy of Jeremiah was put in its present form. It is difficult to find two scholars who agree completely on the process of composition. This means that we should approach the subject with humility, intelligence, and care.

The really important thing is that we have the book. It was given by inspiration of God. It has within it the divine word for our day (as well as Jeremiah's), if we will allow the Spirit to communicate it to us.

Outline

[33] Volz regarded Baruch as responsible for chs. 1—45 (he designated 46—51 a later work). P. P. Saydon considers chs. 1—45 to be the parallel work of Jeremiah (1—25) and Baruch (26—36, 37—45), "Il libro di Geremia. Strutura e composizione," *Rivista Biblica*, 5, 1957, 141–162.

Library of
Calvary Baptist Church
Alton, Illinois

Selected Bibliography

ANDERSON, B. W., and HARRELSON, WALTER, eds. *Israel's Prophetic Heritage.* New York: Harper & Row, 1962.

BRIGHT, JOHN. *Jeremiah,* "The Anchor Bible." New York: Doubleday & Company, Inc., 1965.

BUTTRICK, GEORGE A., ed. *The Interpreter's Dictionary of the Bible.* Vols. I–IV. New York: Abingdon Press, 1962.

CUNLIFFE-JONES, H. *Jeremiah,* "The Torch Bible Commentaries." New York: The Macmillan Company, 1961.

CLEMENTS, R. E. *Prophecy and Covenant.* London: SCM Press, 1965.

EISSFELDT, OTTO. *The Old Testament.* Trans. Peter Ackroyd. New York: Harper & Row, 1965.

HYATT, J. PHILIP, and HOPPER, STANLEY R. "Jeremiah," *The Interpreter's Bible,* Vol. V. New York: Abingdon Press, 1956.

LESLIE, E. A. *Jeremiah.* New York: Abingdon Press, 1954.

LINDBLOM, JOHANNES. *Prophecy in Ancient Israel.* Philadelphia: Muhlenberg Press, 1962.

MORGAN, G. C. *Studies in the Prophecy of Jeremiah.* New York: Fleming H. Revell Company, 1931.

PEAKE, A. S. "Jeremiah and Lamentations," *The New Century Bible.* Edinburgh: T. C. & B. C. Jack, 1910.

RUDOLPH, WILHELM. *Jeremia*. Tubingen: Mohr, 1958.

SKINNER, JOHN. *Prophecy and Religion*. Cambridge: University Press, 1926.

SMITH, G. A. *Jeremiah*. New York: Harper & Brothers, 1929.

STREANE, A. W. *Jeremiah and Lamentations*, "The Cambridge Bible." Cambridge: The University Press, 1926.

VOLZ, PAUL. *Jeremia*. Leipzig: Deichert, 1922.

VON RAD, GERHARD. *Old Testament Theology*, Vol. II. Trans. D. M. G. Stalker. New York: Harper & Row, 1965.

WEISER, ARTUR. *Das Buch des Propheten Jeremia*. Göttingen: Vandenhoeck and Ruprecht, 1955.

Commentary on the Text

The Preface (1:1–3)

¹ **The words of Jeremiah, the son of Hilkiah, of the priests who were in Anathoth in the land of Benjamin, ² to whom the word of the LORD came in the days of Josiah the son of Amon, king of Judah, in the thirteenth year of his reign. ³ It came also in the days of Jehoiakim the son of Josiah, king of Judah, and until the end of the eleventh year of Zedekiah, the son of Josiah, king of Judah, until the captivity of Jerusalem in the fifth month.**

The first three verses of chapter 1 serve as a preface or title page for the first chapter and also for the chapters which follow. The preface shows signs of having been expanded as the size of the book increased. It provides important information concerning the prophet. It gives his name and the name of his hometown, states that he was of priestly descent, and indicates that he exercised his ministry in Judah over a period of four decades (627–587 B.C.).

The primary function of the preface, however, is to set forth a central emphasis of the book: God speaks to men through men, and what he says he does—*The words of Jeremiah, . . . to whom the word of the Lord came.* Over and over we find in Jeremiah such statements as: "The word of the Lord came to me" and "Thus said the Lord to me."

The Hebrew term *dabar* may be translated either "word" or "deed." This fact illustrates the dynamic conception which the Hebrews had of the "word." Once spoken, it could not be recalled. It became an objective entity, endowed with energy from the speaker which propelled it toward actualization—hence the close connection between word and act. The uttering of the word was an event.

Since the preface covers both the record of Jeremiah's utterances and the account of various incidents in his life, the initial phrase *the words of Jeremiah* might be freely rendered "the story of Jeremiah" (cf. Moffatt). The important thing here is the stress on the reality and the vitality of the word of God which comes to men through men in specific life situations and which is decisive in those situations. Observe the striking repetition of the word *until* in v. 3.

I. The Prophet's Call and Consecration (1:4–19)

The remainder of the first chapter is a literary unit with a central theme. It is in the form of a call account. The account contains the prophet's own story of the crucial experience which in large measure explains his remarkable career and contribution as a servant of God.

1. Divine Call Through Ecstatic Vision (1:4–10)

Lindblom states that "without doubt Jeremiah's experience was . . . ecstatic and visionary" (p. 189). It is important to note that, though the experience recounted in vv. 4–10 was visionary, the ecstatic elements are not played up in it. When the record of Jeremiah's call is compared with that of Isaiah or Ezekiel, it becomes obvious that the former is marked by modesty and simplicity. It is different, deep, dynamic. This has serious implications for the spiritual pilgrimage of the prophet and for our understanding of his ministry and message.

We are dealing, then, with a firsthand account of a divine-human encounter. In all probability, the encounter does not take place in the sanctuary but in some ordinary spot. Assuming the initiative, God accosts Jeremiah and says in effect: "I've had my eye on you for a long time. I have something for you to do."

The vision begins as an audition and quickly takes the form of a dialogue. The implication is that it is quite natural for God and man to have conversation with each other. This communion with God is central in Jeremiah's conception of what religion is all about.

(1) God's Revelation of His Purpose (1:4–5)

4 Now the word of the LORD came to me saying,
5 "Before I formed you in the womb I knew you,
  and before you were born I consecrated you;
  I appointed you a prophet to the nations."

The dialogue is introduced by the "revelation formula" (v. 4). Jeremiah is likely engaged in prayer when *the word of the Lord* becomes an active, living reality to him. God declares: *I knew you.* The word know in Hebrew does not signify primarily academic (or cultic) head knowledge, but dynamic, heart knowledge —i.e., the kind of knowledge that comes from firsthand contact between two persons or parties. The one knowing unites with or appropriates that which he knows (cf. Gen. 4:1; Amos 3:2). Since God is God, he can know that which has not yet come into being and can create that which he knows.

Recent study of ancient international treaties or covenants has added a new dimension to the meaning of "know" (*yada'*). At times, in the Akkadian and

Hittite texts, it signifies on the part of the suzerain the recognition of the subject or vassal as his legitimate servant to whom alone he has given the covenant or treaty —hence, recognize, care for, or choose. From the subject's standpoint, it means the recognition of one legitimate suzerain and of the binding character of the treaty or covenant stipulations—hence, acknowledge, recognize, or be subject or loyal to.[34]

In the present context, the word means that God has thought about, been intimately aware of, cared for, and chosen Jeremiah since before his birth.

God continues: *I formed you.* This verb is used of the craftsman, and the picture is that of a potter shaping a vessel (cf. Gen. 2:7). While yet in his mother's womb, Jeremiah was being fashioned by God for special service.

A third thing is said about God's activity prior to Jeremiah's appearance on the human scene: *I consecrated you.* Used only here of a prophet in the Old Testament, this expression means "I set you apart for a special function or mission." The concept of holiness is wrapped up in the verb. Holiness is something which has to do with God (his Godhead) or with someone or something belonging exclusively to God or directly related to him in some way. God places total claim upon Jeremiah's entire being for that which he has in mind for him to do.

Jeremiah's mission is to be a mission to mankind: *a prophet to the nations* is emphatic in Hebrew and does not overstate the case. Jeremiah is to serve as the divinely appointed messenger from the heavenly court to an age in ferment. The international situation is such in his day that to preach at all is to preach to or about his nation and the nations. This is precisely what he does (cf. chs. 25; 27; 36; 46—51), as others had done before him (cf. Amos 1—2; Isa. 13—23). He does it as

---

[34] Cf. D. R. Hillers, *Covenant: The History of a Biblical Idea* (Baltimore: Johns Hopkins Press, 1969), pp. 120–124; H. H. Huffmon, "The Treaty Background of Hebrew Yada'," BASOR, 181, 1966, pp. 31–37.

the accredited spokesman of the sovereign Lord of world history. He knows that God is ruler of all nature and all nations and that the destinies of all peoples are in his hands (Lindblom, pp. 332, 270). The book throughout bears witness to his awareness of this great commission.

(2) Jeremiah's Response (1:6)

⁶ Then I said, "Ah, Lord GOD! Behold, I do not know how to speak, for I am only a youth."

Jeremiah's reaction is recoil. There is a certain inner reluctance (cf. Ex. 3–4). He exclaims: *Ah, Lord God!* This is a sharp ejaculation of awe and anguish. It is not so much the expression of a longing to change things as a lamentation over the fact that they are as they are.

The word for *youth*—unfortunately rendered "child" in some versions—is not to be pressed too literally. It ordinarily denotes a young, unmarried man in his teens or early twenties. Most scholars think that Jeremiah was around 20 to 25 at the time of his call.

It was customary in local assemblies in those days for young men not yet married to keep quiet, while the heads of households did the talking. The primary reference in Jeremiah's reply to God, however, is not to his social status or chronological age but to a deep sense of inadequacy. In his cry of weakness (not unwillingness) he discloses two things: his consciousness of inferiority and inexperience and his awareness of the size of the task to which God is summoning him. Here is a prime prerequisite of effective service for God. It is the person most aware of his own insufficiency who will usually be most dependent upon God's all-sufficiency.

As one reads the account of Jeremiah's call, he begins to sense something new stirring, something struggling toward the surface, something which marks a sort of turning point in Hebrew prophecy. On the one hand, there is in Jeremiah the almost overwhelming conviction that God has set him apart to be his messenger. But also there is in him a strong consciousness of his

humanity, his existence as a human being. At times there is a terrific tension between the two: divine compulsion and human inclination. Jeremiah gets caught in the distress and dilemmas of inner conflict, and he speaks about it to God—sometimes in a very daring manner (cf. his confessions). To his cries God replies.

Jeremiah's relationship to God, therefore, is one of dialogue. Prayer becomes a prime factor in it. At times we see him on his knees, as it were, struggling with God in prayer over the problems that so painfully perplex him. At other times we behold him on his feet, speaking for God in fearless proclamation of his word. A foreshadowing of this new element in prophetic experience we find in the record of Jeremiah's call, especially in the response he makes to God in v. 6.

(3) God's Rejoinder (1:7–10)

⁷ But the LORD said to me,
"Do not say, 'I am only a youth';
    for to all whom I send you you shall go,
    and whatever I command you you shall
        speak.
⁸   Be not afraid of them,
    for I am with you to deliver you,
                        says the LORD."
⁹ Then the LORD put forth his hand and touched my mouth; and the LORD said to me, "Behold, I have put my words in your mouth.
¹⁰   See, I have set you this day over nations
        and over kingdoms,
    to pluck up and to break down,
    to destroy and to overthrow,
    to build and to plant."

Verses 7–10 deal with two things: the preparation of the prophet and the portrayal of the nature and scope of his work. First, God speaks of the preparation of the prophet (vv. 7–9). Whom God calls he always equips. Three elements in Jeremiah's equipment are here specified.

The first is a conviction of divine authority (v. 7). God speaks in this vein: "Jeremiah, you are not to concern yourself greatly with where you preach or what you are to say when you preach or whether you are equal to the responsibility of preaching. You are under orders now—

a conscript! Your obligation is to obey. The remainder is to be left with me." God's servants in our day also need a strong conviction that the ministry exercised is based upon and backed by divine authority.

The second element in the prophet's equipment is a consciousness of the divine presence (v. 8). God continues: "Be not afraid by reason of their faces" (lit. rendering). Faces there will be—empty faces, hard faces, bored faces, indifferent faces, antagonistic faces, leering faces. But Jeremiah is not to fear these faces (i.e., not to be afraid in the presence of his opponents), *for I am with you to deliver you, says the Lord.* The Hebrew emphasizes God's presence with Jeremiah. God may be stern in dealing with his servant. In effect he says, "You must go on my terms, not yours." He may assign his servant a difficult task. But he *never* sends forth his servant alone (cf. Matt. 28:20). Here is the source of the servant's security and strength.

The third part of the prophet's preparation is the communication of the divine word (v. 9). Here is the most concrete evidence of the ecstatic character of Jeremiah's call. God puts forth his hand and touches the mouth of the young man, saying, *Behold, I have put my words in your mouth* (cf. Isa. 6:7; Ezek. 2:8; 3:3; Dan. 10:16). The touch of the hand is not so much to purify, as in Isaiah's case—though this is not excluded—as it is to inspire and empower. It is symbolic of the bestowal of the gift of prophecy.

The touch of God's hand is the supreme qualification of the prophet in any generation. His primary responsibility is the proclamation of the divine word. He receives it from God. He communicates it to the people for God.

The initial dialogue ends with a portrayal of the scope and nature of the prophet's work (v. 10). First, God tells Jeremiah that his ministry is to be extensive in its reach: *See, I have set you this day over nations and over kingdoms*— i.e., "I have made you my overseer, my deputy, my representative with authority to proclaim my purpose and the principles of my government, by which the destinies of the peoples of the earth are determined." What a powerful representation of the range and responsibility of the prophet's task!

Second, God informs Jeremiah that his ministry is to be destructive in its near-term objective. At the close of v. 10 are six infinitives. The first four are concerned with the work of destruction. In the four infinitives, there are only two figures of speech. Jeremiah is to pull up and allow to perish all evil growths not of God's planting. He is to pull down and pulverize all structures not of God's building. He is to be a prophet of judgment.

Third, God indicates to Jeremiah that his ministry is to be constructive in the end result. There are two infinitives which depict the work of construction. The same two figures are present: *to build and to plant.* It is not enough for a prophet to deal in "the destruction of the devilish." He must have a positive program to present. A certain motto reads: "We can wreck anything." That may be an appropriate motto for a demolition crew, but it is not appropriate for the prophet of God, for he is not to be altogether a specialist in the wrecking business. He is to pluck up and pull down in order *to build and to plant.*

Jeremiah is to be not only a prophet of judgment but also a prophet of salvation. He would lay the foundation for a new faith and plant new conceptions of God, religion, and life. He would have a part in preparing God's people for the coming crisis, the restoration, and the new age.

There is an unusually heavy emphasis on the word of the Lord in vv. 4–10. It is something which becomes a dynamic subjective reality to the recipient. It also has an objective character. God communicates it to the prophet. The prophet proclaims it to the people. It will effect judgment. It will also bring salvation. There is always this twofold activity of the divine word.

The prophet's first responsibility is faithfully to preach that word.

2. Divine Communication Through Symbolic Perception (1:11–16)

This section is dynamically related to the passage preceding it. It records two inaugural "visions": the vision of the blossoming almond branch and the vision of the boiling pot.

Scholars are in disagreement as to the date and nature of the experiences here described. Some think that considerable time elapsed between the call and the visions (e.g., Bright, p. 7). Others have a different view. Hyatt observes: "The present position of the two visions in the book suggests that they probably came to Jeremiah at the time of his call or in the days which immediately followed" (pp. 805 f.). We believe that Hyatt is right.

It is customary to refer to the experiences in vv. 11–16 as visions. In a sense, they are. In another, they are not. They are symbolic perceptions (von Rad, p. 66; Lindblom, pp. 139 f.). The difference between the symbolic perception and the vission is that the former has a basis in outward reality, whereas the latter does not. In the former, one beholds a material object with his natural eye, and it becomes the medium of revelation. In the latter, that which takes place transpires entirely in the inner realm, and that which is seen is seen only with the inner eye. In either case, something is "seen." There is insight. There *is* revelation.

(1) The Blossoming Almond Branch (1:11–12)

11 And the word of the Lord came to me, saying, "Jeremiah, what do you see?" And I said, "I see a rod of almond." 12 Then the Lord said to me, "You have seen well, for I am watching over my word to perform it."

The introductory formula here is the same as in vv. 4 and 13. The stylistic form employed in recounting the experience is one likely influenced in some way by the teaching methods of the wisdom schools (cf. question–answer–elaboration pattern).

Perhaps Jeremiah went for a walk one day in the vicinity of Anathoth. It was late winter. Possibly he was meditating upon his recent experience of call and upon conditions prevalent in his country. There was corruption everywhere. It seemed that God was completely inactive. God had promised to do something about the situation nearly a century earlier through the preaching of some of the great prophets. Yet nothing had happened. And now God was calling him to a titanic task. How could he face it? What would he say? The landscape outstretching before him was in harmony with the tone and temper of his thoughts. Deadness all about—was God also dead? Perish the thought! Remember the call! But was he not at least unconcerned or unable to correct the situation?

Jeremiah may have found himself gazing intently at an almond branch beginning to burst into bloom. The word of the Lord came: *Jeremiah, what do you see?* The young man replied: *A rod* (twig) *of almond* (cf. marg.). To this God responded, *I am watching* (cf. marg.) *over my word to perform it.* There is a powerful wordplay in this passage. The Hebrew term was sometimes used to designate the almond as the "wake-tree." It was called this because it was the first to awake out of the long winter's sleep. Its flowers appeared before its foliage (cf. our peach or cherry tree)—sometimes as early as January. A blossoming almond was the early token of spring.

God's response to Jeremiah's reply to his question is quite arresting: "Awake continually am (*shaqed*) I over my word to perform it." *Word* is God's ethical purpose. More specifically, it is likely the prophetic word of judgment upon Judah for her sin, uttered by Isaiah and Micah in the eighth century. By implication it probably includes the word to be received and proclaimed by Jeremiah.

Thus an ordinary sight along some country lane became the medium of an extraordinary insight. There is a conceptual connection, as well as an impressive assonance, in the paronomasia (a play on words). The "wake-tree" suggested the God who is awake. The same God who is awake in the realm of nature, as shown by the blossoming almond branch, is also awake in the realm of history, watching over his word to carry it out.[35]

The truth communicated in this striking way was one that would stand Jeremiah in good stead throughout his long and stormy ministry. It was a word of assurance and hope. If he faithfully communicated the divine word, God would watch over him and it. We need the same stabilizing assurance today. God is not emeritus. He is certainly not dead. This is his world, and he is very much awake and at work in it, watching over his purpose to perform it.

(2) A Boiling Pot (1:13-16)

13 The word of the LORD came to me a second time, saying, "What do you see?" And I said, "I see a boiling pot, facing away from the north." 14 Then the LORD said to me, "Out of the north evil shall break forth upon all the inhabitants of the land. 15 For, lo, I am calling all the tribes of the kingdoms of the north, says the LORD; and they shall come and every one shall set his throne at the entrance of the gates of Jerusalem, against all its walls round about, and against all the cities of Judah. 16 And I will utter my judgments against them, for all their wickedness in forsaking me; they have burned incense to other gods, and worshiped the works of their own hands.

The experience here is somewhat similar and supplementary to the first. Possibly on the same walk Jeremiah may have observed a pot such as was usually present somewhere about a Hebrew house—probably a fairly large, wide-mouthed wash pot or cooking pot.[36]

The pot was resting on rocks on three sides. The other side was open, so that fuel might be placed under the pot and the fire might get air. The unusual thing about this pot was that it was not level. Its face (lip, opening) was tilted away from the north. It was boiling and might at any moment empty its seething contents in a southerly direction.

As Jeremiah was caught up in his contemplation of this phenomenon, the word of the Lord *came* (happened) to him to ask, literally, "What are you looking at?" He responded that he saw a *boiling* (bubbling) *pot,* turned away from the north. Then God said: *Out of the north evil will break forth* (lit., the evil will be opened) upon all who dwell in the land.[37] Although the details are not completely clear, the picture appears to be that of a boiling pot in the north, tilted in the opposite direction and about to spill its contents southward. The point is apparent. Out of the north God will bring an avalanche of retribution upon his people because of their persistent rebellion against his righteous will, as shown by their constant apostasy and idolatry. *The tribes of the kingdoms of the north* will invade and devastate Judah and Jerusalem and will set up their thrones at the gates of the holy city to inflict proper penalties upon the captives. This is God's sentence upon his people for their breach of their covenant relationship with him.

In this prophecy of disaster to the nation we have Jeremiah's first allusion to one of his basic concepts (cf. Int.) The concept of the coming of an enemy from the north pervades his preaching throughout his prophetic career. Apart from it we cannot understand either his ministry or his message.

The foe is not identified. The entire Fertile Crescent was in ferment. But the north in particular was boiling with possibilities. It "held the forces for the fulfilling of the Word" (Smith, p. 85). It was from there that the trouble would be expected to come. Though Jeremiah may

---

[35] Though contested by Kimchi, Schmidt, Stone, Bright, and others, the interpretation here presented has the support of a host of lexicographers and other scholars: GT, BDB, KB, Keil, Peake, Smith, Streane, Skinner, Robinson, Leslie, Cunliffe-Jones, Harrelson, Hopper, Muilenburg, *et al.*

[36] James L. Kelso, *The Ceramic Vocabulary of the Old Testament* (New Haven: American Schools of Oriental Research, 1948), pp. 27, 48, Fig. 16.

[37] On the textual problem, see G. R. Driver, "Linguistic and Textual Problems: Jeremiah," JQR, 28, 1937-38, 97.

have had in mind the Neo-Babylonians, the important thing was that the real foe was God, who was coming to execute judgment against the whole land and the people in it. And the real revelation in this experience was that God was in control and would use the movements of the nations for the achievement of his purpose.

This was a truth which Jeremiah would greatly need. In a world of crisis and change, it helps to realize that the Lord God omnipotent reigns and that he has a purpose which he is working out in history and which he means to accomplish.

It is interesting to observe that, like the account of the call, the symbolic perceptions are in the form of dialogue. That which was central in Jeremiah's relationship with God and his conception of religion was also one of the cardinal characteristics of his style.

3. Divine Charge Through Admonition and Assurance (1:17–19)

¹⁷ But you, gird up your loins; arise, and say to them everything that I command you. Do not be dismayed by them, lest I dismay you before them. ¹⁸ And I, behold, I make you this day a fortified city, an iron pillar and bronze walls, against the whole land, against the kings of Judah, its princes, its priests, and the people of the land. ¹⁹ They will fight against you; but they shall not prevail against you for I am with you, says the LORD, to deliver you."

The record of the entire call-experience closes with words of challenge and comfort. *But you* (emphatic), *gird up your loins.* God is the speaker. He is saying, "Get ready for strenuous action!" The long robe worn by the Oriental male had to be gathered up about the waist to make possible vigorous exertion (as in running a race). Jeremiah was in for a struggle. Following the charge to gird up his loins, come these words: "Stand up and speak to them (your countrymen, my people) everything which I (emphatic) command you (to speak)." Leave nothing out! In view of the situation and his disposition, Jeremiah might be tempted at this point. The charge continues to paraphrase:

"Don't play the coward before them (lit. be broken down before them), lest I surrender you to the consequences of your cowardice (lit. break you down before them). Your message will cut squarely across the character and conduct of your countrymen. Your ministry will be opposed by kings, governmental personnel, priests, and the people of the land. They will fight against you, but they shall not prevail over you ('Attack you they will; overcome you they can't,' Bright, p. 5), for I am with you to deliver you. Oracle of the Lord, this! And I will make you a fortified city, an iron pillar, and a wall of bronze, a person of such strength that nothing and no one can down you. You aren't that now, but you will be one day."

An attempt has been made through this combination of translation and paraphrase to convey the elements of challenge and comfort in the divine charge in vv. 17–19. Jeremiah was not promised sympathy or success, but suffering and strength—and victory.

The phrase oracle of the Lord, usually translated *says the Lord,* means "whisper of the Lord." The reference is to an intimate, authoritative revelation from God.

Equipped with his call, the two tremendous truths communicated through symbolic perception, and words of divine challenge and comfort, Jeremiah launched out into the hardest, most hopeless, and most heroic ministry of any of the Hebrew prophets.

To sum up, Jeremiah had a distinct call from God. It came in a time of impending world crisis—just the sort of situation requiring a true spokesman for God. It came, in all likelihood, as the consummation of a growing experience which crystallized one day in the conviction, in confrontation with God, that all that had come to him through heredity and environment had worked together under God to get him ready for the tremendous task to which he was being summoned. Moreover, the call took the form of a conversation between God and Jeremiah. It was

accompanied by the communication of
needed insights through experiences of
symbolic perception. It was concluded
with a divine charge, involving both challenge and comfort.

The call was real. The account of it is
not merely the recital of a collection of
cultic texts.[38] It is the record of an authentic encounter with God.

When and why did Jeremiah write out
this record? We do not know. He may
have written it out soon after the event,
or later, and have placed it at the beginning of the original scroll (ch. 36) as the
certification of his right to speak for God.
As the book expanded, it remained in the
same position for the same reason.

It is a dynamic account of a profound
experience which has much to say to us
today. It reminds us that God is alive and
active in his world. He is at work in nature, as seen in the blossoming almond
branch; in history, as is stated in the passage about the boiling pot and elsewhere;
and in the human heart, as is indicated in
his dealings with the young countryman
from Anathoth (1:4 ff.).

God's word is still effective—both in
exposing evil, toppling structures of selfishness, overthrowing the forces of unrighteousness, and also for building faith
in the midst of defeatism and despair.
If the church today is to serve effectively
as God's people in redeeming a broken
and sinful humanity, it must hear and
heed the dual notes of that word: incisive,
shaking criticism of the present and sure,
unshakable hope for the future.

Not only is God at work, but he also
has work for us to do in his world. And
we should be about it.

II. The Prophet's Earliest Preaching (2:1—6:30)

Insofar as we possess it and are able to
pinpoint it, the record of the early preaching of Jeremiah is preserved in chapters
2—6. Most of the material in these chapters can, with reasonable assurance, be
dated in the reign of Josiah (cf. Rudolph,
Lindblom, Couturier, von Rad, Weiser,
Eissfeldt). More specifically, it appears to
come from the period between the prophet's call (627 B.C.) and the Josianic reform (622).

This writer finds no conclusive evidence
against the authenticity of any of the
prophecies in these five chapters. The most
questionable passage is 3:14b–18, but
even in it the imagery employed and the
ideas expressed are not at all out of harmony with Jeremiah's thought and outlook.

It is important to note that there is some
ambiguity in the use of the word Israel in
this section. Sometimes it refers to God's
covenant people in totality. At times it
signifies the Northern Kingdom. At other
times it designates Judah as representative
of the continuing covenant community.[39]

Almost all the material in the section
under consideration is in poetry. It is
poetry of the highest order, marked by
vividness, variety, and vitality. At times
it becomes intensely dramatic and even
takes on lyric and epic qualities. Jeremiah's ability as a poet is matched by his
ingenuity in the use of literary forms current among his countrymen. In 2:1—4:4
the lawsuit motif is predominant.[40] By
implication, this motif may carry over into

---

[38] Contra H. G. Reventlow, who considers the call
to be an ordination ritual, involving cultic acts and
texts. Cf. *Liturgie und Prophetisches Ich bei Jeremia*
(Gutershah: Mohn, 1963), pp. 24 ff. The visionary
character of the call refutes such a view. To reject it,
however, is not to say that Jeremiah did not use any
cultic language in his call account and confessions,
but that he went far beyond any traditional forms.
(See John Bright, "Jeremiah's Complaints: Liturgy, or
Expressions of Personal Distress," Durham and Porter,
op. cit., pp. 189–214).

[39] For a similar ambiguity in Hosea, see James M.
Ward, *Hosea: A Theological Commentary* (New York:
Harper & Row, 1966), pp. 239–242.

[40] James Muilenburg, "Form Criticism and Beyond,"
JBL, 88, 1969, p. 5; cf. Int. See the excellent article
by H. H. Huffmon, "The Covenant Lawsuit in the
Prophets," JBL, 78, 1959, 285–295; also, Clements,
op. cit., p. 79; G. E. Wright, *Israel's Prophetic Heritage*, pp. 26–67; D. R. Hillers, *op. cit.*, pp. 124–142;
for further study, see James Limburg, "The Root
Ribh and the Prophetic Lawsuit Speeches," JBL, 88,
1969, 291–304; also, the work of Boecker, Korosec,
Wiseman, et. al.

4:5—6:30. The prophet employed the borrowed literary pattern with flexibility and force. He enriched it by modifying it and introducing other forms into it. The result is a masterful creative synthesis which serves as a most effective means of getting over to the people the truth that they are guilty of a breach of the covenant and must experience terrible judgment if they do not repent.

Mention of the covenant calls to mind that Jeremiah was soundly grounded in the Mosaic faith and the Exodus–Sinai–wilderness–conquest traditions. Like his spiritual mentor, Hosea, he was profoundly influenced by the covenant theology.

There is an obvious theological logic in the arrangement of the prophecies in chapters 2—6. This is indicated by the fact that there are three major units of material, each dealing with a separate but consecutive theme: the sin of the people (2:1–37), the need and nature of repentance (3:1—4:4), and the certainty of judgment if repentance is not forthcoming (4:5—6:30). In brief, the people have betrayed the love of God, whose covenant with them they have broken. The broken relationship cannot be repaired apart from radical repentance, a sincere and complete return to God. Barring this, retribution is inevitable. It will take the form of a ravaging of the land by a foe from the north.

Whether Jeremiah or someone else was responsible for this logic is not known. It is possible that the prophet was and that the arrangement itself was intended to give weight and effectiveness to what he said.

1. The Sin of the People (2:1–37)

Chapter 2 exhibits a remarkable coherence. It centers around a single subject: the sin of Israel, God's people. Four aspects of that sin are stressed.

(1) The Essence of Sin (2:1–13)

¹ The word of the Lord came to me, saying,
² "Go and proclaim in the hearing of Jerusalem, Thus says the Lord,

I remembered the devotion of your youth,
  your love as a bride,
how you followed me in the wilderness,
  in a land not sown.
³ Israel was holy to the Lord,
  the first fruits of his harvest.
All who ate of it became guilty;
  evil came upon them,
                            says the Lord."
⁴ Hear the word of the Lord, O house of Jacob, and all the families of the house of Israel. ⁵ Thus says the Lord:
"What wrong did your fathers find in me
  that they went far from me,
and went after worthlessness, and became
    worthless?
⁶ They did not say, 'Where is the Lord
  who brought us up from the land of
    Egypt,
who led us in the wilderness,
  in a land of deserts and pits,
in a land of drought and deep darkness,
  in a land that none passes through,
  where no man dwells?'
⁷ And I brought you into a plentiful land
  to enjoy its fruits and its good things.
But when you came in you defiled my land,
  and made my heritage an abomination.
⁸ The priests did not say, 'Where is the
    Lord?'
Those who handle the law did not know
    me;
  the rulers transgressed against me;
  the prophets prophesied by Baal,
  and went after things that do not profit.
⁹ "Therefore I still contend with you,
                            says the Lord,
  and with your children's children I will
    contend.
¹⁰ For cross to the coasts of Cyprus and see,
  or send to Kedar and examine with care;
  see if there has been such a thing.
¹¹ Has a nation changed its gods,
  even though they are no gods?
But my people have changed their glory
  for that which does not profit.
¹² Be appalled, O heavens, at this,
  be shocked, be utterly desolate,
                            says the Lord,
¹³ for my people have committed two evils:
  they have forsaken me,
the fountain of living waters,
  and hewed out cisterns for themselves,
broken cisterns,
  that can hold no water.

When stripped of all its outer trappings, the sin of Israel is seen to be that of unfaithfulness to the covenant God. This infidelity has manifested itself in two primary forms: apostasy and idolatry. To Jeremiah, this turning away from the true God to false gods is utter folly.

The prophet starts out with a sharp contrast between Israel's early devotion and her later defection. By means of this contrast he is presenting the accusation. As stated above, the overall form is that of the covenantal lawsuit. This form is used with consummate skill. As plaintiff and prosecutor, God takes Israel to court. The heavens (elsewhere, the earth also) constitute a "special type of 'jury'" (Wright, cf. Anderson and Harrelson, p. 47). They are witnesses to the original covenant now broken. The prophet is the divinely appointed messenger who speaks for the plaintiff and suzerain, as he brings the indictment, the decision of the heavenly King and council—first by implication and then by open declaration. It is possible that he does this at the covenant renewal festival in Jerusalem (cf. v. 1; according to some scholars [e.g., Weiser], the Feast of Tabernacles in the fall was the occasion of an annual renewal of the covenant between the Israelites and God).

Israel's early devotion (vv. 1-3).— Following the introductory formula and the summons of the prophetic messenger to give heed to what the Lord says, there is a poignant and powerful poem in the dirge rhythm, a poetic measure of haunting beauty (see Int.). The literary form sets the tone of the speech, that of sadness. God is speaking through his servant. His words are warm with emotion and tender with affection.

As he speaks, he says, in effect: "I remember the honeymoon days—*the devotion of your youth, your love as a bride.* I recall how in the early days of our marriage you followed me, not for selfish advantage, but out of sincere affection. You were still *in the wilderness, in a land not sown.* You had not yet come into contact with the Baals, the gods of the fertility cult of the Canaanites, in the cultivated country. In those days you were *holy to*

the Lord—my special possession, my chosen people set apart for my service— and *the first fruits of his harvest*—my portion to be touched by no one unauthorized by me. Any who dared to violate the sanctity of this relationship suffered retribution."

Jeremiah has chosen one of Hosea's distinctive figures to describe God's relationship to Israel, the husband-wife metaphor, termed by Emil Brunner "the most daring parable of the love of God." [41] Later, in 3:19, he will use the other of those figures, the father-son metaphor. Though quite daring, these figures are particularly appropriate, for they are strongly suggestive of the sacred intimacy and social implications of the covenant faith. Also, the covenant between God and Israel is a suzerainty covenant, i.e., a covenant between a superior, who "gives" the covenant, and an inferior who "receives" it.[42] The appropriateness of the metaphors becomes more apparent when one recalls that in the ancient Hebrew family the wife occupied a position of dependence upon her husband, and the father, quite naturally, was prior and superior to the son.

Verse 2 contains two words for *love.* One (*'ahabah*) connotes choice. It is love that springs from the inner self and seeks out the beloved. Here it speaks of Israel's love as a bride for her husband, Yahweh. When used of God, it refers to his election love (31:3) and is a foreshadowing of the New Testament affirmation: "God is love."

The other word (*chesed*, rendered *devotion*) combines the elements of love and loyalty. It, too, is a covenant word. Here it signifies Israel's affectionate faithfulness to the God of the covenant relationship. When employed of God, it is his loving loyalty to his people, even though

41 *The Christian Doctrine of God* (Philadelphia: The Westminster Press, 1950), I, 184.
42 G. E. Wright, "History and Reality," *The Old Testament and the Christian Faith*, ed. B. W. Anderson (London: SCM Press, 1964), pp. 192 f.; Hillers, *op. cit.,* pp. 29 ff.

they are unworthy. It may be translated "grace" (31:3). It is replete with fore-gleams of the New Testament revelation of God's redeeming grace.

The term *chesed* sums up perhaps better than any other word the character and claims of the covenant. On the Godward side, it is grace. God "gives" the covenant and is under obligation—without in any way compromising his sovereignty—to provide for the needs of his people: redemption, guidance, discipline, forgive-ness, an order of life, a land.

On the manward side, *chesed* means loyal love, devotion. Israel "receives" the covenant and is under obligation to take what God offers with faith and gratitude and to give him her undivided love and loyalty.[43]

Although Jeremiah does not use the word covenant here, it is evident that he is talking about the covenant relationship. The great prophets before him tended to shy away from the term itself because the people sought to pervert the covenant into a parity covenant, a covenant between equals, and to tether God to their own desires and ends. As we shall see later, Jeremiah does not share their reluctance.

Israel's later defection (vv. 4–13).— Once again there is the call to give atten-tion to the word of the heavenly King. As plaintiff and prosecutor, God is still em-ploying the method of indirection in bringing his indictment.

This time he starts, not with a plaintive lamentation, but with a probing question: *What wrong. . . ? Worthlessness,* one of Jeremiah's devastating nicknames for the pagan deities of Palestine and a deliberate pun on Baal, signifies breath or nothing-ness, that bit of vapor which appears briefly before one's mouth on a frosty morning and is then gone forever. The

same word in verbal form is translated *became worthless,* suggesting that people become like that which they worship, in this case, empty and unreal. God's search-ing question gives us another glimpse into his burdened heart of suffering love.

As his "judgment-speech" continues, God introduces some of the basic facts of salvation-history: he delivered Israel from Egyptian bondage, led her through the wilderness, brought her into a good land, and raised up religious guides to instruct her in the covenant faith (vv. 6–8). In his grace, he went all out for the sake of his chosen people.

But they did not ask, *Where is the Lord,* who had performed all these mighty acts on their behalf? This is likely a liturgi-cal question, used in the ceremony of covenant renewal and intended to make the historical revelation of the past a living reality of the present. Only through such retrospective inquiry and fresh commit-ment could the continuity of the covenant relationship and community be maintained and sustained. In their apostasy and their preoccupation with the more attractive and less exacting nature religion of their neighbors, the Israelites had not only for-saken their covenant God but had also forgotten him.

The leaders have had much to do with the unfaithfulness of the people. *The priests* (emphatic) have not discharged their responsibility for keeping the faith alive and pure by a proper discharge of their duties. *Those who handle the law* (emphatic; those skilled in teaching and interpreting the holy *torah*) have be-trayed the trust reposed in them. They have not recognized the sole sovereignty of God and have had no vital relation-ship with him (cf. 1:5). *The rulers* (em-phatic) have rebelled against the sovereign will of their God. *The prophets* (emphatic) have prophesied by Baal—i.e., they have drawn their inspiration and message from the syncretistic, paganized cult rather than from the God of the covenant faith. Fur-

---

43 In the international treaties, the major stress in the term love was upon loyalty, as shown in conduct; cf. Hillers, *op. cit.,* p. 130; W. L. Moran, "The An-cient Near Eastern Background of the Love of God in Deuteronomy," CBQ, 25, 1963, 77–87.

ther, they have gone after *things that do not profit* (another nickname for the gods of the Canaanites and an indirect pun on the Baals).

The people, on their part, have polluted their God-given "garden" land by their ungodly behavior. Hence God is presenting his case against them (v. 9). He has now moved to outright, open indictment. What Israel has done is unprecedented (v. 10). Nations do not (ordinarily and voluntarily) change their gods, which are *no gods*—have no substance, no real existence. Yet Israel has exchanged her *glory* (the presence of the true God, a moral being of majesty and might) for *that which does not profit* (a sarcastic designation of the utter uselessness of the pagan gods, v. 11).

Here we must exercise care in interpretation. There is a certain ambiguity present in the allusion to the conduct of the people. In some cases they have actually gone over to the worship of Baal, the god of fertility (the Baals of the various areas were local manifestations of the "big" Baal). But, for the most part, they have simply so "baalized" (paganized) the worship of the covenant God that their worship has become, in reality, nothing more than Baal worship.

Israel's defection is a fact fit to shock the *heavens,* the witnesses (v. 12). Following the address to the witnesses, the charge comes to a climax in v. 13, one of the many great verses in the book of Jeremiah: *"Two evils* (the pagans are guilty of one, idolatry; God's people are guilty of two, apostasy *and* idolatry) my people have committed: *me* they have left, *the fountain of the waters of life,* to hew out for themselves *cisterns, cracked cisterns that can hold no water"* (literal translation; italics seek to bring out the force of what is said).

Three things strike us in v. 13. The first is an arresting portrayal of God. He is represented as *the fountain of living waters.* This is one of Jeremiah's most majestic and meaningful metaphors. It is

quite suggestive. It suggests that God is the source of life, that he is sufficient for life, and that he satisfies in life.

The second thing we note is an amazing fact. The staggering fact, which has brought grief to the heart of God (vv. 2–3,5) and horror to the heavens (vv. 10–12), is that Israel has forsaken the *fountain* for the *cisterns,* the living God for empty breaths, do-nothing deities. This has resulted in national deterioration (vv. 5–9).

A third thing stands out: a compensating activity. When Israel left the fountain, she began to cut out cisterns. This is always the case. When men depart from God, they must find a substitute because of deep inner desires and needs that demand attention. Thus they go here and there, digging their cisterns. The water in these cisterns may taste good for a time, but it tends to become stale and stagnant. Also, cisterns have a way of developing a fatal leak and letting one down in the hour of supreme need.

For Israel, the cisterns were idols, primarily. But what is an idol? It is that which represents the totality of reality for man, that which occupies the place in his life which only God can rightly occupy. For us today, therefore, there may be many "cisterns": sensual pleasure, material possessions, social prestige, political power, scholarship, science, formal religion—anything short of God to which we give our ultimate devotion. These cisterns can never satisfy, and they will eventually run dry. But the fountain is there, and the invitation is there (cf. John 4:14; Isa. 55:1; Rev. 22:17).

In summary, the opening section (2: 1–13) lays bare the essence of the people's sin. They have broken the covenant. The prophet drives this truth home with terrific force through a masterful modification of the lawsuit motif and through the use of two powerful metaphors: the unfaithfulness of a wife to her husband and the forsaking of a fountain of living water for cracked cisterns that can hold no water.

(2) The Suffering Caused by Sin (2:14–19)

14 "Is Israel a slave? Is he a homeborn servant?
    Why then has he become a prey?
15 The lions have roared against him,
    they have roared loudly.
   They have made his land a waste;
    his cities are in ruins, without inhabitant.
16 Moreover, the men of Memphis and Tahpanhes
    have broken the crown of your head.
17 Have you not brought this upon yourself
    by forsaking the LORD your God,
    when he led you in the way?
18 And now what do you gain by going to Egypt,
    to drink the waters of the Nile?
   Or what do you gain by going to Assyria,
    to drink the waters of the Euphrates?
19 Your wickedness will chasten you,
    and your apostasy will reprove you.
   Know and see that it is evil and bitter
    for you to forsake the LORD your God;
    the fear of me is not in you,
        says the Lord GOD of hosts.

This is a prophecy which continues the accusation of 2:1–13, with particular stress on the suffering which the people have experienced because of their apostasy. It starts with three short, sharp questions. The answer to the first two questions is, "No. He is a son!" Then what is the explanation of the hardship endured by God's covenant people at the hands of the Assyrians and the Egyptians (vv. 15–16; cf. the Assyrian invasions under Tiglath-pileser, Shalmaneser, Sargon, and Sennacherib; on the lion as a symbol of Assyria, see Nah. 2:12 f.)?

Many scholars think that v. 16 is a later insertion which refers to Judah's subservience to Egypt from 609 to 605 B.C. (e.g., Bright, pp. 17 f.). Since Jeremiah first dictated his prophecies in 605 (ch. 36), this is certainly possible. However, it is not necessary to insist on it, for God's people had taken some rough treatment from the Egyptians in the past. Also, since the verb is in the imperfect tense, it is possible that the prophet is predicting.

Memphis was in lower Egypt, near Cairo. It was an ancient capital of the country. *Tahpanhes* was a frontier town

on the northeastern border of Egypt. *The men of Memphis and Tahpanhes* would therefore be Egyptians.

Verse 17 provides the answer to the question in the latter part of v. 14. It is in the form of another question. The explanation of the people's becoming *prey* to the plundering invaders, Assyria and Egypt, is their apostasy. Jeremiah refers here to one of the cardinal concepts of the prophets: the dynamic relationship between sin and judgment. These were regarded as two sides of the same coin, as two parts of a single process. Rebellion against the sovereign will of the covenant God resulted in inevitable retribution. This retribution was usually represented as taking a very tangible form.

The allusion in v. 18 is to the advice and activities of the pro-Egyptian and pro-Assyrian parties in Judah. These advocated a national policy of military preparedness and the making of political pacts—drinking *the waters* [44] *of the Nile* or *the Euphrates* rather than the waters of "the fountain" (cf. v. 13). In short, they were seeking security in man-made alliances rather than in reliance on God. Jeremiah opposed such alliances as poor politics and worse religion—just another evidence and expression of apostasy.

Having lost her central loyalty, Israel is caught in a web of her own weaving (v. 19). She is going to learn anew that it is a *bitter* thing to leave the Lord. She will discover that sin is a hard taskmaster who pays a dreadful wage.

The artistry and ingenuity of Jeremiah continue to manifest themselves in vv. 14–19, as he employs—in the larger context of the covenantal lawsuit motif—a modified form of the prophecy of disaster,

---

[44] Ancient suzerainty treaties or covenants were sealed in various ways: by smearing oil on the skin and drinking water, by killing a young donkey, by cutting up a calf (cf. 34:18), etc. The retribution (curse) invoked upon the one violating the covenant stipulations was often portrayed in terms of the sending of wild animals (bears, panthers, etc.—cf. 5:6) and snakes (8:17), and/or as the withdrawal of joy (cf. 7:34; 16:9; 25:10; 33:11). See Hillers, *op. cit.,* pp. 40 f., 132–135.

with the basic elements of the accusation (v. 17) and the announcement of the penalty (v. 19) present, but with an unusual introduction and with strong stress on the suffering encountered by the people because of their sin (on prophecy of disaster, see Int.).

(3) The Seriousness of Sin (2:20-29)

20 "For long ago you broke your yoke
  and burst your bonds;
  and you said, 'I will not serve.'
Yea, upon every high hill
  and under every green tree
  you bowed down as a harlot.
21 Yet I planted you a choice vine,
  wholly of pure seed.
How then have you turned degenerate
  and become a wild vine?
22 Though you wash yourself with lye
  and use much soap,
  the stain of your guilt is still before me,
                    says the Lord GOD.
23 How can you say, 'I am not defiled,
  I have not gone after the Baals'?
Look at your way in the valley;
  know what you have done—
  a restive young camel interlacing her tracks,
24   a wild ass used in the wilderness,
  in her heat sniffing the wind!
  Who can restrain her lust?
None who seek her need weary themselves;
  in her month they will find her.
25 Keep your feet from going unshod
  and your throat from thirst.
But you said, 'It is hopeless,
  for I have loved strangers,
  and after them I will go.'
26 "As a thief is shamed when caught,
  so the house of Israel shall be shamed:
they, their kings, their princes,
  their priests, and their prophets,
27 who say to a tree, 'You are my father,'
  and to a stone, 'You gave me birth.'
For they have turned their back to me,
  and not their face.
But in the time of their trouble they say,
  'Arise and save us!'
28 But where are your gods
  that you made for yourself?
Let them arise, if they can save you,
  in your time of trouble;
for as many as your cities
  are your gods, O Judah.
29 "Why do you complain against me?
  You have all rebelled against me,
                    says the LORD.

Israel's sin is deep-seated and of long standing. Her loss of her ultimate loyalty through her breach of the covenant has resulted in a tragic fragmentation and deterioration of life. This idea is set forth in superb fashion under seven figures of speech. The prophet is not guilty of redundancy but is calling upon a graphic and forceful diversity of images in his attempt to emphasize the truth he wishes to get over. There are nuances in the cryptic, compact statements which only the sensitive reader can catch.

The first figure is that of an ox which has broken its yoke, burst its bonds, and is bolting (v. 20a). The yoke suggests that the covenant faith involved obligation as well as redemption, demand as well as deliverance. The people liked the grace side of religion, but did not care for the discipline side of it. Accordingly, Israel said, I will not serve.

Service is at the very center of biblical faith. Salvation is a gift of God's grace. Out of gratitude for that salvation, and love for the God who makes it possible, man is to serve God and his fellowman. This is not easy, and some refuse. Israel did.

The second figure is that of a wife who has played her husband false and fallen for the seductive enticements of other lovers (v. 20b). The rites of the fertility cult of Canaan were usually observed on hilltops and in groves of trees or near a sacred tree or pole (a tree and a stone represented the male and female deities in the nature religion, cf. v. 27). Once again Jeremiah uses Hosea's metaphor of the husband-wife relationship and speaks of sin as spiritual adultery. In the last analysis, that is what sin is—a willful breach of personal relations with God.

The third figure is that of a choice vine which has gone bad (v. 21). The allusion is to the Sorek vine, grown in the valley of Sorek to the west of Jerusalem, a valley famous for its fine vines and wines. This particular kind of vine was about the best to be had (cf. Isa. 5:1 f.). But, for some reason, the vine turned into a strange, wild vine.

Two thoughts stand out: first, sin is an

unnatural thing; second, the source of Israel's trouble is not to be found in God's planting but in the people's perversity.

The fourth figure is that of a person scrubbing himself with *much soap* but unable to remove *the stain* (v. 22). The stain is that which is left by sin. No cheap, self-administered process will cause it to come clean. In v. 23a Jeremiah expresses amazement: how can the people deny that they have been defiled by Baalism in the face of their conduct in *the valley?* The valley in the prophet's mind is the valley of Hinnom, to the west and southwest of Jerusalem. There pagan rites were performed, including sacred prostitution and the practice of human sacrifice (7:31; 2 Kings 23:10).

The fifth figure is that of *a restive camel* that has broken away from the rest of the herd and is wandering about with no discernible pattern in her actions (v. 23b). Her tracks lead nowhere. The picture is that of the confusion, indecision, and frustration which characterize life that is divorced from direction by God.

The sixth figure is that of *a wild ass* in heat, racing here and there, beyond the control of her master, seeking and not needing to be sought (vv. 24–25). Jeremiah is introducing some raw facts of rural life to portray the passionate plunge of the people into paganism. It is apparent that his figures are becoming sharper and stronger. This is perhaps the severest of all.

Somewhat ironically he calls out, in effect: "Don't run the shoes off your feet, and don't cry out till your throats are parched, in your pursuit of the religion of the Baals and the rewards it offers: prosperity, security, felicity!" The people instantly answer: "Preacher, it's no use! You need not talk to us. We are in love with these foreign deities and the comforting and comfortable religion they sponsor. After them we must go!"

The final figure is that of *a thief* who is caught and is unable to keep what he has stolen but is overcome with a sense of shame (vv. 26 ff.). When real trouble comes, the people will be like that thief.

They will experience frustration and desperation. In their extremity, they, who have ascribed their existence to pagan gods and have turned their backs and not their faces to their own God, will cry out to the covenant God for help. He will answer: "Let the gods whom you have served save you in your time of trouble."

It is evident that vv. 20–29 contain a strong indictment of the people for their religious syncretism and rank paganism. To be sure, they have not renounced their bond to their ancestral God, Yahweh. They have acknowledged him in a formal way on special days and occasions. But to get their fields blessed and their flocks multiplied, they have introduced pagan elements into their worship and way of life. They have turned their backs to Yahweh and their faces to the Baals, agricultural deities of their local communities. They have tried to have one God for the sabbath, as it were, and other gods for the other days of the week. When a crisis comes, they call out to Yahweh for assistance. They even feel that they have a legal claim on him. But God says: *Why do you complain* (present a court case) *against me? You have all* (emphatic) *rebelled against me* (v. 29).

Note the surfacing of the lawsuit concept in v. 29. The Lord of the covenant could rightly declare: "You don't have a case against me. I have a case against you."

(4) The Stubbornness with Which the People Persist in Sin (2:30–37)

30 In vain have I smitten your children,
    they took no correction;
   your own sword devoured your prophets
    like a ravening lion.
31 And you, O generation, heed the word of
    the LORD.
   Have I been a wilderness to Israel,
    or a land of thick darkness?
   Why then do my people say, 'We are free,
    we will come no more to thee'?
32 Can a maiden forget her ornaments,
    or a bride her attire?
   Yet my people have forgotten me
    days without number.
33 "How well you direct your course
    to seek lovers!

So that even to wicked women
    you have taught your ways.
34 Also on your skirts is found
    the lifeblood of guiltless poor;
you did not find them breaking in.
Yet in spite of all these things
35 you say, 'I am innocent;
    surely his anger has turned from me.'
Behold, I will bring you to judgment
    for saying, 'I have not sinned.'
36 How lightly you gad about,
    changing your way!
You shall be put to shame by Egypt
    as you were put to shame by Assyria.
37 From it too you will come away
    with your hands upon your head,
for the Lord has rejected those in whom
    you trust,
    and you will not prosper by them.

The concluding portion of the chapter is argumentative in character. It follows the reproach-threat pattern.

God has sought to correct his people through chastisement, but his efforts have been in vain. Even the severe trials which they underwent during the reign of Manasseh have not brought a return to God (v. 30). In spite of God's great goodness to them, they have continued to do as they desire (v. 31). Their conduct has been completely incomprehensible. A young girl could never forget her ornaments nor a bride her wedding sash (the symbol of her status as a married woman); yet Israel, the wife of the Lord, has forgotten her husband *days without number* (v. 32). So far has she gone in her unfaithfulness to him that she has even been able to teach others some immoral techniques (v. 33). There is blood on her skirts, too (v. 34). It is not the blood of criminals caught in the criminal act and killed (Ex. 22:1 f.), but the blood of the innocent (children offered as human sacrifices, or the poor and oppressed, or prophets?).

Yet the people claim *I am innocent.* Neither their protestations of innocence (v. 35b) nor their political planning and plotting (v. 36) can avert the inevitable penalty of their apostasy. As they have flitted to the court of Assyria, so they have flirted in the court of Egypt in a frantic search for security. But they will come away with their hands on their heads in distress and disgrace. God has rejected the objects of their trust (v. 37). As judge, he pronounces sentence: *Behold, I will bring you to judgment.* In the covenantal lawsuit, God can be plaintiff, prosecutor, and judge.

So ends a chapter which illustrates in unusual measure the remarkable ability of Jeremiah both as a poet and as a prophet.

2. The Need and Nature of Repentance (3:1—4:4)

The second major unit in the larger complex (2:1—6:30) is 3:1—4:4. Though many scholars see more than one unit here, the present writer feels that 3:1—4:4 is a marvelous composition—mostly in poetry but partly in prose—made up mainly of materials from Jeremiah's early ministry and centering around the motif of repentance. The key word is "turn" or "return" (*shub*). The prophet uses this word in its various forms and meanings, in different contexts and constructions, and in strategic combinations.

Also, the lawsuit pattern is still noticeably present. In addition, the passage contains the lament, the exhortation, and the promise, and comes to a close with the convenantal conditional and a clarion call to repentance. In sum, the section is "an Exhibit A in ancient Hebrew rhetoric." [45]

The theological logic is apparent. The people are guilty of terrible sin. Sin leads to judgment. The only way the judgment can be averted and a right relationship with God restored is through real repentance. Hence the plea for a radical turnabout in conduct.

(1) A Condemnation of the People (3:1-5)

1 "If a man divorces his wife
    and she goes from him
    and becomes another man's wife,
      will he return to her?
    Would not that land be greatly polluted?
    You have played the harlot with many
      lovers;

45 James Muilenburg, JBL, 88, 10.

and would you return to me?
    says the LORD.
2 Lift up your eyes to the bare heights, and
    see!
  Where have you not been lain with?
  By the waysides you have sat awaiting
    lovers
  like an Arab in the wilderness.
  You have polluted the land
    with your vile harlotry.
3 Therefore the showers have been withheld,
    and the spring rain has not come;
  yet you have a harlot's brow,
    you refuse to be ashamed.
4 Have you not just now called to me,
    'My father, thou art the friend of my
    youth—
5   will he be angry for ever,
    will he be indignant to the end?'
  Behold, you have spoken,
    but you have done all the evil that you
    could."

In this passage there is an incisive indictment of the prevailing attitude of the
covenant people. Israel has played the
harlot. How can she dream of an easy,
effortless return to God?

Many scholars are persuaded that the
prophet is referring in v. 1 to a Hebrew
law concerning marriage and divorce
found in Deuteronomy 24:1–4 (e.g.,
Hyatt, p. 824; Bright, p. 23). According
to that law, if a woman was divorced by
her husband, then married another man
and he died or divorced her, she could
not return to her first husband. He was
not permitted to take her back. Such an
action would be an abomination before
God and would bring pollution upon the
land.

To be sure, Jeremiah was deeply influenced by the Deuteronomic style, language, and teaching. This does not necessarily presuppose the discovery of "the
book of the law" in the Temple in 622.
However, it is doubtful that in the passage
before us the prophet is thinking primarily about the legal conditions under which
a man could or could not receive back a
divorced wife. To begin with, Israel
(Judah) had not been divorced. Furthermore, we should probably read with the
LXX "Can she return to him?" instead of

will he return to her? and "that woman"
instead of *that land* (cf. Peake, Smith,
Streane).

Is it not possible that Jeremiah is appealing more to normal human emotion
than to any legal enactment? In that case,
we might paraphrase and expound the
content of vv. 1–5 as follows: "Do you
men show the same ethical insensitivity
in the intimate relations of family life
that you manifest in the realm of your
relationship with God? *You* there—if your
wife should leave you, enter into an
adulterous union with another man, and
then seek to return to you, would *you* take
her back, especially if there was no indication whatever of any real change in her?
I think not. Yet you, all of you, have left
your God of your own volition. You have
gone after many lovers, not one (v. 1).
Lift up your eyes round about and look at
the harlotry practiced on the hills. The
altars and the licentious acts there bear
effective testimony to your infidelity to
your lawful husband, your covenant God
(v. 2). You have, in fact, been 'as harlots
waiting beside the road to entice paramours, and . . . as predatory Arab robbers lying in ambush to rush upon cara-
vans' (Leslie, p. 35). In the face of such
flagrant faithlessness, how can you possibly
think of a return to your God which requires no real change of heart and life? It
is true, you do retain a certain relation to
him (v. 4). Just now (in an emergency
situation resulting from a drought?) you
chased up to the sanctuary and went
through the ceremonial, saying to Yahweh, 'My father, you are the dear bridegroom of my youth.' Thus you acknowledge him in profession but not in practice.
You do not give him your undivided devotion. You say, 'He gets angry at times and
withholds the rain. But give him time and
he gets over it. There is no need to become
all worked up about it' (vv. 3,5). These
things you have *said*, but you have *done*
evil to the utmost. Your words and deeds
don't gibe. And so, you continue in your
apostasy and your adultery. You have the

brazen forehead of a harlot. You refuse to be ashamed—and have lost the capacity to love."

In this biting invective, in which he employs Hosea's favorite figure again, Jeremiah cuts through to the core of the problem of the people. As a consequence of their pagan or semipagan worship, they have no adequate conception of the character and the claims of their God. Therefore they have no real consciousness of the need for a radical inner change. They do not recognize that the living God will permit no rival, that the true covenant faith requires complete commitment, and that the only way back to a right relationship with God for a sinful people is through genuine repentance.

(2) A Comparison of Judah and Israel (3:6–18)

6 The Lord said to me in the days of King Josiah: "Have you seen what she did, that faithless one, Israel, how she went up on every high hill and under every green tree, and there played the harlot? 7 And I thought, 'After she has done all this she will return to me'; but she did not return, and her false sister Judah saw it. 8 She saw that for all the adulteries of that faithless one, Israel, I had sent her away with a decree of divorce; yet her false sister Judah did not fear, but she too went and played the harlot. 9 Because harlotry was so light to her, she polluted the land, committing adultery with stone and tree. 10 Yet for all this her false sister Judah did not return to me with her whole heart, but in pretense, says the Lord."

11 And the Lord said to me, "Faithless Israel has shown herself less guilty than false Judah. 12 Go, and proclaim these words toward the north, and say,
'Return, faithless Israel,
                           says the Lord.
I will not look on you in anger,
   for I am merciful,
                           says the Lord;
I will not be angry for ever.
13 Only acknowledge your guilt,
   that you rebelled against the Lord your
      God
and scattered your favors among strangers
   under every green tree,
   and that you have not obeyed my voice,
                           says the Lord.
14 Return, O faithless children,
                           says the Lord;

for I am your master;
   I will take you, one from a city and two
      from a family,
   and I will bring you to Zion.
15 " 'And I will give you shepherds after my own heart, who will feed you with knowledge and understanding. 16 And when you have multiplied and increased in the land, in those days, says the Lord, they shall no more say, "The ark of the covenant of the Lord." It shall not come to mind, or be remembered, or missed; it shall not be made again. 17 At that time Jerusalem shall be called the throne of the Lord, and all nations shall gather to it, to the presence of the Lord in Jerusalem, and they shall no more stubbornly follow their own evil heart. 18 In those days the house of Judah shall join the house of Israel, and together they shall come from the land of the north to the land that I gave your fathers for a heritage.

This passage poses some problems. In the first place, all of it except vv. 12b–14 is written in prose. Moreover, it interrupts the sequence of thought: 3:5 ties in with 3:19. Also, the term Israel is used in conjunction with the word Judah; it designates the Northern Kingdom, and that kingdom is compared to the Southern Kingdom, to the disadvantage of the latter. Further, vv. 14b–18 are said by many to presuppose the exile and to contain exilic and postexilic ideas.

Many scholars reject the passage in part or in entirety. Hyatt, for instance, holds that vv. 12–14a are genuine. He deletes the rest on the following grounds: (1) Jeremiah ordinarily uses the word Israel to refer to all of the people of God or to Judah; (2) nowhere else does he state that Judah was more guilty than Israel; (3) vv. 6–11 show close affinities with Ezekiel 16:44–63 and 23:1–49; (4) vv. 14b–18 contain ideas which "are generally foreign to Jeremiah but are frequently found in exilic and postexilic apocalyptic passages" (pp. 826 f.).

Reference has been made to the ambiguity present in the use of the word Israel in both Hosea and Jeremiah. There is no obvious reason for saying that Jeremiah, a northerner of the tribe of Benjamin, could not and did not occasionally employ the term to designate the Northern Kingdom.

This would have been particularly appropriate at the time when Josiah, in pursuit of a policy of national independence and reunion, was seeking to push his power into the area of the former northern state and reestablish the Davidic kingdom (cf. 2 Chron. 34:3–7).

Moreover, to state that a passage should be regarded as secondary because it gives expression to an idea not mentioned elsewhere by the prophet is, to say the least, quite subjective. If this rule were applied to the entire Old Testament, it would be a lot shorter! Maybe one allusion was enough for the prophet's purpose.

Further, the affinities between 6:6–11 and Ezekiel 16:44–63; 23:1–49 are real, but the line of influence and development seems to run from Hosea to Jeremiah to Ezekiel (cf. Bright, p. 26).

Again, the exile is not necessarily presupposed in vv. 14b–18. It may be predicted. Jeremiah did forecast the captivity, often. Who knows exactly when he started, or whether the oracle (prophecy) in vv. 14b–18 may have originated later than the one preceding it? Because of the nature of the concept of hope present in them, it is highly probable that, in their present form, vv. 14b–18 date from the late ministry of the prophet.

As for the universalism expressed in v. 17 and the reunion of Judah and Israel referred to in v. 18, these ideas are found elsewhere in Jeremiah and can in no case be categorically catalogued as exilic or postexilic ideas.

On the other side, it may be said that there is much in vv. 14–18 that is Jeremianic in both language and ideas. This is expressly declared by some scholars and is indirectly demonstrated by the sharp disagreement among others as to what is genuine and what is not in these verses.

In my judgment, the material in this section is authentic and, with the probable exception of 3:14b–18, comes from the reign of Josiah (v. 6) and probably, though not certainly, from the early ministry of Jeremiah. It was likely composed

and/or delivered at a time other than that during which 3:1–5 and 3:19—4:4 originated and was incorporated here because of the centrality of the concept of "turning" in it. The possibility of later additions and/or expansions is not to be ruled out.

The guilt of Judah greater than that of Israel (6–11).—This is a prose monologue addressed by God to Jeremiah. Hosea's figure of the unfaithful wife is further developed. *Israel* and *Judah* are referred to as adulterous (apostate) sisters. They are compared with each other, and Judah is found to be the more guilty of the two. The stated reason for this conclusion is that Judah has had the warning example of Israel and has given no heed to it.

Israel had played the harlot. She had become "apostasy personified." She had embraced fully the fertility cult—*on every high hill and under every green tree* (cf. 2:20; Hos. 4:13). God had expected that she would *return* to him, but she did not *return* (note the play on turning away from God to the gods and then turning back to God from the gods). Jeremiah is asked whether he has noticed what Israel had done and what had happened as a consequence of what she had done. Of course he has *seen* it; it happened a hundred years earlier (721 B.C.). It was then that God sent Israel away to Assyria *with a decree of divorce.*

Judah has also been aware of the apostasy and punishment of the Northern Kingdom. Like her adulterous sister, she also was unfaithful to the covenant God. So great a tragedy as that which overtook Israel should have caused Judah to repent. But she did not. Instead, she took her harlotry so lightly that she polluted the whole land with it. She even "surpassed by her levity and lustfulness the whoredoms of her sister" (Calvin). Under the impact of the preaching of Isaiah and Micah and the masterful leadership of Hezekiah, she "returned" to God—but not *with her whole heart.* The reform was partial and temporary, and there was a terrible relapse under Manasseh. Consequently, since she has not learned from the fate of her sister, her guilt is greater than that of her sister (if the passage dates after 622, the reference could also be to the Josianic reformation).

An earnest summons to return to God (vv. 12–13).—Jeremiah is enjoined to direct his gaze northward, where the Israelites had gone in 721, and declare: *Return, faithless* (turning away) *Israel.* Note the wordplay and the covenantal use of *shub* in v. 12a. The reason for the call is stated (v. 12b). God is a God of grace, who will not keep his anger forever. The appeal to return emanates from his love and desire to save. If the people will repent—will acknowledge their guilt in turning to other gods (*strangers*) and will change their loyalty—then he will restore them to their former true covenantal relationship.

A plea and a promise (vv. 14–18).— Once more the cry rings out: *"Return, O faithless children* (the same sort of play on the word turn as above, both in sound and sense), . . . *for I am your master* (*ba'al,* owner). Also, there is a pun on Baal. "Yahweh, not Baal, is the ture *ba'al* (lord) of Israel" (Bright, p. 24).

After the plea comes the promise. There are several elements in it: First, restoration (v. 14b); second, true Davidic rulers (*shepherds*), who will feed their people *with knowledge and understanding* (v. 15); third, the removal of the ark of the covenant (v. 16; a very daring statement and a very penetrating insight); fourth, the reign of God over people of all nations (v. 17a; cf. Isa. 2:1–4; Mic. 4:1–4); fifth, the regeneration of the people (v. 17b; no longer will they *stubbornly follow their own evil heart,* a favorite expression of Jeremiah); sixth, the reunion of the people of God (v. 18; cf. Hos. 1:11; Isa. 11:12 f.; Ezek. 37:16–28; Ezekiel develops the idea).

Jeremiah looks forward to the day when God will rule through men after his own heart over a reunited, redeemed, regenerated, community, made up of Israel-ites, Judahites, and Gentiles who will have such a mature conception of God and such a dynamic relation to him that they will not need to depend upon external forms and supports but upon "a direct and first-hand knowledge of God" (Peake, I, p. 110). Even the ark of the covenant, the most sacred symbol of God's presence in ancient Israel, will no longer be remembered or missed!

(3) A Contrast in Conduct (3:19–20)

19 " 'I thought
    how I would set you among my sons,
and give you a pleasant land,
    a heritage most beauteous of all nations.
And I thought you would call me, My Father,
    and would not turn from following me.
20 Surely, as a faithless wife leaves her husband,
    so have you been faithless to me, O house of Israel,
        says the LORD' "

This is a brief but beautiful poem in which God speaks. It is a continuation of 3:1–5. In a tender and touching lament, God states that he had it in his mind to treat Israel as *sons* (cf. Num. 27:1–8), and so he did. He gave her a position of great privilege among the peoples of the world and also *a pleasant land,* the most beauteous heritage of all the nations. Naturally he expected the reverence and response which dutiful sons owe a loving father. Instead, Israel behaved as a faithless wife. She betrayed her husband (cf. Hos. 2; 11; note the mixing of Hosea's two great metaphors).

J. R. Gillies has an illuminating remark concerning the use of the plural *sons* and the singular *wife* to designate *Israel:* "The nation, as individuals, were Jahweh's apostate children; as a community, His faithless wife." [46]

One catches the plaintive tone and the note of heartbreak as the contrast is drawn between the way God has treated his

---

[46] *Jeremiah, The Man and His Message* (London: Hodder & Stoughton, 1907), p. 59.

people and the way they have treated and are treating him.

(4) The People's Cry and God's Call (3:21—4:4)

21 A voice on the bare heights is heard,
the weeping and pleading of Israel's sons,
because they have perverted their way,
they have forgotten the LORD their God.
22 "Return, O faithless sons,
I will heal your faithlessness."
"Behold, we come to thee;
for thou art the LORD our God.
23 Truly the hills are a delusion,
the orgies on the mountains.
Truly in the LORD our God
is the salvation of Israel.
24 "But from our youth the shameful thing has devoured all for which our fathers labored, their flocks and their herds, their sons and their daughters. 25 Let us lie down in our shame, and let our dishonor cover us; for we have sinned against the LORD our God, we and our fathers, from our youth even to this day; and we have not obeyed the voice of the LORD our God."

1 "If you return, O Israel,
says the LORD,
to me you should return.
If you remove your abominations from my presence,
and do not waver,
2 and if you swear, 'As the LORD lives,'
in truth, in justice, and in uprightness,
then nations shall bless themselves in him,
and in him shall they glory."
3 For thus says the LORD to the men of Judah and to the inhabitants of Jerusalem:
"Break up your fallow ground,
and sow not among thorns.
4 Circumcise yourselves to the LORD,
remove the foreskin of your hearts,
O men of Judah and inhabitants of Jerusalem;
lest my wrath go forth like fire,
and burn with none to quench it,
because of the evil of your doings."

This passage of great punguncy and emotional power brings the pleading begun in chapter 2 to a climax. The prophet's use of the form of the liturgy shows again his remarkable versatility as a poet. The penetrating insight into the nature of true repentance—as over against a shallow, superficial "return"—demonstrates his unusual powers of prophetic perception. Peake says that vv. 3 and 4 of chapter 4 are "among the grandest in the prophetic literature and comprise Jeremiah's whole theology in a couple of brief sentences" (p. 45). Though the latter part of the statement is an exaggeration, it is true that 4:1–4 takes us to the heart of what biblical repentance really is.

The cry of the people (v. 21).—From the heights, the hotbeds of heathenism, the prophet hears, as it were, the sound of his people weeping. They are confused, frustrated, disillusioned, yearning. They know that *they have perverted their way* by going after other gods and, in so doing, setting themselves against both the true God and themselves. Also, they are aware that *they have forgotten the Lord* and thereby have progressively departed from him. They are now gripped by a sense of shame. Whether this actually happened or whether the prophet envisions it in imagination or anticipation is not known. The latter is likely, though the people doubtless experienced disappointment in their worship and way of life.

The command of God (v. 22a).—In love, God responds to the cry of his bewildered, sorrowful people: "Turn back, O back-turning sons! I will heal your back-turnings" (author's translation). If the people will truly turn to God in real penitence, he will turn to them in pardoning, healing grace (cf. Hos. 14:1–4).

The confession of the people (vv. 22b–25). Some regard this as a liturgy of penitence—a prescribed rite or set of rites for the confession of sin—placed on the lips of the people by the prophet. The change of speakers is obvious from the pronouns used.

The phrase *the orgies on the mountains* refers to all the hubbub on the heights—the feasting, drinking, sacred prostitution —all that went with the fertility cult, or the cult of Israel as infiltrated by it. The people recognize that the sort of thing in which they are engaging is *a delusion.* It can bring no real and abiding satisfaction, strength, and salvation. God alone is the source of these.

Bright correctly renders vv. 24–25 as poetry (p. 20). In these verses the people state that *from our youth,* the early part of their history as God's elect, *the shameful thing* (Baal, the fertility cult) has claimed both them and their possessions. They have been disloyal and disobedient to their God. They will therefore *lie down* in their *shame* (there is a clever play on both the word Baal and the idea of shame here).

Some scholars feel that vv. 22b–25 contain a sincere expression of penitence on the part of the people (Peake, pp. 113 ff.; Cunliffe-Jones, pp. 62 f.). Others are persuaded that the penitence is superficial—more regret or remorse than real repentance. A. C. Welch argues for the latter interpretation at some length and with considerable strength. He observes: "Their false relation to God and their failure to obey Him have destroyed in the people the power to return and to lay hold on that which is better." [47]

The present writer's view is that Jeremiah is imitating a liturgy and that in a masterful manner he is contrasting a shallow "turning" (vv. 22b–25) with the true "turning" (v. 22a; 4:1–4) which God requires.

God's clarion call for real repentance (4:1–4).—These verses begin with the covenantal conditional and end with an earnest exhortation (see Int.). They are tremendously important verses.

We translate verse 1a thus: "If you would return (change your loyalty, turn away from your present loyalty and back to your former loyalty), O Israel—oracle of Yahweh—to me you should return." The phrase "to me" is emphatic (*shub* is used in covenantal sense). God is saying, "If you have it in mind to return, *to me* return! Come all the way back to me!"

Two more "ifs" follow to form a tremendous triad (vv. 1b–2a). *The abominations* are the idolatrous practices of

which the people are guilty. These must be utterly done away. There can be no wavering, no halfheartedness or halfway measures.

The taking of an oath was a fairly frequent practice and a very serious business among the Israelites. When one swore *As the Lord lives,* he concentrated "the whole substance and strength of his soul" into the words which he spoke.[48] Moreover, to swear by a god was to acknowledge his claim to be god and his claim as god upon the one swearing. Swearing '*As the Lord lives' in truth, in justice, and in uprightness* involved a sincere acknowledgment of the character of the covenant God and an honest acceptance of his sovereign claims.

If the people will do the things spoken of in the covenantal conditional in vv. 1–2a, then God's promise to them will be fulfilled, and their destiny will be realized (v. 2b; cf. the promise made to Abraham and his descendants, Gen. 12:3; see also Rev. 21:22–26).

Following the introductory "messenger formula," the prophet uses two figures in his exhortation, which emphasize the truth that if repentance is to be real it must be painful. One of the figures is taken from agricultural life, the other from the religious practice of the people. *Fallow ground* is unplowed ground which has been hardened by the sun or become covered over with weeds and bushes (cf. Hos. 10:12). It must be cleared off and broken up—the fallow ground of unconfessed sin, of impure or unreal worship, of uncommitted living.

The second figure comes from the "sacred" rather than the "secular" realm (though the Old Testament does not draw any real distinction between the two—it speaks in terms of totalities). Circumcision was the sign of the Abrahamic covenant and was an external requirement for membership in the covenant community. Jere-

---

[47] *Op. cit.,* p. 68.

[48] J. Pedersen, *Israel, Its Life and Culture,* trans. Aslang Møller, I–II (London: Oxford University Press, 1954), 407.

miah indicates that to be a part of the true people of God requires not only an outer circumcision but also an inner circumcision, a circumcision of the heart. He is calling for a radical change at the center of man's being, an inner transformation that will express itself in outer action.

The alternative to repentance is ruin: *lest my wrath go forth like fire, and burn with none to quench it.* Jeremiah is no starry-eyed sentimentalist. Like the other true prophets, he is a hardheaded realist. He tells things as they are. He has much to say about the wrath of God. Fairly frequently he associates *fire* with *wrath* (cf. 15:14; 17:4; 21:2; etc.). In speaking of God's wrath, he does not mean to say that God is vindictive and vengeful. Rather, he is referring to the retribution which follows one's refusal to make a proper response to God's righteous purpose and loving pleas. In short, God's wrath is the other side of the coin of his grace. Nor is Jeremiah using "spiritual blackmail" on his people. He is simply telling it as it is: repentance or ruin.

Since this is such an important passage and since repentance is a central theme in the prophet's preaching,[49] it is proper to pause to summarize what he says about it. It is not mere regret or remorse (3: 19–25); it is not a perfunctory ritualism (suggested in 3:4–5 and elsewhere); it is a real return to God (4:1a). Moreover, this return involves three things: a repudiation of idolatry (4:1b), a recognition of the lordship of God (4:2), and a radical revision and rearrangement of life (4:3–4).

It seems appropriate to say that repentance is the supreme need of the present hour. That need is acute, desperate, tragic. Through the practice of our idolatries and the application of the philosophy of self-assertion, humanity has been pushed to the edge of a precipice of unprecedented

disaster. Only repentance and God can save us. It is, repent or perish.

3. The Certainty and Necessity of Judgment (4:5—6:30)

Up to this point in the prophecy, Jeremiah has spoken of the sin of the people. They have broken the covenant. The next logical step is to depict the judgment which is bound to come, if the people do not turn back to God in genuine penitence, trust, and obedience, and to delineate in more detail the moral basis for that judgment. This Jeremiah does in 4:5—6:30, thereby developing the note struck in 4:4b.

This new section, like the two preceding units (2:1–37; 3:1—4:4), contains a unique mixture of forms: cries of alarm, threats, reproaches, lyric poetry, prophetic reflections, and exhortations. This blending of forms is characteristic of Jeremiah, as we have noted. There is much that is new in the experience of this man of God. It is not surprising, therefore, that new methods of expression and communication are required and used.

One of the most arresting features in 4:5—6:30 is a series of powerful poems portraying the coming of a foe from the north against Judah. There are eight of these: 4:5–10,11–18,19–22,23–28,29–31; 5:15–19; 6:1–8,22–26. As brilliant and as vivid as these poems are, the primary stress in them is not on the description of the enemy but on the indictment of the prophet's countrymen. The devastation of the land by the unnamed foe is represented as coming through the action of God as his judgment upon his people for their apostasy. The disaster, though still in the future, is pictured as though it were already taking place (Eissfeldt, p. 358). Both God and his spokesman sing a funeral song about it.

There is a difference among scholars as to the psychological factor in the poems. Some hold that the poems record ecstatic visions (e.g., von Rad, p. 67). Others

---

49 In 3:1—4:4 alone, the verb *shub* appears 10 times (3:1,7,10,12,14,22; 4:1); the noun *shubah*, 4 times (3:6,8,11,12); and the adjective *shobah*, 2 times (3:14,22).

classify them as visual poetry (e.g., Lindblom, pp. 141 ff.). Perhaps a mediating position is more tenable. Most of the poems are examples of revelation through an inspired imagination. Some are graphic descriptions of actual visionary experiences (e.g., 4:19–22 and 23–28).

It should be remembered that Jeremiah began his ministry with the conviction that calamity was coming from the north as divine judgment upon an unrepentant, apostate covenant people. It should also be kept in mind that this conviction remained with him throughout his ministry and that it is impossible to understand his preaching apart from it.

(1) The Ruin That Threatens (4:5–31)

The section starts with five poems which are very artistically arranged and, at points, are quite lyrical in character. They describe the successive stages in the invasion of the land, from the initial sounding of the alarm to the final sinking of the city with a death-shriek before the invader.

a. The Watchman's Warning (4:5–10)

5 Declare in Judah, and proclaim in Jerusalem, and say,
"Blow the trumpet through the land;
  cry aloud and say,
'Assemble, and let us go
  into the fortified cites!'
6 Raise a standard toward Zion,
  flee for safety, stay not,
for I bring evil from the north,
  and great destruction.
7 A lion has gone up from his thicket,
  a destroyer of nations has set out;
he has gone forth from his place
  to make your land a waste;
your cities will be ruins
  without inhabitant.
8 For this gird you with sackcloth,
  lament and wail;
for the fierce anger of the LORD
  has not turned back from us."
9 "In that day, says the LORD, courage shall fail both king and princes; the priests shall be appalled and the prophets astounded." 10 Then I said, "Ah, Lord GOD, surely thou hast utterly deceived this people and Jerusalem, saying, 'It shall be well with you'; whereas the sword has reached their very life."

Verse 5a refers to the responsibility of the prophetic messenger and suggests, as do 2:1 and 4:3, that Jeremiah's messages may have been delivered in Jerusalem, possibly at the covenant renewal festival.

There follows the cry of the watchman on the wall (v. 5b). He calls upon the people to flee to the fortified cities for safety, for a foe is coming from the north, spreading havoc as he comes and threatening the entire land with ruin (vv. 5c–7). He urges them to lament and wail, for this imminent disaster is divine retribution sent because of their sin (v. 8; on *anger*, see the comment on 4:4). In the face of the catastrophe, the leaders of the land will stand horrified and helpless. They will protest to God that he has *deceived* them through assuring them of the inviolability of Jerusalem and the indestructibility of the elect (vv. 9–10).[50]

b. The Approach of the Adversary (4:11–18)

11 At that time it will be said to this people and to Jerusalem, "A hot wind from the bare heights in the desert toward the daughter of my people, not to winnow or cleanse, 12 a wind too full for this comes for me. Now it is I who speak in judgment upon them."
13 Behold, he comes up like clouds,
  his chariots like the whirlwind;
his horses are swifter than eagles—
  woe to us, for we are ruined!
14 O Jerusalem, wash your heart from wickedness,
  that you may be saved.
How long shall your evil thoughts
  lodge within you?
15 For a voice declares from Dan
  and proclaims evil from Mount Ephraim.
16 Warn the nations that he is coming;
  announce to Jerusalem,
"Besiegers come from a distant land;
  they shout against the cities of Judah.
17 Like keepers of a field are they against her round about,
  because she has rebelled against me,
                              says the LORD.

---

[50] Along with Bright and others, the writer regards vv. 9–10 as poetry and a part of the poem. He also accepts the LXX reading of "they shall say" for "I said." The protest is based upon a perversion of the covenant concept and of Isaiah's preaching, particularly the emphasis on the royal Davidic theology.

18 Your ways and your doings
    have brought this upon you.
  This is your doom, and it is bitter;
    it has reached your very heart."

The penetration and power of Jeremiah as a poet-prophet are evident here in the vividness of his imagery, his economy of words, his skill in achieving a "maximum of effect with a minimum of specific description," his earnestness of exhortation, and his skillful blending of the lyrical and the ethical in his dynamic portrayal of imminent destruction as the consequence of revolt against God.

The advance of the enemy is compared to the coming of a wind—not a gentle westerly breeze used in winnowing grain, but a burning sirocco blowing in hot off the desert to the east, filling the air with sand and carrying off both wheat and chaff (the judgment will spare neither good nor bad).[51] The graphic imagery of vv. 11–12 continues in v. 13.

At this point, the prophet injects a call to repentance (v. 14). Note that he speaks of the cleansing of the heart (cf. 4:4) and that he still has hope. His God is a God of love and stands ready to forgive, if the people will turn from their apostasy in true penitence.

The dramatic quality of Jeremiah's early poetry is evident. Note how, for example, he pictures the watchman from *Dan*—on the northern border of the country—relaying the message of warning to watchers on *Mount Ephraim*, in the south, not far from Jerusalem.[52]

That the central thrust in these poems on the foe from the north is not the identity or description of the enemy but the indictment of the people and the imminence of judgment is evidenced by the way in which this second poem closes (vv. 17–18).

c. The Anguish of the Prophet (4:19–22)

19 My anguish, my anguish! I writhe in pain!
    Oh, the walls of my heart!
  My heart is beating wildly;
    I cannot keep silent;
  for I hear the sound of the trumpet,
    the alarm of war.
20 Disaster follows hard on disaster,
    the whole land is laid waste.
  Suddenly my tents are destroyed,
    my curtains in a moment.
21 How long must I see the standard,
    and hear the sound of the trumpet?
22 "For my people are foolish,
    they know me not;
  they are stupid children,
    they have no understanding.
  They are skilled in doing evil,
    but how to do good they know not."

The third poem is a personal lament (contra Eissfeldt), in which Jeremiah gives voice to his inner agony as he contemplates the catastrophe coming upon his countrymen. Claus Westermann calls attention to the fact that the lament is developed more extensively and used more effectively in Jeremiah than in any other prophet.[53]

Just as the *heart* was considered to be primarily the seat of the intellect and the will, so the bowels (v. 19, Heb. "my bowels," not *my anguish*) were regarded as the seat of the emotions (along with the kidneys). *The walls* of the *heart* are the sides of the cavity of the heart against which it beats.

In this very important passage we have the first direct indication of Jeremiah's deep identification with his people in their sin and their suffering. In some degree, he speaks as a representative of the people. *My tents* may be the tents of his countrymen, as well as his own (the *curtains* are the tent hangings). The anguish, which he will experience and express again and again, stems from his love for his people. Already we see the shadow of a cross falling across the soul of the servant of God.

The personal lament culminates in a prophetic oracle (v. 22), which itself is

---

51 Bright renders vv. 11–12 as poetry (p. 29). The lawsuit concept is more apparent in his translation of v. 12b: "Now it's I myself who utter sentence upon them."

52 On the sending of fire-signals, see the Lachish Letters, Pritchard, ANET, pp. 321 f.

53 Westermann, *op. cit.*, p. 202.

also a lament, the lament of God. The stupidity of the people in playing God false is the bitterest part of their apostasy. Once again the closing emphasis is ethical indictment, not the identity of the enemy (cf. vv. 8 ff.,17–18).

The poems heretofore are probably literary visions, i.e., poetry of a visual type, which is the creation of a gifted imagination under inspiration. However, this third poem has the earmarks of an ecstatic vision. Hans Schmidt classifies it "among the best descriptions of a vision in the Old Testament, nay in all literature" (cf. Skinner, p. 49, quotation from *Die grossen Propheten und ihre Zeit*, p. 205).

d. The Cosmos Reverting to Chaos (4: 23–28)

23 I looked on the earth, and lo, it was waste
  and void;
    and to the heavens, and they had no light.
24 I looked on the mountains, and lo, they
  were quaking,
    and all the hills moved to and fro.
25 I looked, and lo, there was no man,
    and all the birds of the air had fled.
26 I looked, and lo, the fruitful land was a
  desert,
    and all its cities were laid in ruins
    before the Lord, before his fierce anger.
27 For thus says the Lord, "The whole land
shall be a desolation; yet I will not make a full
end.
28 For this the earth shall mourn,
    and the heavens above be black;
    for I have spoken, I have purposed;
    I have not relented nor will I turn back."

There is much difference of opinion as to the authenticity, character, and length of this poem, but none, apparently, concerning its literary excellence. It is a masterpiece.

It is not possible or advisable to present a detailed discussion of the problems mentioned. Suffice it to say that, in full awareness of all that is involved, the authenticity of the passage is accepted (cf. Duhm, Rudolph, Peake, Skinner, Lindblom, and von Rad). As to its character, it is not apocalyptic in the technical, critical sense, but in the poetic, existential sense. It speaks of a world catastrophe (cf. Isa.

2:12 ff.). It is no blueprint for a particular historical event, such as an invasion of Judah. It expresses a deep awareness of impending crisis, "a poetic sense of the devastation which man brings on himself by opposing God's purpose for him" (Cunliffe-Jones, p. 67). In some respects, it is similar to much of what we find in contemporary poetry concerning the human predicament. As for the length, vv. 27–28 are poetry and belong to the poem (Bright, p. 31).

The poem is a remarkable piece of writing. As to structure, there are three things about it that are very striking. The first is the repetition in Hebrew of the combination *ra'iti . . . w°hinneh: I looked . . . and lo.* Four times these musical words occur. The second arresting feature is a rather radical change of poetic meter. The dirge rhythm is deliberately varied. Third, there is a descending parallelism from the more general to the more specific, until the individual (the poet) is seen standing alone in the midst of chaos: *earth—heavens; mountains—hills; man—birds; fruitful land—cities.*

Cosmos has reverted to chaos (cf. Gen. 1:2). Light is gone. The mountains and the hills, symbols of strength and stability, are no longer stable and secure, but are shaking and swaying and sinking. There is no man about, and the birds have fled. The cultivated land is a desert, and fortified cities are in ruins. And Jeremiah is looking on—as man faces the ultimate outcome of his choosing to live as a rebel against God. What a picture!

The picture was seen in vision, and the clue to understanding it is to recognize that the prophet views the destruction of the universe. This, in turn, becomes symbolic for him of the destruction of Judah.

This poem of unusual power speaks to our contemporary situation. It pictures the shaking of the foundations. We, too, live in a time of crisis. Chaos threatens to invade and destroy the cosmos.

But we should remember that if sin leads to desolation, repentance leads to salvation; also that the same Bible which contains the picture of chaos also contains the promise of a new heaven and a new earth (cf. Isa. 65:17–25; Rev. 21–22).

e. The Assault of the Adversary and the Death Agony of Zion (4:29–31)

29 At the noise of horseman and archer
    every city takes to flight;
    they enter thickets; they climb among rocks;
    all the cities are forsaken,
    and no man dwells in them.
30 And you, O desolate one,
    what do you mean that you dress in scarlet,
    that you deck yourself with ornaments of gold,
    that you enlarge your eyes with paint?
    In vain you beautify yourself.
    Your lovers despise you;
    they seek your life.
31 For I heard a cry as of a woman in travail,
    anguish as of one bringing forth her first child,
    the cry of the daughter of Zion gasping for breath,
    stretching out her hands,
    "Woe is me! I am fainting before murderers."

The final poem in the series begins with a vivid picture of the people in precipitate flight before the foe (v. 29). They flee to the hills—"scuttle for the caves, crouch in the thickets, scramble up the cliffs." The day of reckoning with the righteous Ruler of this world has come!

The opening picture is followed by a graphic and dramatic portrayal of Jerusalem primping and prettying herself up (vv. 30 f.). She puts on her gorgeous garments and golden *ornaments* and paints her eyes with black powder to make them look bigger and brighter. All this she does in order to allure her *lovers* (the people who make up the army of the invader). But she discovers, much to her chagrin, that they are not interested in her love but her life. As the section comes to a close, she spreads out her hands in a desperate plea, shrieks with terror, and sinks to the ground, saying (Bright, p. 32):

"Ah, me! I'm dying.
The murderers—they've killed me!"
By means of vivid imagery, a variety in parallelism, an effective use of sound pat-

terns, a creative synthesis of forms, dramatic momentum, the employment of symmetries, sober realism, and penetrating prophetic insight, Jeremiah hammers home the truth that there will be a "payday someday." It is written into the structure of things. Apart from real repentance, persistent rebellion against God will result in ruin.

(2) The Reason for the Ruin (5:1–31)

Chapter 5 is a unique chapter. It tells about "a private prophetic project" by means of which the imperative necessity for judgment was indelibly impressed upon the prophet (Volz). God sent him through the streets of Jerusalem in search of a man (v. 1). Jeremiah went on the quest. He first made his way *to the poor*— the peddlers, shopkeepers, donkey drivers, ordinary laborers, the uneducated masses. His search was in vain. Then he made his way to *the great*—the upper class, the "jet set" of Jerusalem. He doubtless thought: The "down-and-outers" are ignorant. They have no time or opportunity to learn *the way of the Lord*. But the "up-and-outers" do. Surely among them could be found one man of piety and integrity. The result was the same.

As a consequence of this experience and his reflection upon it, the prophet brought one of the sharpest, most incisive critiques of a decadent society to be found anywhere in the Bible or outside it. Chapter 5 contains that critique. There are four major elements in it, four evidences of the deterioration that comes when there is no dynamic covenant relationship with the living God.

a. Corruptness of Conduct (5:1–9)

1 Run to and fro through the streets of Jerusalem,
    look and take note!
    Search her squares to see
    if you can find a man,
    one who does justice
    and seeks truth;
    that I may pardon her.
2 Though they say, "As the LORD lives,"
    yet they swear falsely.

3 O Lord, do not thy eyes look for truth?
  Thou hast smitten them,
    but they felt no anguish;
  thou hast consumed them,
    but they refused to take correction.
  They have made their faces harder than
      rock;
    they have refused to repent.
4 Then I said, "These are only the poor,
    they have no sense;
  for they do not know the way of the Lord,
    the law of their God.
5 I will go to the great,
    and will speak to them;
  for they know the way of the Lord,
    the law of their God."
  But they all alike had broken the yoke,
    they had burst the bonds.
6 Therefore a lion from the forest shall slay
      them,
    a wolf from the desert shall destroy them.
  A leopard is watching against their cities,
    every one who goes out of them shall be
      torn in pieces;
  because their transgressions are many,
    their apostasies are great.
7 "How can I pardon you?
    Your children have forsaken me,
    and have sworn by those who are no
      gods.
  When I fed them to the full,
    they committed adultery
    and trooped to the houses of harlots.
8 They were well-fed lusty stallions,
    each neighing for his neighbor's wife.
9 Shall I not punish them for these things?
                              says the Lord;
    and shall I not avenge myself
    on a nation such as this?

Wanted: *a man!* What kind of man?
One who does justice (*mishpat*) *and seeks
truth* (*'emunah*). The word *mishpat* is
variously rendered in the Old Testament.
It may refer to the place where justice is
administered (the court), the execution of
justice in the court (right decision), etc.
Here it signifies covenant religion on its
practical side as a divine ordering of life—
God's true way of life for his people.

The basic idea of *'emunah* is that of
firmness. As one of its primary meanings,
it designates a state or condition of steadi-
ness resulting from steadying oneself upon
someone or something other than self.
Hence it can mean both faith and faithfulness, both trust and trustworthiness, both

reliance and reliability. In relation to the
covenant, it speaks of a firmness in one's
relationship to God which shows itself in a
stability or integrity or fidelity in one's
relationship to others in the community.

So, the kind of man God wants and
Jeremiah is seeking—so that God may perchance pardon the people for their apostasy (cf. Gen. 18:22–33)—is a man who
has a firm faith in and fidelity to the covenant God and who demonstrates this in
his conformity in daily life to the code of
behavior befitting a person in covenant
relationship with God. The man sought by
God must be marked by true piety and
real integrity.

Jeremiah searches through the streets,
the squares, and the shops of the capital
city, peering into faces, observing attitudes
and actions, going both to small and great.
But the result is disappointment. The people are corrupt in conduct. They are guilty
of perjury, a very serious offense (v. 2; cf.
4:2). They are in a state of apostasy. They
have *broken the yoke* and *burst the bonds*
(v. 5b; cf. 2:20). In fact, they have shaken
off the restraints of the covenant faith and
strayed so far that they are in peril of
being pounced upon by *a lion . . . a
wolf . . . a leopard . . . because their
transgressions are many* (v. 6; see comment on 2:18, fn.). They have forsaken the
Lord and *sworn by those who are no gods*
(v. 7a). They have *refused . . . correction* and *made their faces harder than
rock.* They will not *repent* (v. 3b). They
do not know *the way of the Lord,* though
they should (vv. 4–5).

In addition to perjury and apostasy,
they are practicing *adultery.* They are like
*well-fed lusty stallions, each neighing for
his neighbor's wife* (vv. 7b–8). Prosperity
has not brought gratitude and godliness
but depravity (v. 7b).

Verses 1–9 record the shattering disillusionment of the prophet and a frank
and fearless exposure of the moral corruption pervading and poisoning the life
of the people. The accusation brought
concludes with a brief, indirect, but force-

ful announcement of judgment in the form of two questions (v. 9). Corruption will end in retribution.

b. Complacency (5:10–19)

10 "Go up through her vine-rows and destroy,
   but make not a full end;
   strip away her branches,
   for they are not the LORD's.
11 For the house of Israel and the house of Judah
   have been utterly faithless to me,
                     says the LORD.
12 They have spoken falsely of the LORD,
   and have said, 'He will do nothing;
   no evil will come upon us,
   nor shall we see sword or famine.
13 The prophets will become wind;
   the word is not in them.
   Thus shall it be done to them!' "
14 Therefore thus says the LORD, the God of hosts:
   "Because they have spoken this word,
   behold, I am making my words in your mouth a fire,
   and this people wood, and the fire shall devour them.
15 Behold, I am bringing upon you
   a nation from afar, O house of Israel,
                     says the LORD.
   It is an enduring nation,
   it is an ancient nation,
   a nation whose language you do not know,
   nor can you understand what they say.
16 Their quiver is like an open tomb,
   they are all mighty men.
17 They shall eat up your harvest and your food;
   they shall eat up your sons and your daughters;
   they shall eat up your flocks and your herds;
   they shall eat up your vines and your fig trees;
   your fortified cities in which you trust
   they shall destroy with the sword."
18 "But even in those days, say the LORD, I will not make a full end of you. 19 And when your people say, 'Why has the LORD our God done all these things to us?' you shall say to them, 'As you have forsaken me and served foreign gods in your land, so you shall serve strangers in a land that is not yours.' "

This portion of the chapter begins with a threat (v. 10), which is followed by a reproach (vv. 11–13). Then comes a second threat or warning of judgment (v. 14), which is expanded into a sixth poem on the foe from the north (vv. 15–19).

God speaks directly in vv. 10–11. He commands unspecified destroyers to *ravage his vineyard*. It is his vineyard, but the branches are not his, for they are bearing the wrong kind of fruit (cf. Isa. 5:1 ff.). Therefore they are to be stripped away (cf. comment on 2:21). However, the stock of the vine is not to be removed. A *full end* is not to be made. A remnant will survive the judgment, and the vineyard of the Lord will one day become fruitful again for his glory. One almost misses this note of hope because of the emphasis on reproach and retribution.

The branches in the Lord's vineyard are to be stripped away because of the fact that *the house of Israel and the house of Judah* have been unfaithful to their covenant relationship with him (v. 11). The particular manifestation of that unfaithfulness pinpointed here is that of apathy (vv. 12–13). Lacking in integrity, the people are guilty of indifference.

The primary reason for this apathy is that the people have perverted the doctrine of election. Instead of regarding it as a moral act subject to moral criticism and control, they have come to look upon it as an unconditioned relationship which guarantees for them national victory and glory. They have made it the basis of grandiose dreams. In these dreams they have been supported by the popular prophets, purveyors of a superficial and baseless optimism.

Thus they have settled down into a comfortable sense of false security, saying, in effect, "It can't happen here—not to *us*, God's elect. Election and destruction are mutually exclusive" (cf. v. 12). When the true prophets like Jeremiah seek to correct this dangerous perversion of a great concept and the apathy growing out of it, the people counter with the retort: "You are just windbags. Your statements about judgment are meaningless. God's word is not in you" (v. 13).

The deft touch of the master of rhetorical devices is felt in the introduction of the word *ruach*. The probable root idea behind this word is power—air in motion. Hence it can be translated both as "spirit" and as "wind." "Spirit" is power. Ordinarily in the Old Testament—except in the early stages of the development of the concept—the Spirit of God is God present in power, carrying out his purpose or endowing someone else with the power to carry it out. A wind can also be a thing of power.

The self-complacent people who have dubbed the true prophetic word of judgment *wind* (*ruach*), an empty thing, are going to find that it will prove to be a thing of tremendous power. A wind will fan it into a flame, and it will burn like fire. The people will be as *wood,* and *the fire* will *devour them* (v. 14).

A difficult thing to deal with, this sin of the settled and satisfied (cf. Amos 6:1; Zeph. 1:12)! Jeremiah knows that the people must be shaken out of their complacency and made to face up to reality. They must be flogged by the prophetic word. And so there is an extended prophecy of judgment, beginning with v. 14. This prophecy includes a picture of the coming of the enemy from the north (vv. 15–17) and a forecast of captivity (vv. 18–19). Since the people have insisted on serving foreign gods in their own land, they must serve foreign masters in a strange land (like 3:14b–18, the reference to the captivity here and to the survival of a remnant in verse 10—also in 4:27; 5:18 —probably comes from a later period in Jeremiah's ministry). Again, it is indicated that sin leads to judgment.

c. Callousness (5:20-29)

20 Declare this in the house of Jacob,
    proclaim it in Judah:
21 "Hear this, O foolish and senseless people,
    who have eyes, but see not,
    who have ears, but hear not.
22 Do you not fear me? says the Lord;
    Do you not tremble before me?
    I placed the sand as the bound for the sea,
    a perpetual barrier which it cannot pass;
    though the waves toss, they cannot prevail,
    though they roar, they cannot pass over
    it.

23 But this people has a stubborn and rebellious heart;
    they have turned aside and gone away.
24 They do not say in their hearts,
    'Let us fear the Lord our God,
    who gives the rain in its season,
    the autumn rain and the spring rain,
    and keeps for us
    the weeks appointed for the harvest.'
25 Your iniquities have turned these away,
    and your sins have kept good from you.
26 For wicked men are found among my people;
    they lurk like fowlers lying in wait.
    They set a trap;
    they catch men.
27 Like a basket full of birds,
    their houses are full of treachery;
    therefore they have become great and rich,
28 they have grown fat and sleek.
    They know no bounds in deeds of wickedness;
    they judge not with justice
    the cause of the fatherless, to make it prosper,
    and they do not defend the rights of the needy.
29 Shall I not punish them for these things?
                        says the Lord.
    and shall I not avenge myself
    on a nation such as this?"

After the introductory summons to the prophet to proclaim and to the people to hear the word of the Lord (v. 20) comes a lengthy reproach (vv. 21–28), followed by a brief threat (v. 29).

The aspect of the sin of the people which stands out here is their sheer callousness. They *have eyes, but see not.* They *have ears, but hear not* (v. 21b). They have no sense of awe in the presence of the God of majesty and might, who set *the sand as the bound for the sea, a perpetual barrier which it cannot pass* (v. 22). They have no gratitude for God's goodness, which has shown itself in his protection of them and provision for them (v. 24). They have no regard for God's laws. Like fowlers, who through their cleverness fill their cages with trapped birds, they, in violation of covenant laws, have filled their coffers with wealth by setting traps for the defenseless members of society (vv. 26–28). Their wickedness knows no bounds (v. 28a). They have become *fat and sleek* (v. 28a) and *stubborn and rebellious* (v. 23a), i.e., prosperous and proud—and defiant of God. Neither his power nor his grace nor his law can get to them. They are hardened, encrusted, calloused.

God must therefore deal with them (v. 29). Sin's penalty must be paid.

d. A Conspiracy of Evil in the Life of the Community (5:30–31)

30 An appalling and horrible thing
      has happened in the land:
31 the prophets prophesy falsely,
      and the priests rule at their direction;
   my people love to have it so,
      but what will you do when the end
      comes?

The chapter comes to a climactic conclusion with a brief passage which pictures "an appalling and disgusting situation" (v. 30, A. R. Johnson's translation). There is an element of lament as well as accusation here. Something horrible has *happened in the land*: "*The prophets* prophesy by the lie (the reference being either to Baal or to the falseness of the message because it is the word of man rather than the word of God), and *the priests* rule at their hands,[54] and *my people* love it so" (literal translation; italics for the Hebrew emphasis).

Here is the conspiracy of evil standing at the center of community life and reaching out to its circumference. Such a conspiracy can have but one consequence, if there is no radical change, catastrophe. Thus the chapter and the critique conclude with the searching, sobering question: *What will you do when the end comes?* A very good question for the beginning!

This is an important chapter. A major item of interest in it is God's method in impressing indelibly upon his servant the moral necessity for the judgment. He put him out where the people were. God's man needs to spend time with God. He

also must spend time with people, "where cross the crowded ways of life." Jeremiah became involved with the people, and when he spoke they got the point.

The picture of the prophet moving about the city, gazing intently at this person and that, in his search for "a man" characterized by genuine piety and integrity, suggests that the individual was coming more and more into the center of his thinking. It is recognized that in Jeremiah and Ezekiel there is a shift from the nation to the individual as the basic unit in religious experience (though this must not be overpressed). Foregleams of this appear in Jeremiah's experience described in chapter 5.

Under God's guidance and through his engagement with life, the prophet came to the conclusion that a collection of corrupt individuals produces a corrupt society and that corrupt structures and institutions perpetuate that society and breed more corrupt individuals. And so the vicious cycle continues.

Jeremiah presents in chapter 5 a catalogue of crimes, a critique of a decadent urban society. The source of the trouble was the loss of the ultimate loyalty, the lack of a right relationship with God. When this goes, life begins to fall apart. Unless something is done about it, calamity is sure and certain.

But what can be done, when the members of the society are corrupt, complacent, calloused, and there is a conspiracy of evil at the core of it all? The only hope lies in the change of the human heart through the grace of God. Jeremiah seems to move toward this conclusion.

(3) Rebellion, Ritual, and Retribution (6:1–30)

This section lacks the coherence of the two preceding sections (4:5–31; 5:1–31). It is more miscellaneous in character. It contains both reproach and threat, but with variations and additions. There are five parts to it.

---

[54] This could mean "at their side" or "by their authority"; Rudolph's idea is appealing: "The priests work 'hand in hand' with them" (p. 37).

a. The Siege of the City (6:1–8)

1 Flee for safety, O people of Benjamin,
   From the midst of Jerusalem!
   Blow the trumpet in Tekoa,
      and raise a signal on Bethhaccherem;
   for evil looms out of the north,
      and great destruction.
2 The comely and delicately bred I will de-
      stroy,
      the daughter of Zion.
3 Shepherds with their flocks shall come
      against her;
   they shall pitch their tents around her,
   they shall pasture, each in his place.
4 "Prepare war against her;
      up, and let us attack at noon!"
   "Woe to us, for the day declines,
      for the shadows of evening lengthen!"
5 "Up, and let us attack by night,
      and destroy her palaces!"
6 For thus says the LORD of hosts:
   "Hew down her trees;
      cast up a siege mound against Jerusalem.
   This is the city which must be punished;
      there is nothing but oppression within
      her.
7 As a well keeps its water fresh,
      so she keeps fresh her wickedness;
   violence and destruction are heard within
      her;
   sickness and wounds are ever before me.
8 Be warned, O Jerusalem,
      lest I be alienated from you;
   lest I make you a desolation,
      an uninhabited land."

This is the seventh in the series of the poems about the foe from the north. It reflects the same skill and versatility seen elsewhere. One is impressed with the cry of alarm, the sharp call for exodus, the alliteration (e.g., Heb. for "blow" and "Tekoa"), the graphic imagery, the element of the dramatic in the conversation of the commanders and the outcry of the citizens of the city, and the earnest plea to turn before it is too late.

The fact that Jeremiah was a Benjamite may explain his use of the term *Benjamin* in his vigorous summons to the people of the city to seek safety in the hill country to the south. *Tekoa*, hometown of Amos, was some 12 miles south of Jerusalem. Recent excavations suggest Ramat Rachel (on the road from Jerusalem to Bethlehem) as the possible site of *Beth-hacherem*.[55]

55 Y. Aharoni, BA, 24, 1961, 98–118.

The reason for the summons to get out of Jerusalem is that "evil (emphatic) peers forth (lit., bends forward in order to see or fall upon) from the north, even a great shattering" (v. 1b.). The word *evil* may refer to natural evil (disaster, calamity) or to moral evil—sin and/or the judgment it brings. Both meanings are likely implied here, for Jeremiah is referring to a calamity which is coming as retribution for rebellion against God (cf. 4:5–31; 5: 15 ff.).

There is a textual problem in v. 2. With Volz, Cornhill, Rudolph, Bright, and others, we probably should read "Daughter-Zion, have I likened you to a meadow [pasture] delightful?" Verse 3 then picks up the figure, as the approaching invaders are compared to shepherds bringing their flocks to graze in that meadow (the *shepherds* are the commanders, and *their flocks* are the soldiers in the army).

Verses 4–5 take the reader into camp. A vigorous conversation is in progress, as the commanders debate when to attack. Having let the opportunity to seize the city during the noon siesta slip by, they decide to assault it at night. The description of the coming of the enemy and the imminent siege of the city ends with a declaration by *the Lord of hosts* (vv. 6–8). This declaration is an oracle made up of a reproach and a threat. God joins in, as it were, on the conversation of the commanders, telling them to cut down trees and cast up mounds against Jerusalem (a common practice among the Assyrians and Babylonians in siege operations), for, he continues, *This is the city which must be punished.*

Two aspects of the situation calling forth this statement are stressed. First, the city is like *a well* (self-replenishing) that *keeps fresh her wickedness* (a very strong and suggestive simile). Second, she is guilty of various specific sinful acts: *violence and destruction.* These specific acts flow forth from the central fountain of unfaithfulness to the covenant relationship.

Like the other poems about the foe from the north, this one closes with a prediction of judgment to come. The words *Be warned, O Jerusalem, lest I be alienated from you* (lit., be torn away or pulled out from you) indicate that the prophet still has hope.

b. The Sinfulness of the City's Citizens (6:9–15)

9 Thus says the LORD of hosts:
"Glean thoroughly as a vine
   the remnant of Israel;
like a grape-gatherer pass your hand again
   over its branches."
10 To whom shall I speak and give warning,
   that they may hear?
Behold, their ears are closed,
   they cannot listen;
behold, the word of the LORD is to them an
   object of scorn,
they take no pleasure in it.
11 Therefore I am full of the wrath of the
   LORD;
I am weary of holding it in.
"Pour it out upon the children in the street,
   and upon the gatherings of young men,
   also;
both husband and wife shall be taken,
   the old folk and the very aged.
12 Their houses shall be turned over to others,
   their fields and wives together;
for I will stretch out my hand
   against the inhabitants of the land,"
                              says the LORD.
13 "For from the least to the greatest of them,
   every one is greedy for unjust gain;
and from prophet to priest,
   every one deals falsely.
14 They have healed the wound of my people
   lightly,
   saying, 'Peace, peace,'
   when there is no peace.
15 Were they ashamed when they committed
   abomination?
No, they were not at all ashamed;
   they did not know how to blush.
Therefore they shall fall among those who
   fall;
at the time that I punish them, they shall
   be overthrown,"
                              says the LORD.

This portion of the chapter is in the form of a dialogue between God and Jeremiah. It starts out with a private oracle, in which the prophet is told to resume his search for a godly man (v. 9; cf. 5:1 ff.). This takes the form of a command to glean the vineyard of the Lord (Judah), as a grape-gatherer would carefully *glean* a

vine to make sure that he had not missed some cluster of grapes concealed by the thick foliage.

The prophet replies to God's request. He states that it is no use, for the people are totally corrupt (v. 10). Like their hearts (4:4), *their ears are closed* (not open and responsive), and they will not receive and respond to *the word of the Lord.* . . . *An object of scorn,* a thing in which they *take no pleasure,* is this *word* of judgment.

Though it is having little effect on the people, that *word* is having a tremendous effect on Jeremiah. He is about to explode! Verse 11a is an illuminating statement. From the human standpoint, it suggests that the rejection of the prophet's message by a corrupt, contemptuous "covenant community" (?) is becoming hard to take. Indignation burns within him. Also, it shows that he shares what A. Heschel calls the pathos of God, i.e., his feeling.[56]

Revelatory experiences not only affected the intellect and the imagination, but also aroused the emotions: sometimes anguish (4:19); occasionally exultation (15:16); at times anger (v. 11a). The prophets lived in intimate communion with the God who called them and whose word they communicated. Accordingly, they partook in some measure of his love and his wrath (Lindblom, pp. 179, 298 f.). This is true of Jeremiah (cf. von Rad, p. 63).

God's response to the prophet's outburst follows in vv. 11b–15. His initial words *Pour it out upon* them (this *wrath,* cf. 4:4) constitute the first foreshadowing of the figure of the cup of the Lord's wrath (cf. 13:12–14; 25:15 ff.). In this outpouring of the disturbing, destructive word of divine wrath, none are to be missed, for all are guilty *from the least to the greatest of them.* But none are more guilty than the religious leaders. The priests and the prophets—and the people they lead —"everyone acteth the fraud" (v. 13b, A. R. Johnson's translation).

There are three elements in the indictment of the priests, the prophets, and the

---

56 *The Prophets* (New York: Harper & Row, 1963).

people. The first is greed for unjust gain (v. 13a). They are money-mad. The second is a spirit of superficial optimism (v. 14). This is especially encouraged by the traffickers in peace-oracles. The nation is suffering from a deadly disease. Yet no skilled surgery is being used, only baseless assurance. The popular religious leaders are applying a soothing salve to the surface of the skin, whereas underneath that surface a fatal cancer is at work. They shout, in effect, "It's all right!" when it isn't "all right" (*peace* refers to rich harmonious relationships with God and men, or to the well-being resulting from such relationships). The third thing of which the people and their religious guides are guilty is a lack of shame in the presence of sins committed. They have lost their ability *to blush.* Nothing shocks them or shakes them up. In their self-righteousness, they claim, "there's nothing wrong with us" (v. 15a). And thus they must suffer punishment (v. 15b).

c. Sacrifice and Ceremony No Substitute for Surrender to God (6:16–21)

16 Thus says the Lord:
"Stand by the roads, and look,
  and ask for the ancient paths,
where the good way is; and walk in it,
  and find rest for your souls.
But they said, 'We will not walk in it.'
17 I set watchmen over you, saying,
  'Give heed to the sound of the trumpet!'
But they said, 'We will not give heed.'
18 Therefore hear, O nations,
  and know, O congregation, what will
    happen to them.
19 Hear, O earth; behold, I am bringing evil
  upon this people,
  the fruit of their devices,
because they have not given heed to my
  words;
  and as for my law, they have rejected it.
20 To what purpose does frankincense come to
  me from Sheba,
  or sweet cane from a distant land?
Your burnt offerings are not acceptable,
  nor your sacrifices pleasing to me.
21 Therefore thus says the Lord:
'Behold, I will lay before this people
  stumbling blocks against which they
    shall stumble;
fathers and sons together,
  neighbor and friends shall perish.' "

Here, too, is an oracle of the reproach-threat type—like so many in Jeremiah—changed, expanded, enriched. It proclaims, in effect, that God has called his people to return to the ancient paths of the Mosaic covenant faith, but they have refused to respond to the call. They have paid no heed to his warnings (vv. 16–17), have spurned his *law* (v. 19), and have sought to meet his covenant requirements by substituting sacrifice and ceremony for surrender and service (vv. 19–20). God is not going to allow this to continue. He will bring *evil* upon them. He will place *stumbling blocks* in their path, so that they will stumble and fall—all (v. 21)! They will reap *the fruit of their own devices.* The calamity which God is going to send as chastisement will be the inevitable consequence of their choices and conduct.

Observe that *my words* and *my law* are set in parallelism in v. 19b. Word and law (instruction, revelation) are sometimes synonymous. The prophets were "regarded as teachers of torah" (Lindblom, pp. 156 f.). The *frankincense* and *sweet cane* mentioned in v. 20 were used in worship. The latter came from India; the former, from Sheba, a country in southwest Arabia. The attitude of Jeremiah toward the cult will not be discussed here. Suffice it to say that, he is not objecting to the cult as such but to the form it took and the way it was being used in his day.

Verse 16 is one of the outstanding verses in the prophecy of Jeremiah. Several things stand out in it. The first is a challenge to serious thought: "Stand by the roads (lit. upon the ways—i.e., at the place where they meet or part), and look (gaze at the guideposts). See where it is that you are headed, lest you wind up in a wilderness or over a precipice. Think upon your way. Ponder your paths!" This is a challenge which needs to be issued to many today: those who follow the crowd, those who go in for novelty for novelty's sake, those who choose pleasure or money as the highest good in life, those who worship at the shrine of science or scholarship or institutional religion.

Second, there is a command to careful inquiry into the old paths, with a view to ascertaining the good way. This is no brief for an unthinking conservatism. Jeremiah was a "rebel prophet," who dared to cut across many established customs and conventions of his day. At the same time, he was soundly grounded in the covenant faith of Moses and the fathers. *The ancient paths* were paths of faith, spiritual worship, ethical conduct, and obedience. Among these would be found *the good way*, God's way—good because it was ordained of God from eternity and set in the structure of reality, good because it had been tested and found to be true. It was not necessarily the easiest way or the most popular way or the shortest way. But it was God's way and therefore good—in its commencement, its continuation, and its consummation.

In the third place, there is the call to action: *walk in it*. It is not enough to think and inquire. There must be a positive response. The only way to salvation in Jeremiah's day—or ours—was that of a turning back to the eternal paths of God.

Next comes the accompanying promise: *and find rest for your souls*. Soul refers to the total life of the person. *Rest* signifies freedom from anxiety after wandering around. The allusion is to the settling down or relaxation of the whole of life—of the individual or the group—in a situation which makes this possible. The concept of "rest" in the Scriptures is rich and suggestive—richer, of course, and more personal in the New Testament than in the Old (cf. Matt. 11:28–30; Heb. 3:18; 4:9; etc.). Man's rest involves sharing the rest of God.

Like the ancient Israelites, people today seek rest in various directions, but there is only one path that leads to it, that of commitment to the God of covenant grace, who has manifested himself supremely in the Incarnation, crucifixion, and resurrection of Jesus Christ, our Savior and Lord.

Finally, there is the people's choice: *We will not walk in it*. According to Jeremiah,

there are two ways men can take (cf. Deut. 30:15–20). One leads to rest, the other to ruin. Each person, each nation must choose the path he or it will follow. Israel chose the road to ruin.

d. A Sound Like the Roaring of the Sea (6:22–26)

22 Thus says the LORD:
    "Behold, a people is coming from the north country,
        a great nation is stirring from the farthest parts of the earth.
23 They lay hold on bow and spear,
        they are cruel and have no mercy,
        the sound of them is like the roaring sea;
    they ride upon horses,
        set in array as a man for battle,
        against you, O daughter of Zion!"
24 We have heard the report of it,
        our hands fall helpless;
    anguish has taken hold of us,
        pain as of a woman in travail.
25 Go not forth into the field,
        nor walk on the road;
    for the enemy has a sword,
        terror is on every side.
26 O daughter of my people, gird on sackcloth,
        and roll in ashes;
    make mourning as for an only son,
        most bitter lamentation;
    for suddenly the destroyer
        will come upon us.

This is the final poem in the series about the invasion and devastation of Judah by a foe from the north. It is in the form of a speech by God (vv. 22–23) and a lament by the people (vv. 24–26). Although it is an exceedingly vigorous and vivid piece of poetic composition, it does not add anything distinctively new or different to the portrait already painted. It stresses the cruelty of the enemy and the terror and anguish which his presence will create— *terror . . . on every side* (one of Jeremiah's favorite expressions) and agony like that of a woman in labor. Also, there will be *mourning as for an only son*—about the bitterest sorrow that could come to an Israelite family.

e. An Assay of the Attitudes and Actions of the People (6:27–30)

27 "I have made you an assayer and tester among my people,
        that you may know and assay their ways.

²⁸ They are all stubbornly rebellious,
  going about with slanders;
  they are bronze and iron,
  all of them act corruptly.
²⁹ The bellows blow fiercely,
  the lead is consumed by the fire;
  in vain the refining goes on,
  for the wicked are not removed.
³⁰ Refuse silver they are called,
  for the LORD has rejected them."

This passage is in the form of a dialogue. In v. 27 God speaks. Verses 28–30 contain Jeremiah's answer.

There is a difference of opinion concerning the date of this section and its relation to the context. Some scholars date it much later than most of the material in chapters 2–6 and maintain that it has no direct connection with what precedes it (e.g., Skinner, pp. 156 ff.).

The passage may well recount an experience which transpired early in the ministry of the prophet—probably before 622 B.C.—and which is dynamically tied in with that which comes before it, especially in chapters 5—6. Someone felt that it belonged where it is. Since its link is not with the verses immediately preceding it (vv. 22–26) but with the larger context, that person would not likely be a compiler or an editor. Why not Jeremiah? Perhaps he inserted the passage here because it recorded an experience which clarified and enlarged his understanding of his role as a prophet at a strategic time in his career, the period shortly before the Josianic reformation.

By means of a metaphor of unusual force, God reassures Jeremiah of his divine commission and gives him a new conception of his work (v. 27). Not only is he a proclaimer and an exhorter, but also an assayer. The figure is that of testing or refining metal. Back in the days before quick silver, the refining process required that lead be mixed with the alloy containing silver. The two were fused into a molten mass in a furnace. A current of air was turned upon that mass. The lead, acting as an oxidizing agent, carried off the alloy or dross, leaving the pure silver

Bright, pp. 48,50).

The prophet is to be a tester of the attitudes and actions of the people, an assayer of their character and conduct, "a moral analyst." This may refer in part to what he is already doing. In part, it may be—and likely is—a preparation for an upcoming new stage in his ministry which will involve his relation to the great reform. Jeremiah gives his current assay of the situation in vv. 28–30. The dross is so closely mixed in with the silver in the life of the covenant people that, though the oxidizing takes place, the dross is not removed and that which remains is refuse silver.

There is a tremendous wordplay in v. 30: a people who have persistently rejected God will ultimately be rejected by God—and men.

The prophet is not necessarily indicating that he has given up hope for the nation. He may be doing what prophets often do: stating the case in absolute and shocking terms with the hope of shaking the people into a sense of reality and into a sincere return to God. Prophetic absolutes can be incentives to action. The question here is whether Jeremiah is speaking only as "a prophet of denunciation," or also as "a prophet of grace through denunciation" (Cunliffe-Jones, p. 80). Why could it not be the latter?

In his early years as a prophet Jeremiah delivered the message of the Lord with great earnestness, ingenuity, and force. He pleaded with the people to repent and return to a right relationship with God. He proclaimed that if there was no covenantal return retribution was certain to come. He was persuaded that unless the foe within was conquered the foe without would conquer.

III. A Collection of Oracles of Diverse Character (7:1—10:25)

As the reader moves from chapter 6 to chapter 7, he becomes aware of a rather abrupt change. There is continuity, to be sure, in the reiterated emphasis on the central theme of chapters 2—6: Israel's betrayal of God's love in the breach of the covenant and her punishment for her sin, if she does not repent. Yet, though there is continuity, there is also a fairly sharp break.

There is a shift in chronology. The clue to the understanding of this shift is to be found in 26:1 ff. It is now generally agreed that chapters 7 and 26 deal with the same incident. From 26:1 we learn that the sermon in 7:3 ff. was delivered in 609 B.C. (see comment on 26:1). This means that the reader has suddenly been transported from the period prior to the Josianic reform to the early part of Jehoiakim's reign, a timespan of some 14 years during which some very important things have happened (see Int.).

In addition to the lack of chronological continuity between chapters 6 and 7, there is also a noticeable change in language and style. The language has a Deuteronomic flavor, and the style is "a prose style akin to the sermon" (Eissfeldt, p. 352). One finds that he is reading the first of "the prose sermons of Jeremiah" (see Int.). Insofar as the material in chapters 7—10 can be dated, it appears to come from the reign of Jehoiakim.

1. Religious Rites and Right Relationships (7:1—8:3)

Eissfeldt terms this unit "the great Temple sermon" and treats it in three parts: 7:1-15, 16–20, and 7:21—8:3 (p. 351). Although it is possible that 7:1—8:3 constitutes a single sermon preached by the prophet at one time in the Temple in 609, this is probably not the case (cf. 26:3–6). A slightly different analysis is suggested here.

(1) A Sermon on the Source of Security (7:1–15)

¹ The word that came to Jeremiah from the LORD: ² "Stand in the gate of the LORD's house, and proclaim there this word, and say, Hear the word of the LORD, all you men of Judah who enter these gates to worship the LORD. ³ Thus says the LORD of hosts, the God of Israel, Amend your ways and your doings, and I will let you dwell in this place. ⁴ Do not trust in these deceptive words: 'This is the temple of the LORD, the temple of the LORD, the temple of the LORD.'

⁵ "For if you truly amend your ways and your doings, if you truly execute justice one with another, ⁶ if you do not oppress the alien, the fatherless or the widow, or shed innocent blood in this place, and if you do not go after other gods to your own hurt, ⁷ then I will let you dwell in this place, in the land that I gave of old to your fathers for ever.

⁸ "Behold, you trust in deceptive words to no avail. ⁹ Will you steal, murder, commit adultery, swear falsely, burn incense to Baal, and go after other gods that you have not known, ¹⁰ and then come and stand before me in this house, which is called by my name, and say, 'We are delivered!'—only to go on doing all these abominations? ¹¹ Has this house, which is called by my name, become a den of robbers in your eyes? Behold, I myself have seen it, says the LORD. ¹² Go now to my place that was in Shiloh, where I made my name dwell at first, and see what I did to it for the wickedness of my people Israel. ¹³ And now, because you have done all these things, says the LORD, and when I spoke to you persistently you did not listen, and when I called you, you did not answer, ¹⁴ therefore I will do to the house which is called by my name, and in which you trust, and to the place which I gave to you and to your fathers, as I did to Shiloh. ¹⁵ And I will cast you out of my sight, as I cast out all your kinsmen, all the offspring of Ephraim.

The occasion was likely the fall festival of 609. Jeremiah had watched the growth of "the temple superstition," the hardening of the people's trust in the external forms of religion. His advocacy of the Josianic reformation at the start had given way to caution, then to criticism, and now to an open break.

This break may have been precipitated, in part, by a possible call by the cultic personnel for a great religious rally, in the context of the crisis brought on by the death of Josiah, the deportation of Jehoahaz, and the designation of Jehoiakim as king by Neco, the new overlord of Judah. The priests and the prophets may have said: "The Temple of the Lord! The Temple of the Lord! The Temple of the Lord! Here is the thing that has stood through all the storms. Let us rally around it. Let us attend its services with greater regularity, and let us observe its ceremonies with greater conscientiousness and care. It is the foundation of our faith, the source of our security, a bulwark never failing!" If there was such a rally, as some suggest, it may have been in connection with covenant renewal in the autumn.

With a holy fire in his heart, the prophet appeared in the Temple area. Taking his life in his hands, he denounced the cherished Temple worship, indicated that an ethical religion alone is acceptable to God, and declared that God was going to destroy both Temple and city, if the people did not return to a proper covenant relationship with him. Is it any wonder that the "temple sermon" caused a terrific uproar and almost cost Jeremiah his life (26:7 ff.)?

The sermon seems to be in the form of a legal brief. First, there is a vigorous denunciation of the whole priestly program (vv. 1–4). This is the statement of the case.

Verses 1 and 2 are introductory (cf. 26:1–3). The sermon proper starts with vv. 3–4. These verses may be summarized thus: "Don't listen to the pious lies being peddled by the priests and prophets concerning trust in the Temple as the basis of security. Their entire program is a delusion. There is one and only one way to security: you must change your ways. Then God will be with you and bless you."

There follows a pointed declaration of God's demands (vv. 5–7). This is a résumé of what God expects and has promised.

Here Jeremiah says, in effect: "God desires and requires ethical and spiritual transformation, not mere cultic activity and conformity. You must *really* execute justice—must govern yourselves by the code of conduct proper to a covenant people—in your daily dealings with one another. You must also *really* refrain from serving other gods and give your covenant God the kind of steadfast devotion he demands."

Next comes an indignant indictment of worship divorced from life (vv. 8–11). This is the direct accusation: "You engage in theft, murder, adultery, perjury, and idolatry, and then dare to come to this house and say, 'We're secure. We've got it made'—only to go your way in flagrant violation of the covenantal laws of God. You have made the Lord's house a robber's hideout, a place of refuge, a quiet retreat to which you can go for safety after perpetrating your crimes. And God is sick of it! Wickedness and worship he cannot take."

Allusion is made in v. 9 to the Eighth, Sixth, Seventh, Ninth, First, and Second commandments. The breaking of these amounted to "an almost total breach of the covenantal stipulations" (Bright, p. 56). Moreover, here is further evidence of Jeremiah's deep anchorage in the Mosaic faith and the Exodus traditions. The Mosaic law—particularly the Decalogue—was the expression of the will of the covenant Lord for his covenant people.[57]

Finally, there is a graphic description of the destruction which is impending (vv. 12–15). Jeremiah concludes the indictment with an announcement of judgment: We may summarize as follows: "Because you are indulging in religion unrelated to life and devoid of any real faith in or fidelity to me, *says the Lord*, therefore I am going to destroy *the house which is called by my name* and *in which you trust*, and *the place which I gave to you and to your fathers*, as I destroyed Shiloh in the days of Samuel. Also, I will send you into captivity, as I sent your *kinsmen*, the citizens of the Northern Kingdom, into exile —unless you repent."

Shiloh, the center of worship for the tribal confederacy for a time, was located approximately 20 miles north of Jerusalem. Archeological discovery and biblical study indicate that it was demolished about 1050 B.C. The destruction probably took

---

[57] Apart from Moses, one cannot understand Jeremiah. Cf. Fohrer, JBL, 80, 309 ff.; Holladay, JBL, 83, 1964, 153–164; JBL, 85, 1966, 17–27.

place in connection with the victory of the Philistines referred to in 1 Samuel 4.

The expression *I will cast you out of my sight* is an accommodation to the view that God dwelt in his house in his land. Thus, if his people were taken into exile in a foreign country, they were out of his sight. The *kinsmen* had been carried into Assyrian captivity in 721.

That the "temple sermon" ends with v. 15 is strongly suggested by the fact that the parallel account of it (26:3–6) terminates with the threat of the destruction of the Temple, *the* thing which angered the crowd—especially the clergy—and caused them to seek to kill Jeremiah.

The basic issue in this great sermon is the question of security. Like the people of our day, Jeremiah's countrymen were frantically searching for security. The prophet told them that they were looking in the wrong place. Security was not to be found in mere reverence for a holy book, however important this might be. It was not to be had through external reformation of life, as significant as this might be. It would not come through an elaborate ritualism in religion, as necessary as ritual is, in its proper place.

The only security there is, said Jeremiah, lies in a right relationship with God, expressing itself in right relationships with one's fellowmen. This can come only through the acceptance of God's call to repentance, faith, and obedience. No "foxhole" religion—only an ethical fellowship with the living God!

(2) A Prohibition of Prayer for a Profligate People (7:16–20)

16 "As for you, do not pray for this people, or lift up cry or prayer for them, and do not intercede with me, for I do not hear you. 17 Do you not see what they are doing in the cities of Judah and in the streets of Jerusalem? 18 The children gather wood, the fathers kindle fire, and the women knead dough, to make cakes for the queen of heaven; and they pour out drink offerings to other gods, to provoke me to anger. 19 Is it I whom they provoke? says the LORD. Is it not themselves, to their own confusion? 20 Therefore thus says the LORD GOD:

Behold, my anger and my wrath will be poured out on this place, upon man and beast, upon the trees of the field and the fruit of the ground; it will burn and not be quenched."

This is an arresting passage for at least two reasons. First, it starts with God's initial command to Jeremiah to cease praying for his people (v. 16; cf. 11:14; 14:-11). A. R. Johnson [58] has called to our attention that the prophet had two major functions: proclamation and prayer—facing the people with God's message and facing God with the needs of the people.

Jeremiah was a man of prayer. Among the prophets he was the supreme intercessor. In no other prophetic book are there "so many . . . expressions of compassion for the people" (Lindblom, p. 205). Out of this central fountain of loving compassion flowed the stream of intercession.

Yet because the people were so corrupt that repentance was seemingly impossible and judgment inevitable, further intercession was forbidden by God. In spite of this prohibition, Jeremiah felt that his call involved prayer for the people, and apparently persisted in it (cf. 15:11; 18:20; Bright, p. 56).

In the second place, the passage provides a striking example of the creativity and versatility of prophetic speech in Jeremiah's unusual variation and adaptation of the basic reproach-threat pattern. The fundamental elements are present, but the form is employed with much freedom.

In this case, the accusation begins with God's prohibition of intercession (v. 16). This prohibition is followed by two probing questions addressed to the prophet (vv. 17, 19). These questions focus attention on the fact that the people are guilty of idolatry of the rankest sort. The spotlight centers on the practice of the cult of Ishtar or Astarte, *the queen of heaven*, the goddess of the planet Venus, worshiped by the Assyrians and Babylonians as the goddess of love and fertility. This form of idolatry had been removed—certainly re-

[58] *The Cultic Prophet in Ancient Israel* (Cardiff: University of Wales Press, 1962), pp. 56 ff.

pressed—by the reform under Josiah. But Josiah was dead, and Ishtar worship must have revived under Jehoiakim (cf. 8:1–3; 44:15–30). The *cakes* used in the worship were probably made in the likeness of the goddess, or of a star, her symbol.

The expression *provoke me to anger* is a favorite with Jeremiah (cf. 8:9; 11:17; 25:6 f.; 32:29; 44:8). God asks whether the people think they *provoke* him by their actions. In reality, they provoke themselves, *to their own confusion*—i.e., God is not knocked off balance by their conduct; they will be, it will recoil upon their own heads!

There is a brief but forceful prediction of retribution in v. 20: *Therefore!* God's *anger* and his *wrath*—the reaction of his holy love to human sin—*will be poured out on this place* (Jerusalem, or the Temple?).

(3) Cultic Conformity or Complete Commitment (7:21–28)

21 Thus says the LORD of hosts, the God of Israel: "Add your burnt offerings to your sacrifices, and eat the flesh. 22 For in the day that I brought them out of the land of Egypt, I did not speak to your fathers or command them concerning burnt offerings and sacrifices. 23 But this command I gave them, 'Obey my voice, and I will be your God, and you shall be my people; and walk in all the way that I command you, that it may be well with you.' 24 But they did not obey or incline their ear, but walked in their own counsels and the stubbornness of their evil hearts, and went backward and not forward. 25 From the day that your fathers came out of the land of Egypt to this day, I have persistently sent all my servants the prophets to them, day after day; 26 yet they did not listen to me, or incline their ear, but stiffened their neck. They did worse than their fathers.

27 "So you shall speak all these words to them, but they will not listen to you. You shall call to them, but they will not answer you. 28 And you shall say to them, 'This is the nation that did not obey the voice of the LORD their God, and did not accept discipline; truth has perished; it is cut off from their lips.

These words, like those in 7:1–15 and 16–20, were likely spoken in the Temple during the fall festival. They constitute a reproach-threat prophecy, with the threat implied (according to Westermann, a special modification of the speech form by Jeremiah).

There has been sharp debate about the genuineness and the meaning of this passage. For the present writer, there is no question about the former, and little about the latter. The big issue among scholars has been: Does Jeremiah reject the sacrificial system root and branch as something of purely human origin and of no value? This commentator does not believe that he does. He is convinced that Jeremiah is stressing the truth that God's first and fundamental requirement is not cultic conformity but complete commitment, expressing itself in obedience.[59]

The prophet begins sarcastically (v. 21). The *burnt offerings* were completely consumed by fire on the altar. The *sacrifices* (other animal offerings) were, for the most part, eaten by the worshipers.

Jeremiah says, in effect: "*Add your burnt offerings to your sacrifices, and eat the whole of it, for all the good it does!* These offerings have no sanctity, for they are brought by guilty hands. They have lost their real significance, for your hearts are not in them. Therefore they are mere *flesh!* What I really want, as I have persistently emphasized since the day I brought you out of Egypt, is wholehearted devotion. My first desire and demand at the very beginning of your history as my covenant people was: *Obey my voice, and I will be your God, and you shall be my people.* This was my requirement then, and it is my requirement now. But you have refused to comply. Instead, you have followed *the stubbornness* of your *evil hearts.* You have refused to *listen* or to *accept discipline. Truth* (cf. 5:1) *has perished.* You are altogether unfaithful to me."

59 Clements, *op. cit.,* pp. 86–102; Rowley, *From Moses to Qumran,* pp. 111–140; Couturier, *op. cit.,* p. 310; Roland de Vaux, *Ancient Israel* (New York: McGraw-Hill, 1961), pp. 428, 454–456; A. S. Kapelrud, *Central Ideas in Amos* (Oslo: W. Nygaard, 1956), pp. 68–81.

The reproach closes on a plaintive note —God yearning and pleading, and the people refusing and rebelling.

The clue to the interpretation of this difficult and controversial passage appears to be the preservation of a balance between vv. 22 and 23. Jeremiah does not mean that there was no sacrifice in the days of Moses. There was. Nor does he repudiate the cult lock, stock, and barrel. He is not objecting to the cult as such, but to a cult emptied of its original content and real purpose.

Evidence of a more positive attitude toward the cult is seen in his reverence for the Temple and in the fact that he was preaching in the Temple. As God's house, the Temple was holy. As a robber's hideout, it must be destroyed. In like manner, the ritual was a means of grace. But when turned into magic, it became an abomination before God. No amount of sacrifice or ceremony could suffice as a substitute for simple self-surrender.

(4) The Valley of Sacrifice (7:29—8:3)

29 Cut off your hair and cast it away;
    raise a lamentation on the bare heights,
for the LORD has rejected and forsaken
    the generation of his wrath.'

30 "For the sons of Judah have done evil in my sight, says the LORD; they have set their abominations in the house which is called by my name, to defile it. 31 And they have built the high place of Topheth, which is in the valley of the son of Hinnom, to burn their sons and their daughters in the fire; which I did not command, nor did it come into my mind. 32 Therefore, behold, the days are coming, says the LORD, when it will no more be called Topheth, or the valley of the son of Hinnom, but the Valley of Slaughter: for they will bury in Topheth, because there is no room elsewhere. 33 And the dead bodies of this people will be food for the birds of the air, and for the beasts of the earth; and none will frighten them away. 34 And I will make to cease from the cities of Judah and from the streets of Jerusalem the voice of mirth and the voice of gladness, the voice of the bridegroom and the voice of the bride; for the land shall become a waste.

1 "At that time, says the LORD, the bones of the kings of Judah, the bones of its princes, the bones of the priests, the bones of the prophets, and the bones of the inhabitants of Jerusalem shall be brought out of their tombs; 2 and they shall be spread before the sun and the moon and all the host of heaven, which they have loved and served, which they have gone after, and which they have sought and worshiped; and they shall not be gathered or buried; they shall be as dung on the surface of the ground. 3 Death shall be preferred to life by all the remnant that remains of this evil family in all the places where I have driven them, says the LORD of hosts.

Here the prophet attacks the people again for their apostasy. They are commanded to *cut off* their *hair* and *cast it away*—an act ominous of death. Cutting the hair was a sign of grief, the reason for the mourning here being God's rejection of his people. They are told to *raise a lamentation on the bare heights* (centers of idolatrous worship), *for the Lord has rejected . . . the generation of his wrath* (i.e., the one with which he is angry).

So the reproach begins with a lament. The basis of the lament is twofold: the people have defiled the Temple *with their abominations,* and they have practiced child sacrifice at *Topheth* in *the valley of . . . Hinnom,* just south or southwest of Jerusalem (cf. 2 Kings 23:10).

The bell of judgment tolls in vv. 32–34. In the valley where the people have slaughtered their children they themselves will be slaughtered. The slaughter will be so great that, with the burial grounds full, *Topheth, the valley of Slaughter,* will be used. With bruial space still inadequate, unburied bodies will be left lying on the ground in dishonor and disgrace. All joy will cease (cf. 16:9; 25:10; 33:11).

At that time (the time of divine retribution), the bodies of the dead will be brought forth from the graves, not to be stripped of any ornaments or treasures with which they have been buried, but to be exposed in death to the heavenly bodies which they have worshiped. This—the very deepest shame—would mean restless wandering in the underworld (8:1–3).

The connectedness and, at points (cf. 8:1–3; 7:32–34), disconnectedness are probably the consequence of editorial work. Materials have been brought together which reflect a common theme and situation.

To sum up, in 7:1—8:3, Jeremiah launches a vigorous attack against the cult on two grounds: the syncretistic additions to it from the nature religion of the neighbors, and the superstitions substitution of it for sincere devotion to God. He emphasizes that God's primary concern is not religious rites but right relationships.

2. The Incurable Condition of the People (8:4—10:25)

This new section is related to 7:1—8:3 in that it deals with the same theme and dates, in all probability, from the same general period. It represents a variety of circumstances, moods, and literary forms.

(1) The Prophet's Perplexity (8:4–7)

4 "You shall say to them, Thus says the LORD:
When men fall, do they not rise again?
If one turns away, does he not return?
5 Why then has this people turned away
in perpetual backsliding?
They hold fast to deceit,
they refuse to return.
6 I have given heed and listened,
but they have not spoken aright;
no man repents of his wickedness,
saying, 'What have I done?'
Every one turns to his own course,
like a horse plunging headlong into battle.
7 Even the stork in the heavens
knows her times;
and the turtledove, swallow, and crane
keep the time of their coming;
but my people know not
the ordinance of the LORD.

Jeremiah is staggered by the mystery of evil. Not only in this passage but also in the passages that follow, the burning question keeps troubling his heart and rising to his lips, "Why?" The persistence of the people in their apostasy is so unnatural and incomprehensible.

The prophet begins (to translate vv. 4–5 literally): "You shall say to them, Thus says the Lord, 'Does one fall and not *rise* (*return* to the point he left)? If one *turns*

(away), does he not *return* (to the place of departure)? Why (then) has this people *turned away* in perpetual *back-turning*? They cling strongly to deceit, they refuse to *return* (to me)."

There is a deliberate, designed, skillful ambiguity in the play on the Hebrew *shub* (turn, return). As noted earlier, *shub* can mean turn away from or turn back to. Jeremiah employs both meanings here. In v. 5 he moves from the idea of physical direction to that of spiritual relation: turning from God (in apostasy)—turning back to God (in penitence).

The verb occurs again in v. 6. The prophet expresses his amazement and bewilderment that *no man repents of his wickedness, . . . every one turns to his own course.* Jeremiah is grieved, as well as perplexed, by the headlong plunge of the people toward destruction, *like a horse plunging* (overflowing) *. . . into battle.*

He contrasts the behavior of the people with that of migratory birds (v. 7). Birds know the *times* of their coming and going, and observe them. They obey the God-given law of their being (a marvelous mystery and metaphor). *But* God's people not only do not govern themselves by the revealed law of their being and well-being—*the ordinance of the Lord*—they do not even *know* it!

Know is a dynamic and meaningful word (1:5). In using it here, the prophet is speaking of both an intimate acquaintance with and a wholehearted obedience to the covenantal commands or stipulations, God's order of life for Israel.[60]

(2) Wisdom and the Word of God (8:8–13)

8 "How can you say, 'We are wise,
and the law of the LORD is with us'?
But, behold, the false pen of the scribes
has made it into a lie.
9 The wise men shall be put to shame,
they shall be dismayed and taken;

[60] On the knowledge of God, see the comment on 1:5; cf. J. L. McKenzie, JBL, 74, 1955, 22 ff.; see also Hillers, *op. cit.*, pp. 120–124.

lo, they have rejected the word of the
Lord,
and what wisdom is in them?
10 Therefore I will give their wives to others
and their fields to conquerors,
because from the least to the greatest
every one is greedy for unjust gain;
from prophet to priest
every one deals falsely.
11 They have healed the wound of my people
lightly,
saying, 'Peace, peace,'
when there is no peace.
12 Were they ashamed when they committed
abomination?
No, they were not at all ashamed;
they did not know how to blush.
Therefore they shall fall among the fallen;
when I punish them, they shall be overthrown,
says the Lord.
13 When I would gather them, says the Lord,
there are no grapes on the vine,
nor figs on the fig tree;
even the leaves are withered,
and what I gave them has passed away
from them."

Stung by the statement made in v. 7,
the people probably retort: "We do have
wisdom. We know how God rules. We
have it in writing—in a book!" Jeremiah
expresses further amazement. How can the
people claim to have wisdom when *they
have rejected the word of the Lord?* There
is no wisdom apart from God's *word* (his
revelation of his will—and a proper response to that revelation). They have
spurned that word.

Their rejection of the *word* of God is
seen in their greed for gain, their spirit of
superficial optimism, and the absence of
any sense of shame in the presence of their
sins (vv. 10–12; see comment on 6:12–15).
Because they have rejected his word, God
has rejected them. They will experience
retribution (vv. 10a,12b,13).

There has been much difference of opinion concerning the reference to the making
of *the law* into *a lie* by *the false pen of
the scribes* (v. 8). It seems apparent that
the scribes were perverting *the law* in the
interests of sacerdotalism. They were
stressing the external and ecclesiastical to
the exclusion of the ethical and spiritual

(cf. Rudolph and Weiser). This was leading to ritual rigidity instead of ethical integrity and spiritual vitality.

It is highly probable that there is a direct relation between the activity spoken
of in v. 8 and the Deuteronomic reform
and the prophet's assessment of it.

(3) The Collapse of the Spirit of the Peo-
ple (8:14–17)

14 Why do we sit still?
Gather together, let us go into the fortified
cities
and perish there;
for the Lord our God has doomed us to
perish,
and has given us poisoned water to drink,
because we have sinned against the
Lord.
15 We looked for peace, but no good came,
for a time of healing, but behold, terror.
16 "The snorting of their horses is heard from
Dan;
at the sound of the neighing of their
stallions
the whole land quakes.
They come and devour the land and all
that fills it,
the city and those who dwell in it.
17 For behold, I am sending among you serpents,
adders which cannot be charmed,
and they shall bite you,"
says the Lord.

The mood of the people is one of despair (v. 14a). The reason for the despair
is that they are under the judgment of
God and feel that they are doomed to perish because of their sin (v. 14b). Things
have not turned out as they hoped and
expected (v. 15; cf. 7:10). They have
been quite unrealistic. It is a time of terror. The *snorting* of the war horses can be
heard from the northern part of Palestine
or *Dan. The whole land quakes.*

At the close of the lament, God speaks.
Whereas the judgment is portrayed above
under the figure of the gathering of a crop,
it is pictured here under the figure of the
bite of poisonous snakes. Snake-charming
was an art practiced in the Near East, including Israel. But no one skilled in this
art will be able to charm *the serpents* coming against God's people. Some crises have

been averted by various devices, such as faithless intriguing in foreign courts. Not this one! These adders are going to bite! This is the oracle of the Lord.

(4) The Compassion of the Prophet (8:18—9:1)

18 My grief is beyond healing,
  my heart is sick within me.
19 Hark, the cry of the daughter of my people
  from the length and breadth of the land:
  "Is the LORD not in Zion?
  Is her King not in her?"
  "Why have they provoked me to anger with
  their graven images,
  and with their foreign idols?"
20 "The harvest is past, the summer is ended,
  and we are not saved."
21 For the wound of the daughter of my people is my heart wounded,
  I mourn, and dismay has taken hold on
  me.
22 Is there no balm in Gilead?
  Is there no physician there?
  Why then has the health of the daughter
  of my people
  not been restored?
1 O that my head were waters,
  and my eyes a fountain of tears,
  that I might weep day and night
  for the slain of the daughter of my people!

Jeremiah is heartsick and sorrow-stricken. The reason for his great grief is *the cry* of his countrymen *from the length and breadth of the land*. They want to know why God has forsaken them. God counters with an inquiry as to why they have provoked him with their idolatry (v. 19*b*; cf. Holladay, JBL, 81, pp. 48–49).

The statement in v. 20 is probably a popular saying that was going the rounds. It is a striking and suggestive sentence. To get the force of it, one has to remember that *the harvest* and *the summer* were two different seasons. The former was the time for the gathering of the grain. The latter was the time for the gathering of the fruit. If one of these harvests was a failure, the other was usually a success. If both were unsuccessful, stark tragedy stared the people in the face. The proverb speaks of the tragedy of wasted opportunity. There

comes a time when it is too late!

After voicing his grief again (v. 21), the prophet raises three penetrating questions (v. 22). The answer expected to each of the first two is yes. Gilead was noted for its medicinal herbs and the resin of the storax tree and for its physicians. The answer to the third question is not that no remedy is available but that the remedy has not been applied.

Observe the recurrence of the word *Why?* in this section. The prophet is experiencing more and more inner conflict and anguish. He "scales the peak of pain" in 9:1 (Heb. 8:23), as he brings his lament to a close.

A tragic misrepresentation of Jeremiah is based, in part, upon this verse. He has been termed "the weeping prophet." This is one of the ironies of biblical interpretation. One should avoid this gross error. He may call Jeremiah the reluctant prophet, or the praying prophet, or the suffering prophet, or the preaching prophet, but not the weeping prophet. He never wasted time weeping when there was work to be done (though he loved greatly and suffered deeply), and he is one of the greatest minds and spirits of all time.

It is difficult to date a passage like 8:14—9:1, but for this writer, "the point of greatest illumination" for this double lament seems to be the situation that developed after the death of Josiah at the hands of Pharaoh Neco in 609 B.C. Neco established his headquarters at Riblah, in northern Palestine. The Egyptians used horses extensively in their military operations. Neco was the new overlord of Judah. The great experiment under Josiah had failed. Many people were gripped by fear, consternation, grief, and despair. The sky had fallen. Their dreams were shattered. Had God let them down?

The brief reign of Jehoahaz or the early part of Jehoiakim's reign appears to provide a better background for this passage than 587, 598, or the time prior to 622 B.C.

(5) The Prophet's Despair (9:2–9)

2   O that I had in the desert
      a wayfarers' lodging place,
    that I might leave my people
      and go away from them!
    For they are all adulterers,
      a company of treacherous men.
3   They bend their tongue like a bow;
      falsehood and not truth has grown strong
        in the land;
    for they proceed from evil to evil,
      and they do not know me, says the LORD.
4   Let every one beware of his neighbor,
      and put no trust in any brother;
    for every brother is a supplanter,
      and every neighbor goes about as a
        slanderer.
5   Every one deceives his neighbor,
      and no one speaks the truth;
    they have taught their tongue to speak lies;
      they commit iniquity and are too weary
        to repent.
6   Heaping oppression upon oppression, and
      deceit upon deceit,
    they refuse to know me, says the LORD.
7   Therefore thus says the LORD of hosts:
    "Behold, I will refine them and test them,
      for what else can I do, because of my
        people?
8   Their tongue is a deadly arrow;
      it speaks deceitfully;
    with his mouth each speaks peaceably to
      his neighbor,
    but in his heart he plans an ambush for
      him.
9   Shall I not punish them for these things?
      says the LORD;
    and shall I not avenge myself
      on a nation such as this?

This is another lament of the prophet, coming most likely out of the early period of Jehoiakim's administration. The mood is radically different from that in 8:18—9:1. There Jeremiah identifies himself with his people in their suffering and their sin. Here he wishes to separate himself from them and have no responsibility for them—to be done with them!

In many ways, Jeremiah is the most human of the prophets. He runs the gamut of emotion and frankly and honestly expresses what he feels.

Here he voices a very human desire, the desire to run away (v. 2). He longs for an inn for traveling men, a wayfarer's

lodge, in the desert. Such a place was usually sparsely furnished, for people only spent the night there. Sometimes there was an innkeeper. He had no responsibility for the guests. He could talk and trade stories with them. Then the next morning they would be gone.

Perhaps Jeremiah wishes to be such an innkeeper. He wants human intercourse without responsibility. He longs for a seat in the balcony, to be a looker-on at life.

Why? The people are just "a bunch of rascals" (v. 2b—"a gang of crooks," Bright, p. 67). In the invective which follows v. 2a, certain things are pinpointed: adultery, duplicity, dishonesty, mendacity, and cruelty. All are traced to their source in a lack of true piety (vv. 3b,6b). The lack of a right relationship with God results in wrong relationships with men.

This passage, like so many in Jeremiah, blends the reproach-threat form with another. In this case, it is the lament. The lament (vv. 2–6) leads up to an oracle of the Lord, announcing judgment (vv. 7–9).

Jeremiah knew that the inn in the desert did not exist. He was aware that there can be no escape from reality and responsibility. Momentarily, he wanted to run away and be rid of it all. And the people would have been glad if he had! But he could not and did not. One cannot run away—from sin, self, suffering, or the sovereignty of God. The inn simply isn't there! The great souls are those who stick through, when they really want to run.

(6) Impending Ruin (9:10–16)

10 "Take up weeping and wailing for the moun-
      tains,
      and a lamentation for the pastures of the
        wilderness,
    because they are laid waste so that no one
      passes through.
    and the lowing of cattle is not heard;
    both the birds of the air and the beasts
      have fled and are gone.
11   I will make Jerusalem a heap of ruins,
      a lair of jackals;

and I will make the cities of Judah a desolation,
without inhabitant."
12 Who is the man so wise that he can
understand this? To whom has the mouth of
the LORD spoken, that he may declare it? Why
is the land ruined and laid waste like a wilderness, so that no one passes through? 13 And the
LORD says: "Because they have forsaken my
law which I set before them, and have not
obeyed my voice, or walked in accord with it,
14 but have stubbornly followed their own
hearts and have gone after the Baals, as their
fathers taught them. 15 Therefore thus says the
LORD of hosts, the God of Israel: Behold, I will
feed this people with wormwood, and give
them poisonous water to drink. 16 I will scatter
them among the nations whom neither they nor
their fathers have known; and I will send the
sword after them, until I have consumed
them."

This unit starts with a short lament by
the prophet (v. 10), in which there is a
graphic picture of a wasteland and in
which we detect again Jeremiah's deep involvement with God, his message, and the
people. The reading "For the mountains I
will take up a wailing . . ." is to be preferred to that in the RSV (cf. MT, KJV,
ASV; Bright, p. 72).

After the opening lament comes a fairly
lengthy prophecy (vv. 11–16), which
continues the description of imminent destruction and, in a rather unique way, designates the cause of it. God speaks, first
in direct declaration (v. 11), and then by
way of interrogation (v. 12).

The explanation if it all—the mystery
of iniquity and its penalty—is the action
of the people (vv. 13–14). They have forsaken God's *law*, refused to listen to his
voice (i.e., word), and have followed the
Baals. Hence God must feed them *wormwood* (a bitter experience) and give them
poisonous water to drink (a deadly po-
tion). He will scatter them among the nations and slay them with the sword (vv.
15–16).

Once again, the apostasy-idolatry-pun-
ishment pattern appears. There is always
an interaction between God and man in
history and human life. God is sovereign.

Man has freedom of choice under the divine sovereignty. He can choose his course,
but not the consequences of his choice.
Here, and elsewhere, Jeremiah brings out
both God's part and man's part in the human situation, especially in the retribution
process. But, in his preaching as a whole,
the prophet stresses man's part—the human element of responsibility—in the
judgment he experiences, more than do
the prophets who precede him.

Some scholars consider vv. 12–16 to be
"a prose commentary," which was added
later by an editor to explain the Exile, already a reality (e.g., Hyatt, p. 891), and
which distorts the message of Jeremiah
(e.g., Cunliffe-Jones, p. 95). With Bright
(p. 73), we see no distortion here. There
is the possibility of a free recall or some
expansion of the prophet's thought (by
Baruch?). During Jehoiakim's reign Jeremiah began frequently to forecast the
coming of judgment at the hands of Nebuchadnezzar.

(7) Raise a Dirge (9:17–22)

17 Thus says the LORD of hosts:
"Consider, and call for the mourning women
to come;
send for the skilful women to come;
18 let them make haste and raise a wailing
over us,
that our eyes may run down with tears,
and our eyelids gush with water.
19 For a sound of wailing is heard from Zion:
'How we are ruined!
We are utterly shamed,
because we have left the land,
because they have cast down our dwellings.' "
20 Hear, O women, the word of the LORD,
and let your ear receive the word of his
mouth;
teach to your daughters a lament,
and each to her neighbor a dirge.
21 For death has come up into our windows,
it has entered our palaces,
cutting off the children from the streets
and the young men from the squares.
22 Speak, "Thus says the LORD:
'The dead bodies of men shall fall
like dung upon the open field,
like sheaves after the reaper,
and none shall gather them.' "

This is a communal lament, a dirge over the demolition of Jerusalem. It has been termed "perhaps the most brilliant example of the prophetic elegy which the Old Testament contains" (Skinner, p. 124).

The *mourning women . . . skilful women* are those who stimulate mourning in others or recite dirges over the dead (see Int.). Now they *really* have something to grieve over: the destruction of houses and human life. Death is loose in the land. Not even the strongest houses can keep him out.[61] As he goes, the Reaper cuts down children in the streets and youth in the squares. There is no one to gather up the dead bodies and bury them.

Here the prophet is at his poetic best in graphic, creative, dramatic portrayal. This powerful poem contains a threat in the form of a lament, the reproach being present only by implication. Bright dates the masterful composition prior to the siege of Jerusalem and the captivity of 598–597 (i.e., in the reign of Jehoiakim).

(8) The True Basis for Boasting (9:23–24)

23 Thus says the LORD: "Let not the wise man glory in his wisdom, let not the mighty man glory in his might, let not the rich man glory in his riches; **24** but let him who glories glory in this, that he understands and knows me, that I am the LORD who practice steadfast love, justice, and righteousness in the earth; for in these things I delight, says the LORD."

Although this rich passage bears no obvious relation to the immediate context, there is no real reason for questioning its authenticity, as some have done (e.g., Volz, Schmidt). Peake, Cunliffe-Jones, Hyatt, Hopper, Bright, Couturier, and others accept it as genuine. It is quite in keeping with Jeremiah's emphasis (cf. 2:8; 4:22; 9:2–5; 22:16; 31:3 f.). Its proverbial style need not trip us. Jeremiah used methods and forms drawn from many sources, including the wisdom schools.

Some date the passage prior to the coming of Nebuchadnezzar to deal with Jehoiakim's revolt against him (601). Perhaps the men of wisdom (court counselors, etc.) were congratulating themselves upon the arrangements they had made—with Egypt and others—for breaking free from Babylon. The men of might (political and military leaders) may have been bragging about the strength, skill, and strategy with which they could protect the people. Possibly the men of wealth were rejoicing in their riches and in the prospect of greater gain, should the nation regain its independence.

Against this false pride Jeremiah launched a blistering broadside. Men are never to boast in wisdom, power, or wealth as such. These things are not bad in themselves. They are good. The prophet is employing a Hebrew idiom: "not this but that" in the sense of "this more than that." Wisdom, power, and wealth are good, when properly used; but the thing so much more important than either of them or all of them put together is the knowledge of God—i.e., a dynamic relationship with the God who is sovereign Lord and who delights in and practices *steadfast love* (*chesed*, grace, loyal love), *justice* (*mishpat*, right decision), and *righteousness* (*ts°dhaqah*, action in conformity with his character and covenant).

These are covenant words. Covenant (*b°rit*) referred to a dynamic relationship between God and Israel, a relationship grounded in God's grace (cf. 2:2) and expressing itself in loyal love of the people for God and each other. The relationship was sustained by the practice of justice and righteousness (cf. 5:1), i.e., conformity to the code of conduct required by the covenant. The maintenance of the relationship resulted in a state of peace (*shalom*, completeness, totality, and hence harmony within the self and with God and others, the condition necessary for

---

61 In the Ras Shamra texts, it is stated that Baal did not want any windows in his palace, lest Mot the god of death come through them and kidnap his wives.

growth toward fulfillment).[62] From this "totality"—this state of rich harmonious relationships—flowed "blessing," i.e., inner vitality or life-force and that to which this led for the individual and the community: joy, fertility, prosperity, victory. In this, one could *glory* (boast).

Every generation has its set of values, its system of priorities. As in Jeremiah's day, so in our day some place wisdom (culture, scientism, education) at the head of the list. In this they glory. Others give first place to power (personal or collective). This means everything. It gets all their attention and allegiance. Still others put wealth, the accumulation of things, at the top of the ladder of value. But there is no true basis for boasting in these.

The only authentic basis for boasting is to be found in God. A right relationship with him is the thing that matters supremely. We are to put him first in our lives and let him fill us with those qualities which he has and which he only can bestow. This is what abides—God, the knowledge of him, grace, justice, righteousness—and in this we should boast.

Although vv. 23–24 do not link directly with the context, they may have been included in this complex because of similarity in content to 8:8–13. They constitute a kind of "climax in the religion of Israel."[63]

(9) Circumcised—Yet Uncircumcised (9:25–26)

25 "Behold, the days are coming, says the LORD, when I will punish all those who are circumcised but yet uncircumcised—26 Egypt, Judah, Edom, the sons of Ammon, Moab, and all who dwell in the desert that cut the corners of their hair; for all these nations are uncircumcised, and all the house of Israel is uncircumcised in heart."

---

62 See excellent essay by John I Durham on "*Shalom* and the Presence of God," in Durham and Porter, *op. cit.*, pp. 272–293. He stresses the cultic connection of *shalom* (peace) and assigns it a rich content. As the gift of God, "peace" can be received only in the presence of God. This gives a new dimension to a word already rich with meaning.

63 Couturier, JBC, p. 311.

All who do not have the kind of knowledge of God spoken of in 9:23–24 are uncircumcised spiritually, even though they may be circumcised physically. All the peoples referred to in vv. 25–26 practiced circumcision. But no mere outward mark or sign is enough. There must be an inner reality.

Jeremiah has already called for a circumcision of heart (4:4). He has said that the ears of the people are uncircumcised (6:10). He now states that, like the pagans, they are uncircumcised in their hearts as well (v. 26). Because of this, they, like all others in a similar state, will experience divine judgment (cf. Matt. 5:8; Rom. 2:25; 1 Cor. 7:19).

We are back to the essence of the "temple sermon" (7:1–15): not rites, but right! And, by implication, we have a remarkable anticipation of Paul's position, expressed in his epistle to the Galatians, where he states that what is needful in man is "a new creation" and "faith working through love" (Gal. 6:15; 5:6). This new creation is made possible in Christ, who can bring us into a dynamic, life-changing relationship with the God of grace, justice, and righteousness (2 Cor. 5:17).

(10) God and the Gods (10:1–16)

1 Hear the word which the LORD speaks to you, O house of Israel. 2 Thus says the LORD:
"Learn not the way of the nations,
    nor be dismayed at the signs of the heavens
    because the nations are dismayed at them,
3 for the customs of the peoples are false.
A tree from the forest is cut down,
    and worked with an axe by the hands of a craftsman.
4 Men deck it with silver and gold;
    they fasten it with hammer and nails
    so that it cannot move.
5 Their idols are like scarecrows in a cucumber field,
    and they cannot speak;
they have to be carried,
    for they cannot walk.
Be not afraid of them,
    for they cannot do evil,
    neither is it in them to do good."
6 There is none like thee, O LORD;

thou art great, and thy name is great in
might.

7 Who would not fear thee, O King of the
nations?
For this is thy due;
for among all the wise ones of the nations
and in all their kingdoms
there is none like thee.

8 They are both stupid and foolish;
the instruction of idols is but wood!

9 Beaten silver is brought from Tarshish,
and gold from Uphaz.
They are the work of the craftsman and of
the hands of the goldsmith;
their clothing is violet and purple;
they are all the work of skilled men.

10 But the LORD is the true God;
he is the living God and the everlasting
King.
At his wrath the earth quakes,
and the nations cannot endure his indignation.

11 Thus shall you say to them: "The gods
who did not make the heavens and the earth
shall perish from the earth and from under the
heavens."

12 It is he who made the earth by his power,
who established the world by his wisdom,
and by his understanding stretched out
the heavens.

13 When he utters his voice there is a tumult
of waters in the heavens,
and he makes the mist rise from the ends
of the earth.
He makes lightnings for the rain,
and he brings forth the wind from his
storehouses.

14 Every man is stupid and without knowledge;
every goldsmith is put to shame by his
idols;
for his images are false,
and there is no breath in them.

15 They are worthless, a work of delusion;
at the time of their punishment they shall
perish.

16 Not like these is he who is the portion of
Jacob,
for he is the one who formed all things,
and Israel is the tribe of his inheritance;
the LORD of hosts is his name.

A rather sharp break occurs between
9:26 and 10:1. Chapters 7—9 speak
mainly of the depravity and destruction
of God's covenant people as a national entity and of the prophet's distress and despair over this prospect. This theme is
taken up again in 10:17. Chapter 10:1–16
is a separate and striking section which

focuses on the folly of idolatry. This forceful exposure of the absurdity and irra-
tionality of idolatry takes the form of a
contrast between the power of the God of
Israel and the powerlessness of the gods of
the pagans.

Because of the interruption of the sequence of thought, an alleged presupposition of an advanced stage of the experience of exile, and affinities with passages
in Isaiah 40—55, most scholars question
the authenticity of the section under consideration. While the present writer recognizes the strength of the case against its
genuineness, he is not persuaded that that
case is assured.

As already suggested, there is a shift of
emphasis as one moves from chapter 9 to
chapter 10. Two things may be said, however. First, there are other passages in
chapters 7—10 which sit loosely in their
context. Second, there are points of contact
between 10:1–16 and its context. In
9:23–24 Jeremiah has spoken about the
true basis of boasting, a right relationship
with the true God, who practices and delights in grace, justice, and righteousness.
In 9:25–26 he has indicated that all who
are not rightly related to this God are
"uncircumcised in heart" and are going to
encounter judgment. He has mentioned
several pagan peoples.

Moreover, that 10:1–16 presupposes the
Babylonian exile as a present reality is
more the case than in other passages already considered. The Assyro-Babylonian
forms of superstition and astral worship
were well known in Judah. The prophet's
countrymen did not have to go to Babylon
to find out about them or be warned
against them. Further, the first captivity
came in 597. It is known that Jeremiah
was deeply concerned about the Jewish
exiles and that he communicated with
them (chs. 24,29). He could have warned
them against falling under the spell of the
Babylonian brand of idolatry.

By far the strongest argument against
the authenticity of 10:1–16 is the presence
in it of striking similarities to passages

which critical scholars assign to the exile (cf. Isa. 40:18–20; 41; 44:9–20; 46:1–7). There is no doubt that similarities are there—both in ideas and in imagery. Lindblom maintains that absolute monotheism originated in the exile with Second Isaiah and that, in connection with this development, a new literary form emerged: the idol satire (p. 378).

One needs to be reminded that when it comes to the question of literary influence it is difficult—and precarious—to be dogmatic about which way the line runs (see remarks on 3:6 ff.). With Graf, Volz, Rudolph, and others, the present writer feels that Jeremiah may have influenced the author of Isaiah 40 ff., or that both were drawing from a common cultic store of language and ideas. Moreover, it is impossible to be certain that the idol satire was a distinct literary form, or, if it was, when it first appeared. Also, Second Isaiah had no monopoly on monotheism.

It should be indicated that though there are similarities between 10:1–16 and passages in Isaiah 40—55, there are also similarities between 10:1–16 and other passages in Jeremiah. In 2:1–37 Jeremiah brings a polemic against idolatry. There are other references to the same subject. The prophet constantly pinpoints apostasy and idolatry—of various types—as the explanation of the necessity for judgment. His presuppositions in his approach to idolatry are the same elsewhere as in 10:1–16 and in the passages in Isaiah. This demonstrates how accurately and profoundly he "penetrated to the root of this particular species of human defection" (Hopper, p. 897).

So, though he is aware of the strength of the arguments advanced by brilliant scholars against the genuineness of 10:1–16, this writer is not at all certain that the case is closed.[64]

Much more important than the ques-

tion of authorship, however, is the matter of meaning and relevance. The crucial question about any passage of Scripture always is not whether a particular person wrote it, but whether the voice of God is heard in it and, if so, what it is saying.

There are two parts to the passage under study: vv. 1–5 and 6–16. There are three major emphases in it: first, a warning to God's people not to adopt the superstitious practices of the pagan peoples around them; second, an exposure of the folly of trying to materialize deity; third, a strong stress on the reality, sovereignty, and power of the God of Israel.

The prophet begins with an injunction to God's people not to *learn* (adopt, copy) *the way* (religious practices) *of the nations* nor to be afraid of celestial omens (such as meteors, comets, eclipses), for all of *the customs* (religious beliefs and behavior) of the peoples are *false* (emptiness, nothingness; cf. 2:5). To commit oneself to these customs is to commit oneself to emptiness, and leads to dismay and dread.

With a superb sarcasm, the prophet proceeds to expose the folly of idolatry. The idol is constructed from a tree. The tree is cut down by a man. The idol is shaped by a man. It is overlaid with silver and gold by a man. It is decked out in lavish dress by a man. It is securely fastened to the wall with chains by a man (no god should be allowed to fall on its face!). When finished and fastened in place, it is like a scarecrow in a cucumber field (a devastating figure). It cannot talk or walk. It has to be carried. It cannot do good or evil—nothing! Why? Because it is a nothing. Its *instruction* is *but wood;* i.e., it robs the worshiper of a sense of the reality of the divine and of a reverence for the divine. It leads to woodenness.

Not so the God of Israel! There is none like him—unique, supreme, the God of the universe, a God of infinite power and wisdom, *the true God, the living God and the everlasting King.* He is in charge of nature and the nations. *The Lord of hosts is his name.*

---

[64] It is interesting that recently Weiser (*op. cit*) and Ackroyd (*Journal of Theological Studies,* 14, 1963, 385–390) have maintained that 10:1–16 contains a reworked form of a Jeremianic attack on idols.

This is the God who is *the portion of Jacob* and whose *inheritance* (possession, people) is *Israel*. In short, this great God of wisdom and power is a God of grace, who redeemed Israel and entered into covenant with her. He is the only God. Why leave him for an empty breath, a mere nothing, a piece of wood? Why forsake an overflowing fountain for a cracked cistern that can hold no water (cf. 2:13)?

The temptation to idolatry is powerful and ever-present. Men today, as in the prophet's day, have a flair for idolatry. Their idolatry takes many forms (not necessarily metal, maybe mental—less tangible, but nonetheless real): sensual pleasure, lust for power, love of money, a hunger for fame, formal religion, professing one thing and practicing another (giving one's ultimate allegiance to something other than that which he worships with his lips)— anything short of God that represents the totality of reality for those involved. The folly of idolatry is that men fashion their gods with care, fasten them securely in place, fall down before them, and find that they are nothingness. They give their worshipers no help; instead they become like their gods. Wooden deities! Wooden devotees! Hollow "scarecrow" gods! Hollow men!

(11) The Coming Calamity (10:17–22)

17 Gather up your bundle from the ground,
    O you who dwell under siege!
18 For thus says the Lord:
"Behold, I am slinging out the inhabitants of
    the land at this time,
and I will bring distress on them,
    that they may feel it."
19 Woe is me because of my hurt!
    My wound is grievous.
But I said, "Truly this is an affliction,
    and I must bear it."
20 My tent is destroyed,
    and all my cords are broken;
my children have gone from me,
    and they are not;
there is no one to spread my tent again,
    and to set up my curtains.
21 For the shepherds are stupid,
    and do not inquire of the Lord;
therefore they have not prospered,
    and all their flock is scattered.

22 Hark, a rumor! Behold, it comes!—
    a great commotion out of the north country
to make the cities of Judah a desolation,
    a lair of jackals.

These verses contain a short oracle (vv. 17–18), a lament (vv. 19–21), and a brief ejaculation (v. 22). The oracle starts with a command addressed by the prophet to a personified Jerusalem to get ready for departure. This leads up to the direct announcement of judgment: God is going to cast his people out of the land. In response to the oracular utterance, there is a touching communal lament in which the people voice their pain over the prospect of imminent ruin and the reason for it. The *shepherds* and the *flock* are the rulers and the people of Judah. The stupidity of the leaders, as seen in their failure to find and follow the will of God for the nation, is the principal explanation of the impending catastrophe.

The passage ends with a brief ejaculation about a commotion in the north and the coming of an invader from that direction *to make the cities of Judah a desolation.* The invader is Babylon.

(12) A Cry for Compassion in Chastisement (10:23–25)

23 I know, O Lord, that the way of man is not
    in himself,
that it is not in man who walks to direct
    his steps.
24 Correct me, O Lord, but in just measure;
    not in thy anger, lest thou bring me to
    nothing.
25 Pour out thy wrath upon the nations that
    know thee not,
and upon the peoples that call not on thy
    name;
for they have devoured Jacob;
    they have devoured him and consumed
    him,
and have laid waste his habitation.

The dialogue style of vv. 23–25 (cf. 10: 17–22) is evident. It is also apparent that out of his conversations with God come some of Jeremiah's deepest insights and most outstanding statements.

Verse 23—the beginning of a prayer— gives expression to the paradox of the human situation, recognized by Job, Augustine, Kierkegaard, and modern depth psychologists. *The way of man is not in himself.* In a profound sense, he belongs to Another. Therefore, *it is not in man . . . to direct his steps.* Apart from a recognition of the priority of his relationship to God, man cannot find freedom and fulfillment but experiences increasing self-deception and frustration. Or as Jung [65] puts it, "Whoever is unable to lose his life by the same token will never gain it."

Recognizing that *the way of man is not in himself* and that when he refuses to recognize this reality and rebels—becomes arrogantly self-sufficient—his way is perverted, the prophet is aware of the necessity for correction by God. He also knows that man's state apart from God is so serious that the dispensation of pure justice in divine discipline would result in destruction. Accordingly, he prays that God will not *correct in just measure* (with mathematical exactness), but that in wrath he will remember mercy (v. 24).

The prayer closes with a request for retribution to be poured out upon those who have ravaged God's people and their land (v. 25). Some deny this to Jeremiah because of its vindictive spirit (cf. 11:20; 12:3; 15:15; 17:18; 18:19–23; etc.).

In sum, chapters 7—10 constitute a collection of oracles of diverse character, coming mainly from Jeremiah's middle ministry. They emphasize various aspects of the apostasy of the people and the punishment inherent in it. They show a diversity of form, include an increasing amount of pure poetry, and reveal a greater suffering and a growing inwardness of conception on the part of the prophet.

IV. Jeremiah and the Covenant (11:1—12:17)

The superscription (11:1) indicates the start of a new section. The reader encounters immediately the "prose sermon"

style met for the first time in the book in 7:1—8:3.

Although the content of the new section is somewhat diverse in character, it constitutes an editorial unit. The unit has an autobiographical framework (cf. 7:1–8:3), and much of it is in the form of a dialogue between God and Jeremiah. The major emphasis is on the prophet and the covenant.

In the Old Testament the term covenant first occurs in Genesis 9:8–17 (7 times) in connection with the covenant between God and mankind. It appears in Genesis 17: 1–21 (13 times) in connection with the covenant with Abraham and his descendants.

Though both of these covenants are important, the most important covenant in Old Testament days is the Mosaic covenant made at Sinai (Ex. 19—24). It was definitely of the suzerainty type (see 2:2–3). It was grounded in the grace of God and gave tangible form to the election of Israel, now historically confirmed in the Exodus event (Ex. 1—18). Though based upon the beneficence of the Giver, it involved obligation on the part of the receiver. This is where the law came in, as the covenant on its human side.[66]

It is now accepted by many scholars that there were periodic covenant renewals in ancient Israel. It is quite possible that these were annual affairs in the autumn. A study of Exodus 19—24, Joshua 24, 2 Kings 22—23, and Nehemiah 8—10 will reveal the basic pattern of renewal: a rehearsal of God's mighty acts, a call for decision, the response of the people in rededication, the reading of the law, and a recital of the curses of disobedience and the blessings of obedience.

The covenant renewal of 622 b.c. followed this pattern (2 Kings 22—23). It issued in an all-out effort at purification

---

65 Carl Gustav Jung, *The Integration of Personality*, trans. S. M. Dell (London: Routledge & Paul, 1950), p. 304.

66 On the covenant concept, the covenant with Israel, and recent study in the area, see Eichrodt, *op. cit.*, pp. 36–69; George Mendenhall, "Covenant," IDB, 1, 714 ff.; Walter Harrelson, "Law in the OT," IDB, pp. 77–89; Hillers, *op. cit.*, pp. 46–71.

and centralization of worship in Judah. That effort is referred to as the Josianic or Deuteronomic reformation.

1. Crusader for the Covenant (11:1–14)

¹ The word that came to Jeremiah from the LORD: ² "Hear the words of this covenant, and speak to the men of Judah and the inhabitants of Jerusalem. ³ You shall say to them, Thus says the LORD, the God of Israel: Cursed be the man who does not heed the words of this covenant ⁴ which I commanded your fathers when I brought them out of the land of Egypt, from the iron furnace, saying, Listen to my voice, and do all that I command you. So shall you be my people, and I will be your God, ⁵ that I may perform the oath which I swore to your fathers, to give them a land flowing with milk and honey, as at this day." Then I answered, "So be it, LORD."

⁶ And the Lord said to me, "Proclaim all these words in the cities of Judah, and in the streets of Jerusalem: Hear the words of this covenant and do them. ⁷ For I solemnly warned your fathers when I brought them up out of the land of Egypt, warning them persistently, even to this day, saying, Obey my voice. ⁸ Yet they did not obey or incline their ear, but every one walked in the stubbornness of his evil heart. Therefore I brought upon them all the words of this covenant, which I commanded them to do, but they did not."

⁹ Again the LORD said to me, "There is revolt among the men of Judah and the inhabitants of Jerusalem. ¹⁰ They have turned back to the iniquities of their forefathers, who refused to hear my words; they have gone after other gods to serve them; the house of Israel and the house of Judah have broken my covenant which I made with their fathers. ¹¹ Therefore, thus says the LORD, Behold, I am bringing evil upon them which they cannot escape; though they cry to me, I will not listen to them. ¹² Then the cities of Judah and the inhabitants of Jerusalem will go and cry to the gods to whom they burn incense, but they cannot save them in the time of their trouble. ¹³ For your gods have become as many as your cities, O Judah; and as many as the streets of Jerusalem are the altars you have set up to shame, altars to burn incense to Baal.

¹⁴ "Therefore do not pray for this people, or lift up a cry or prayer on their behalf, for I will not listen when they call to me in the time of their trouble.

Following the introductory formula (v. 1; cf. 7:1) is the command to Jeremiah to deliver God's message to *the men of Judah*

and the inhabitants of Jerusalem (v. 2). That message concerns *the words* (terms) *of this covenant* (vv. 3,6,8; *my covenant,* v. 10). The crucial question is: What covenant? Some maintain that the Deuteronomic covenant is meant. Others insist with equal vigor that the reference is to the Sinaitic covenant.

Much of this debate seems to be somewhat off center, for both covenants were essentially the same. Deuteronomy is a great book. It contains the only extended exposition of the covenant faith of Israel in the Old Testament. That faith goes back to the Exodus event, the holiest of all events, the pivotal event in Israel's religion and life.

To be sure, there is a lengthy "code" of law in Deuteronomy 12—26, but it is "preached" law. Also, it is preceded by chapters 1—11, in which we have a rehearsal of God's mighty acts of grace on behalf of his people, coupled with an earnest exhortation to the people to give their God their undivided devotion. Then comes the law—the revealed order of life for the people in covenant relationship with God—and it is not a code but a proclamation, an exposition of the law. The central thrust of Deuteronomy, as of the covenant at Sinai, is God's revelation and redemption, and man's response in faith and obedience.

In view of this fact and of the historical situation, it is a reasonable conjecture that the phrase *this covenant* refers to the Mosaic covenant of Sinai, as renewed in 622 under the leadership of Josiah and the guidance of Deuteronomy.

If this conclusion has validity, 11:1 ff. bears "witness to the view that Jeremiah . . . gladly welcomed the reform of Josiah." ⁶⁷ and went on a preaching mission, promoting its principles and program. Those who take this position are not agreed as to whether that mission came in the early stages of the reformation (622

⁶⁷ Eissfeldt, *op. cit.,* p. 360; Rowley, *From Moses to Qumran,* pp. 187–210.

B.C. and years immediately following), or at a later time, when the prophet saw the people lapsing from their commitment (ca. 609). In view of the paucity of information on the subject, it may not be inappropriate to suggest that both groups could be right. The prophet may have advocated the reform in its early stages. Later, when he saw the people slipping, he may have preached to them again about the stipulations of the covenant.

In vv. 1–5 Jeremiah is enjoined to *hear the words of this covenant* and to herald them to the people, with particular emphasis on the curse that comes from not giving heed to them (cf. Deut. 11:28; 27:26; 28:15–68). He is to remind the Judahites that he is speaking of the covenant which God made with them at the time of their deliverance from Egypt, *from the iron furnace* (a graphic metaphor for great suffering; cf. Deut. 4:20), and that their well-being in the land God gave them is dependent upon their obedience to his will (cf. Deut. 2:30; 6:3; 7:8; 26:15).

In response to this divine injunction, Jeremiah says: *So be it* (amen), *Lord* (cf. Deut. 27:11–26). Never did a sincere "amen" to God cost a prophet more.

Verses 6–8 reiterate a part of what is said in vv. 1–5. The prophet is told more specifically to go through the city and the country, impressing upon the people God's requirement of obedience, their refusal in the past to obey, and the retribution which followed that disobedience.

For reasons not known, most of vv. 7–8 is omitted by the LXX. The phrase *the stubbornness of his evil heart* is a favorite with Jeremiah, as are other words and phrases found in the larger context, confirming the view expressed earlier that there is no essential difference between the Jeremiah of the poetry and the Jeremiah of the prose portions of the prophecy.

Verses 9–14 suggest that there was resistance to the preaching of the prophet and to the reform movement. When this opposition came is not known, but it made clear to Jeremiah that the people were not rightly related to God, were bent on backsliding, and must suffer for it.

It is possible that, if vv. 1–8 refer primarily to the activity of the prophet in 622 and thereafter, vv. 9–14 may refer to a subversive campaign which came later, possibly reaching its peak in the early part of Jehoiakim's reign. In any case, it seems that in the days of Josiah Jeremiah supported the renewal and reactivation of the covenant entered upon at Sinai and expounded in Deuteronomy, the probable guidebook of the reformation. This support stirred up opposition. The people stubbornly refused to comply with the covenant demands. This meant judgment. Jeremiah was forbidden again to intercede in their favor (cf. 7:16).

2. Empty Cultus and Inescapable Catastrophe (11:15–17)

15 What right has my beloved in my house, when she has done vile deeds? Can vows and sacrificial flesh avert your doom? Can you then exult? 16 The LORD once called you, 'A green olive tree, fair with goodly fruit'; but with the roar of a great tempest he will set fire to it, and its branches will be consumed. 17 The LORD of hosts, who planted you, has pronounced evil against you, because of the evil which the house of Israel and the house of Judah have done, provoking me to anger by burning incense to Baal."

This passage, though important, presents a number of textual difficulties. Any attempt at a solution will involve conjecture. The Hebrew is quite obscure. The RSV follows the LXX (so Rudolph). We offer a translation of vv. 15–16 which combines the LXX reading with some suggested emendations, chiefly from G. R. Driver[68]

What right has my beloved in my house?
    You have done wicked deeds!
Can fatlings and holy flesh remove
    Your evil from upon you?
        Then you could exult!
'A luxuriant olive tree, fair of form/fruit'
    The Lord called your name.
He will kindle a fire against it
    And its branches will be consumed
        With the sound of a great roaring.'

68 *Op. cit.*, p. 108.

The phrase *my beloved* refers to the people of God. *My house* is the Temple. *Vows* (fatlings) *and sacrificial flesh* represent the sacrificial system. Olive trees grew in the Temple area (Psalm 52:8; cf. Hos. 14:7). *Fire* is a symbol of judgment.

If the text of the passage is in bad repair, fortunately the meaning is fairly clear. God's people have fallen away from him. Therefore, in their present state, they have no business in his house. He addresses them in the second person: "You have sinned. Do you think that mere ritual can get rid of your guilt and the penalty which it involves? If this were the case, you could certainly rejoice. But not so!"

Jeremiah is using a touch of irony, a rhetorical device of which he is fairly fond. He is stating that under existing conditions the observance of a round of sacrifice and ceremony is pure cant and will accomplish nothing. Hence there is no basis for exultation. Instead, there is going to be divine visitation. It would appear that the prophet is becoming critical of the form the Deuteronomic reform is taking.

Verse 17 is an expansion of the idea set forth in v. 16. God planted the *tree*. Now he must deal drastically with it. His people have provoked him to *anger*. Therefore he must punish them.

This idea of divine discipline does not appeal to modern man. It is biblical nonetheless. The God of both the Old and the New Testaments is a God of holy love. If we do not accept his live as forgiving mercy, we must eventually confront it as judgment. We tend to forget that there are two types of severity. There is the severity that stems from cruelty and desires to destroy. There is also the severity that springs from love and seeks to save. The God of Jeremiah—and of Jesus—is a God of saving severity.

3. Conspiracy and Complaint (11:18—12:6)

This is Jeremiah's first confession. Although some scholars consider the passage to consist of two separate confessions (11: 18–23; 12:1–6), it is better to regard it as one, with 11:18–23 relating the story of the prophet's maltreatment as the background, and 12:1–6 recording his protest and God's reply (on the confessions, see Int. and the conclusion of the treatment of 20:7–18).

Because of textual difficulties in the first confession, some scholars make rather radical rearrangements of the verses in it (see technical commentaries). The rearrangements often result in a smoother sequence of thought. However, textual rearrangement can become a very subjective affair. This writer prefers, for the most part, to treat the passage as it appears in the prophecy.

(1) The Conspiracy (11:18–23)

18 The LORD made it known to me and I knew;
  then thou didst show me their evil deeds.
19 But I was like a gentle lamb
  led to the slaughter.
I did not know it was against me
  they devised schemes, saying,
"Let us destroy the tree with its fruit,
  let us cut him off from the land of the living,
  that his name be remembered no more."
20 But, O LORD of hosts, who judgest righteously,
  who triest the heart and the mind,
let me see thy vengeance upon them,
  for to thee have I committed my cause.
21 Therefore thus says the LORD concerning the men of Anathoth, who seek your life, and say, "Do not prophesy in the name of the LORD, or you will die by our hand"—22 therefore thus says the LORD of hosts: "Behold, I will punish them; the young men shall die by the sword; their sons and their daughters shall die by famine; 23 and none of them shall be left. For I will bring evil upon the men of Anathoth, the year of their punishment."

We have here the story of a plot to take the prophet's life (see also 12:6).

The place—Anathoth. The prophet had stirred up "the brethren" in his hometown by his proclamation of the word of God— and, in particular, by his advocacy of the Josianic reform. The reform meant the shutting down of the local sanctuary. This put Jeremiah's priest relatives out of a job.

So the priests of Anathoth decided to deal with the meddling kinsman and fellow townsman.

Possibly the prophet had just returned from a preaching trip to Jerusalem. How refreshing to be home again and to relax among family members and familiar surroundings! However, as he went about the village, he detected a difference in atmosphere. Then, with dramatic suddenness, the revelation came: a plot was afoot, and he was the target (vv. 18–19a; 12:6).

The purpose—to bring about Jeremiah's decease. The schemers had warned Jeremiah to curtail his kind of preaching. He had refused. Now they set about to do it for him. He had called them a lovely "olive tree" (11:16) which God was going to set fire to and finish off. Well, to them he was a *tree* that bore an undesirable *fruit.* Therefore they would cut down the tree, so that the fruit would cease—the prophetic "word" which cut so sharply into their consciences and compensation. They would dispense with both the man and the message (v. 19b)!

The plea—*O Lord of hosts, . . . let me see thy vengeance upon them* (Mendenhall, "thy deliverance from them") Jeremiah was shocked and shaken up. He had been caught off guard, like *a gentle lamb* (lit., "a familiar or domesticated lamb"), playing with its master in hope of a bit of sugar or a bunch of leaves—some show of affection—only to meet the slaughterer's knife. Weary in body and spirit, the prophet was now broken in heart. He was suffering from some self-pity too—a middle-aged man comparing himself to a pet lamb about the place! And so he lashed out at those who in opposing him were opposing the God he served (v. 20).

This is Jeremiah's first imprecation against his personal enemies. There will be others. The problem posed by the imprecations for the Christian will be discussed in connection with 18:18–23.

The promise—*Behold, I will punish them.* The prophet was told that the wicked would be judged (vv. 21–23).

With this assurance of just retribution for his opposition, Jeremiah became more calm and reflective.

(2) The Complaint (12:1–4)

1 Righteous art thou, O Lord,
   when I complain to thee;
      yet I would plead my case before thee.
   Why does the way of the wicked prosper?
      Why do all who are treacherous thrive?
2 Thou plantest them, and they take root;
      they grow and bring forth fruit;
   thou art near in their mouth
      and far from their heart.
3 But thou, O Lord, knowest me;
      thou seest me, and triest my mind toward thee.
   Pull them out like sheep for the slaughter,
      and set them apart for the day of slaughter.
4 How long will the land mourn,
      and the grass of every field wither?
   For the wickedness of those who dwell in it
      the beasts and the birds are swept away,
      because men said, "He will not see our latter end."

The lawsuit motif shows up again in this section. Already the prophet has spoken of committing his "case" to God (11:20). Now, under the terrific tension of an intense struggle with the mysteries of divine providence, he earnestly desired to present his case before God.[69] And so he made his complaint.

In the complaint, he revealed several things: he was confused by the inequities of life (v. 1); he was concerned about God's reputation (v. 2); he was conscious of his own integrity (v. 3); he came to God with his case and committed it to him (vv. 1–4).

Perhaps a paraphrase of his prayer will give some insight into its meaning and the agonizing struggle through which the prophet was passing: "Lord, you are right-

---

[69] W. L. Holladay advances the view that Jeremiah wished to sue God for breach of contract ("Jeremiah's Lawsuit with God," *Interpretation*, 17, 1963, 280). Though his thesis has some things to commend it, it is to be rejected. The prophet was presenting his case *to* God, not *against* him (cf. Duhm, Volz, Rudolph, Hyatt, *et al.*). He did not question the righteousness of God.

eous—in all ways and at all times in the right. I cannot bring a valid suit against you. But I must honestly disclose my inner difficulty and distress. There are some cases which I wish to discuss with you." The word rendered *case* in v. 1*a* is in the plural (*mishpatim*). It refers here to judicial decisions made by God in his administration of affairs on earth.

Jeremiah became specific (v. 1*b*): "Why do the wicked prosper? Why is crookedness the prime prerequisite for success in this world? You plant these scoundrels and they grow (note the play on the figure of the tree: 11:16,19; 12:2). Why? They are pious frauds who mouth words of religion but have no real love for you in their hearts."

The emotional temperature of God's servant began to rise again, as he thought about those who had sought to kill him: "You know me through and through, Lord. You are aware that there is no such hypocrisy in me. Therefore, judge these men. Snatch them out and sanctify them for the slaughter. How long will this intolerable situation go on? The land is suffering from drought and famine. The grass is withering, and the birds and beasts are dying—all because of the evil conduct of these people. They are saying that you don't know or care about any of it. Deal with them!"

The prophet was in deep distress. He was wrestling with "the dark enigma of suffering," the problem of the contrast between the prosperity of the wicked and the persecution and pain of the righteous (and, in particular, of God's messenger). In short, his complaint was directed at the rectitude of divine providence, the justice of God in his dealings with men.

Some think that this is the first direct articulation of this problem in the Old Testament. The same problem is faced in Habakkuk, Job, and Psalms 37; 49; 73. The only solution for it is to be found in the shape of a cross, firmly planted in the earth, reaching up toward the sky, on a hill called Calvary.

(3) The Challenge (12:5-6)

5 "If you have raced with men on foot, and
   they have wearied you,
      how will you compete with horses?
And if in a safe land you fall down,
      how will you do in the jungle of the Jordan?
6 For even your brothers and the house of
   your father,
      even they have dealt treacherously with
      you;
   they are in full cry after you;
believe them not,
      though they speak fair words to you."

Jeremiah received a reply to his plea. It was not the kind he wanted but the kind he needed. He was in need of reinforcement, not reassurance—a strong challenge, not soothing comfort.

There is a textual problem in v. 5, one of the great verses in Jeremiah. It centers around the participle *boteach* (are trusting, are confident). The Masoretic Text reads: "if in a land of peace you are confident, how will you do in the jungle of the Jordan?" Volz proposed the insertion of the negative particle *lo'* before *boteach*. Some scholars accepted but some rejected his emendation. The verb *batach* is closely connected with an Arabic root signifying "lie with face downward, tumble down." To throw oneself down before an individual or a deity was to throw oneself on him for protection—hence, to put trust in him. The RSV translation (*fall down*) relies on the Arabic as an aid in solving the problem.

God was saying to his servant (to paraphrase): "If a few footrunners have worn you out in your race for me, what will you do when you come up against thoroughbred horses? And if you fall flat on your face on level ground in a pleasant meadowland as you move for me, what will you do in the tangled, lion-infested jungles of the Jordan? The days are coming which will make these days look like easy days. There are higher hurdles ahead. You are up against boys now. There are men farther down the road, and farther still, giants. Cheer up, Jeremiah, the worst is yet to come!"

This was a call to courage, a challenge to heroic endurance. The prophet must learn that the problem of theodicy must be solved in a personal way and that he must be able to live without having all of the answers to the enigmas of life. This is the kind of challenge—this call to courage —to which real men respond, and, in responding, they become better men for it.

There were implications in this challenge for Jeremiah. There was a recognition of past service. There was also a revelation of future suffering. God was declaring, in effect; "You have done well with the footmen (under Josiah). I have confidence in you. You can and must place your confidence in me. The way will become increasingly hard (under Jehoiakim and Zedekiah), but I will be with you in the race with the horses."

There is something here for us, too. Life is full of testing times. The trials of the human pilgrimage tend, in the providence of God, to be graduated—the footmen before the horses, the land of peace before the jungle of the Jordan. The lesser trials are intended to prepare us for the greater. Victory in the lesser is a pledge and promise of triumph in the greater, for the same God who helps us with the footmen and in the land of peace will also aid us with the horses and in the jungle of the Jordan. Nothing is too hard for him. If we move with him, we will become stronger in character and service.

The first confession of Jeremiah introduces to a new form. It is not found elsewhere in the prophetical literature. Patterned somewhat after the individual lament in the Psalter, it is nonetheless distinctive as the expression of an intimate personal struggle of the prophet with his call, his communication of the "word," and the consequences encountered (contra Gerstenberger and Reventlow).[70] We see him here, not as the courageous proclaimer

of God's message in public (which he was), but as a lonely, sensitive, suffering man, pouring out his complaint, his criticism, and his questions in the presence of God, and calling for answers and vindication. It is easy to see why he is referred to as the most human of the prophets.

In the dialogue of prayer, he discloses that he is caught in the tension between surrender to God and surrender to the world. To the outburst of a deeply wounded heart God responds with a stern challenge. This experience is the prelude to others (15:10–21; 17:9–10, 14–18; 18:18–23; 20:7–14). Together they portray a spiritual crisis that came to Jeremiah during the days of Jehoiakim.

4. The People of God and the Pagans (12:7–17)

This section is said by some scholars to have no connection with the context. This is not the case. Hopper is right in pointing out that there is a deep, dynamic, and poetic relationship between it and that which precedes it (p. 919). The section itself has a common theme: Israel's relationship to the neighboring nations.

(1) God's Dirge over the Devastation of His Heritage (12:7–13)

7 "I have forsaken my house,
    I have abandoned my heritage;
  I have given the beloved of my soul
    into the hands of her enemies.
8 My heritage has become to me
    like a lion in the forest,
  she has lifted up her voice against me;
    therefore I hate her.
9 Is my heritage to me like a speckled bird
    of prey?
  Are the birds of prey against her round
    about?
  Go, assemble all the wild beasts;
    bring them to devour.
10 Many shepherds have destroyed my vineyard,
    they have trampled down my portion,
  they have made my pleasant portion
    a desolate wilderness.
11 They have made it a desolation;
    desolate, it mourns to me.
  The whole land is made desolate,
    but no man lays it to heart.

---

70 E. Gerstenberger, "Jeremiah's Complaints: Observations on Jer. 15:10–21," JBL, 82, 393–408; H. G. Reventlow, Liturgie und prophetisches Ich bei Jeremia (Gutersloh: Mohn, 1968).

¹² Upon all the bare heights in the desert
    destroyers have come;
for the sword of the LORD devours
    from one end of the land to the other;
    no flesh has peace.
¹³ They have sown wheat and have reaped
    thorns,
    they have tired themselves out but profit
    nothing.
They shall be ashamed of their harvests
    because of the fierce anger of the LORD."

The complaint of Yahweh in these verses corresponds to the complaint of Jeremiah in 12:1–4. Here Jeremiah is following in the footsteps of Hosea in interpreting the heart of God in terms of his own experience. He has experienced great pain because of his rejection by his people. God also experiences great pain because of his people's rejection of him and the retribution which this inevitably entails.

The historical background of this lament of the Lord was likely Nebuchadnezzar's sending contingents of soldiers from neighboring countries to put down Jehoiakim's revolt in 601 B.C. (cf. 2 Kings 24:1–2). The terms *birds of prey* and *many shepherds* (leaders) apply more to an attack by several small groups than to an assault by a world power (Nebuchadnezzar himself in 598).

As one reads the lament, he feels the pathos in it. He notes the warmth in the varied imagery employed to designate Israel as God's possession, his people—note the several terms: *my house, my heritage, beloved of my soul, a speckled bird of prey, my vineyard,* and *my pleasant portion.*

Israel has abandoned her God. Therefore he is abandoning her to the consequences of her action (v. 7). She has roared angry defiance at him *like a lion* roaring through a forest. Therefore he is leaving her to the solitude she has created for herself like some savage beast (v. 8). *Like a speckled bird of prey,* attacked by other *birds of prey,* she is being attacked by mixed hordes of pagans. Like an unprotected *vineyard,* she is being trampled by invading *shepherds,* who are making it

a waste. God's *pleasant portion* is being despoiled. The land is being ravaged (vv. 11 f.).

All this has come through the activity of God (the portrayal in vv. 7–13 is probably description rather than prediction). *The sword of the Lord devours.* Central to all Jeremiah's preaching is his concept of God as Lord of history, with a purpose which he is working out and a goal toward which he is moving. Israel is, in a very special sense, the people of his purpose. But she has rebelled against his purpose. In so doing, she has brought trouble upon herself. God's *fierce anger*—the basic antagonism of his nature to sin—makes it necessary that she suffer. But he suffers too. This poem gives vivid expression to his pain over the punishment of his people for their apostasy.

(2) God's Dealings with the Devastators (12:14–17)

¹⁴ Thus says the LORD concerning all my evil neighbors who touch the heritage which I have given my people Israel to inherit: "Behold, I will pluck them up from their land, and I will pluck up the house of Judah from among them. ¹⁵ And after I have plucked them up, I will again have compassion on them, and I will bring them again each to his heritage and each to his land. ¹⁶ And it shall come to pass, if they will diligently learn the ways of my people, to swear by my name, 'As the LORD lives,' even as they taught my people to swear by Baal, then they shall be built up in the midst of my people. ¹⁷ But if any nation will not listen, then I will utterly pluck it up and destroy it, says the LORD."

Here Jeremiah has something to say about the neighboring nations who have invaded Israel. Though unaware of it, they have served the purpose of God. It is also a part of God's plan that they too, along with the Judeans, be carried into captivity by the Babylonians (cf. 25:8–9; 27:4–11; etc.). Through Nebuchadnezzar, God *will pluck them up from their land,* just as he *will pluck up the house of Judah from among them.* But when this has been done, they will also experience restoration to their own area.

If they respond to God, acknowledge his character and sovereign claims, and learn *the ways* (religious practices) of his people, they will *be built up in the midst of* his *people*. If not, then he will *pluck* them up and *destroy them* (cf. play on words from 1:10). They have a place in God's redemptive plan. That place—and their future—depends upon their response to him.

As Cornill observes, this is "highly original." [71] Leslie calls it "a fresh new word of great spiritual breadth and international tolerance" (p. 187).

Though some reject the passage because of the universalism in it (e.g., Lindblom), the present writer accepts it as essentially Jeremianic and feels that it demonstrates the profound insight of the great prophet.

Chapters 11 and 12 constitute a complex of materials of various types centering around the general subject, Jeremiah and the covenant. They provide much insight into the heart of the prophet and the heart of God. They recount the incident which may mark the start of the martyrdom of God's servant.

V. Two Parables, a Plea, and Some Pessimistic Predictions (13:1–27)

This new section (indicated by the formula in v. 1) is partly in prose and partly in poetry. It consists of prophecies of various types coming mainly from the reign of Jehoiakim. The connecting link is the continuing emphasis on the apostasy of the people and the punishment which they are experiencing and will encounter as a penalty for it.

1. The Linen Loincloth (13:1–11)

[1] Thus said the LORD to me, "Go and buy a linen waistcloth, and put it on your loins, and do not dip it in water." [2] So I bought a waistcloth according to the word of the LORD, and put it on my loins. [3] And the word of the LORD came to me a second time, [4] "Take the waistcloth which you have bought, which is upon your loins, and arise, go to the Euphrates, and hide it there in a cleft of the rock." [5] So I went,

[71] *Jeremia*, p. 165.

and hid it by the Euphrates, as the LORD commanded me. [6] And after many days the LORD said to me, "Arise, go to the Euphrates, and take from there the waistcloth which I commanded you to hide there." [7] Then I went to the Euphrates, and dug, and I took the waistcloth from the place where I had hidden it. And behold, the waistcloth was spoiled; it was good for nothing.

[8] Then the word of the LORD came to me: [9] "Thus says the LORD: Even so will I spoil the pride of Judah and the great pride of Jerusalem. [10] This evil people, who refuse to hear my words, who stubbornly follow their own heart and have gone after other gods to serve them and worship them, shall be like this waistcloth, which is good for nothing. [11] For as the waistcloth clings to the loins of a man, so I made the whole house of Israel and the whole house of Judah cling to me, says the LORD, that they might be for me a people, a name, a praise, and a glory, but they would not listen.

The section starts with a prose account of an acted out parable (vv. 1–7), followed by a prophetic oracle which provides the explanation of the parable (vv. 8–11).

The prophets were called to communicate the word of God. They performed their task in various ways. Ordinarily they did it through proclamation in public address. In delivering the divine word in public discourse, they could and did employ many literary forms and stylistic devices. The articulate word, however, was not their only means of getting the message across. They sometimes engaged in symbolic acts (e.g., 1 Kings 11:20 ff.; Isa. 20:1 ff.; Ezek. 4—5; 12). Since this method was also used in law, medicine, and worship, it was familiar to the people.

Why did the prophets employ the acted out parable? The answer to this question is that the symbolic act was an intensified declaration of the divine word. It therefore partook of the character and characteristics of that word. It was both illustrative and effective. It not only pictured or prefigured that which was to take place, but also propelled it toward actualization. It was strongly reinforced by that which was said in connection with it.

Obviously this means that the symbolic

act was charged with power and that it roots back into primitive ideas of mimetic magic: like produces like. But, though this was its origin, its character was transformed by the great prophets by taking it up into the will of God, to which they were so completely committed. They never used the symbolic act for personal ends but always for the illustration and realization of God's purposes, and it was the power of God—not some magical power—which was at work through the word proclaimed, whether by public utterance or acted out symbolism or both.[72]

Symbolic acts played a fairly prominent role in the ministry of Jeremiah (chs. 13; 16; 19; 27; 28; 32; 43; 51). The first of his symbolic acts is recorded in 13:1–11.

The passage begins with the story of the act itself (vv. 1–7). Jeremiah received a command to purchase *a linen waistcloth,* to *put it* on his *loins,* and not to permit it to come into contact with *water.* This he did. Then came a second divine directive to take the loincloth and conceal it in *a cleft of the rock* on *the Euphrates.* He complied with this order. After *many days* had passed, he was told to go and get the loincloth. When he did so, he discovered that it *was spoiled . . . good for nothing.*

According to Leslie, the loincloth was "man's principal ornament" in Oriental life —something highly prized and worn close to his person (p. 86). In this case, it was new and was made of linen. It was important that it be new (Lindblom, p. 52). Why it was specified that it was to be made of linen is not known. Was it because linen was cooler (KB), because it would be more readily ruined by dampness than leather (Peake), or because linen was worn by the priests (Streane; cf. Ex. 28: 42)? Since the loincloth represents Israel in the symbolism and since Israel was called to be "a kingdom of priests" (Ex.

19:6), the last-mentioned theory has much to commend it.

Verses 8–11 announce, in the form of a prophetic oracle, the significance of the symbolic act. God is going to *spoil* (crush) *the pride of Judah and . . . Jerusalem.* Through their arrogant disobedience and flagrant idolatry his people have become *good for nothing.* Like *the waistcloth* which *clings to the loins* of its wearer, God gave them a position of intimacy and honor. He bound them to himself in covenant relationship, that they might be for him *a people, a name, a praise, and a glory,* i.e., a redeemed community among whom he would be present and through whom he would be revealed and praised. But they refused to *listen* (i.e., to comply with the covenant stipulations). Therefore they have become spoiled.

This acted out parable is somewhat perplexing both as to the action described in it and as to the interpretation to be given of it. A few scholars have denied its authenticity, either because of its "childish" character (Duhm), or because of its "contradiction" of the prophet's attitude in 24:1 ff. (Welch). Duhm's position is quite subjective. We cannot judge the actions of the prophets by modern standards. As for Welch, his objection can be met by the simple recognition of the fact that the parable of 13:1–11 comes out of the reign of Jehoiakim and that of 24:1 ff. dates from the days of Zedekiah and presupposes the captivity of 597.

Though most scholars accept the genuineness of 13:1–11, there are two questions about which there is much disagreement. First, did Jeremiah make two round trips to the Euphrates—a total distance of some 1400 miles? Lindblom denies categorically that he did. He classifies the whole experience as an ecstatic vision (p. 131; cf. Peake, Rudolph, Weiser). The great weakness of this view is that for a symbolic act to have much effect it had to be witnessed. The same objection applies to Couturier's theory, namely, that the story is an allegory, a literary invention.

---

[72] H. Wheeler Robinson, "Prophetic Symbolism," ed. T. H. Robinson, *Old Testament Essays* (Oxford: University Press, 1927), pp. 1–17; Lindblom, *op. cit.,* pp. 165–172; Georg Fohrer, *Die Symbolischen Handlungen der Propheten,* Zurich, 1953.

Other scholars hold that Jeremiah made two trips, but not to the Euphrates. Instead, he went to the Wadi Farah, a little village in a rocky valley about four miles northeast of Anathoth (Josh. 18:23). This conclusion is made possible either by emendation or by representation. Following Aquila's translation and the suggestion made by Schick and Ewald, some change the Hebrew slightly so that *Perathah* reads *Farah.* Others say that, because of the similarity in the sound of the words, *Farah* was understood to "represent" *Perathah*— or the other way round. Cunliffe-Jones simply observes that Jeremiah made two "acted out token trips." He fails to say where he went. The trouble with all of this —aside from the arbitrary textual change and the fact that *Perathah* always means the Euphrates in the Hebrew Bible—is that a trip to a small town in Palestine would hardly get across the point of the parable.

The experience was real, not visionary or imaginary (cf. Cornill, Giesebrecht, Erbt, Birmingham, Leslie, *et al.*). The record reads like a simple, matter-of-fact narrative. In all probability, Jeremiah made the trips to the Euphrates as proof positive of his deep earnestness in the exercise of his ministry, and as evidence of his complete readiness to do whatever God wanted him to do to get his message over to the people. He was underscoring his words with his deeds.

This brings us to the second question: What is the meaning of the parable? Again, there is a diversity of answers. To Volz, the point is that the exile would last a long time (cf. v. 6). Weiser thinks that it is that the Jews would return from the exile (cf. vv. 6–7). Others suggest that it is that the corruption of the people was the cause of the captivity (e.g., Graf, Cornill, Rudolph, Peake). Baumann maintains that it lies in the degrading power of Babylonian polytheism and the tragic consequences of this in and for the life of the nation (cf. Cunliffe-Jones, *et al.*).

Just what was God saying through his servant in this bit of acted out symbolism? The Euphrates evidently stands for the Mesopotamian area. Jeremiah represents God. The loincloth symbolizes Israel. Israel was God's treasured possession, his covenant people. At one time there had been a very intimate and beautiful relation between him and them. But that relationship had been corrupted by pagan influences which began to pour into Israel and Judah from the "Land between the Rivers" as early as the eighth century, continued to exert their power during the days of Manasseh and Amon, and reasserted themselves in the reign of Jehoiakim. These pagan influences had separated God's people from him and made them good for nothing, for Israel's existence had no meaning apart from God's purpose for her as his elect, a people in covenant relationship with him. So, as this writer sees it, the parable deals with election, corruption, rejection, and destruction—but primarily with the second, corruption (cf. Couturier).

It is well to remember that to the extent that God's people permit anything —pride, paganism, or whatever—to rob them of a right relationship with God they become "good for nothing"—i.e., ineffective for the carrying out of his kingdom purposes.

2. The Wine Jars (13:12–14)

12 "You shall speak to them this word: 'Thus says the Lord, the God of Israel, "Every jar shall be filled with wine." ' And they will say to you, 'Do we not indeed know that every jar will be filled with wine?' 13 Then you shall say to them, 'Thus says the Lord: Behold, I will fill with drunkenness all the inhabitants of this land: the kings who sit on David's throne, the priests, the prophets, and all the inhabitants of Jerusalem. 14 And I will dash them one against another, fathers and sons together, says the Lord. I will not pity or spare or have compassion, that I should not destroy them.' "

This is the second parable in prose. It is of particular interest in that in it the prophet presents "the first sketch of his image of the cup of wine of the wrath of God which the nations are to drink" (Cunliffe-Jones, p. 111; recall 6:11; cf. 25:15–

28; Ezek. 23:31–34; Isa. 51:17; Rev. 14:
8,10).

Here Jeremiah takes a popular proverb or a portion of a drinking song and uses it for his purposes. The setting for the delivery of the prophecy is likely a sacrificial feast at which considerable drinking is taking place. There may be some "talkback" in the preaching situation.

Let the reader exercise his imagination. A festival is in progress. The prophet appears. He starts his message. Seeing some empty jars nearby, he recites a saying expressive of faith in future well-being: *Every jar shall be filled with wine.* Possibly some listeners begin to heckle because of being confronted with such a commonplace (cf. Isa. 28:9–10). They scoff at the preacher: "We know, of course, don't we, that every jar will be filled with wine (literal translation)?" The prophet fires back: "Yes, you're right! And just as empty jars (possibly pointing to some close at hand) are destined to be filled with wine, so all of you—the entire lot—are going to be filled with *drunkenness* (horror, stupefaction, inability to act) during the coming crisis when I smash you against one another without mercy" (author's interpretative summary).

These are stern words of warning, spoken most probably during the reign of Jehoiakim. They do not refer so much to God's intention as to the inevitable retribution which is coming as the inescapable consequence of the people's choice and course of action. Their way of life is stultifying their moral and spiritual faculties. When the day of reckoning dawns, they will not have the spiritual insight or moral energy to deal with it. Reeling against each other, they will perish together.

3. An Appeal to Give Up Pride (13:15–17)

15 Hear and give ear; be not proud,
    for the LORD has spoken.
16 Give glory to the LORD your God
    before he brings darkness,

before your feet stumble
    on the twilight mountains,
and while you look for light
    he turns it into gloom
    and makes it deep darkness.
17 But if you will not listen,
    my soul will weep in secret for your pride;
my eyes will weep bitterly and run down with tears,
    because the LORD's flock has been taken captive.

A common characteristic of Hebrew is the quick switch that can be made from prose to poetry (and vice versa). This is true in everyday speech even today in the Near East. Fairly recently a traveler in Southern Arabia said of the Bedouin: "When moved, Arabs break easily into poetry. I have heard a lad spontaneously describe in verse some grazing which he had just found: he was giving natural expression to his feelings." [73]

This switching is fairly common in the Old Testament.[74] Especially is it the case that one can glide from prose to poetry when deeply moved or when approaching a climax in a composition. In the latter case, it may even become a rhetorical device. An example of switching from prose to poetry is to be seen in the shift from 13:1–14 to 13:15 ff.

In a passage of great pathos and power (vv. 15–17), Jeremiah pleads with his people to give up their arrogance and to grant glory to God—i.e., the worship of true obedience. He paints a graphic picture. The people are like travelers who are caught in a storm in the mountains, run for cover under a rock or in a cave, and wait for the storm to pass, only to be overtaken by the coming of night. In short, it is getting very late for Judah. The actual historical situation may be that of 598–597 B.C.

Read the wistful words of v. 17 and feel the pain in them. The people are suffering. God is suffering. Jeremiah is suffering. The

[73] W. Thesiger, *Arabian Sands* (Harmondsworth: Penquin, 1964), p. 87.
[74] Koch, *op. cit.*, p. 97.

prophet is already walking the way of a cross.

4. Degradation and Deportation (13:18–19)

18 Say to the king and the queen mother:
"Take a lowly seat,
for your beautiful crown
has come down from your head."
19 The cities of the Negeb are shut up,
with none to open them;
all Judah is taken into exile,
wholly taken into exile.

This brief, deeply moving poetic prophecy is addressed to Jehoiachin and his mother, Nehushta. The occasion is the captivity of 597. Jeremiah tells the young king and the queen-mother that they must accept their fate with humility and grace. There is no possibility of help from the Egyptians to the south. The exile is a reality.

Verse 19b is not to be taken literally. It is prophetic hyperbole. Many Judeans were carried off in 597. Others would have to go later.

5. Retribution for a Reprobate People (13:20–27)

20 "Lift up your eyes and see
those who come from the north.
Where is the flock that was given you,
your beautiful flock?
21 What will you say when they set as head
over you
those whom you yourself have taught
to be friends to you?
Will not pangs take hold of you,
like those of a woman in travail?
22 And if you say in your heart,
'Why have these things come upon me?'
it is for the greatness of your iniquity
that your skirts are lifted up,
and you suffer violence.
23 Can the Ethiopian change his skin
or the leopard his spots?
Then also you can do good
who are accustomed to do evil.
24 I will scatter you like chaff
driven by the wind from the desert.
25 This is your lot,
the portion I have measured out to you,
says the LORD,
because you have forgotten me
and trusted in lies.

26 I myself will lift up your skirts over your
face,
and your shame will be seen.
27 I have seen your abominations,
your adulteries and neighings, your lewd
harlotries,
on the hills in the field.
Woe to you, O Jerusalem!
How long will it be
before you are made clean?"

The date of the final portion of this complex is probably 605, shortly after the battle of Carchemish. The prophecy is addressed to Jerusalem, personified as a woman.

In it Jeremiah calls upon the lady shepherdess to give account of her stewardship of the flock entrusted to her, as she gazes upon the foe approaching from the north (v. 20). He asks her what she will say and feel when her former *friends* become her rulers (v. 21). He tells her that the reason for her fate is her apostasy (v. 22). In fact, *so accustomed to do evil* has she become that it is second nature with her (v. 23). Because of her corruptness of conduct she is to be scattered like chaff before a strong desert wind (v. 24). This is to be her measured portion because of her wanton spiritual adultery (vv. 25–27). There is much pathos in the closing question (v. 27b): *"O Jerusalem! How long . . . ?"*

Verses 23–24, considered to be out of place by some (incorrectly, the writer thinks), stress the ability of sin to get a stranglehold on man and squeeze out all that is worthwhile, eventually leading to catastrophe. Verse 23 contains a penetrating, pictorial portrayal of the power of habit, especially evil habit. The impossibility which it suggests becomes a glorious possibility through the grace of God in Jesus Christ (2 Cor. 5:17).

VI. The Great Drought and Other Impending Disasters (14:1—15:4)

Von Rad calls this section "the liturgy of the great drought" (p. 198). It is a carefully integrated composition (contra Weiser) in dialogue form and prepared most probably in imitation of a liturgy (see Int.; for varying views see Bright, pp. 102 f.; Eissfeldt, p. 356).

The occasion was a great natural calamity (cf. Joel 1—2). This natural calamity suggested to the prophet a greater national catastrophe: captivity. The two disasters, drought and destruction through invasion and deportation, are intertwined in a superb blend of poetry and prose in a literary production which partakes of the character of a penitential liturgy. It is possible that Jeremiah uttered these words at the Temple in a time of penitence and prayer during the crisis caused by the drought. The stress on the certainty of captivity points to the reign of Jehoiakim as the historical setting for the incident. Apparently the prophet had lost hope for the preservation of the nation.

1. The People's Plight (14:1-6)

1 The word of the LORD which came to Jeremiah concerning the drought:
2 "Judah mourns
    and her gates languish;
  her people lament on the ground,
    and the cry of Jerusalem goes up.
3 Her nobles send their servants for water;
    they come to the cisterns,
  they find no water,
    they return with their vessels empty;
  they are ashamed and confounded
    and cover their heads.
4 Because of the ground which is dismayed,
    since there is no rain on the land,
  the farmers are ashamed,
    they cover their heads.
5 Even the hind in the field forsakes her
    newborn calf
  because there is no grass.
6 The wild asses stand on the bare heights,
    they pant for air like jackals;
  their eyes fail
    because there is no herbage.

Verse 1 is the preface. It is unlike any introductory formula used thus far (cf. 46:1; 47:1; 49:34).

The preface is followed by a piece of pure poetry which pictures the land in the grip of grief because of a great drought. The country and its cities mourn. The capital sends up its cry. The citizens are unable to secure water from their cisterns.

Farmers have to cease their labors for lack of rain. Even the animals are suffering. The female deer, famed for her faithful and affectionate care of her young, abandons them because there is no grass. The wild ass, noted for its endurance, stands on the hilltop, panting for air, with eyes glazed from weakness because of a lack of fodder. It is a national emergency brought on by a natural calamity.

2. The People's Plea (14:7-9)

7 "Though our iniquities testify against us,
    act, O LORD, for thy name's sake;
  for our backslidings are many,
    we have sinned against thee.
8 O thou hope of Israel,
    its savior in time of trouble,
  why shouldst thou be like a stranger in the
    land,
  like a wayfarer who turns aside to tarry
    for a night?
9 Why shouldst thou be like a man confused,
    like a mighty man who cannot save?
  Yet thou, O LORD, art in the midst of us,
    and we are called by thy name;
    leave us not."

The description of national distress is followed by a prayer in the form of a communal lament. The people confess their sins and cry out to God for help in their extremity. The phrase *for thy name's sake* may mean "out of concern for thy reputation" or "in keeping with thy character." It appears often in penitential hymns, as do interrogations of Yahweh (see comment on 14:20-22). The name of God signifies his nature, his being, his presence, particularly as revealed in the covenant relationship.

After addressing God as *the hope of Israel* and *its savior in time of trouble,* the people direct two pointed questions to him, asking why in their desperate situation he has shown so little concern for them and why he has failed to come to their aid. "After all," they say, "you are our covenant God. Your name has been called over us. We are yours. Then do not forsake us. Save us—now!"

It is interesting to observe that the people do not inquire, "Why are we letting God down?" but, "Why is God letting us down?" This is quite indicative. Here is the popular perversion of the covenant referred to earlier. The people are seeking to put God in a corner, to press legal claim upon him, to bind him to a contract.

"Foxhole" religion did not originate during World War II. It has been in vogue a long time. Men may give their loyalty to the gods of their choosing when the sun is shining, but when the storm strikes they strike out toward the temple and the God of grace and glory. Here we uncover the basic difference between pagan religion— of whatever name—and biblical faith. Pagan religion seeks to put God, or the gods, at man's disposal. Biblical faith endeavors to place man at God's disposal.

3. God's Reply (14:10)

10 Thus says the LORD concerning this people:
"They have loved to wander thus,
  they have not restrained their feet;
therefore the LORD does not accept them,
  now he will remember their iniquity
  and punish their sins."

God's answer to the people's plea is brief and pointed. They have sought his help, not in a spirit of true repentance nor out of real love for him and a sincere desire to do his will, but in an attitude of desperation. They are in a hole, and they want out! This crisis-situation-sort of repentance on the part of a people who *have loved to wander* and *have not restrained their feet* cannot suffice as a substitute for a real turning back to God. Hence God rejects their lamentation and petition.

4. The People's Punishment (14:11–16)

11 The LORD said to me: "Do not pray for the welfare of this people. 12 Though they fast, I will not hear their cry, and though they offer burnt offering and cereal offering, I will not accept them; but I will consume them by the sword, by famine, and by pestilence."
13 Then I said: "Ah, Lord GOD, behold, the prophets say to them, 'You shall not see the sword, nor shall you have famine, but I will give you assured peace in this place.' " 14 And the LORD said to me: "The prophets are prophesying lies in my name; I did not send them, nor did I command them or speak to them. They are prophesying to you a lying vision,

worthless divination, and the deceit of their own minds. 15 Therefore thus says the LORD concerning the prophets who prophesy in my name although I did not send them, and who say, 'Sword and famine shall not come on this land': By sword and famine those prophets shall be consumed. 16 And the people to whom they prophesy shall be cast out in the streets of Jerusalem, victims of famine and sword, with none to bury them—them, their wives, their sons, and their daughters. For I will pour out their wickedness upon them.

This oracle is primarily a prophecy of judgment. It is in prose, and it takes the form of a conversation between God and the prophet. It begins in a very personal way with an injunction to the prophet to cease praying for a people who are beyond redemption (v. 11; cf. 7:16; 11:14). God rejects mere ritual, however elaborate, as a substitute for right relationships (v. 12a; cf. 6:20; 7:21–26; 11:15–16). Those who cling to this kind of religion and continue in their stubborn refusal to return to the covenant God are headed for catastrophe (v. 12b).

At this juncture Jeremiah intercedes for the people he loves so much, pleading that the popular purveyors of peace-oracles are responsible for the position in which the people find themselves (v. 13). Note the short, sharp ejaculation of pain at the beginning of the prayer (cf. 1:6). Also, observe that *the prophets* are promising the people *assured peace* (i.e., guaranteed well-being).

One of the greatest problems that Jeremiah faced in his ministry was posed by the preaching of the false prophets. Some of these men were consciously and deliberately insincere and sometimes immoral. But, in all probability, most were not. They were self-deceived, or had inadequate or inaccurate conceptions of God and his claims upon his people, or were motivated by a mistaken patriotism. Jeremiah had to combat the influence of their ministry throughout his ministry (e.g., 2:8; 5:11,30 f.; 6:13–15; 8:10–12). It all came to a head in 594–593, as we shall see later (chs. 27—28).

Verses 13–16 extend the boundaries of concern in the passage beyond the drought to include an even greater disaster: the horrors of war and famine. The prophets of peace have been saying that the people will not see the sword nor experience famine. God states that this is a lie, a divination that adds up to zero, a product of wishful thinking. Sword and famine will come upon the land. Both prophets and people will share in the judgment which is to be poured out upon them because of their wickedness.

An increasing note of severity is noticeable in these prophecies. So radical is the people's corruption that it is irreparable. They are incapable of repentance and reformation. And God is going to do something about the situation. God is as active in judgment now as then.

5. The Prophet's Pain (14:17–18)

¹⁷ "You shall say to them this word:
'Let my eyes run down with tears night and
    day,
    and let them not cease,
for the virgin daughter of my people is
    smitten with a great wound,
    with a very grievous blow.
¹⁸ If I go out into the field,
    behold, those slain by the sword!
And if I enter the city,
    behold, the diseases of famine!
For both prophet and priest ply their trade
    through the land,
    and have no knowledge.' "

This brief, poignant passage is more a poem than a prophecy (cf. 14:2–6), though prophecy was often in poetic form. The prophet is distressed to the depths of his being. He pours out his pain in the form of a funeral dirge, the force of which can best be felt by simply reading it thoughtfully. As one reads, he gets a glimpse into the soul of God's suffering servant.

The word *virgin* designates God's people as yet "unravished, unconquered by a foreign foe." On the intricate textual problem in verse 18b, see Bright, pp. 101 f. Note the shift from prose back to poetry and the continuing fusion of the present

disaster (drought) with a greater one to come (destruction), with increasing emphasis on the latter.

6. A Second Petition (14:19–22)

¹⁹ Hast thou utterly rejected Judah?
    Does thy soul loathe Zion?
Why hast thou smitten us
    so that there is no healing for us?
We looked for peace, but no good came;
    for a time of healing, but behold, terror.
²⁰ We acknowledge our wickedness, O LORD,
    and the iniquity of our fathers,
    for we have sinned against thee.
²¹ Do not spurn us, for thy name's sake;
    do not dishonor thy glorious throne;
    remember and do not break thy covenant
        with us.
²² Are there any among the false gods of the
        nations that can bring rain?
    Or can the heavens give showers?
Art thou not he, O LORD our God?
    We set our hope on thee,
    for thou doest all these things.

Following the heartrending personal lament comes another communal lament. The people probe God with questions which imply that he has let them down. They present a perfunctory acknowledgement of their sin. They press upon the Lord his obligation to protect his name (honor), his *glorious throne* (power), and his *covenant* (contract); they have a threefold basis for their plea. They proclaim that he is God, their God, and that he is their hope. It is as though they said, "We're in trouble God. Get us out!"

Here is a group of people who have gone so far in sin and ceremonial worship that they are ignorant of the character of God and the claims of true religion. Their attitude is: "All you have to do to get forgiveness is to chase up to the 'church,' go through some ceremonies and offer some sacrifices—then you can go your way, free once again to do as you please."

How can people be such fools? We share the prophet's perplexity—and pain. All over this land and in many parts of the world there are multitudes acting in the same way, totally forgetful of the fact that the great Saviour-God is also a God of righteousness and that biblical religion, which begins with redemption, also involves an ethical exaction.

7. God's Response (15:1-4)

¹ Then the LORD said to me, "Though Moses and Samuel stood before me, yet my heart would not turn toward this people. Send them out of my sight, and let them go! ² And when they ask you, 'Where shall we go?' you shall say to them, 'Thus says the LORD:
"Those who are for pestilence, to pestilence,
   and those who are for the sword, to the
      sword;
   those who are for famine, to famine,
   and those who are for captivity, to captivity." '
³ "I will appoint over them four kinds of destroyers, says the LORD: the sword to slay, the dogs to tear, and the birds of the air and the beasts of the earth to devour and destroy. ⁴ And I will make them a horror to all the kingdoms of the earth because of what Manasseh the son of Hezekiah, king of Judah, did in Jerusalem.

The people expected a no in response to their questions in 14:19a, but they got a resounding yes.

God says to Jeremiah, in effect: "It's no use! They are too far gone! Even if Moses and Samuel, your two great intercessors of the past, should stand in the gap before me for the people, it could do no good. I would still have to say, 'Get them out of my presence.' If they ask, 'Where are we to go?' You are to say that I have marked some for the plague, some for the sword, some for starvation, and some for *captivity*. Judah's doom is sealed!"

So ends one of the most dramatic and dynamic portions of the prophecy.

VII. Prophecies and Prayers in Poetry and Prose (15:5—17:27)

The "patchwork" pattern of arrangement, so perplexing at times to the one who studies the prophecy of Jeremiah, is exceedingly apparent in this portion of the book. We have here a miscellaneous collection of prophetic utterances and personal experiences which are rather loosely put together in places but which have at least three things in common with each other and with the larger context. First, they seem, for the most part, to emanate from the reign of Jehoiakim. Second, they stress the prophet's increasing isolation and suffering. Third, they ring the changes on the certainty and severity of the judgment that is coming upon Judah because of her sin.

1. Judah's Winnowing and Jeremiah's Woes (15:5-21)

The material is this part of the complex is genuine. It is all in poetry (on vv. 10–14, see Bright, pp. 106, 114; cf. Weiser, pp. 135–136, 148). It contains some of the most poignant and important passages in the prophecy.

(1) The Punishment of an Apostate People (15:5-9)

⁵ "Who will have pity on you, O Jerusalem,
   or who will bemoan you?
Who will turn aside
   to ask about your welfare?
⁶ You have rejected me, says the LORD,
   you keep going backward;
so I have stretched out my hand against
      you and destroyed you;—
   I am weary of relenting.
⁷ I have winnowed them with a winnowing
      fork
   in the gates of the land;
I have bereaved them, I have destroyed my
      people;
   they did not turn from their ways.
⁸ I have made their widows more in number
      than the sand of the seas;
I have brought against the mothers of
      young men
   a destroyer at noonday;
I have made anguish and terror
   fall upon them suddenly.
⁹ She who bore seven has languished;
   she has swooned away;
her sun went down while it was yet day;
   she has been shamed and disgraced.
And the rest of them I will give to the
      sword
   before their enemies,
            says the LORD."

In a personal lament the prophet pictures the pathetic plight of Jerusalem. The lament includes the major elements of the prophecy of disaster, but, as usual, Jeremiah exercises great liberty in his use of the literary form.

The first few verbs (v. 5) and the last

verb (v. 9) are in the imperfect tense. Most of the rest are perfects. They are prophetic perfects. They portray that which has not yet happened as though it has already transpired, so certain is the prophet that it is going to come about.

The lament starts with three startling questions (v. 5). The substance of the questions is: "When calamity comes as a consequence of your sin (cf. 15:1–4), who will show any real concern for your well-being?" In vv. 6 ff. the oracular lament moves from questions to affirmations and predictions. God speaks through the prophet by way of indictment: "*You* (emphatic) left me, . . . *backward* (emphatic) you keep walking" (v. 6a). The first verb here is in the perfect tense. It is a very strong verb. It means smite, beat, or break in pieces, then cast off or reject. The people have cast God aside like something broken in bits and no longer desirable or usable. The second verb is an imperfect. It is frequentative in force. Not only have the people left the Lord, but they also keep walking backward, i.e., away from him.

Reproach changes to threat in v. 6b. God announces the penalty of this apostasy. Here the verbs are prophetic perfects. Because the people will not turn back to him with that sincerity and seriousness which alone can bring forgiveness and fullness of life, God is worn out with altering his intention or course of action (repenting or *relenting*) concerning them and is going to lash out and smash them.

The forecast of judgment continues in v. 7a with the use of a very strong figure, that of winnowing. One who has seen the process will get the impact of the metaphor. With his *winnowing fork* God will take the people (the chaff) to the gates of the cities (or the border of the country), pitch them into the air, and let the wind carry them off into captivity.

God goes on: "I will bereave, I will destroy my people. *From their ways* (emphatic position) they have not returned (i.e., to me; convenantal use of *shub*)."

The imagery becomes more pathetic and pointed. *Widows* will be multiplied, so that they outnumber *the sand of the seas.* A *destroyer* will be *brought* unexpectedly (*at noonday;* cf. 6:1–8) *against* defenseless *mothers* of young soldiers slain in battle. There will be *anguish, terror,* dismay, death. It is the oracle of the Lord (vv. 8–9).

(2) The Price of Being a Prophet (15:10–12)

This is Jeremiah's second confession. Verses 13–14 are obviously out of context. They are repeated in 17:3–4, where they have a suitable setting. How and why they were incorporated here is not known.

a. The Prophet's Pain and Perplexity (15:10–14)

10 Woe is me, my mother, that you bore me, a man of strife and contention to the whole land! I have not lent, nor have I borrowed, yet all of them curse me. 11 So let it be, O LORD, if I have not entreated thee for their good, if I have not pleaded with thee on behalf of the enemy in the time of trouble and in the time of distress! 12 Can one break iron, iron from the north, and bronze?
13 "Your wealth and your treasures I will give as spoil, without price, for all your sins, throughout all your territory. 14 I will make you serve your enemies in a land which you do not know, for in my anger a fire is kindled which shall burn for ever."

Jeremiah bemoans his birth because he appears to be at odds with everybody, *a man of strife and contention to the whole land! Strife* and *contention* are legal terms. Here is the lawsuit motif again, but in a different dress. Jeremiah has spoken of God's convenantal suit against Israel, his suit before God, and the people's feeling that they have a case against the Lord. Here he represents himself as one forever at law with his countrymen, forever taking them to court.

He refers to his *mother* in v. 10. In v. 9 mention was made of a mother of "seven" (symbolic of completeness) who lost her sons prematurely. Is Jeremiah subtly suggesting that he wishes his mother had lost him prematurely, too? In any case, he is having "soul-trouble." With a bit of wit— or sarcasm (?)—he observes that he has not lent nor borrowed money (a very effective way to turn a friend or family member into an enemy), yet all are cursing him.

Verse 11 presents a textual problem. There has to be some reconstruction of the Hebrew. The RSV is probably correct in following the LXX, Old Latin, Cornill, and others in its solution of the problem and rendering of the verse: *So let it be* (Amen to their curses, let them be carried out), *O Lord, if I have not entreated thee for their good.*

The prophet is experiencing tremendous agony because of bitter antagonism and active opposition. His stinging attacks upon the pet prejudices and sins of the people, his scorching exposures of their religious hypocrisy and hollowness, and his severe forecasts of terrible judgment have provoked aggressive and open hostility. He could understand the ridicule and the rough treatment except that he has not engaged in lending or borrowing money (and not paying it back), and he has not done anything that was not prompted by a compassionate concern for his countrymen. To top it off, he has poured out his heart before God for his adversaries in their times of need, these same people who are hurling curses at him.

Verse 12 is also somewhat obscure. Condamin gives up on it as hopeless. Rothstein casts it out as a gloss. Giesebrecht thinks it was brought in from some other place in the prophecy. Bright acts as if it doesn't exist. Others propose various emendations and suggestions. Again, the best reading is probably that of the RSV.

But what does it mean in this context? There are two possibilities. First, it may refer to the impossibility of withstanding the advance of the foe from the north. Resistance is useless, and the prophet must realize this and relay it to his people. Second, it may express an uncertainty on

Jeremiah's part as to whether his strength is sufficient to stand against the opposition he is facing: "Can iron (i.e., my strength) break iron from the north and bronze (i.e., the power of my opponents)." Peake says: "The point of the reference to iron from the North is that the best and hardest iron came from the Black Sea" (p. 211). In this connection, Duhm [75] suggests an emendation which is on the right track: "Is an arm of iron on my shoulder, is my brow brass?" There is a parallel in Job 6:12: "Is my strength the strength of stones? or is my flesh of brass?"

In short, Jeremiah is saying to God: "Am I am iron man? Can I, in my frailty, face an unlimited amount of antagonism and opposition? I am human, you know!" And he was. This brings him close to us. The nobility of the man lies in the fact that, though he had such feelings and expressed them freely, he never quit but kept on "keeping on" for God.

Verses 13–14 (a doublet) deal with the penalty of Judah's apostasy, are addressed to Judah (not God), and appear in 17:3–4, where they are in context. They will be treated there.

b. The Prophet's Prayer (15:15–18)

15 O LORD, thou knowest;
　　remember me and visit me,
　　and take vengeance for me on my persecutors.
　In thy forbearance take me not away;
　　know that for thy sake I bear reproach.
16 Thy words were found and I ate them,
　　and thy words became to me a joy
　　and the delight of my heart;
　for I am called by thy name,
　　O LORD, God of hosts.
17 I did not sit in the company of merrymakers,
　　nor did I rejoice;
　I sat alone, because thy hand was upon me,
　　for thou hadst filled me with indignation.
18 Why is my pain unceasing,
　　my wound incurable,
　　refusing to be healed?
　Wilt thou be to me like a deceitful brook,
　　like waters that fail?

[75] *Op. cit., in loc.*

This is one of the most unorthodox prayers ever published. It is certainly not a pretty polished speech, politely presented to God. It is a pouring out of the prophet's heart in divine presence—dregs and all. At times it almost borders on blasphemy. Its intensity reveals the depth of Jeremiah's communion with God and concern for God, himself, his people, his vocation, and the foundation of his faith and ministry— his woes over the winnowing!

There is no reason to question the authenticity of this prayer or to regard it as a conglomerate of traditional cultic texts. It is the record of an intimate, authentic experience with God. Here is a man at prayer, a man who is greatly troubled by the failure of his people, and by the frustration of his preaching—and God's relation to it all.

In the prayer, Jeremiah first pleads with God to remember him—this he needs, this he lives by—and to wreak vengeance (or work deliverance) for him upon (or from) his persecutors (v. 15a). Listen: "Do not *through your patience* (emphatic; lit. through a tardiness of your anger, i.e., your lengthening of the grace-period for my enemies) let me be taken away (get killed). Know! My bearing of abuse is for you" (v. 15b). The prophet is concerned about two things primarily at this point: vindication in relation to his adversaries (cf. 11:20; 12:3; 17:18; 18:23; 20:11), and communion with God (God's remembering him and visiting him, the very source of life's meaning for him).

Next, Jeremiah proclaims his joy in belonging to God and in becoming the medium of his revelation (v. 16). He indicates that at times for him, God's man, the preaching of "the word" is a great delight. Elsewhere he states that sometimes it was an almost intolerable burden.

The prophet protests the loneliness which is his lot (v. 17). A warm, sensitive, affectionate individual is suffering anguish because of isolation. The necessity of proclaiming a message of condemnation has alienated him from others. He has not had the privilege of laughing with his fellows (they have laughed at him). He has had to sit alone—by reason of the pressure of the presence and power of God, and filled with the pathos of God.

At the close of the prayer, Jeremiah plumbs the depths of pain (v. 18). The figure of the *deceitful brook* is devastating. In Palestine there are wadis in abundance. During the rainy season they are full to overflowing. But in the hot summer months they are bone dry. Woe to that person who goes looking in one of them for water for personal or agricultural purposes! As Jeremiah gazes into the face of God, he asks, "Are you like such a wadi?"

God's man is in the agony of uncertainty. He wonders whether he may be wrong. There is no external verification of the truth he has been proclaiming, and he is terribly lonely. And so the same person who declared that God is "the fountain of living waters" (2:13) now wonders whether this God is a dry wadi, which is quite promising in good times but fails to produce in hard times, times of real need.

What is Jeremiah's trouble? Two things it seems—aside from the fact that he is human and is undergoing inner and outer distress. First, he is the victim of self-concern. He has "I-trouble." Encircle the pronouns of the first person singular, and you will find that they appear 18 times in four verses. Self has moved in toward the center of the stage. Second, the prophet is momentarily interpreting his commission in terms of comfort more than in terms of character and kingdom service. God had told him that he would have a hard time but that he would be with him and deliver him (1:8,17–19).

Does God fail his servants. No! Inadequate conceptions of him do. The wrong brand of religion does. But God—never!

c. God's Reply (15:19–21)

19 Therefore thus says the LORD:
  "If you return, I will restore you,
    and you shall stand before me.

If you utter what is precious, and not what
    is worthless,
    you shall be as my mouth.
They shall turn to you,
    but you shall not turn to them.
20 And I will make you to this people
    a fortified wall of bronze;
they will fight against you,
    but they shall not prevail over you,
for I am with you
    to save you and deliver you,
                        says the LORD.
21 I will deliver you out of the hand of the
    wicked,
    and redeem you from the grasp of the
        ruthless."

For Jeremiah prayer is a practice in
honesty. God always answers that kind of
prayer. He does in this case. But, as in
12:5, it is not an easy answer. He tells
Jeremiah that he has betrayed his high
calling and that he must now do two
things. First, he must repent. His attitude
is one of resentment and rebellion. This is
sin. It has impaired his relationship with
God. He must return to God. He has
preached repentance. He must now practice what he has preached. Second, he
must rid himself (and his message) of all
that is unworthy. He must separate the
precious from the worthless, do away with
the worthless, and dedicate the precious
to the Lord. The tester, the assayer (6:27),
is not all pure metal. The dross must go.

If Jeremiah will do these two things,
four results will follow (Leslie, pp. 145 f.).
First, he will be God's true messenger to
the people. Second, he will not conform
to the wishes of the crowd, but will cause
the crowd to turn to him ultimately for
the word of God. Third, he will become
what God promised in his call-experience,
a fortified wall of bronze. Fourth, God will
defend and deliver him from evil men.
Duhm, Streane, and others see an allusion
to Jehoiakim and his cohorts in the reference to the wicked and the ruthless (v.
21).

Jeremiah's skill in the use of language
and literary devices is noticeably present
in v. 19, in which he plays with the ingenuity of a master upon the various

shades of meaning in the word shub. Note
a literal translation: "Therefore thus has
the Lord said: 'If you return (turn back
to me), I will cause you to return (will restore you to a right relationship with me);
before me (in my presence as a trusted,
faithful servant) you will stand. And if
you cause to go forth the precious from
the common (cheap), as my mouth you
will be. They (emphatic) will turn to you,
but you (emphatic) will not turn to
them.'"

When a servant of God is in the throes
of doubt and distress, the real question becomes: Will he run away? or, Will he stick
and struggle through? The only way out is
through a deeper surrender to God and a
more sincere service of God. A greater
commitment leads to greater certainty.
This proved to be the case with the
prophet.[76]

2. The Great Renunciation (16:1-21)

This passage—partly in prose and partly
in poetry—is autobiographical in character. In the judgment of this commentator, it is authentic. The links with the
context are not too obvious, but they are
there: the highlighting of the loneliness of
the prophet, the heavy emphasis on severe
judgment because of terrible sin, the presence of key terms such as "sword and
famine," etc.

(1) Jeremiah Forbidden to Marry (16:1-
    4)

1 The word of the LORD came to me: 2 "You
shall not take a wife, nor shall you have sons or
daughters in this place. 3 For thus says the
LORD concerning the sons and daughters who
are born in this place, and concerning the
mothers who bore them and the fathers who
begot them in this land: 4 They shall die of
deadly diseases. They shall not be lamented,
nor shall they be buried; they shall be as dung
on the surface of the ground. They shall perish
by the sword and by famine, and their dead

76 Some scholars who regard the confessions as the
record of a spiritual crisis during Jeremiah's middle
ministry are persuaded that that crisis was resolved in
the experience described in 15:15-21 (e.g., Skinner
and Fohrer).

bodies shall be food for the birds of the air and for the beasts of the earth.

The prophet is denied the delights of family life. There is to be no wife to greet him and there are to be no children to meet him when he returns exhausted—and sometimes exasperated—from his exacting preaching forays into the city or other parts of the country. This tremendous denial is a part of God's plan for him. His giving up of a life made bright by the presence of wife and children is to be a sign that catastrophe is coming upon the country and that parents and children will die horrible deaths from sword, starvation, and disease.

(2) Jeremiah Restricted in Social Practices (16:5–9)

5 "For thus says the LORD: Do not enter the house of mourning, or go to lament, or bemoan them; for I have taken away my peace from this people, says the LORD, my steadfast love and mercy. 6 Both great and small shall die in this land; they shall not be buried, and no one shall lament for them or cut himself or make himself bald for them. 7 No one shall break bread for the mourner, to comfort him for the dead; nor shall any one give him the cup of consolation to drink for his father or his mother. 8 You shall not go into the house of feasting to sit with them, to eat and drink. 9 For thus says the LORD of hosts, the God of Israel: Behold, I will make to cease from this place, before your eyes and in your days, the voice of mirth and the voice of gladness, the voice of the bridegroom and the voice of the bride.

The prophet is to be deprived of participation in the normal social practices in times of sadness and of gladness. He is not to enter the house of mourning or the house of feasting. In short, he is not to weep with those who weep nor to rejoice with those who rejoice—and this, too, as a part of his witness and work for God.

(3) Judah to Be Punished for Her Sin (16:10–13)

10 "And when you tell this people all these words, and they say to you, 'Why has the LORD pronounced all this great evil against us? What is our iniquity? What is the sin that we have committed against the LORD our God?' 11 then you shall say to them: 'Because your fathers have forsaken me, says the LORD, and have gone after other gods and have served and worshiped them, and have forsaken me and have not kept my law, 12 and because you have done worse than your fathers, for behold, every one of you follows his stubborn evil will, refusing to listen to me; 13 therefore I will hurl you out of this land into a land which neither you nor your fathers have known, and there you shall serve other gods day and night, for I will show you no favor.'

Jeremiah is told that when the people inquire—as inquire they will—as to why such a horrible calamity is coming upon them, he is to tell them that the reason is their sin: apostasy and idolatry. There is a clever play on the name of the prophet in v. 13: Yahweh will hurl the people out of the land.

(4) A Second Exodus Greater than the First (16:14–15)

14 "Therefore, behold, the days are coming, says the LORD, when it shall no longer be said, 'As the LORD lives who brought up the people of Israel out of the land of Egypt,' 15 but 'As the LORD lives who brought up the people of Israel out of the north country and out of all the countries where he had driven them.' For I will bring them back to their own land which I gave to their fathers.

The dark night of captivity is coming, but one day the sun will shine again. Just as God brought the fathers out of slavery in Egypt into the promised land, so he will bring a disciplined people out of Babylonian bondage and back to the land of the fathers. These verses are repeated in 23:7–8. They fit more snugly there.

(5) No Escape from God (16:16–18)

16 "Behold, I am sending for many fishers, says the LORD, and they shall catch them; and afterwards I will send for many hunters, and they shall hunt them from every mountain and every hill, and out of the clefts of the rocks. 17 For my eyes are upon all their ways; they are not hid from me, nor is their iniquity concealed from my eyes. 18 And I will doubly recompense their iniquity and their sin, because they have polluted my land with the carcasses of their detestable idols, and have filled my inheritance with their abominations."

There is much stress upon God's activity in the process of judgment and upon the thoroughness of that process. The two figures employed, fishing and hunting, do not necessarily refer to two captivities (597, 587). They may represent two stages of the captivity, with particular emphasis upon the impossibility of escaping encounter with God (cf. Amos 9:2–4). Since the *idols* are considered to be lifeless, they are ceremonially unclean and therefore pollute the land. A double punishment is one of unusual severity.

(6) Yahweh, God of All the Earth and the Light of All Men (16:19–21)

19 O LORD, my strength and my stronghold,
   my refuge in the day of trouble,
to thee shall the nations come
   from the ends of the earth and say:
"Our fathers have inherited nought but lies,
   worthless things in which there is no profit.
20 Can man make for himself gods?
   Such are no gods!"
21 "Therefore, behold, I will make them know, this once I will make them know my power and my might, and they shall know that my name is the LORD."

The genuineness of this great promise passage has been questioned because of its universalism. But the concept of the conversion of the pagan nations to Yahwism has a solid basis in a very old tradition (Weiser, Holladay, Condamin, Wolff, *et al.*). The passage "swarms with Jeremianic phrases" (Bright, p. 113), and its poetic structure and style are quite similar to those of Jeremiah (Holladay). The writer believes it to be authentic.

In the passage, the prophet speaks first, affirming that Yahweh is his *strength* and *stronghold* and that to Yahweh will come *nations . . . from the ends of the earth.* They will confess that they have been worshiping *worthless things* (nonentities). He will respond, saying that he will teach them now—at once—and will bring them into a dynamic life-changing relationship with him (v. 21, also in poetic form; cf. Bright, p. 109; Weiser, p. 142).

There are many parallels between Jeremiah and Jesus. One is that neither was privileged to marry. Jeremiah did not re-

nounce marriage because of an aversion to it but because of a conviction that this renunciation was a part of God's purpose for him. Other prophets married and had children (cf. Hos. 1–3; Isa. 8:1–4,18; Ezek. 24:15–27). There was nothing wrong with marriage, as far as the prophets were concerned.

But Jeremiah was gripped by the conviction that giving up marriage and family was God's will for him and a part of his witness to his people. There is a parallel between him and Paul at this point, and there is something in the apostle's counsel against marriage "in view of the impending distress" (1 Cor. 7:26) which is reminiscent of Jeremiah 16. The point is that each person should commit himself to God's will for his life. This may mean one thing for one, another for another. But only in the doing of his will do we find peace and power.

3. Miscellaneous Materials (17:1–27)

One has referred to this chapter as a "miscellaneous file." It is common among commentators to call attention to its heterogenous character and its complete lack of organic unity. This seems to be an inaccurate assessment of the situation. As this expositor looks beneath the surface, he sees what he believes to be a dynamic relation of the chapter to its context and of the different parts of the chapter to each other. In strategy and structure it is somewhat like the conclusion of T. S. Eliot's *The Waste Land.* In short, this chapter may not be a catchall after all, but a great climax. As to the date of the material in it, we cannot be sure, but the reign of Jehoiakim provides the most likely historical setting.

(1) Judah's Sin and the Certainty of Her Punishment (17:1–4)

1 "The sin of Judah is written with a pen of iron; with a point of diamond it is engraved on the tablet of their heart, and on the horns of their altars, 2 while their children remember their altars and their Asherim, beside every green tree, and on the high hills, 3 on the mountains in the open country. Your wealth

and all your treasures I will give for spoil as the price of your sin throughout all your territory. 4 You shall loosen your hand from your heritage which I gave to you, and I will make you serve your enemies in a land which you do not know, for in my anger a fire is kindled which shall burn for ever."

The sin of Judah is deep-seated (cf. 2:22 ff.). It is indelibly inscribed upon *the tablet* of her *heart* (the citadel of personality) and upon *the horns* of her *altars* (symbolic of the whole system of ceremony and sacrifice)—i.e., at the very center of her being and in the cult which she is observing.

Volz suggests that this message was delivered on the Day of Atonement, which came before the fall festival of covenant renewal. On that day the blood of the sin offering was placed on *the horns* of the altar (probably metal projections from the four corners of the altar; cf. Lev. 4—5, especially 4:4,18,25,30,34; 16:18). Jeremiah was saying that the sin of the people could not be washed away by blood offered with no heart in it and no godly quality of life to back it up.

Whether Volz is right or not, the prophet here states that the guilt of his countrymen is so great that it cannot be removed by an empty, elaborate ritualism. Later he will indicate that God alone can eradicate sin and guilt through his grace by changing the heart of the individual (31:33–34).

In vv. 3–4 he states that sin, so indelibly and openly written upon heart and altar, has a price that must be paid. The penalty is captivity. Since the people have refused to serve their covenant Lord in their God-given homeland, they must serve a foreign overlord in another land (cf. 5:18–19; 15:13–14; etc). God's holy love requires this (*anger, fire,* etc.).

(2) A Psalm Contrasting Two Types of Character (17:5–8)

5 Thus says the LORD:
"Cursed is the man who trusts in man
and makes flesh his arm,
whose heart turns away from the LORD.
6 He is like a shrub in the desert,
and shall not see any good come.

He shall dwell in the parched places of the wilderness,
in an uninhabited salt land.
7 "Blessed is the man who trusts in the LORD,
whose trust is the LORD.
8 He is like a tree planted by water,
that sends out its roots by the stream,
and does not fear when heat comes,
for its leaves remain green,
and is not anxious in the year of drought,
for it does not cease to bear fruit."

Scholars have been inclined at times to question the authenticity of this wisdom poem, largely because of "a prejudice, essentially long outmoded, that psalm composition is later than Jeremiah" (Eissfeldt, p. 359). Along with Eissfeldt, Lindblom, Holladay, and others, the present writer accepts the genuineness of the passage without hesitation.

The picture in the poem is that of two trees (cf. Psalm 1). One is *a shrub in the desert.* It dwells *in the parched places of the wilderness, in an uninhabited salt land,* and eventually dries up. The other is *a tree planted by water.* It flourishes, *does not fear when heat comes,* has an evergreen foliage, and bears a valuable fruit continually.

By way of sharp contrast, this psalm pictures two types of persons. The first places his trust *in man, makes flesh* (the self-centered, frail, creaturely substance which man has in common with beasts) *his arm* (strength), and at the core of his being *turns away from the Lord.* This secularization of life lands him in a desert of dryness and death (v. 6).

The second person puts his faith *in the Lord.* The basic orientation of his life toward that which is spiritual and eternal rather than that which is material and temporal leads to life, joy, beauty, stability, strength, and fruitfulness.

An astute scholar, A. S. Peake, while maintaining that there is no question about the Jeremianic origin of this beautiful passage, asserts that there is "no close connection with the context" (p. 221). But there is. It is not of the surface sort but of a deeper kind. Jeremiah is talking about an "either-or" situation. There are two ways in life. Man may take either the one or the other. He may choose the way of faith or the way of "unfaith," the way of submission to God or the way of rebellion against God. There is no other alternative, and he must decide which way he will go. His choice will have consequences. One way will lead to distress, the other to delight. One will bring death, the other life.

Judah has chosen the way of rebellion against the will of her covenant God. She has put her trust in the *flesh* rather than in *the Lord*. Therefore she will experience the curse instead of the blessing. She will end up in a desert of dryness and death (cf. the strong emphasis in the preceding passages on the terrible penalty in store for her because of her apostasy).

(3) The Prophet's Penetration of the Human Predicament (17:9–10)

9 The heart is deceitful above all things,
  and desperately corrupt;
   who can understand it?
10 "I the Lord search the mind
  and try the heart,
   to give to every man according to his ways,
   according to the fruit of his doings."

The prophet is gripped by the agonizing conviction that his people are increasingly set in their sins and are therefore headed for catastrophe. But what is the explanation? Surely there must be something radically wrong with man.

We see Jeremiah, as it were, peering into the depths of *the heart*—his heart, the heart of Judah, the human heart. He is appalled at what he beholds. He then lays bare in a single sentence the secret of the human predicament, the source of the world's woe: the heart is deceitful and desperately diseased. Only God can fully know and understand it.

The prophet has several times spoken of the fact that his countrymen followed the stubborn inclinations of their evil hearts. Here he sums it all up as he declares that the root of the problem is a deceitful, diseased heart, defiant of God's control.

We have here a striking anticipation of the "discovery" of modern depth psychology and the emphasis of certain contemporary writers and theologians. The human heart seeks to cover up its real problems and motivations, suffers from a fatal sickness, and, in living in revolt against God, becomes the center of conflict, which, if not resolved, means disaster.

So all roads, for Jeremiah lead to the same end. Judah is headed for ruin because her *heart* is not right.

(4) A Proverb About a Partridge (17:11)

11 Like the partridge that gathers a brood
   which she did not hatch,
    so is he who gets riches but not by right;
   in the midst of his days they will leave
    him,
   and at his end he will be a fool.

The meaning of the metaphor employed by Jeremiah in this verse is that just as a mother partridge that takes over another bird's nest and hatches the eggs discovers that later the young abandon her because they are "an alien brood," so the man who acquires wealth in the wrong way will find that it will leave him one day and fly away.

Surely this succinct statement can have no connection with the context. But wait! Is it not possible that it presents an illustration of the principle that is being stressed? Jehoiakim and Judah have chosen the way of trust in the arm of flesh. They will discover that all activity not in conformity with the will of the covenant Lord will bring them into a desert, a saltland, and that the evil brood collected through that activity will be lost. Back again to Judah's fate and the reason for it!

(5) A Passage on the True Place of Sanctuary (17:12–13)

12 A glorious throne set on high from the
   beginning
   is the place of our sanctuary.

13 O Lord, the hope of Israel,
   all who forsake thee shall be put to
     shame;
  those who turn away from thee shall be
     written in the earth,
   for they have forsaken the Lord, the
     fountain of living water.

Jeremiah has reiterated that anything and everything outside a right covenant relationship with God will end in frustration and failure—and ultimate catastrophe. Here he turns the coin over and says that the true place of sanctuary is a throne of glory *set on high from the beginning!*

The phrase *glorious throne* is a pregnant phrase, which probably refers, in part, to the ark of the covenant, the Shekinah, and possibly certain aspects of an enthronement ritual. But it reaches beyond all of this (which Jeremiah considered to be quite real but representative) to refer to the transcendent Being whose spiritual presence fills the universe (cf. 23:23–24). In this God—and him alone—are to be found salvation and security. All who forsake him will be *written in the earth* (dust; a forceful figure for the fragile, futile existence of sinners) rather than in the "book of life" (cf. Ex. 32:32; Isa. 4:3; Rev. 20:5).

God's "throne of glory," the symbol of his personal presence and universal sovereignty, is *the place of our sanctuary,* our *hope,* the center and source of salvation and security in every situation. One scholar says that this passage is "altogether central to Jeremiah's attitude" and "one of the pivotal utterances of his book" (Hopper, p. 955). Another writes: "This, then, is the first of Jeremiah's great thoughts about God, and it means—'The Lord God omnipotent reigneth,' there is none other but He, and His will runs authoritative and supreme into all corners of the universe." [77] This God who reigns also redeems. He has revealed himself supremely in Jesus Christ, our Saviour and Lord.

---

[77] A. MacLaren, *Isaiah and Jeremiah* (Grand Rapids: Wm. B. Eerdmans Publishing Co., 1932), p. 313.

(6) A Prayer for Healing and Help (17:14–18)

14 Heal me, O Lord, and I shall be healed;
   save me, and I shall be saved;
   for thou art my praise.
15 Behold, they say to me,
   "Where is the word of the Lord?
   Let it come!"
16 I have not pressed thee to send evil,
   nor have I desired the day of disaster,
     thou knowest;
  that which came out of my lips
     was before thy face.
17 Be not a terror to me;
   thou art my refuge in the day of evil.
18 Let those be put to shame who persecute
     me,
   but let me not be put to shame;
  let them be dismayed,
   but let me not be dismayed;
  bring upon them the day of evil;
   destroy them with double destruction!

The reader who has pursued the study of the prophecy to this point is aware that Jeremiah is having times of great inner agony. From chapter 10 onward, in particular, there have been fairly frequent outbursts of anger, outcries of anguish, and expressions of perplexity and pain. The prophet is on a *via dolorosa.*

Of the many passages revealing Jeremiah's inner struggles, five are known as his "confessions." We have examined two; we now come to the third. There is a difference of opinion concerning its length. Some scholars limit it to vv. 14–18; others include vv. 12–13; still others link vv. 9–10 to 14–18 to form the confession. The present writer can easily see how vv. 9–10 are dynamically related to the prayer in vv. 14–18. With regard to vv. 12–13, he has more reservation, though he recognizes definite links between these verses and the ones that follow.

Jeremiah has gazed into the human heart, his heart, and has been staggered by what he has seen. As he unveils his inner being in the white light of God's holy presence, he becomes painfully conscious of the potentialities for evil in him. He earnestly desires to be purged of all selfishness and sin, that he may be a true witness for God.

It is quite interesting to note the point at which his prayer focuses, as he pleads for help and healing: his proclamation of judgment (vv. 14–16). His stern sermons have provoked anger and antagonism. We may imagine audience outbursts: "His message isn't true. No judgment is coming. He's just trying to scare us. Let us see the 'word' actualized, if it is authentic!" "He preaches doom because he enjoys it. This gloomy misfit of a prophet with enough emotional problems to give a first class psychiatrist a fit gets pleasure out of skinning us alive from the pulpit!"

The vengeful goading of his foes (vv. 16–17) and the glorious vision of the greatness of God (17:12–13) send him to his knees. He wonders whether he may have crossed the line between a sincere dedication to the glory of God and the good of his people, and a desire for personal vindication. He feels that he has been honest and that all the words that have come from his lips concerning *the day of disaster* have come from God and have passed the test of his holy presence. But—can he be sure? Above all else, he longs to be pure in his motives, lest he be unworthy of his high calling.

(7) A Proclamation About the Sanctity of the Sabbath (17:19–27)

19 Thus said the LORD to me: "Go and stand in the Benjamin Gate, by which the kings of Judah enter and by which they go out, and in all the gates of Jerusalem, 20 and say: 'Hear the word of the LORD, you kings of Judah, and all Judah, and all the inhabitants of Jerusalem, who enter by these gates. 21 Thus says the LORD: Take heed for the sake of your lives, and do not bear a burden on the sabbath day or bring it in by the gates of Jerusalem. 22 And do not carry a burden out of your houses on the sabbath or do any work, but keep the sabbath day holy, as I commanded your fathers. 23 Yet they did not listen or incline their ear, but stiffened their neck, that they might not hear and receive instruction.

24 " 'But if you listen to me, says the LORD, and bring in no burden by the gates of this city on the sabbath day, but keep the sabbath day holy and do no work on it, 25 then there shall enter by the gates of this city kings who sit on the throne of David, riding in chariots and on

horses, they and their princes, the men of Judah and the inhabitants of Jerusalem; and this city shall be inhabited for ever. 26 And people shall come from the cities of Judah and the places round about Jerusalem, from the land of Benjamin, from the Shephelah, from the hill country, and from the Negeb, bringing burnt offerings and sacrifices, cereal offerings and frankincense, and bringing thank offerings to the house of the LORD. 27 But if you do not listen to me, to keep the sabbath day holy, and not to bear a burden and enter by the gates of Jerusalem on the sabbath day, then I will kindle a fire in its gates, and it shall devour the palaces of Jerusalem and shall not be quenched.' "

The diverse character of the contents of chapter 17 is evident. The vital connection between the various parts is not so apparent, but quite real. The material in vv. 19–27 is certainly different from that which precedes it. These verses have to do with sabbath observance. Because of an alleged anticultic attitude of Jeremiah and an assumption that sabbath observance began with seriousness during the exile, most commentators have ascribed this passage to a late editor or redactor.

There is something to be said for this point of view. There is a stress on the ceremonial side of religion in the section on the sabbath which, on the surface at least, seems to be "out of harmony with Jeremiah's thought." [78] But as one studies the passage carefully, he begins to wonder. In the first place, it is full of Jeremianic expressions. Moreover, sabbath observance did not begin with the exile. We have evidence of it in preexilic days (e.g., Amos 8:5; Isa. 1:13; Hos. 2:11). In fact, as an institution the sabbath goes back to Moses (Ex. 20:8; 31:15; 34:21), and ultimately roots in the action of God at the time of the creation (Gen. 2:1–3).

Moses had a tremendous influence on Jeremiah. This is seen in his diction, in his understanding of his ministry, and in his emphasis on the Mosaic covenant and traditions. Since the commandment about

---

[78] R. Calkins, *Jeremiah the Prophet* (New York: The Macmillan Co., 1930), p. 161.

sabbath observance is a part of the Decalogue and fundamental to the Mosaic covenant, and in view of Jeremiah's constant emphasis on the breach of the covenant as the reason for the impending doom of the nation, it would be passing strange if he had no reverence for the sabbath and never made any reference to it.

This becomes even more apparent when one recognizes the significance of the sabbath. Volz speaks of it as the grandest institution in the religion of Israel. Some regard it as the sign of the Mosaic covenant. If this be the case, it was an outer token of Israel's relationship to God and tantamount to dedication to and worship of him. Its proper observance symbolized her loyalty to her covenant God.

Originally, too, the sabbath was a day of delight, a day of rest, rejoicing, and renewal through cessation of secular activity and through social and spiritual fellowship (cf. Isa. 58:13–14). It was a part of the torah, which was covenant law, always set in the context of the "good news" of what God in his grace and power had done for his people. The motive for obedience to the demands of grace was gratitude and love. Hence the law was not considered to be a burdensome code, but a thing of joy (cf. Psalms 1:2; 19:7–14; 119). The injunction concerning the sabbath was a part of that law. The sabbath was to be kept holy, and this was a delightsome thing, when done in the right spirit and with the right motivation.

The change came during the postexilic and interbiblical periods, when the law was multiplied ad infinitum, externalized, and divorced from gratitude, penitence, love, and spiritual worship. Legalism developed, as the law became an end in itself, a means of escaping rather than meeting God's demands, and therefore a burdensome chore, so that Jesus had to remind the Pharisees that the sabbath was made for man, not man for the sabbath (Mark 2:27).

Was Jeremiah a legalist? Certainly not. Could he, then, speak about the sabbath as he does in 17:19–27? The writer thinks that there is the real possibility that he could and did. Would he make "the fate of Jerusalem depend on a formal ritual observance not necessarily related to a transformed way of living" (Cunliffe-Jones, p. 137)? The writer doubts that he does this. The emphasis throughout the passage is on holiness and obedience. The people are to keep the sabbath day holy—he does not say, in a formal way—as a symbol of their dedication as a nation to God and of their obedience to his covenant demands. To be sure, Jeremiah states the obligation with unusual force.

And there is the conditional character of the proclamation: if the people will properly observe the sabbath, then they will continue as the covenant community, governed by Davidic rulers and engaging in religious devotion; if they don't, they will face disaster. Preceding prophecies have stressed the certainty of doom—no "ifs" about it.

Three things can be said. First, there are occasional indications in chapters 7—20 that Jeremiah has not lost hope entirely. Second, the fact that a passage is set down in the midst of others does not mean necessarily that it dates from the same day, month, or year as they. Verses 19–27 could have come from that part of Jehoiakim's reign when the prophet still had hope for the nation. Third, absolute declarations such as appear in this section and elsewhere can sometimes be incentives to action rather than categorical absolutes.

Rudolph, Weiser, Penna, and Bright admit that in the passage under consideration are almost certainly actual words of Jeremiah and that he must have had a deep respect for the sabbath and have regarded the breaking or desecrating of it as very serious. However, they believe that his words have been expanded and somewhat modified by someone else (not late).

With Condamin and others, the writer feels that Jeremiah probably uttered these words on the sabbath—even *he* could be prosaic at times! If they are authentic, it is not too difficult to see the connection with the context. With regard to what precedes, it is clear that the prophet has been continually emphasizing that obedience to God's will as expressed in the covenant stipulations is the condition on which the continuance of the nation depends. The law of the sabbath was one of those stipulations, possibly involving the very sign of the covenant itself. The breach of this law will result in ruin. This is what the prophet has been forecasting.

With respect to what follows, the episode in 17:19 ff. introduces a trio of symbolic acts taking place in different parts of Jerusalem (17:19 ff.; 18:1 ff.; 19:1 ff.).

Jeremiah declares, in effect: "Your fathers broke the covenant, as indicated by their desecration of the sabbath. Learn from their example. Do not follow in their steps. If you do, you are going to suffer."

Proper sabbath observance is not synonymous with puritanical legalism, and there is much to be said for corporate worship and personal renewal—physical and spiritual—on a set day, and also for an open public witness to the reality of inner dedication of life to God.

VIII. Parable, Proclamation, and Persecution (18:1—20:18)

Chapters 18—20 constitute an editorial unit. The unit contains valuable materials of various types, coming most probably from the reign of Jehoiakim.

1. The Potter and the Clay (18:1-12)

¹ The word that came to Jeremiah from the LORD: ² "Arise, and go down to the potter's house, and there I will let you hear my words." ³ So I went down to the potter's house, and there he was working at his wheel. ⁴ And the vessel he was making of clay was spoiled in the potter's hand, and he reworked it into another vessel, as it seemed good to the potter to do. ⁵ Then the word of the LORD came to me: ⁶ "O house of Israel, can I not do with you as this potter has done? says the LORD. Behold, like the clay in the potter's hand, so are you in my hand, O house of Israel. ⁷ If at any time I declare concerning a nation or a kingdom, that

I will pluck up and break down and destroy it, ⁸ and if that nation, concerning which I have spoken, turns from its evil, I will repent of the evil that I intended to do to it. ⁹ And if at any time I declare concerning a nation or a kingdom that I will build and plant it, ¹⁰ and if it does evil in my sight, not listening to my voice, then I will repent of the good which I had intended to do to it. ¹¹ Now, therefore, say to the men of Judah and the inhabitants of Jerusalem: 'Thus says the LORD, Behold, I am shaping evil against you and devising a plan against you. Return, every one from his evil way, and amend your ways and your doings.' ¹² "But they say, 'That is in vain! We will follow our own plans, and will every one act according to the stubbornness of his evil heart.'

This personal experience of Jeremiah is one of the most interesting and important in the Bible. A part of its importance stems from the fact that it provides real insight into the matter of inspiration and revelation. Here the Bible takes us into its confidence and indicates how God caused a truth to be born in a prophet's brain. It pulls back the curtain and grants us a momentary glimpse into the revelatory process. Strangely enough, the revelation did not come in a prayer closet or a sanctuary but through an ordinary occurrence in a common workshop. Then the prophet, under inspiration, put the revelation in words which the people could understand and which would fit their situation.

The pottery episode is also significant because the parable of the potter and the clay became "the classical illustration of the divine sovereignty" and "the fitting emblem for the highest conception man can form of the divine sovereignty in relation to human freedom" (Skinner, pp. 162, 164). God is sovereign, but he works with free men. Man is free, but only to choose the response he will make to God. Irenaeus put it thus: "To make is the property of God, but to be made that of man."

The experience of Jeremiah at the potter's house is important, too, because it teaches God's patience and love. Though some scholars find in the parable only a threat of coming calamity for Judah, the present writer is persuaded that the note of hope is struck (cf. also Cornill, Smith, Skinner, Streane, Leslie, Cunliffe-Jones, von Rad, Couturier, *et al.*). God, in his sovereign grace, was giving his people another chance to rise to his purpose.

A fourth reason for the tremendous significance of the pottery experience is that it constitutes a turning point in the prophet's career. He was now convinced that the nation was doomed, but this did not mean the absolute end. Through the discipline of captivity God would fashion another vessel which he could use for the carrying forward of his work in the world. Beyond the judgment that must come upon Judah there lay a future of hope. In short, the experience at the pottery meant the entry of a new element into Jeremiah's message and marked the beginning of a new epoch in his ministry. From this time forward he began "to build and to plant."

Verses 1–4 tell about the trip to the potter's house. *The potter's house* could be either a worshop or a factory, including the workshop, a kiln, a place for keeping and treading clay, and a refuse dump. The probable location of the pottery was in the southern section of the city, overlooking or even in the valley of Hinnom, with easy access to drainage and to the water of the Siloam pools.

The potter's *wheel* (lit., two stones) consisted of two circular discs of stone connected by a vertical rod. The lower disc was larger to give it momentum as it was activated by the feet. The upper disc was lighter and was used for shaping the clay into the vessel the potter wished to make.

The application of the parable follows in vv. 5–12. God can do as the potter does: he can adjust to a changed situation. If his people cooperate with him, he can make of them the kind of people he wants them to be, a true covenant community. If they refuse to cooperate, he must deal drastically with them in loving discipline in order that, if possible, they may be made over into a people he can use effectively for the achievement of his purpose.

Some scholars object to the allusion to nations other than Israel (vv. 7–10) as unJeremianic. Since Jeremiah was appointed "a prophet to the nations" (1:5), this objection seems unjustified. There may be here merely a broadening by the prophet —possibly later—of the application to include any nation, since his God is Lord over all nations and is working out a purpose in history which involves all nations.

It is interesting to note the skill with which key words of Jeremiah especially prominent in the account of his call are interwoven into this parable and its application. Also, it is instructive to observe that in the call to repentance (v. 11) the door is left open, though the people refuse to enter it (v. 12). The important Hebrew *shub* appears twice in a covenantal sense (vv. 8,11).

Now for a bit further exposition. Even the strongest and best of men have their times of torturing uncertainty. Jeremiah had entered such a period. About a quarter of a century earlier, under the impetus of a dynamic call-experience, he had gone forth into a terribly upset world, through which the winds of change were fiercely blowing. Charged with the responsibility of proclaiming the divine word, he had used almost every method imaginable: proclamation, condemnation, lamentation, exhortation, intercession. Yet the people had become worse instead of better. Now (probably after 605 B.C., during the reign of Jehoiakim) the conviction crystallized in the prophet's mind that the situation was hopeless and captivity certain. But this posed a problem. Was God defeated? Was he casting Israel off forever? If so, what would become of his purpose and promises?

As Jeremiah sat—thinking, wrestling, praying—a divine directive arose within: *Arise, and go down to the potter's house, and there I will let you hear my words.* A strange command! A fine fellow, the potter perhaps, but not the sort likely to impart much insight concerning a profound problem! Yet Jeremiah went. First, he saw that the potter had a purpose. In a flash, it dawned on Jeremiah: Here is a picture of God; he is the potter at the wheel. As potter, he is sovereign over life. Despite the crisis, confusion, and change, God is in control. Since God has a purpose for life, the highest wisdom of man is to seek to find and fit into that purpose.

Second, there is ever the possibility of perverting the potter's purpose. When the potter finished the vessel he was making, he examined it carefully. His keen eyes and sensitive fingers detected a flaw. It was *spoiled* in his hand. Because some gritty substance or stubborn quality in the clay had resisted his touch, he had failed. Israel had perverted the purpose of the potter God.

Thus, at the potter's workshop, it was unforgettably impressed upon Jeremiah that there is always the possibility of man's perverting the purpose of the divine Potter.

Third, Jeremiah learned something of the patience and perseverance of the potter. When the potter discovered that his vessel was marred, he crushed it. What now? thought Jeremiah, Will he throw it on the dump for discards, give up, lock up, and go home? No. The potter placed the clay on the wheel again and shaped it into another vessel, as seemed best to him to do. The revelation dawned: "Here is the explanation of the exile. God is not casting Israel off. He is giving her another chance. Captivity does not mean doom but discipline."

God offered Israel—and he offers us— a new beginning, a fresh start. We, as the Israelites, have only to turn to him in penitence, faith, and obedience. This was the "gospel" for Jeremiah.

It was this third insight which was new and which had tremendous consequences for the preaching of the great prophet.

2. The Unnaturalness of the People's Apostasy (18:13-17)

13 "Therefore thus says the LORD:
Ask among the nations,

who has heard the like of this?
The virgin Israel
has done a very horrible thing.
14 Does the snow of Lebanon leave
the crags of Sirion?
Do the mountain waters run dry,
the cold flowing streams?
15 But my people have forgotten me,
they burn incense to false gods;
they have stumbled in their ways,
in the ancient roads,
and have gone into bypaths,
not the highway,
16 making their land a horror,
a thing to be hissed at for ever.
Every one who passes by it is horrified
and shakes his head.
17 Like the east wind I will scatter them
before the enemy.
I will show them my back, not my face,
in the day of their calamity."

This poetic oracle incorporates both reproach and threat. It stresses the unnaturalness and incomprehensibility of Israel's sin (cf. 2:10-13,32; 5:20-25; 8:7). Her defection is contrary to the practice of pagans and the established patterns in nature.

God's *virgin* daughter (cf. 14:17) has done *a very horrible thing*. She has forsaken the Lord, has in fact *forgotten* him, and has followed after *false gods*. Her behavior stands in sharp contrast to that of other nations—who do not change their gods (cf. 2:11)—and to that of nature— the snows of Hermon (*Sirion*) are always there, and the mountain streams ceaselessly flow, meeting the needs below.

Because Israel has refused to walk *the ancient roads* (cf. 6:16) and is traveling on *bypaths, not the highway* (cf. 18:12), her *land* will become *a horror, a thing to be hissed at forever*. God *will scatter* her *before the enemy*, as the sirocco scatters the sand in the desert. As she has turned her back and not her face to God (cf. 2:27), so he will show his *back* and *not* his *face* to her in the time of her *calamity*. In sum, because of her conduct, so unnatural and so incomprehensible, Israel will experience the judgment of a holy God.

3. A Plot and a Protest (18:18-23)

18 Then they said, "Come, let us make plots against Jeremiah, for the law shall not perish

from the priest, nor counsel from the wise, nor the word from the prophet. Come, let us smite him with the tongue, and let us not heed any of his words."

19 Give heed to me, O LORD,
  and hearken to my plea.
20 Is evil a recompense for good?
  Yet they have dug a pit for my life.
  Remember how I stood before thee
    to speak good for them,
    to turn away thy wrath from them.
21 Therefore deliver up their children to famine;
    give them over to the power of the sword,
    let their wives become childless and widowed.
  May their men meet death by pestilence,
    their youths be slain by the sword in battle.
22 May a cry be heard from their houses,
    when thou bringest the marauder suddenly upon them!
  For they have dug a pit to take me,
    and laid snares for my feet.
23 Yet, thou, O LORD, knowest
    all their plotting to slay me.
  Forgive not their iniquity,
    nor blot out their sin from thy sight.
  Let them be overthrown before thee;
    deal with them in the time of thine anger.

Verse 18 tells about the plot against the prophet (cf. 11:18—12:6). The chief culprits were the religious leaders. The intensity of the mounting opposition to Jeremiah is reflected in the collusion of these men in a concerted effort to get rid of him. There were three groups of them: sages, priests, and prophets (cf. Ezek. 7:26). Jeremiah had been caustic in his criticism of all three groups (cf. 2:8; 4:9 f.; 5:30 f.; 6:13–15; 8:8 f.; 14:13 f.; etc.). It is no surprise that they desired to dispense with him.

The plot put the prophet in a dither. First, he pleads his innocence (vv. 19–20). Next, he prays that God will destroy those who are opposing him (vv. 21–23). Here the prophet is at the peak of passion. This is his bitterest imprecation. The spirit of vindictiveness shown in this fourth "confession" presents a problem for the Christian.

It has also constituted a problem for scholars. Several have denied the authenticity of vv. 21–23 because they are "unworthy of Jeremiah." Such a position is highly subjective and reprehensible. Jeremiah was a servant of the Lord, but he was also a human being—sometimes exceedingly human. "It is only as we accept him as a human being that we can rightly hear the prophetic word that he spoke" (Bright, p. 126).

From the Christian point of view, there is no justification for the prophet's attitude toward his enemies, but there is an explanation. There are at least three factors that should be kept in mind.

First, so far as we know, Jeremiah never really succeeded at anything significant he ever undertook. He was constantly baffled and bewildered, frustrated and fouled up, by the people whom he loved, served, and sought to save. He was opposed by governmental personnel, priests, prophets, "philosophers," and the people generally—including friends and family members. He was constantly constrained from within to preach a message of judgment. He had to watch the destruction of all a Hebrew treasured most. He was conspired against and, according to tradition, killed by his countrymen. He would have been more than human if occasionally he had not had something to say about it all.

Second, like other Israelites, he thought concretely, not abstractly. He, like them, did not distinguish between sin and the sinner. Moreover, he was convinced that he was serving God with sincerity. In opposing him, his foes were opposing God. If they won, God lost. So, in praying for their destruction, he was doing more than giving vent to personal passion. He was expressing his devotion to God and his desire for the vindication of his cause. As an Old Testament believer, he could do this with good conscience.

Third, he nowhere refers to a belief in a future life. He must have had one, but he didn't make much of it. He thought in terms of earthly retribution. The doctrine of the resurrection and final judgment emerges quite late in the Old Testament. It was now or never for Jeremiah. He had no risen Christ who plainly taught that there will be a final judgment, when all things will be set right. This reminds us that we are still in the Old Testament and that Christ makes a difference.

Though as Christians we need Jeremiah's capacity for righteous indignation against entrenched evil, we must use such passages as 18:19–23 with the greatest of care. We know to distinguish between sin and the sinner. We are to hate sin, but we are to love sinners, including our enemies, and seek to bring them into a saving knowledge of the grace of God in Christ.

4. A Parable and a Proclamation (19:1–15)

There is something quite different about this chapter. It contains a literary type which has not yet appeared in the book: biographical narration. Someone else, probably Baruch, is telling a story about Jeremiah.

Up to this point in the prophecy, we have had autobiographical accounts, prophecies, and prayers. Here we have the start of a source in which the primary concern is not what the prophet says but what he does, with particular stress on the suffering he encounters because of what he does. There are oracles, but usually they are presented in prose and with brevity. And all of it—this "biography"—is related in the third person. A comparison of chapters 7 and 26 will disclose the difference in form and emphasis.

The material in chapter 19 is concerned with events which probably transpired in the first part of Jehoiakim's reign. It is included here because of the symbolic act and the allusion to a potter's vessel.

(1) The Parable of the Potter's Pitcher (19:1–13)

¹ Thus said the LORD, "Go, buy a potter's earthen flask, and take some of the elders of the people and some of the senior priests, ² and go out to the valley of the son of Hinnom at the entry of the Potsherd Gate, and proclaim there the words that I tell you. ³ You shall say, 'Hear the word of the LORD, O kings of Judah and inhabitants of Jerusalem. Thus says the LORD of hosts, the God of Israel, Behold, I am

bringing such evil upon this place that the ears of every one who hears of it will tingle. ⁴ Because the people have forsaken me, and have profaned this place by burning incense in it to other gods whom neither they nor their fathers nor the kings of Judah have known; and because they have filled this place with the blood of innocents, ⁵ and have built the high places of Baal to burn their sons in the fire as burnt offerings to Baal, which I did not command or decree, nor did it come into my mind; ⁶ therefore, behold, days are coming, says the LORD, when this place shall no more be called Topheth, or the valley of the son of Hinnom, but the valley of Slaughter. ⁷ And in this place I will make void the plans of Judah and Jerusalem, and will cause their people to fall by the sword before their enemies, and by the hand of those who seek their life. I will give their dead bodies for food to the birds of the air and to the beasts of the earth. ⁸ And I will make this city a horror, a thing to be hissed at; every one who passes by it will be horrified and will hiss because of all its disasters. ⁹ And I will make them eat the flesh of their sons and their daughters, and every one shall eat the flesh of his neighbor in the siege and in the distress, with which their enemies and those who seek their life afflict them.'

¹⁰ "Then you shall break the flask in the sight of the men who go with you, ¹¹ and shall say to them, 'Thus says the LORD of hosts: So will I break this people and this city, as one breaks a potter's vessel, so that it can never be mended. Men shall bury in Topheth because there will be no place else to bury. ¹² Thus will I do to this place, says the LORD, and to its inhabitants, making this city like Topheth. ¹³ The houses of Jerusalem and the houses of the kings of Judah—all the houses upon whose roofs incense has been burned to all the host of heaven, and drink offerings have been poured out to other gods—shall be defiled like the place of Topheth.' "

Jeremiah is commanded to purchase a *baqbuq*, "the most artistic and expensive member of the pitcher family" and thus "well fitted to typify Jerusalem in Jeremiah's illustrated sermon," for its neck was so narrow that "it could never be mended." [79] The prophet is then told to take the pitcher, along with some of the leaders of the people, and go to *the valley of the son of Hinnom at the entry of the Potsherd Gate*. There he is to make a double proclamation: in symbol and in

---

[79] Kelso, *op. cit*, p. 175.

speech. As he and his "audience" look out over the valley and see Tophet in particular, the place where human sacrifice was offered to Baal (32:35, Molech), he is to smash the costly, delicate, unmendable pitcher and make the pronouncement in v. 11 (cf. 13:1–11). Jeremiah does what he is told to do.

Interwoven with his vivid announcement of judgment is an oracle of reproach, called by some "the Tophet sermon." The symbolic act is dealt with in vv. 1,2,10, and 11. The "sermon" appears in vv. 3–9, 12–13 (cf. 7:29–34). The former is a prediction of destruction. The latter is a denunciation of the people for their apostasy. There is a bit of awkwardness in the mingling of the two, but a prophecy of disaster usually included both accusation and an announcement of retribution, the one being the reason for the other. The awkwardness might conceivably be accounted for by the fact that someone else other than the prophet is telling the story (though many scholars maintain that there has been a mixing of "the Tophet sermon" and the symbolic act by an editor).

The point is clear. There comes a time when God's patience runs out. When it does, religious opportunity passes, and God's grace gives way to his wrath.

(2) A Proclamation in the Temple (19:14–15)

¹⁴ Then Jeremiah came from Topheth, where the LORD had sent him to prophesy, and he stood in the court of the LORD's house, and said to all the people: ¹⁵ "Thus says the LORD of hosts, the God of Israel, Behold, I am bringing upon this city and upon all its towns all the evil that I have pronounced against it, because they have stiffened their neck, refusing to hear my words."

The prophet went from Tophet to the Temple, and there he preached essentially the same sermon again—briefly but pointedly. Pashhur got the point! Apparently some others did too.

5. Persecution and Reaction (20:1–18)

Here we have one of the earliest references to open, outright persecution of the prophet because of his preaching. Also, in this chapter is preserved the last and greatest of the confessions.

(1) The Persecution of the Prophet (20:1–6)

¹ Now Pashhur the priest, the son of Immer, who was chief officer in the house of the LORD, heard Jeremiah prophesying these things. ² Then Pashhur beat Jeremiah the prophet, and put him in the stocks that were in the upper Benjamin Gate of the house of the LORD. ³ On the morrow, when Pashhur released Jeremiah from the stocks, Jeremiah said to him, "The LORD does not call your name Pashhur, but Terror on every side. ⁴ For thus says the LORD: Behold, I will make you a terror to yourself and to all your friends. They shall fall by the sword of their enemies while you look on. And I will give all Judah into the hand of the king of Babylon; he shall carry them captive to Babylon, and shall slay them with the sword. ⁵ Moreover, I will give all the wealth of the city, all its gains, all its prized belongings, and all the treasures of the kings of Judah into the hand of their enemies, who shall plunder them, and seize them, and carry them to Babylon. ⁶ And you, Pashhur, and all who dwell in your house, shall go into captivity; to Babylon you shall go; and there you shall die, and there you shall be buried, you and all your friends, to whom you have prophesied falsely."

Jeremiah's sermon at Tophet and in the Temple drew fire. *Pashhur,* the chief of the temple police (not the Pashhur of 21:1; 38:1 ff.), *beat . . . the prophet, and put him in the stocks . . .* (on *the upper Benjamin Gate,* cf. 2 Kings 15:35). There he was left for perhaps as many as 24 hours. It is thought that he had to lie in a very cramped position (cf. the Hebrew root of the word for *stocks;* also the LXX and Targum translation: "a cramped room") and that for much of the time he was subject to much ridicule and rough treatment. There is a veiled wordplay here: the Temple "overseer" (20:1, *paqid*) was seeking to silence God's "overseer" (1:10, *paqad;* cf. Amos 7:10–17).

When Pashhur decided to release the prophet the next day, Jeremiah drenched him with denunciation. He said to the priest, in effect: "Your parents gave you one name. God is giving you another. It is

Magor-missabib, which means 'Terror-all-around.' I'm making you a double sign of my preaching, which you have tried to silence. You will be a sign to yourself and to your people—a sign that the doom I have predicted is going to become a reality and a sign that a nameless dread will be the dominant emotion in both you and them when it arrives. God is going to give this country into the hand of the king of Babylon, and he will carry its inhabitants into captivity to Babylon. You and your family will be in the crowd, and you will die and be buried in Babylon." The reason: *you have prophesied falsely.* This prophecy of disaster was apparently fulfilled in 597 B.C. (cf. 29:26).

A bad night had not blunted Jeremiah's prophetic powers. He did a daring thing in making Pashhur "a walking sermon," a living sign of the essence of the message he preached in the Temple, the certainty of coming calamity (19:15). He called Pashhur's hand for playing the prophet and causing the people to trust in a lie ("No calamity shall befall us!"). He became so excited and confident that he even identified the foe from the north and the place of captivity for the first time: Babylon.

(2) Agony and Victory (20:7–18)

7 O LORD, thou hast deceived me,
  and I was deceived;
 thou art stronger than I,
  and thou hast prevailed.
 I have become a laughingstock all the day;
  every one mocks me.
8 For whenever I speak, I cry out,
  I shout, "Violence and destruction!"
 For the word of the LORD has become for me
  a reproach and derision all day long.
9 If I say, "I will not mention him,
  or speak any more in his name,"
 there is in my heart as it were a burning fire
  shut up in my bones,
 and I am weary with holding it in,
  and I cannot.
10 For I hear many whispering.
  Terror is on every side!
 "Denounce him! Let us denounce him!"
  say all my familiar friends,
  watching for my fall.

"Perhaps he will be deceived,
  then we can overcome him,
  and take our revenge on him."
11 But the LORD is with me as a dread warrior;
  therefore my persecutors will stumble,
  they will not overcome me.
 They will be greatly shamed,
  for they will not succeed.
 Their eternal dishonor
  will never be forgotten.
12 O LORD of hosts, who triest the righteous,
  who seest the heart and the mind,
 let me see thy vengeance upon them,
  for to thee have I committed my cause.
13 Sing to the LORD;
  praise the LORD!
 For he has delivered the life of the needy
  from the hand of evildoers.
14 Cursed be the day
  on which I was born!
 The day when my mother bore me,
  let it not be blessed!
15 Cursed be the man
  who brought the news to my father,
 "A son is born to you,"
  making him very glad.
16 Let that man be like the cities
  which the LORD overthrew without pity;
 let him hear a cry in the morning
  and an alarm at noon,
17 because he did not kill me in the womb;
  so my mother would have been my grave,
  and her womb for ever great.
18 Why did I come forth from the womb
  to see toil and sorrow,
  and spend my days in shame?

Peake calls this poem "one of the most powerful and impressive passages in the whole of the prophetic literature, a passage which takes us, as no other, not only into the depths of the prophet's soul, but into the secrets of the prophetic consciousness" (p. 241).

This last confession is made up of two parts: vv. 7–13 and 14–18. Some regard these two parts as two separate confessions uttered at different times. This may be a true view of them. They are dissimilar, especially in the final note sounded. In vv. 7–13 the prophet reaches a lofty peak of victory. In vv. 14–18 he descends to the deepest level of despair yet attained.

However, many scholars consider 20: 7–18 to be a single confession in two parts.

They explain the sharply contradictory moods with which the two parts end in one of three ways. Some are convinced that Jeremiah never emerged from the dark night of the soul but, instead, walked a road which led step by step to a deeper despair. Yet he was obedient in spite of it all (e.g., von Rad, p. 204). Others believe that the prophet was a very sensitive, highly emotional individual and that he had "violent alternations of feeling, so that he could commit himself to God, be gripped by the conviction that God was with him and would give him the victory, burst into a hymn of praise, and then drop into the depths of despondency—only to come out again later.[80]

There is a third possibility. It is that the words in vv. 14–18 were spoken before those in vv. 7–13. This is conjecture—as is much of what anyone says about the confessions—but the present writer thinks that it is possible and even tenable. It is his view that Jeremiah went through a spiritual crisis during his middle ministry and that by God's grace he emerged from his gloom into the sunshine again, God's iron man, whom nothing and nobody could down, a prophet of courage and hope, committed to the will of God whatever it might cost.

Three of the several reasons for this view are: (1) there are no records of any more debates between Jeremiah and God; (2) he moves with the firm tread of a man who has centered down in God; (3) his portrayals of the future of God's people get brighter as the situation around him grows blacker.

The writer is aware of the fact that one cannot safely date a passage in Jeremiah by its location in the book. He knows, too, that some scholars see no connection between vv. 7–18, or 7–13, and 1–6, and that some affirm categorically that such staccato expressions of cursing, resentment, commitment, assurance, and singing could

not possibly emanate from the same situation and occasion. He often wonders how these scholars who have not spent a day and night in stocks in physical, mental, and spiritual torment can be so sure as to what a man who has, could and would feel and say. He sees no reason whatever for objecting to the idea that vv. 1–6 provide the setting for vv. 7–13 and possibly 7–18.

Jeremiah was in deep distress. He was undergoing indignity, physical torture, and terrific mental anguish. He had, in fact, reached a dead end—and this for doing the will of God. His enemies were in the saddle. All looked hopeless. Black despair gripped him. Assuming that vv. 14–18 come before vv. 7–13, the prophet burst forth into a bitter outcry, in which he *cursed . . . the day* of his birth and *the man who brought the news to* his father from the women's quarters concerning his new *son* (it was customary to reward such a bearer of good news). *The man* should have been destroyed like ancient Sodom and Gomorrah (since Jeremiah would not know who the man was, this is largely a rhetorical device). As for himself, once born, why was he permitted to live, to spend his days in sorrow and shame (cf. vv. 14–18 with Job 3, which is influenced by them)?

Having given vent to his feelings about his coming into the world, Jeremiah got down to the matter of his call, i.e., his work in the world. He addressed God directly in vv. 7 ff. The depth of his emotion is evident in the words used in v. 7. The verb translated "deceive" really means seduce, and the verb rendered "be strong" signifies seize or overpower. Jeremiah was bordering on blasphemy again (cf. 15:18). However, in fact, his extreme frankness was a testimony to the intimacy of his fellowship with God.

One of the cardinal characteristics of the great classical prophets was their strong sense of inner constraint—at times, as here, even of coercion. This rooted back in a conviction of divine call. No prophet gave

---

[80] H. T. Kuist, *Jeremiah and Lamentations* (Richmond: John Knox, 1961), p. 66; cf. Rudolph, *op. cit., in loc.*

a clearer or more forceful expression of this feeling of call and constraint than Jeremiah, and nowhere did he express that feeling more strongly than in 20:7,9. Having reached a dead end, he went back to the call and cried out, in effect: "Lord, you got me into this. You took advantage of my naive simplicity. You seduced me, forced me, overpowered me—and didn't disclose the seriousness of the responsibility or the extent of the suffering involved. *I have become a laughingstock all the day.*"

Could there be a reference here to the treatment he got in the stocks during the daytime? The tormentors went to bed at night, during which time some of the bitter words of vv. 14–18 and the strong words of vv. 13 ff. could have come from Jeremiah's lips.

If a major mark of a true prophet was his sense of call, his chief responsibility was the communication of the divine word. Jeremiah had faithfully fulfilled this function (v. 8). The result? He was a day-long joke to the people. They continually reviled him. Why? Because he brought a word of woe rather than a word of weal.

The agonizing prayer continued to pour forth in v. 9. The prophet had been considering—especially in recent hours—giving up the ministry and going back to the life of the layman. But, when he thought like that, something caught fire inside him and burned in his bones. He could not put it out or hold it in! Talk about prophetic constraint and compulsion, this is it! We are reminded of Paul's words: "Woe is me if I do not preach the gospel" (1 Cor. 9:16)!

Jeremiah was painfully conscious of the taunts of the crowd (v. 10). One can imagine the motley crew milling about the suffering servant of God in the stocks. Recalling his favorite expression, so recently given by him as a symbolic name to Pashhur, the priest in charge of law and order at the Temple, some of them would whisper with sizzling sarcasm: "There's old Terror-all-around! He's denounced us aplenty! Let's denounce him!"

It is amazing how brave some people can be when they have the upper hand and are in no danger. The thing that hurt Jeremiah the most was that *familiar friends* were among those seeking revenge upon him—and this for his seeking, through prayer and preaching, to save them from a tragic fate!

Now comes the assurance: agony followed by victory (vv. 11–13). Confidence in God's saving presence and sovereign power caused the prophet to move upward out of the depths. His foes were on the losing side, not he. God was going to win, and his servant would be vindicated. A dead end became a doorway to victory.

Listen: "O Lord of hosts, thou righteous Assayer (cf. 6:27; 17:10), who art continually seeing (vivid participial construction) the inner emotions and thoughts (lit. the kidneys and the heart), I will see thy deliverance from them, for *to thee* I have committed my case (a legal term)!"

This personal translation differs from that of the RSV. The verb rendered *let me see* is a simple imperfect in form. It is possible that it could be a cohortative in force. It may also be a simple imperfect. The word translated *vengeance* may also signify deliverance (cf. 11:20; 15:15). In the writer's judgment, it is likely that Jeremiah was voicing a conviction more than a petition here.

Verse 13 brings the confession to a triumphant close. This verse is a problem to critical scholars. Some reject it (e.g., Duhm, Cornill, Giesebrecht, Volz, Peake). Others accept it (e.g., Rothstein, Rudolph, Condamin, Bright, Holladay). The basis for the rejection is chiefly the use of the "psalm-word" *needy* and the hymnic form of the verse.

With regard to the former, it may be said that Jeremiah uses the word elsewhere (2:34; 5:28; 22:16) and that he no doubt was familiar with psalms, for they were employed in worship. With respect to the latter, need we remind ourselves that Jeremiah was a poet of tremendous versatility and that he has shown his capacity for psalm composition already (e.g., 17:5–8)?

But the clincher consists of two pieces of evidence which put the authenticity of the verse almost beyond any question.[81] The phrase "deliver from the hand of" occurs in 15:21 and 21:12 (authentic oracles), but it is not found elsewhere in the Old Testament. The same can be said for the phrase "from the hand(s) of evildoers" also used in 23:14 (a genuine passage).

The writer has stated his belief that Jeremiah here moved through agony to victory. The struggle, which had been going on for some time, came to a crisis and was resolved through a commitment to God.[82] This is not to say that the prophet would have no difficulties or uncertainties in the future. But it does mean that never again would he endure such a dark night of the soul. He had made his way through the valley of struggle and suffering to the highlands of a richer, more far-reaching service than he had known before. The promise of his call had been fulfilled. He was now "an iron pillar, a fortified city, and a wall of bronze" (1:18), and was on his way to becoming the spiritual giant among the Hebrew prophets. He could now serve his people amid the gathering shadows, minister to them in their darkest hour, and help prepare them to survive the political and theological crisis which the captivity would precipitate. A fire burned within which nothing—not even he—could put out!

The confessions of Jeremiah are without parallel in the prophetical literature of the Old Testament. In some ways, they are the most valuable part of his prophecy. Since we have now examined all of them, it is in order to indicate something of their significance (also see Int.).

First, they shed considerable light on the personality of the prophet. They indicate that he was sensitive, shrinking, intensely human, somewhat impatient, rather introspective, quite emotional, torn by a sense of inadequacy—a man of conflicts, both without and within. The confessions inform us that the secret of the power of his personality was his strong consciousness of God's call and sufficiency.

Second, the confessions shed a great deal of light on the psychology of prophecy. They point up the fact that there were two elements in the revelatory process: the human and the divine. On the one side, there was divine constraint; on the other, human complaint. The divine compulsion did not rob Jeremiah of his human freedom—to protest, to pray, to employ various literary forms and stylistic and symbolic devices to get the divine word across. God spoke through him, but it was through a very human person, not a puppet, that he spoke.

Third, the confessions shed a lot of light on the practice of prayer. Not that Jeremiah ever delivered a sermon or essay on the subject. He simply prayed. From his experience we can learn a great deal. His prayers teach us that prayer is an individual thing—not the special prerogative of any person or profession. It is a two-way affair, not a monologue but a dialogue.

He made prayer a practice in honesty. For him prayer was no magical formula by which he sought to get from God what he wanted but a moral fellowship through which he poured out his heart before God and sought to bring all of his motives and emotions into the white light of divine presence and his life into harmony with the divine purpose.

Finally, the confessions shed much light on piety in the Old Testament period. For Jeremiah religion was a dynamic personal fellowship with God, rooted in redeeming

---

81 W. L. Holladay, JBL, 81, 1962, p. 52.

82 Skinner (p. 214) and Fohrer (*Introduction to the Old Testament*, pp. 395, 401) hold that there was a crisis resolved through surrender, but they arrange the confessions so that the victory came in 15:1–21. Couturier maintains that the peak of the crisis was reached in 20:7–18 (*op. cit.*, pp. 301, 315, 319). For further study of the confessions and various views about them, see Skinner, pp. 201–230; Smith, pp. 317–334; Leslie, pp. 137–154; G. von Rad, "Die Konfessionen Jeremias," *Evangelische Theologie*, 3, 1936, 265–276; and others.

grace and expressing itself in right relationships, a life of obedience and service. Foregleams of this appear in his call-experience. Nowhere is it more prominent than in his confessions.

We have discussed his imprecations (cf. 18:18–23). This aspect of his piety—and of that of Old Testament believers generally—falls short of the Christian ideal. The major defect in Jeremiah's piety was "an incomplete possession of the spirit of love, which is the medium of perfect communion with God . . . Jeremiah had not learned the lesson of the Cross" (Skinner, pp. 229 f.; cf., however, Jeremiah's intercession for those who opposed him and his injunction to the exiles in 29:7). He could not truly pray: "Father, forgive them, for they do not know what they do." It would take one greater than Jeremiah—One who reminded people of Jeremiah—to teach men to pray in that spirit. And we have not learned it yet!

IX. Jeremiah and the Rulers of Judah (21:1—23:8)

As the reader passes from chapter 20 to chapter 21, he experiences a jolt. Timewise, he jumps from the early part of the reign of Jehoiakim to the latter part of the reign of Zedekiah. This chronological leap could cover as many as 20 years.

In addition, the character of the material changes. To be sure, some of it has the same Deuteronomic cast as has been seen in such passages as 7:1 ff.; 11:1 ff.; 16:1 ff.; 18:1 ff.; and 19:1 ff. Also, there is the combination of prose and poetry already encountered in various places. But there is a difference. The material here is concerned with Jeremiah's experiences with and prophecies to the kings of Judah. It is true that two of the prophecies are not beamed at any particular king but at the royal house generally, and that one predicts the coming of the messianic king. But it is obvious that the primary connecting link is the prophet's attitude and utterances with regard to the Davidic kings.

Although the material is biographical in the manner of its presentation, in its basic form it likely goes back to Jeremiah. With respect to the "Deuteronomic passages," there is the same divergence of opinion and conclusion among scholars as in the case of similar passages appearing elsewhere in the prophecy.

1. Zedekiah's Request and Jeremiah's Reply (21:1-10)

Well-meaning, weak-willed Zedekiah became king in 597 B.C. During his reign he was torn between two pressures: the influence of Jeremiah and that of the nationalistic party. The latter advocated revolt against the Babylonian overlord, in reliance on Egypt. Zedekiah came close to rebelling in 594–593, but apparently held off. With the accession of Pharaoh Hophra in 589, trouble started. The king of Judah was deeply involved. By late summer or early fall, the Babylonian legions arrived in Judah and began their suppression of the revolt. They blockaded Jerusalem, sought to divide the people and drive them into their towns and cities, and then pick the strongholds off one by one. This went on for several months before the real siege of Jerusalem started. The incident recorded in 21:1–10 took place during the blockade and before the beginning of the siege.

(1) Zedekiah's Request (21:1-2)

¹ This is the word which came to Jeremiah from the Lord, when King Zedekiah sent to him Pashhur the son of Malchiah and Zephaniah the priest, the son of Maaseiah, saying, ² "Inquire of the Lord for us, for Nebuchadrezzar king of Babylon is making war against us; perhaps the Lord will deal with us according to all his wonderful deeds, and will make him withdraw from us."

Quite distraught no doubt, Zedekiah sent to Jeremiah a delegation of two men, *Pashhur* (38:1) and *Zephaniah* (37:3) both probably members of the pro-Egyptian party. The purpose in their coming was to ask the prophet to *inquire* of the Lord concerning the situation which the city and country were facing. Evidently Zedekiah was expecting the same sort of assurance of divine aid and deliverance as Hezekiah received from Isaiah during the Assyrian crisis of 701 (cf. Isa. 37:36 f.).

Jeremiah is revealed here in a new role. No longer is he hated and hounded by "the higher-ups." The strong confirmation of his preaching by the captivity of 597 has made him a national figure whom the king consults in the hour of crisis.

(2) Jeremiah's Reply (21:3-10)

3 Then Jeremiah said to them: 4 "Thus you shall say to Zedekiah, 'Thus says the Lord, the God of Israel: Behold, I will turn back the weapons of war which are in your hands and with which you are fighting against the king of Babylon and against the Chaldeans who are besieging you outside the walls; and I will bring them together into the midst of this city. 5 I myself will fight against you with outstretched hand and strong arm, in anger, and in fury, and in great wrath. 6 And I will smite the inhabitants of this city, both man and beast; they shall die of a great pestilence. 7 Afterward, says the Lord, I will give Zedekiah king of Judah, and his servants, and the people in this city who survive the pestilence, sword, and famine, into the hand of Nebuchadrezzar king of Babylon and into the hand of their enemies, into the hand of those who seek their lives. He shall smite them with the edge of the sword; he shall not pity them, or spare them, or have compassion.'
8 "And to this people you shall say: 'Thus says the Lord: Behold, I set before you the way of life and the way of death. 9 He who stays in this city shall die by the sword, by famine, and by pestilence; but he who goes out and surrenders to the Chaldeans who are besieging you shall live and shall have his life as a prize of war. 10 For I have set my face against this city for evil and not for good, says the Lord: it shall be given into the hand of the king of Babylon, and he shall burn it with fire.'

The prophet's response consists of two parts. In the first part (vv. 3-7), he states that the people will find it impossible to repel the enemy. Instead, they will retreat within the city. For God himself will fight against them. Many will die by plague, sword, and starvation. Those who survive will be turned over to Nebuchadnezzar. The second part of the reply is addressed more directly to the populace (vv. 8-10).

They are offered a choice between *the way of life and the way of death. The way of death* is to stay in the city and seek to save it. *The way of life* is to surrender to the enemy. Jeremiah counsels the latter course and forecasts that the city will be captured and consumed by fire.

The unusual expression *his life as a prize of war* (cf. 38:2; 39:18; 45:5) is an idiom which probably originated in the army. When an army came home in triumph, it brought booty. But when it came in defeat, there was none. The returning soldiers were likely asked, "What booty or prize of war do you have?" After an unsuccessful campaign, the answer may have been a shrug of the shoulders and something like this: "Booty? My life is my booty. I managed to get back alive. That is my prize of war."

The courage of Jeremiah in the crisis situation is impressive. He faithfully delivers the word of the Lord to the king and his countrymen, even though that word is unpleasant and undesirable.

2. The Responsibility and Delinquency of the Royal House (21:11-14)

11 "And to the house of the king of Judah say, 'Hear the word of the Lord, 12 O house of David! Thus says the Lord:
" 'Execute justice in the morning,
     and deliver from the hand of the oppressor
     him who has been robbed,
lest my wrath go forth like fire,
     and burn with none to quench it,
     because of your evil doings.' "
13 "Behold, I am against you, O inhabitant of the valley,
O rock of the plain,
                 says the Lord;
you who say, 'Who shall come down against us,
     or who shall enter our habitations?'
14 I will punish you according to the fruit of your doings,
                 says the Lord;
I will kindle a fire in her forest,
     and it shall devour all that is round about her."

This poetic oracle, addressed to the royal house of Judah, would be especially appropriate during the reign of Jehoiakim. In it there is the proclamation of a principle: the Davidic dynasty is responsible, under God, for the establishment of justice in society in keeping with covenant law (vv. 11–12; Ex. 22:20–23). Stability and continuity are dependent upon a faithful discharge of this responsibility.

Since there has been delinquency in this area, the royal house is under the judgment of God. Retribution will come upon both court and city (vv. 13–14; on the textual problem in v. 13, see especially Weiser and Bright). The maintenance of justice was a major duty attached to sacral kingship in the Near East. In Judah, the obligation was intrinsic to both the Mosaic and the Davidic covenants.

3. First Encounter with Jehoiakim (22:1–9)

¹ Thus says the LORD: "Go down to the house of the king of Judah, and speak there this word, ² and say, 'Hear the word of the LORD, O King of Judah, who sit on the throne of David, you, and your servants, and your people who enter these gates. ³ Thus says the LORD: Do justice and righteousness, and deliver from the hand of the oppressor him who has been robbed. And do no wrong or violence to the alien, the fatherless, and the widow, nor shed innocent blood in this place. ⁴ For if you will indeed obey this word, then there shall enter the gates of this house kings who sit on the throne of David, riding in chariots and on horses, they, and their servants, and their people. ⁵ But if you will not heed these words, I swear by myself, says the LORD, that this house shall become a desolation. ⁶ For thus says the LORD concerning the house of the king of Judah:
" 'You are as Gilead to me,
    as the summit of Lebanon,
yet surely I will make you a desert,
    an uninhabited city.
⁷ I will prepare destroyers against you,
    each with his weapons;
and they shall cut down your choicest cedars,
    and cast them into the fire.
⁸ " 'And many nations will pass by this city, and every man will say to his neighbor, "Why has the LORD dealt thus with this great city?" ⁹ And they will answer, "Because they forsook the covenant of the LORD their God, and worshiped other gods and served them." ' "

It is the writer's belief that this prophecy, in which the basic principle stated in 21:11–14 is reiterated, was delivered by Jeremiah to Jehoiakim soon after his accession (Eissfeldt, p. 352; Fohrer, op. cit., p. 396). This is the first recorded case of the prophet's appearance at court.

As God's messenger, Jeremiah is told to *go down* (from the standpoint of the Temple) *to the house of the king of Judah* (i.e., the palace, located a little lower on the hill than the Temple, which crowned its crest), *and speak there this word. This word* is a prophecy of disaster, but not of the orthodox variety. There is a conditional element in it.

The king and his countrymen—both *servants* (court officials) and subjects (*people*)—are enjoined to practice *justice and righteousness*. In particular, they are to rescue the robbed from the power of the ruthless oppressor, to refrain from doing harm to the defenseless members of society (cf. Ex. 22:20–26; Lev. 19:33–34; Deut. 10:18–19), and to refuse to shed innocent blood—whether through actual murder, unjust judicial decisions, or oppressive practices. If the word of the covenant Lord in these matters is obeyed, both king and country will enjoy well-being. But if not, God will make the Temple *a desolation* and Jerusalem *a desert*. When the people of the nations ask why he has done this incredible thing (destroyed his own city and center of worship), the answer will be: the people broke their *covenant* with him by their apostasy and idolatry.

The unnamed *destroyers* are the Babylonians. They will *cut down* the *choicest cedars* (the timbers in the Temple and the House of the Forest of Lebanon, 1 Kings 3:2–5; 7:2–4; Isa. 22:8) and will *cast them into the fire* (cf. 39:8; 52:13).

In the dramatic situation here depicted, a shy countryman about 40 years of age corners the wicked king in the statehouse and lays down the gauntlet to him. The significance of the encounter between Jeremiah and Jehoiakim is stressed in the Introduction.

4. Lament over Jehoahaz (22:10–12)

10 Weep not for him who is dead,
   nor bemoan him;
   but weep bitterly for him who goes away,
   for he shall return no more
   to see his native land.

11 For thus says the LORD concerning Shallum the son of Josiah, king of Judah, who
reigned instead of Josiah his father, and who
went away from this place: "He shall return
here no more, 12 but in the place where they
have carried him captive, there shall he die,
and he shall never see this land again."

The prophecy concerning Jehoahaz
(Shallum) consists of two parts: a poetic
lamentation (v. 10) and a prose amplification (vv. 11–12). It is possible that while
mourning rites were still in process over
the premature passing of Josiah the
prophet appeared among the mourners
and chanted a *qinah* (dirge). In it he
called upon his countrymen *not to weep
for him that is dead* (i.e., Josiah, who had
had a fine administration and had died
gloriously fighting for his country), but
rather to *weep bitterly for him who goes
away* (i.e., young Jehoahaz, who had no
chance to show his ability as an administrator), for he (Jehoahaz) would not see
his native land again but would die in
Egypt (v. 10).

The prose expansion (vv. 11–12) may
be a later addition by Jeremiah or someone
else.

This prophecy is best interpreted, not as
the reflection of any political bias, but as
the spontaneous expression of the prophet's sympathy for one in trouble.

5. Judgment-Speech to Jehoiakim (22:13–19)

13 "Woe to him who builds his house by un-
      righteousness,
   and his upper rooms by injustice;
   who makes his neighbor serve him for
      nothing,
   and does not give him his wages;
14 who says, 'I will build myself a great house
      with spacious upper rooms,'
   and cuts out windows for it,
      paneling it with cedar,
      and painting it with vermilion.
15 Do you think you are a king
      because you compete in cedar?

Did not your father eat and drink
   and do justice and righteousness?
   Then it was well with him.
16 He judged the cause of the poor and needy;
   then it was well.
   Is not this to know me?
                              says the LORD.
17 But you have eyes and heart
   only for your dishonest gain,
   for shedding innocent blood,
   and for practicing oppression and vio-
      lence."
18 Therefore thus says the LORD concerning
Jehoiakim the son of Josiah, king of Judah:
   "They shall not lament for him, saying,
      'Ah my brother!' or 'Ah sister!'
   They shall not lament for him, saying,
      'Ah lord!' or 'Ah his majesty!'
19 With the burial of an ass he shall be
      buried,
   dragged and cast forth beyond the gates
      of Jerusalem."

The prophet may have accosted the
king in front of an unfinished structure and
proclaimed to him these words of woe
(Volz, p. 222). Others may have been
standing nearby. The passion-packed inter-
jection translated *Woe to* may also be
rendered "Accursed be!" or "Shame upon!"
The singular pronouns in the first part of
this prophecy of disaster indicate the self-
centeredness and cruelty of the king (cf. 2
Kings 23:34 ff. and the Int.).

His house—in v. 14, *a great house*—has
been thought to be an imposing addition to
the palace complex in Jerusalem. Recent
excavations have uncovered at Ramat
Rachel a pretentious building dating
around 600 B.C.[83] This could be the *great
house.*

The upper rooms were the roof chambers
(penthouse), which were more comfortable in hot weather than the lower rooms
because the air could come through the
lattice work. Forcing subjects to serve without wages was the hated corvee, which
had caused so much discontent during
Solomon's administration and immediately
after his death. *Cedar* was rare and expensive.

Martin Buber states that the prophecies
in 22:1—23:8 are "unparalleled in the

[83] Cf. Y. Aharoni, BA, 24, 1961, 118.

literature of the ancient Orient for their liberty of spirit." [84] Jeremiah is certainly speaking with plenty of freedom—and force—in vv. 13 ff.

After pronouncing upon the *injustice* and *unrighteousness* employed in the king's building operation and upon his preoccupation with *paneling* and *painting*, the prophet asks Jehoiakim whether he thinks that a capacity for choosing the right kind of material for decorating a statehouse constitutes that which makes a real king (v. 15a). He proceeds to contrast father and son (vv. 15b–17). He recalls that the father (Josiah) ate and drank. According to some, this refers to his conscientious participation in the covenant meal.[85] Whether this be the precise meaning of the terminology here or not, Josiah is represented as a person of true piety and genuine integrity, a man who enjoyed life but also took his responsibilities as ruler seriously. He faithfully executed the covenant stipulations in his dealings with his subjects. This, says Jeremiah, is what a king ought to be and do. This, in fact, is what it means to *know* God. This is *real* religion: *not* selfish preoccupation with one's own wishes *but* active participation in life, carrying out God's covenant will.

But the son, a selfish, heartless oppressor! He was a typical tyrant with no concern for anybody but himself.

In the final part of his impassioned philippic (vv. 18–19), Jeremiah declares that when the godless despot dies no one will grieve, for everybody will be glad he is dead. Furthermore, he will not be given an honorable burial such as any decent person ought to have, to say nothing of a king, but rather will be dragged outside Jerusalem like a donkey to the city dump and left on the ground to be fed on by the vultures and to fertilize the soil. No modern reader can begin to imagine the horror

such a fate would hold for the ancient Semite!

The exclamations *Ah my brother! Ah sister! Ah lord! Ah his majesty!* are cries of lamentation, addressed by the mourners to each other at the time of death, when mourning rites were observed. M. J. Dahood makes *lord* mean "father" (as head of the house), and by means of a slight emendation (*horah* for *hodah;* "r" and "d" look much alike in Hebrew) gets "mother" out of *his majesty.* He further observes that all of these terms could aptly apply to Jehoiakim, for the king was father, mother, brother, and sister to his subjects.[86]

As to the precise fulfillment of the prophecy in v. 19, scholars are uncertain, largely because of the statement made in 2 Kings 24:6. Peake shows pretty conclusively that 2 Kings 24:6 does not necessarily mean that Jehoiakim was given a place in the royal tombs. He also demonstrates to this writer's satisfaction that the prediction in 22:19 and 36:30 was fulfilled. Otherwise it would have been suppressed (p. 256).

It is doubtful that Jeremiah ever uttered words more scorching and scathing than those which he addressed to a young king who was more concerned about constructing a palace for himself than he was about carrying out the purpose of God for his people. One is amazed at both the prophet's capacity for righteous indignation and at his raw courage. We can be sure that he incurred the hatred of the monarch. The marvel is that Jehoiakim failed to have him killed. The fact that Jeremiah got off alive is likely a tribute to his force and influence. Another prophet was not so fortunate in his clash with the king (26:20–23).

6. A Dirge over Jerusalem's Disaster (22:20–23)

20 "Go up to Lebanon, and cry out,
    and lift up your voice in Bashan;
  cry from Abarim,
    for all your lovers are destroyed.

84 *The Prophetic Faith* (New York: Harper & Row, 1960), p. 174.

85 J. Pedersen, *Israel: Its Life and Culture,* trans. Annie I. Fausbøll (Copenhagen: Bonner Og Korch, 1953), III–IV, 389 ff.; cf. Cunliffe-Jones, Hopper, et. al.

86 *Catholic Biblical Quarterly,* 23, 1961, 462–464.

21 I spoke to you in your prosperity,
 but you said, 'I will not listen.'
This has been your way from your youth,
 that you have not obeyed my voice.
22 The wind shall shepherd all your shepherds,
 and your lovers shall go into captivity;
then you will be ashamed and confounded
 because of all your wickedness.
23 O inhabitant of Lebanon,
 nested among the cedars,
how you will groan when pangs come upon
 you,
 pain as of a woman in travail!"

This is a poignant lament over Jerusalem, a deeply loved but disobedient city. The date is about 598, close to the time of the capture of the city and the first Babylonian captivity. Since Jehoiakim died prior to the siege and since his son Jehoiachin succeeded to the throne for a short time before deportation to Babylon, the passage is appropriately placed—after the invective against Jehoiakim and before the oracles concerning Jehoiachin.

Personified as a woman, Jerusalem is told to go up in the mountains and mourn over her fate. The reason for the terrible tragedy about to befall her is her stubborn refusal to listen to the voice of God. She who is perched upon the elevation among the Lebanese cedars (i.e., the buildings made from them) will experience great pain when the calamity comes, *pain as of a woman in travail.*

There is a word play in v. 22, picked up somewhat by the RSV translation. The *wind* which the people have held in contempt (5:13) will *shepherd* their *shepherds* (their *lovers*, their leaders) and will blow them into captivity. This actually happened a little later, in early 597.

7. *Oracles Against Jehoiachin* (22:24–30)

24 "As I live, says the LORD, though Coniah the son of Jehoiakim, king of Judah, were the signet ring on my right hand, yet I would tear you off 25 and give you into the hand of those who seek your life, into the hand of those of whom you are afraid, even into the hand of Nebuchadrezzar king of Babylon and into the hand of the Chaldeans. 26 I will hurl you and the mother who bore you into another country, where you were not born, and there you shall

die. 27 But to the land to which they will long to return, there they shall not return."
28 Is this man Coniah a despised, broken pot,
 a vessel no one cares for?
Why are he and his children hurled and
 cast
 into a land which they do not know?
29 O land, land, land,
 hear the word of the LORD!
30 Thus says the LORD:
"Write this man down as childless,
 a man who shall not succeed in his days;
for none of his offspring shall succeed
 in sitting on the throne of David,
 and ruling again in Judah."

We have two prophecies from Jeremiah which pertain to Jehoiachin. The first (vv. 24–27) was probably composed shortly after his capitulation; the second (vv. 28–30), soon after his deportation. The first oracle states in strong terms, but with deep pathos, that the king and his mother are going to be hurled into captivity and that they will never return. The second oracle declares that no descendant of Jehoiachin will sit on David's throne. Jehoiachin has been stripped of all rights as far as the kingship is concerned. This is the meaning of the word rendered *childless.* It is a technical term, signifying "deprived of all honor," "entered as childless in the census list." Jehoiachin actually had seven sons (1 Chron. 3:17–18) and is named as one of the ancestors of Jesus (Matt. 1:11 f.).

8. *False Rulers and a True Ruler* (23:1–8)

1 "Woe to the shepherds who destroy and scatter the sheep of my pasture!" says the LORD. 2 Therefore thus says the LORD, the God of Israel, concerning the shepherds who care for my people: "You have scattered my flock, and have driven them away, and you have not attended to them. Behold, I will attend to you for your evil doings, says the LORD. 3 Then I will gather the remnant of my flock out of all the countries where I have driven them, and I will bring them back to their fold, and they shall be fruitful and multiply. 4 I will set shepherds over them who will care for them, and they shall fear no more, nor be dismayed, neither shall any be missing, says the LORD.

5 "Behold, the days are coming, says the LORD, when I will raise up for David a righteous Branch, and he shall reign as king and deal wisely, and shall execute justice and right-

eousness in the land. [6] In his days Judah will be saved, and Israel will dwell securely. And this is the name by which he will be called: 'The LORD is our righteousness.'

[7] "Therefore, behold, the days are coming, says the LORD, when men shall no longer say, 'As the LORD lives who brought up the people of Israel out of the land of Egypt,' [8] but 'As the LORD lives who brought up and led the descendants of the house of Israel out of the north country and out of all the countries where he had driven them.' Then they shall dwell in their own land."

There is a close connection between this passage and the one preceding it in that it, too, refers to the *shepherds* or rulers of Judah (cf. 22:22). In fact, it brings the entire section on the kings of the country to a strong climax. Since there have been oracles dealing with Josiah (by indirection), Jehoahaz, Jehoiakim, and Jehoiachin, we would expect at the end an oracle concerning Zedekiah, the last king of Judah.

We have this oracle in 23:1–8. It is true that Zedekiah is not referred to directly by name. Yet there is a veiled allusion to him in the play on his name in v. 6. This indirectness is in harmony with Jeremiah's general policy in his relations with Zedekiah. He knew that Zedekiah had a real respect for him. He was aware that the king was a good man but at the same time a rather weak man. He recognized that the bad government the people were getting under his administration was largely the result of the immaturity and aggressive activity of the governmental officials. Much of this, Jeremiah realized, was occasioned by Zedekiah's vacillation and indecision. Yet the prophet had a great deal of pity for the king and refrained from launching a polemic against him. His vigorous attack was leveled at the *shepherds*, Zedekiah's associates. This probably explains the absence of any direct reference to the king by name in this passage.

Though there has been serious question among some scholars concerning the authenticity of the passage or some part thereof, the present writer finds no valid reason for taking any portion of it from Jeremiah. In this position he is supported by men like Giesebrecht, Rothstein, Cornill, Peake, Cunliffe-Jones, Eissfeldt, von Rad, Couturier, Weiser, Bright (except for vv. 7–8), and others.

The readers will recognize that in the RSV the entire passage is in prose. Bright renders vv. 5–6 as poetry (p. 140; cf. Weiser, *Jeremia*, p. 202). Volz and Condamin discover poetry in vv. 1–4, and recently Holladay has defended the poetic structure of these verses and offered a strophic analysis of them.[87] At the present stage of study, it seems safe to say that 23:1–8 is a blend of poetry and prose, with poetry predominating.

We date the prophecy early in Zedekiah's reign (some think that it was read at his coronation). Hopes centering around his administration were running high. With penetrating insight and forthright candor, Jeremiah stated that the hopes of the people would never be realized in Zedekiah, but only in an ideal king yet to come.

The prophecy falls into three parts: vv. 1–4, 5–6, and 7–8. The dominant note is hope, in contrast to that of doom, which prevails up to this point in the complex on the kings. This assurance about the future builds up in crescendo fashion in three stages. From the literary standpoint, there is movement from a prophecy of disaster to oracles of salvation.

Verses 1–4 contain a proclamation of retribution for the false *shepherds* and a promise of restoration of God's *flock* to their own land. The prophet starts with a sharp denunciation of the *shepherds* (political leaders), who have betrayed the trust placed in them (cf. Ezek. 34: 1 ff.). They have reversed their role. Instead of leading the sheep to the pasture or fold, they have scattered them abroad. They must suffer for their delinquency in their responsibility. Since they have not *attended to* (taken care of) God's flock, God will *attend to* (take care of) them for their *evil doings*.

[87] "The Recovery of the Poetic Passages of Jeremiah," JBL, 85, 1966, 420–424.

Following the pronouncement of judgment upon the false shepherds is God's promise. He will restore a *remnant* of his *flock* and will raise up true *shepherds* to take care of that remnant. The remnant will be the saving factor in his program for the future.

Note that, in keeping with his theology of history, the prophet continues to preserve the polarity between God's activity and man's responsibility: *You have scattered my flock, and have driven them away*, v. 2; *I have driven them*, v. 3.

In vv. 5-6 there is a prophecy concerning the messianic king. He is spoken of as *a righteous Branch* (better, "Shoot"). This Shoot will spring up from the stump of a tree, or a root running out from that stump (cf. Isa. 11:1; 53:2), and will become, a stately tree, a great ruler. The king will *deal wisely* (will have the insight and ability to carry through to effective conclusion that which he undertakes) and will *execute justice and righteousness* (will properly discharge covenantal obligations). Under his rule, both Judahites and Israelites will experience security and salvation, and they will call his name *The Lord is our righteousness* (the basis of our acceptability and acceptance before God; a deft play on "Zedekiah"). In short, the righteous ruler of the future will succeed in his service to God and men, will make possible salvation and security, and will completely carry out all covenant stipulations in his relationship with God's people as king.

The oracle closes with a prediction of a new Exodus which will so outshine the first in splendor that the people will no longer take oaths by the first but only by the second. In other words, the first will be completely eclipsed in glory and significance by the second (vv. 7-8; cf. 16: 14-15).

The present writer believes that Weiser is correct in his position that Jeremiah's presentation of this picture of the wonder of the new Exodus in contrast to the old marks a new epoch in salvation-history. Jeremiah is moving toward the new covenant concept. He perceives that in the experience of suffering in exile God is testing and refining his people and that through it all his purpose of grace will be carried forward, eventuating in a second Exodus which will so far surpass the first that the first will scarcely be remembered.

The complex has now come full circle: beginning and ending with a prophecy to Zedekiah (21:3 ff.; 23:1 ff.). It has a distinctive character in that it is the only portion of the book containing a collection of Jeremiah's utterances to and about the Davidic kings. It gives strong expression to the prophet's conviction that through Nebuchadnezzar God was going to bring about tremendous changes in the national and international situation. It comes to a powerful climax and close on the note of hope. Through the darkness Jeremiah saw a light shining. God was in charge. As he read history in the light of God's purpose, he was certain that God would win in the end.

X. The Polemic Against the Prophets (23:9-40)

Jeremiah was a sensitive, poetic spirit. By birth and background he was a priest. He was a prophet by divine appointment. He had many trials during his ministry as God's messenger. Doubtless one of the greatest was the necessity of combating the evil influence of both the priests and the prophets of his day. He said little about the priests but a very great deal against the prophets, more in fact than any other canonical prophet.

This ecclesiastical conflict began early in his career and continued to the end (cf. 2:8; 5:13,30 f.; 6:13-14; 8:10-12; 14: 13-15; 18:18-23; 26:8,11,16; 27—29; 23: 9-40). It resulted in an open clash in 594-593 B.C., in connection with the proposed revolt against Babylon and all the activity and agitation in relation to it in Jerusalem at that time (chs. 27—28).

Though the date of 23:9-40 is controversial and uncertain, it is the present writer's judgment that this remarkable collection of utterances comes from the late period of the prophet's career and is best viewed in the context of the dramatic situation described in chapters 27—28 (cf. Volz, Leslie, Bright, Fohrer, *et al.;* contra Rudolph).

More important than the date is the character of the collection. Says Leslie: "Nowhere in the Old Testament is the true nature of prophecy expounded with greater insight than in this section" (p. 324). This is the case. We have here the most penetrating analysis of true and false prophecy to be found in the Bible.

In form, the polemic is a combination of poetry and prose. Bright renders all of it as poetry except vv. 25–27 and 30–40. This fits in with the present trend (cf. Notscher, Rudolph, Weiser, *et al.*). In his article, "The Recovery of Poetic Passages of Jeremiah," W. L. Holladay makes a case for taking all of vv. 25–32 as poetry (see fn. 87).

1. Deep Distress (23.9–12)

9 Concerning the prophets:
My heart is broken within me,
    all my bones shake;
I am like a drunken man,
    like a man overcome by wine,
because of the LORD
    and because of his holy words.
10 For the land is full of adulterers;
    because of the curse the land mourns,
    and the pastures of the wilderness are
        dried up.
Their course is evil,
    and their might is not right.
11 "Both prophet and priest are ungodly;
    even in my house I have found their
        wickedness,
                        says the LORD.
12 Therefore their way shall be to them
    like slippery paths in the darkness,
    into which they shall be driven and fall;
for I will bring evil upon them
    in the year of their punishment,
                        says the LORD.

We have found it to be true of Jeremiah that he suffers pain, that he shares the pain of the people and the pain of God, and that he speaks freely about his pain. He begins the section *concerning the prophets* with a graphic expression of inner pain.

What is it that has *broken* his *heart,* caused his *bones* to *shake,* and made him feel or act *like a man overcome by wine?* Why all the anguish? The answer comes in v. 9b. Jeremiah is in agony because of his realization of the awfulness of sin and because of the revelation of God's antagonism to it—the *holy words* of denunciation and doom which he must utter (cf. 4:19–22; 5:1–5, 30–31; 9:2 ff.).

He becomes more specific in vv. 10–11. He is undergoing terrible inner distress because of the general corruption that is so widespread and because of the tragic consequences to which it will inevitably lead. The bitterest part of it all is that the priests and the prophets share and support that corruption.

The question is often raised as to whether the allusion in v. 10 is spiritual adultery or to physical adultery. Probably both, for the one tended to promote the other. Baalism was a near-deification of sex. Sacred prostitution was a part of its ritual of worship.

In verse 11 Jeremiah states that the priests and prophets are polluting the Temple, possibly by pagan or semi-pagan practices. In short, they are corrupt, lacking in that "aloofness of character which creates power to touch national life healingly" (Morgan, p. 131). Such men will discover that they will be propelled by their transgressions and inner compulsions down a slippery path that will lead into ever-deepening darkness and distress until ultimately they fall (v. 12).

2. A Sharp Distinction (23:13–15)

13 In the prophets of Samaria
        I saw an unsavory thing:
    they prophesied by Baal
        and led my people Israel astray.
14 But in the prophets of Jerusalem
        I have seen a horrible thing:
    they commit adultery and walk in lies;
        they strengthen the hands of evildoers,
        so that no one turns from his wickedness;
    all of them have become like Sodom to me,
        and its inhabitants like Gomorrah."

15 Therefore thus says the LORD of hosts concerning the prophets:

"Behold, I will feed them with wormwood,
and give them poisoned water to drink;
for from the prophets of Jerusalem
ungodliness has gone forth into all the land."

In each of the four subsections there is an indictment followed by a pronouncement of judgment. The latter is introduced by the word "therefore" (vv. 12,15,30, 39).

Here the indictment begins with a comparison of the prophets of Israel and the prophets of Judah, to the disadvantage of the latter. *The prophets of Samaria* (Israel) had *prophesied by Baal,* a false god —*an unsavory thing! The prophets of Jerusalem* (Judah) have been prophesying by the true God, but in a false way—*a horrible thing!* Hence their guilt is greater. Jeremiah spells out what he means: *they commit adultery and walk in lies* (especially the big lie about unconditional divine protection). The contrast with the prophets of Israel would indicate that *adultery* here is primarily physical.

The prophets' way of life is an insult and a hindrance to true worship. Lacking in moral character, they are also lacking in the capacity for moral leadership. Instead of directing the people into a deeper fellowship with God and a more ethical relationship with their fellowmen,

*they strengthen the hand of evildoers,
so that no one turns from his wickedness.*

Here is the Hebrew *shub* again, so fundamental to Jeremiah's prophetic vocabulary. As he saw it, the central need of man is a crucial turning from the way of wickedness to a right relationship with God, and the supreme responsibility of true prophecy is to seek to bring about that turning. Jeremiah believed in the importance of repentance.

Because *the prophets of Jerusalem* are false and the prophetic spirit has been poisoned, out of this central fountain of falseness *ungodliness has gone forth into all the land.* All of the people of the city and the country *have become like Sodom* and *Gomorrah*—i.e., morally and spiritually corrupt. A poisoned prophetic spirit gradually poisons the life of a nation. Retribution is inevitable. Here the judgment is set forth under two metaphors: *wormwood* (something very bitter) and *poisoned water* (something deadly).

3. An Incisive Indictment (23:16–32)

16 Thus says the LORD of hosts: "Do not listen to the words of the prophets who prophesy to you, filling you with vain hopes; they speak visions of their own minds, not from the mouth of the LORD. 17 They say continually to those who despise the word of the LORD, 'It shall be well with you'; and to every one who stubbornly follows his own heart, they say, 'No evil shall come upon you.'"

18 For who among them has stood in the council of the LORD
to perceive and to hear his word,
or who has given heed to his word and listened?

19 Behold, the storm of the LORD!
Wrath has gone forth,
a whirling tempest;
it will burst upon the head of the wicked.

20 The anger of the LORD will not turn back
until he has executed and accomplished
the intents of his mind.
In the latter days you will understand it clearly.

21 "I did not send the prophets,
yet they ran;
I did not speak to them,
yet they prophesied.

22 But if they had stood in my council,
then they would have proclaimed my words to my people,
and they would have turned them from their evil way,
and from the evil of their doings.

23 "Am I a God at hand, says the LORD, and not a God afar off? 24 Can a man hide himself in secret places so that I cannot see him? says the LORD. Do I not fill heaven and earth? says the LORD. 25 I have heard what the prophets have said who prophesy lies in my name, saying, 'I have dreamed, I have dreamed!' 26 How long shall there be lies in the heart of the prophets who prophesy lies, and who prophesy the deceit of their own heart, 27 who think to make my people forget my name by their dreams which they tell one another, even as their fathers forgot my name for Baal? 28 Let the prophet who has a dream tell the dream, but let him who has my word speak my

word faithfully. What has straw in common with wheat? says the LORD. 29 Is not my word like fire, says the LORD, and like a hammer which breaks the rock in pieces? 30 Therefore, behold, I am against the prophets, says the LORD, who steal my words from one another. 31 Behold, I am against the prophets, says the LORD, who use their tongues and say, 'Says the LORD.' 32 Behold, I am against those who prophesy lying dreams, says the LORD, and who tell them and lead my people astray by their lies and their recklessness, when I did not send them or charge them; so they do not profit this people at all, says the LORD.

Lacking in moral character and in the capacity for moral leadership, the popular prophets are also lacking in an authentic message. Their message is devoid of moral content or challenge. Hence it is the word of man and not the word of God. It originates in the human cranium—or subconscious—and not in the council of the Lord.

This is by far the most important and illuminating part of this polemic. It consists of five parts: vv. 16–17,18–20,21–22, 23–24, and 25–32.

Jeremiah starts his indictment by saying that the prophets of the day preach peace and prosperity rather than punishment. They proclaim to the people "All is well" (*shalom*, peace),[88] regardless of the condition of their hearts or the tenor of their lives. They feed the people on *vain* (empty, baseless) *hopes.* They fill their hearts with *visions of their own minds* self-induced "revelations," containing much wishful thinking. To *those who despise the* (true) *word of the Lord—* such as Jeremiah delivers—*they say continually,* "Everything is in order," and *to everyone who stubbornly follows his own heart* (the set of his will against God's will), *they say, 'No evil shall come upon you.'* They tailor their sermons to fit their desires and the desires of their listeners (vv. 16–17).

The root of the trouble is that they have not been *in the council of the Lord.* Had they been there, they would have per-

ceived what the true word of the Lord is and would be proclaiming it. They would know that for such a situation as that in which they serve the word of the Lord would have to be a word of judgment. The essence of that word is vividly depicted in vv. 19–20. But since the pseudo-prophets have not stood in the council of the Lord and therefore do not know what the true word of the Lord is, they palm off on the people peace-oracles, which pander to them in their passions (vv. 18–20).

The council of the Lord is a forceful phrase, embodying a profound concept. God is portrayed as a great King, surrounded by his council or court. The members of the council are his intimate associates and servants who do his bidding (cf. 1 Kings 22:19–22; Amos 3:7; Isa. 6; Psalms 82:1; 89:7; Job 1–2; 15:8).

True prophets are represented as standing in the court of the King. They have a dynamic communion with him and a direct commission from him. They get *his word* from him and go forth as faithful messengers to deliver that word. The word may involve a reproach and a pronouncement of judgment. It may contain a proclamation of salvation. They often begin the message (word) with the "messenger formula": "Thus says (lit., 'has said') the Lord."

With slight variations, vv. 19–20 also appear in 30:23–24. On the assumption that they interrupt the flow of thought, some scholars delete them from the discourse on the prophets. But it seems to this writer that these verses fit the context quite well. They tie in with v. 18 and plainly indicate that if the prophets of the day were in close relation with God they would know that the need of the hour and the true word of God for the hour was not a message devoid of moral character or criticism, but a message that would cut and condemn and convict—in order to save.

But, sad to say, such is not the case (vv. 21–22). These men are not in the council of the Lord because they have no divine call, and are not therefore under any sense of divine constraint. It is no surprise that they preach as they do, or that their preaching has the effect it has. Yet it could have been so different. Had they had a true relationship with God and a true message from God, *then,* says the Lord, *they would have proclaimed my words to my people, and they would have turned them from their evil way.* In short, prophetic preaching of the right sort has transforming power.

The presence of true, God-called, committed, courageous prophets among God's people is a token of his love for them. Sad is the day when the sun goes down on the prophets in any land—including our own —and when there is "no vision" (no true prophetic perception, Mic. 3:6 f.). For "where there is no vision (no prophetic perception leading to ethical transformation), the people perish" (Prov. 29:18, KJV).

Verses 23–24 stand out rather sharply. The connection with the context is not too obvious but nonetheless real. The first two questions expect a negative answer (vv. 23–24a). The third question requires an affirmative answer (v. 24b).

What is the prophet saying here? The true God, his God, the God of the covenant faith, is not a little local god, whose presence, purpose, and power are limited to a particular place and people. Nor is he a "next-door-neighbor" sort of deity, with whom one can be quite "chummy" and from whom he can easily escape. But he is a majestic, sovereign God, whose spiritual presence pervades the entire universe. He is *a God at hand*—yes, but also *a God afar off.* He is both immanent and transcendent. Woe to those who presume to go when he has not sent them, to speak when he has not called them, to proclaim as his word to his people a pack of baseless hopes and lies! If they think they can escape encounter with him, they are wrong [89] (cf. Amos 9:2–4; Bright, p. 140: "Can any-

one hide in some hole, and not see him?" v. 24a). This passage is very provocative. It suggests the question: "How big is your God?"

Verses 25–32 bring this subsection and the entire complex to a climax, Jeremiah is still attacking the prophets at the point of the message they proclaim. The crux of what he is saying is that the prophets have no real revelation from God because they have no real relation to him. Since they have no authentic revelation from God, their sermons are either stolen from others or spun out of their own heads. They have dreams and identify these as the word of the Lord.[90] They use the tongue and say, *'Says the Lord'* (oracle an oracle, v. 31; effective wordplay). This means that they seek to simulate inspiration. They use "the particular intonation . . . supposed to be due to supernatural inspiration, and . . . no doubt characteristic of ecstatic speech" (Skinner, p. 193). They employ "the holy whine," "the ministerial voice," as they hand out *their lies* (false ideas about God, religion, and life) and *their recklessness* (better, "their loose talk" or, with Bright, "their mendacious claptrap," v. 32a).

As a consequence of this kind of preaching, *they do not profit the people at all* (v. 32 f.), *lead* them *astray* (v. 32b), and cause them to *forget* God's *name,* i.e., his real character and claims upon them (v. 27a).

A very incisive and suggestive contrast is drawn by the prophet between the word of man and the word of God in vv. 28–29. The word of man is *straw* (chaff); it has no substance and provides no sustenance— a strong wind will blow it away. The word of God is like *wheat,* which gives life; like a *fire,* which consumes anything and everything contrary to God's character and will; and like *a hammer,* that breaks in bits all opposition and smashes any and all illusions and falsehoods in which men place their confidence. The word of the

[89] For two unusual interpretations, see Skinner, pp. 198 f., and Lindblom, p. 334.

[90] On dreams, see I. Mendelsohn, IDB, 1, 868–869.

living God is a dynamic, creative, powerful thing!

4. A Prophetic Discourse (23:33-40)

33 "When one of this people, or a prophet, or a priest asks you, 'What is the burden of the LORD?' you shall say to them, 'You are the burden, and I will cast you off, says the LORD.' 34 And as for the prophet, priest, or one of the people who says, 'The burden of the LORD,' I will punish that man and his household. 35 Thus shall you say, every one to his neighbor and every one to his brother, 'What has the LORD answered?' or 'What has the LORD spoken?' 36 But 'the burden of the LORD' you shall mention no more, for the burden is every man's own word, and you pervert the words of the living God, the LORD of hosts, our God. 37 Thus you shall say to the prophet, 'What has the LORD answered you?' or 'What has the LORD spoken?' 38 But if you say, 'The burden of the LORD,' thus says the LORD, 'Because you have said these words, "The burden of the LORD," when I sent to you, saying, "You shall not say, 'The burden of the LORD,' " 39 therefore, behold, I will surely lift you up and cast you away from my presence, you and the city which I gave to you and your fathers. 40 And I will bring upon you everlasting reproach and perpetual shame, which shall not be forgotten.' "

This discourse revolves around a wordplay. The Hebrew word for *burden* (*massa'*) comes from a verb meaning "lift up or off." The noun literally signifies "a lifting up, a thing lifted off." Thus it can refer either to the lifting of a load (burden) or to the lifting up of the voice (oracle, usually doom-oracle).

Jeremiah's preaching was a bit burdensome and boring to some of the "brethren," it seems. He talked a lot about sin and judgment—he had, in fact, a sizable store of doom-oracles to his credit. So, when they would see him, some began asking, in effect: "What's the *massa'* ('burden') of the Lord today? We know it's got to be a heavy doom-oracle. So what is it this time?" One day, when the question came, Jeremiah turned it on the questioners. With a touch of irony and a deft use of the ambiguity in the term, he replied: "*You* are the *burden* (*massa'*) of the Lord! And he's tired of carrying you and is going to

cast you off!" Recall all the references the prophet had made through the years to God's loving care in bearing his people.

Many scholars believe that vv. 34–40 represent an expansion of the wordplay in v. 33 at a later time and in a different direction. Of these, some hold that there is radical distortion; others, amplification and slight modification. There are other scholars who regard the passage as a prohibition by Jeremiah of the use of the phrase because of its misuse. Because of the sarcastic spirit shown in their reference to *the burden of the Lord*, the people are forbidden to employ the expression at all and are told that the Lord is going to send them into exile.

It is abundantly clear that Jeremiah censured the "false" prophets very strongly (the term false prophet occurs in the LXX, but not in the Hebrew Bible). He was convinced that they were largely responsible for the superficial optimism, the insensitivity to social and ethical issues, and the moral and spiritual corruption so widely prevalent among his countrymen. They were supporters of the established order and the chief obstacle to his preaching.

But how could one tell the difference between a "true" prophet and a "false" prophet? [91] Both spoke in the name of the covenant God. Both spoke with conviction. Both appealed to inspiring experiences to authenticate their preaching. How could Jeremiah *know*? How could the people see the differences? It was not easy, and they were not always sure. There are degrees of falseness and different forms, and some of it may get into all at times, unless great care is exercised.

How can we tell the difference between the two? Because the subject is so impor-

[91] See Skinner, pp. 185–200; Smith, pp. 245–266; Eichrodt, *op. cit.*, pp. 332 ff.; A. S. van der Woude, "Micah in Dispute with the Pseudo-Prophets," *Vetus Testamentum*, 19, 1969, 244–260; also, G. von Rad, "Die falschen Propheten," *ZAW*, 31, 1933; E. F. Siegman, *The False Prophets of the Old Testament*, 1939; G. Quell, *Wahre und falsche Propheten*, 1952; E. Oswald, *Falsche Prophetie in Alten Testament*, 1962; Bruce Vawter, "Introduction to Prophetic Literature," *The Jerome Bible Commentary*, 1968.

tant and relevant, we present, for purposes of self-examination, a list of criteria which may be helpful. It has been compiled from the study of pertinent passages in Jeremiah and from the comments of scholars on those passages.

First, the true prophet has a genuine call from God and a vital personal communion with God, as a consequence of which he comes to have a clear insight into the character of God and his claims upon his people. The false prophet has no such call, fellowship or insight.

Second, the true prophet has a sensitivity to the reality and nature of sin in himself and in society, and is conscientious and courageous in the application of the principles of revealed religion to his own life and to all areas and relationships of life. The false prophet has no such sensitivity to sin or to social and ethical issues, and is often guilty of deliberate sin in his own life.

Third, the true prophet has what one calls "an eye for events," the ability to interpret the signs of the times in the light of God's purpose. The false prophet is blinded by ambition, a greed for gain, a false patriotism, a bad theology—or something else.

Fourth, the true prophet communicates faithfully a fresh, living word of the living God, beamed at the needs of his own contemporary situation. The false prophet deals in unthinking dogmatism, irrelevant generalities, unoriginal discourses, unexamined traditions, and religious cliches.

Fifth, the true prophet makes his prophecies conditional, recognizing that his God is sovereign Lord whose holy will for his people will result in salvation or retribution, depending on the human response. The false prophet makes his prophecies unconditional, regarding God as a deity who is automatically beneficent toward his people.

Sixth, the true prophet is honest and patient, ever seeking the truth, willing to weigh evidence and respect the views of others. The false prophet sees only one side and knows he is always right.

Seventh, the true prophet is motivated by a loyal love for God and men, and is propelled by an inner constraint from God's Spirit. The false prophet is driven by a desire for position or possessions or by the urge to talk.

Eighth, the true prophet is vindicated by events. The false prophet is proved to be a liar. But this takes time. And the way of the true prophet can be hard.

We have to admit that there is a problem in distinguishing the true prophet from the false prophet. The distinction is often elusive. There is no external criterion—title, office, ecstatic behavior, or forms of expression and communication. The solution of the problem lies partly in the conduct of the man and the content of his message, but primarily in a sense of divine constraint, the deep consciousness of having true insight into the will of God for the present situation. The true "word" from the Lord has a self-authenticating power which is difficult to resist by one who gives it a fair hearing.

To conclude, for the prophet himself and for the people, the true prophet is recognized by a right relationship with God. When the people of God have the Spirit of God within them, they are enabled to recognize the truth of God and those who "are of the truth."

XI. The Two Baskets of Figs (24:1–10)

This passage is of great importance because it discloses the strength of Jeremiah's faith in God and the depth of his insight into God's redemptive purpose. It also indicates the ground and direction of his hope for the future.

Obviously autobiographical in form (vv. 1,3,4), the chapter records an incident which occurred in 597 B.C. or shortly thereafter. At that time there were two groups of Judahites: those in Palestine and those in exile. The more influential and capable people had been carried off to Babylon by Nebuchadnezzar. Those left behind, for the most part, were thought of as a lower class and caliber of people. Inexperienced in politics and immature in religion, they were congratulating themselves that *they* were the remnant who had survived the judgment and had been given the land by God himself (cf. 2 Kings 24:10–17; Ezek. 11:3,5; 33:23–29). As for the exiles, *they* were terrible sinners—good riddance!

Possibly it was the summer of 597. People were bringing their figs to the city. Jeremiah saw two baskets of them, and they became the medium of revelation to him.

1. The Prophet's Experience (24:1–3)

¹ After Nebuchadrezzar king of Babylon had taken into exile from Jerusalem Jeconiah the son of Jehoiakim, king of Judah, together with the princes of Judah, the craftsmen, and the smiths, and had brought them to Babylon, the LORD showed me this vision: Behold, two baskets of figs placed before the temple of the LORD. ² One basket had very good figs, like first-ripe figs, but the other basket had very bad figs, so bad that they could not be eaten. ³ And the LORD said to me, "What do you see, Jeremiah?" I said, "Figs, the good figs very good, and the bad figs very bad, so bad that they cannot be eaten."

While meditating upon the sight and situation before him, the prophet had a profound spiritual experience. The form which the record of the experience took is reminiscent of 1:11–16 and of the didactic method used in the wisdom schools (cf. Amos 7:1–9; 8:1–3). What about the nature of the experience described? Is it an ecstatic vision (Rudolph, Weiser), or a literary invention (Welch), or a symbolic perception (Leslie, Lindblom)?

In the opinion of the present writer, it is a symbolic perception (see comment on 1:11–16). This means that Jeremiah actually saw *two baskets of figs placed before the temple of the Lord.* As he reflected upon what he saw—a basket of delicious, edible figs and a basket of rotting figs, fit only for animal consumption or casting aside—he may have fallen into a trance. In any case, the ordinary objects became the medium of an extraordinary revelation.

The usual time for gathering figs in Palestine is August. Some trees produce two crops: one in June and another later. *First-ripe figs* are a special delicacy.

The reference to the position of the baskets is crucial. It indicates that the central issue in the experience is religious. Penna's [92] conjecture is interesting: the allusion to *first-ripe figs* is suggestive of a firstfruit offering (Deut. 26:2–11); since the figs in one basket are rotting, the implication is that the Temple is not inviolable and therefore is no guarantee of security for those remaining in the land.

It is interesting to observe that some of Jeremiah's most penetrating insights came through the commonplace: a blossoming almond branch, a boiling pot, a potter's work, an ox-yoke, the observation of birds—and here, two baskets of figs. This connection of God with the commonplace reminds us of our Lord. He saw evidence of his reality and activity everywhere—in flowers, trees, birds, children, men.

2. The Explanation of the Experience (24: 4–10)

⁴ Then the word of the LORD came to me: ⁵ "Thus says the LORD, the God of Israel: Like these good figs, so I will regard as good the exiles from Judah, whom I have sent away from this place to the land of the Chaldeans. ⁶ I will set my eyes upon them for good, and I will bring them back to this land. I will build them up, and not tear them down; I will plant them, and not uproot them. ⁷ I will give them a heart to know that I am the LORD; and they shall be my people and I will be their God, for they shall return to me with their whole heart.

⁸ "But thus says the LORD: Like the bad figs which are so bad they cannot be eaten, so will I treat Zedekiah the king of Judah, his princes, the remnant of Jerusalem who remain in this land, and those who dwell in the land of Egypt. ⁹ I will make them a horror to all the kingdoms of the earth, to be a reproach, a byword, a taunt, and a curse in all the places where I shall drive them. ¹⁰ And I will send sword, famine, and pestilence upon them, until they shall be utterly destroyed from the land which I gave to them and their fathers."

92 A. Penna, *Geremia* (Rome: LSB, 1954), *in loc.*

The remainder of the passage provides the interpretation of the prophet's experience. The *good figs* represent *the exiles* in Babylon (vv. 4–7). God looks upon them with friendly eyes. They are the hope of true religion in the future. They have endured the shock of deportation. In the main, they have been stripped of their false securities and have had their illusions shattered. They are undergoing the discipline of divine love. Some will respond to their suffering in a right spirit. They will *return* to God *with their whole heart.* There will be a total turnabout and a complete coming back to God at the center of their beings. God will *give* them *a heart to know* him (here grace is at work; cf. 31:33–34; 33:38–41; Ezek. 36:26–28).

The exiles will come into this dynamic, personal, experiential relationship with God without the usual means of grace— temple, priesthood, ritual—and through them, as they respond, God will carry forward his purpose of salvation. In them is centered the responsibility and hope of a continuing covenant community of the future and with a future: *they shall be my people, and I will be their God.*

Observe how the verbs *build, plant, tear down,* and *uproot* are employed here, as so often in Jeremiah, especially in the prose portions of the prophecy (cf. 1:10).

The *bad figs* symbolize the self-righteous *remnant* left in Judah and the Jews living in Egypt (vv. 8–10). The Judahites, in particular, are characterized by a spirit of arrogant superiority, by scorn for their less fortunate fellow countrymen, and by a superstitious reliance on such sanctified shams as the inviolability of city and Temple and the efficacy of empty formalistic worship. Some are even engaging in rank paganism (cf. Ezek. 8:5 ff.).

The Jews in Egypt were likely Judeans who as active members of the pro-Egyptian party had sought refuge in that land in 609, or 601, or 597.

The strong language of vv. 9–10 is used primarily to shatter the self-complacency of the Judahites and stab them awake to the realities in their situation.

Three things in chapter 24 strike the writer with unusual force. The first is the prophet's conviction that God can be known anywhere—Babylon or Jerusalem —without the usual religious symbols and supports, if he is sought with all the heart (cf. 29:13). The second is Jeremiah's release of his message of hope in the context of a tremendous tragedy. The third is his identification of his hope for the future of biblical faith with the exiles, a point of view which will characterize his preaching from this time forward (cf. chs. 29, 30–33).

His insight was vindicated by historical event. Much that is finest and best in the Old Testament emerged from the Exile and through the exiles. Eventually some of the captives came back to their home country. God restored them. They rebuilt the Temple and reestablished a worshiping community. In the hearts of some of them there was a true knowledge of God which included a broad vision of their world mission as God's people and a deep longing for the coming of the Messiah. In the fullness of God's time, he came!

XII. The Cup of the Wine of God's Wrath (25:1–38)

The battle of Carchemish (605 B.C.) was a pivotal experience in the life of Judah and in the ministry of Jeremiah. Nebuchadnezzar's decisive victory over the Egyptians meant that Babylon was now potential master of the Mediterranean world. It also meant that Jeremiah's forecasts of the coming of the foe from the north could now be easily and quickly fulfilled. It is not surprising that a new note of urgency entered the prophet's preaching at this point. The crisis was at hand. It was now or never. The rebels must repent!

1. A Summation and a Proclamation (25: 1–14)

¹ **The word that came to Jeremiah concerning all the people of Judah, in the fourth year**

of Jehoiakim the son of Josiah, king of Judah (that was the first year of Nebuchadrezzar king of Babylon), ² which Jeremiah the prophet spoke to all the people of Judah and all the inhabitants of Jerusalem: ³ For twenty-three years, from the thirteenth year of Josiah the son of Amon, king of Judah, to this day, the word of the LORD has come to me, and I have spoken persistently to you, but you have not listened. ⁴ You have neither listened nor inclined your ears to hear, although the LORD persistently sent to you all his servants the prophets, ⁵ saying, 'Turn now, every one of you, from his evil way and wrong doings, and dwell upon the land which the LORD has given to you and your fathers from of old and for ever; ⁶ do not go after other gods to serve and worship them, or provoke me to anger with the work of your hands. Then I will do you no harm.' ⁷ Yet you have not listened to me, says the LORD, that you might provoke me to anger with the work of your hands to your own harm.

⁸ "Therefore thus says the LORD of hosts: Because you have not obeyed my words, ⁹ behold, I will send for all the tribes of the north, says the LORD, and for Nebuchadrezzar the king of Babylon, my servant, and I will bring them against this land and its inhabitants, and against all these nations round about; I will utterly destroy them, and make them a horror, a hissing, and an everlasting reproach. ¹⁰ Moreover, I will banish from them the voice of mirth and the voice of gladness, the voice of the bridegroom and the voice of the bride, the grinding of the millstones and the light of the lamp. ¹¹ This whole land shall become a ruin and a waste, and these nations shall serve the king of Babylon seventy years. ¹² Then after seventy years are completed, I will punish the king of Babylon and that nation, the land of the Chaldeans, for their iniquity, says the LORD, making the land an everlasting waste. ¹³ I will bring upon that land all the words which I have uttered against it, everything written in this book, which Jeremiah prophesied against all the nations. ¹⁴ For many nations and great kings shall make slaves even of them; and I will recompense them according to their deeds and the work of their hands."

This is a prophecy of judgment in the characteristic style of Jeremiah's prose sermons (cf. 7:1 ff.; 18:1 ff.; 19:1 ff.). The introductory formula is a bit different. It adds a chronological note to the effect that *the word* came to the prophet *in the fourth year of Jehoiakim king of Judah* and in *the first year of Nebuchadrezzar king*

of Babylon. It also indicates that *the word* was delivered to *all of the people of Judah and all the inhabitants of Jerusalem.* Since Nebuchadnezzar became king in July or August, 605, the occasion for the proclamation could have been the fall festival of that year.

The summation begins with v. 3 and goes through v. 7. It is in the form of a reproach. Speaking from a heart filled with loving compassion and righteous indignation, Jeremiah reminds the people that for 23 years he has faithfully communicated *the word of the Lord* to them. Yet they have stubbornly refused to give heed to it. He has joined his voice to the voices of other God-called prophets in persistently urging upon them the absolute necessity of that fundamental turning so essential to a secure abiding in their God-given land. The only response has been constant disobedience and continual idolatry.

Verses 8–14 contain a proclamation of disaster. This also has been integral to the preaching of Jeremiah through the years. But there are new elements which make the proclamation distinctive. First, the prophet identifies Nebuchadnezzar and his legions as the foe from the north. Second, he predicts that the Babylonian supremacy will last for *seventy years* (cf. 29:10; Zech. 1:12; 2 Chron. 36:21; Dan. 9:2). Third, he states that in time God will bring judgment upon the Babylonians. Fourth, mention is made of a *book.*

In v. 9 Nebuchadnezzar is spoken of by God as *my servant* (cf. 27:6; 43:10). This phrase is omitted from the LXX. The probable reason is that the translators found it to be offensive as the description of a pagan emperor.

This raises a question: In what sense did Jeremiah use the phrase? Z. Zevit has shown that in Hebrew, as in Ugaritic, "servant" can have the technical meaning "vassal" and that the vassal was subject to his liege lord and responsible for placing his army at the service of his lord whenever requested or required.[93] Thus, in using the phrase *my servant*, Jeremiah was not speaking of Nebuchadnezzar as a devout worshiper or servant of Yahweh, but as his vassal, subject to his sovereign will and obligated to provide his army for the carrying out of the sovereign's purpose. This is simply another expression of the prophet's theology of history.

It is pedantic to delete the reference to other *nations* (v. 9) and to change *these nations* to "this nation" (v. 11), as some have done, on the ground that Jeremiah was speaking only of Judah. The prophet had a broad perspective (cf. 1:5; 25:15 ff.; 27:3—11; 46—51).

The allusion to *seventy years* is taken literally by some scholars (e.g., Penna, Whitley, Orr). By others it is treated as a general expression for a lifetime or for two generations.[94]

The mention of *this book* (v. 13), when set in the context of Jeremiah's dictation of his prophecies in 605 (cf. 25:1; 36:1), suggests that the present passage may have been the conclusion to that book (36:4,32; Rudolph, p. 139).

There is a peculiar poignancy in the declaration that the coming calamity will mean the cessation of the sights and sounds of a happy everyday existence (v. 10; cf. 7:34; 16:9; 33:11).

For a treatment of the differences between the Masoretic Text and the LXX in this passage, the reader must be referred to the more technical commentaries (on the insertion of the foreign prophecies after v. 13a by the LXX, see Int.).

2. *The Presentation of the Cup of Wrath to the Nations (25:15-38)*

15 Thus the LORD, the God of Israel, said to me: "Take from my hand this cup of the wine of wrath, and make all the nations to whom I send you drink it. 16 They shall drink and

stagger and be crazed because of the sword which I am sending among them."

17 So I took the cup from the LORD's hand, and made all the nations to whom the Lord sent me drink it: 18 Jerusalem and the cities of Judah, its kings and princes, to make them a desolation and a waste, a hissing and a curse, as at this day; 19 Pharaoh king of Egypt, his servants, his princes, all his people, 20 and all the foreign folk among them; all the kings of the land of Uz and all the kings of the land of the Philistines (Ashkelon, Gaza, Ekron, and the remnant of Ashdod); 21 Edom, Moab, and the sons of Ammon; 22 all the kings of Tyre, all the kings of Sidon, and the kings of the coastland across the sea; 23 Dedan, Tema, Buz, and all who cut the corners of their hair; 24 all the kings of Arabia and all the kings of the mixed tribes that dwell in the desert; 25 all the kings of Zimri, all the kings of Elam, and all the kings of Media; 26 all the kings of the north, far and near, one after another, and all the kingdoms of the world which are on the face of the earth. And after them the king of Babylon shall drink.

27 "Then you shall say to them, 'Thus says the LORD of hosts, the God of Israel: Drink, be drunk and vomit, fall and rise no more, because of the sword which I am sending among you.' 28 "And if they refuse to accept the cup from your hand to drink, then you shall say to them, 'Thus says the LORD of hosts: You must drink! 29 For behold, I begin to work evil at the city which is called by my name, and shall you go unpunished? You shall not go unpunished, for I am summoning a sword against all the inhabitants of the earth, says the LORD of hosts.'

30 "You, therefore, shall prophesy against them all these words, and say to them:

'The LORD will roar from on high,
    and from his holy habitation utter his voice;
he will roar mightily against his fold,
    and shout, like those who tread grapes,
    against all the inhabitants of the earth.
31 The clamor will resound to the ends of the earth,
    for the LORD has an indictment against the nations;
he is entering into judgment with all flesh,
    and the wicked he will put to the sword,
        says the LORD.'
32 "Thus says the LORD of hosts:
Behold, evil is going forth
    from nation to nation,
and a great tempest is stirring
    from the farthest parts of the earth!
33 "And those slain by the LORD on that day shall extend from one end of the earth to the

---

93 "The Use of *Ebedh* in Jeremiah," JBL, 88, 1969, 74–77.

94 For an Assyrian parallel for this usage, see E. Vogt, *Biblica*, 38, 1957, 236; O. Ploger, *Festschrift F. Baumgartel*, 1959, 124–130.

other. They shall not be lamented, or gathered,
or buried; they shall be dung on the surface
of the ground.
34 "Wail, you shepherds, and cry,
    and roll in ashes, you lords of the flock,
for the days of your slaughter and disper-
      sion have come,
    and you shall fall like choice rams.
35 No refuge will remain for the shepherds,
    nor escape for the lords of the flock.
36 Hark, the cry of the shepherds,
    and the wail of the lords of the flock!
For the LORD is despoiling their pasture,
37   and the peaceful folds are devastated,
    because of the fierce anger of the LORD.
38 Like a lion he has left his covert,
    for their land has become a waste
because of the sword of the oppressor,
    and because of his fierce anger."

Though vv. 1–14 are in prose, vv. 15–38
are a combination of prose and poetry.
These verses have been much discussed
and debated and variously dealt with by
scholars (see more detailed commentaries). They relate an experience of the
prophet. In ecstatic vision, Jeremiah is
commanded to take a *cup of the wine of
wrath* from God's *hand* and, as cupbearer,
to present it to particular *nations* that they
may *drink* it and *stagger* like crazy men.
He obeys the order.

What is the significance of this symbolism? The cup of wine represents God's
basic antagonism to the sinfulness of the
nations. The reeling of the nations signifies
the ruin that is coming as divine retribution upon them because of their sin. The
righteous Ruler of the universe will bring
not only Judah but also other nations to
account.

It is possible that Jeremiah originated
this powerful, dreadful image of the cup
of divine wrath (cf. 13:12–14; 49:12;
51:7). If this be the case, here is another example of the creative ability of
this servant of God. The grim figure and
the reality it represented must have caused
horror and anguish in his sensitive soul.

Helmut Ringren advances the view that
the metaphor of the cup of God's wrath
came out of certain ancient cultic prac-

tices.[95] Even if this is true, Jeremiah
brings it into biblical literature, where it is
picked up and used extensively (cf. Hab.
2:16; Ezek. 23:33; Mark 10:39; 14:36;
John 18:11; Rev. 14:10; 16:19).

This is a cup from which we all have to
drink, the cup of the consequences of our
wrong choices. Life places it to our lips,
and its contents can be very bitter—
whether the recipient be a nation or a person.

XIII. Jeremiah and the Religious Leaders (26:1—29:32)

Baruch's "biography" of Jeremiah is an
unusual and exciting work. It is exceedingly significant from both the literary
and the theological standpoints. It has
been referred to as the first biography in
the Old Testament and as the beginning
of a new literary form.

Theologically speaking, it is outstanding.
It relates the story of a man who suffered
great agony in the service of God, a
prophet who walked the way of a cross
because of his commitment to the purpose
of the Lord. Recorded by an eyewitness
and personal friend, that story has profound theological overtones and implications. One of the most far-reaching is
that suffering and the service of God and
man are somehow intertwined: mission
and martyrdom go together. Here there
are foregleams of the Suffering Servant
concept and of the sacrifice on the cross.

As far as the book arrangement is concerned the "biography" begins with chapter 19. Chronologically, it starts with chapter 26. It includes the material in chapters
26—45, with one notable exception, "the
book of consolation" (chs. 30—33). Chapters 26—29 are bound together by a
common cord: the increasing antagonism
between Jeremiah and the religious leaders. This conflict comes out into the open
in the Temple incident (609) and culmi-

---

95 *Svensk exigetish arsbok*, 17, 1952, 19 ff.; cf.
Couturier, *op. cit.*, p 323.

nates in the dramatic clash between the prophet and his colleagues at a Jerusalem caucus (594–593).

1. The Story of the "Temple Sermon" (26: 1–24)

The "temple sermon," one of the greatest in biblical times and of all time, represented, in all probability, Jeremiah's open break with the Deuteronomic reform. In it he trampled upon the patriotism, pet prejudices, and hallowed religious practices of many, perhaps most, of the people.

We are fortunate to possess two versions of this important incident. In chapter 7 the stress is on the sermon itself, as preached by the prophet. Chapter 26 is a biographical account of the experience, giving only the gist of the sermon and majoring on the reception it got and the reaction it provoked. Baruch's special interest centers in the suffering encountered by the prophet in the performance of his God-assigned task.

(1) The Setting of the Sermon (26:1–3)

¹ In the beginning of the reign of Jehoiakim the son of Josiah, king of Judah, this word came from the LORD, ² "Thus says the LORD: Stand in the court of the LORD's house, and speak to all the cities of Judah which come to worship in the house of the LORD all the words that I command you to speak to them; do not hold back a word. ³ It may be they will listen, and every one turn from his evil way, that I may repent of the evil which I intend to do to them because of their evil doings.

The occasion was a religious observance in the accession year of King Jehoiakim. Though it may have been an enthronement festival in the spring of 608, it was most likely the fall festival of September– October, 609 (cf. 7:1 ff.).

The beginning of the reign designates the time between the king's taking the throne and the following New Year, at which time his first regnal year began— hence "accession year." [96]

96 J. Begrich, *Die Chronologie der Konig von Israel und Juda* (Tubingen: Mohr, 1929), pp. 91, 93.

At this time, the *word came from the Lord*. It was a burning, biting word. Jeremiah was commanded to *stand in the court of the Lord's house* and deliver this word—all of it—to *all* the people of *the cities of Judah* who come to the Temple *to worship. Speak . . . all the words that I command you to speak to them; do not hold back a word* (don't leave out a thing!).

There is no contradiction between the command to "stand in the gate of the Lord's house" (7:2) and the command to *stand in the court of the Lord's house* (26:2). The gate led from the outer court to the inner court. The people assembled in the outer court. The position usually occupied by a prophet would be in or near the gate, facing the group gathered in the outer court. Observe the stress on the function of a true prophet. He was God's messenger, commissioned to communicate his message faithfully to the people.

The reason for God's command on this occasion is presented in v. 3: to seek to persuade the people to *turn* from their illusions, their false loves and loyalties, and their sins to a relationship of true devotion to him. This fundamental turning must be done by *every one* of them. God longed to alter his course of action (*repent*) with regard to *the evil* (the retribution bound up with their rebellion) which he was devising for them (vivid participial construction in Heb.).

We note again the polarity between God's activity and man's responsibility. God offers forgiveness, but man must receive it through repentance.

(2) The Substance of the Sermon (26:4– 6)

⁴ You shall say to them, 'Thus says the LORD: If you will not listen to me, to walk in my law which I have set before you, ⁵ and to heed the the words of my servants the prophets whom I send to you urgently, though you have not heeded, ⁶ then I will make this house like Shiloh, and I will make this city a curse for all the nations of the earth.' "

The content of the sermon is presented only in essence here, for the reason already cited. A fuller account of the substance of it is preserved in 7:1 ff.

Succinctly stated, it is simply this. The people are called upon to change their way of life and to commit themselves to God's sovereign will. If they refuse to do this, as they have persistently done, God will destroy the Temple, as Shiloh was destroyed earlier, and will make Jerusalem "a curse word" to all the countries of the earth (i.e., when they wish to pronounce a curse, they will say, "May you become as Jerusalem!").

The divine *law* and the prophetic word are set in parallelism here, as elsewhere. Both were concerned with the articulation of God's will for his people.

(3) The Sequel of the Sermon (26:7-24)

Here Baruch comes to his real concern: the impact the message made and the treatment Jeremiah got.

a. The Determination to Dispense With Jeremiah (26:7-11)

⁷ The priests and the prophets and all the people heard Jeremiah speaking these words in the house of the Lord. ⁸ And when Jeremiah had finished speaking all that the Lord had commanded him to speak to all the people, then the priests and the prophets and all the people laid hold of him, saying, "You shall die! ⁹ Why have you prophesied in the name of the Lord, saying, 'This house shall be like Shiloh, and this city shall be desolate, without inhabitant'?" And all the people gathered about Jeremiah in the house of the Lord.
¹⁰ When the princes of Judah heard these things, they came up from the king's house to the house of the Lord and took their seat in the entry of the New Gate of the house of the Lord. ¹¹ Then the priests and the prophets said to the princes and to all the people, "This man deserves the sentence of death, because he has prophesied against this city, as you have heard with your own ears."

The sermon created quite a commotion, and it is no wonder. It struck at the most cherished dogmas of the day: the people's belief in the inviolability of the Temple and the Holy City and their superstitious trust in the Temple and the Temple worship as a valid source of security.

The "clergy" stirred up a mob scene. They—and others no doubt—began saying, to paraphrase in modern terms: "We don't have to listen to this off-beat preacher from the country. How dare he speak to us as he does! We meet all of the cultic requirements of religion. We are good people, God's elect. Let's stop this subversive heresy. Let's kill the man!"

It is interesting that the LXX calls *the prophets* "false prophets" in vv. 7,8,11,16 and that some translators omit the phrase *and all the people* in the latter part of v. 8: "The priests and the prophets seized (vigorous verb) him, saying, 'You must *surely* die!'" (author's translation). Whether the textual change is justified or not (the case for it is not strong), it becomes increasingly apparent as the story unfolds that the chief agitators in the riot were the prophets and the priests. This recalls a similar scene many years later when the scribes and the Pharisees incited the people to mob fury against our Lord.

The charge against Jeremiah is brought in v. 9. He had prophesied the destruction of the Temple and the city. God had promised the preservation of both. Here was his earthly habitation. How could he demolish the seat of his work and worship? Jeremiah's prediction was a blasphemous lie! He therefore was a false prophet, and the law required that a prophet who prophesied falsely be put to death (Deut. 18:20).

And all the people gathered about Jeremiah in the house of the Lord. They were not shaking the preacher's hand to commend the sermon. The word rendered *gathered about* carries the basic idea of assemble. Often the assembling was for worship. Sometimes it was for launching a military campaign. Fairly frequently, as here, it referred to a coming together with hostile intent. Jeremiah was in deep trouble.

When the governmental personnel (*princes*) heard what was happening—

either through a messenger or because of the noise of the uproar nearby—they came running (v. 10). They disliked this sort of thing, this tumult in the Temple; and they promptly set up court in the area of the New Gate of the Temple (cf. 7:2; 20:2; 2 Kings 15:35). Desiring that the matter be handled legally rather than by "lynching," the prophets and priests brought a formal charge to the court: Jeremiah deserved death because he had prophesied a lie (v. 11). This "lie" was his contradiction of their Zion-theology and their perversion of the covenant concept and Isaiah's preaching.

b. Jeremiah's Self-defense (26:12–15)

12 Then Jeremiah spoke to all the princes and all the people, saying, "The Lord sent me to prophesy against this house and this city all the words you have heard. 13 Now therefore amend your ways and your doings, and obey the voice of the Lord your God, and the Lord will repent of the evil which he has pronounced against you. 14 But as for you, behold, I am in your hands. Do with me as seems good and right to you. 15 Only know for certain that if you put me to death, you will bring innocent blood upon yourselves and upon this city and its inhabitants, for in truth the Lord sent me to you to speak all these words in your ears."

We come to a high and holy moment in the history of biblical faith and of humanity's struggle for freedom. In an extremely tense situation fraught with danger, the prophet retracted nothing but came immediately to grips with the charge: *The Lord* (emphatic) *sent me to prophesy against this house and this city all the words you have heard.* Note that Jeremiah directed his defense to *the princes and . . . the people.*

His next words are immortal: "But *as for me*, behold, I am in your hands (i.e., your power). Do to me what seems good and right to you. Only know *for sure* (emphatic, be absolutely certain; Bright, "Make no mistake about it") that if you *kill* me, truly *innocent blood* you will be bringing upon yourselves, this city, and all its inhabitants, for *in truth* the Lord sent me to you to speak in your ears all these

words" (vv. 14–15, author's translation). What transparent sincerity! What tremendous courage! What total commitment to God's will whatever the cost! One is reminded of the words of Luther at the Diet of Worms.

c. Jeremiah's Deliverance (26:16–24)

16 Then the princes and all the people said to the priests and the prophets, "This man does not deserve the sentence of death, for he has spoken to us in the name of the Lord our God." 17 And certain of the elders of the land arose and spoke to all the assembled people, saying, 18 "Micah of Moresheth prophesied in the days of Hezekiah king of Judah, and said to all the people of Judah: 'Thus says the Lord of hosts,

Zion shall be plowed as a field;
    Jerusalem shall become a heap of ruins,
      and the mountain of the house a wooded height.'
19 Did Hezekiah king of Judah and all Judah put him to death? Did he not fear the Lord and entreat the favor of the Lord, and did not the Lord repent of the evil which he had pronounced against them? But we are about to bring great evil upon ourselves."
20 There was another man who prophesied in the name of the Lord, Uriah the son of Shemaiah from Kiriathjearim. He prophesied against this city and against this land in words like those of Jeremiah. 21 And when King Jehoiakim, with all his warriors and all the princes, heard his words, the king sought to put him to death; but when Uriah heard of it, he was afraid and fled and escaped to Egypt. 22 Then King Jehoiakim sent to Egypt certain men, Elnathan the son of Achbor and others with him, 23 and they fetched Uriah from Egypt and brought him to King Jehoiakim, who slew him with the sword and cast his dead body into the burial place of the common people. 24 But the hand of Ahikam the son of Shaphan was with Jeremiah so that he was not given over to the people to be put to death.

The charge had been brought and the defense made. Now the verdict was given: "No death sentence (a legal term) for this man! For in the name of the Lord our God he has spoken to us" (v. 16, author's translation).

There is a noticeable difference in the attitude of the laity and the clergy on this occasion. The priests and prophets had entrenched interests at stake. The laymen were more free and open. They recognized the ring of reality in what the prophet was saying. Some landed gentry stood up on Jeremiah's behalf and cited the preaching of Micah as a precedent in point. A century earlier, the prophet from Moresheth, a country village, had said essentially the same thing that Jeremiah had said (Mic. 3:12). The people had not put him to death. Instead, King Hezekiah launched a religious reform!

This is a remarkable thing, this quotation from Micah. There is no exact parallel to it in the prophetical literature. Among other things, it indicates that the utterances of the prophets were preserved and were familiar to the people.

A prominent person in governmental circles, Ahikam, also came to Jeremiah's assistance (v. 24; cf. 2 Kings 22:12,14; 25:22). Here is indirect but forceful evidence of Jeremiah's early support of Josiah's reform (cf. also 36:10,25; 39:14; 40:5 ff.).

In the story of Jeremiah's deliverance, as an indication of the danger in which he was, Baruch has inserted the account of another prophet, Uriah, who had prophesied against the city and country as Jeremiah had done and had been killed for it (vv. 20–23). It is a marvel that Jeremiah escaped with his life. Either he had not crossed Jehoiakim yet, or the latter feared him. In any case, he was preserved to preach for many more years.

2. A Sermon in Symbol and Speech (27: 1–22)

Chapter 27 is related to chapter 26 in that it, too, reflects the developing antagonism between Jeremiah and the prophets. The connection with chapters 28—29 is even closer, for the three chapters not only have a common theme but also exhibit common peculiarities of language. These facts suggest that chapters 27—29 once constituted a separate prophetic pamphlet circulated independently for a time before its incorporation into Baruch's

narrative. Rudolph advances the view that this little booklet may have been a polemic against a suspect prophetic movement during the exile (in loco.; the exile began in 597).

Chapters 27—28 are intimately bound to each other by their concern with the same situation and symbol. The situation was the meeting in Jerusalem of diplomats from neighboring nations (594–593), either to persuade Zedekiah to join a revolt against Babylon or to plan the strategy for a rebellion already decided upon. The symbol was the yoke, used by both Jeremiah and Hananiah in their public prophetic proclamations. It represented subjection to Nebuchadnezzar.

There is an involved textual problem in 27:1 and 28:1. For a discussion of the problem, the interested reader is referred to more technical commentaries (e.g., Bright, pp. 199 f.). It is obvious that the two chapters deal with the same general situation. Critical textual study brings 27:1 and 28:1 into harmony, so that both passages refer to the fourth year of the reign of Zedekiah.

(1) A Message Directed to the Rulers of the Nations (27:1–11)

¹ In the beginning of the reign of Zedekiah the son of Josiah, king of Judah, this word came to Jeremiah from the LORD. ² Thus the LORD said to me: "Make yourself thongs and yoke-bars, and put them on your neck. ³ Send word to the king of Edom, the king of Moab, the king of the sons of Ammon, the king of Tyre, and the king of Sidon by the hand of the envoys who have come to Jerusalem to Zedekiah king of Judah. ⁴ Give them this charge for their masters: 'Thus says the LORD of hosts, the God of Israel: This is what you shall say to your masters: ⁵ "It is I who by my great power and my outstretched arm have made the earth, with the men and animals that are on the earth, and I give it to whomever it seems right to me. ⁶ Now I have given all these lands into the hand of Nebuchadnezzar, the king of Babylon, my servant, and I have given him also the beasts of the field to serve him. ⁷ All the nations shall serve him and his son and his grandson, until the time of his own land comes; then many nations and great kings shall make him their slave.

8 " ' "But if any nation or kingdom will not serve this Nebuchadnezzar king of Babylon, and put its neck under the yoke of the king of Babylon, I will punish that nation with the sword, with famine, and with pestilence, says the LORD, until I have consumed it by his hand. 9 So do not listen to your prophets, your diviners, your dreamers, your soothsayers, or your sorcerers, who are saying to you, 'You shall not serve the king of Babylon.' 10 For it is a lie which they are prophesying to you, with the result that you will be removed far from your land, and I will drive you out, and you will perish. 11 But any nation which will bring its neck under the yoke of the king of Babylon and serve him, I will leave on its own land, to till it and dwell there, says the LORD." ' "

Jeremiah provides proof positive of his superb statesmanship in his assessment of the political situation through a penetrating sermon in symbol and speech. Because the situation is so crucial, he resorts to the intensified form of prophetic proclamation used on earlier occasions (cf. 13:1 ff.; 16:1 ff.; 19:1 ff.). There is a difference here. The future is left open. It will be determined by the action of the audience.

One may visualize the situation in Jerusalem. Things are buzzing around the palace. An air of secrecy and excitement is much in evidence. Delegates from the courts of surrounding countries are coming and going, as they have periodic sessions. Suddenly the prophet-preacher shows up at one of their meetings. He is wearing a plowman's ox-yoke about his neck. All have seen such a yoke many times, but not on a man!

We may paraphrase and interpret Jeremiah's declaration to the startled group as follows: "This yoke is the symbol of submission to Nebuchadnezzar of Babylon. I want you to take back to your respective rulers this message: Yahweh, the creator and controller of the world, has a purpose which he is working out in history, and his purpose now is that you submit to the yoke of Babylonian supremacy. That supremacy will last until Babylon's time of reckoning arrives. But for you to resist now is to resist God, and there is no future in that kind of enterprise. Don't listen

to these prophets who are fanning the flames of nationalism and rebellion and who are filling you with false hopes and lies. Submit and survive."

Perhaps you can imagine the reaction. As a demonstrator, a one-man protest movement, Jeremiah doubtless created quite a sensation! You may recall a somewhat similar dramatic action by Isaiah (Isa. 20:1 ff.). For these sensitive, gifted, educated men of God, this sort of thing must have been difficult. But for them the all-important matter was to communicate the message of God as forcefully and faithfully as possible.

It is not recommended that modern ministers wear yokes or go barefoot and "naked" (arrayed in the loincloth of a slave). But that something can be learned and emulated from these great servants of God with regard to commitment and communication seems obvious.

We are not only impressed by Jeremiah's ingenuity in getting his sermon across but also with his consistency in interpreting events in terms of a theology of history.

(2) A Message Delivered to King Zedekiah of Judah (27:12–15)

12 To Zedekiah king of Judah I spoke in like manner: "Bring your necks under the yoke of the king of Babylon, and serve him and his people, and live. 13 Why will you and your people die by the sword, by famine, and by pestilence, as the LORD has spoken concerning any nation which will not serve the king of Babylon? 14 Do not listen to the words of the prophets who are saying to you, 'You shall not serve the king of Babylon,' for it is a lie which they are prophesying to you. 15 I have not sent them, says the LORD, but they are prophesying falsely in my name, with the result that I will drive you out and you will perish, you and the prophets who are prophesying to you."

Still wearing the yoke and seeking to discharge his responsibility as statesman-prophet, Jeremiah preached to Zedekiah essentially the same sermon which he had delivered to the kings of the nations through their representatives—in this summary: "Yield to the authority of Nebuchadnezzar, for this is God's will. The only alternative is disaster. Do not follow the false counsel of the prophets. If you do, both you and they will suffer the same tragic fate."

(3) A Message Addressed to the Priests and the People (27:16–22)

16 Then I spoke to the priests and to all this people, saying, "Thus says the Lord: Do not listen to the words of your prophets who are prophesying to you, saying, 'Behold, the vessels of the Lord's house will now shortly be brought back from Babylon,' for it is a lie which they are prophesying to you. 17 Do not listen to them; serve the king of Babylon and live. Why should this city become a desolation? 18 If they are prophets, and if the word of the Lord is with them, then let them intercede with the Lord of hosts, that the vessels which are left in the house of the Lord, in the house of the king of Judah, and in Jerusalem may not go to Babylon. 19 For thus says the Lord of hosts concerning the pillars, the sea, the stands, and the rest of the vessels which are left in this city, 20 which Nebuchadnezzar king of Babylon did not take away, when he took into exile from Jerusalem to Babylon Jeconiah the son of Jehoiakim, king of Judah, and all the nobles of Judah and Jerusalem—21 thus says the Lord of hosts, the God of Israel, concerning the vessels which are left in the house of the Lord, in the house of the king of Judah, and in Jerusalem: 22 They shall be carried to Babylon and remain there until the day when I give attention to them, says the Lord. Then I will bring them back and restore them to this place."

From both Jeremiah and Ezekiel we learn that after the deportation of 597 there was much agitation in Babylon and Jerusalem centering around Jehoiachin, now in exile and still considered by many to be the true Davidic ruler; stamps discovered at Beth-shemesh and Ramat Rachel and dating after 597 confirm this.[97] The hope was that the power of Babylon would shortly be broken, Jehoiachin restored to power, and the captives and Temple paraphernalia brought back. The prophets were helping keep the hope alive.

It was to shatter this illusion that Jeremiah beamed the message of vv. 16–22 at

[97] Cf. Y. Aharoni, BASOR, 170, 67).

the priests and . . . all this people. The message is the same as the one addressed to Zedekiah and the other kings, with a particular application to the priests, who would be especially interested in the "furnishings" of the Temple.[98]

Jeremiah tells the priests and the people that they must stop listening to the nationalistic prophets. If the prophets are genuinely called and sincerely concerned, let them get busy praying that the country will yield to the will of God, so that the rest of the Temple furnishings will not be carried off by Nebuchadnezzar. Jeremiah's conflict with the prophets is becoming more and more acute.

3. Jeremiah's Clash with Hananiah (28:1–17)

As already suggested, the relationship between chapters 28 and 27 is very close, despite the fact that 28 is cast in a biographical form and 27 is set in an autobiographical framework. Both chapters contain a mixture of literary types: acted out parable, prophecy of disaster (both to an individual and to the nation), oracle of salvation, biographical narration, and autobiographical narration. Actually, there is a blending of forms.

(1) Hananiah's Prophecy of Release and Restoration (28:1–4)

1 In that same year, at the beginning of the reign of Zedekiah king of Judah, in the fifth month of the fourth year, Hananiah the son of Azzur, the prophet from Gibeon, spoke to me in the house of the Lord, in the presence of the priests and all the people, saying, 2 "Thus says the Lord of hosts, the God of Israel: I have broken the yoke of the king of Babylon. 3 Within two years I will bring back to this place all the vessels of the Lord's house, which Nebuchadnezzar king of Babylon took away from this place and carried to Babylon. 4 I will also bring back to this place Jeconiah the son of Jehoiakim, king of Judah, and all the exiles from Judah who went to Babylon, says the Lord, for I will break the yoke of the king of Babylon."

[98] On these furnishings, see 1 Kings 7; G. E. Wright, Biblical Archaeology (Philadelphia: The Westminster Press, 1957), pp. 136–145.

This is an oracle of salvation. It starts with the regular "messenger formula" in an expanded form (v. 2a). There follows a proclamation of a fundamental change in the situation (v. 2b). This has not yet happened, but the decision has been made in the heavenly assembly by the great King. This guarantees its actualization. Next comes the principal part of the prophecy, the promise of deliverance (vv. 3–4). The Hebrew perfect tense gives way to the imperfect, as the prediction is made with more detail and emphasis. This conforms to the basic structure of the prophecy of salvation in its simplest form.

Hananiah of Gibeon, evidently a leader among the prophets, met Jeremiah in the Temple precincts. The latter was still wearing the yoke. In the presence of the priests and the people in the area, Hananiah said to Jeremiah that he had just had a revelation from the Lord. In a short time— *two years*—the Lord was going to break the yoke of Babylon and bring home Jehoiachin, the captives, and the Temple furnishings.

(2) Jeremiah's Reception of the Prophecy and His Response to It (28:5–9)

5 Then the prophet Jeremiah spoke to Hananiah the prophet in the presence of the priests and all the people who were standing in the house of the LORD; 6 and the prophet Jeremiah said, "Amen! May the LORD do so; may the LORD make the words which you have prophesied come true, and bring back to this place from Babylon the vessels of the house of the LORD, and all the exiles. 7 Yet hear now this word which I speak in your hearing and in the hearing of all the people. 8 The prophets who preceded you and me from ancient times prophesied war, famine, and pestilence against many countries and great kingdoms. 9 As for the prophet who prophesies peace, when the word of that prophet comes to pass, then it will be known that the LORD has truly sent the prophet."

The prophet Jeremiah replied immediately to *Hananiah the prophet: Amen! May the Lord do so; may the Lord make the words which you have prophesied come true* . . . (v. 6). Apparently "Amen" was employed when one accepted favor-

ably a message or a commission (cf. 1 Kings 1:36). Jeremiah revealed here both his love for his country and his belief in the sincerity of Hananiah. Was there a possibility that the prophecy was a true message from God and that he was wrong?

Some prophetic reflection caused him to remind Hananiah that as prophets they stood in a stream of tradition in which true prophets spoke about judgment and in which the burden of proof rested upon the prophets who were "peace-proclaimers." History had to vindicate the prophet of salvation, otherwise he would be shown to be a false prophet (vv. 7–9).

Jeremiah did not mean that true prophets never delivered promises of salvation, for they did. Much less did he mean that all promise passages in preexilic prophecy are to be deleted and relegated to the exilic or postexilic age. He meant that true prophecy is ethical in content and ethically conditioned, and that the situation which had existed among the people— persistent rebellion against God—had called for frank, fearless denunciation of sin and proclamation of judgment. Any bright and breezy forecast of well-being without moral content or condition was suspect. Particularly was this the case at the time (594–593).

One must bear in mind Jeremiah's strong conviction from the beginning of his ministry that things were terribly awry in the country and that, barring a radical repentance, the country was headed for catastrophe.

(3) Hananiah's Symbolic Action and Verbal Proclamation (28:10–11)

10 Then the prophet Hananiah took the yoke-bars from the neck of Jeremiah the prophet, and broke them. 11 And Hananiah spoke in the presence of all the people, saying, "Thus says the LORD: Even so will I break the yoke of Nebuchadnezzar king of Babylon from the neck of all the nations within two years." But Jeremiah the prophet went his way.

Possibly in a fit of fury (though this is not certain), *the prophet Hananiah* broke the yoke from the neck of *Jeremiah the prophet* and said: *Thus says the Lord: Even so will I break the yoke of Nebuchadnezzar.* This was also a symbolic act, accompanied by a prophetic pronouncement, consisting of the "messenger formula" and an explanatory statement (cf. 13:8–11; 19:11; 51:64).

Reference has been made to the significance of the prophetic word once uttered —whether of weal or of woe—and of the symbolic act, a more intensified form of prophetic speech. By breaking the yoke which Jeremiah had used to symbolize subjection to Babylon for a long period, and by uttering his prophecy concerning the release from Babylon within two years, Hananiah evidently expected to negate or cancel out Jeremiah's prophecy and set his in motion.

At the end of v. 11 there is a short, interesting, puzzling sentence: *But Jeremiah the prophet went his way.* Was he nonplussed? He had no answer. What was the trouble? Above, it was noted that Jeremiah accepted Hananiah's oracle of salvation at first, for he, too, desired salvation, not only for himself, but also for his people. Upon reflection, he spoke about the prejudice of experience in favor of the prophecy of retribution as over against the prophecy of salvation (of the ethically unconditioned variety). He thereby revealed that he could not wholly accept what Hananiah had said. Yet he could not at the moment find too much against it. Inspiration was lacking at the time, and so he went his way to pray about the thing and wrestle it through (cf. 42:2,7, where he thought and prayed ten days before receiving an authentic revelation).

(4) Jeremiah's Final Declaration and Vindication (28:12–17)

12 Sometime after the prophet Hananiah had broken the yoke-bars from off the neck of Jeremiah the prophet, the word of the LORD came to Jeremiah: 13 "Go, tell Hananiah, 'Thus says the LORD: You have broken wooden bars, but I will make in their place bars of iron. 14 For thus says the LORD of hosts, the God of Israel: I have put upon the neck of all these

nations an iron yoke of servitude to Nebuchadnezzar king of Babylon, and they shall serve him, for I have given to him even the beasts of the field.' " 15 And Jeremiah the prophet said to the prophet Hananiah, "Listen, Hananiah, the LORD has not sent you, and you have made this people trust in a lie. 16 Therefore thus says the LORD: 'Behold, I will remove you from the face of the earth. This very year you shall die, because you have uttered rebellion against the LORD.' "

17 In that same year, in the seventh month, the prophet Hananiah died.

Jeremiah had to reply to Hananiah, and reply he did—when *the word of the Lord came* to him (v. 12). From the literary viewpoint, Jeremiah's answer is an intriguing blend of a prophecy of disaster to an individual (Hananiah) and a prophecy of disaster to a nation (Judah). As elsewhere, the prophet demonstrates his ability to use basic speech forms with freedom and effectiveness.

The message for the nation was that instead of a yoke of wood that might be broken God had forged for the people a yoke of iron which none could break (vv. 13–14). The policy of revolt implied in Hananiah's prophecy would result in total subjection to Nebuchadnezzar.

There is here the statement of a basic principle which is applicable in all of life. We are not islands unto ourselves. We have yokes of responsibility—to ourselves, to others, to God. If we refuse to live under these yokes, it is a law of God, in the very constitution of things, that we forge for ourselves harder and heavier yokes. On the other hand, the yoke of Christ is easy, "because its wearer is yoked to the power of God" (cf. Matt. 11:30; Hopper, p. 1016).

The message for Hananiah was that, since he had not been *sent* by God, *had uttered rebellion against the Lord* (in advocating a policy contrary to the will of God), and had caused the people *to trust in a lie,* he must die (cf. Deut. 13:6; 18:20). And he did. Bright says: "There is no reason whatever to doubt that Hananiah, borne down—we may suppose— by this awful curse, did die as v. 17

tates: the incident would scarcely have
been recorded otherwise" (p. 203). The
incident was viewed as a vindication of
Jeremiah's ministry (cf. 28:5–9).

It is evident that in chapter 28 the
words *the prophet* are constantly used in
connection with the names of Jeremiah
and Hananiah. It seems that this is intentional, not accidental. The two prophets
are being set over against each other. They
engage in open clash. Both speak in the
name of the Lord. Both speak with conviction and apparent sincerity. Both employ the proper formula. Both engage in
symbolic acts. Yet both cannot be right.
We call Jeremiah a "true" prophet and
Hananiah a "false" prophet (here the LXX
supports us). But how do we know? How
could the people know?

In the exposition of 23:9–40, we stated
that, in our opinion, that tremendous passage probably dates from the reign of
Zedekiah and that "the point of greatest
illumination" for it is the clash between
Jeremiah and Hananiah. We also gave a
list of criteria for distinguishing between
true and false prophets. Chapter 28 should
be studied in the light of that list. Such a
study can be quite revealing and a bit
disturbing—for the minister!

4. The Prophet's Communication with the Captives (29:1–32)

This chapter contains one of the most
remarkable and revealing documents in
the Old Testament: Jeremiah's first letter
to the exiles, as recorded in vv. 4 ff. It is
not dated, and there is a difference of
opinion about the date. It is generally
agreed that the date falls between 598
and 587. Some scholars assign it to 594–
593. Others put it a bit earlier; still others,
somewhat later.

The present writer's position is that the
experience recorded in chapter 24 came
soon after the first major Babylonian captivity and that chapter 29 reflects the
situation which developed between that
time and the disturbance in Jerusalem
described in chapters 27—28. In other

words, the correspondence took place between 597 and 594.

Jeremiah was deeply concerned about
the well-being of the exiles. He was aware
of the political unrest among them, unrest which centered around Jehoiachin
and which was cultivated by the prophets.
It was the same sort of unrest as was being
stirred up by the nationalist party in
Jerusalem, including the prophets who supported the policies of the party. Because
of his concern for his fellow countrymen
in captivity, Jeremiah communicated with
them by letter. This resulted in some re-
percussions. The story is related in chapter 29.

(1) Jeremiah's First Communication with the Captives (29:1–23)

¹ These are the words of the letter which
Jeremiah the prophet sent from Jerusalem to
the elders of the exiles, and to the priests, the
prophets, and all the people, whom Nebuchadnezzar had taken into exile from Jerusalem to
Babylon. ² This was after King Jeconiah, and
the queen mother, the eunuchs, the princes of
Judah and Jerusalem, the craftsmen, and the
smiths had departed from Jerusalem. ³ The letter was sent by the hand of Elasah the son of
Shaphan and Gemariah the son of Hilkiah,
whom Zedekiah king of Judah sent to Babylon
to Nebuchadnezzar king of Babylon. It said:
⁴ "Thus says the LORD of hosts, the God of
Israel, to all the exiles whom I have sent into
exile from Jerusalem to Babylon: ⁵ Build
houses and live in them; plant gardens and eat
their produce. ⁶ Take wives and have sons and
daughters; take wives for your sons, and give
your daughters in marriage, that they may bear
sons and daughters; multiply there, and do not
decrease. ⁷ But seek the welfare of the city
where I have sent you into exile, and pray to
the LORD on its behalf, for in its welfare you
will find your welfare. ⁸ For thus says the LORD
of hosts, the God of Israel: Do not let your
prophets and your diviners who are among you
deceive you, and do not listen to the dreams
which they dream, ⁹ for it is a lie which they
are prophesying to you in my name; I did not
send them, says the LORD.

¹⁰ "For thus says the LORD: When seventy
years are completed for Babylon, I will visit
you, and I will fulfil to you my promise and
bring you back to this place. ¹¹ For I know the
plans I have for you, says the LORD, plans for
welfare and not for evil, to give you a future
and a hope. ¹² Then you will call upon me and

come and pray to me, and I will hear you.
[13] You will seek me and find me; when you
seek me with all your heart, [14] I will be found
by you, says the LORD, and I will restore your
fortunes and gather you from all the nations
and all the places where I have driven you,
says the LORD, and I will bring you back to the
place from which I sent you into exile.
[15] "Because you have said, 'The LORD has
raised up prophets for us in Babylon,'—[16] Thus
says the LORD concerning the king who sits on
the throne of David, and concerning all the
people who dwell in this city, your kinsmen
who did not go out with you into exile: [17] 'Thus
says the LORD of hosts, Behold, I am sending
on them sword, famine, and pestilence, and I
will make them like vile figs which are so bad
they cannot be eaten. [18] I will pursue them
with sword, famine, and pestilence, and will
make them a horror to all the kingdoms of the
earth, to be a curse, a terror, a hissing, and a
reproach among all the nations where I have
driven them, [19] because they did not heed my
word of the LORD, all you exiles whom I seat
to you by my servants the prophets, but you
would not listen, says the LORD.'—[20] Hear the
word of the LORD, all you exiles whom I sent
away from Jerusalem to Babylon: [21] 'Thus says
the LORD of hosts, the God of Israel, concerning Ahab the son of Kolaiah and Zedekiah the
son of Maaseiah, who are prophesying a lie to
you in my name: Behold, I will deliver them
into the hand of Nebuchadrezzar king of Babylon, and he shall slay them before your eyes.
[22] Because of them this curse shall be used by
all the exiles from Judah in Babylon: "The
LORD make you like Zedekiah and Ahab, whom
the king of Babylon roasted in the fire,"
[23] because they have committed folly in Israel,
they have committed adultery with their neighbors' wives, and they have spoken in my name
lying words which I did not command them. I
am the one who knows, and I am witness, says
the LORD.' "

Verses 1–3 serve as an introduction to
that which follows. They indicate the circumstances surrounding the sending of the
prophet's first letter to the exiles. The incident occurred after the captivity of 597.
The letter was carried to the captives by
an important delegation with a significant
mission. In all probability, the purpose of
the trip by Elasah and Gemariah was to
take tribute from subject to sovereign and
to assure Nebuchadnezzar of Zedekiah's
allegiance.

Following the introduction is the letter

itself. It is cast in the form of a prophetic
oracle. It starts with the "messenger formula:" *Thus says the Lord.* The most important part of the letter appears in vv. 4–14.
Verses 4–9 contain counsel for the present,
vv. 10–14, a forecast of the future.

Jeremiah is quite frank as he urges the
exiles to face up to the facts. A personal
translation and summary can clarify the
meaning: "You may as well settle down,
for you are going to be there a long
time. Don't put up temporary shacks, but
build permanent structures. *Plant* vineyards and gardens. Have families. Seek
diligently (strong verb) the well-being
(*shalom*) of the city where I have sent
you into exile (the area assigned to you).
And pray on its behalf to the Lord, for
in its peace (well-being) will be your
peace (well-being). And pay no attention
to the prophets, for what they are preaching is *a lie.* God did not send them. Their
message is not his message."

Some scholars delete vv. 8–9. But there
is no real basis for the excision. The verses
undergird what precedes and prepare for
what follows. It was the preaching of the
false prophets concerning the brevity of
the stay in Babylon that created the necessity for the counsel in vv. 4 ff. and the
forecast in vv. 10 ff.

Jeremiah turns from the present to the
future in this paraphrase and summary:
"Although you will not return soon, as
some of your prophets are saying, you
are coming back after *seventy years.* God
has *plans* for you, *plans* which he is making (vivid participial construction), *plans
for welfare* (well-being, resulting from
rich harmonious relationships), plans for a
future of hope. Meanwhile, you are not
necessarily separated from him, for you
can find him (in intimate personal relationship) in Babylon as in Jerusalem—
without land, temple, priests, sacrifice—if
you *seek* him (endeavor to press into fellowship with him) *with all your heart*
(i.e., with intellect and will, with all your
energies). Then, in his own time, God will
turn your turning (*will restore your for-*

tunes), and he will cause you to *return* to the place from which he sent you into exile" (vv. 10–14, author's summary).

The Hebrew phrase *shubh sh°bhut* (*restore the fortunes*) is a bit unusual and is found several times in Jeremiah. Literally, it means "turn the turning." Bauman maintains that the expression had a technical judicial signification: the removal of the sentence of imprisonment. It more likely referred originally and primarily to a restoration of the people to their primal status (Dietrich). Later, it may have come to focus on the restoration from exile.

Verses 15–19 repeat what Jeremiah has said in 24:8–10 concerning the kinsmen of the captives still in Judah. They are like rotten figs which must be cast aside, not by arbitrary decree of a despotic deity, but as the inevitable consequence of their persistent rebellion against the will of a God of righteousness and love. They have steadfastly refused to give heed to the word of the Lord proclaimed to them by by the true prophets whom he has sent.

In vv. 20–23 the exiles are enjoined to hear the word of the Lord spoken by his authorized messenger and are given an oracle of disaster directed against two prophets among them, Ahab and Zedekiah, who are prophesying a lie to them— likely the same lie as the one proclaimed by Hananiah in Jerusalem (ch. 28). These men have been speaking in the name of the Lord, yet he has not sent them. They have *committed folly in Israel*—probably by their political agitation among the people and their machinations against Nebuchadnezzar. Worst of all, they have *committed adultery with their neighbors wives*—they are immoral men. Let not these men think that because they are in a foreign land they are outside the view and beyond the reach of the Lord of hosts. All that they are doing and saying is like an open book before his eyes. He will bring them to account. He has in fact determined to deliver them into the hands of Nebuchadnezzar, who will burn them alive (because of their promotion of re-

bellion). So tragic will be their fate that they will serve as the basis of a curse formula for the Judean exiles in the future.

Nebuchadnezzar executed the two men because of rebellion against his overlordship. As Jeremiah saw it, there was a deeper reason: rebellion against the lordship of God. Both were right.

According to some scholars, vv. 16–20 are not a part of the letter but a later insertion of an expansion of the thought of 24:8–10. About this it is difficult to be dogmatic.

(2) Jeremiah's Second Communication with the Captives (29:24–32)

24 To Shemaiah of Nehelam you shall say: 25 "Thus says the LORD of hosts, the God of Israel: You have sent letters in your name to all the people who are in Jerusalem, and to Zephaniah the son of Maaseiah the priest, and to all the priests, saying, 26 'The LORD has made you priest instead of Jehoiada the priest, to have charge in the house of the LORD over every madman who prophesies, to put him in the stocks and collar. 27 Now why have you not rebuked Jeremiah of Anathoth who is prophesying to you? 28 For he has sent to us in Babylon, saying, "Your exile will be long; build houses and live in them, and plant gardens and eat their produce." ' "
29 Zephaniah the priest read this letter in the hearing of Jeremiah the prophet. 30 Then the word of the LORD came to Jeremiah: 31 "Send to all the exiles, saying, 'Thus says the LORD concerning Shemaiah of Nehelam: Because Shemaiah has prophesied to you when I did not send him, and has made you trust in a lie, 32 therefore thus says the LORD: Behold, I will punish Shemaiah of Nehelam and his descendants; he shall not have any one living among this people to see the good that I will do to my people, says the LORD, for he has talked rebellion against the LORD.' "

As one reads the prophet's letter, he wonders about the possible reaction of people settled in communities along unused canals in swampland infested by mosquitoes, where the heat and humidity were high and the suffering at times intense. He is not surprised to discover that one of the prophets among the people, a certain Shemaiah of Nehelam, wrote letters to people in Jerusalem about Jeremiah's letter. One of these letters went to Zephaniah (21:1; 37:3), chief of the Temple police. In it he said, in effect: "Why don't you muzzle this man Jeremiah? He is a crazy fellow, a dangerous fanatic. Take care of him. It's your job to handle characters like him who disturb the peace."

Apparently in the position once occupied by Pashhur (old "Terror-all-around," now in exile, it would seem, in keeping with Jeremiah's prediction, 20:1–6), Zephaniah read the letter to Jeremiah—and did nothing about it. The implication is that he was favorably disposed toward the prophet.

Jeremiah got busy and sent another message to the exiles warning them of the fundamental falsehood and folly of Shemaiah's viewpoint (resistance to Babylon and the hope of an early release) and predicting that because this man had no mandate from God and had talked *rebellion against the Lord* (the Lord's will being submission to Babylon), no member of his family would participate in the return which God would one day make possible—*the good that I will do to my people* (v. 32).

It is well to remember that there were some true prophets—at least one, Ezekiel—among the exiles. But the pseudo-prophets seemed to be in the ascendancy. Ezekiel had a great deal of difficulty with them, too (cf. Ezek. 13:1 ff.).

Chapter 29 is an important chapter. The most significant portion of it is the first letter written by Jeremiah to the exiles. That letter played a part in bringing about the open clash between Jeremiah and the prophets in Jerusalem in 594–593. But its chief interest lies in the light it sheds on Jeremiah and his conception of God and religion. It is quite revealing. It indicates that the prophet was now an impressive and influential person in the life of the land (cf. 21:1 ff.). The fulfillment of his prophecies in 597 had improved his status.

Moreover, the letter gives us another glimpse of Jeremiah's tremendous courage. He dared to shatter the illusions and false hopes of the people and to stand up against the prophets who were encouraging the people in them.

Also, the letter discloses that Jeremiah was a man of indomitable faith. He was not unrealistic. He knew that the captivity would last a long time. But though pessimistic about the immediate prospect, he was optimistic for the long pull. He was sure that God had plans for the well-being of his people, plans that involved a future of hope. God would one day bring them home.

Further, this meaningful letter reveals that Jeremiah was a man of penetrating insight. He discerned that true faith is not dependent upon geographical locality or cultic conformity. One can know God anywhere, if he meets the conditions.

Finally, Jeremiah is seen pioneering in another direction. The passage in which he enjoins prayer for the Babylonians (v. 7) is said by Volz to be "the only place in the Old Testament where intercession on behalf of enemies and unbelievers is commended" (*Jeremia*, p. 269). To be sure, the motive is self-interest, but this command marks a long step toward the injunction of our Lord: "Love your enemies and pray for those who persecute you" (Matt. 5:44).

The prophet both personalized and universalized the religion of his people. It was not a long way to the conception of a world mission.

XIV. The Book of Consolation (30:1— 33:26)

Chapters 30–33 contain a collection of prophecies of optimistic character. The dominant note is hope. For this reason, the collection is often called "the book of consolation." Why is this "book" of comfort placed at this point in the prophecy? It seems to interrupt Baruch's "biography." A closer look, however, reveals that there are definite links with the context. For one thing, chapter 32 is biographical. It recounts the story of a symbolic act, whereby Jeremiah, during his confinement in the court of the guard, gave concrete expression to his unconquerable faith in the future of God's purpose. Some scholars hold that chapters 30—31, originally a separate unit, were placed before 32 to serve as an introduction to chapters 32—33 (e.g., Eissfeldt, p. 361).

Also, chapter 29 includes prophecies of salvation and concludes with God's reference to "the good that I will do to my people" (29:32). Some think that this explains the position of chapters 30—33 (e.g., Hyatt, p. 1022). It is possible that the prophecies in chapters 30—33 were incorporated here in conscious contrast to the ethically unconditioned oracles of salvation of the pseudo-prophets mentioned in chapters 27—29. The point is that there are biographical and theological ties with the context.

There is much difference of opinion concerning the length, authorship, date, and interpretation of the collection. As to length, it appears obvious to the present writer that chapters 30—33 have a distinctive introduction and a common theme and therefore belong together.

The question of authenticity is so complex and viewpoints about it so varied that it is impossible to enter into a detailed discussion of it. Some attention will be given to the matter in dealing with the different units. The present trend among scholars is toward regarding an increasing amount of the material in chapters 30—33 as genuine.

Sizable deletions are still made, however. The primary reasons are: historical viewpoint, similarities in language and style to Isaiah 40 ff., and a spirit of nationalism considered to be unworthy of Jeremiah. Often a large element of subjectivity enters into the process whereby a scholar reaches his conclusions. The evidence is evaluated quite differently by different men.

Moreover, there is disagreement as to the date of passages accepted as Jeremianic, particularly in chapters 30—31. Some place them quite early in the ministry of the prophet (e.g., Rudolph, Leslie, Weiser,

Gelin). Others are persuaded that they come out of the latter part of Jeremiah's career (e.g., Skinner, Penna, Notscher, Anderson, von Rad). Bright puts some early and some late.

The judgment of this commentator is that the prophecies in chapters 30—33 are Jeremianic, in the sense that they either come directly from Jeremiah, or consist of variations or mediations on Jeremianic themes. These prophecies which come directly from Jeremiah represent the fruit of his rich experience and originated about 587.

1. The Good That I Will Do (30:1-24)

¹ The word that came to Jeremiah from the LORD: ² "Thus says the LORD, the God of Israel: Write in a book all the words that I have spoken to you. ³ For behold, days are coming, says the LORD, when I will restore the fortunes of my people, Israel and Judah, says the LORD, and I will bring them back to the land which I gave to their fathers, and they shall take possession of it."

Verses 1-3 serve as a general introduction to the complex, with each chapter having its individual heading (30:4; 31:1; 32:1; 33:1). The introduction states the theme of the whole: the glorious future of God's people (on *restore the fortunes*, see comment on 29:14).

⁴ These are the words which the LORD spoke concerning Israel and Judah:
⁵ "Thus says the LORD:
We have heard a cry of panic,
of terror, and no peace.
⁶ Ask now, and see,
can a man bear a child?
Why then do I see every man
with his hands on his loins like a woman in labor?
Why has every face turned pale?
⁷ Alas! that day is so great
there is none like it;
it is a time of distress for Jacob;
yet he shall be saved out of it.
⁸ "And it shall come to pass in that day, says the LORD of hosts, that I will break the yoke from off their neck, and I will burst their bonds, and strangers shall no more make servants of them. ⁹ But they shall serve the LORD their God and David their king, whom I will raise up for them.

At the outset, the prophet paints a graphic picture of the day of the Lord. It is a day of distress (vv. 5–7a) and a day of deliverance (vv. 7b–9). Though the people are gripped by anguish and terror as they experience the judgment aspect of God's activity on his day (here, the catastrophe of 587 and the ensuing captivity), they will be saved out of their distress by the Lord, and will serve him and *David their king.*

Observe the use of *Israel and Judah* and *Jacob.* Jacob was the ancestor of all of the Israelites. Attention has been called to the ambiguity in Jeremiah's use of such terms as Jacob, Judah, and Israel (cf. chs. 2— 4). It is the present writer's view that we should not put Jeremiah in a straightjacket and require him to use only one term and mean the same thing by it at all times.

The allusion to *David their king* is messianic (cf. 23:5–6; 30:21; 33:15). The portrayal of the day of the Lord and the prediction about the ideal king are similar to those of other preexilic prophets (cf. Hos. 3:5; Amos 5:18–20; Zeph. 1:14–18; Isa. 11:1–10; Mic. 5:2–5).

10 "Then fear not, O Jacob my servant, says the Lord,
　　nor be dismayed, O Israel;
　for lo, I will save you from afar,
　　and your offspring from the land of their captivity.
　Jacob shall return and have quiet and ease,
　　and none shall make him afraid.
11 For I am with you to save you,
　　　　　　　　　says the Lord;
　I will make a full end of all the nations
　　among whom I scattered you,
　　but of you I will not make a full end.
　I will chasten you in just measure,
　　and I will by no means leave you unpunished.

These verses also occur in 46:27–28. In them God tenderly assures his people that, though he must chasten them *in just measure,* he will not leave them in *captivity* but will *save* them *from afar* (cf. 31:2). Therefore they are *not* to *fear.*

12 "For thus says the Lord:
　Your hurt is incurable,
　　and your wound is grievous.
13 There is none to uphold your cause,

　no medicine for your wound,
　no healing for you.
14 All your lovers have forgotten you;
　　they care nothing for you;
　for I have dealt you the blow of an enemy,
　　the punishment of a merciless foe,
　because your guilt is great,
　　because your sins are flagrant.
15 Why do you cry out over your hurt?
　　Your pain is incurable.
　Because your guilt is great,
　　because your sins are flagrant,
　I have done these things to you.
16 Therefore all who devour you shall be devoured,
　　and all your foes, every one of them,
　　　shall go into captivity;
　those who despoil you shall become a spoil,
　　and all who prey on you I will make a prey.
17 For I will restore health to you,
　　and your wounds I will heal,
　　　　　　　　　says the Lord,
　because they have called you an outcast:
　'It is Zion, for whom no one cares!'

In sharp contrast to a picture of an incurable condition of sin and guilt (vv. 12–15) is set a promise of healing and health (vv. 16–17). *Your lovers* are the political allies of Judah. They have deserted God's people in the day of divine visitation (cf. 588–587). The situation is desperate. From the human standpoint, there is no cure for the people's condition. Yet God in his grace will heal the hurt incurable. He will save his people from within.

Those who hold to the early date of the authentic passages in chapters 30—31 and to their exclusive reference to the Northern Kingdom are hard put to maintain their position here. They have to get rid of the allusion to *Zion* (v. 17). They emend *It is Zion* to "She is our quarry."

18 "Thus says the Lord:
　Behold, I will restore the fortunes of the tents of Jacob,
　　and have compassion on his dwellings;
　the city shall be rebuilt upon its mound,
　　and the palace shall stand where it used to be.
19 Out of them shall come songs of thanksgiving,
　　and the voices of those who make merry.
　I will multiply them, and they shall not be few;

I will make them honored, and they shall
    not be small.
0 Their children shall be as they were of old,
    and their congregation shall be estab-
      lished before me;
    and I will punish all who oppress them.
1 Their prince shall be one of themselves,
    their ruler shall come forth from their
      midst;
    I will make him draw near, and he shall
      approach me,
    for who would dare of himself to ap-
      proach me?
                    says the LORD.
22 And you shall be my people,
    and I will be your God."

In this remarkable passage Jeremiah
sketches an ideal theocracy. He describes
the rebuilding of the city and community,
the overflowing joy of the citizens therein,
and the reign of God among them through
a chosen representative, a *prince* and a
ruler from their midst, who will *approach*
him. In this new theocracy, the covenant
ideal will be realized (v. 22).

There is something very striking about
v. 21. The king referred to here is God's
representative among the people. One of
his privileges by virtue of his position is
that of access to the presence of the great
King. He deals directly with God and is
the "perfect intermediary between Yahweh
and his people." [99] The unique feature in
the picture is the manner of his approach.
It is through "standing bail or surety" (KB)
by the offering of his life in pledge. Says
von Rad: "It seems to me to be extremely
characteristic that even in a Messianic prediction Jeremiah is particularly interested
in the preconditions of the saving event as
these affect the person involved. In my
view—and here again we recognize Jeremiah—the most important thing is that the
anointed one risks his life, and in this way
holds open access to God in the most personal terms possible" (p. 219).[100]

Are there foreshadowings here of something profound and far-reaching?

99 Couturier, *op. cit.*, p. 325.

100 S. Mowinckel calls attention to the connection
between the establishment of the new covenant and
the priestly mediatorial function of the new king, *He
That Cometh*, pp. 179 f.

23 Behold the storm of the LORD!
    Wrath has gone forth,
    a whirling tempest;
      it will burst upon the head of the wicked.
24 The fierce anger of the LORD will not turn
    back
    until he has executed and accomplished
    the intents of his mind.
In the latter days you will understand this.

Jeremiah has been speaking mainly
about the salvation to be experienced by
God's people. Here he refers—and not for
the first time—to the storm of judgment to
be encountered by the people who oppose
God. The alternative? The salvation of the
Lord, or the storm of the Lord!

2. The Optimism of Grace (31:1–40)

1 "At that time, says the LORD, I will be the
    God of all the families of Israel, and
    they shall be my people."
2 Thus says the LORD:
    "The people who survived the sword
      found grace in the wilderness;
    when Israel sought for rest,
3   the LORD appeared to him from afar.
    I have loved you with an everlasting love;
      therefore I have continued my faithful-
      ness to you.
4 Again I will build you, and you shall be
    built,
    O virgin Israel!
    Again you shall adorn yourself with tim-
      brels,
    and shall go forth in the dance of the
      merrymakers.
5 Again you shall plant vineyards
    upon the mountains of Samaria;
    the planters shall plant,
    and shall enjoy the fruit.
6 For there shall be a day when watchmen
    will call
    in the hill country of Ephraim:
    'Arise, and let us go up to Zion,
    to the LORD our God.' "

A variation of the covenant formula, v.
1 stands as the heading of chapter 31. The
phrase *all the families of Israel* refers to the
whole people of God.

Verses 2–6 constitute a poem-prophecy
which in both beauty of expression and
sublimity of conception is one of the greatest in the book. It is replete with Exodus
imagery and terminology and contains in
embryo the concept of a new Exodus (cf.

4:14; 23:7–8). The new and the old are related as type and anti-type.[101]

The passage depicts a great homecoming (vv. 4–6). *Israel,* personified as a *virgin* and representing the entire people of God, will return from exile. The community will be reconstituted. Ruined cities will be rebuilt. Farming will be revived. The people will rejoice, their culminating joy being that of worship in *Zion.*

How appropriate would these words be during the days immediately following the fall of Jerusalem, when Gedaliah was governor and Mizpah was the seat of government! How apt the allusion to *the mountains of Samaria* and *the hill country of Ephraim!* The tone and terminology fit the late period better than the early phase of the prophet's ministry. The basis for Jeremiah's glowing hope for the future is the wondrous love of God, which goes out as grace to those unworthy of it. This brings us back to vv. 2–3.

Verse 2 starts with the "messenger formula," indicating that the speaker is delivering a message from God. *The people who survived the sword* are those in captivity (not Egyptian bondage). The combination *found grace* occurs five times in Exodus 33:12–17. The *wilderness* is a metaphor for a period of deprivation and discipline (cf. Hos. 2:14 f.). The phrase *sought for rest* contains a verb form based on the same root as the noun for "rest" in 6:16 (cf. Ex. 33:14; Deut. 28:65). *From afar* is from the direction of Jerusalem, considered in a popular way to be God's earthly habitation and center of operation. The verbs are prophetic perfects, describing that which is future as though it were past, since it is already a reality in the mind of God.

In v. 3 are two tremendous words for *love.* The first refers to election love, the second to covenant love (see 2:2). The term *everlasting* designates that which is obscure or lies beyond the vanishing point: in space, infinity; in time, indefinite antiq-

uity or futurity. The primary meaning of *mashak* is draw (GT, BDB, KB: seize, lay hold of, drag, draw). A resultant meaning is continue. If something is drawn out it is *continued.* But the RSV translation is too tame.[102] The perfects may be treated as perfects of experience.

The people are suffering for their sins in exile. God appears to them *from afar,* in response to their seeking *rest,* and says:
"With an everlasting love I love thee;
Therefore with grace I draw thee"
(author's translation).

Obviously, this is one of the finest sentences in the Holy Scriptures (cf. Hos. 11:1 ff.). From it we learn that God's love underlies the trying experiences of life. Even his judgment is the instrument of his love: "the pull of his compassion and the push of his purpose."[103] Also, his love is limitless (*everlasting*). Perhaps there is here a faint foreshadowing of the truth referred to in Ephesians 3:18–19. Moreover, God's love is strong, the most powerful force in life. If the realization that he loves us with a limitless love that goes the limit for us will not "draw" us—melt our hearts and wills into contrition and submission—nothing else will. Further, God's love individualizes: "I love *thee.*" To be sure, Jeremiah is addressing a personified Israel. But it is in Jeremiah that the individual begins to come into sharper focus as the basic unit in religious experience. Surely anyone looking back upon this statement through Christ and the cross must recognize that God's love goes out to all men one by one—regardless of color, class, or creed. Jeremiah grounded his hope for the future in the grace of God.

7 For thus says the LORD:
    "Sing aloud with gladness for Jacob,
        and raise shouts for the chief of the
            nations;
    proclaim, give praise, and say,
        'The LORD has saved his people,
            the remnant of Israel.'
8 Behold, I will bring them from the north

---

101 J. Harvey, *Sciences ecclésiastiques,* 15, 1963, 383–405.

102 Cf. A. Feuillet, VT, 12, 1962, 122–124.
103 Paul Scherer, *Event in Eternity* (New York: Harper & Bros., 1945), p. 19.

country,
and gather them from the farthest parts
of the earth,
among them the blind and the lame,
the woman with child and her who is in
travail, together;
a great company, they shall return here.
9 With weeping they shall come,
and with consolations I will lead them
back,
I will make them walk by brooks of water,
in a straight path in which they shall not
stumble,
for I am a father to Israel,
and Ephraim is my first-born.
·0 "Hear the word of the LORD, O nations,
and declare it in the coastlands afar off;
say, 'He who scattered Israel will gather
him,
and will keep him as a shepherd keeps
his flock.'
11 For the LORD has ransomed Jacob,
and has redeemed him from hands too
strong for him.
12 They shall come and sing aloud on the
height of Zion,
and they shall be radiant over the goodness of the LORD,
over the grain, the wine, and the oil,
and over the young of the flock and the
herd:
their life shall be like a watered garden,
and they shall languish no more.
13 Then shall the maidens rejoice in the dance,
and the young men and the old shall be
merry.
I will turn their mourning into joy,
I will comfort them, and give them gladness for sorrow.
14 I will feast the soul of the priests with
abundance,
and my people shall be satisfied with my
goodness,
says the LORD."

God, who is *a father to Israel* and to
Ephraim his *first-born* (cf. Ex. 4:22; Jer.
3:19; 31:20), *will bring* the exiles home
by brooks of water (there will be no suffering from thirst) and *by a straight path* (all
will be smoothed out, so that none will
stumble). He will guide and guard them
as any good shepherd would, having *ransomed* and *redeemed* them from servitude.
With joy in their hearts and songs on
their lips, the returning captives will have
faces aglow *over the goodness of the Lord.*
For them life will be *like a watered* (Peake,

"saturated") *garden* (matchless boon!).
Those who are brought back will experience outer prosperity and peace and inner
joy and tranquility. There will be plenty
for the priests, and God's people *will be
satisfied with his goodness.*

Many scholars regard this passage as
secondary, largely because of parallels in
style, language, and thought between it
and passages in Isaiah 40 ff. The problem
is that some of the language is "Jeremianic"
and some "Isaianic." Noted scholars (e.g.,
Graf, Volz, Rudolph, *et al.*) have argued
for the authenticity of the passage and
have explained the parallels either on the
basis of Jeremiah's influencing Isaiah or of
both employing traditional terminology.

15 Thus says the LORD:
"A voice is heard in Ramah,
lamentation and bitter weeping.
Rachel is weeping for her children;
she refuses to be comforted for her children,
because they are not."
16 Thus says the LORD:
"Keep your voice from weeping,
and your eyes from tears;
for your work shall be rewarded,
says the LORD,
and they shall come back from the land
of the enemy.
17 There is hope for your future,
says the LORD,
and your children shall come back to
their own country.
18 I have heard Ephraim bemoaning,
'Thou hast chastened me, and I was chastened,
like an untrained calf;
bring me back that I may be restored,
for thou art the LORD my God.
19 For after I had turned away I repented;
and after I was instructed, I smote upon
my thigh;
I was ashamed, and I was confounded,
because I bore the disgrace of my youth.'
20 Is Ephraim my dear son?
Is he my darling child?
For as often as I speak against him,
I do remember him still.
Therefore my heart yearns for him;
I will surely have mercy on him,
says the LORD.
21 "Set up waymarks for yourself,
make yourself guideposts;
consider well the highway,

the road by which you went.
Return, O virgin Israel,
    return to these your cities.
22 How long will you waver,
    O faithless daughter?
For the LORD has created a new thing on
    the earth:
a woman protects a man."

This is an exceedingly vivid, dramatic, and eloquent prophecy. It is authentic and fits well the situation following the fall of Jerusalem (40:1–6). It has been suggested that the revelation may have been received and delivered at Ramah as some of Rachel's *children* were being taken from her in 587.

The oldest tradition in the Old Testament locates Rachel's tomb near Ramah, about five miles north of Jerusalem, in the territory of Benjamin, one of Rachel's sons (1 Sam. 10:2 f.; cf. Gen. 35:16–20; 48:7). Jeremiah was a Benjamite.

In this peerless poem-prophecy, mother Rachel is pictured as weeping over her children, now carried into captivity. The allusion could be to Israelites taken away in 721, or in 597 and 587, or both. The spirit of Rachel, long dead in body, weeps and wails and will not be comforted, because her children have been torn from her.

God replies to her expression of grief with words of gracious consolation (vv. 16–17). He assures her that her labor in giving birth to her children and in caring for them has not been in vain. It will *be rewarded. There is hope for* her *future.* Those *children* will one day *come back from the land of the enemy . . . to their own country.*

While the mother is weeping, the children are also weeping. They confess that they deserve the discipline which they have received. They have been stubborn and self-willed *like an untrained calf* (one not yet broken in, v. 18a). They pray a prayer of penitence (vv. 18b–19): "Cause me to *turn* (back to thee), and I will *return* (to thee; *will* return to my former relationship with thee—emphatic; cohortative of resolution)," or "Cause me to *return* (repent) that I *may return* (to my former status or

to my home country—cohortative of desire or entreaty?) *for thou art the Lord my God."*

The play on *shub* continues: "For after my *turning* away (from thee) I repented, and after my being taught (being made submissive through discipline) I smote upon my thigh (a sign of great grief and deep distress)" (author's translation).

We have here the kind of repentance which the people must manifest before they can be restored.

In v. 20 God responds to the penitent prodigal. This heartrending verse grants us a glimpse of the agony of a loving father over his wayward son. There is a surge and conflict of emotions. God has had to *speak against* Israel because of his ingratitude and infidelity, but each time he mentions Israel's name he remembers that he is his *son.* His heart *yearns for him. He will surely have mercy on him* (cf. Luke 15: 11–24).

Two arresting paradoxes appear in the passage. Both penetrate to the heart of reality. The first is found in v. 18: *bring me back that I may be restored* (cause me to turn, that I may return). The second occurs in v. 20: *as often as I speak against him, I do remember him still.*

It is uncertain as to whether the prophet or God speaks directly in vv. 21–22. The people are urged to set their minds on the road back, the road over which they go (or went) into captivity, and to set up guideposts (markers: mental or physical?), for this is the way that will lead them home. Then comes the call: *Return, O virgin Israel / return to these your cities. / How long will you waver* (dilly-dally, keep flitting back and forth in indecision, refuse to accept and act on the promises), / *O faithless* (turnabout, back-turning) *daughter.*

Verse 22 brings the passage to a climax by calling attention to God's creation of a wonderful *new thing,* which, in turn, necessitates a ready and radical response on the part of the people. Unfortunately, textual difficulties somewhat blunt the force of the climax. The problem lies in the last clause of v. 22 (LXX reading: "men will walk in salvation"). There have been many and varied suggestions, emendations, and attempts at translation and explanation. None is totally satisfactory.

We may dismiss Duhm's changing of *tesobeb* to *tissob*: "A woman is turned into a man—" supposedly the witty comment of a scribe, the *new thing* being the transformation, in the space of two verses, of Israel from a *son* (v. 20) into a *virgin . . . daughter* (v. 22). Condamin's [104] suggested emendation to *tashubh* (requiring a slight alteration) is the best of several efforts in the direction of change: "The woman (faithless Israel) *returns* to the man (Yahweh, her husband)."

The RSV follows the Masoretic Text. As translated, the statement is usually interpreted to mean that, whereas ordinarily a man must protect a woman, in God's new society things will be so different that if any protecting is done a woman can protect a man (one might wonder why there would be need for this). Since the verb rendered *protects* signifies encompass or surround, the reference could be to the faithful adherence of God's people to him in sincere devotion—certainly a new, unheard of thing!

23 Thus says the LORD of hosts, the God of Israel: "Once more they shall use these words in the land of Judah and in its cities, when I restore their fortunes:
'The LORD bless you, O habitation of righteousness,
O holy hill!'
24 And Judah and all its cities shall dwell there together, and the farmers and those who wander with their flocks. 25 For I will satisfy the weary soul, and every languishing soul I will replenish."
26 Thereupon I awoke and looked, and my sleep was pleasant to me.
27 "Behold, the days are coming, says the LORD, when I will sow the house of Israel and the house of Judah with the seed of man and the seed of beast. 28 And it shall come to pass that as I have watched over them to pluck up and break down, to overthrow, destroy, and

bring evil, so I will watch over them to build and to plant, says the LORD. 29 In those days they shall no longer say:
'The fathers have eaten sour grapes,
and the children's teeth are set on edge.'
30 But every one shall die for his own sin; each man who eats sour grapes, his teeth shall be set on edge.

Here is the great reversal. The God who is awake and watchful over his word to perform it, and who has promised not only to pluck up and pull down but also to build and to plant, will effect the reversal. That reversal will involve both parts of the people of God (vv. 23-28).

But the renewal which the reversal entails will be on the basis of individual response. Each must assume responsibility for his own acts and must act in response to God's call to repentance and participation in his redemption. Jeremiah is pointing to a new order in human affairs (vv. 29-30)—an order of individual ethical responsibility—as he moves toward the prophecy of the new covenant, possibly the loftiest peak in the Old Testament revelation.

The genuineness of all three smaller units in the larger passage (vv. 23-26, 27-28, 29-30) has been questioned by various scholars for different reasons: the presumed impossibility of Jeremiah's speaking so glowingly of the Temple hill as in v. 23, too much of a nationalistic emphasis in vv. 23-28, and an assumed dependence of vv. 29-30 on Ezekiel. In the present writer's judgment, these reasons are not conclusive, if indeed they are valid. Further, it should be noted that there are many Jeremianic expressions scattered through the section.

Verse 26 is a puzzle. It has been variously interpreted. Many have regarded it as a marginal comment of a scribe who fell asleep while copying the script, awoke, and voiced his gratitude for his refreshing slumber. Later his comment crept into the text. Some believe that the verse involves a quotation or citation of a familiar song (Rudolph, Weiser). Others find here an expression of despondency by one who

104 A. Condamin, *Le Livre de Jeremie*, 1936, *in loc.*

awakes from a lovely dream, only to face the raw, rugged realities of life. Lindblom says that the reference is to "the end of an inspired state of mind in which the preceding revelation was composed by Jeremiah" (p. 256).

In v. 29 Jeremiah quotes a popular saying which was going the rounds. In it the people were seeking to excuse themselves from responsibility for their predicament and pass the buck to their forebears—and ultimately to God. The prophet employs this saying as the occasion for the enunciation of a new truth.

Ezekiel, a colleague deeply influenced by Jeremiah and active among the captives, used the saying as the starting point for a great sermon on the dignity, competency, and responsibility of the individual before God (Ezek. 18).[105]

31 "Behold, the days are coming, says the LORD, when I will make a new covenant with the house of Israel and the house of Judah, 32 not like the covenant which I made with their fathers when I took them by the hand to bring them out of the land of Egypt, my covenant which they broke, though I was their husband, says the LORD. 33 But this is the covenant which I will make with the house of Israel after those days, says the LORD: I will put my law within them, and I will write it upon their hearts; and I will be their God, and they shall be my people. 34 And no longer shall each man teach his neighbor and each his brother, saying, 'Know the LORD,' for they shall all know me, from the least of them to the greatest, says the LORD; for I will forgive their iniquity, and I will remember their sin no more."

In this, the noblest of Jeremiah's prophecies, we have "the Gospel before the Gospel." It is the earliest and closest approach to the New Testament faith in the Old Testament.

Some have doubted or denied its genuineness, but its authenticity "ought never to have been questioned . . ." as Bright observes: "It represents what might well be

considered the high point of his [Jeremiah's] theology. It is certainly one of the profoundest and most moving passages in the Bible" (p. 287).

In the writer's opinion, Jeremiah alone could have been used to give this revelation. It represents the essence of his experience and the apex of his spiritual pilgrimage. It is the peak toward which the whole trend of outer and inner developments in his ministry had been moving. The revelation came during or shortly after the tragedy of 587, when the man who had been walking the way of a cross stood in the midst of the destruction of all that he treasured—save his relationship to God.

The passage under consideration is a separate unit with a striking, symmetrical, and suggestive structure. The key to the structure centers in the introductory formula, the fourfold use of ne'um yahweh (says the Lord), and the three appearances of the particle ki (but or for).

The structure suggests that this is revelation. Four times the expression says the Lord (lit., whisper of Yahweh, an intimate, authoritative communication from Yahweh) occurs (vv. 31,32,33,34). Some prosaic souls think that this is too many and proceed with the process of excision. This misses the point. God's new thing is to be radically different. The sulking, cynical captives would be skeptical. Hence its announcement gets a heavy stamp of divine authority: "This is revelation!"

Moreover, the revelation came in a particular life situation. Jeremiah and the Jews were faced with a problem. The old covenant had collapsed because the people had persistently broken it (v. 32). It had been made with the nation. The nation had crashed on the rock of God's law. Now the question arose: How can a holy God maintain a relationship with a sinful people who, because of collective guilt, have been deprived of country and sent into captivity? The answer came in the concept of a new covenant, the nature of which would be such as to guarantee it against failure.

Further, the revelation involves both

---

[105] J. Harvey has a fine study of the new emphasis on individual responsibility in Jeremiah and Ezekiel and its relation to the old concept of corporate responsibility—*Sciences ecclésiastiques*, 10, 1958, 167–202. On the significance of Jeremiah for Ezekiel's preaching, see J. W. Miller, *Das Verhältnis und Hezekiels*, 1955.

continuity and discontinuity. There will be continuity. Like the old, the new covenant will be rooted in and rest on the divine initiative. God will act in sovereign grace: *I will make . . . , I will put . . . write . . . , I will forgive* (*salach*, a word uniquely expressive of divine action). . . .

Like the old, the new covenant will have as its intent the realization of a dynamic relationship between God and man. It will fulfill the purpose of the old covenant: *I will be their God, and they shall be my people.*

Like the old, the new covenant will include at its center the *law* (*torah*)—not a new *law*—as the articulation of God's will for a people in covenant relationship with him (v. 33b).

Like the old, the new covenant will be made with *the house of Israel,* the whole people of God (vv. 31,33a). It will transcend the national entity but not community and group solidarity. Though, as we shall see, the individual becomes the focal point of religious experience in the new covenant, it is not the individual apart from community. The Old Testament never divorces the individual from the group. Nor should we. Rugged individualism in religion is not biblical.

If there is continuity between the old and the new, there is also discontinuity. But in what sense is the new *not like* the old? Wherein is it really *new?*

First, the new covenant is incorporated into the promise.[106] Formerly, covenants were made, not promised. The taking up of the covenant into the promise meant a radical change. The new covenant would mark the end of the history of God's previous dealings with his people.

Second, it includes an eschatological dimension. The opening formula *Behold, the days are coming* (v. 31) refers to "the new form of the God-relation in the salvation-time" (Weiser, p. 294).

---

106 Claus Westermann, "The Way of the Promise in the Old Testament," *The Old Testament and the Christian Faith,* ed. B. W. Anderson (London: SCM Press, 1964), p. 219.

Third, the new covenant involves the creation of a new man through a new divine deed. This brings us to the crux of what is said in vv. 33–34. God is going to *write* his *law* (the revelation of his order of life for his people), not on tablets of stone, but on the *heart* (the inner being of the individual).

Here is where the distinctively new factor begins to enter. God will *put* his will straight into man's *heart,* so that the necessity of communication through external methods will be circumvented. This does not mean that the ministry of teaching is to be removed. It is Jeremiah's way of speaking of the work of the Holy Spirit in the making of a new man, who not only has illumination as to what God's will is, but also has the power to respond in obedience to that will. This new man knows God firsthand.

For (*ki*): The reason for this inner illumination and transformation is that the individual is brought into fellowship with God. One needs to recall what Jeremiah means by knowing God. One can *know* the law in a formal sense and not *know* God (2:8). To *know* God one must refrain from wrongdoing (4:22; 9:3,6) and practice justice, righteousness, and love (9:24; 22:16). To *know* God one must have a pure and regenerate heart that turns to him in loyal obedience (24:7). To *know* God is not a formal affair, but a direct, dynamic, intimate, personal fellowship with God which controls the course of one's life. This does not come through creed and ceremony but through contact and communion. Under the new covenant this fellowship with God will be possible for everybody—*from the least of them to the greatest.*

But how does a sinner enter fellowship with God? *For* (*ki*) *I will forgive . . .* There can be no life-changing fellowship with God apart from the forgiveness of sins. Just as Jeremiah's reference to the heart and to the knowledge of God should be set against the background of such statements as 24:7 and 32:39, so his allusion to forgiveness of sins should be viewed in the context of his frequent mention of the stubbornness of man's evil heart and his earnest calls to repentance. Only God can do anything about man's tragic predicament. But he can and will.

How he will do it Jeremiah does not say. That he will do it he asserts without equivocation. He adds a beautiful feature. God will not only forgive, but also forget—the *only* thing in the Bible which he is represented as forgetting and that which we would most like for him to forget—our sin!

If we reverse the prophet's order and move from cause to effect, we have in the "faith" of the future: the forgiveness of sins through Christ ("the grace of our Lord Jesus Christ"), the fellowship with the Father in love ("the love of God the Father"), and the fullness of the Spirit ("the communion of the Holy Spirit"). And God's new thing is "the picture of a new man, a man who is able to obey . . . because of a miraculous change of his nature" (von Rad, pp. 213 f.).

In some measure, we have anticipated the tremendous impact and ultimate fulfillment of this great prophecy (cf. 32: 37 ff.; Ezek. 11:19; 18:31; 36:25–31; John 3:32; 2 Cor. 5:17; also, 1 Cor. 11:25; 2 Cor. 3:1 ff.). The prophecy points to the cross, and its actualization comes in Jesus Christ. There is deep discontinuity. Yet within that discontinuity is a wonderful continuity, for the same marvelous grace which brought Israel into being and directed her toward her destiny also creates the new Israel in Christ and guides her toward the great consummation.

It is astounding that 600 years before Christ, in the midst of the greatest loneliness, tragedy, and grief, Jeremiah could proclaim a teaching so profound, so spiritual, and so true, that soon after Christianity had taken root in history it could be quoted as a good description of the gospel (Heb. 8:8–12; 10:16–17). This has been called "the supreme achievement of Israel's religion, and its author . . . the loftiest

religious genius who adorned the lives of the prophets" (Peake, I, p. 46).

35 Thus says the Lord,
　who gives the sun for light by day
　　and the fixed order of the moon and the
　　　stars for light by night,
　who stirs up the sea so that its waves roar—
　　the Lord of hosts is his name:
36 "If this fixed order departs
　　from before me, says the Lord,
　then shall the descendants of Israel cease
　　from being a nation before me for ever."

37 Thus says the Lord:
　"If the heavens above can be measured,
　　and the foundations of the earth below
　　　can be explored,
　then I will cast off all the descendants of
　　Israel
　for all that they have done,
　　　　　　　　　　says the Lord."
38 "Behold, the days are coming, says the Lord, when the city shall be rebuilt for the Lord from the tower of Hananel to the Corner Gate. 39 And the measuring line shall go out farther, straight to the hill Gareb, and shall then turn to Goah. 40 The whole valley of the dead bodies and the ashes, and all the fields as far as the brook Kidron, to the corner of the Horse Gate toward the east, shall be sacred to the Lord. It shall not be uprooted or overthrown any more for ever."

At the close of the forecast of the new covenant he will make and the new man he will create, God sets a double seal. The first part of the seal is placed directly by the hand of God (vv. 35–37). It involves his faithfulness, as seen in the *fixed order* of nature. This faithfulness—frequently referred to by Jeremiah—is a guarantee of the permanence of the "new Israel," the redeemed, restored people of God.

This is "a rhetorical climax." The prophet moves quickly from the inner world to the outer, and declares that as long as the *fixed order* of the universe and the God behind it stand, the new covenant community will stand. "In salvation there is something inviolable, something of the eternity of God" (Leslie, p. 108).

The second part of the seal is the promise of the new Jerusalem (vv. 38–40). This involves the action of man. Note that this final word of God in chapter 31 is introduced by the same words which introduce the prophecy of the new covenant (31:31). Observe also that the city is to *be rebuilt for the Lord* and that it *shall be sacred to the Lord* and *shall not be uprooted or overthrown any more forever.* Now the temporal Jerusalem has been built, destroyed, and rebuilt time and again. In view of this, there must be eschatological implications here. Moreover, there is an indirect stress on "the anthropological side" of God's work of salvation, so characteristic of Jeremiah (von Rad, p. 214).

Both the beautiful poem in vv. 35–37 and the prose passage in vv. 38–40 have been deleted from the authentic utterances of Jeremiah by some scholars because of too much preoccupation with the "nation" and the "city." In some degree, the same indictment might be brought against vv. 31–34.

3. "And I Bought the Field" (32:1–44)

¹ The word that came to Jeremiah from the LORD in the tenth year of Zedekiah king of Judah, which was the eighteenth year of Nebuchadrezzar. ² At that time the army of the king of Babylon was besieging Jerusalem, and Jeremiah the prophet was shut up in the court of the guard which was in the palace of the king of Judah. ³ For Zedekiah king of Judah had imprisoned him, saying, "Why do you prophesy and say, 'Thus says the LORD: Behold, I am giving this city into the hand of the king of Babylon, and he shall take it; ⁴ Zedekiah king of Judah shall not escape out of the hand of the Chaldeans, but shall surely be given into the hand of the king of Babylon, and shall speak with him face to face and see him eye to eye; ⁵ and he shall take Zedekiah to Babylon, and there he shall remain until I visit him, says the LORD; though you fight against the Chaldeans, you shall not succeed'?"
⁶ Jeremiah said, "The word of the LORD came to me: ⁷ Behold, Hanamel the son of Shallum your uncle will come to you and say, 'Buy my field which is at Anathoth, for the right of redemption by purchase is yours.' ⁸ Then Hanamel my cousin came to me in the court of the guard, in accordance with the word of the LORD, and said to me, 'Buy my field which is at Anathoth in the land of Benjamin, for the right of possession and redemption is yours; buy it for yourself.' Then I knew that this was the word of the LORD.

Here we get back to biography and to a specific historical situation. Two things are emphasized: the prophet's imprisonment (vv. 1–5) and the prophet's presentiment (vv. 6–8).

The tenth year of Zedekiah would be 588–587. *The court of the guard* was a portion of the palace where prisoners with dangerous views were kept under the direct supervision of the king. Confinement was semipublic.

Had chapter 32 been placed with 37 and 38, where it belongs chronologically, the parenthetical explanation of the prophet's imprisonment would not have been essential. But because of the element of hope in it, it has been incorporated in "the book of consolation." Therefore vv. 1–5 are necessary to give the historical context.

Verses 6–8 tell of Jeremiah's presentiment concerning the coming of a cousin to confer with him about the redemption of some family property at Anathoth. The prophet identified this presentiment as *the word of the Lord.* When Hanamel arrived, Jeremiah said: *Then I knew that this was the word of the Lord.* The presentiment had been confirmed in experience.

⁹ "And I bought the field at Anathoth from Hanamel my cousin, and weighed out the money to him, seventeen shekels of silver. ¹⁰ I signed the deed, sealed it, got witnesses, and weighed the money on scales. ¹¹ Then I took the sealed deed of purchase, containing the terms and conditions, and the open copy; ¹² and I gave the deed of purchase to Baruch the son of Neriah son of Maaseiah, in the presence of Hanamel my cousin, in the presence of the witnesses who signed the deed of purchase, and in the presence of all the Jews who were sitting in the court of the guard. ¹³ I charged Baruch in their presence, saying, ¹⁴ 'Thus says the LORD of hosts, the God of Israel: Take these deeds, both this sealed deed of purchase and this open deed, and put them in an earthenware vessel, that they may last for a long time. ¹⁵ For thus says the LORD of hosts, the God of Israel: Houses and fields and vineyards shall again be bought in this land.'

The incident here recorded is most instructive. First, it is an illuminating illustration of an ancient business transaction. We are given a wealth of information about the procedure in such a deal: the weighing out of the silver in payment, the securing of *witnesses*, the signing in duplicate of the *deed of purchase* with its *terms and conditions*, the sealing of one copy and the leaving of the other open, and the placing of the deeds in a jar for preservation (cf. the Dead Sea Scrolls).

But, though the detailed description of a property transfer is of great interest, the really important thing is the revelation which came through this symbolic act and the accompanying pronouncement (v. 15): God had a future for his people, and Jeremiah had faith in that future. The prophet gave tangible token of his faith in one of the most eloquent actions in the Bible: *And I bought the field!* How the Jews must have jeered in that jailhouse! Land was worthless around Jerusalem and Anathoth at that time. But Jeremiah was certain that the day was coming when God would restore his people to their homeland and when property now worthless would be bought and sold again. He gave feet to the idea: "It's dark today. It may be dark tomorrow. But there is always light ahead."[107]

In Judah's darkest hour Jeremiah was her supreme optimist. No trafficker in tears and tragedy this man, but a true prophet of gallant courage and gigantic faith! For him, nothing could ultimately defeat the purpose of God.

16 "After I had given the deed of purchase to Baruch the son of Neriah, I prayed to the LORD, saying: 17 'Ah Lord GOD! It is thou who hast made the heavens and the earth by thy great power and by thy outstretched arm! Nothing is too hard for thee, 18 who showest steadfast love to thousands, but dost requite the guilt of fathers to their children after them, O great and mighty God whose name is the LORD of hosts, 19 great in counsel and mighty in

107 Charles E. Jefferson, *Cardinal Ideas of Jeremiah* (New York: The Macmillan Company, 1928), pp. 194–214.

deed; whose eyes are open to all the ways of men, rewarding every man according to his ways and according to the fruit of his doings; 20 who hast shown signs and wonders in the land of Egypt, and to this day in Israel and among all mankind, and hast made thee a name, as at this day. 21 Thou didst bring thy people Israel out of the land of Egypt with signs and wonders, with a strong hand and outstretched arm, and with great terror; 22 and thou gavest them this land, which thou didst swear to their fathers to give them, a land flowing with milk and honey; 23 and they entered and took possession of it. But they did not obey thy voice or walk in they law; they did nothing of all thou didst command them to do. Therefore thou hast made all this evil come upon them. 24 Behold, the siege mounds have come up to the city to take it, and because of sword and famine and pestilence the city is given into the hands of the Chaldeans who are fighting against it. What thou didst speak has come to pass, and behold, thou seest it. 25 Yet thou, O Lord GOD, hast said to me, "Buy the field for money and get witnesses"—though the city is given into the hands of the Chaldeans.' "

This is an agonizing but beautiful prayer. Some scholars—perhaps most—are persuaded that though it has a Jeremianic base it has been expanded. It starts out with a brief ejaculation of pain, *Ah Lord God!* and ends with a note of expectancy, *Yet thou, O Lord God, . . .*

Apparently this is one of those afterthought situations. Jeremiah awoke to the realization of what he had done, to the stark realism of the situation around him, and to the seeming contradiction between the two. Had he misinterpreted God's guidance in buying the field? Deeply distressed, he sought "ultimate clarity" from God, as he unburdened his soul in prayer (Rudolph, p. 193).

The prayer is remarkable in its revelation of God. It also reminds us of Jeremiah's characteristic practice in receiving and responding to disturbing and difficult revelations.

26 The word of the LORD came to Jeremiah: 27 "Behold, I am the LORD, the God of all flesh; is anything too hard for me? 28 Therefore, thus says the LORD: Behold, I am giving this city into the hands of the Chaldeans and into the hand of Nebuchadrezzar king of Babylon, and

he shall take it. ²⁹ The Chaldeans who are fighting against this city shall come and set this city on fire, and burn it, with the houses on whose roofs incense has been offered to Baal and drink offerings have been poured out to other gods, to provoke me to anger. ³⁰ For the sons of Israel and the sons of Judah have done nothing but evil in my sight from their youth; the sons of Israel have done nothing but provoke me to anger by the work of their hands, says the LORD. ³¹ This city has aroused my anger and wrath, from the day it was built to this day, so that I will remove it from my sight ³² because of all the evil of the sons of Israel and the sons of Judah which they did to provoke me to anger—their kings and their princes, their priests and their prophets, the men of Judah and the inhabitants of Jerusalem. ³³ They have turned to me their back and not their face; and though I have taught them persistently they have not listened to receive instruction. ³⁴ They set up their abominations in the house which is called by my name, to defile it. ³⁵ They built the high places of Baal in the valley of the son of Hinnom, to offer up their sons and daughters to Molech, though I did not command them, nor did it enter into my mind, that they should do this abomination, to cause Judah to sin.

³⁶ "Now therefore thus says the LORD, the God of Israel, concerning this city of which you say, 'It is given into the hand of the king of Babylon by sword, by famine, and by pestilence': ³⁷ Behold, I will gather them from all the countries to which I drove them in my anger and my wrath and in great indignation; I will bring them back to this place, and I will make them dwell in safety. ³⁸ And they shall be my people, and I will be their God. ³⁹ I will give them one heart and one way, that they may fear me for ever, for their own good and the good of their children after them. ⁴⁰ I will make with them an everlasting covenant, that I will not turn away from doing good to them; and I will put the fear of me in their hearts, that they may not turn from me. ⁴¹ I will rejoice in doing them good, and I will plant them in this land in faithfulness, with all my heart and all my soul.

⁴² "For thus says the LORD: Just as I have brought all this great evil upon this people, so I will bring upon them all the good that I promise them. ⁴³ Fields shall be bought in this land of which you are saying, It is a desolation, without man or beast; it is given into the hands of the Chaldeans. ⁴⁴ Fields shall be bought for money, and deeds shall be signed and sealed and witnessed, in the land of Benjamin, in the places about Jerusalem, and in the cities of Judah, in the cities of the hill country, in the cities of the Shephelah, and in the cities of the

Negeb; for I will restore their fortunes, says the LORD."

God's reply, which starts on the same note as that with which the prayer began (vv. 27,17), dwells on two things. First, because the guilt of Jerusalem is so great, her destruction is sure. Second, because her God is a God of grace, her restoration is certain. Verses 37–41 are very important. They are not a mere copy of 31:31–34. There are too many points of difference. There is a particular emphasis on God's *giving* his people *one heart and one way,* as he makes with them *an everlasting covenant.* The *fear* of the Lord is equivalent to obedience to God's will (von Rad, p. 215).

4. Happy Days Ahead (33:1–26)

¹ The word of the LORD came to Jeremiah a second time, while he was still shut up in the court of the guard: ² "Thus says the LORD who made the earth, the LORD who formed it to establish it—the LORD is his name: ³ Call to me and I will answer you, and will tell you great and hidden things which you have not known. ⁴ For thus says the LORD, the God of Israel, concerning the houses of this city and the houses of the kings of Judah which were torn down to make a defense against the siege mounds and before the sword: ⁵ The Chaldeans are coming in to fight and to fill them with the dead bodies of men whom I shall smite in my anger and my wrath, for I have hidden my face from this city because of all their wickedness. ⁶ Behold, I will bring to it health and healing, and I will heal them and reveal to them abundance of prosperity and security. ⁷ I will restore the fortunes of Judah and the fortunes of Israel, and rebuild them as they were at first. ⁸ I will cleanse them from all the guilt of their sin against me, and I will forgive all the guilt of their sin and rebellion against me. ⁹ And this city shall be to me a name of joy, a praise and a glory before all the nations of the earth who shall hear of all the good that I do for them; they shall fear and tremble because of all the good and all the prosperity I provide for it.

The overall emphasis in chapters 30—32 continues in 33. The outlook is bright. The subject is the happy future of God's people. Critical opinion varies with regard to the authenticity of the material in chapter 33, but it is fair to say that most scholars consider that most of the material consists of later mediations on Jeremianic themes.

The first part of the chapter (vv. 1–9) gives us a glimpse into the mind and heart of the great preacher during the final days of the siege of Jerusalem. Two things stand out. First, Jeremiah is convinced that all of the suffering and the severity of the judgment has been caused by the persistent rebellion of the people against God. Second, the prophet is certain that though God's face is hidden now he will ultimately show it and save his people. He will forgive, heal, cleanse, and rebuild. *And this city will become . . . a name of joy, a praise and a glory* (v. 9).

10 "Thus says the LORD: In this place of which you say, 'It is a waste without man or beast,' in the cities of Judah and the streets of Jerusalem that are desolate, without man or inhabitant or beast, there shall be heard again 11 the voice of mirth and the voice of gladness, the voice of the bridegroom and the voice of the bride, the voices of those who sing, as they bring thank offerings to the house of the LORD:
'Give thanks to the LORD of hosts,
    for the LORD is good,
    for his steadfast love endures for ever!'
For I will restore the fortunes of the land as at first, says the LORD.
12 "Thus says the LORD of hosts: In this place which is waste, without man or beast, and in all of its cities, there shall again be habitations of shepherds resting their flocks. 13 In the cities of the hill country, in the cities of the Shephelah, and in the cities of the Negeb, in the land of Benjamin, the places about Jerusalem, and in the cities of Judah, flocks shall again pass under the hands of the one who counts them, says the LORD.

The city has fallen (v. 10). The prophet, who has often referred to the removal of joy when the judgment came, speaks of the rebirth of joy in the day of renewal in words almost antiphonal (v. 11a). He uses a portion of a cultic hymn, which dwells on the enduring goodness and grace of God (v. 11b). The thought here is very similar to that in 31:2–6.

In the new age, there will be pastoral peace in the land. As the people go about their daily pursuits, they will be secure and unafraid (cf. 30:19; 31:4,12–14).

14 "Behold, the days are coming, says the LORD, when I will fulfil the promise I made to the house of Israel and the house of Judah. 15 In those days and at that time I will cause a righteous Branch to spring forth for David; and he shall execute justice and righteousness in the land. 16 In those days Judah will be saved and Jerusalem will dwell securely. And this is the name by which it will be called: 'The LORD is our righteousness.'
17 "For thus says the LORD: David shall never lack a man to sit on the throne of the house of Israel, 18 and the Levitical priests shall never lack a man in my presence to offer burnt offerings, to burn cereal offerings, and to make sacrifices for ever."
19 The word of the LORD came to Jeremiah: 20 "Thus says the LORD: If you can break my covenant with the day and my covenant with the night, so that day and night will not come at their appointed time, 21 then also my covenant with David my servant may be broken, so that he shall not have a son to reign on his throne, and my covenant with the Levitical priests my ministers. 22 As the host of heaven cannot be numbered and the sands of the sea cannot be measured, so I will multiply the descendants of David my servant, and the Levitical priests who minister to me."
23 The word of the LORD came to Jeremiah: 24 "Have you not observed what these people are saying, 'The LORD has rejected the two families which he chose'? Thus they have despised my people so that they are no longer a nation in their sight. 25 Thus says the LORD: If I have not established my covenant with day and night and the ordinances of heaven and eath, 26 then I will reject the descendants of Jacob and David my servant and will not choose one of his descendants to rule over the seed of Abraham, Isaac, and Jacob. For I will restore their fortunes, and will have mercy upon them."

This section is omitted from the LXX. The reason is not known. It is included here because of the element of hope in it. It stresses God's abiding faithfulness to his people, as seen particularly in his restoration of them and in his raising up of *a righteous Branch* of the line of David to rule over them in *justice and righteousness* (cf. 23:5–6). Once again the prophet speaks of the basic stability of the natural order and uses this to indicate the enduring quality of God's new spiritual order (cf. 31:35–37).

XV. Experiences of the Prophet During the Siege of the City (34:1–22)

Here Baruch's "biography" is resumed, following the insertion of "the book of consolation" (chs. 30—33).

The chapter under consideration has no obvious relation to the chapters immediately preceding it. There are linguistic parallels between it and chapters 35—36. This, plus the fact that it is integral to the account of the prophet's experiences during the time of Baruch's association with him, may explain its present position in the prophecy.

1. Counsel for the King (34:1–7)

¹ The word which came to Jeremiah from the LORD, when Nebuchadrezzar king of Babylon and all his army and all the kingdoms of the earth under his dominion and all the peoples were fighting against Jerusalem and all of its cities: ² "Thus says the LORD, the God of Israel: Go and speak to Zedekiah king of Judah and say to him, 'Thus says the LORD: Behold, I am giving this city into the hand of the king of Babylon, and he shall burn it with fire. ³ You shall not escape from his hand, but shall surely be captured and delivered into his hand; you shall see the king of Babylon eye to eye and speak with him face to face; and you shall go to Babylon.' ⁴ Yet hear the word of the LORD, O Zedekiah king of Judah! Thus says the LORD concerning you: 'You shall not die by the sword. ⁵ You shall die in peace. And as spices were burned for your fathers, the former kings who were before you, so men shall burn spices for you and lament for you, saying, "Alas, lord!" ' For I have spoken the word, says the LORD."
⁶ Then Jeremiah the prophet spoke all these words to Zedekiah king of Judah, in Jerusalem, ⁷ when the army of the king of Babylon was fighting against Jerusalem and against all the cities of Judah that were left, Lachish and Azekah; for these were the only fortified cities of Judah that remained.

The incident here recorded occurred after the one referred to in 21:1–10. In the exposition of that passage, the early strategy and activity of Nebuchadnezzar in Palestine were briefly depicted. By the spring of 588 B.C., except for Jerusalem, only two strongholds remained uncon-

quered: Lachish and Azekah (v. 7).[108]

Under the leadership of the Lord, in early 588, Jeremiah confronted King Zedekiah and gave him some counsel in the form of a prophetic oracle. The message was that resistance to the enemy was hopeless. Jerusalem would be taken and put to the torch. The only wise course was to surrender to Nebuchadnezzar in compliance with the will of God, in which case the king might get leniency of treatment, an honorable funeral, and lamentation befitting a ruler (vv. 2–5).

Two things stand out in this passage. One is Jeremiah's relatively gentle and sympathetic treatment of Zedekiah (cf. comment on 23:1–8). The other is the prophet's consistency. For years he had known that the Babylonians were the appointed agents of God's judgment on Judah. He stuck by that conviction. He might complain, "curse" his enemies, or cry out in agony or anger to God, but he would not compromise in his preaching.

It would be a great mistake and a gross misrepresentation to interpret the advice given by Jeremiah as an indication that he was a coward who was unwilling to defend his country or that he was a fifth columnist in the employ of the Babylonians to undermine the morale of his countrymen. It would be equally wrong to maintain that he was acting as a counselor who was pointing out a course to be followed in all emergency situations involving national defense. He was speaking as a servant of God in terms of a conviction which had come to him from God concerning his particular situation.

2. A Covenant Violation and an Oracle of Condemnation (34:8–22)

⁸ The word which came to Jeremiah from the LORD, after King Zedekiah had made a covenant with all the people in Jerusalem to make a proclamation of liberty to them, ⁹ that every one should set free his Hebrew slaves, male and female, so that no one should enslave a Jew, his brother. ¹⁰ And they obeyed, all the

---

[108] See Lachish Letters IV, Pritchard, op. cit., p. 382.

princes and all the people who had entered into the covenant that every one would set free his slave, male or female, so that they would not be enslaved again; they obeyed and set them free. 11 But afterward they turned around and took back the male and female slaves they had set free, and brought them into subjection as slaves. 12 The word of the LORD came to Jeremiah from the LORD: 13 "Thus says the LORD, the God of Israel: I made a covenant with your fathers when I brought them out of the land of Egypt, out of the house of bondage, saying, 14 'At the end of six years each of you must set free the fellow Hebrew who has been sold to you and has served you six years; you must set him free from your service.' But your fathers did not listen to me or incline their ears to me. 15 You recently repented and did what was right in my eyes by proclaiming liberty, each to his neighbor, and you made a covenant before me in the house which is called by my name; 16 but then you turned around and profaned my name when each of you took back his male and female slaves, whom you had set free according to their desire, and you brought them into subjection to be your slaves. 17 Therefore, thus says the LORD: You have not obeyed me by proclaiming liberty, every one to his brother and to his neighbor; behold, I proclaim to you liberty to the sword, to pestilence, and to famine, says the LORD. I will make you a horror to all the kingdoms of the earth. 18 And the men who transgressed my covenant and did not keep the terms of the covenant which they made before me, I will make like the calf which they cut in two and passed between its parts—19 the princes of Judah, the princes of Jerusalem, the eunuchs, the priests, and all the people of the land who passed between the parts of the calf; 20 and I will give them into the hand of their enemies and into the hand of those who seek their lives. Their dead bodies shall be food for the birds of the air and the beasts of the earth. 21 And Zedekiah king of Judah, and his princes I will give into the hand of their enemies and into the hand of those who seek their lives, into the hand of the army of the king of Babylon which has withdrawn from you. 22 Behold, I will command, says the LORD, and will bring them back to this city; and they will fight against it, and take it, and burn it with fire. I will make the cities of Judah a desolation without inhabitant."

As the siege of the city continued, the picture became blacker and blacker for the country. Then the king took an unusual step. He led the beleaguered citizens of Jerusalem in the making of a covenant to free all Hebrew slaves, male and female.

There was a covenantal law concerning the release of a Hebrew slave after six years (Ex. 21:2–6; Deut. 15:1–18). But this law had suffered neglect. In their desperation, the people decided to go beyond the law and let all slaves go, including those whose time of service was not up. It was specifically agreed that they would not force the freed slaves back into slavery again. The royal decree was issued in covenantal form, and the covenant was sealed in a very solemn fashion (vv. 18–20; cf. Gen. 15:7–17; Ex. 24:6–8).[109]

What was the motive behind this move? It was likely mixed: fewer mouths to feed, freeing slaves from labor to fight, seeking the favor of God. There was definite economic pressure, and there was a need for fighting men. But the primary motive appears to have been religious. The outlook was dark, and the people desired a divine deed of deliverance, as in 701. They needed God. So they got busy complying with his covenantal commands!

Then it happened. The Babylonians left (v. 22; 37:1 ff.). They lifted the seige temporarily in order to deal with the Egyptian army advancing from the south. Remember that Egypt was behind this fracas. She must show some semblance of support.

But the Jews thought it was over. God had done it again! The city was delivered —as in the old days! There must have been rejoicing. The people could use their former slaves now. There was work to be done. So they promptly reversed their earlier action and reenslaved those who had been released. This, of course, was plain hypocrisy and treachery. Peake refers to the affair as "a death-bed repentance, with the usual sequel on recovery" (p. 139).

This flagrant act of treachery and blasphemy stirred Jeremiah's prophetic spirit. He delivered a sizzling oracle of condemnation: a people so corrupt deserved the terrible fate which was going to be theirs!

The oracle begins with the "revelation formula" and the "messenger formula" (vv.

109 See also Couturier, op. cit., p. 329.

12–13*a*). Then comes the indictment (vv. 13*b*–16), followed by the announcement of judgment (vv. 17–22).

In the indictment, reference is made to God's redemption of his people from servitude in Egypt, his articulation of his will in his holy law (including the law about slaves), and the rebellion of the *fathers* against his will. Then Jeremiah becomes painfully specific. In speaking of the recent violation of the covenant in slapping the former servants back into slavery, he lets go on his leitmotif of "turning:" "Then *you* (emphatic) recently *turned back* (to me) and did the thing that was right in my eyes in proclaiming emancipation, each to his fellow, and you cut a covenant (cf. v. 18) before me in the house over which my name is called (i.e., in *my* house). But you *turned back* (from me) and profaned my name, and *caused to return* (to servitude), every one of you, his male and female slaves, whom you had set free . . . " (author's translation).

The prediction of disaster is specific and strong (vv. 17–22). It starts with a word-play: *kara' d*e*ror* (proclaim emancipation): the people proclaimed emancipation for their slaves and then revoked the proclamation; God is now proclaiming emancipation for the people to destruction.

Observe the frequent occurrence of the word *covenant* in vv. 8–22. Jeremiah did not avoid the term as did his predecessors. Note, too, that the covenant with Israel is connected with the Exodus event (v. 13). Though there has been much debate and disagreement on the subject, scholarly study has shown that the covenant is as old as Yahwism.[110]

In the dynamic account of a dishonest deal Jeremiah makes it clear that, while rooted in redeeming grace, biblical faith must express itself in ethical conduct.

XVI. A Lesson in Loyalty (35:1–19)

Although the symbolic act described in chapter 35 is not dated with precision, vv.

[110] For a summary of the study, see D. J. McCarthy, *op. cit.,* pp. 217–240; Hillers, *op. cit.,* pp. 1–71.

1 and 11 suggest the historical situation which serves as its background. The defeat of Nebuchadnezzar by the Egyptians in 601 B.C. apparently gave Jehoiakim courage to rebel against his overlord. It was necessary that the Babylonian ruler send soldiers from neighboring vassal states to crush the revolt. They were unsuccessful. Nebuchadnezzar came in 598 (cf. Int.).

During this turbulent period, *ca.* 600 to 598, the Rechabites moved into Jerusalem for safety. Who were these people? They were a protest group. Distant relatives of the Israelites (1 Chron. 2:55; Judg. 1:16) and ardent Yahwists (2 Kings 10: 15–17), they had dwelt through the centuries in the southern part of Palestine (Judg. 4:17; 5:24; 1 Sam. 15:6). What was unusual about them? They took a vow which required that they refrain from planting vineyards, drinking wine, and living in houses. Instead, they stayed in tents away from "the sown," as the Israelites had done during the desert sojourn.[111]

The Rechabites represented a vigorous repudiation of the pagan elements that had infiltrated the faith and life of Israel from the Canaanite cult and culture, and a radical reversion toward the simplicity and purity of religion and life in "the good old days." Since wine was and is considered a food beverage in the Near East, these "teetotalers" must have been quite a curiosity in the capital city.

One day Jeremiah felt constrained to use the group as an object lesson for his people. The story and its significance are set down in prose with a Deuteronomic coloring (cf. 7:1 ff.; 11:1 ff.; 16:1 ff.). The passage has both an autobiographical cast and a biographical framework. It belongs to Baruch's memoirs.

1. The Story of the Symbolic Act (35:1–11)

¹ The word which came to Jeremiah from the LORD in the days of Jehoiakim the son of Josiah, king of Judah: ² "Go to the house of the Rechabites, and speak with them, and bring them to the house of the LORD, into one of the chambers; then offer them wine to drink." ³ So

[111] See M. H. Pope, IDB, 4, 14–16.

I took Jaazaniah the son of Jeremiah, son of Habazziniah, and his brothers, and all his sons, and the whole house of the Rechabites. 4 I brought them to the house of the LORD into the chamber of the sons of Hanan the son of Igdaliah, the man of God, which was near the chamber of the princes, above the chamber of Maaseiah the son of Shallum, keeper of the threshold. 5 Then I set before the Rechabites pitchers full of wine, and cups; and I said to them, "Drink wine." 6 But they answered, "We will drink no wine, for Jonadab the son of Rechab, our father, commanded us, 'You shall not drink wine, neither you nor your sons for ever; 7 you shall not build a house; you shall not sow seed; you shall not plant or have a vineyard; but you shall live in tents all your days, that you may live many days in the land where you sojourn.' 8 We have obeyed the voice of Jonadab the son of Rechab, our father, in all that he commanded us, to drink no wine all our days, ourselves, our wives, our sons, or our daughters, 9 and not to build houses to dwell in. We have no vineyard or field or seed; 10 but we have lived in tents, and have obeyed and done all that Jonadab our father commanded us. 11 But when Nebuchadrezzar king of Babylon came up against the land, we said, 'Come, and let us go to Jerusalem for fear of the army of the Chaldeans and the army of the Syrians.' So we are living in Jerusalem."

Acting under divine direction, Jeremiah went to the community (*house*) of the Rechabites and asked them to accompany him to the Temple. This they did. At the Temple, they entered *the chamber* (Knox, "apartment") *of the sons of Hanan . . . the man of God*. Since the phrase *the man of God* usually designates a prophet in the Old Testament, Hanan may have been a prophet, and his *sons* may have been his disciples. Evidently he was friendly toward Jeremiah.

Jeremiah proceeded to set before the Rechabites pitchers full of wine. He urgently invited them to partake. They politely but firmly refused. They gave their reason: faithfulness to a vow taught by their founder and taken by them. The vow prohibited drinking wine and living in houses. They stressed that they had been obedient to the teaching of their founder in all particulars. They were very careful to explain that their presence in Jerusalem, a city of houses and walls, was in no sense

due to a deviation from any ancestral practice or principle but only to the danger posed by the presence of invading enemy soldiers. They were simply seeking temporary security.

2. The Significance of the Act (35:12–19)

12 Then the word of the LORD came to Jeremiah: 13 "Thus says the LORD of hosts, the God of Israel: Go and say to the men of Judah and the inhabitants of Jerusalem, Will you not receive instruction and listen to my words? says the LORD. 14 The command which Jonadab the son of Rechab gave to his sons, to drink no wine, has been kept; and they drink none to this day, for they have obeyed their father's command. I have spoken to you persistently, but you have not listened to me. 15 I have sent to you all my servants the prophets, sending them persistently, saying, 'Turn now every one of you from his evil way, and amend your doings, and do not go after other gods to serve them, and then you shall dwell in the land which I gave to you and your fathers.' But you did not incline your ear or listen to me. 16 The sons of Jonadab the son of Rechab have kept the command which their father gave them, but this people has not obeyed me. 17 Therefore, thus says the LORD, the God of hosts, the God of Israel: Behold, I am bringing on Judah and all the inhabitants of Jerusalem all the evil that I have pronounced against them; because I have spoken to them and they have not listened, I have called to them and they have not answered."

18 But to the house of the Rechabites Jeremiah said, "Thus says the LORD of hosts, the God of Israel: Because you have obeyed the command of Jonadab your father, and kept all his precepts, and done all that he commanded you, 19 therefore thus says the LORD of hosts, the God of Israel: Jonadab the son of Rechab shall never lack a man to stand before me."

Ordinarily a symbolic act was accompanied by a pronouncement. Here the pronouncement is longer than usual. In fact, it includes two oracles, both dynamically related to the act.

The first is a prophecy of disaster, addressed to the covenant community (vv. 12–17). Following the introduction (vv. 12–13a) comes the reproach (vv. 13b–16). Here Jeremiah sets the fidelity of the Rechabites and the infidelity of the Judahites in sharp contrast. The Rechabites have been obedient to the letter to the teachings of a human founder. But the Judahites have been consistently and persistently disobedient to the teachings of the eternal God. With urgency and constancy this God has sent his servants the prophets to call his people to repentance (covenantal *shub*, v. 15). He has also shown his love by dealing out discipline (*instruction*, involving chastisement; cf. 2:30). They have not only rejected correction and refused to repent—they have not paid God any attention at all. The thunder of judgment is heard in v. 17: such a course of action can lead to but one end—the destruction of the nation.

The second prophecy is an oracle of salvation, directed to the Rechabite community (vv. 18–19). Because of their fidelity, the Rechabites are promised stability and continuity.

The problem of the relation of religion and culture is a perennial problem. Through the ages it has been solved in different ways by different groups. In Jeremiah's day, the Rechabites took the position that religion stands against culture. They said: "Return to the simple life of the fathers in the wilderness." Jeremiah took the position that religion stands over culture as conscience and critic. He preached: "Repent and return to a right relationship with God, and let that relationship express itself in all areas of life."

Jeremiah was not advocating the practices of the Rechabites but the principle behind those practices: "the moral quality of loyalty" (Volz, *Jeremia*, p. 323; cf. Clements, p. 48). He lived in a house. He probably drank wine as a part of the daily diet. But he was convinced that the supreme concern of every person and nation should be to enter into a right relationship with God and to be faithful to all the requirements of that relationship.

In this day of relativism and religious compromise, do we not need the prophet's emphasis on "the moral quality of loyalty —" loyalty to our best selves, to family, to country (in an enlightened sense), to the church, to the highest ideals for mankind, and, above all, to God in Christ?

XVII. *The Indestructible Word* (*36:1–32*)

It was a crucial hour. Jeremiah was sensitive to this fact. Nebuchadnezzar had just defeated the Egyptians at Carchemish and was pressing southward into Palestine. For 23 years the prophet had proclaimed that divine judgment was coming upon his country if the people did not return to a life of faith and obedience as a covenant community. Now the crisis was at hand! It was the psychological moment for making a last minute appeal for real repentance.

Since Jeremiah was *debarred* from the Temple area and could not proclaim God's message in person, he dictated his prophecies to Baruch, that he might read them to the Judahites on the occasion of a fast, when many would be present at the house of the Lord and in a sober mood.

When the fast was decreed (likely because of the national emergency), the scroll on which the prophecies were recorded was read three times. On the third reading it was destroyed by the king. When Jeremiah heard about this development, he produced a new and enlarged edition of his prophecies.

The story of all of this is preserved in chapter 36. This chapter, a part of Baruch's "biography" of Jeremiah, is an intensely interesting and tremendously important chapter.

For one thing, it is characterized by literary excellence.[112] The story which it relates is told with consummate skill. With real artistry the author allows the reader to feel the situation building toward a climax. Also, the chapter records a pivotal experience of the prophet, his first dictation of his prophecies. It is probable that he had written records which he used in the dictation process. But this is conjecture. In any case, what we have here is a definite, designed, divinely directed recording in writing of the prophetic word de-

112 Cf. E. Neilsen, *Oral Tradition* (Chicago: Alec R. Allenson, 1954), pp. 64–79.

livered over a period of almost a quarter of a century. This was something new in the ministry of Jeremiah, and it has implications which are new in the story of Old Testament prophecy.

More important still, chapter 36 is unique in that it is the only detailed account of the production of a prophetical "book" in the Old Testament. It sheds much light on the process whereby prophetical literature came into being and, as suggested in the Introduction, is the starting point both for the composition of the prophecy and for the critical study of its composition.

Isaiah had also written out his prophecies against the background of failure to get the spoken word across (Isa. 8:16–18; 30:8). But there is something new in Jeremiah's action. Not only is there a further step in the reduction of oral proclamation to writing in order to have a permanent record of it, but also there is the conviction that God's word is indestructible. Once uttered, it will not return void. It will endure and be effective. It must be handed on. Even when it is fulfilled, it will still have—will ever have—new meaning and relevance.

The striking and significant chapter under study is easy to analyze and needs little exposition.

1. The Word Recorded (36:1–8)

¹ In the fourth year of Jehoiakim the son of Josiah, king of Judah, this word came to Jeremiah from the Lord: ² "Take a scroll and write on it all the words that I have spoken to you against Israel and Judah and all the nations, from the day I spoke to you, from the days of Josiah until today. ³ It may be that the house of Judah will hear all the evil which I intend to do to them, so that every one may turn from his evil way, and that I may forgive their iniquity and their sin."
⁴ Then Jeremiah called Baruch the son of Neriah, and Baruch wrote upon a scroll at the dictation of Jeremiah all the words of the Lord which he had spoken to him. ⁵ And Jeremiah ordered Baruch, saying, "I am debarred from going to the house of the Lord; ⁶ so you are to go, and on a fast day in the hearing of all the people in the Lord's house you shall read

the words of the Lord from the scroll which you have written at my dictation. You shall read them also in the hearing of all the men of Judah who come out of their cities. ⁷ It may be that their supplication will come before the Lord, and that every one will turn from his evil way, for great is the anger and wrath that the Lord has pronounced against this people." ⁸ And Baruch the son of Neriah did all that Jeremiah the prophet ordered him about reading from the scroll the words of the Lord in the Lord's house.

Verse 1 provides the setting: *the fourth year* of the reign of Jehoiakim (cf. 25:1; 45:1; 46:2). This was 605. In that year, likely soon after the battle of Carchemish, *this word came to Jeremiah from the Lord.*

Verses 2 and 3 contain a private oracle. In it Jeremiah was commanded to secure "a book-scroll," on which he was to inscribe *all of the words* which God had spoken through him *against Israel* (LXX, "Jerusalem") *and Judah and all the nations* from his call (627) up to the present crisis (605). The purpose was to persuade the people to *turn* (repent, covenantal use of *shub*), in order that God might *forgive their iniquity and their sin.*

Verses 4–8 record Jeremiah's compliance with the commands in the oracle. Instead of writing out the prophecies himself, he dictated them to Baruch (cf. 32:12,13,16; 43:3,6; 45:1–5). The word rendered *debarred* means surrounded or enclosed, then hindered, held back, or restrained. Since Jeremiah was free to move about in the city (36:19,26,32), he was evidently not in prison but simply unable to go to the Temple area, probably because of an ecclesiastical interdict resulting from his "temple sermon" and/or his "Tophet sermon" (26; 19:1—20:6). In v. 6 allusion is made to *a fast day.* At this time it appears that fasts could be called whenever an occasion of crisis arose. Later, following the fall of Jerusalem, they became fixed events.

2. The Word Read and Rent (36:9–26)

Here is where the story really starts to build up in suspense. There were three readings of *the scroll.* The first is recounted very briefly, the second more at length, and the third in greater detail—with the focus of interest all the way through being the fate of the scroll.

(1) The Reading in the Presence of the People (36:9–10)

9 In the fifth year of Jehoiakim the son of Josiah, king of Judah, in the ninth month, all the people in Jerusalem and all the people who came from the cities of Judah to Jerusalem proclaimed a fast before the LORD. 10 Then, in the hearing of all the people, Baruch read the words of Jeremiah from the scroll, in the house of the LORD, in the chamber of Gemariah the son of Shaphan the secretary, which was in the upper court, at the entry of the New Gate of the LORD's house.

Baruch had to wait some months for the occasion for the public reading to present itself. During the delay he was having his difficulties (cf. 45:1 ff.). Finally the time came. It was a fast day proclaimed either because of a drought or because of the danger posed by the presence of the Babylonian army in Palestine (or both). Since it was December, there could have a lack of rain (Volz). But it was December, 604. In that same month the Babylonians assaulted and sacked the city of Ashkelon in the Philistine plain.[113] This in itself would be cause enough for the fast.

The reading of *the scroll* to the people took place *in the chamber* (apartment) *of Gemariah,* which was in the upper court of the Temple near the New Gate (the same court in which Jeremiah had been put on trial for his life, 26:7 ff.). Gemariah belonged to a prominent family which was apparently quite friendly to Jeremiah. This was a great day in the life of Baruch and something new in the life of Judah—the public reading of the prophetic word.

(2) The Reading in the Presence of the Princes (36:11–19)

11 When Micaiah the son of Gemariah, son of Shaphan, heard all the words of the LORD from the scroll, 12 he went down to the king's house, into the secretary's chamber; and all the princes were sitting there: Elishama the secretary, Delaiah the son of Shemaiah, Elnathan

113 D. J. Wiseman, *op. cit.,* p 69.

the son of Achbor, Gemariah the son of Shaphan, Zedekiah the son of Hananiah, and all the princes. 13 And Micaiah told them all the words that he had heard, when Baruch read the scroll in the hearing of the people. 14 Then all the princes sent Jehudi the son of Nethaniah, son of Shelemiah, son of Cushi, to say to Baruch, "Take in your hand the scroll that you read in the hearing of the people, and come." So Baruch the son of Neriah took the scroll in his hand and came to them. 15 And they said to him, "Sit down and read it." So Baruch read it to them. 16 When they heard all the words, they turned one to another in fear; and they said to Baruch, "We must report all these words to the king." 17 Then they asked Baruch, "Tell us, how did you write all these words? Was it at his dictation?" 18 Baruch answered them, "He dictated all these words to me, while I wrote them with ink on the scroll." 19 Then the princes said to Baruch, "Go and hide, you and Jeremiah, and let no one know where you are."

Gemariah's son reported what he had heard to the ministers of state, who were in session in the secretary's chamber in the palace, just down from the Temple. Then there was a stir. The *princes* were alarmed. They sent Jehudi posthaste to get Baruch and the scroll. When Baruch arrived, they were quite deferential: *Sit down and read it.* As they listened, they looked around at each other in fear. They crossexamined Baruch with regard to the origin of the scroll. They wanted to make sure that these were not Baruch's words but God's words. When they became satisfied about the matter, they showed affectionate regard for the safety of Baruch and Jeremiah. They felt that they must make a report to the king. But they knew Jehoiakim! Accordingly, they counseled that Baruch and Jeremiah conceal themselves. Their lives were in danger.

Observe the much fuller account of this second reading: the concern, the caution, and the counsel. And now—to the king the scroll must go. What will he do?

(3) The Reading in the Presence of Jehoiakim (36:20–26)

20 So they went into the court to the king, having put the scroll in the chamber of Elishama the secretary; and they reported all the

words to the king. [21] Then the king sent Jehudi to get the scroll, and he took it from the chamber of Elishama the secretary; and Jehudi read it to the king and all the princes who stood beside the king. [22] It was the ninth month, and the king was sitting in the winter house and there was a fire burning in the brazier before him. [23] As Jehudi read three or four columns, the king would cut them off with a penknife and throw them into the fire in the brazier, until the entire scroll was consumed in the fire that was in the brazier. [24] Yet neither the king, nor any of his servants who heard all these words, was afraid, nor did they rend their garments. [25] Even when Elnathan and Delaiah and Gemariah urged the king not to burn the scroll, he would not listen to them. [26] And the king commanded Jerahmeel the king's son and Seraiah the son of Azriel and Shelemiah the son of Abdeel to seize Baruch the secretary and Jeremiah the prophet, but the LORD hid them.

Having put the scroll in a safe place. the ministers of state sought audience with the monarch. They received it and reported what happened. Jehoiakim sent for the scroll. Jehudi read it to him.

The king was *in the winter house* (the part of the palace exposed to the sun) sitting before a fire *burning in the brazier.* As he heard the words, he had mixed emotions: curiosity and anger. After listening to the reading of three or four columns, he would slash them off with his penknife and cast them into the fire. Naturally, when the reading was completed, the scroll was consumed.

In this way he indicated his contempt for the words read. He "rent the roll his father would have reverenced." But there was more. He was seeking a cancellation of the effectiveness of those words. He made the fundamental mistake of thinking that the penknife is more powerful than the pen and that the word of God can be negated by the act of man.

3. The Word Rewritten (36:27–32)

[27] Now, after the king had burned the scroll with the words which Baruch wrote at Jeremiah's dictation, the word of the LORD came to Jeremiah: [28] "Take another scroll and write on it all the former words that were in the first scroll, which Jehoiakim the king of Judah has burned. [29] And concerning Jehoiakim king of

Judah you shall say, 'Thus says the LORD, You have burned this scroll, saying, "Why have you written in it that the king of Babylon will certainly come and destroy this land, and will cut off from it man and beast?" [30] Therefore thus says the LORD concerning Jehoiakim king of Judah, He shall have none to sit upon the throne of David, and his dead body shall be cast out to the heat by day and the frost by night. [31] And I will punish him and his offspring and his servants for their iniquity; I will bring upon them, and upon the inhabitants of Jerusalem, and upon the men of Judah, all the evil that I have pronounced against them, but they would not hear.' "
[32] Then Jeremiah took another scroll and gave it to Baruch the scribe, the son of Neriah, who wrote on it at the dictation of Jeremiah all the words of the scroll which Jehoiakim king of Judah had burned in the fire; and many similar words were added to them.

What now? When Jeremiah heard about the destruction of the written record of his prophecies, he received a second private oracle, instructing him to secure another scroll and inscribe on it all the words that were on the first scroll. He was also given a prophecy of disaster for Jehoiakim. Because of his dastardly deed, the king would experience a tragic end.

In obedience to the divine command, Jeremiah dictated his prophecies to Baruch a second time (both men had been preserved through the good providence of God, 36:26), and *many similar words were added to them.* This time the purpose was not to persuade the people to repent, but to preserve the revelation in permanent form for future generations. This was God's word. It is always relevant and powerful. Therefore it must be passed on.

From this dramatic and important story come insights of abiding value. First, the God of the Bible is a God who communicates with man. He is a God of grace who is ever-present among his people, seeking to reveal himself and redeem them.

Second, God speaks to man in various ways. He spoke to Jehoiakim through a godly father, Josiah. Most of us have at least one "Josiah" in our lives through whom God communicates challenge and/or comfort. Moreover, God spoke to

Jehoiakim through trouble. The king had an abundance of it, particularly in 604. But he would not listen. God also addresses us at times through trial. Our response determines whether we are made better or bitter. Further, God spoke to Jehoiakim through the written word. The king cut the "scriptures" into bits and cast them into the fire. Today God still communicates through his "word." We hear the spoken word. We see the living Word, the word made flesh in Christ. We have the written word, the Holy Bible.

Third, God's word may be accepted or rejected. Man has the power of choice. God does not override the human will. We can say yes or no to him. Jehoiakim said no.

Fourth, though God's word can be rejected—even rent—it cannot be abrogated. It is indestructible. It is going on. This is true of the spoken word, the written word, and the living Word. This is not magic. It is reality. "The grass withers, the flower fades; but the word of our God will stand forever" (Isa. 40:8).

XVIII. Jeremiah During the Siege and Sack of the City (37:1—40:6)

We come now to the longest single section in Baruch's "biography" of Jeremiah. The materials in chapters 37—44 are arranged in chronological order. At the end is Baruch's signature and seal (ch. 45). It seems wise to treat this lengthy section in two segments, the first (37:1—40:6) centering around the prophet's activities during the siege and immediately after the sack of Jerusalem, and the second (40:7—44:30) focusing on his latter days.

The story of Jeremiah's behavior in the midst of Judah's supreme tragedy is one of the most stirring and inspiring in all literature. To get the full story, the reader will need to study again 21:1 ff. and 34:1 ff.

1. The Prophet in Prison (37:1-21)

Sometimes it is a bit difficult to shift gears in one's journey through Jeremiah.

There are sudden transitions both in chronology and in kind of material. Verses 1 and 2 seek to aid the reader in orienting himself and also serve as a superscription to 37:1—44:30. One discovers that he has moved from the reign of Jehoiakim (chs. 35—36) on to the reign of Zedekiah (ch. 34). The specific situation is the siege of Jerusalem.

(1) A Request for Prayer (37:1-10)

¹ Zedekiah the son of Josiah, whom Nebuchadrezzar king of Babylon made king in the land of Judah, reigned instead of Coniah the son of Jehoiakim. ² But neither he nor his servants nor the people of the land listened to the words of the LORD which he spoke through Jeremiah the prophet.

³ King Zedekiah sent Jehucal the son of Shelemiah, and Zephaniah the priest, the son of Maaseiah, to Jeremiah the prophet, saying, "Pray for us to the LORD our God." ⁴ Now Jeremiah was still going in and out among the people, for he had not yet been put in prison. ⁵ The army of Pharaoh had come out of Egypt; and when the Chaldeans who were besieging Jerusalem heard news of them, they withdrew from Jerusalem.

⁶ Then the word of the LORD came to Jeremiah the prophet: ⁷ "Thus says the LORD, God of Israel: Thus shall you say to the king of Judah who sent you to me to inquire of me, 'Behold, Pharaoh's army which came to help you is about to return to Egypt, to its own land. ⁸ And the Chaldeans shall come back and fight against this city; they shall take it and burn it with fire. ⁹ Thus says the LORD, Do not deceive yourselves, saying, "The Chaldeans will surely stay away from us," for they will not stay away. ¹⁰ For even if you should defeat the whole army of Chaldeans who are fighting against you, and there remained of them only wounded men, every man in his tent, they would rise up and burn this city with fire.'"

Immediately after the general introduction, it is stated that Zedekiah sent a second delegation (cf. 21:1) of two men—Jehucal (cf. 38:1) and Zephaniah (21:1; 29:25,29; 52:24)—to the prophet with an earnest entreaty that he pray for the people. This was during the time of the temporary withdrawal of the Babylonians to deal with the Egyptians, who were marching up from the south (cf. vv. 7-10). Evidently the king and the people were still expecting some sort of miraculous divine intervention to save them—or they may have thought that it might have already happened, but were not sure. In any case, we have here another eloquent testimony to the position Jeremiah occupied as intercessor supreme.

Whatever the king and the people may have thought and hoped, Jeremiah knew that time had run out. His response was that the Babylonians would be back and that, if after their engagement with the Egyptians and the Jews they had nothing but wounded soldiers left, they would still destroy the city. Though suffering greatly, the prophet was still faithfully proclaiming the word of God in a difficult and dangerous situation.

(2) Accusation and Arrest (37:11-15)

11 Now when the Chaldean army had withdrawn from Jerusalem at the approach of Pharaoh's army, 12 Jeremiah set out from Jerusalem to go to the land of Benjamin to receive his portion there among the people. 13 When he was at the Benjamin Gate, a sentry there named Irijah the son of Shelemiah, son of Hananiah, seized Jeremiah the prophet, saying, "You are deserting to the Chaldeans." 14 And Jeremiah said, "It is false; I am not deserting to the Chaldeans." But Irijah would not listen to him, and seized Jeremiah and brought him to the princes. 15 And the princes were enraged at Jeremiah, and they beat him and imprisoned him in the house of Jonathan the secretary, for it had been made a prison.

While the siege was still lifted, Jeremiah decided to go to Anathoth to transact some business. The exact nature of the mission is not known. The Hebrew reads: "to divide there among the people;" the LXX: "to do business." Some have thought that the reason for the trip was to arrange for funds for the exacting days ahead (e.g., Cornill). It seems more reasonable to suppose that the situation referred to in 32:6 ff. caused the prophet to start the journey, i.e., the redemption of some family property.

As he was going out the Benjamin Gate on the north side of the city, Irijah, an officer on duty, accused him of deserting

to the enemy. Jeremiah had been preaching that this was the thing to do (cf. 21: 8-10). Apparently quite a few had complied with his counsel, and there was considerable concern about it. Now he was confronted with the charge that he was practicing what he had been preaching.

He stoutly disavowed the charge, but the sentry would not accept his defense. Instead, he *seized* the prophet and turned him over to the government officials (*the princes*). They *beat* him and placed him in a dungeon under the house of the "secretary of state" (possibly "a maximum-security prison," Bright, p. 229). There, if left long enough, he would die.

(3) Jeremiah's Conference with the King (37:16-21)

16 When Jeremiah had come to the dungeon cells, and remained there many days, 17 King Zedekiah sent for him, and received him. The king questioned him secretly in his house, and said, "Is there any word from the LORD?" Jeremiah said, "There is." Then he said, "You shall be delivered into the hand of the king of Babylon." 18 Jeremiah also said to King Zedekiah, "What wrong have I done to you or your servants or this people, that you have put me in prison? 19 Where are your prophets who prophesied to you, saying, 'The king of Babylon will not come against you and against this land'? 20 Now hear, I pray you, O my lord the king: let my humble plea come before you, and do not send me back to the house of Jonathan the secretary, lest I die there." 21 So King Zedekiah gave orders, and they committed Jeremiah to the court of the guard; and a loaf of bread was given him daily from the bakers' street, until all the bread of the city was gone. So Jeremiah remained in the court of the guard.

After the prophet had been in prison *many days,* possibly weeks, Zedekiah sent for him. It was a very dramatic situation. Duhm has a classic passage about it.[114]

As the emaciated servant of God, now more and more walking the way of a cross, confronted the weak, vascillating king, Zedekiah asked, *Is there any word from the Lord?* Jeremiah answered, *There*

114 *Jeremia,* p. 301.

is. Then he preached him the same sermon he had preached many times: *You shall be delivered into the hands of the king of Babylon.*

In this secret conference, several things stand out. For one thing, Jeremiah retracted nothing. He stood by his conviction as to what God's will was. He was now "an iron pillar" and "a wall of bronze." In the second place, he asserted his innocence and argued for the integrity and truthfulness of his preaching as over against the falsity of that of the "king's preachers." Further, he urgently asked for clemency. He begged the king not to send him back to the dungeon, for there he would die. Jeremiah was a martyr, but he had no martyr complex. He had a healthy desire to live and would do anything honorable and right to insure the realization of that desire.

This leads to a final observation: there was one thing the prophet would not do, namely, compromise his conscience. The only way to stop a man like that is to kill him. This is what the officials intended to do.

Zedekiah granted the prophet's request for gentler treatment. He put him in *the court of the guard* (cf. 32:2), and he assured him of a daily food ration for as long as it lasted, which was until the city fell (cf. 52:6 f.).

2. Final Experiences of Jeremiah Before the Fall of the City (38:1–28)

The events in this chapter took place after those referred to in 37:1 ff. and shortly before the capitulation and destruction of the city. As ever, the central interest of Baruch in reporting them is the suffering of God's servant.

Following Steuernagel, Skinner and Bright have set forth the view that 37:11–21 and 38:1–28 are variant but complimentary accounts of the same happenings. It is true that there are parallels between them. In both, Jeremiah is hauled before the princes and is treated with violence. In both, his imprisonment is related to a cistern. In both, Jeremiah requests leniency. In both, he ends up in the court of the guard.

However, though there are similarities, there are some very marked differences. In the first account, we learn of Jeremiah's arrest. In the second, there is no allusion to this. In the first account, the prophet is placed in a dungeon in a cistern house beneath the home of Jonathan the secretary. In the second, he is cast into a cistern belonging to Malkiah and located in the court of the guard. In the first account, there is no reference to any rescue from a cistern. In the second, there is, and the story is related in detail. In the two interviews with the king the attitude of the prophet is not the same. In the second, he is much more cautious, implying greater disillusionment with Zedekiah and longer suffering on his part. In the second account, Zedekiah is more desperate and asks Jeremiah not to divulge to the princes the real reason for the interview.

It is true that in both confrontations reference is made to Jeremiah's request that he not be sent back to the dungeon, but in the second encounter he is merely asked to state that he made this request. In both accounts, Jeremiah winds up in the court of the guard, but in the second instance it is stated that he remained there *until the day that Jerusalem was taken.* The next verse indicates the exact time when that happened.

It is the present writer's view that chapters 37 and 38 present events in sequence and not in parallel accounts. He has no aversion to the idea that the prophet could have had two interviews with the king instead of one, or to the idea that the princes made a second attempt to dispense with Jeremiah when foiled in the first.

(1) A Dauntless Prophet and a Determined Opposition (38:1–6)

¹ Now Shephatiah the son of Mattan, Gedaliah the son of Pashhur, Jucal the son of Shelemiah, and Pashhur the son of Malchiah heard the words that Jeremiah was saying to all the people, ² "Thus says the Lord, He who stays in

this city shall die by the sword, by famine, and by pestilence; but he who goes out to the Chaldeans shall live; he shall have his life as a prize of war, and live. ³ Thus says the Lord, This city shall surely be given into the hand of the army of the king of Babylon and be taken." ⁴ Then the princes said to the king, "Let this man be put to death, for he is weakening the hands of the soldiers who are left in this city, and the hands of all the people, by speaking such words to them. For this man is not seeking the welfare of this people, but their harm." ⁵ King Zedekiah said, "Behold, he is in your hands; for the king can do nothing against you." ⁶ So they took Jeremiah and cast him into the cistern of Malchiah, the king's son, which was in the court of the guard, letting Jeremiah down by ropes. And there was no water in the cistern, but only mire, and Jeremiah sank in the mire.

In the court of the guard Jeremiah enjoyed a measure of freedom. Though he was confined and kept under watch, he could keep talking. And he did. He spoke to soldiers, palace officials, visitors, and any and all of the people to whom he had opportunity to express himself. He was uttering the same sort of "seditious" words which he had said on other occasions (cf. v. 2 with 21:8–10 and v. 3 with 34:2,22).

The princes in positions of responsibility were fed up with this kind of treasonous talk. They went to the king with the demand that the prophet must die. He was *weakening the hands* (morale) of all who were seeking to defend the city by saying constantly that the cause was hopeless and by counseling the defenders to desert to the Babylonians and thereby receive their lives *as a prize of war* (cf. 21:9).

It is interesting that one of the Lachish Letters (VI) contains a similar charge made earlier in the siege by the commander of an outpost concerning some of the officials in Jerusalem. Apparently there was a division among the princes as to what policy should be pursued. A similar division is reflected in the days of Jehoiakim with regard to Jeremiah and the scroll (ch. 36).

The weakness of Zedekiah stands out sharply in his response to the demand of the officials (v. 5; cf. the words of Pilate

centuries later in a similar situation, Matt. 27:23–24). Friendly toward Jeremiah and, deep down, favorably disposed toward following his advice, he was, at the same time, pathetically afraid of the princes. As Duhm observed, he was more a prisoner than the prisoner before him.

Armed with royal permission to dispose of the traitorous prophet, the princes placed him in *the cistern of Malchiah, the king's son, which was in the court of the guard, . . . and there was no water in the cistern, but only mire, and Jeremiah sank in the mire* (v. 6). It was meant that he should die of suffocation and/or starvation.

Since there were many cisterns in Jerusalem for collecting water during the rainy season (the winter months) to be used during the dry months (May to October), the fact that there was only mire in the cistern would suggest that this incident transpired shortly before the fall of Jerusalem (July, 587).

This passage, coupled with 21:8–10, raises two important and related questions: Did Jeremiah love his country? and, Was he a patriot or a traitor? The answer to the first is easy for one who knows Jeremiah. He loved his country so much that he was willing to suffer for it and to sacrifice everything he held near and dear, if by any chance the soul of the nation might be saved. His preaching was determined by his perspective. He believed in a righteous sovereign God who in his grace had chosen Israel to be the people of his great purpose of revelation and redemption. This God had entered into covenant with Israel after saving her from servitude. But Israel had broken the covenant. Therefore she must be disciplined, in order that, if possible, she might be brought back into a right relationship with her God and made more amenable to his purpose. Captivity was a part of the disciplinary process. The carrying forward of God's great purpose was more important than the preservation of the state.

But was Jeremiah a patriot—or a traitor?

The answer depends upon what one means by patriotism. If he means uncritical, unqualified support of one's country "right or wrong," Jeremiah was no patriot. If he means one who is so devoted to his country that he is not content until it becomes the embodiment of the highest social, moral, and spiritual ideals, Jeremiah was a splendid example of the enlightened type of patriotism so badly needed today.

(2) A Daring Deliverance (38:7–13)

7 When Ebedmelech the Ethiopian, a eunuch, who was in the king's house, heard that they had put Jeremiah into the cistern—the king was sitting in the Benjamin Gate—8 Ebedmelech went from the king's house and said to the king, 9 "My lord the king, these men have done evil in all that they did to Jeremiah the prophet by casting him into the cistern; and he will die there of hunger, for there is no bread left in the city." 10 Then the king commanded Ebedmelech, the Ethiopian, "Take three men with you from here, and lift Jeremiah the prophet out of the cistern before he dies." 11 So Ebedmelech took the men with him and went to the house of the king, to a wardrobe of the storehouse, and took from there old rags and worn-out clothes, which he let down to Jeremiah in the cistern by ropes. 12 Then Ebedmelech the Ethiopian said to Jeremiah, "Put the rags and clothes between your armpits and the ropes." Jeremiah did so. 13 Then they drew Jeremiah up with ropes and lifted him out of the cistern. And Jeremiah remained in the court of the guard.

The episode recounted in this passage is "one of the fairest in the Old Testament." [115] It is the account of a strategic act on the part of an unknown character of great courage. Ebed-melech, an Ethiopian eunuch and a palace official of some importance, discovered the prophet's predicament and went immediately to the king to secure permission and aid, that he might rescue Jeremiah before it was too late. Due to the timely and decisive intervention of an otherwise unknown and unsung hero, the prophet's life was preserved.

The Hebrew text of v. 9 suggests that Jeremiah was as good as dead, if he remained in the cistern. The vacillating Zedekiah was as responsive to the appeal of the Ethiopian on the prophet's behalf as he had been to the pressure brought by the princes against him. Ebed-melech was granted a detail of thirty men (the RSV emends slightly to "three" on the basis of one Hebrew manuscript and the seeming superabundance of aid), and Jeremiah was gently and safely removed from the mire and back to the court of the guard. By this time he must have been in a very weakened state.

(3) A Desperate Individual (38:14–28)

14 King Zedekiah sent for Jeremiah the prophet and received him at the third entrance of the temple of the LORD. The king said to Jeremiah, "I will ask you a question; hide nothing from me." 15 Jeremiah said to Zedekiah, "If I tell you, will you not be sure to put me to death? And if I give you counsel, you will not listen to me." 16 Then King Zedekiah swore secretly to Jeremiah, "As the LORD lives, who made our souls, I will not put you to death or deliver you into the hand of these men who seek your life."

17 Then Jeremiah said to Zedekiah, "Thus says the LORD, the God of hosts, the God of Israel, If you will surrender to the princes of the king of Babylon, then your life shall be spared, and this city shall not be burned with fire, and you and your house shall live. 18 But if you do not surrender to the princes of the king of Babylon, then this city shall be given into the hand of the Chaldeans, and they shall burn it with fire, and you shall not escape from their hand." 19 King Zedekiah said to Jeremiah, "I am afraid of the Jews who have deserted to the Chaldeans, lest I be handed over to them and they abuse me." 20 Jeremiah said, "You shall not be given to them. Obey now the voice of the LORD in what I say to you, and it shall be well with you, and your life shall be spared. 21 But if you refuse to surrender, this is the vision which the LORD has shown to me: 22 Behold, all the women left in the house of the king of Judah were being led out to the princes of the king of Babylon and were saying,

'Your trusted friends have deceived you
    and prevailed against you;
now that your feet are sunk in the mire,
    they turn away from you.'

23 All your wives and your sons shall be led out to the Chaldeans, and you yourself shall not escape from their hand, but shall be seized by the king of Babylon; and this city shall be burned with fire."

115 Smith, op. cit., p. 281.

²⁴ Then Zedekiah said to Jeremiah, "Let no one know of these words and you shall not die. ²⁵ If the princes hear that I have spoken with you and come to you and say to you, 'Tell us what you said to the king and what the king said to you; hide nothing from us and we will not put you to death,' ²⁶ then you shall say to them, 'I made a humble plea to the king that he would not send me back to the house of Jonathan to die there.'" ²⁷ Then all the princes came to Jeremiah and asked him, and he answered them as the king had instructed him. So they left off speaking with him, for the conversation had not been overheard. ²⁸ And Jeremiah remained in the court of the guard until the day that Jerusalem was taken.

Zedekiah was now in deep distress. The siege, one of the most horrible in history, had lasted a long time. Provisions were low. People were dying of disease and starvation. Some were deserting. The king was desperate. He sent for Jeremiah. The clandestine conference was held *at the third entrance of the temple of the Lord.* This was probably the king's personal entrance from the palace to the Temple. Zedekiah was so frantic that he was grabbing for any available straw.

The scene is full of pathos. On the one side is a man who is in trouble as a ruler, but who has consistently refused the only course that could lead to any degree of safety and security, largely because of his weak-kneed submission to the influence of "hot-headed" princes and "empty-headed" prophets. On the other side is an emaciated man, an "iron pillar" of a man, who has suffered terribly and sought constantly to bring the king to the point of doing God's will. Evidently Zedekiah is still looking for some ray of hope, some favorable word from the Lord. He asks Jeremiah to tell him the truth and hide nothing from him.

The prophet is cautious. He knows his man, and his reservation is born of bitter experience. He says, in effect: "What's the use? If I tell you the truth, you will kill me (or allow someone to). If I give you the word of the Lord, you will not obey it." The king promises that he will not slay Jeremiah or turn him over to those who

might. Then the prophet speaks. It is the same message as before (vv. 17–18).

There is a touching tenderness and solemnity in the prophet's final appeal to his monarch. When Zedekiah discloses that fear of those who have gone over to the enemy keeps him from following the prophet's counsel, Jeremiah assures him that the thing he dreads will not happen and begs him to heed the voice of God.

The prophet reveals his artistry as a poet again in the satire in the *qinah* rhythm in v. 22, in which he weaves together his recent experience in the cistern with Zedekiah's experience with his inexperienced, irresponsible leaders (*trusted friends*), who have landed him in the *mire* and taken to their heels. Jeremiah has been in *the mire* because of faithfulness to God; Zedekiah is in *the mire* because of unfaithfulness to God!

This interview, in which the prophet delivers his last recorded words to his king, ends with Zedekiah urgently requesting Jeremiah not to make known to the princes the real reason for their meeting. Instead, he is to tell them, when they ask, that he *made a humble plea to the king that he would not send* him *back to the house of Jonathan to die there.*

Jeremiah complies with this request. Does he prevaricate? Tell a "little white lie"? He certainly does not disclose the whole truth. This reminds us again of his gentleness toward Zedekiah and his kinship with us. He returns to the court of the guard and remains there until the fall of the city.

3. The Fall of Jerusalem and the Fate of Jeremiah (39:1—40:6)

¹ In the ninth year of Zedekiah king of Judah, in the tenth month, Nebuchadrezzar king of Babylon and all his army came against Jerusalem and besieged it; ² in the eleventh year of Zedekiah, in the fourth month, on the ninth day of the month, a breach was made in the city. ³ When Jerusalem was taken, all the princes of the king of Babylon came and sat in the middle gate: Nergalsharezer, Samgarnebo, Sarsechim the Rabsaris, Nergalsharezer the Rabmag, with all the rest of the officers of the

king of Babylon. 4 When Zedekiah king of Judah and all the soldiers saw them, they fled, going out of the city at night by way of the king's garden through the gate between the two walls; and they went toward the Arabah. 5 But the army of the Chaldeans pursued them, and overtook Zedekiah in the plains of Jericho; and when they had taken him, they brought him up to Nebuchadrezzar king of Babylon, at Riblah, in the land of Hamath; and he passed sentence upon him. 6 The king of Babylon slew the sons of Zedekiah at Riblah before his eyes; and the king of Babylon slew all the nobles of Judah. 7 He put out the eyes of Zedekiah, and bound him in fetters to take him to Babylon. 8 The Chaldeans burned the king's house and the house of the people, and broke down the walls of Jerusalem. 9 Then Nebuzaradan, the captain of the guard, carried into exile to Babylon the rest of the people who were left in the city, those who had deserted to him, and the people who remained. 10 Nebuzaradan, the captain of the guard, left in the land of Judah some of the poor people who owned nothing, and gave them vineyards and fields at the same time.

11 Nebuchadrezzar king of Babylon gave command concerning Jeremiah through Nebuzaradan, the captain of the guard, saying, 12 "Take him, look after him well and do him no harm, but deal with him as he tells you." 13 So Nebuzaradan the captain of the guard, Nebushazban the Rabsaris, Nergalsharezer the Rabmag, and all the chief officers of the king of Babylon 14 sent and took Jeremiah from the court of the guard. They entrusted him to Gedaliah the son of Ahikam, son of Shaphan, that he should take him home. So he dwelt among the people.

15 The word of the LORD came to Jeremiah while he was shut up in the court of the guard: 16 "Go, and say to Ebedmelech the Ethiopian, 'Thus says the LORD of hosts, the God of Israel: Behold, I will fulfil my words against this city for evil and not for good, and they shall be accomplished before you on that day. 17 But I will deliver you on that day, says the LORD, and you shall not be given into the hand of the men of whom you are afraid. 18 For I will surely save you, and you shall not fall by the sword; but you shall have your life as a prize of war, because you have put your trust in me, says the LORD.' "

1 The word that came to Jeremiah from the LORD after Nebuzaradan the captain of the guard had let him go from Ramah, when he took him bound in chains along with all the captives of Jerusalem and Judah who were being exiled to Babylon. 2 The captain of the guard took Jeremiah and said to him, "The LORD your God pronounced this evil against this place; 3 the LORD has brought it about, and has done as he said. Because you sinned against the LORD, and did not obey his voice, this thing has come upon you. 4 Now, behold, I release you today from the chains on your hands. If it seems good to you to come with me to Babylon, come, and I will look after you well; but if it seems wrong to you to come with me to Babylon, do not come. See, the whole land is before you; go wherever you think it good and right to go. 5 If you remain, then return to Gedaliah the son of Ahikam, son of Shaphan, whom the king of Babylon appointed governor of the cities of Judah, and dwell with him among the people; or go wherever you think it right to go." So the captain of the guard gave him an allowance of food and a present, and let him go. 6 Then Jeremiah went to Gedaliah the son of Ahikam, at Mizpah, and dwelt with him among the people who were left in the land.

The sad story of the long siege of the city comes to a close with its capitulation in July, 587. This tremendous tragedy had been foreshadowed in Jeremiah's call-experience (1:13-16), and its possibility had been an integral part of his preaching for 40 years. It is only appropriate and proper that Baruch's story of his ministry should include an account of the great catastrophe, and that he should interweave with the record of the fate of Jerusalem that of the fate of Jeremiah, who loved the city so much and had served it so faithfully and suffered so deeply in his efforts to save it (cf. the account in 52: 4-16; 2 Kings 25:1-12).

Verses 1-10 deal with the capitulation and destruction of the city and with the dispensation made of the king and the citizenry. Verses 1 and 2 are introductory. They indicate that the siege of the city began in January, 588, and ended in July, 587, at which time a breach was finally made in its walls by the Babylonians.

Following the surrender of the city, some of the chief Babylonian officers set up a center of military government *in the middle gate* (likely the principal eastern gate of the Temple, now known as the Golden Gate) to administer the affairs of the conquered country.

When Zedekiah and his soldiers saw that the walls were breached, they fled by night *by way of the king's garden* (in the southern section of the city), through the Tyropoeon and Kidron valleys, toward the Jordan. They were headed for high country beyond the river! But they were caught and brought before Nebuchadnezzar at Riblah on the Orontes, north of Damascus. There Zedekiah's sons and nobles were slain before his eyes. Then his eyes were put out, and he was placed in chains and carried to Babylon. The city was demolished about a month later (cf. 39:1; 52:4,12). Most of the people were deported. A few peasants, *who owned nothing*, were left to look after the fields and vineyards.

So much for the city, the king, and the citizens, but what about Jeremiah? Here we run headlong into a problem. The problem is whether 39:11–14 and 40:1–6 are variant and contradictory accounts of the same event or separate and authentic accounts of different events. The present writer holds that they are the latter. He is aware that there is some confusion present in the stories (there was a good deal in and around Jerusalem also!), but he is convinced that the difficulties can be resolved.

When the city was captured and put to the torch, Jeremiah was released by order of Nebuchadnezzar through Nebuzaradan. The order was probably carried out by a subordinate officer. Later, when the captives were being collected, by some mishap the prophet was bound along with the rest of the prisoners—likely by someone not acquainted with him or his special status. They were herded off to Ramah, the headquarters for getting the captives ready for the long trek to Babylon. There Nebuzaradan learned of Jeremiah's plight, set him free, and offered him the choice described in 40:4–5, using language (somewhat Deuteronomic) which he had heard Jeremiah use or which reflects, in some measure, the theology of the biographer.

Verses 15–18 contain an oracle of prom-

ise to Ebed-melech. Obviously, the prophecy is out of place, chronologically speaking, for it is stated that it was received by the prophet during his stay in the court of the guard. Some question its authenticity, but on subjective grounds: it was "a late editor," they say, not Jeremiah, who thought the man ought to be rewarded for his act of generosity.

Though out of chronological order, there may be method in the biographer's "madness." A sharp contrast is implied here between the tragic fate of Zedekiah because of his unfaithfulness to God and the brighter future of Ebed-melech because of his faithfulness to God. Ebed-melech is promised his life *as a prize of war* (cf. 21:9), because he has put his trust in the Lord. But this is Deuteronomic (law of retribution), and some say that a prophet, especially Jeremiah, would rather be caught dead than Deuteronomic!

The present writer believes this to be an authentic oracle of promise, which expresses both the gratitude and good will of Jeremiah toward one who had helped him, and a fundamental tenet of the biblical faith: those who trust in God have in them the principle of permanence (Hab. 2:4). They have staying power. They will win in the end. Ebed-melech's faith was "accounted to him for righteousness" (cf. Rom. 4:3; Gen. 15:6).

At Ramah, Jeremiah was given a choice. He could go to Babylon and spend his declining days in ease and honor, or he could stay with the people left in Palestine: *Go wherever you think it right to go* (40:5).

There follows one of the most eloquent and revealing sentences in the book (v. 6). The action of the prophet was in keeping with his character. At one difficult juncture in his ministry he had given expression to a desire to run away from his people and all responsibility for them, for they were all faithless (9:2). But he did not run. Now he had a golden opportunity to go, but he refused it. He chose to stay with Gedaliah and the unpromising crowd left behind—and this despite his view that the future of true biblical faith lay with the exiles. Here is the greatness of this man. Because of a deep devotion to God, a love for people, and a sensitivity to human need, he chose to walk the way of a cross.

XIX. The Latter Days of Jeremiah (40: 7—44:30)

Concerning Jeremiah's decision to cast his lot with Gedaliah and the group left behind, Rudolph says: "That is proof not only of love for his native home and of the absurdity of the charge that he was deserting to the Chaldeans (37:13), but also of his belief in the future (32:15), which is for him bound up with the person of Gedaliah" (*Jeremia*, p. 228).

Jeremiah did have a deep love for his country. Although his faith for the future of true religion was bound up with the Jews in Babylonian bondage, he also had faith that God would one day restore them to their homeland. He had given tangible proof of this faith by his purchase of a plot of land at Anathoth (cf. 32:9–15). Perhaps, in addition to his desire to support Gedaliah and serve where the need was greatest (Ezekiel was actively ministering to the exiles), there was also a desire to die in peace in his homeland. But this was not to be. The story of Jeremiah's latter days is related in a section beginning with 40:7 and going through 44:30.

1. The Failure of the Fresh Start (40:7— 41:18)

⁷ When all the captains of the forces in the open country and their men heard that the king of Babylon had appointed Gedaliah the son of Ahikam governor in the land, and had committed to him men, women, and children, those of the poorest of the land who had not been taken into exile to Babylon, ⁸ they went to Gedaliah at Mizpah—Ishmael the son of Nethaniah, Johanan the son of Kareah, Seraiah the son of Tanhumeth, the sons of Ephai the Netophathite, Jezaniah the son of the Maacathite, they and their men. ⁹ Gedaliah the son of Ahikam, son of Shaphan, swore to them and their men, saying, "Do not be afraid to serve the Chaldeans. Dwell in the land, and serve the king of Babylon, and it shall be well with you. ¹⁰ As for me, I will dwell at Mizpah, to stand for you before the Chaldeans who will come to us; but as for you, gather wine and summer fruits and oil, and store them in your vessels, and dwell in your cities that you have taken." ¹¹ Likewise, when all the Jews who were in Moab and among the Ammonites and in Edom and in other lands heard that the king of Babylon had left a remnant in Judah and had appointed Gedaliah the son of Ahikam, son of Shaphan, as governor over them, ¹² then all the Jews returned from all the places to which they had been driven and came to the land of Judah, to Gedaliah at Mizpah; and they gathered wine and summer fruits in great abundance.

¹³ Now Johanan the son of Kareah and all the leaders of the forces in the open country came to Gedaliah at Mizpah ¹⁴ and said to him, "Do you know that Baalis the king of the Ammonites has sent Ishmael the son of Nethaniah to take your life?" But Gedaliah the son of Ahikam would not believe them. ¹⁵ Then Johanan the son of Kareah spoke secretly to Gedaliah at Mizpah, "Let me go and slay Ishmael the son of Nethaniah, and no one will know it. Why should he take your life, so that all the Jews who are gathered about you would be scattered, and the remnant of Judah would perish?" ¹⁶ But Gedaliah the son of Ahikam said to Johanan the son of Kareah, "You shall not do this thing, for you are speaking falsely of Ishmael."

¹ In the seventh month, Ishmael the son of Nethaniah, son of Elishama, of the royal family, one of the chief officers of the king, came with ten men to Gedaliah the son of Ahikam, at Mizpah. As they ate bread together there at Mizpah, ² Ishmael the son of Nethaniah and the ten men with him rose up and struck down Gedaliah the son of Ahikam, son of Shaphan, with the sword, and killed him, whom the king of Babylon had appointed governor in the land. ³ Ishmael also slew all the Jews who were with Gedaliah at Mizpah, and the Chaldean soldiers who happened to be there.

⁴ On the day after the murder of Gedaliah, before any one knew of it, ⁵ eighty men arrived from Shechem and Shiloh and Samaria, with their beards shaved and their clothes torn, and their bodies gashed, bringing cereal offerings and incense to present at the temple of the LORD. ⁶ And Ishmael the son of Nethaniah came out from Mizpah to meet them, weeping as he came. As he met them, he said to them, "Come in to Gedaliah the son of Ahikam." ⁷ When they came into the city, Ishmael the son of Nethaniah and the men with him slew them, and cast them into a cistern. ⁸ But there

were ten men among them who said to Ishmael, "Do not kill us, for we have stores of wheat, barley, oil, and honey hidden in the fields." So he refrained and did not kill them with their companions.

⁹ Now the cistern into which Ishmael cast all the bodies of the men whom he had slain was the large cistern which King Asa had made for defense against Baasha king of Israel; Ishmael the son of Nethaniah filled it with the slain. ¹⁰ Then Ishmael took captive all the rest of the people who were in Mizpah, the king's daughters and all the people who were left at Mizpah, whom Nebuzaradan, the captain of the guard, had committed to Gedaliah the son of Ahikam. Ishmael the son of Nethaniah took them captive and set out to cross over to the Ammonites. ¹¹ But when Johanan the son of Kareah and all the leaders of the forces with him heard of all the evil which Ishmael the son of Nethaniah had done, ¹² they took all their men and went to fight against Ishmael the son of Nethaniah. They came upon him at the great pool which is in Gibeon. ¹³ And when all the people who were with Ishmael saw Johanan the son of Kareah and all the leaders of the forces with him, they rejoiced. ¹⁴ So all the people whom Ishmael had carried away captive from Mizpah turned about and came back, and went to Johanan the son of Kareah. ¹⁵ But Ishmael the son of Nethaniah escaped from Johanan with eight men, and went to the Ammonites. ¹⁶ Then Johanan the son of Kareah and all the leaders of the forces with him took all the rest of the people whom Ishmael the son of Nethaniah had carried away captive from Mizpah after he had slain Gedaliah the son of Ahikam—soldiers, women, children, and eunuchs, whom Johanan brought back from Gibeon. ¹⁷ And they went and stayed at Geruth Chimham near Bethlehem, intending to go to Egypt ¹⁸ because of the Chaldeans; for they were afraid of them, because Ishmael the son of Nethaniah had slain Gedaliah the son of Ahikam, whom the king of Babylon had made governor over the land.

This is an authentic historical account in which there is straight reporting of events with a minimum of dialogue. One of the most unusual features of the record of Gedaliah's administration and assassination is that there is no allusion in it to Jeremiah and no information about his activity during the period involved.

Some scholars have used this remarkable silence about the prophet's role as an argument against the authenticity of the passage. Since the biographer was chiefly concerned about the prophet's participation in the life of the people—especially his "passion" which came as a consequence of that participation—the logic runs that he could not have composed this portion of the prophecy. Therefore it had to come from a later hand.

But this reasoning is fallacious, for, although Jeremiah is not mentioned in the passage, he was committed to Gedaliah, and the murder of the man caused his hope of ending his days in the homeland to come crashing down around him and set the stage for his being carried by force to Egypt by frightened fugitives. In other words, it was another in the long line of tragedies in his ministry, another of "the stations of the cross." The account could, therefore, be a part of Baruch's memoirs.

The section requires little explanation or exposition. The ability and magnanimity of Gedaliah as a man and as an administrator stand out sharply, though briefly. He persuaded the guerrilla groups scattered about over the country to join the Judean community, now a province of the Babylonian Empire, and promised their commanders that he would stand between them and the *Chaldeans.* Hearing about the promising new start back home, Jews who had fled to Moab, Ammon, and Edom—neighboring nations—returned to Gedaliah at Mizpah, and they gathered the late summer fruit harvest *in great abundance.*

Things were looking bright. It appeared to be the beginning of a period of peace and prosperity. As for Jeremiah, this may have been the easiest, happiest time of his ministry. For a short season he was free from the burden of proclaiming judgment and was at liberty to set forth the glowing prospect and glorious promises regarding the future of God's people, redeemed, reunited, restored—a new community with a new covenant and a new king.

It is the writer's conviction that from this period, in all probability, came some of the grandest products of Jeremiah's genius as a poet-prophet, i.e., portions of "the book of consolation," notably chapters 30–31. How appropriate to set the powerful poem-prophecy about Rachel's weeping against the background of Jeremiah's experience at Ramah (near which was her grave), and the greatest prophecy of them all, that of the new covenant, at the apex of his spiritual pilgrimage and in the context of the complete failure of the old covenant, which had been made with Israel as a nation, now destroyed!

How long the promising situation lasted we cannot tell. The biblical account in Jeremiah suggests that the time was short. This much we know: It came to an end. There were rumors of a plot. It was being worked up by Ishmael in collusion with Baalis, king of the Ammonites. Ishmael was of the seed royal and was likely a nationalist and a "Chaldean-hater" (Duhm). This made him a willing instrument of Baalis for extending his influence and control in Palestine.

When a friendly colleague, Johanan, acquainted Gedaliah with the rumors, the latter assessed them "a pack of lies" (*sheqer*). But they were not. In violation of all laws of Near Eastern hospitality, Ishmael and his men, while eating with the governor, rose up and slew him with the sword, and also struck down in cold blood all other Jews who were there and *the Chaldean soldiers who happened to be there*.

There followed a piece of dastardly treachery and sadism: the pretended cordiality of Ishmael and the cruel slaughter of all but ten of eighty worshipers from Shechem, Shiloh, and Samaria, who were going up in deep mourning to the ruins of the Temple in Jerusalem for cultic observance.

In 41:1 we are told that it was the seventh month (October, Hebrew sacred calendar). This was the month in which came the great fall festival, the Day of Atonement, and the enthronement (or New Year) ceremony. One has to keep in mind the two methods of reckoning

time: the Babylonian, the civil calendar, with the year starting and stopping in the spring; and the Hebrew, the sacred calendar, with the year beginning and ending in the fall.

As the story unfolded, Ishmael took the entire population of Mizpah, the seat of government, and took off toward Ammon. When Johanan heard about the terrible tragedy, he gave chase, overtook and overcame Ishmael's band at Gibeon, and recovered the Jewish captives. However, Ishmael, along with eight colleagues, escaped to safety in the country of his chief cohort in crime, the king of Ammon. There Ishmael "disappeared from history, a right royal villain."[116]

Quite understandably, the recovered Jews were afraid, afraid of reprisals from Nebuchadnezzar, their overlord. They did not return to Mizpah. Instead, they started south. They stopped for shelter at Geruth Chimham, near Bethlehem.

2. The Flight to Egypt (42:1—43:7)

¹ Then all the commanders of the forces, and Johanan the son of Kareah and Azariah the son of Hoshaiah, and all the people from the least to the greatest, came near ² and said to Jeremiah the prophet, "Let our supplication come before you, and pray to the LORD your God for us, for all this remnant (for we are left but a few of many, as your eyes see us), ³ that the LORD your God may show us the way we should go, and the thing that we should do." ⁴ Jeremiah the prophet said to them, "I have heard you; behold, I will pray to the LORD your God according to your request, and whatever the LORD answers you I will tell you; I will keep nothing back from you." ⁵ Then they said to Jeremiah, "May the LORD be a true and faithful witness against us if we do not act according to all the word with which the LORD your God sends you to us. ⁶ Whether it is good or evil, we will obey the voice of the LORD our God to whom we are sending you, that it may be well with us when we obey the voice of the LORD our God."

⁷ At the end of ten days the word of the LORD came to Jeremiah. ⁸ Then he summoned Johanan the son of Kareah and all the commanders of the forces who were with him, and all the people from the least to the greatest, ⁹ and said to them, "Thus says the LORD, the

116 Gillies, *op. cit.*, p. 325.

God of Israel, to whom you sent me to present your supplication before him: ¹⁰ If you will remain in this land, then I will build you up and not pull you down; I will plant you, and not pluck you up; for I repent of the evil which I did to you. ¹¹ Do not fear the king of Babylon, of whom you are afraid; do not fear him, says the LORD, for I am with you, to save you and to deliver you from his hand. ¹² I will grant you mercy, that he may have mercy on you and let you remain in your own land. ¹³ But if you say, 'We will not remain in this land,' disobeying the voice of the LORD your God ¹⁴ and saying, 'No, we will go to the land of Egypt, where we shall not see war, or hear the sound of the trumpet, or be hungry for bread, and we will dwell there,' ¹⁵ then hear the word of the LORD, O remnant of Judah. Thus says the LORD of hosts, the God of Israel: If you set your faces to enter Egypt and go to live there, ¹⁶ then the sword which you fear shall overtake you there in the land of Egypt; and the famine of which you are afraid shall follow hard after you to Egypt; and there you shall die. ¹⁷ All the men who set their faces to go to Egypt to live there shall die by the sword, by famine, and by pestilence; they shall have no remnant or survivor from the evil which I will bring upon them.

¹⁸ "For thus says the LORD of hosts, the God of Israel: As my anger and my wrath were poured out on the inhabitants of Jerusalem, so my wrath will be poured out on you when you go to Egypt. You shall become an execration, a horror, a curse, and a taunt. You shall see this place no more. ¹⁹ The LORD has said to you, O remnant of Judah, 'Do not go to Egypt.' Know for a certainty that I have warned you this day ²⁰ that you have gone astray at the cost of your lives. For you sent me to the LORD your God, saying, 'Pray for us to the LORD our God, and whatever the LORD our God says declare to us and we will do it.' ²¹ And I have this day declared it to you, but you have not obeyed the voice of the LORD your God in anything that he sent me to tell you. ²² Now therefore know for a certainty that you shall die by the sword, by famine, and by pestilence in the place where you desire to go to live."

¹ When Jeremiah finished speaking to all the people all these words of the LORD their God, with which the LORD their God had sent him to them, ² Azariah the son of Hoshaiah and Johanan the son of Kareah and all the insolent men said to Jeremiah, "You are telling a lie. The LORD our God did not send you to say, 'Do not go to Egypt to live there'; ³ but Baruch the son of Neriah has set you against us, to deliver us into the hand of the Chaldeans, that they may kill us or take us into exile in Baby-

lon." ⁴ So Johanan the son of Kareah and all the commanders of the forces and all the people did not obey the voice of the LORD, to remain in the land of Judah. ⁵ But Johanan the son of Kareah and all the commanders of the forces took all the remnant of Judah who had returned to live in the land of Judah from all the nations to which they had been driven— ⁶ the men, the women, the children, the princesses, and every person whom Nebuzaradan the captain of the guard had left with Gedaliah the son of Ahikam, son of Shaphan; also Jeremiah the prophet and Baruch the son of Neriah. ⁷ And they came into the land of Egypt, for they did not obey the voice of the LORD. And they arrived at Tahpanhes.

Light had suddenly turned to darkness. The fresh start had resulted in failure. What now? Enter Jeremiah!

To go or not to go—that was the question. Should the fugitives remain in the homeland, with uncertainty and possible danger, or should they flee to a foreign land? It was not an easy choice. They came to the prophet—one and all, *from the least to the greatest.* They asked that he go to God in prayer to discover what God's will for them was. When Jeremiah promised that he would pray for them, they pledged to him by solemn oath that they would abide by the answer, whether it was pleasing to them or not.

The prophet prayed for *ten days* before *the word of the Lord* came to him (v. 7). Then he communicated it to the people. The *word* was that they should not go to Egypt but back to their home community.

By implication, much is said here about Jeremiah and prayer. For one thing, it is made apparent again that Jeremiah was known as a man of prayer. Also, it is evident that the king and the people turned to him in times of trouble with earnest requests that he pray for them. But the thing that stands out is that prayer was preparation for the receiving of revelation (this does not exclude reflection) and that Jeremiah persisted in it *until* the revelation was clear (observe his threefold repetition of *thus says the Lord,* vv. 9,15,18). When the word came and he was inwardly certain, he told it as it was. A great man, this man!

When the message of the Lord was relayed to the people, they rejected it. Public opinion and mass emotion are fickle things. Apparently the people had changed during the intervening ten days. They not only refused Jeremiah's counsel but also accused him of passing on to them words of Baruch as the word of God (43:3). This is an unexpected and unusual twist, which provides an indirect tribute to the influence of a man who kept himself in the background at all times in his writing (save for ch. 45). And so the leaders and the people took Jeremiah and Baruch by force and fled to Egypt. They eventually arrived at Tahpanhes (cf. 2:16).

Because of its length, some repetition, and a Deuteronomic flavor, the response of the prophet in 42:9–22 has been rejected by some and assigned to a later editor. This seems to the present writer unwarranted. The thought is quite definitely in harmony with that of Jeremiah. From the earliest days of his prophetic career he had considered the breaking of a covenant a very serious business. Such flagrant violation of the people's pledge made in solemn oath before God could have but one result: a widening of the chasm between them and him. This, in turn, would bring down upon them the very calamities they were trying to avert. Their promise to do God's will when disclosed and their refusal to abide by that promise could mean only trouble.

The denunciation of the people for disobedience in 42:19–22 before the disobedience is directly indicated in 43:1–3 creates a sort of special problem. Some solve it by placing 43:1–3 before 42:19–22 (e.g., Cunliffe-Jones, Bright, *et al.*). This may be necessary. However, a perceptive prophet like Jeremiah could likely sense and had sensed, in various ways (facial expressions, mutterings, inner feelings, etc.), what the reaction and decision of the group was before he had finished speaking.

3. The Finale (43:8—44:30)

8 Then the word of the LORD came to Jeremiah in Tahpanhes: 9 "Take in your hands large stones, and hide them in the mortar in the pavement which is at the entrance to Pharaoh's palace in Tahpanhes, in the sight of the men of Judah, 10 and say to them, 'Thus says the LORD of hosts, the God of Israel: Behold, I will send and take Nebuchadrezzar the king of Babylon, my servant, and he will set his throne above these stones which I have hid, and he will spread his royal canopy over them. 11 He shall come and smite the land of Egypt, giving to the pestilence those who are doomed to the pestilence, to captivity those who are doomed to captivity, and to the sword those who are doomed to the sword. 12 He shall kindle a fire in the temples of the gods of Egypt; and he shall burn them and carry them away captive; and he shall clean the land of Egypt, as a shepherd cleans his cloak of vermin; and he shall go away from there in peace. 13 He shall break the obelisks of Heliopolis which is in the land of Egypt; and the temples of the gods of Egypt he shall burn with fire.' "

1 The word that came to Jeremiah concerning all the Jews that dwelt in the land of Egypt, at Migdol, at Tahpanhes, at Memphis, and in the land of Pathros, 2 "Thus says the LORD of hosts, the God of Israel: You have seen all the evil that I brought upon Jerusalem and upon all the cities of Judah. Behold, this day they are a desolation, and no one dwells in them, 3 because of the wickedness which they committed, provoking me to anger, in that they went to burn incense and serve other gods that they knew not, neither they, nor you, nor your fathers. 4 Yet I persistently sent to you all my servants the prophets, saying, 'Oh, do not do this abominable thing that I hate!' 5 But they did not listen or incline their ear, to turn from their wickedness and burn no incense to other gods. 6 Therefore my wrath and my anger were poured forth and kindled in the cities of Judah and in the streets of Jerusalem; and they became a waste and a desolation, as at this day. 7 And now thus says the LORD God of hosts, the God of Israel: Why do you commit this great evil against yourselves, to cut off from you man and woman, infant and child, from the midst of Judah, leaving you no remnant? 8 Why do you provoke me to anger with the works of your hands, burning incense to other gods in the land of Egypt where you have come to live, that you may be cut off and become a curse and a taunt among all the nations of the earth? 9 Have you forgotten the wickedness of your fathers, the wickedness of the kings of Judah, the wickedness of their wives, your own

wickedness, and the wickedness of your wives, which they committed in the land of Judah and in the streets of Jerusalem? 10 They have not humbled themselves even to this day, nor have they feared, nor walked in my law and my statutes which I set before you and before your fathers.

11 "Therefore thus says the Lord of hosts, the God of Israel: Behold, I will set my face against you for evil, to cut off all Judah. 12 I will take the remnant of Judah who have set their faces to come to the land of Egypt to live, and they shall all be consumed; in the land of Egypt they shall fall; by the sword and by famine they shall be consumed; from the least to the greatest, they shall die by the sword and by famine; and they shall become an execration, a horror, a curse, and a taunt. 13 I will punish those who dwell in the land of Egypt, as I have punished Jerusalem, with the sword, with famine, and with pestilence, 14 so that none of the remnant of Judah who have come to live in the land of Egypt shall escape or survive or return to the land of Judah, to which they desire to return to dwell there; for they shall not return, except some fugitives."

15 Then all the men who knew that their wives had offered incense to other gods, and all the women who stood by, a great assembly, all the people who dwelt in Pathros in the land of Egypt, answered Jeremiah: 16 "As for the word which you have spoken to us in the name of the Lord, we will not listen to you. 17 But we will do everything that we have vowed, burn incense to the queen of heaven and pour out libations to her, as we did, both we and our fathers, our kings and our princes, in the cities of Judah and in the streets of Jerusalem; for then we had plenty of food, and prospered, and saw no evil. 18 But since we left off burning incense to the queen of heaven and pouring out libations to her, we have lacked everything and have been consumed by the sword and by famine." 19 And the women said, "When we burned incense to the queen of heaven and poured out libations to her, was it without our husbands' approval that we made cakes for her bearing her image and poured out libations to her?"

20 Then Jeremiah said to all the people, men and women, all the people who had given him this answer: 21 "As for the incense that you burned in the cities of Judah and in the streets of Jerusalem, you and your fathers, your kings and your princes, and the people of the land, did not the Lord remember it? Did it not come into his mind? 22 The Lord could no longer bear your evil doings and the abominations which you committed; therefore your land has become a desolation and a waste and a curse, without inhabitant, as it is this day. 23 It is because you burned incense, and because you sinned against the Lord and did not obey the voice of the Lord or walk in his law and in his statutes and in his testimonies, that this evil has befallen you, as at this day."

24 Jeremiah said to all the people and all the women, "Hear the word of the Lord, all you of Judah who are in the land of Egypt, 25 Thus says the Lord of hosts, the God of Israel: you and your wives have declared with your mouths, and have fulfilled it with your hands, saying, 'We will surely perform our vows that we have made, to burn incense to the queen of heaven and to pour out libations to her.' Then confirm your vows and perform your vows! 26 Therefore hear the word of the Lord, all you of Judah who dwell in the land of Egypt: Behold, I have sworn by my great name, says the Lord, that my name shall no more be invoked by the mouth of any man of Judah in all the land of Egypt, saying, 'As the Lord God lives.' 27 Behold, I am watching over them for evil and not for good; all the men of Judah who are in the land of Egypt shall be consumed by the sword and by famine, until there is an end of them. 28 And those who escape the sword shall return from the land of Egypt to the land of Judah, few in number; and all the remnant of Judah, who came to the land of Egypt to live, shall know whose word will stand, mine or theirs. 29 This shall be the sign to you, says the Lord, that I will punish you in this place, in order that you may know that my words will surely stand against you for evil: 30 Thus says the Lord, Behold, I will give Pharaoh Hophra king of Egypt into the hand of his enemies and into the hand of those who seek his life, as I gave Zedekiah king of Judah into the hand of Nebuchadrezzar king of Babylon, who was his enemy and sought his life."

The story of Israel has come full circle. It started in Egypt, when a crowd of slaves experienced deliverance from servitude by God's grace and power and moved out in a venture of faith toward the Promised Land. Jeremiah had spoken about that from the earliest days of his ministry (cf. 2:2–3; etc.). Now a crowd of Jewish fugitives has returned to Egypt in fear. This was not the kind of covenant community God had intended to create.

The story of Jeremiah reaches its close. We are granted two glimpses of him in Egypt. In both situations he is doing what he has done so very long: puncturing illusions and preaching reality.

The first illusion was that since the people were now in Egypt they were safe. They were beyond the reach of the arm of Babylon. By means of a symbolic act at night, the prophet shattered this illusion (43:8–13). Nebuchadnezzar would invade and ravage Egypt.

A fragmentary Babylonian text in the British Museum recounts an invasion of Egypt by Nebuchadnezzar in the thirty-seventh year of his reign (568–567).[117] It is so fragmentary that little information is provided concerning the outcome of the invasion. Josephus speaks of an invasion of Egypt by Nebuchadnezzar five years after the fall of Jerusalem in 587, at which time he killed one pharaoh and replaced him with another.[118] The paucity of knowledge concerning the period is such that it is impossible to know exactly what happened.

The skepticism of Duhm and some other scholars concerning this incident (43:8–13) is unwarranted and is not shared by the present writer. He agrees with Bright that "the incident is undoubtedly authentic" (p. 265). The allusion in this acted out parable to *Pharaoh's palace in Tahpanhes* is not to the royal palace but to some sort of statehouse or government building, likely used by the pharaoh when he came to town. The Elephantine Papyri refer to "the king's house" at Tahpanhes.

The second illusion which Jeremiah exploded was that the people could worship other gods alongside their covenant God and get away with it. They could not. In seeking to do so, they were in grave peril of losing God altogether (44:1–30).

By implication, the prophet had already denounced idolatry in the symbolic act and accompanying oracle in 43:8–13. In the lengthy prose discourse in chapter 14, he really gets down to brass tacks on the subject. It was no new subject. We recognize the boom of the same old artillery. Will the fire never go out in this man's bones and being—now in his sixties?

The discourse in 44:1–30 is basically

authentic and is made up of two addresses by Jeremiah, with an audience response in between. The prophet spoke to all the Jews of the dispersion in Egypt, probably at some festival.

In his opening address (vv. 2–14), he reminded the people of the desolation of Jerusalem and Judah and of the persistent disobedience of the people to the will of their covenant Lord which brought it about. Then he rebuked them for continuing to engage in idolatry in Egypt. Finally he referred to the terrible retribution which was coming because of their sin.

The audience reaction in vv. 1–519 is most interesting. The prophet had said that idolatry was the prime reason for the disaster that had befallen the city and the country. The people replied that, the way they saw it, it was the other way round. Things had gone well with them during the time when they were worshiping other gods, especially *the queen of heaven* (a prominent Assyrian goddess, whose worship was especially popular among women). It was when they gave all this up and had the big cleanup campaign under Josiah that things started to go wrong.

This is a very unusual popular slant on the Josianic reformation. Weiser suggests that, in talking about the time when things went well with them, the people were thinking of the long reign of Manasseh, a reign marked by peace and reasonable prosperity and also by an unprecedented wave of paganism, especially of the Assyrian variety—but also of almost every other variety as well. Then came the vigorous Deuteronomic reform, followed by one catastrophe after another and culminating in the destruction of the nation. What contrast: from blaming the supreme tragedy of 587 on the apostasy and idolatry of the people to blaming it on the purification and centralization of the worship of Yahweh!

In his last recorded message (44:20–30), Jeremiah fired a broadside. He reiterated the real reason for the calamity

117 Pritchard, *op. cit.*, p. 308.
118 *Antiq.*, X.9,7.

that had come, referred sarcastically to the people's response to his denunciation of their idolatrous practices ("We plan to keep right on with our worship of the queen of heaven;" "Then keep it up! But!" v. 25), and recounted again the terrible fate in store for them. They were going to pay an awful price for their apostasy.

This is a stern note on which to end. It must be set in the context of the total ministry of the man, a long ministry of service, suffering, and sacrifice, motivated by loyal love for God and people. It must also be set in the context of the history of the people, a history of persistent apostasy and rebellion.

With an appeal to history as the judge as to who will prove to be right (v. 28b), the greatest prophet of ancient Israel drops from sight. Tradition holds that the Jews killed him. Then, as is so often the case, they canonized him. When Jesus walked the highways and byways of Palestine and some said that he reminded them of "the prophet," they were talking about Jeremiah. Next to Jesus, he was the most successful "failure" of biblical days, and in many ways, the most Jesus-like man in the Old Testament.

XX. Jeremiah and Baruch (45:1-5)

Baruch consistently remains in the background as he relates the story of the suffering of God's servant. Only here does he step forth from the shadows and show something of himself as a human being. This short but significant passage, in which he gives expression to his personal feelings, has been called "the confession of Baruch."

The "confession" is dated *in the fourth year of Jehoiakim* and is connected with the dictation of Jeremiah's prophecies in that year (v. 1). Some scholars have questioned the reliability of this information, largely on the basis of the chapter's position in the book and the nature of its contents. There are those who hold that the oracle is Jeremiah's charge to his faithful companion while the aged prophet was on his death bed (e.g., Skinner), or

as he was sending him off to the exiles in Babylon to bear his witness there (e.g., Erbt). A few scholars question not only the accuracy of the date but also the authenticity of the oracle.

The present writer accepts both the reliability of the date and the genuineness of the passage (along with Cornill, Volz, Rudolph, Peake, Couturier. Bright, Eissfeldt, et al.). The position in the book may be due to Baruch's modesty, as some suggest, or, as this writer thinks, to his desire to make it a sort of seal and personal signature to his account of the prophet's "passion" and to provide some theological insight into the reason for his preservation of the stories about the prophet's martyrdom. The destruction which the prophet proclaimed at great price and which was coming to pass was not coming by accident but by the action of God. This action was causing God great heartache, and a man—two men—got caught up in the divine pathos and pain (cf. Weiser, von Rad, et al.). By implication, it is indicated that mission and martyrdom belong together.

¹ The word that Jeremiah the prophet spoke to Baruch the son of Neriah, when he wrote these words in a book at the dictation of Jeremiah, in the fourth year of Jehoiakim the son of Josiah, king of Judah: ² "Thus says the LORD, the God of Israel, to you, O Baruch: ³ You said, 'Woe is me! for the LORD has added sorrow to my pain; I am weary with my groaning, and I find no rest.' ⁴ Thus shall you say to him, Thus says the LORD: Behold, what I have built I am breaking down, and what I have planted I am plucking up—that is, the whole land. ⁵ And do you seek great things for yourself? Seek them not; for, behold, I am bringing evil upon all flesh, says the LORD; but I will give you your life as a prize of war in all places to which you may go."

The Occasion (v. 1).—Jeremiah's preaching was vindicated by the outcome of the battle of Carchemish in 605. His forecasts of nearly a quarter of a century could now very easily and quickly become reality. He determined to make an earnest eleventh-hour effort to bring the nation to repentance in the face of the impending crisis and imminent catastrophe. Acting under the guidance of God, he dictated his prophecies to be read in the Temple at the time of a fast (36).

That was the situation. Chapter 45 fits into the time-gap between 36:8 and 36:9.

The Complaint (*vv. 2–3*).—Baruch's lament is set in the context of divine address (v. 2). It is a very frank expression of deep despondency (v. 3). The reader is not informed as to the reasons for the complaint Streane suggests that the *pain* came from Baruch's contemplation of the sins of his countrymen and the judgment coming as a consequence of those sins and that the *sorrow* was caused by his concern about what was going to happen to him (p. 261).

Although admittedly it is somewhat conjectural, it is likely that there were at least three grounds for the complaint. First, Baruch was overwhelmed by the words dictated to him concerning the seriousness of the people's sin and the shattering consequences of their sin. Second, he had probably suffered some difficulties and indignities already because of his association with the prophet of doom, and no doubt he envisioned in his imagination yet greater suffering to come when he read the prophecies in public. Third, he saw his aircastles of ambition and advancement come crashing down.

To be sure, he had never spoken of any personal desire for popularity and prestige in so many words. But he was a man of unusual ability and family background.[119] Apparently he had joined Jeremiah early in Jehoiakim's reign, after the prophet had become a national figure. It is reasonable to suppose that a man of his caliber and connections could have had some plans for position or promotion in mind, or at least could have entertained some hopes in that direction (so Bright, Blank, *et al.*).

Moreover, the lament is shot through with self-concern and self-pity: "*Woe is me!* In effect, he says: "I'm having a terribly hard time of it. Things are not turning out as I expected. The way is rough. I'm worn out with my groaning, and I can find no rest." Self-pity, a temptation which often besets God's servants, is frequently indicative of frustrated ambition.

The Challenge (*vv. 4–5*).—Because Jeremiah "had been there" too (cf. 11:18– 12:6; 15:10–21), God could use him to help his friend in the hour of need. The medicine administered was somewhat the same as that given Jeremiah in his times of "soul-trouble."

First, God made clear to Baruch that what he was suffering paled into insignificance when set alongside what he (God) was suffering. He was having to pull up that which he had planted and pull down that which he had built (cf. 1:10). And there was much pain in the pulling up and pulling down. In a rather daring and disturbing way, God was matching his servant's complaint with his own, as though he said: "O Baruch, what is your hurt compared to mine?"

There is here a most unusual revelation. Wheeler Robinson says: "There is hardly a passage in the Old Testament which gives us a more impressive glimpse of the eternal cross in the heart of God, the bitterness of his disappointment with man." [120]

Second, God called to Baruch's attention that if he was going to serve him he must serve on his terms. He charged him to stop putting self at the center, to give God and his cause priority, and to be prepared to take the consequences: "*Do you seek great things for yourself? Seek them not* (*or*, "Would you seek personal advancement? Desist!"). God was saying: "This is no time for personal ambition. This is a time for true greatness. All I can promise you is my presence and protection. *I will give you your life as a prize of war*" (cf. 21:9).

The occasion, the complaint, the challenge—the consequence? The story has a

---

119 Cf. Josephus; 43:3; 51:59; 2 Chron. 24:8.

120 H. W. Robinson, *The Cross in the Old Testament* (Philadelphia: The Westminster Press, 1955), p. 143.

sequel (cf. chs. 36—44). Baruch was at
life's crossroads. He had to decide whether
he would live for self or stick by God and
his servant. He made his choice, and it
was the right one. He accepted the divine
challenge and carried on faithfully to the
end. The way got rougher and the going
tougher, but he refused to give up. He
was with the prophet during all his trials
in the reigns of Jehoiakim and Zedekiah,
during the horrible siege and sack of Jerusalem, during the failure of the new start
after the fall of the city, and during the
flight to Egypt. He was still beside him
when the curtain came down in the land
of the pharaohs. He had much to do, under God, with the composition, preservation, and transmission of the prophecy of
Jeremiah. He made an enduring and inestimable contribution to the kingdom of
God. God's word to Baruch may have a
peculiar personal relevance for many just
now. For the world's supreme need today
is life that is totally committed to the will
of God in Christ whatever the cost.

XXI. Prophecies Concerning Other Peo-
ples (46:1—51:64)

This is a separate "book" with its own
superscription (46:1), containing a collection of prophecies against foreign nations.
It is the least read part of Jeremiah. This is
unfortunate for at least two reasons: It
has in it some of the best poetry in the
prophecy, and it is essential to an adequate
understanding of the prophet.

There is a great variety of viewpoint
concerning the date and authorship of
chapters 46—51. Because of style, tone,
viewpoint, and much extraneous material,
some deny that Jeremiah had anything to
do with them and date them late in the
exilic period or in the postexilic age (cf.
Volz, Pfeiffer, Rost). Bardtke posits an
original book of foreign prophecies from
the early ministry of Jeremiah, who, in
his view, appeared first as a nationalistic
prophet and later underwent a radical
change. Many scholars today hold that
Jeremiah was responsible for the nucleus

of the collection, that he incorporated or
used older traditional materials, and that
additions and expansions were made later.

The section deals mainly with judgment
upon pagan peoples. That judgment is consistently portrayed in terms of war. But
the primary stress is upon the activity of
God. It is "the sword of the Lord" that
rages among the nations. Only occasionally
is the human agent brought sharply into
the foreground (cf. 49:30).

The collapse of nation after nation is
dramatically and magnificently depicted.
But that is not the whole story. Alongside
extended pictures of destruction are promises of restoration (cf. 46:27 ff.; 48:47;
49:6,39; etc.). All of it is an emphatic expression of the concept of Yahweh's lordship over history. It is not a partial view,
either, for it includes God's activity in
both retribution and salvation for other
nations as well as Judah. In fact, judgment, a moral necessity, is the prelude to
salvation (this may account for the position of the chapters in the book).

Although it is rather widely accepted
that the Sitz im Leben of the foreign
prophecies was warfare, evidence in the
Old Testament suggests that the prophecies were employed in multiple contexts in
the life of the people: military situations,
court life, and services at the sanctuary
(cf. Mowinckel, Kraus, Johnson, von Rad,
Weiser, Reventlow).

1. Concerning Egypt (46:1-28)

The first in the collection of prophecies
against the nations is a chapter containing two oracles concerning Egypt.

(1) The Defeat of the Egyptians (46:1-
12)

¹ The word of the Lord which came to
Jeremiah the prophet concerning the nations.
² About Egypt. Concerning the army of
Pharaoh Neco, king of Egypt, which was by
the river Euphrates at Carchemish and which
Nebuchadrezzar king of Babylon defeated in
the fourth year of Jehoiakim the son of Josiah,
king of Judah:
3 "Prepare buckler and shield,
    and advance for battle!

4 Harness the horses;
        mount, O horsemen!
   Take your stations with your helmets,
        polish your spears,
        put on your coats of mail!
5 Why have I seen it?
   They are dismayed
        and have turned backward.
   Their warriors are beaten down,
        and have fled in haste;
   they look not back—
        terror on every side!
                                    says the LORD.
6 The swift cannot flee away,
        nor the warrior escape;
   in the north by the river Euphrates
        they have stumbled and fallen.
7 "Who is this, rising like the Nile,
        like rivers whose waters surge?
8 Egypt rises like the Nile,
        like rivers whose waters surge.
   He said, I will rise, I will cover the earth,
        I will destroy cities and their inhabitants.
9 Advance, O horses,
        and rage, O chariots!
   Let the warriors go forth:
        men of Ethiopia and Put who handle the
        shield,
        men of Lud, skilled in handling the bow.
10 That day is the day of the Lord GOD of
        hosts,
        a day of vengeance,
        to avenge himself on his foes.
   The sword shall devour and be sated,
        and drink its fill of their blood.
   For the Lord GOD of hosts holds a sacrifice
        in the north country by the river Euphra-
        tes.
11 Go up to Gilead, and take balm,
        O virgin daughter of Egypt!
   In vain you have used many medicines;
        there is no healing for you.
12 The nations have heard of your shame,
        and the earth is full of your cry;
   for warrior has stumbled against warrior;
        they have both fallen together."

Verse 2 provides the preface to the
poem-prophecy which follows. It indicates
that the occasion which constitutes the
background was the defeat of the Egyptians by the Babylonians at Carchemish
(605 B.C.).

When the prophet learned of the outcome of the crucial battle, he was deeply
moved and composed a poem (vv. 3–12)
which for vividness and power is scarcely
surpassed by anything in the book. The
poem begins with a portrayal of the prep-

aration of the Egyptians for the struggle.
One can hear the officers as they issue
their sharp orders (vv. 3–4). He observes
the collapse of the courage of the Egyptians as they confront the Babylonians,
and notes their panic in the presence of
the superior power of the enemy (v. 5).
He sees their failure in the attempt at flight
and watches them fall to the ground
(v. 6). He listens to the prophet as he
taunts Pharaoh Neco for his pride and
pompous aspirations, which rise like the
River Nile at floodstage (cc. 7–8a). He
is fascinated as the resurgence of Egypt
under a new dynasty is pictured (vv.
8b–9), only to be brought to a complete
stop by a decisive setback on the banks of
another river, the Euphrates (v. 10), a
tragedy without remedy (vv. 11–12).

Aside from its sheer poetic quality, this
passage is noteworthy in that, in keeping
with his theology of history, Jeremiah represents the new turn in human affairs as
something under divine control and in
line with the divine purpose (v. 10).

(2) A Description of the Consequences of the Defeat (46:13–28)

13 The word which the LORD spoke to Jeremiah the prophet about the coming of Nebuchadrezzar king of Babylon to smite the land
of Egypt:
14 "Declare in Egypt, and proclaim in Migdol;
        proclaim in Memphis and Tahpanhes;
   Say, 'Stand ready and be prepared,
        for the sword shall devour round about
        you.'
15 Why has Apis fled?
        Why did not your bull stand?
        Because the LORD thrust him down.
16 Your multitude stumbled and fell,
        and they said one to another,
   'Arise, and let us go back to our own people
        and to the land of our birth,
        because of the sword of the oppressor.'
17 Call the name of Pharaoh, king of Egypt,
        'Noisy one who lets the hour go by.'
18 "As I live, says the King,
        whose name is the LORD of hosts,
   like Tabor among the mountains,
        and like Carmel by the sea, shall one
        come.
19 Prepare yourselves baggage for exile,
        O inhabitants of Egypt!
   For Memphis shall become a waste,

a ruin, without inhabitant.
20 "A beautiful heifer is Egypt,
but a gadfly from the north has come
upon her.
21 Even her hired soldiers in her midst
are like fatted calves;
yea, they have turned and fled together,
they did not stand;
for the day of their calamity has come upon
them,
the time of their punishment.
22 "She makes a sound like a serpent gliding
away;
for her enemies march in force,
and come against her with axes,
like those who fell trees.
23 They shall cut down her forest,
says the Lord,
though it is impenetrable,
because they are more numerous than
locusts;
they are without number.
24 The daughter of Egypt shall be put to
shame,
she shall be delivered into the hand of a
people from the north."
25 The Lord of hosts, the God of Israel, said:
"Behold, I am bringing punishment upon
Amon of Thebes, and Pharaoh, and Egypt and
her gods and her kings, upon Pharaoh and
those who trust in him. 26 I will deliver them
into the hand of those who seek their life, into
the hand of Nebuchadrezzar king of Babylon
and his officers. Afterward Egypt shall be inhabited as in the days of old, says the Lord.
27 "But fear not, O Jacob my servant,
nor be dismayed, O Israel;
for lo, I will save you from afar,
and your offspring from the land of their
captivity.
Jacob shall return and have quiet and ease,
and none shall make him afraid.
28 Fear not, O Jacob my servant,
says the Lord,
for I am with you.
I will make a full end of all the nations
to which I have driven you,
but of you I will not make a full end.
I will chasten you in just measure,
and I will by no means leave you unpunished."

This is a separate prophecy. For the
most part, it also is in poetry. It, too, has
a preface (v. 13). The preface would appear to place the composition of the
prophecy a bit later than the one preceding it—either during Nebuchadnezzar's
push southward after his victory in 605,
or during his activity in the Philistine
plain in 604.

At the start, Jeremiah warns Migdol
(an Egyptian border city) and Memphis
(the capital of Lower Egypt, near Cairo)
that the Babylonian army has been working havoc on all sides and surely will not
make an exception of Egypt (v. 14). The
sacred bull Apis, highly revered as the
incarnation of a god, has left the land because Yahweh has driven him out (v.
15). This means that the country will collapse. Accordingly, foreigners who have
settled in Egypt will decide to return to
their own people (v. 16). Since the pharaoh cannot protect them, they will nickname him "Big Noise who has missed his
chance" (v. 17). As Tabor overtops the
nearby mountains and Carmel the sea and
plain about it, so will the Babylonian
tower over the Egyptians (v. 18). Let the
Egyptians get ready for exile, for the invader is coming (v. 19).

In a series of arresting similes and metaphors Jeremiah pictures the invasion and
devastation of the country (vv. 20–26).
In sharp contrast to the fate of Egypt is
the future of Israel (vv. 27–28; cf. 30:10-
11). Instead of destruction, there will be
deliverance. Egyptians will be carried into
exile; Israelites will come back from exile.

Once again the prophet expresses his
conviction that God reigns and that he is
active in history, directing and overruling
the movements of the nations to his own
glory and the vindication of his moral
government of his universe.

2. Concerning Philistia (47:1–7)

1 The word of the Lord that came to Jeremiah the prophet concerning the Philistines
before Pharaoh smote Gaza.
2 Thus says the Lord:
"Behold, waters are rising out of the north,
and shall become an overflowing torrent;
they shall overflow the land and all that fill
it,
the city and those who dwell in it.
Men shall cry out,
and every inhabitant of the land shall
wail.
3 At the noise of the stamping of the hoofs of
his stallions,
at the rushing of his chariots, at the rumbling of their wheels,
the fathers look not back to their children,

so feeble are their hands,
4 because of the day that is coming to destroy
   all the Philistines,
   to cut off from Tyre and Sidon
   every helper that remains.
   For the LORD is destroying the Philistines,
   the remnant of the coastland of Caphtor.
5 Baldness has come upon Gaza,
   Ashkelon has perished.
   O remnant of the Anakim,
   how long will you gash yourselves?
6 Ah, sword of the LORD!
   How long till you are quiet?
   Put yourself into your scabbard,
   rest and be still!
7 How can it be quiet,
   when the LORD has given it a charge?
   Against Ashkelon and against the seashore
   he has appointed it."

The second in the series of prophecies against foreign nations is directed against the Philistines, Judah's immediate neighbors. It is quite different both in imagery and emphasis from other oracles against these neighbors (cf. Amos 1:6–8; Isa. 14:29–31; Ezek. 25:15–17; Zeph. 2:4–7; Zech. 9:5–7).

The date of the passage is much debated. Verse 1 connects the coming of this *word of the Lord* with the smiting of *Gaza* by *Pharaoh*. The trouble is that we do not know when Gaza was smitten or who smote it.

Some scholars believe that the allusion is to an attack by Neco on Kadytis (ordinarily identified with Gaza) in 609. This incident is mentioned by Herodotus (II, 159). A. Malamat has lent recent support to the view that Gaza was taken by the Egyptians at that time.[121] Other scholars surmise that the assault on Gaza took place in 605, 604, or 601.

Like the oracles on Egypt, this authentic poem-prophecy possesses unusual literary power. Its theme is the disaster that is coming upon the Philistines from the north. It begins by picturing the predicted invasion as a great flood which will overflow the entire country and all the cities in it, so that the citizens will cry out in consternation and lamentation (v. 2). Min-

gled with the weeping and wailing will be the noise of the stamping of stallions, the rushing of chariots, and the rumbling of wheels. Gripped by terror, fathers will forsake their children and flee (v. 3). The alliance with the Phoenicians will prove to be of no help (v. 4a).

Why? The answer is that the Lord is going to bring destruction upon the Philistines (v. 4b). Gaza will feel the icy grip of grief (cf. 16:6; 41:5). Ashkelon will be silenced (struck dumb). The question leaps out: *O remnant of the Anakim* (giants), *how long will you gash yourselves* (self-mutilation, like shaving the head, was a sign of grief and distress; on the textual problem in v. 5b, see Bright, p. 309).

The passage comes to a forceful close with an apostrophe to the sword of the Lord, a question from the people as to when that sword will cease its activity, and the reply of the prophet in the form of another question: *How can it be quiet* (at rest), *when the Lord has given it a charge* (vv. 6–7)?

Jeremiah has referred elsewhere to the sword of the Lord. Like the image of the cup of God's wrath, this is one of the prophet's strongest, most awesome figures. Here, as elsewhere, the sword of the Lord symbolizes God's righteous judgment. That judgment, which is coming upon Judah, is also coming upon other countries. The Philistines, too, must drink of the cup of divine wrath (cf. 25:17–20).

3. Concerning Moab (48:1–47)

The oracle concerning the Moabites differs from the preceding prophecies against foreign nations in three ways: its unusual length, its abundant use of material from other sources, and the large number of place names in it.[122]

The prophecy is obviously a collection of utterances concerning Moab by different

---

[121] *Israel's Exploration Journal*, **1**, 1950–1951, 154–159.

[122] The last-mentioned characteristic makes the prophecy invaluable for the geographical study of Moabite territory. Cf. G. E Wright and F. V. Filson, *The Westminster Historical Atlas of the Bible*, rev. ed., 1956; or L. H. Grollenberg, *Atlas of the Bible*, trans. Joyce M. H. Reid and H. H. Rowley, 1956.

prophets at various times. Most of the borrowed material is found in the latter part of the chapter (vv. 29–46), and the chief passages involved are vv. 29–39 (cf. parts of Isa. 15—16), vv. 43–44 (cf. Isa. 24:17–18), and verses 45–46 (cf. Num. 21:28–29). It is possible that Jeremiah was using material from other men—primarily Isaiah—or that both Jeremiah and others were employing anonymous sayings treasured and transmitted by the fellowship of the faithful. We do not know.

The exact setting of the present prophecy is difficult to determine because of the lack of internal evidence and because of the inadequacy of our knowledge of Moabite history.[123] If our assumption that Jeremiah's grasp of the political and religious significance of the victory of the Babylonians at Carchemish is the primary explanation of his preoccupation with the future of surrounding nations is true, then the oracle against Moab dates from the period shortly after that victory and deals with Moab in the light of the significance of Nebuchadnezzar's triumph for her. And all of it is set in the context of Jeremiah's deep conviction that Yahweh is sovereign Lord of history and is working out his righteous purpose in history.

(1) The Downfall of Moab (48:1–10)

¹ Concerning Moab.
Thus says the LORD of hosts, the God of Israel:
"Woe to Nebo, for it is laid waste!
    Kiriathaim is put to shame, it is taken;
    the fortress is put to shame and broken down;
²   the renown of Moab is no more.
In Heshbon they planned evil against her:
    'Come, let us cut her off from being a nation!'
You also, O Madmen, shall be brought to silence;
    the sword shall pursue you.
³ "Hark! a cry from Horonaim,
    'Desolation and great destruction!'
⁴ Moab is destroyed;

---

123 On the involvement of Moab with Judah during Jeremiah's ministry, see 2 Kings 24:2; Jer. 12:7–13; 27:1–11; on Moabite history, read A H. van Zyl's *The Moabites,* 1960.

---

    a cry is heard as far as Zoar.
⁵ For at the ascent of Luhith
    they go up weeping;
for at the descent of Horonaim
    they have heard the cry of destruction.
⁶ Flee! Save yourselves!
    Be like a wild ass in the desert!
⁷ For, because you trusted in your strongholds and your treasures,
    you also shall be taken;
and Chemosh shall go forth into exile,
    with his priests and his princes.
⁸ The destroyer shall come upon every city,
    and no city shall escape;
the valley shall perish,
    and the plain shall be destroyed,
    as the LORD has spoken.
⁹ "Give wings to Moab,
    for she would fly away;
her cities shall become a desolation,
    with no inhabitant in them.
¹⁰ "Cursed is he who does the work of the LORD with slackness; and cursed is he who keeps back his sword from bloodshed.

The opening part of the prophecy presents a description of the laying waste of the land, with major cities named. The invasion comes from the north. Heshbon, Nebo, and Kiriathaim constituted the northern defense of the country. These places are represented as having been taken.

The reason for Moab's downfall is given in v. 7: she has trusted in material things rather than in the true and living God. Because of this, she is going to experience disaster (vv. 7b–9).

Chemosh is the name of the Moabite deity. Like all false, man-made gods, he is the projection of human limitations, imperfections, and desires and cannot help in the time of trouble.

Verse 10 is in prose. It has been called a "bloodthirsty verse" (Peake) and was Pope Gregory VII's favorite. It is this sort of scriptural statement that must be used with care by the Christian. The work of the Lord is not to be done with indolence, but it must be the work of the Lord.

(2) Disaster and Disillusionment (48: 11–17)

¹¹ "Moab has been at ease from his youth
    and has settled on his lees;

he has not been emptied from vessel to
    vessel,
  nor has he gone into exile;
so his taste remains in him,
  and his scent is not changed.
12 "Therefore, behold, the days are coming,
says the LORD, when I shall send to him tilters
who will tilt him, and empty his vessels, and
break his jars in pieces. 13 Then Moab shall be
ashamed of Chemosh, as the house of Israel
was ashamed of Bethel, their confidence.
14 "How do you say, 'We are heroes
  and mighty men of war'?
15 The destroyer of Moab and his cities has
    come up,
   and the choicest of his young men have
     gone down to slaughter,
    says the King, whose name is the LORD of
     hosts.
16 The calamity of Moab is near at hand
   and his affliction hastens apace.
17 Bemoan him, all you who are round about
    him,
   and all who know his name;
  say, 'How the mighty scepter is broken,
   the glorious staff.'

Moab is pictured as a land whose people are characterized by a spirit of self-
complacency. They have not known
trouble, and therefore have not learned
through discipline. Instead of being poured
from vessel to vessel, they have settled
upon their lees (v. 11).

But Moab's complacency is going to be
disturbed, and she will experience disappointment and disillusionment (v. 12).
The things in which she has trusted—including her army and her deity—will let
her down in the hour of crisis, just as
Israel's formalistic observance of her system of ceremony and sacrifice at Bethel,
the shrine of the Northern Kingdom, failed
to save her from the Assyrians (vv. 13 ff.).

The sin of the settled is a common sin
among the prosperous and proud and is
very difficult to deal with. It is subtle and
deadly. Someone has observed that God's
causes are not defeated so much by open
opposition as by being sat on by number-
less, nameless nobodies. Complacency does
clog the wheels of life and leads eventually
to catastrophe. For God does not allow it
to continue indefinitely. There comes a
tilting, a pouring out, a shaking up, a

shattering. Man is compelled to reckon
with reality.

(3) Devastation and Derision (48:18-28)

18 "Come down from your glory,
  and sit on the parched ground,
  O inhabitant of Dibon!
 For the destroyer of Moab has come up
   against you;
  he has destroyed your strongholds.
19 Stand by the way and watch,
   O inhabitant of Aroer!
  Ask him who flees and her who escapes;
   say, 'What has happened?'
20 Moab is put to shame, for it is broken;
   wail and cry!
  Tell it by the Arnon,
   that Moab is laid waste.
21 "Judgment has come upon the tableland,
upon Holon, and Jahzah, and Mephaath, 22 and
Dibon, and Nebo, and Bethdiblathaim, 23 and
Kiriathaim, and Bethgamul, and Bethmeon,
24 and Kerioth, and Bozrah, and all the cities of
the land of Moab, far and near. 25 The horn of
Moab is cut off, and his arm is broken, says the
LORD.
26 "Make him drunk, because he magnified
himself against the LORD; so that Moab shall
wallow in his vomit, and he too shall be held
in derision. 27 Was not Israel a derision to you?
Was he found among thieves, that whenever
you spoke of him you wagged your head?
28 "Leave the cities, and dwell in the rock,
  O inhabitants of Moab!
 Be like the dove that nests
  in the sides of the mouth of a gorge.

The poet-prophet continues his graphic
portrayal of the destruction of Moab (vv.
18 ff.). The nation's power (*horn, arm*)
will be broken (v. 25), and the country
will become the object of ridicule, a laughingstock among the nations (vv. 26–27).
Therefore, let the people leave the land
and live the difficult, dangerous lives of
fugitives, like doves which build their
nests high up on the steep rocky side of a
gorge (v. 28).

(4) A Dirge over a Land Now Desolate
      (48:29-39)

29 We have heard of the pride of Moab—
   he is very proud—
  of his loftiness, his pride, and his arrogance,
   and the haughtiness of his heart.
30 I know his insolence, says the LORD;
   his boasts are false,

his deeds are false.
31 Therefore I wail for Moab;
    I cry out for all Moab;
    for the men of Kirheres I mourn.
32 More than for Jazer I weep for you,
    O vine of Sibmah!
    Your branches passed over the sea,
    reached as far as Jazer;
    upon your summer fruits and your vintage
    the destroyer has fallen.
33 Gladness and joy have been taken away
    from the fruitful land of Moab;
    I have made the wine cease from the wine
    presses;
    no one treads them with shouts of joy;
    the shouting is not the shout of joy.
34 "Heshbon and Elealeh cry out; as far as
Jahaz they utter their voice, from Zoar to
Horonaim and Eglathshelishiyah. For the waters of Nimrim also have become desolate.
35 And I will bring to an end in Moab, says the
LORD, him who offers sacrifice in the high
place and burns incense to his god.
36 Therefore my heart moans for Moab like a
flute, and my heart moans like a flute for the
men of Kirheres; therefore the riches they
gained have perished.
37 "For every head is shaved and every
beard cut off; upon all the hands are gashes,
and on the loins is sackcloth. 38 On all the
housetops of Moab and in the squares there is
nothing but lamentation; for I have broken
Moab like a vessel for which no one cares, says
the LORD. 39 How it is broken! How they wail!
How Moab has turned his back in shame! So
Moab has become a derision and a horror to all
that are round about him."

These verses contain a lament over
Moab, whose land lies desolate because of
her arrogant pride. Her vineyards are to
be despoiled. Joy will depart. Sacrificial
worship will cease (vv. 29–35). Heads
will be shaved and beards shorn. Hands
will be mutilated and sackcloth worn. The
reason for these signs of outer grief? God
will smash Moab "like an unwanted pot"
(vv. 37–39; cf. 22:28). The prophet expresses his inner pain at the dark prospect
for a neighboring people (v. 36).

(5) Destruction and Restoration
    (48:40–47)

40 For thus says the LORD:
"Behold, one shall fly swiftly like an eagle,
    and spread his wings against Moab;
41 the cities shall be taken
    and the strongholds seized.

The heart of the warriors of Moab shall be
    in that day
    like the heart of a woman in her pangs;
42 Moab shall be destroyed and be no longer
    a people,
    because he magnified himself against the
    LORD.
43 Terror, pit, and snare
    are before you, O inhabitant of Moab!
                                   says the LORD.
44 He who flees from the terror
    shall fall into the pit,
    and he who climbs out of the pit
    shall be caught in the snare.
    For I will bring these things upon Moab
    in the year of their punishment,
                                   says the LORD.
45 "In the shadow of Heshbon
    fugitives stop without strength;
    for a fire has gone forth from Heshbon,
    a flame from the house of Sihon;
    it has destroyed the forehead of Moab,
    the crown of the sons of tumult.
46 Woe to you, O Moab!
    The people of Chemosh is undone;
    for your sons have been taken captive,
    and your daughters into captivity.
47 Yet I will restore the fortunes of Moab
    in the latter days, says the LORD."
Thus far is the judgment on Moab.

Like a great eagle, the enemy will
spread his wings over Moab (v. 40). Few
will escape destruction, because the people
magnified themselves against the Lord (v.
42). Along with the proclamation of retribution, however, there is presented a
promise of restoration (v. 47).

Two things stand out here. The first is
that the nation that magnifies itself against
the Lord—usurps the position and prerogatives of God—is headed for disaster. God
is the supreme fact and factor in life. Man's
relationship with him determines his future
and his ultimate fate. This raises the burning question: How can a nation—our nation—be brought to a dynamic faith in the
living God and a life of obedience to his
sovereign will—before it is too late?

The second thing that is arresting in the
closing part of this chapter is that God's
purpose is not that nations should be destroyed—for destruction's sake—but that
they might be redeemed, in order to live
together in rich harmonious relationships
in his kingdom.

4. Concerning Ammon (49:1-6)

¹ Concerning the Ammonites.
Thus says the LORD:
"Has Israel no sons?
　　Has he no heir?
Why then has Milcom dispossessed Gad,
　　and his people settled in its cities?
² Therefore, behold, the days are coming,
　　says the LORD,
when I will cause the battle cry to be
　　heard
　　against Rabbah of the Ammonites;
it shall become a desolate mound,
　　and its villages shall be burned with fire;
then Israel shall dispossess those who dis-
　　possessed him,
　　says the LORD.
³ "Wail, O Heshbon, for Ai is laid waste!
　　Cry, O daughters of Rabbah!
Gird yourselves with sackcloth,
　　lament, and run to and fro among the
　　hedges!
For Milcom shall go into exile,
　　with his priests and his princes.
⁴ Why do you boast of your valleys,
　　O faithless daughter,
who trusted in her treasures, saying,
　　'Who will come against me?'
⁵ Behold, I will bring terror upon you,
　　says the Lord GOD of hosts,
　　from all who are round about you,
and you shall be driven out, every man
　　straight before him,
　　with none to gather the fugitives.
⁶ But afterward I will restore the fortunes of
the Ammonites, says the LORD."

Like the Moabites, the Ammonites were
related to the Israelites, and, like them,
they were involved in the disturbances in
Palestine after 601 and in 594–593. Another fact is relevant. When Tiglath-
pileser III invaded Galilee and Gilead in
733, he took captives as he went. The
Gadites dwelt in Gilead, just north of
Ammon. After Tiglath's invasion and deportation, the Ammonites took over their
territory. This explains the way in which
the present poem-prophecy begins.

Knowing the right of the Israelites to
the land, the prophet asks why it is in the
hands of a pagan people who worship
Milcom as their patron deity (v. 1).
Then he forecasts judgment for the Ammonites and *afterward*—mercy (vv. 2–6).
The same two notes are struck here as in

chapter 48.

Observe the characterization and charge
in v. 4. It is basically the same as in the
case of the Moabites: arrogant self-
sufficiency and secularism. The precise date
of the prophecy cannot be determined. It
probably comes out of the period between
605 and 598.

5. Concerning Edom (49:7-22)

⁷ Concerning Edom.
Thus says the LORD of hosts:
"Is wisdom no more in Teman?
　　Has counsel perished from the prudent?
　　Has their wisdom vanished?
⁸ Flee, turn back, dwell in the depths,
　　O inhabitants of Dedan!
For I will bring the calamity of Esau upon
　　him,
　　the time when I punish him.
⁹ If grape-gatherers came to you,
　　would they not leave gleanings?
If thieves came by night,
　　would they not destroy only enough for
　　themselves?
¹⁰ But I have stripped Esau bare,
　　I have uncovered his hiding places,
　　and he is not able to conceal himself.
His children are destroyed, and his broth-
　　ers,
　　and his neighbors; and he is no more.
¹¹ Leave your fatherless children, I will keep
　　them alive;
　　and let your widows trust in me."
¹² For thus says the LORD: "If those who did
not deserve to drink the cup must drink it, will
you go unpunished? You shall not go unpunished, but you must drink. ¹³ For I have sworn
by myself, says the LORD, that Bozrah shall become a horror, a taunt, a waste, and a curse;
and all her cities shall be perpetual wastes."
¹⁴ I have heard tidings from the LORD,
　　and a messenger has been sent among
　　the nations:
"Gather yourselves together and come
　　against her,
　　and rise up for battle!"
¹⁵ For behold, I will make you small among
　　the nations,
　　despised among men.
¹⁶ The horror you inspire has deceived you,
　　and the pride of your heart,
you who live in the clefts of the rock,
　　who hold the height of the hill.
Though you make your nest as high as the
　　eagle's,
　　I will bring you down from there,
　　　　　　　　　　　　　says the LORD.
¹⁷ "Edom shall become a horror; every one

who passes by it will be horrified and will hiss because of all its disasters. [18] As when Sodom and Gomorrah and their neighbor cities were overthrown, says the LORD, no man shall dwell there, no man shall sojourn in her. [19] Behold, like a lion coming up from the jungle of the Jordan against a strong sheepfold, I will suddenly make them run away from her; and I will appoint over her whomever I choose. For who is like me? Who will summon me? What shepherd can stand before me? [20] Therefore hear the plan which the LORD has made against Edom and the purposes which he has formed against the inhabitants of Teman: Even the little ones of the flock shall be dragged away; surely their fold shall be appalled at their fate. [21] At the sound of their fall the earth shall tremble; the sound of their cry shall be heard at the Red Sea. [22] Behold, one shall mount up and fly swiftly like an eagle, and spread his wings against Bozrah, and the heart of the warriors of Edom shall be in that day like the heart of a woman in her pangs."

Like the prophecy against Moab, the one against Edom is a combination of poetry and prose, and of authentic sayings by Jeremiah and anonymous utterances taken from older sources.

There is a close relationship between this prophecy and the prophecy of Obadiah (cf. vv. 9–10a with Obad. 5–6; vv. 14–16 with Obad. 1–4). Who is quoting whom? The probability is that Obadiah is quoting Jeremiah, or, more likely still, that both are using an older source.

Another striking aspect of this prophecy is that much of it appears elsewhere in Jeremiah (cf. vv. 12–13 with 25:15–19; v. 19 with 19:18; v. 18 with 50:40; vv. 19–20 with 50: 44–46; v. 22 with 48: 40b). The fact is that there is little in vv. 17–22 which does not occur elsewhere—either within or without the prophecy of Jeremiah—and not too much in vv. 7–16 (vv. 7–8,10b–11,13).

The oracle is a prophecy of the utter destruction of Edom. God has decreed it, and nothing can avert it. Neither her sages nor her soldiers can save her. Neither her friends nor her mountain fortress can protect her (cf. vv. 7,10,16,22). God has set the time of her doom (v. 8b). Like an eagle, he will swoop down upon her (v. 22). Like a lion, he will pounce upon her

(v. 19). He will give her the cup of his wrath to drink (v. 12). The judgment will be thorough. The destruction will be complete—as *when Sodom and Gomorrah and their neighbor cities were overthrown.* (v. 8). When the harvesters go through the vineyards, they leave gleanings. Thieves at night do not take everything in sight. But God will strip Edom bare (vv. 9–10). He will bring her down from her eagle's nest (v. 16). As a result, she will be a shocking sight (v. 17), and Bozrah, her chief city, will become *a horror, a taunt, a waste, and a curse* (v. 13).

Is this "a hymn of hate?" Is it merely an expression of personal passion, or of intense patriotism or nationalism? Or is there in it a proclamation of a principle? To understand the prophecy, one must study the relationship between the Israelites and the Edomites throughout their history. They provide the classic case of fratricidal hatred and strife in Old Testament times. The struggle between their ancestors, Jacob and Esau, in their mother's womb continued among their descendants down through the centuries.

Like their forefather Esau, the Edomites were "profane" (cf. Heb. 12:16). Insensitive to the holy, they were noted for worldly wisdom and for highway robbery. They were secularists. There is only one mention of Edomite gods in the Old Testament, so far as the writer knows (2 Chron. 25:20). They had a religion, but apparently they did not give it much place in their lives.

Despite their earthiness and evil, the Israelites, the descendants of Jacob, could never escape from their hunger for the things of God. At the center of their life was a temple. They had their priests, their prophets, their psalmists. They gave us our Bible and our Christ. The Edomites left nothing of abiding value.

Edom came to represent evil incarnate, secularism in essence. The struggle between these two peoples was more than a personal feud. In some sense and measure, it symbolizes the fundamental antagonism between sin and righteousness, between faith and "unfaith," between God and the flesh. In this struggle that rages through the ages, God is going to win. Every entrenched evil will one day come down!

When the present writer served as preacher for the Christian Leadership Training Conference at Berchtesgaden, Germany, in June, 1965, he met each morning for prayer and briefing at eight o'clock with other program personnel in the room in which Hitler wrote part of *Mein Kampf*. During the week he often gazed up at "the eagle's nest" and thought of Jeremiah 49:16 and Obadiah 1–4. It kept ringing in his ears: What an irony of history! The place from which Hitler planned to rule the world, now a place for religious retreats! Here is another evidence that God reigns, and that it is embedded in the basic order of the universe that what is of God will last and what is against God will not!

One who has visited ancient Edom has found eloquent testimony to this truth.

6. Concerning Damascus (49:23–27)

23 Concerning Damascus.
"Hamath and Arpad are confounded,
 for they have heard evil tidings;
they melt in fear, they are troubled like the
  sea
  which cannot be quiet.
24 Damascus has become feeble, she turned to
  flee,
 and panic seized her;
anguish and sorrows have taken hold of
  her,
 as of a woman in travail.
25 How the famous city is forsaken,
 the joyful city!
26 Therefore her young men shall fall in her
  squares,
 and all her soldiers shall be destroyed in
  that day,
             says the LORD of hosts.
27 And I will kindle a fire in the wall of Damascus,
 and it shall devour the strongholds of
  Benhadad."

Damascus, the capital of Syria, is not mentioned in 25:17–26. Nor do we know of any event which directly involved the city with Judah during the ministry of

Jeremiah (but cf. 1 Kings 24:2). No specific occasion is given for the prophecy here. Perhaps the oracle is simply another indication of the prophet's grasp of the broad scope and significance of the Babylonian victory at Carchemish and of Nebuchadnezzar's role in the plan of God.

The import of the prophecy is that the Syrian cities are paralyzed by fear in the face of the approaching foe (vv. 23 f.). The calamity that is coming (vv. 25 f.) is represented as the judgment of a holy God (v. 27).

7. Concerning Kedar and Hazor (49:28–33)

28 Concerning Kedar and the kingdoms of Hazor which Nebuchadrezzar king of Babylon
smote.
 Thus says the LORD:
 "Rise up, advance against Kedar!
  Destroy the people of the east!
29 Their tents and their flocks shall be taken,
  their curtains and all their goods;
 their camels shall be borne away from
  them,
  and men shall cry to them: 'Terror on
  every side!'
30 Flee, wander far away, dwell in the depths,
 O inhabitants of Hazor!
             says the LORD.
For Nebuchadrezzar king of Babylon
 has made a plan against you,
 and formed a purpose against you.

31 "Rise up, advance against a nation at ease,
  that dwells securely,
             says the LORD,
 that has no gates or bars,
 that dwells alone.
32 Their camels shall become booty,
  their herds of cattle a spoil.
 I will scatter to every wind
  those who cut the corners of their hair,
 and I will bring their calamity
  from every side of them,
             says the LORD.
33 Hazor shall become a haunt of jackals,
  an everlasting waste;
 no man shall dwell there,
  no man shall sojourn in her."

Kedar was the name of a nomadic tribe, dwelling in the desert to the east of Palestine (cf. 2:10; Isa. 21:16; 60:7; Ezek. 27:21). *Hazor* appears to be a collective name either for the semi-nomadic Arabs or for the villages in which they lived.

The prophecy opens with a divine command to an unnamed person to advance against the Arabian tribes (v. 28). All of Kedar's belongings will be borne away by the enemy. Men will cry out *Terror on every side!* The unnamed person is Nebuchadnezzar. He has *a plan* against the dwellers in the east (v. 30). God calls upon him to rise up and carry it out (v. 31). He is promised an easy victory (v. 32). Hazor will become a perpetual desolation where no one dwells (v. 33).

8. Concerning Elam (49:34–39)

34 The word of the Lord that came to Jeremiah the prophet concerning Elam, in the beginning of the reign of Zedekiah king of Judah.
35 Thus says the Lord of hosts: "Behold, I will break the bow of Elam, the mainstay of their might; 36 and I will bring upon Elam the four winds from the four quarters of heaven; and I will scatter them to all those winds, and there shall be no nation to which those driven out of Elam shall not come. 37 I will terrify Elam before their enemies, and before those who seek their life; I will bring evil upon them, my fierce anger, says the Lord. I will send the sword after them, until I have consumed them; 38 and I will set my throne in Elam, and destroy their king and princes, says the Lord.
39 "But in the latter days I will restore the fortunes of Elam, says the Lord."

This prophecy is dated in the accession year of Zedekiah (597). There is no basis for questioning the reliability of the date. Elam was a strong state to the east of Babylonia in the area now known as Iran. We have no direct knowledge of any relationship between Elam and Judah or between Elam and any revolt against Babylon during the reign of either Jehoiakim or Zedekiah.

As in the case of Egypt, Moab, and Ammon, the oracle concerning Elam is both a prophecy of destruction and a prophecy of restoration. The Elamites were outstanding archers. This is the reason for the reference to the breaking of *the bow* (military strength) of Elam. Though retribution will come upon the Elamites, God will one day restore their fortunes.

9. Concerning Babylon (50:1—51:64)

1 The word which the Lord spoke concerning Babylon, concerning the land of the Chaldeans, by Jeremiah the prophet:
2 "Declare among the nations and proclaim,
set up a banner and proclaim,
conceal it not, and say:
'Babylon is taken,
Bel is put to shame,
Merodach is dismayed.
Her images are put to shame,
her idols are dismayed.'
3 "For out of the north a nation has come up against her, which shall make her land a desolation, and none shall dwell in it; both man and beast shall flee away.
4 "In those days and in that time, says the Lord, the people of Israel and the people of Judah shall come together, weeping as they come; and they shall seek the Lord their God. 5 They shall ask the way to Zion, with faces turned toward it, saying, 'Come, let us join ourselves to the Lord in an everlasting covenant which will never be forgotten.'
6 "My people have been lost sheep; their shepherds have led them astray, turning them away on the mountains; from mountain to hill they have gone, they have forgotten their fold. 7 All who found them have devoured them, and their enemies have said, 'We are not guilty, for they have sinned against the Lord, their true habitation, the Lord, the hope of their fathers.'
8 "Flee from the midst of Babylon, and go out of the land of the Chaldeans, and be as he-goats before the flock. 9 For behold, I am stirring up and bringing against Babylon a company of great nations, from the north country; and they shall array themselves against her; from there she shall be taken. Their arrows are like a skilled warrior who does not return empty-handed. 10 Chaldea shall be plundered; all who plunder her shall be sated, says the Lord.
11 "Though you rejoice, though you exult,
O plunderers of my heritage,
though you are wanton as a heifer at grass,
and neigh like stallions,
12 your mother shall be utterly shamed,
and she who bore you shall be disgraced.
Lo, she shall be the last of the nations,
a wilderness dry and desert.
13 Because of the wrath of the Lord she shall not be inhabited,
but shall be an utter desolation;
everyone who passes by Babylon shall be appalled,
and hiss because of all her wounds.
14 Set yourselves in array against Babylon round about,
all you that bend the bow;

shoot at her, spare no arrows,
  for she has sinned against the LORD.
15 Raise a shout against her round about,
  she has surrendered;
her bulwarks have fallen,
  her walls are thrown down.
For this is the vengeance of the LORD:
  take vengeance on her,
  do to her as she has done.
16 Cut off from Babylon the sower,
  and the one who handles the sickle in
    time of harvest;
because of the sword of the oppressor,
  every one shall turn to his own people,
  and every one shall flee to his own land.
17 "Israel is a hunted sheep driven away by
lions. First the king of Assyria devoured him,
and now at last Nebuchadrezzar king of Babylon has gnawed his bones. 18 Therefore, thus
says the LORD of hosts, the God of Israel:
Behold, I am bringing punishment on the king
of Babylon and his land, as I punished the king
of Assyria. 19 I will restore Israel to his pasture,
and he shall feed on Carmel and in Bashan,
and his desire shall be satisfied on the hills of
Ephraim and in Gilead. 20 In those days and in
that time, says the LORD, iniquity shall be
sought in Israel, and there shall be none; and
sin in Judah, and none shall be found; for I
will pardon those whom I leave as a remnant.
21 "Go up against the land of Merathaim,
  and against the inhabitants of Pekod.
Slay, and utterly destroy after them,
                          says the LORD,
  and do all that I have commanded you.
22 The noise of battle is in the land,
  and great destruction!
23 How the hammer of the whole earth
  is cut down and broken!
How Babylon has become
  a horror among the nations!
24 I set a snare for you and you were taken,
  O Babylon,
  and you did not know it;
you were found and caught,
  because you strove against the LORD.
25 The LORD has opened his armory,
  and brought out the weapons of his
    wrath,
for the Lord GOD of hosts has a work to do
  in the land of the Chaldeans.
26 Come against her from every quarter;
  open her granaries;
pile her up like heaps of grain, and destroy
    her utterly;
  let nothing be left of her.
27 Slay all her bulls,
  let them go down to the slaughter.
Woe to them, for their day has come,
  the time of their punishment.
28 "Hark! they flee and escape from the land

of Babylon, to declare in Zion the vengeance of
the LORD our God, vengeance for his temple.
29 "Summon archers against Babylon, all
those who bend the bow. Encamp round about
her; let no one escape. Requite her according
to her deeds, do to her according to all that she
has done; for she has proudly defied the LORD,
the Holy One of Israel. 30 Therefore her young
men shall fall in her squares, and all her
soldiers shall be destroyed on that day, says the
LORD.
31 "Behold, I am against you, O proud one,
  says the Lord GOD of hosts;
for your day has come,
  the time when I will punish you.
32 The proud one shall stumble and fall,
  with none to raise him up,
and I will kindle a fire in his cities,
  and it will devour all that is round about
    him.
33 "Thus says the LORD of hosts: The people
of Israel are oppressed, and the people of Judah with them; all who took them captive
have held them fast, they refuse to let them go.
34 Their Redeemer is strong; the LORD of hosts
is his name. He will surely plead their cause,
that he may give rest to the earth, but unrest
to the inhabitants of Babylon.
35 "A sword upon the Chaldeans, says the
    LORD,
  and upon the inhabitants of Babylon,
  and upon her princes and her wise men!
36 A sword upon the diviners,
  that they may become fools!
A sword upon her warriors,
  that they may be destroyed!
37 A sword upon her horses and upon her
    chariots,
  and upon all the foreign troops in her
    midst,
  that they may become women!
A sword upon all her treasures,
  that they may be plundered!
38 A drought upon her waters,
  that they may be dried up!
For it is a land of images,
  and they are mad over idols.
39 "Therefore wild beasts shall dwell with
hyenas in Babylon, and ostriches shall dwell in
her; she shall be peopled no more for ever, nor
inhabited for all generations. 40 As when God
overthrew Sodom and Gomorrah and their
neighbor cities, says the LORD, so no man shall
dwell there, and no son of man shall sojourn
in her.
41 "Behold, a people comes from the north;
  a mighty nation and many kings
  are stirring from the farthest parts of the
    earth.
42 They lay hold of bow and spear;
  they are cruel, and have no mercy.

The sound of them is like the roaring of the
    sea;
  they ride upon horses,
  arrayed as a man for battle
    against you, O daughter of Babylon!
43 "The king of Babylon heard the report of
    them,
  and his hands fell helpless;
  anguish seized him,
    pain as of a woman in travail.
44 "Behold, like a lion coming up from the
jungle of the Jordan against a strong sheepfold,
I will suddenly make them run away from her;
and I will appoint over her whomever I choose.
For who is like me? Who will summon me?
What shepherd can stand before me? 45 Therefore hear the plan which the Lord has made
against Babylon, and the purposes which he
has formed against the land of the Chaldeans:
Surely the little ones of their flock shall be
dragged away; surely their fold shall be appalled at their fate. 46 At the sound of the capture of Babylon the earth shall tremble, and
her cry shall be heard among the nations."

1 Thus says the Lord:
"Behold, I will stir up the spirit of a de-
    stroyer
  against Babylon,
  against the inhabitants of Chaldea;
2 and I will send to Babylon winnowers,
  and they shall winnow her,
  and they shall empty her land,
    when they come against her from every
    side
  on the day of trouble.
3 Let not the archer bend his bow,
  and let him not stand up in his coat of
    mail.
  Spare not her young men;
  utterly destroy all her host.
4 They shall fall down slain in the land of
    the Chaldeans,
  and wounded in her streets.
5 For Israel and Judah have not been for-
    saken
    by their God, the Lord of hosts;
  but the land of the Chaldeans is full of guilt
    against the Holy One of Israel.
6 "Flee from the midst of Babylon,
  let every man save his life!
  Be not cut off in her punishment,
    for this is the time of the Lord's venge-
    ance,
  the requital he is rendering her.
7 Babylon was a golden cup in the Lord's
    hand,
    making all the earth drunken;
  the nations drank of her wine,
    therefore the nations went mad.
8 Suddenly Babylon has fallen and been

    broken;
  wail for her!
  Take balm for her pain;
    perhaps she may be healed.
9 We would have healed Babylon,
  but she was not healed.
  Forsake her, and let us go
    each to his own country;
  for her judgment has reached up to heaven
    and has been lifted up even to the skies.
10 The Lord has brought forth our vindica-
    tion;
  come, let us declare in Zion
    the work of the Lord our God.
11 "Sharpen the arrows!
  Take up the shields!
The Lord has stirred up the spirit of the kings
of the Medes, because his purpose concerning
Babylon is to destroy it, for that is the vengeance of the Lord, the vengeance for his temple.
12 Set up a standard against the walls of
    Babylon;
  make the watch strong;
  set up watchmen;
    prepare the ambushes;
  for the Lord has both planned and done
    what he spoke concerning the inhabitants
    of Babylon.
13 O you who dwell by many waters,
    rich in treasures,
  your end has come,
    the thread of your life is cut.
14 The Lord of hosts has sworn by himself:
  Surely I will fill you with men, as many as
    locusts,
    and they shall raise the shout of victory
    over you.
15 "It is he who made the earth by his power,
  who established the world by his wisdom,
  and by his understanding stretched out
    the heavens.
16 When he utters his voice there is a tumult
    of waters in the heavens,
  and he makes the mist rise from the
    ends of the earth.
  He makes lightnings for the rain,
    and he brings forth the wind from his
    storehouses.
17 Every man is stupid and without knowl-
    edge;
  every goldsmith is put to shame by his
    idols;
  for his images are false,
    and there is no breath in them.
18 They are worthless, a work of delusion;
  at the time of their punishment they shall
    perish.
19 Not like these is he who is the portion of
    Jacob,
  for he is the one who formed all things,
  and Israel is the tribe of his inheritance;

the LORD of hosts is his name.

20 "You are my hammer and weapon of war:
with you I break nations in pieces;
with you I destroy kingdoms;

21 with you I break in pieces the horse and
his rider;
with you I break in pieces the chariot
and the charioteer;

22 with you I break in pieces man and woman;
with you I break in pieces the old man
and the youth;
with you I break in pieces the young man
and the maiden;

23 with you I break in pieces the shepherd
and his flock;
with you I break in pieces the farmer and
his team;
with you I break in pieces governors and
commanders.

24 "I will requite Babylon and all the inhabitants of Chaldea before your very eyes for
all the evil they have done in Zion, says the
LORD.

25 "Behold, I am against you, O destroying
mountain,
says the LORD,
which destroys the whole earth;
I will stretch out my hand against you,
and roll you down from the crags,
and make you a burnt mountain.

26 No stone shall be taken from you for a
corner
and no stone for a foundation,
but you shall be a perpetual waste,
says the LORD.

27 "Set up a standard on the earth,
blow the trumpet among the nations;
prepare the nations for war against her,
summon against her the kingdoms,
Ararat, Minni, and Ashkenaz;
appoint a marshal against her,
bring up horses like bristling locusts.

28 Prepare the nations for war against her,
the kings of the Medes, with their governors and deputies,
and every land under their dominion.

29 The land trembles and writhes in pain,
for the LORD's purposes against Babylon
stand,
to make the land of Babylon a desolation,
without inhabitant.

30 The warriors of Babylon have ceased fighting,
they remain in their strongholds;
their strength has failed,
they have become women;
her dwellings are on fire,
her bars are broken.

31 One runner runs to meet another,
and one messenger to meet another,
to tell the king of Babylon

that his city is taken on every side;

32 the fords have been seized,
the bulwarks are burned with fire,
and the soldiers are in panic.

33 For thus says the LORD of hosts, the God of
Israel:
The daughter of Babylon is like a threshing
floor
at the time when it is trodden;
yet a little while
and the time of her harvest will come."

34 "Nebuchadrezzar the king of Babylon has
devoured me,
he has crushed me;
he has made me an empty vessel,
he has swallowed me like a monster;
he has filled his belly with my delicacies,
he has rinsed me out.

35 The violence done to me and to my kinsmen be upon Babylon,"
let the inhabitant of Zion say.
"My blood be upon the inhabitants of
Chaldea,"
let Jerusalem say.

36 Therefore thus says the LORD:
"Behold, I will plead your cause
and take vengeance for you.
I will dry up her sea
and make her fountain dry;

37 and Babylon shall become a heap of ruins,
the haunt of jackals,
a horror and a hissing,
without inhabitant.

38 "They shall roar together like lions;
they shall growl like lions' whelps.

39 While they are inflamed I will prepare them
a feast
and make them drunk, till they swoon
away
and sleep a perpetual sleep
and not wake, says the LORD.

40 I will bring them down like lambs to the
slaughter,
like rams and he-goats.

41 "How Babylon is taken,
the praise of the whole earth seized!
How Babylon has become
a horror among the nations!

42 The sea has come up on Babylon;
she is covered with its tumultuous waves.

43 Her cities have become a horror,
a land of drought and a desert,
a land in which no one dwells,
and through which no son of man passes.

44 And I will punish Bel in Babylon,
and take out of his mouth what he has
swallowed.
The nations shall no longer flow to him;
the wall of Babylon has fallen.

45 "Go out of the midst of her, my people!
Let every man save his life

from the fierce anger of the LORD!

46 Let not your heart faint, and be not fearful
at the report heard in the land,
when a report comes in one year
and afterward a report in another year,
and violence is in the land,
and ruler is against ruler.

47 "Therefore, behold, the days are coming
when I will punish the images of Babylon;
her whole land shall be put to shame,
and all her slain shall fall in the midst
of her.

48 Then the heavens and the earth,
and all that is in them,
shall sing for joy over Babylon;
for the destroyers shall come against
them out of the north, says the LORD.

49 Babylon must fall for the slain of Israel,
as for Babylon have fallen the slain of
all the earth.

50 "You that have escaped from the sword,
go, stand not still!
Remember the LORD from afar,
and let Jerusalem come into your mind:

51 'We are put to shame, for we have heard
reproach;
dishonor has covered our face,
for aliens have come
into the holy places of the LORD's house.'

52 "Therefore, behold, the days are coming,
says the LORD,
when I will execute judgment upon her
images,
and through all her land
the wounded shall groan.

53 Though Babylon should mount up to
heaven,
and though she should fortify her strong
height,
yet destroyers would come from me upon
her,
says the LORD.

54 "Hark! a cry from Babylon!
The noise of great destruction from the
land of the Chaldeans!

55 For the LORD is laying Babylon waste,
and stilling her mighty voice.
Their waves roar like many waters,
the noise of their voice is raised;

56 for a destroyer has come upon her,
upon Babylon;
her warriors are taken,
their bows are broken in pieces;
for the LORD is a God of recompense,
he will surely requite.

57 I will make drunk her princes and her wise
men,
her governors, her commanders, and her
warriors;
they shall sleep a perpetual sleep and not

wake,
says the King, whose name is the LORD
of hosts.

58 "Thus says the LORD of hosts:
The broad wall of Babylon
shall be leveled to the ground
and her high gates
shall be burned with fire.
The peoples labor for nought,
and the nations weary themselves only
for fire."

59 The word which Jeremiah the prophet
commanded Seraiah the son of Neriah, son of
Maaseiah, when he went with Zedekiah king of
Judah to Babylon, in the fourth year of his
reign. Seraiah was the quartermaster.
60 Jeremiah wrote in a book all the evil that
should come upon Babylon, all these words
that are written concerning Babylon. 61 And
Jeremiah said to Seraiah: "When you come to
Babylon, see that you read all these words,
62 and say, 'O LORD, thou hast said concerning
this place that thou wilt cut it off, so that
nothing shall dwell in it, neither man nor
beast, and it shall be desolate for ever.'
63 When you finish reading this book, bind a
stone to it, and cast it into the midst of the
Euphrates, 64 and say, 'Thus shall Babylon
sink, to rise no more, because of the evil that I
am bringing upon her.' "
Thus far are the words of Jeremiah.

This a long prophecy, or collection of
prophecies, directed against Babylon, the
world power from 605 till 539. It is a
very difficult section, about which there
has been and is much debate. Most of the
debate has centered about the question of
date and authorship. It is almost universally
agreed among scholars today that, in its
present form, it did not come from Jeremiah. Some go so far as to say that no part
of it is Jeremianic. Others maintain that, although there is a Jeremianic core in the
collection, the collection as it is contains
much material which is taken from older
sources or which was composed after Jeremiah's career had come to a close.

There are several reasons for the position
taken by scholars with regard to the passage on Babylon. First, it is marked by
unusual length, repetition, and lack of
sequence of thought. In the measure in
which these occur here, they are not
characteristic of Jeremiah. Second, the pas-

sage is said to presuppose a situation considerably later and different than that which constituted the background of Jeremiah's preaching—the situation shortly before the fall of Babylon and the restoration of Israel. Third, the viewpoint and spirit reflected in the passage are different from those in the authentic prophecies of Jeremiah. Fourth, there is a heavy literary dependence in the passage on other parts of Jeremiah and other parts of the Old Testament.

The present writer recognizes that the case against the authenticity of this passage is strong—some arguments are much stronger than others. Here, he can only state his conclusions. First, there is a core of Jeremianic material in 50:1—51:58 (cf. Eissfeldt, Bright, *et al.*). Second, there is material in 50:1—51:58 that has been borrowed from other parts of Jeremiah or of the Old Testament. Third, the material in 50:1—51:58 is not late (the overthrow of Babylon is still in the future, and there is mention of the Medes but not of the Persians). Beyond this it is almost impossible to go with any assurance. There is the probability that Jeremianic and other materials were adapted and added to by someone else, in God's providence, after Jeremiah's ministry had come to a close. But to say that all of it is from Jeremiah or that all of it is not, or that this part is and this part is not, is simply to say what one thinks on the basis of his evaluation of the evidence. No one can speak with absolute certainty on the subject.

As for the spirit manifested in places in the passage, this is found elsewhere in Jeremiah and the Old Testament, and reminds us that we are still in the Old Testament. Jesus would remind us that we are not permanently to reside there. We are to learn to pray, "Father, forgive them, for they do know not what they do." However, this reminder is not meant to remove the comfort that comes from the realization that the powers of evil must ultimately go to the wall and that the purpose of God will eventually prevail.

Because of the length and looseness of connection of the passage, it is impossible to outline it with any degree of satisfaction. Perhaps a good starting point for the study is the symbolic act recorded at the end (51:59–64). There is no valid reason for questioning either the act or the account of it (Bright, pp. 212,359). The account is in prose. The act is dated in the fourth year of Zedekiah's reign (594–593).

This is a very dramatic and significant incident. It seems that it became necessary for Zedekiah to go to Babylon to assure Nebuchadnezzar of his allegiance (probably a consequence of the caucus in Jerusalem, 27:1 ff.). Doubtless the king had with him a coterie of important state officials. Jeremiah took advantage of this trip to get a message across to the people. He wrote out a prophecy and gave it to Seraiah, a brother of Baruch and a member of the king's entourage, with the instruction that he was to take it to Babylon, to read it aloud after arrival, to tie a rock to it, and then to cast it into the Euphrates River. As he did this, he was to issue a pronouncement (v. 64). This intensified form of prophetic proclamation would indicate that the word of destruction had been set in motion (cf. 13:1 ff.; 19:1 ff.; 27:1 ff.; 32:1 ff.; 43:9).

There is a parallel between the acted out parable in 51:59–64 and the one in 32:9–15. In the first act, the prophet proclaimed his firm belief in the ultimate fall of the great pagan world power, which God was using as the instrument of his purpose. In the second act, he declared his faith in the preservation of God's people and the ultimate triumph of his purpose.

At the close of this simple story stands the sentence: *Thus far are the words of Jeremiah.*

One's approach to the study of the remainder of the passage on Babylon may be made in one of two ways. First, he may group the various parts of 50:1—51:58 around major motifs, as does H. Cunliffe-Jones (pp. 270–280). Or, second, he may come at the material in the passage by observing an alternation which begins with 50:1-7 and continues through the entire passage to 51:58. It is the alternation between the emphasis on the doom of Babylon and the emphasis on the deliverance of Israel: two sides of the same coin, God's action in setting the situation sraight. Howard Kuist [124] uses this approach. To some extent, Leslie does the same thing. He has a rather detailed and helpful treatment of the section on Babylon which the reader may wish to consult (pp. 295-312).

Because of the nature of the material and space limitations, it is not possible or advisable to attempt a minute examination of the contents of 50:1—52:64. For this sort of study, the reader must be referred to Leslie's work or to the more detailed verse-by-verse commentaries.

However, certain key ideas may be singled out for special stress. First, kingdoms built on force and fear and fraud must and will one day fall. "The mills of God grind slowly, yet they grind exceedingly small." This emphasis pervades the entire passage (cf. 50:2-3,13-16,39-40; 51:5,7-8,13,24,26,33,39-40, et al.).

Second, the way to the restoration of a right relationship with God is repentance. Hopper calls attention to the beauty and the significance of the picture of the people in penitence, weeping as they return (50: 4-5). Nothing is said about the possibility of repentance on the part of the Babylonians, but time had run out for them. They were past the point of repentance and redemption. This happens. It is a part of reality.

Third, the true God of this world is infinitely great, the majestic creator and controller of the universe (51:15-16). He is *the portion* of his people (51:19). Alexander Maclaren points out the reciprocal character of this possession-relationship: "We possess God, He possesses us, we are his inheritance, He is our portion . . . this mutual ownership is the very living center of all religion. Without it there is no rela-

tion of any depth between God and us." [125]

Fourth, anything short of God, any man-made deity, any idol will prove to be "a work of delusion" and will perish—and, along with it, the one who gives it his allegiance (51:17-18). Idolatry is absurdity.

Fifth, God is a *goel* (50:33-34). This word means a near kinsman, vindicator, or redeemer. This concept of God as Redeemer (*goel*) is prominent in "the Isaiahan Rhapsody on Redemption" (cf. Isa. 43:14; 44:6; 47:4; 48:17; 49:7; 54:5). It is best known to most because of the familiar statement of Job in his struggle with the mystery of God's dealings with him: "I know that my Redeemer [*goel*] lives" (Job 19:25). The full revelation of God as Redeemer comes in Christ, "in whom we have our redemption, the forgiveness of our sins" (Col. 1:14).

The Appendix (52:1-34)

[1] Zedekiah was twenty-one years old when he became king; and he reigned eleven years in Jerusalem. His mother's name was Hamutal the daughter of Jeremiah of Libnah. [2] And he did what was evil in the sight of the LORD, according to all that Jehoiakim had done. [3] Surely because of the anger of the LORD things came to such a pass in Jerusalem and Judah that he cast them out from his presence.

And Zedekiah rebelled against the king of Babylon. [4] And in the ninth year of his reign, in the tenth month, on the tenth day of the month, Nebuchadrezzar king of Babylon came with all his army against Jerusalem, and they laid siege to it and built siegeworks against it round about. [5] So the city was besieged till the eleventh year of King Zedekiah. [6] On the ninth day of the fourth month the famine was so severe in the city, that there was no food for the people of the land. [7] Then a breach was made in the city; and all the men of war fled and went out from the city by night by the way of a gate between the two walls, by the king's garden, while the Chaldeans were round about the city. And they went in the direction of the Arabah. [8] But the army of the Chaldeans pursued the king, and overtook Zedekiah in the plains of Jericho; and all his army was scattered from him. [9] Then they captured the king, and brought him up to the king of Babylon at Riblah in the land of Hamath, and he passed sentence upon him. [10] The king of Babylon

---

[124] *op. cit.*, pp. 135-137.

[125] *Op. cit.*, p. 268.

slew the sons of Zedekiah before his eyes, and also slew all the princes of Judah at Riblah. 11 He put out the eyes of Zedekiah, and bound him in fetters, and the king of Babylon took him to Babylon, and put him in prison till the day of his death.

12 In the fifth month, on the tenth day of the month—which was the nineteenth year of King Nebuchadrezzar, king of Babylon—Nebuzaradan the captain of the bodyguard who served the king of Babylon, entered Jerusalem. 13 And he burned the house of the LORD, and the king's house and all the houses of Jerusalem; every great house he burned down. 14 And all the army of the Chaldeans, who were with the captain of the guard, broke down all the walls round about Jerusalem. 15 And Nebuzaradan the captain of the guard carried away captive some of the poorest of the people and the rest of the people who were left in the city and the deserters who had deserted to the king of Babylon, together with the rest of the artisans. 16 But Nebuzaradan the captain of the guard left some of the poorest of the land to be vinedressers and plowmen.

17 And the pillars of bronze that were in the house of the LORD, and the stands and the bronze sea that were in the house of the LORD, the Chaldeans broke in pieces, and carried all the bronze to Babylon. 18 And they took away the pots, and the shovels, and the snuffers, and the basins, and the dishes for incense, and all the vessels of bronze used in the temple service; 19 also the small bowls, and the firepans, and the basins, and the pots, and the lampstands, and the dishes for incense, and the bowls for libation. What was of gold the captain of the guard took away as gold, and what was of silver, as silver. 20 As for the two pillars, the one sea, the twelve bronze bulls which were under the sea, and the stands, which Solomon the king had made for the house of the LORD, the bronze of all these things was beyond weight. 21 As for the pillars, the height of the one pillar was eighteen cubits, its circumference was twelve cubits, and its thickness was four fingers, and it was hollow. 22 Upon it was a capital of bronze; the height of the one capital was five cubits; a network and pomegranates, all of bronze, were upon the capital round about. And the second pillar had the like, with pomegranates. 23 There were ninety-six pomegranates on the sides; all the pomegranates were a hundred upon the network round about.

24 And the captain of the guard took Seraiah the chief priest, and Zephaniah the second priest, and the three keepers of the threshold; 25 and from the city he took an officer who had been in command of the men of war, and seven men of the king's council, who were found in the city; and the secretary of the commander of the army who mustered the people of the land; and sixty men of the people of the land, who were found in the midst of the city. 26 And Nebuzaradan the captain of the guard took them, and brought them to the king of Babylon at Riblah. 27 And the king of Babylon smote them, and put them to death at Riblah in the land of Hamath. So Judah was carried captive out of its land.

28 This is the number of the people whom Nebuchadrezzar carried away captive: in the seventh year, three thousand and twenty-three Jews; 29 in the eighteenth year of Nebuchadrezzar he carried away captive from Jerusalem eight hundred and thirty-two persons; 30 in the twenty-third year of Nebuchadrezzar, Nebuzaradan the captain of the guard carried away captive of the Jews seven hundred and forty-five persons; all the persons were four thousand and six hundred.

31 And in the thirty-seventh year of the captivity of Jehoiachin king of Judah, in the twelfth month, on the twenty-fifth day of the month, Evilmerodach king of Babylon, in the year that he became king, lifted up the head of Jehoiachin king of Judah and brought him out of prison; 32 and he spoke kindly to him, and gave him a seat above the seats of the kings who were with him in Babylon. 33 So Jehoiachin put off his prison garments. And every day of his life he dined regularly at the king's table; 34 as for his allowance, a regular allowance was given him by the king according to his daily need, until the day of his death as long as he lived.

The prophecy of Jeremiah ends in a very strange and surprising way. Nothing is said about the prophet's death. There is no word from him or about him. He is not even mentioned in the final chapter.

That chapter consists of an excerpt from 2 Kings 24:18—25:30, with minor variations, one major omission (2 Kings 25: 22–26), and one significant addition (vv. 28–30). The addition is quite important because it contains material from an unknown source and not found elsewhere in the Bible (either MT or LXX).

Since Jeremiah is nowhere referred to in the excerpt from 2 Kings, the question arises: Why was it added at the end of the prophecy that bears his name? Perhaps there are two reasons. First, the appendix closes on a note of hope. It tells of the deliverance of Jehoiachin after 37 years of imprisonment. Jehoiachin was a Davidic ruler who, though he ruled only three months, gets considerable attention in Jeremiah (13:18–19; 22:24–30; 24:1–10; 27: 16–22; 29:1 ff.). His release by Evilmerodach, son and successor to Nebuchadnezzar, in the first year of his reign (561) was probably regarded as a symbol of promise, a foregleam of the fulfillment of the beautiful forecasts of the glorious future of God's people given by Jeremiah.

Second, the appendix may have been included to emphasize that Jeremiah's prophecies concerning the fate of Jerusalem and Judah came true.

In short, "the chapter seems to say: the divine word both has been fulfilled—and will be fulfilled" (Bright, p. 370; cf.

Fohrer, Weiser, et al.).

The concluding chapter deals with five things primarily: the destruction of Jerusalem (vv. 1–16), the despoiling of the Temple (vv. 17–23), the death of many instigators and supporters of the revolt (vv. 24–27; note the prominence of the priests here), the three deportations of the Jews (vv. 28–30; 597,587,582), and the deliverance of Jehoiachin (vv. 31–34).

Thus the book ends. In the last recorded sermon that Jeremiah preached, he made his appeal to history (44:24–30). Calm and confident in God, he was certain that events would vindicate the word of the Lord, which he so faithfully and fearlessly proclaimed. And they did! and would! So says chapter 52.

Lamentations

ROBERT B. LAURIN

Introduction

Is it possible to believe in God anymore? This is a question repeatedly asked today in one way or another. And for a significant number of people the answer is no! Why? Because the circumstances of life seem to many to have led us beyond faith in God. The endless succession of wars, countless shattered lives and marriages, tragedies of body and mind, coupled with startling developments in the sciences, have all tended to make faith in a divine presence more difficult. And so our age has demonstrated a frantic search for alternatives to belief in God, for some other loyalty around which to orient one's life.

The problem is not new, and the question about faith in the gods or in God has found many expressions in the literature of the ages. The book of Lamentations is a contribution to this problem. It is a specifically Israelite attempt to preserve faith in God (Yahweh) in the midst of the immensely tragic destruction of Jerusalem in the sixth century B.C.

I. Name and Authorship

The English versions of this book are headed by the title: "The Lamentations of Jeremiah." There are two things about this, however, that must be clarified. First, the name "Lamentations" probably arose from the reference in 2 Chronicles 35:25 to a collection called "the Laments." Subsequent Jewish tradition continued to refer to the book by this title (e.g., the Talmud and rabbinic commentators), and this was also

followed by the Greek and Latin versions which are the basis of our English translations. However, most Hebrew manuscripts and printed editions title the book by the first word of chapters 1, 2, and 4—"How." Actually the designation "How" is not really different from calling the book "Lamentations," since this is the characteristic word in funeral laments in the Old Testament (cf. 2 Sam. 1:19,25,27; Isa. 1:21; Jer. 48:17). So either title projects the mood of the whole book, namely, that of woe and weeping over the downfall of Jerusalem.

Second, the ascription of authorship to Jeremiah does not arise out of the book itself, since the text gives us no definite clues in this regard. This tradition probably also arose from 2 Chronicles 35:25, which speaks not only of the collection of "Laments" but also of the fact that Jeremiah uttered a lament for Josiah. This reference, however, is difficult to associate with the book of Lamentations, since it contains no laments about Josiah. Nevertheless, tradition has continued to associate authorship with Jeremiah. The Greek translation (LXX) even places the following preface before the regular text of Lamentations: "And it came to pass after the captivity of Israel and the desolation of Jerusalem that Jeremiah sat weeping, and he lamented this lament over Jerusalem and said . . . ." And this association with Jeremiah has persisted through the years in Jewish, Catholic, and Protestant tradition. The latter two groups have stressed this by placing the book immediately after Jeremiah in the collection of prophetic books.

It is not easy to determine the author of Lamentations. Although it is possible that the book is related to the work of Jeremiah, it is not very likely. Furthermore, when one compares various passages in each book, the differences in tone and idea are striking. Jeremiah had proclaimed that King Zedekiah would be captured by the king of Babylon (Jer. 37:17), yet Lamentations 4:20 expresses shock that this has happened. Jeremiah had denounced the people's trust in help from an Egyptian army during the siege of Jerusalem (Jer. 34:21; 37:3–10), yet the author of Lamentations 4:17 speaks pathetically of his frustrated hope for help from Egypt as if he had actually expected them to give aid.

Who then wrote the poems of Lamentations? Although there are some differences in style and imagery that suggest the possibility of more than one author, the overriding linguistic and theological unity make more probable a single writer. Who he was we do not know. His words in 4:17 suggest that he was in that group of confused Jerusalemites who believed up to the last minute that the Lord would not let the capital city fall to the Babylonians. He had heard the words of Jeremiah condemning the idolatrous worship of the priests and the misleading prophecy of the prophets, and he had accepted this judgment (cf. Lam. 2:14; 4:13). Thus he was probably not one of the official priests or prophets, for he speaks in these passages as one outside these groups. Yet he apparently could not quite believe, with Jeremiah, that the city would be destroyed.

Perhaps the author was a political official, a member of Zedekiah's court, or a military figure in the king's army. If so, this would explain the reference in 4:18–20 that he joined in the flight with Zedekiah from Jerusalem during the siege of the city by the Babylonians (2 Kings 25:4–5). Whatever public position he held, if any, it is clear that he was a man of faith in the midst of a political and personal situation that threatened to destroy faith. So the book is a record of his spiritual struggle in which he seeks to share with his suffering contemporaries the victory he won over doubt and unfaith.

II. Time and Place

It is clear from the context that the time of the book of Lamentations is after the invasion of Jerusalem by the Babylonian armies in 597 B.C. and after their destruction of Jerusalem in 587. This situation strikes one immediately on reading the text (1:1–3). That this refers to the Babylonian capture of the city, and not to some later destruction, such as by Antiochus IV Epiphanes in 168, is apparent from various evidences. First, the author threatens Edom with punishment (4:22). This has its most natural reference to the treachery practiced by Edom at the time of the Babylonian siege (cf. Obad.). Second, the description in Lamentations of the last days of Judah parallels in many points the references in 2 Kings and Jeremiah. One can compare, for example, the accounts of the siege of the city (2 Kings 25:1–2; Lam. 2:22; 3:5.7), the resultant famine (2 Kings 25:3; Jer. 37:21; Lam. 1:11,19; 2:11–12, 19–20; 4:4–5,9–10), the looting of the Temple (2 Kings 25:13–15; Lam. 1:10; 2:6–7), the slaughter of the leaders (2 Kings 25:18–21; Jer. 39:6; Lam. 1:15; 2:2,20;4:16).[1]

There has been some discussion about whether or not all five chapters of the book come from the same time. All do have a common theme, and all have a sense of immediacy about the catastrophe, yet the exact time after the downfall is not clear. Some scholars have thought that chapter 1, because it does not mention the destruction either of the city or the Temple, must date from the period between the first onslaught on the city in 597 and the final invasion in 587 B.C. However, in spite of lack of explicit mention of city or Temple in this regard, the general situation depicted (cf.

[1] For further details, cf. N. Gottwald, "Lamentations, Book of," IDB, K-Q, p. 62.

1:3,10,17–20) is of widespread deportation and carnage. We know that even after 587 the city was not depopulated, so the verses that show a groaning, starved populace (cf. 1:4,11) would be consonant with this later period. Thus, it seems best to date all five chapters after 587 B.C., but sometime before the release from Babylonian captivity in 538 B.C. The fact that there is nothing in the chapters that indicates any expectation of immediate relief (except perhaps 4:22) suggests a time close to 587.

Where were the chapters written? Here again there is uncertainty. It is possible that the poems all come out of Babylonia during the exile. However, there is no clear reference to the exilic situation, and there are so many explicit descriptions of the desolated city of Jerusalem, that it seems difficult not to give the weight of evidence to exilic Jerusalem as the place where the book was written.

III. Literary Structure and Form

It is readily apparent that the book is a collection of five separate songs or poems, each of which comprises a chapter. This is not so easily identified in English, but it is obvious in the Hebrew text. Chapters 1—4 are each a complete acrostic, that is, each chapter uses all 22 letters of the Hebrew alphabet in successive order as the first letters of lines and stanzas (ch. 3) or of stanzas alone (chs. 1, 2, 4). Chapter 5, while not an acrostic, is still alphabetical in that it contains 22 verses, that is, the same number as there are letters in the Hebrew alphabet.

All of this can be noticed in the English text to the extent that the editors have separated the stanzas in the various chapters. They have also numbered the verses so that chapters 1, 2, 4, and 5 all contain 22 verses, while chapter 3 has 66.

Why did the author use the acrostic method? It is not the only example of the use of acrostic composition in the Old Testament, although it may be the earliest (cf. Psalms 9; 10; 25; 34; 37; 111; 112; 119; 145; Prov. 31:10–31; Nah. 1:2–8).

The author may have been attempting to indicate the idea of completeness by the use of the acrostic. He would be communicating, in other words, that his grief was totally poured out, his world was completely at an end. If, as we shall see, these poems were used in worship, then the acrostic form would also provide the symbolic means of expressing one's full confession of sin and despair, and thus provide for the expectation of God's full forgiveness and restoration.

The book of Lamentations overall is a collection of laments over Jerusalem and Judah, expressing both individual and community sorrow. The lament form is associated in the Old Testament with some difficulty that has arisen due to disease, famine, enemy invasion, treachery of friends, and so on. Jeremiah 20:7–13 and Psalm 69 are good examples of the "individual" form, while Psalms 44 and 79 illustrate the "community" form. This type of expression probably arose for use in formal worship services at a temple or shrine. In expressing its lament the book often utilizes elements from the funeral dirge, as well as incorporating such things as confessions of sin (1:5,8,14,18,20; 3:39–42; 4:6), wisdom sayings (3:25–37), and hymns of praise (3:22–24; 5:19). Thus each of the chapters may be given a general literary classification—a lament—but always with the recognition that to the author the important thing was to communicate the theological significance of the disaster to the community as a whole.

IV. Liturgical Use

Were the poems composed originally for use in cultic worship, or were they written as personal expressions of grief, intended to be used by others to help them live through the loss and heartache of those days? It is clear that the five chapters are not a unified whole. Each chapter is a complete poem in itself, as indicated both by the repeated acrostic pattern and the fact that the material does not move to a climax in chapter 5. So each poem can communicate effectively apart from the context of the other four. It seems best, therefore, to think of each poem as having been composed and sung, perhaps as a kind of folk song, during the grim days between the destruction of Jerusalem in 587 B.C. and the release of the slaves from Babylonia in 538.

Through the years, perhaps even during the days of exile, these poems were selected out of a larger collection of laments to be used for communal worship in commemoration of the desolation of Jerusalem in 587 (cf. Zech. 7:1–7 and 8:18–19). One scholar believes that there was such a cultic lamentation ceremony conducted among the ruins of the Temple in Jerusalem.[2] After A.D. 70 the book was also used in the synagogues to remember the conquest of Jerusalem by the Romans and the resultant dispersion of the Jews. The Christian church has also found a place for Lamentations. In its liturgical tradition it has used the poems during Holy Week to reflect the sufferings of Jesus Christ.

Those who collected these poems for liturgical use were apparently trying to create a sense of suffering, sin, and grief in the worshipers, but also a feeling of hope and continued trust in the Lord. This could be achieved both because of the inventive use of literary forms by the author and because of the way the book was structured by the collectors. On the one hand, as we have seen, the author of the poems used the lament form overall but incorporated into it a variety of feelings. Thus the person truly involved in worship would run the gamut of emotions and responses to life and to the Lord. On the other hand, the collectors wisely did not seek to rewrite the separate poems into a unified whole. They left the inevitable redundancies and repetitions in collecting four acrostics and one alphabetic poem. This has the effect of stressing and driving home to the worshiper the immensity of the tragedy and the pos-

sibilites of hope. Thus this fluctuation back and forth of moods made an impact not possible with only one description.

V. Theological Message

The theological importance of the book of Lamentations lies in its forthright evaluation of national calamity. It seeks to bring about an honest examination of the (1) historical causes, (2) present responsibilites, and (3) future possibilities inherent in social disaster. In the days of Judah the book spoke to the disruptive and terrible events of the Babylonian conquest in 597 and 587 B.C. Why did it happen? What part did Yahweh play in it? What could the people do in response? What was the future of the divine promises and love? The book is thus addressed to the problem of continuing faith in God during circumstances that seemed to make faith impossible.

In modern times the book retains its importance, not just for those who have undergone national collapse, but also for those who face the great possibility of disaster if they do not heed the personal and social conditions of continuing corporate solidity and security. In a word, the book proclaims the theological reasons why, to use the words of Eliphaz the Temanite (author's translation), "affliction does not come from the dust, . . . but man brings trouble on himself" (Job 5:6–7).

The book of Lamentations, therefore, has three dominant themes. (1) National disaster is integrally linked with national responsibility for years of social neglect. Here is the historical cause of present tragedy. The book is surprisingly sparse in its delineation of specific sins. Perhaps this is because the prophetic teaching was assumed (e.g., Isa. 1:10–20; Jer. 7:1–15; Hos. 4:1–3,6; Amos 5:14–15,21–24), for the book is permeated by the prophetic mood of doom when social responsibilities are neglected.

Most of the time the book is content to affirm the cause of disaster and suffering rather generally by describing Judah's "transgressions" (better, rebellions; 1:5,14,

2 H.-J Kraus, *Klagelieder (Threni)* (Neukirchen: Neukirchener, 1960) 2., erweiterte Auflage, 9–13

22; 3:42), "sins" (i.e., failure to achieve a standard of behavior; 1:8; 3:39; 4:6,13,22; 5:7,16), "rebellion" (better, stubbornness; 1:18,20; 3:42), "iniquity" (i.e., wandering from the path; 2:14; 4:6,13,22; 5:7), and "uncleanness" (i.e., with reference to ritual purity; 1:9; 4:15). But on two occasions a specific charge is leveled against the leadership of the prophets and priests. In 2:14 they are condemned for failure to warn the people that their ways were wrong and would inevitably lead to disaster. And in 4:13 they are indicted for killing those who opposed their policies. These are perhaps meant to be paradigms for the behavior of all the people, for as the community confessions of sin show, all the populace shared in the guilt. Thus the book speaks to any nation that social inequality and oppression are basic causes of national disintegration.

(2) Present response must lie in simple return to trustful obedience to the Lord. The book of Lamentations is no revolutionary document counseling violent revolt against the enemy. There is not a single word about any subversive activity, although there are expressions of passionate longing for vengeance (1:21–22; 3:64–66; 4:21–22). Probably this was due partly to the political circumstances of the time. Revolt could not possibly succeed and would only bring needless further suffering. But there was a more important reason. Jeremiah had earlier counseled the people to surrender to the Babylonians as a sign that they had accepted their fate as a just divine punishment for sins (cf. Jer. 24:1–10; 25:8–14; 38:17–18). This is the mood of Lamentations.

One of the dominant thrusts of the book is its demand that the destruction of Jerusalem and Judah be seen for what it was—the direct hand of Yahweh on his people to punish them for their sins. The years of sin had aroused his wrath. One cannot miss this insistent note (e.g., 1:5,12–15; 2:1–8,17; 3:37–39,43–45; 4:11,16). One may speak of secondary causes in the defeat of Judah —political machinations, social oppressions,

and so on—and rightly so, but the book wishes to make abundantly clear that it was Yahweh's will that was flaunted and thus his wrath that was poured out.

All this, however, raised a fundamental problem of faith. The people had been nurtured on the book of Deuteronomy. Its great code had been the basis of Josiah's reform movement in the years following 622 B.C. Central to Deuteronomy's concept is the affirmation of Yahweh's control of history, rewarding righteousness and punishing evil (cf. Deut. 30). But in the book of Lamentations there is an implied difficulty with this. Punishment was one thing, but the measure of judgment was another. The severity of destruction in Jerusalem apparently went beyond the bounds of what was thought just. And it was compounded by the continuing exaltation of the heathen enemies, who cared nothing about Yahweh. Chapter 3 moves particularly with this confusion over faith, as do the concluding verses of chapter 5.

It is against all this that we should read the agonized cries and vivid descriptions of carnage in the city. These are not simply outpourings of physical pain. They are more the pathetic cries of spiritual confusion. Yahweh seemed to have deserted his people. So this is why the book calls for quiet trust in the compassionate Lord (3:22–26), and why it takes pains to stress the divine judgment. It wishes to make abundantly clear that the present desolation is due deliberately to Yahweh and not to some weakness or failure on his part. Yet at the same time it wants to stress that Yahweh still had steadfast love for his people, still was faithful, still was working out his purposes. Thus they could continue to trust him, for his ways might be mysterious, but they were not monstrous.

(3) Future blessing lies only in the Lord. Interspersed throughout the book are prayers for a change of fortune (2:9,11,20; 3:56,59; 5:22). Sometimes they betray their human character by implying that God will not help unless he is worn down by insistent appeals (e.g., 3:49–50). Per-

haps this is part of the reason for the repeated and detailed descriptions of Jerusalem's destruction. But beneath it all is the recognition that, if Yahweh is still the Lord of history, he can do something about evil and sorrow. Indeed, he not only can, but will, since "he does not willingly afflict" (3:33). The Lord's basic purpose is to bring good to man. So the book advises the people to wait quietly for salvation (3:26), since hope was founded on the character of the Lord.

There is another facet to this. Although the book expects the end of exile (4:22), longs for political restoration (5:21), and waits for personal vengeance (1:21-22; 4:21-22), yet it is content to leave the future in the hands of Yahweh. Since his present actions are mysterious, so his future actions will be as well. This is a vital contribution of the book of Lamentations. It sets no dates, prescribes no patterns. It simply says that the future is bright with promise for those who have overcome doubt in trustful reliance upon the Lord.

So for the Christian church the book is a needed corrective to any naive view that walls off faith from life, or that seeks to project the way God must work (cf. Acts 1:7). But Lamentations is still incomplete. It lacks the knowledge of Jesus Christ, who demonstrates most convincingly and concretely the abiding steadfast love of God, and so answers the plaintive question of 5:21. And in his call to all those who are "heavy laden" to come to him and find "rest" (Matt. 11:28), he changes the uncertain "there may yet be hope" (Lam. 3:29) to confident promise.

Outline

I. The misery of Jerusalem (1:1-22)
   1. Condition of the city (1:1-11)
   2. Cry for compassion (1:12-19)
   3. Prayer for deliverance (1:20-22)
II. The anger of the Lord (2:1-22)
   1. Savagery of God (2:1-10)
   2. Agony of the poet (2:11-17)
   3. Call for relief (2:18-22)
III. The example of personal response (3:1-66)
   1. Experience of God's wrath (3:1-18)
   2. Reality of God's love (3:19-36)
   3. Call to repentance (3:37-41)
   4. Prayer of repentance (3:42-47)
   5. Expectation of relief (3:48-66)
IV. The magnitude of judgment (4:1-22)
   1. Horrors in the city (4:1-16)
   2. Failure of help (4:17-20)
   3. Fateful future for Edom (4:21-22)
V. The cry for salvation (5:1-22)
   1. Details of destruction (5:1-18)
   2. Prayer for restoration (5:19-22)

Selected Bibliography

BRIGHT, JOHN. A History of Israel. Philadelphia: The Westminster Press, 1959, pp. 302–355.

EISSFELDT, OTTO. The Old Testament. An Introduction. Oxford: Basil Blackwell, 1965, pp. 91–98, 111–120, 500–505.

GOTTWALD, NORMAN. Studies in the Book of Lamentations. London: SCM Press Ltd., 1954.

———, "Lamentations, Book of," The Interpreter's Dictionary of the Bible, K-Q. Nashville: Abingdon Press, 1962.

HARRISON, ROLAND. Introduction to the Old Testament. Grand Rapids: Wm. B. Eerdmans Publishing Co., 1969, pp. 1065–1071.

MEEK, THEOPHILE, "The Book of Lamentations," The Interpreter's Bible, Vol. VI. Nashville: Abingdon Press, 1956.

PEAKE, ARTHUR. Jeremiah and Lamentations. Edinburgh: T. C. & E. C. Jack, 1910.

STREANE, ANNESLEY. The Book of the Prophet Jeremiah Together with the Lamentations. Cambridge: Cambridge University Press, 1903.

VON RAD, GERHARD. Old Testament Theology, Vol. I. New York: Harper & Brothers, 1962, pp. 383–418.

Commentary on the Text

I. The Misery of Jerusalem (1:1–22)

The book begins with a haunting funeral dirge in which Jerusalem's miserable condition after the Babylonian destruction is graphically depicted. At first (vv. 1–11) the city is described as a widow, weeping and wailing over the loss of position, beauty, and children. Then (vv. 12–22) the widowed city herself speaks (also briefly in the last lines of vv. 9,11), pleading for someone to help and praying for the Lord to intervene. Throughout the chapter there is expressed the honest acceptance of the city's own sinfulness that brought the disaster (1:5,8–9,14,18,22). But the implication in this confession is clear: the city has suffered enough; now it is time for the Lord to forgive. In order to understand this and succeeding chapters we need to keep constantly in mind not only the people's centuries-long belief in the Lord as *their* sovereign, merciful, electing God, but also the terrible carnage that surrounded them each day. Ruined homes, stripped vines, fresh graves, decimated families, and above all the destroyed Temple, seemed incompatible with the presence of the Lord.

1. Condition of the City (1:1–11)

1 How lonely sits the city
  that was full of people!
 How like a widow has she become,
  she that was great among the nations!
 She that was a princess among the cities
  has become a vassal.
2 She weeps bitterly in the night,
  tears on her cheeks;
 among all her lovers
  she has none to comfort her;
 all her friends have dealt treacherously with her,
  they have become her enemies.
3 Judah has gone into exile because of affliction
  and hard servitude;
 she dwells now among the nations,
  but finds no resting place;
 her pursuers have all overtaken her
  in the midst of her distress.

4 The roads to Zion mourn,
  for none come to the appointed feasts;
 all her gates are desolate,
  her priests groan;
 her maidens have been dragged away,
  and she herself suffers bitterly.
5 Her foes have become the head,
  her enemies prosper,
 because the LORD has made her suffer
  for the multitude of her transgressions;
 her children have gone away,
  captives before the foe.
6 From the daughter of Zion has departed
  all her majesty.
 Her princes have become like harts
  that find no pasture;
 they fled without strength
  before the pursuer.
7 Jerusalem remembers
  in the days of her affliction and bitterness
 all the precious things
  that were hers from days of old.
 When her people fell into the hand of the foe,
  and there was none to help her,
 the foe gloated over her,
  mocking at her downfall.
8 Jerusalem sinned grievously,
  therefore she became filthy;
 all who honored her despise her,
  for they have seen her nakedness;
 yea, she herself groans,
  and turns her face away.
9 Her uncleanness was in her skirts;
  she took no thought of her doom;
 therefore her fall is terrible,
  she has no comforter.
 "O LORD, behold my affliction,
  for the enemy has triumphed!"
10 The enemy has stretched out his hands
  over all her precious things;
 yea, she has seen the nations
  invade her sanctuary,
 those whom thou didst forbid
  to enter thy congregation.
11 All her people groan
  as they search for bread;
 they trade their treasures for food
  to revive their strength.
 "Look, O LORD, and behold,
  for I am despised."

The dirge begins with the characteristic *How* (cf. Isa. 1:21), which is not really a question, but rather a moaning statement: "O my, how solitary sits the city!" The passage then moves on to describe the tremendous contrast between what was and what is. Once she was bustling with people, a powerful capital city, receiving tribute from other nations. Now she is bereft; only a few survivors creep around the city which has itself become a vassal. The use of the term *widow* is particularly well chosen, since throughout the Old Testament the widow was often both rejected and harshly treated. Long life was considered to be a blessing for righteous living, and so a widow and any orphans shared in the reproach felt to have fallen on a family struck by death, and thus by a supposed divine judgment on sin (Deut. 10:18; 14:29; 24:19–21; 26:12).

The rest of the section spells out the details of the events that led up to Jerusalem's present chaos. Since Jerusalem is depicted as a woman (*princess*), v. 2 can speak of *lovers* who have forsaken her and *friends* who have acted treacherously with her. The reference is to those surrounding nations—Edom, Moab, Ammon, Tyre, and Sidon—which had initially cooperated with Judah in her resistance against the Babylonian armies (cf. Jer. 27:3 ff.) but who had abandoned her in her time of need (Jer. 49:7–22; Ezek. 25:1–17).

In v. 3 the author turns for a moment from Jerusalem to speak of the nation as a whole, *gone into exile.* Many feel that this refers to those who had fled before the Babylonians to the land of Egypt or elsewhere in order to escape the *affliction and hard servitude.* Jeremiah himself was forced to accompany such a group (Jer. 42—43). But the more natural meaning of the context is a reference to the "exile" with which the whole book deals, namely, in Babylonia.

The author then returns in 1:4–11 to describe the situation in Jerusalem in further detail. The roads to Zion are no longer crowded with happy throngs on their way to the festivals, since Temple worship is at an end. The unclean enemy has desecrated the sanctuary (v. 10). So the *priests groan,* and the maidens who sang and danced at worship (cf. Psalm 68:25; Jer. 31:4,13)

are grieved (v. 4). The RSV reads *her maidens have been dragged away,* but the Hebrew text is better read as it stands: "the maidens are grieved."

In vv. 5,8–9 we have the first mention of the prophetic theme that will be stressed throughout the book, namely, that the terrible suffering of Jerusalem and Judah does not mean that Yahweh has lost his power to foreign gods or that he is absent and cannot hear or see his people's agony. On the contrary, even here Yahweh is demonstrating his might, for the exile is the deliberate judgment of God for Judah's sins. This is important to remember, for it provides a basic argument by the author for the maintenance of faith. Yahweh is not at fault; it is because of *the multitude of her transgressions* (1:5), and because *Jerusalem sinned grievously* (v. 8), that she has been stripped naked by the enemy.

And what was this sin? The text is not definite, but the context seems to suggest that her problem was political machinations. Verse 2 had spoken of her "lovers" who had abandoned her, and vv. 8 and 9 speak similarly of *all who honored her despise her,* so that *she has no comforter.* The people of Israel had been called to be a spiritual power (Gen. 12:1–3), but they consistently attempted to be a political power. But they had neither the geographical strength, nor the economic resources to achieve this. Their greatness was intended to lie in their message about God. So in their attempt to play power politics they were building their own downfall. Thus, the prophets so often condemned their treaty-making; they were neglecting the very reason for their existence.

This then is why *Jerusalem sinned grievously* (v. 8). They consistently refused to be what they were called to be, and so judgment fell of their own making. In graphic fashion the author speaks of this in v. 9: *Her uncleanness was in her skirts; she took no thought of her doom.* Since Jerusalem had already been likened to a woman, the author here boldly compares her sin to the stain of menstrual blood (cf. Lev. 15:

19–20). Normally this would be covered up, and no one would know. So Jerusalem thought her sin was unknown, and thus *took no thought of her doom* (or, fate). She thought she was getting away with her political dealings. But she was not; the stain was clear for all to see. This is why she is now so shocked: *her fall is terrible.*

2. Cry for Compassion (1:12–19)

12 "Is it nothing to you, all you who pass by?
    Look and see
  if there is any sorrow like my sorrow
    which was brought upon me,
  which the LORD inflicted
    on the day of his fierce anger.
13 "From on high he sent fire;
    into my bones he made it descend;
  he spread a net for my feet;
    he turned me back;
  he has left me stunned,
    faint all the day long.
14 "My transgressions were bound into a yoke;
    by his hand they were fastened together;
  they were set upon my neck;
    he caused my strength to fail;
  the Lord gave me into the hands
    of those whom I cannot withstand.
15 "The Lord flouted all my mighty men
    in the midst of me;
  he summoned an assembly against me
    to crush my young men;
  the Lord has trodden as in a wine press
    the virgin daughter of Judah.
16 "For these things I weep;
    my eyes flow with tears;
  for a comforter is far from me,
    one to revive my courage;
  my children are desolate,
    for the enemy has prevailed."
17 Zion stretches out her hands,
    but there is none to comfort her;
  the LORD has commanded against Jacob
    that his neighbors should be his foes;
  Jerusalem has become
    a filthy thing among them.
18 "The LORD is in the right,
    for I have rebelled against his word;
  but hear, all you peoples,
    and behold my suffering;
  my maidens and my young men
    have gone into captivity.
19 "I called to my lovers
    but they deceived me;
  my priests and elders
    perished in the city,
  while they sought food
    to revive their strength.

The widowed Jerusalem now breaks in and speaks for herself. She had spoken briefly at the end of vv. 9 and 11. Here she cries out to those *who pass by* (v. 12) for some understanding and sympathy for the magnitude of her sorrow. If she could feel that someone understood and cared, then she could revive her courage (v. 16). This is similar to Job's longing for an "umpire" (9:33) who would understand his side as well as God's. Job admitted that he was not perfect, but wondered if the severity of his misery was just punishment for sins. This is the mood here. Has anyone ever seen *any sorrow* (agony) *like my sorrow* (agony) . . . *which the Lord inflicted* (NEB, "cruelly punished") *on the day of his fierce anger?*

The personified Jerusalem then moves on to describe the severity of her punishment by Yahweh. Throughout there is the implication: Is all this just? First, in v. 13, a series of three calamities is listed: a *fire* that destroyed the structure of the city (cf. 4:11; 2 Kings 25:9), *a net* thrown over her feet that *turned* the inhabitants *back* from escape (cf. Hos. 7:12; Ezek. 12:13), and a continual sickness that left her *faint.* In v. 14 he adds another figure of speech, *a yoke.* The Lord burdened Jerusalem down with the punishment for her *transgressions,* so that she is like an animal bearing a heavy, depressing burden. Then in v. 15 the imagery reaches its greatest intensity. The Lord is pictured as sending a deliberately-called group of invaders (*assembly*) to squeeze the lifeblood out of Jerusalem's inhabitants.

In v. 17 the author breaks in, and, as in vv. 1–11, confirms the desolation of Jerusalem. Then Jerusalem herself speaks again in vv. 18–19, repeating the basic theme of the section: *The Lord is in the right . . . but hear, all you peoples, and behold my suffering.* Jerusalem accepts the fact that God caused her suffering, and that she deserved to be punished. But—and this is important to notice—she protests against its severity. The Hebrew text uses an emphatic imperative in v. 18 (*but hear*) to express this. So the author is raising the question of faith in the Lord ever so subtly. Is it still possible to believe in Yahweh in the face of such apparent overreaction to Israel's wickedness?

3. Prayer for Deliverance (1:20-22)

20 "Behold, O Lord, for I am in distress,
  my soul is in tumult,
  my heart is wrung within me,
    because I have been very rebellious.
  In the street the sword bereaves;
    in the house it is like death.
21 "Hear how I groan;
    there is none to comfort me.
  All my enemies have heard of my trouble;
    they are glad that thou hast done it.
  Bring thou the day thou hast announced,
    and let them be as I am.
22 "Let all their evil doing come before thee;
    and deal with them
  as thou hast dealt with me
    because of all my transgressions;
  for my groans are many
    and my heart is faint."

Finally the city turns to Yahweh, and pleads for help in terms that show that common mixture of faith in God and desire for personal vengeance. The city calls upon the Lord to notice the depth of her agony. *Behold, O Lord, for I am in distress* is better read "Look, O Lord, what distress I have." Why? Not just because of the slaughter in the city (v. 20), but because of the rejoicing of the enemies (vv. 21–22). So Jerusalem prays that the Lord will strike them down as severely as he punished her (cf. Psalm 69:22–29). There is no question that the note of personal vengeance is strong here, but there is also another perspective. If Yahweh is truly lord of the world, then no evildoers can ever escape. If his own people are punished, then those who reject him must not escape.

II. The Anger of the Lord (2:1-22)

In this second dirge the chaotic situation in Jerusalem is once again described. The basic difference from chapter 1 is at the point of emphasis. While in chapter 1 the focus is on the condition of the city, in chapter 2 the stress is on Yahweh, who caused this grim situation. All the elements of chapter 1 are here—the terrible suffering of the people, the mocking laughter of the enemies, the judgment for sin, and the deliberate purpose of Yahweh—but because of the emphasis on Yahweh the problem of faith is raised more directly. Throughout, it is the poet who speaks except in the closing prayer of vv. 20–22 where Zion is the subject.

1. Savagery of God (2:1-10)

1 How the Lord in his anger
    has set the daughter of Zion under a cloud!
  He has cast down from heaven to earth
    the splendor of Israel;
  he has not remembered his footstool
    in the day of his anger.
2 The Lord has destroyed without mercy
    all the habitations of Jacob;
  in his wrath he has broken down
    the strongholds of the daughter of Judah;
  he has brought down to the ground in dishonor
    the kingdom and its rulers.
3 He has cut down in fierce anger
    all the might of Israel;
  he has withdrawn from them his right hand
    in the face of the enemy;
  he has burned like a flaming fire in Jacob,
    consuming all around.
4 He has bent his bow like an enemy,
    with his right hand set like a foe;
  and he has slain all the pride of our eyes
    in the tent of the daughter of Zion;
  he has poured out his fury like fire.
5 The Lord has become like an enemy,
    he has destroyed Israel;
  he has destroyed all its palaces,
    laid in ruins its strongholds;
  and he has multiplied in the daughter of Judah
    mourning and lamentation.
6 He has broken down his booth like that of a garden,
    laid in ruins the place of his appointed feasts;
  the Lord has brought to an end in Zion
    appointed feast and sabbath,
  and in his fierce indignation has spurned
    king and priest.
7 The Lord has scorned his altar,
    disowned his sanctuary;
  he has delivered into the hand of the enemy
    the walls of her palaces;
  a clamor was raised in the house of the Lord
    as on the day of an appointed feast.
8 The Lord determined to lay in ruins
    the wall of the daughter of Zion;
  he marked it off by the line;

he restrained not his hand from destroying;
he caused rampart and wall to lament,
they languish together.
Her gates have sunk into the ground;
he has ruined and broken her bars;
her king and princes are among the nations;
the law is no more,
and her prophets obtain
no vision from the LORD.
) The elders of the daughter of Zion
sit on the ground in silence;
they have cast dust on their heads
and put on sackcloth;
the maidens of Jerusalem
have bowed their heads to the ground.

In this first section the poet deliberately
stresses the fact that Yahweh has caused
the present suffering in Jerusalem in order
to leave a dominant impression—without
mercy or care Yahweh has savagely, almost
sadistically, crushed the life out of his
people. *The Lord has destroyed without
mercy* (v. 2) is the theme.

The song begins in v. 1 with the familiar
"how" of lament, and then moves on to
describe how the Lord in his anger has
brought a sweeping destruction to the
people of Jerusalem (*the daughter of
Zion*), to the city itself (*the splendor of
Israel;* cf. overthrow of Babylon in Isa.
13:19), and to the Temple (*his footstool;*
cf. Isa. 60:13; Ezek. 43:7; Psalm 132:7).
There is an unmistakable allusion in the
expression *He has cast down from heaven
to earth* to the fall of Babylon described in
Isaiah 14:12–20. Jerusalem has been dealt
with by Yahweh as if she were a heathen
nation, challenging his rule.

In vv. 2–5 the poet raises his gaze to the
whole country, and sees a similar ferocious
Yahweh at work. *The Lord has destroyed
without mercy all the habitations of Jacob.*
More graphically this phrase may be translated: "the Lord has swallowed up without
any compassion." The same verb swallow,
expressing utter annihilation, reoccurs in
vv. 5, 8, and 16. And so the poet depicts
the events prior to the downfall of Jerusalem when the fortified towns throughout
the country were "swallowed up" one by
one (cf. Jer. 34:7). The *might of Israel*

(v. 3), literally the "horn of Israel," is then
a reference to all the defences and fortifications around the country (cf. Psalm 75:11;
Jer. 48:25). These fell to the Babylonians
because Yahweh withdrew his *right hand
in the face of the enemy,* that is, withheld
his strong help (cf. Psalm 74:11).

And not only did Yahweh keep back his
protection; he actively engaged in warfare
against Judah (vv. 4–5), destroying *all the
pride* of Israel's eyes. This last phrase is
literally "all the desirable ones" and probably refers to all the particularly-prized
inhabitants—leaders, wives, and children.
In 1:10–11 the same word occurs, but
there it refers to desirable *things.*

Finally in vv. 6–10 the poet returns to
his description of Yahweh's vengeance on
Jerusalem, and as a climax focuses on the
grimmest deed of all—the destruction of
temple, priest, king, and worship. The
Lord destroyed the Temple (*his booth*) as
easily as one knocks down a temporary hut
in the harvest field. He *spurned* both king
and priest, the two main cultic officials. He
gave the Temple buildings (*palaces*) into
the enemy's hands, so that it was their shout
of triumph (*clamor*) that was heard instead of the usual joyous sounds of worshipers. And to show that the rejection of
the Lord was complete, he no longer spoke
through his official priests or cultic prophets. This is the import of the last part of
v. 9, more clearly translated: "there is no
more teaching, and her prophets cannot
find a vision from the Lord" (cf. 2:14;
Ezek. 7:26).

2. Agony of the Poet (2:11–17)

11 My eyes are spent with weeping;
     my soul is in tumult;
   my heart is poured out in grief
     because of the destruction of the daughter
     of my people,
   because infants and babes faint
     in the streets of the city.
12 They cry to their mothers,
     "Where is bread and wine?"
   as they faint like wounded men
     in the streets of the city,
   as their life is poured out
     on their mothers' bosom.

¹³ What can I say for you, to what compare
    you,
 O daughter of Jerusalem?
What can I liken to you, that I may comfort
    you,
 O virgin daughter of Zion?
For vast as the sea is your ruin;
 who can restore you?
¹⁴ Your prophets have seen for you
 false and deceptive visions;
they have not exposed your iniquity
 to restore your fortunes,
but have seen for you oracles
 false and misleading.
¹⁵ All who pass along the way
 clap their hands at you;
they hiss and wag their heads
 at the daughter of Jerusalem;
"Is this the city which was called
 the perfection of beauty,
 the joy of all the earth?"
¹⁶ All your enemies
 rail against you;
they hiss, they gnash their teeth,
 they cry: "We have destroyed her!
Ah, this is the day we longed for;
 now we have it; we see it!"
¹⁷ The LORD has done what he purposed,
 has carried out his threat;
as he ordained long ago,
 he has demolished without pity;
he has made the enemy rejoice over you,
 and exalted the might of your foes.

In stark contrast with the previous verses, the poet now pours out his own feelings about the people who have undergone such grim suffering. The impact is: I am in agony about the people of Judah, but Yahweh does not seem to notice our plight. This, of course, is intended to raise the problem of faith. What grieves the poet particularly is his inability to do anything. In vv. 11–12 he piles up metaphors to express his frustration and sorrow. Then in vv. 13–17 he speaks of his agony over being unable to comfort the inhabitants of the city in their shame and despair. He says in v. 13, *What can I say for you?* The heart of his problem is here, and only comes out clearly when we translate this more literally: "What can I bear witness to you?" In other words, "How can I cheer you?" (NEB). He is asking how he might be able to help the people understand and cope with their catastrophe.

He wants to be able to announce a message of hope from the Lord. But the circumstances are so without precedent—*for vast as the sea is your ruin*—that he has nothing to say. He cannot speak a good word from the Lord, because he is confused about the goodness of the Lord's intentions. This is in contrast with the deceptive words of the *prophets* (v.14), who refused to be honest with the people and who were the cause of Judah's calamity. They did not speak the truth, and so did not expose Judah's *iniquity* in time for the people to avoid the disaster. They saw, rather, *false and deceptive visions* (lit., worthless and whitewashed visions).

So the result is that Jerusalem is in ruins, the laughingstock of the nations (vv. 15–16), for a holy Yahweh has had no other recourse than to punish for disobedience. He has *carried out his threat* (better, fulfilled his word; cf. Lev. 26:23–39; Deut. 28:15–68). Still, behind all of this, one senses the poet's own troubled spirit. Yahweh had to punish; this the poet can accept. But did Yahweh have to punish so severely?

3. Cry for Relief (2:18–22)

¹⁸ Cry aloud to the Lord!
 O daughter of Zion!
Let tears stream down like a torrent
 day and night!
Give yourself no rest,
 your eyes no respite!
¹⁹ Arise, cry out in the night,
 at the beginning of the watches!
Pour out your heart like water
 before the presence of the Lord!
Lift your hands to him
 for the lives of your children,
who faint for hunger
 at the head of every street.
²⁰ Look, O LORD, and see!
 With whom hast thou dealt thus?
Should women eat their offspring,
 the children of their tender care?
Should priest and prophet be slain
 in the sanctuary of the Lord?
²¹ In the dust of the streets
 lie the young and the old;
my maidens and my young men
 have fallen by the sword;
in the day of thy anger thou hast slain them,
 slaughtering without mercy.

22 Thou didst invite as to the day of an ap-
      pointed feast
    my terrors on every side;
   and on the day of the anger of the LORD
      none escaped or survived;
    those whom I dandled and reared
      my enemy destroyed.

In vv. 18–19 the summons is given to raise a ceaseless lament to the Lord, particularly on behalf of the children dying in the streets. Following hard on the previous verses the implication is: Without understanding of the Lord's actions, with confusion over his reasons for such suffering, the only recourse is to seek to cajole him, to plead with him, or to agonize before him. He must surely respond to the horror of dead children. The RSV reads: *Cry aloud to the Lord! O daughter of Zion!* (v.18). But the text is read more literally in the last phrase "O wall of the daughter of Jerusalem," and is a reference to v. 8, where "rampart and wall" lament their destruction. It is a bold personification, but certainly not uncommon (cf. Isa. 14:31).

The actual prayer itself is then uttered in vv. 20–22 by the destroyed city. It plays in detail on the horrible conditions of the city. The cannibalism of those days is mentioned elsewhere in Scripture (4:10; 2 Kings 6:26–29; Jer. 19:9). The prayer then moves on to speak also of the slaughter of priest and prophet, young and old, maidens and young men (vv. 20–21). But what gives the prayer force, and what raises the implicit question of faith, is the stress on Yahweh's involvement. In typical Old Testament fashion, since Yahweh is lord of history and punishes sin, everything that happened in Jerusalem was his work (v. 21). And even further, Yahweh deliberately invited the Babylonians into Jerusalem to a time of savage rejoicing as on a feast day (v. 22). The song closes in deep sorrow and confusion over the actions of an apparently unjust God—or so the writer felt.

III. *The Example of Personal Response (3:1–66)*

This chapter moves from an individual lament (vv. 1–39) to a community lament (vv. 40–47) back to an individual lament (vv. 48–66). In light of the fact that the author seems to set himself apart from the rest of the people in v. 48 (cf. vv. 14,27), this suggests that we are to interpret the chapter as basically an individual poem, in which in vv. 40–41 he calls upon the people as a whole to pray, and then in vv. 42–47 gives the prayer. Later the whole poem was used for corporate worship. In chapter 2 the poet had expressed his longing to comfort Jerusalem (2:13), yet spoke of his confusion over how faith could survive in the midst of such great suffering. Now in chapter 3 he has the answer. It is summed up in vv. 21–27. Trust in the Lord, even though circumstances seem to deny his care, for "the steadfast love of the Lord never ceases" (v. 22).

1. *Experience of God's Wrath (3:1–18)*

1 I am the man who has seen affliction
    under the rod of his wrath;
2 he has driven and brought me
    into darkness without any light;
3 surely against me he turns his hand
    again and again the whole day long.
4 He has made my flesh and my skin waste
      away,
    and broken my bones;
5 he has besieged and enveloped me
    with bitterness and tribulation;
6 he has made me dwell in darkness
    like the dead of long ago.
7 He has walled me about so that I cannot
      escape;
    he has put heavy chains on me;
8 though I call and cry for help,
    he shuts out my prayer;
9 he has blocked my ways with hewn stones,
    he has made my paths crooked.
10 He is to me like a bear lying in wait,
    like a lion in hiding;
11 he led me off my way and tore me to pieces;
    he has made me desolate;
12 he bent his bow and set me
    as a mark for his arrow.
13 He drove into my heart
    the arrows of his quiver;
14 I have become the laughingstock of all
      peoples,
    the burden of their songs all day long.
15 He has filled me with bitterness,
    he has sated me with wormwood.
16 He has made my teeth grind on gravel,
    and made me cower in ashes;

17 my soul is bereft of peace,
    I have forgotten what happiness is;
18 so I say, "Gone is my glory,
    and my expectation from the LORD."

We see here, and in later portions of the chapter, why traditionally Jeremiah has been identified as the author of the book. Many of the expressions and experiences can be paralleled in the life of the prophet (e.g., Jer. 20:7/Lam. 3:14; Jer. 14:11–12/ Lam. 3:8). The poet's purpose throughout these verses is to present a variety of images that depict how severely he himself has felt the judgment of Yahweh. He is no stranger to suffering, and so when later he proclaims his continued faith, he cannot be charged with misunderstanding. He pictures himself as an animal *driven* cruelly and repeatedly out into the darkness (vv. 1–3). The Lord has given him a crippling illness (vv. 4–6), so that he is as good as dead. The last phrase of v. 6 is better translated, "like a man long dead" (NEB).

The Lord has also made him feel like a helpless prisoner (vv.7–9), unable to move because of *heavy chains,* unheard by the Lord when he prays for help. He has become like a hunted animal whom God pursues, catches, and either tears to pieces like another animal would (vv. 10–11) or else drives an arrow through (vv. 12–13). In such a condition he is naturally judged by others to have been punished by God, and so becomes the object of their scorn (v. 14). And the Lord has acted as a deceitful host to a weary traveller. He gave him something to drink, indeed he *sated* him, but it was *bitterness* and *wormwood* (a bitter herb). He offered him food, but it was stones and ashes (vv. 15–16). So quite naturally the poet exclaims: *my soul is bereft of peace* (or, well-being) *"Gone is my glory* (better, my strength), *and my expectation from the Lord."*

The poet has thus been speaking to the beleaguered people of Jerusalem. I know what it is to experience *the rod of his wrath* (v. 1), he says, and to feel that all hope has been lost. It is important to notice clearly what he is stressing. He does not say that

he lost his faith; he only says that he *thought* he had lost it. He is attempting to identify with his contemporaries, but at the same time to prepare them for the encouraging words that follow.

2. Reality of God's Love (3:19–36)

19 Remember my affliction and my bitterness,
    the wormwood and the gall!
20 My soul continually thinks of it
    and is bowed down within me.
21 But this I call to mind,
    and therefore I have hope:
22 The steadfast love of the LORD never ceases,
    his mercies never come to an end;
23 they are new every morning;
    great is thy faithfulness.
24 "The LORD is my portion," says my soul,
    "therefore I will hope in him."
25 The LORD is good to those who wait for him,
    to the soul that seeks him.
26 It is good that one should wait quietly
    for the salvation of the LORD.
27 It is good for a man that he bear
    the yoke in his youth.
28 Let him sit alone in silence
    when he has laid it on him;
29 let him put his mouth in the dust—
    there may yet be hope;
30 let him give his cheek to the smiter,
    and be filled with insults.
31 For the Lord will not
    cast off for ever,
32 but, though he cause grief, he will have compassion
    according to the abundance
    of his steadfast love;
33 for he does not willingly afflict
    or grieve the sons of men.
34 To crush under foot
    all the prisoners of the earth,
35 to turn aside the right of a man
    in the presence of the Most High,
36 to subvert a man in his cause,
    the Lord does not approve.

Now the poet moves to the second step in his argument. *Remember my affliction—* I cannot forget it—but also remember that there are other aspects to reality; these can give a person *hope* (v. 21). The word for *hope* here is the same word translated "expectation" in 3:18. The author is really saying: I thought all hope was gone, but my problem was that I had a very narrow view of God; I thought only of the judgment of God and of my sin; I forgot about the mercy of God and his forgiveness. And so in this section the poet seeks to encourage faith and hope.

The affirmation of faith is given in vv. 22–24. There is particular significance to the words *steadfast love* of the Lord. The Hebrew term that lies behind this is difficult to translate, for it implies a combination of ideas: love, faithfulness, kindness, loyalty, and strength. It is the basic word that is used to describe the covenant relationship (cf. Mic. 7:20), and it is this idea that is in mind here. One of the major judgments of the prophets on Israel was that she failed to show this kind of *steadfast love* for Yahweh; she broke her relationship by serving other gods (cf. Hos. 6:6–7). But, at the same time, one of the basic affirmations that gave Israel security was that Yahweh would never be fickle or unfaithful. This is the great promise of Isaiah 54:10. So it is with his knowledge in mind that the poet proclaims his trust in Yahweh. He has never failed Israel yet. His steadfast love and "mercies" (compassionate tendernesses) can be counted on to be as reliable as the dawning of every day (cf. Jer. 33:25–26). So the poet shouts: *great is thy faithfulness.*

Here is the important "in spite of" that is the foundation of every faith affirmation. Yahweh has been pictured at some length by the poet as wreaking his vengeance in awful measure. But "in spite of" it all—the loss of families, land, and life—the poet says: *The Lord is my portion.* The background to this expression is the conquest of Palestine. At that time each of the tribes was given a territory as his "portion," but the priests did not receive any land. Their portion was Yahweh (Num. 18:20). This is the impact here. There was no land to claim; there was only the Lord. He was the only one who remained permanent in the midst of change. He was the only one in whom they could live.

With this in mind the poet then moves on to speak of the necessity for patient waiting (vv. 25–26), enduring quietly any suffering that might come (vv. 27–30), knowing

that it will not last forever because the Lord will not let evil have the last word (vv. 31–36). It is interesting to notice how the poet speaks of patience. It is not a dull, resigned, bitter waiting. As someone said: "When God says wait, he does not mean loiter!" It is, rather, an eager, expectant, uncomplaining waiting for the Lord to act in his own good time. Here is why knowledge is such an important part of faith. Only if we know what kind of God it is we trust—one with an *abundance of steadfast love* (v. 32)—can we leave the baffling aspects of life in his hands.

3. Call to Repentance (3:37–41)

37 Who has commanded and it came to pass,
   unless the Lord has ordained it?
38 Is it not from the mouth of the Most High
   that good and evil come?
39 Why should a living man complain,
   a man, about the punishment of his sins?
40 Let us test and examine our ways,
   and return to the LORD!
41 Let us lift up our hearts and hands
   to God in heaven:

The poet has made the point that though Yahweh punishes sin, he is primarily concerned to benefit man, not afflict him (3:33). Here he follows out the logic of this point of view. He calls the people to examine their lives, to determine where their sin lies, and to ask for the Lord's forgiveness, so that they might be ready to receive his favor.

The force of the author's argument comes out in his opening words in vv. 37–39. In terms that are reminiscent of the prophet Amos (3:6), he asks the question, Who else than Yahweh is responsible for the events of our day? The people were tempted, in the extremity of their situation, to ascribe the evil times to another power, or to doubt the ability of God to change things (cf. Jer. 5:12). The poet wishes to make it plain that there is no other sovereignty in the world (cf. Isa. 45:7). If this were not true, if there were some rival, malignant power in the world, then there could be no hope, no security. But since both *good and evil* come from the Lord, and since "he does not willingly afflict" mankind (3:33), one can have hope that repentance will bring blessing. And so the poet calls for this repentance in vv. 40–41.

4. Prayer of Repentance (3:42–47)

42 "We have transgressed and rebelled,
    and thou hast not forgiven.
43 "Thou hast wrapped thyself with anger and
    pursued us,
    slaying without pity;
44 thou hast wrapped thyself with a cloud
    so that no prayer can pass through.
45 Thou hast made us offscouring and refuse
    among the peoples.
46 "All our enemies
    rail against us;
47 panic and pitfall have come upon us,
    devastation and destruction;

The actual prayer is now raised. It was either recited in worship on behalf of the congregation, or else the people voiced it themselves. But it begins significantly with a contrast: *We have transgressed and rebelled, and thou has not forgiven.* In Hebrew these pronouns are in the emphatic position. The point is that the people are accepting the fact that up to this moment Yahweh, in order to remain just, could not forgive, since the people had not admitted their sin. So the last phrase of v. 42 means: "thou hast justly not forgiven." This is why *no prayer can pass through* (v. 44); it was only a cry for help, not also a word of repentance. Thus this prayer is a true prayer of repentance—the acceptance of God's judgment on oneself.

5. Expectation of Relief (3:48–66)

48 my eyes flow with rivers of tears
    because of the destruction of the daugh-
    ter of my people.
49 "My eyes will flow without ceasing,
    without respite,
50 until the Lord from heaven
    looks down and sees;
51 my eyes cause me grief
    at the fate of all the maidens of my city.
52 "I have been hunted like a bird
    by those who were my enemies without
    cause;
53 they flung me alive into the pit
    and cast stones on me;
54 water closed over my head;
    I said, 'I am lost.'

55 "I called on thy name, O Lord,
    from the depths of the pit;
56 thou didst hear my plea, 'Do not close
    thine ear to my cry for help!'
57 Thou didst come near when I called on
    thee;
    thou didst say, 'Do not fear!'
58 "Thou hast taken up my cause, O Lord,
    thou hast redeemed my life.
59 Thou hast seen the wrong done to me, O
    Lord;
    judge thou my cause.
60 Thou hast seen all their vengeance, all their
    devices against me.
61 "Thou hast heard their taunts, O Lord,
    all their devices against me.
62 The lips and thoughts of my assailants
    are against me all the day long.
63 Behold their sitting and their rising;
    I am the burden of their songs.
64 "Thou wilt requite them, O Lord,
    according to the work of their hands.
65 Thou wilt give them dullness of heart;
    thy curse will be on them.
66 Thou wilt pursue them in anger and destroy
    them
    from under thy heavens, O Lord."

The poet now breaks into the middle of a stanza (notice the change of person in v. 48), and for the rest of the chapter he expresses his continued prayer for Jerusalem (vv. 48–51) and his confidence in divine vengeance (vv. 52–66). In the last section the poet describes how the Lord once delivered and showed his love when he was in the "pit" (v. 55; cf. v. 47). The situation is now similar, and so with confidence the poet prays for the Lord again to take vengenace on his foes (vv. 62–66). These final words show us once more the human character of God's servants. He was cruelly treated, so he wants his foes to be tortured too. The verbs in vv. 64–66 probably should be translated as entreaties rather than as indicatives: *Requite them, O Lord, according to the work of their hands. . . .* It is possible of course, that they should remain as in the RSV, namely as indicative statements of confidence.

IV. The Magnitude of Judgment (4:1–22)

This chapter moves in three parts, each with its own particular form. In vv. 1–10 we see the reappearance of the funeral dirge (*How*) over the destroyed Jerusalem

Then in vv. 17–20 comes a community lament, noticed by the shift to the first person plural. Finally in vv. 21–22 the singer of the first section returns with an ironic "announcement of salvation" (*rejoice and be glad*), which turns out to be actually a proclamation of doom for Edom.

1. Horrors in the City (4:1–16)

1 How the gold has grown dim,
   how the pure gold is changed!
  The holy stones lie scattered
   at the head of every street.
2 The precious sons of Zion,
   worth their weight in fine gold,
  how they are reckoned as earthen pots,
   the work of a potter's hands!
3 Even the jackals give the breast
   and suckle their young,
  but the daughter of my people has become cruel,
   like the ostriches in the wilderness.
4 The tongue of the nursing cleaves
   to the roof of its mouth for thirst;
  the children beg for food,
   but no one gives to them.
5 Those who feasted on dainties
   perish in the streets;
  those who were brought up in purple
   lie on ash heaps.
6 For the chastisement of the daughter of my
   people has been greater
   than the punishment of Sodom,
  which was overthrown in a moment,
   no hand being laid on it.
7 Her princes were purer than snow,
   whiter than milk;
  their bodies were more ruddy than coral,
   the beauty of their form was like sapphire.
8 Now their visage is blacker than soot,
   they are not recognized in the streets;
  their skin has shriveled upon their bones,
   it has become as dry as wood.
9 Happier were the victims of the sword
   than the victims of hunger,
  who pined away, stricken
   by want of the fruits of the field.
10 The hands of compassionate women
   have boiled their own children;
  they became their food
   in the destruction of the daughter of my people.
11 The Lord gave full vent to his wrath,
   he poured out his hot anger;
  and he kindled a fire in Zion,
   which consumed its foundations.
12 The kings of the earth did not believe,
   or any of the inhabitants of the world,

that foe or enemy could enter
   the gates of Jerusalem.
13 This was for the sins of her prophets
   and the iniquities of her priests,
  who shed in the midst of her
   the blood of the righteous.
14 They wandered, blind, through the streets,
   so defiled with blood
  that none could touch
   their garments.
15 "Away! Unclean!" men cried at them;
   "Away! Away! Touch not!"
  So they became fugitives and wanderers;
   men said among the nations,
   "They shall stay with us no longer."
16 The Lord himself has scattered them,
   he will regard them no more;
  no honor was shown to the priests,
   no favor to the elders.

The poet begins with a kind of summary (vv. 1–2), in which he makes a contrast between the loss of Temple treasures and the destruction of Jerusalem's inhabitants. He does this by an interesting expression of double meaning. In v. 1 he begins by ostensibly speaking of the Temple; its *gold* and *holy stones* are tarnished and scattered. But as we see in v. 2 he has been speaking of the people of the city, *the precious sons of Zion*. This is the point he will be stressing throughout the chapter. The golden treasures have indeed been plundered, but the real treasures of the city are the inhabitants. This is what is really important —people, not things—and why the destruction is so tragic and horrible. The rest of the section then speaks of these people.

First, in vv. 3–6, the poet speaks of the torture suffered by the babes and little children. Mothers, because of the privation of the siege, had their milk dry up, and so were unable to suckle their young. Thus they appeared to be as uncaring about their young as the ostrich (cf. Job 39:13–18). Both poor and rich alike suffered (v. 5). And the reason? Sin—greater even than that of Sodom (v. 6). Next, in vv. 7–11, the singer describes the young people. The word *princes* (v. 7) is probably better read "youth." Once they were beautiful, now they are only shriveled skin and bones. It would have been better for them if they had been slain by the sword. And once again, Why? Sin, which caused the Lord to pour out his *hot anger* on Jerusalem.

Finally, in vv. 12–16, the cause of this sin is identified—the leadership: *prophets* and *priests*. The *kings of the earth* shared with the Israelites, says the poet, the belief that Jerusalem was inviolable. Was it not the city of the sovereign Yahweh? But the nation's stability and security lay not in some automatic religious relationship with Yahweh, but rather in her obedience socially and personally. In 2:14 the prophets were condemned for not exposing the people's sins. But here they are denounced for their own iniquities; in particular, their shedding of *the blood of the righteous*.

The book of Jeremiah describes in many places the wildly corrupt and deadly circumstances in the city of Jerusalem, as the leaders sought to destroy anyone who opposed their policies (Jer. 6:13–15; 8:10; 23:11; 26:7–22). Rotted within by such crimes, when the Babylonians drew near, Jerusalem had no unity by which she might withstand the advance. Indeed by that time it was too late, since the leadership had long since followed policies in their greed that were destructive to the nation. And so this poet pictures the prophets and priests scattered and homeless, like lepers, doomed to continual rejection.

2. Failure of Help (4:17–20)

17 Our eyes failed, ever watching
 vainly for help;
 in our watching we watched
 for a nation which could not save.
18 Men dogged our steps
 so that we could not walk in our streets;
 our end drew near; our days were numbered;
 for our end had come.
19 Our pursuers were swifter
 than the vultures in the heavens;
 they chased us on the mountains,
 they lay in wait for us in the wilderness.
20 The breath of our nostrils, the LORD's anointed,
 was taken in their pits,
 he of whom we said, "Under his shadow
 we shall live among the nations."

In 597 B.C. the Babylonians made their first capture of Jerusalem, taking the king, the queen mother, various officials and citizens, and enormous booty back to Babylon (2 Kings 24:10–17). A puppet ruler was put on the throne, but the following years saw various pressures and plots for revolt. In 588 it broke out into open rebellion, perhaps in cooperation with Tyre and Ammon, and certainly with the urging of Egypt. The Babylonians reacted quickly, and placed Jerusalem under siege (2 Kings 25:1 ff.). Apparently King Zedekiah of Judah appealed for help from the Egyptians, who sent an army in response (Jer. 37:5). The Babylonians left off besieging Jerusalem, and routed the Egyptians, as Jeremiah predicted they would (Jer. 37:6–10; 34:21–22). Returning to Jerusalem the Babylonians breached the walls, forcing King Zedekiah, with some of his soldiers, to flee. But the king was pursued, captured, blinded, and taken off to Babylon, where he died (2 Kings 25:3–7; Jer. 52:7–11).

It is this series of events that lies behind vv. 17–20. The anxious waiting for help that never came (v. 17), the siege of the city (v. 18), the attempted escape of King Zedekiah (v. 19), and his capture and death (v. 20) are all pictured. It should be realized how paradoxical was the loss of the king. As *the Lord's anointed* the king was felt to be inviolable. His divine protection was celebrated in cultic song (Psalms 2:1–11; 45:2–7). Now the king was dead, and so the divine promises seemed also dead (cf. similarly Psalm 89).

3. Fateful Future for Edom (4:21–22)

21 Rejoice and be glad, O daughter of Edom,
 dweller in the land of Uz;
 but to you also the cup shall pass;
 you shall become drunk and strip yourself bare.
22 The punishment of your iniquity, O daughter of Zion, is accomplished,
 he will keep you in exile no longer;
 but your iniquity, O daughter of Edom, he will punish,
 he will uncover your sins.

In these concluding lines Israel is given hope by the poet. But, in typical fashion, it is proclaimed in the midst of doom for someone else, namely, Edom. The Edomites, descendants of Esau, and long the enemies of Israel, played a particularly reprehensible role during the destruction of Jerusalem. Apparently they took an active part in it, plundering the city, and capturing escaping refugees (cf. Obad. 10–16; Psalm 137:7; Jer. 49:7–22). They would therefore have to drink the *cup* of God's wrath (cf. Jer. 25:15; Psalm 11:6), becoming drunk and disgraced (cf. Hab. 2:15–16). But the people of Judah had drunk enough; no more of her sons and daughters would be forcibly taken off to Babylonia. The promise in v. 22 is probably better read: "never again shall he send you into exile." This may reflect the rejoicing in Jerusalem after 581 B.C., when, according to Jeremiah 52:28–30, the last group of people was deported.

V. The Cry for Salvation (5:1–22)

1 Remember, O LORD, what has befallen us;
    behold, and see our disgrace!
2 Our inheritance has been turned over to
        strangers,
    our homes to aliens.
3 We have become orphans, fatherless;
    our mothers are like widows.
4 We must pay for the water we drink,
    the wood we get must be bought.
5 With a yoke on our necks we are hard
        driven;
    we are weary, we are given no rest.
6 We have given the hand to Egypt,
    and to Assyria, to get bread enough.
7 Our fathers sinned, and are no more;
    and we bear their iniquities.
8 Slaves rule over us;
    there is none to deliver us from their
        hand.
9 We get our bread at the peril of our lives,
    because of the sword in the wilderness.
10 Our skin is hot as an oven
    with the burning heat of famine.
11 Women are ravished in Zion,
    virgins in the towns of Judah.
12 Princes are hung up by their hands;
    no respect is shown to the elders.
13 Young men are compelled to grind at the
        mill;
    and boys stagger under loads of wood.
14 The old men have quit the city gate,
    the young men their music.
15 The joy of our hearts has ceased;
    our dancing has been turned to mourning.

16 The crown has fallen from our head;
    woe to us, for we have sinned!
17 For this our heart has become sick,
    for these things our eyes have grown dim,
18 for Mount Zion which lies desolate;
    jackals prowl over it.

Once again we have pictured for us the miserable conditions of Jerusalem after its capture. This time it is in the form of a community lament. As always through the book, the song is permeated with confusion and agony, not just over the loss of life, but also over the threatened loss of faith.

1. Details of Destruction (5:1–18)

The opening cry *Remember* is common throughout the Old Testament for God to recall his promises (Ex. 32:13; Psalms 25:6; 74:2). It presupposes faith that refuses to give up, even though it may be severely tested. So the people seek to stir up the Lord's loving action by graphically describing the carnage. The Promised Land (*our inheritance;* cf. Deut. 4:21) has been taken over by others. This is what brought special disgrace, since the land had been promised to the Israelites by the Lord (Gen. 12:7; Deut. 6:18). What Israel forgot, of course, was that continued existence in the land had its conditions (Deut. 4:25–31). It did not belong to Israel, but to Yahweh. Israel was only permitted to live there as "sojourners" (Lev. 25:23), so long as they kept the commandments of the Lord. The fact that the land was now taken over by *strangers*, who had ousted them from their *homes* (v. 2), was the sign of their disobedience and shame.

Because they were no longer God's tenants on the land, but were the vassals of aliens, they had to suffer the rigors of servitude. They had to *pay for the water* they drank, as well as for the *wood* they burned. The pathos of the situation is seen when the Hebrew is translated: "our *own* water . . . our *own* wood." They bore the burden of unyielding forced service (v. 5) that demanded labor of even the very young (v. 13). Their vassalage to Babylonian *slaves* (the military officials, v. 8; cf.

2 Kings 24:10–11; 25:24) brought humiliation to the *women* (v. 11) and shameful death to the leaders (v. 12; *their hands* refers to the "slaves" of v. 8). To be hung up after death was a particular sign of humiliation (cf. Deut. 21:22–23). Because of the risk from marauding Bedouin bands, emboldened by the downfall of the state, it was difficult to get food from outside the walls (v. 9). So food was scarce, and starvation caused a raging fever (v. 10).

In the midst of this exclamation of woe over the conditions, the people once again admit the cause—sin. At first, they put the blame on their *fathers* (v. 7). Instead of seeking their economic security in obedience to the covenant with Yahweh (Deut. 8:3), they sought to enter into economic alliances with Egypt and Assyria (v. 6; cf. Hos. 7:11; 11:5; Jer. 2:18,36). They played the deadly game of power politics, contrary to the will of the Lord, and brought suffering on their descendants. Later in the song, however, the people admit their own sin. The loss of statehood (*crown;* cf. Jer. 13:18) was due to their own continued sin (v. 16). This sin we have already seen (2:14; 4:13).

2. Prayer for Restoration (5:19–22)

19 But thou, O LORD, dost reign for ever;
    thy throne endures to all generations.
20 Why dost thou forget us for ever,
    why dost thou so long forsake us?
21 Restore us to thyself, O LORD, that we may
    be restored!
    Renew our days as of old!
22 Or hast thou utterly rejected us?
    Art thou exceedingly angry with us?

The song concludes with a haunting question that pervades the whole book, and depicts the struggle of faith. Referring to the call to "remember" with which the poem began (5:1), the people affirm: In the midst of a changing and oft-destructive world, Yahweh's promises and rulership remain constant (cf. Psalms 9:8; 93:2; 102:13; 103:19). So how can he allow the desolation to endure? (vv. 19–20). The

question is not so much one of doubt, as it is one of perplexity. For the people move on to ask for a restoration of the good, old days, concluding with the statement (not a question as in the RSV): "For if thou hast utterly rejected us (as some might say), thou hast been angry with us too much."

The RSV translation is possible, and if retained would express the author's final despairing conclusion that the break between the Lord and his people was final. However this does not seem to be the mood of the rest of the book. The author, like Job, faces circumstances that seem to show total rejection by God. But his faith is too strong, and so he only says "if."

The confusion of the people is not hard to understand. They lived in a world where one's faith was tied closely to one's political fortunes. When one nation conquered another, it was attributed to the conquest of one set of gods over another. The prophet of Isaiah 40:27–31 had to deal with this problem among those who were living in Babylonian exile. If Yahweh were really sovereign, why would he continue to allow his people to suffer? This has always been the question that challenges biblical faith in the midst of evil. If God is the sovereign, loving one the Bible claims, then he would not allow evil to exist. This can only be the conclusion of those who judge superficially. For the Bible responds: Do not let appearances deceive you. If God is God, then his ways must be mysterious; he is a God who "hides himself" (Isa. 45:15). He may still be loving, and yet not act in ways we assume he should (Isa. 55:8).

The "stumbling block" of the cross is a prime example. Our response must be loving trust. It is this that the poet stated in chapter 3, and it is the answer Yahweh gave to Job as well (Job 38—42). This faith is implicit in the concluding statement of chapter 5, but the grim circumstances of that day did not allow it to overcome the doubt that always hangs around the edges of belief.

Ezekiel

JOHN T. BUNN

Introduction

The book of Ezekiel constitutes a watershed in biblical literature, for it is a book reflecting major transitions in religious thought. While it maintains a firm anchoring in previous Israelite religious tradition, novel insights mark it with originality. As such it stands in the middle of a major shift from traditional prophetic to newer apocalyptic thought. This new apocalyptic thought emphasizes an imminent battle in which Yahweh destroys evil, raises the righteous to power, and effects a messianic-type kingdom. These acts on the part of Yahweh are expressed in symbolic manner and are thus quite puzzling.

Why then do we have this virtually unique approach in Ezekiel? The message of God to man has ever been one directed toward man's needs brought about by changed conditions. In Ezekiel's day Israel was confronted with a combination of problems never before encountered. The Temple was destroyed. The most of the faithful had been exiled from the land of promise. Israelite nationalism had come to an abrupt end. The very promises of Yahweh to Israel seemed to have been shattered. Hopelessness and despair were rampart. In the light of this, Yahweh through Ezekiel proclaims an eternal message in an unaccustomed manner.[1]

For Ezekiel the changed condition of Israel required a contemporary message,

one which would speak to them in their alien situation. This would out of necessity demand fresh insights, striking interpretations, and the casting of Yahweh's injunctions in unprecedented patterns. Thus we shall find the book to be extraordinarily different and quite baffling.

I. Historical Setting

A most formative influence upon the prophetic message is the flux of history. Above all a prophet is a forth-teller, one who speaks forth the oracles of God to man in his life situation. Prophetic validity has its very origin in the *sitz im leben* (i.e., situation in time).

Ezekiel proclaimed his message during the tragic and climactic end of Israelite nationalism, an event preceded by some fifty years of diminished political power and deepening religious apostasy. In Judah Manasseh (*ca.* 687–642 B.C.) had reversed the trends toward political and religious reform instituted by Hezekiah (*ca.* 715–687). Manasseh restored the high places, permitted resurgence of corrupt local Yahweh cults, placed royal approval upon the restoration of Baalism, and as an official act welcomed a deluge of Assyrian idolatrous practices. Divination and magic, the twin hallmarks of Assyrian religion, were grafted onto Israelite religion.

No perceptible change occurred during the brief reign of Manasseh's son, Amon (*ca.* 642–640 B.C.). Only the accession of Josiah (*ca.* 640) slowed for a while the

[1] Cf. Ernest Sellin and Georg Fohrer, *Introduction to the Old Testament*, trans. David E. Green (Nashville: Abingdon Press, 1968), p. 408.

gross defection of the people of Judah and Jerusalem from traditional Yahwism. As bold as were the reforms of Josiah, especially those of 621, they were not sufficient to reverse the headlong plunge of Judah into national and redemptive oblivion. The death of Josiah in 609 prefigured the death of Judah.

Following the battle of Carchemish in 605 B.C., the dominant power was Babylonia or Chaldea. Judah became a tribute-paying province with its native kings ruling according to the dictates of Nebuchadnezzar. A rebellious Jehoiakim (*ca.* 609–598 B.C.) incurred the wrath of his Chaldean overlord. Nebuchadnezzar's response, though swift, was not timely enough to exact punishment of Jehoiakim. Jehoiakim died leaving the throne to Jehoiachin (3 months, 598), who assumed leadership just in time to receive the punishment intended for his father. Judah and Jerusalem were subdued by the Babylonian armies. Jehoiachin and the country's leadership were taken into captivity, and Zedekiah (*ca.* 598–589) was placed upon the throne as a puppet ruler.

Zedekiah promptly initiated a hazardous policy for Judah involving the tiny nation in intrigues with Psammetichus II and Apries of Egypt. The intent was to throw off Chaldean domination. Such audacity on the part of Zedekiah was superseded only by his political clumsiness. Reaction by Nebuchadnezzar was prompt and catastrophic. The Chaldean armies ravaged Judah, decimated the population, and turned Jerusalem into a holocaust. Thus in August, 587 B.C., Judah and Jerusalem were no more. The land lay a mutilated corpse, and the remnant of the population was deported to the land of Babylon.

If the priestly ministry of Ezekiel began a decade or so prior to Jehoiakim and if the prophetic ministry began shortly before 592 B.C., then in the most intimate way the prophet was exposed to these chaotic events. It was from the standpoint of priest and prophet that Ezekiel addressed the people, spoke to the times, weighed the causative agents for the judgment of Yahweh, and interpreted the mighty acts of Yahweh in history in new ways.

II. The Man Ezekiel

As with most Old Testament prophets little is known of the intimate personal life of Ezekiel. He was the son of Buzi (1:3), a priest presumably attached to the Jerusalem Temple. It is assumed by some that the prophet, prior to the Exile of 598/599 B.C., also served as a member of the Temple priesthood.[2]

He was married. His wife, in the word of the Lord, was the "delight of your eyes" (24:16). Apparently this wife was his companion in flight and exile maintaining a private home (cf. 8:1; 14:1; 20:1) near "the great canal" (i.e., Chebar) at the location of Tel-abib. That the home was a center of Ezekiel's prophetic activity is attested to by allusions to frequent visits by the exiled Israelite leadership and its central place in certain of the symbolic prophetic pantomimes (cf. 8:1; 12:18; 14:1; 20:1).

Although careful readers note a general lack of reference in Ezekiel to harsh treatment by the Babylonian overlords, the very location of their settlement implies a status of forced labor for the rank and file but with concessions granted to those of leadership among the exiles.[3]

The two greatest personal tragedies for Ezekiel, whose name means "God strengthens," occurred at the same time; the death of his wife and the destruction of Jerusalem (24:15 ff.). Both events transpired on the same day of the year about 587 B.C.

Apart from these scant facts concerning his life, the stature of the man and the complexity of his ministry are best revealed in the nature of his message and the lasting influence of his religious thought.

In this one man there is the perfect mat-

2 Emil Kraeling, *Commentary of the Prophets* (New Jersey: Thomas Nelson and Sons, 1966).
3 W. F. Albright, "King Jehoiachin in Exile," *The Biblical Archaeologist*, 4 (1942), 49–55; cf. also Isa. 2 and Psalm 137 for idyllic views of the Exile.

ing of the fiery evangel and tender pastor. His pronouncements of judgment tear the mind and lacerate the spirit, while his oracles of hope salve the soul and bind up the broken heart. About Ezekiel there was a wall of separation from his fellowmen and an abrasive harshness in human relationships. But within the core of his being there resided a most sensitive spirit alert to the slightest demand of Yahweh upon him.

That, however, which is normally interpreted as hardness in Ezekiel is but an iron self-discipline. His rigid judgments and stern self-control denote no lack of humanness. To the contrary they are evidences of his understanding of himself and others in the light of his divinely appointed task. He had been called to vindicate the name of Yahweh. Among an apostate people, this both required and demanded incredible obedience to his task. Thus he could on the occasion of the death of his beloved wife avoid all signs of mourning for this was required of him as a sign to the people (24:15 ff.).

Nor can we overlook the perceptive insights into contemporary affairs issuing from an exceptionally broad knowledge of the ancient Near East. His prophetic utterances reveal an amazing store of information related to historical event, geography, maritime trade, compositions of armies, political alliances, mythology, and wisdom literature. Ezekiel, as few others, utilized this vast store of knowledge to illuminate national and international conditions as they related to the Israelite concept of God.

His literary talent is striking from the standpoint of originality. Types and symbols, parables and allegory signalize his poetical oracles, and tremendous facility in descriptive narration marks his accounts. Attention to detail in describing the vision theophanies (1:4—3:15; 37:1—14) marks Ezekiel as a rudimentary phenomenologist. Yet the meticulous recording of the new temple vision (chs. 40—48) reveals his ingrained priestly predisposition.

No other prophet of the Old Testament demonstrates such an acute sympathy for priestly theology and cultic rite. There was in Ezekiel an abhorrence of anything unclean. Conditions which would restrict or deny the full implementation of an expanded body of statutes and ordinances were to be overcome. Yet with all of the priestly concern for organized cultic religion within Ezekiel there was the strong pulse of pastoral care. He felt a personal responsibility for each of his exiled countrymen. And he looked upon himself as called, not only to proclaim judgment, but to be a watchman over them. Ezekiel with all of his outward aloofness, ecstatic detachment, and stark discipline did give to Israel for the first time a concrete demonstration of the genuine pastor.

Fiery ecstatic prophet, legalist, ritualist, priest, sympathetic pastor, imaginative literary artist, flamboyant preacher, stern disciplinarian were all components of this highly complex man. Yet he was much more, he was a prophet caught up in a whirlwind of change. He was in the vanguard of the shift from prophecy to apocalyptic, from monarchial nationalism to a religious state, from highly organized ceremonial Temple religion to loosely organized exilic communities of faith, from set patterns of Israelite orthodoxy to unique departures in religious thought.

Caught up in the crucible of change Ezekiel strove mightily to maintain Yahwism as the religious option for a people devoid of hope. The events of history required new modes of thought and methods of presentation for the message of God. Thus it is little wonder that Ezekiel would be designated as the Calvin of the Old Testament by Kittel; the most influential man in Israelite history by Smith; prophet and theologian by von Rad; or the father of Judaism and apocalyptic by many other writers.[4]

4 Perhaps the words of Kraeling imply even more: "What *Pilgrim's Progress* meant to Protestants, that Ezekiel must have meant to many Jews in the Exile and afterwards." Kraeling, *op. cit.*, 401.

III. The Psychology of Ezekiel

Attempts to explain the psychic aspects of Ezekiel are legion. He has been defined as a clairvoyant, a medium, an ecstatic mystic, a cataleptic, a catatonic, and a psychotic.[5]

Only the most insensitive reader would deny the problems associated with Ezekiel's unique experiences. When one accepts the position that Ezekiel resided physically among the exiles in Babylonia and at one and the same time periodically resided spiritually in Jerusalem, he is confronted with a significant problem.

Additionally there is question concerning the periods of aphasia (3:26; 24:27; 33:21 ff.) and the curious attack of paralysis (4:4 ff.). Ezekiel's violent bodily movements and extreme vocalization of feelings seem to point to some type of extreme mental processes (cf. 6:11; 21:12,14). Prolonged periods of unusual visionary experience (i.e., chs. 8—11 and 40—48) infer unique frames of mind for this prophet. When these are coupled with atypical and certainly non-traditional methods for presentation of the prophetic message in pantomime form, the problem is compounded.

For insight into the mental states of Ezekiel one must deal with two all-important considerations: the total sweep of the prophetic mind-set in Israel and the concept of spirit. With Ezekiel we see a return to the earliest period of Israelite prophetism, the period of the ecstatic prophet.[6] The phrases "hand of Yahweh" and "word of Yahweh came unto me" are used in those contexts, which imply sudden seizures. These expansive ecstatic states closely link Ezekiel with the experiences of the earliest ecstatic prophets (cf. 1 Sam. 10:5–6; 19:20–24; 2 Sam. 6:16–23).

Even more important is the attributing of these states to the force of the Spirit of Yahweh and the belief that the Spirit served not only as the medium of revelation but the fountainhead of messages conveyed.

No other prophet so frequently or forcefully sees or refers to "spirit" as a massive power initiated by Yahweh which moves upon the prophet with overwhelming effect. This produced a dynamic revelatory state within which context Ezekiel responded. The Spirit was a wholly other power that broke upon the prophet as a gigantic storm and under whose influence he received a call to a task, was transported in the spirit from a Babylonian exilic community to the Jerusalem community, experienced the vision of the valley of dry bones, saw future events as consummated, witnessed hidden events, perceived what was within the minds of men, and in auditions received instructions on methods for presentation of the message of Yahweh.

The point of fact seems to be that Ezekiel stood in a unique revelatory state not once but many times during his ministry. And within these ecstatic states, which were to be shared experiences, he found Yahweh revealed. Upon release from the state he conveyed the impressions received to the people. Thus ecstaticism was for Ezekiel a vehicle of revelation, objective in nature. "In the white heat of intense preoccupation and emotion he fused these materials into unity, stamped them with the marks of his own personality and sent them forth as coin of the prophetic realm." [7]

Certainly the psychic experiences of Ezekiel were abnormal. However, they were not psychotic aberrations. All prophetic experience is, in a sense, abnormal; if it were not so, all normal religious men would in effect be prophets. That which seems to be so different in the mentality of Ezekiel is but the presentation of a man

---

[5] Cf. Edwin Broome, Jr., "Ezekiel's Abnormal Personality," JBL, LXV (1946), 277–292.

[6] Cf. W. F. Albright, *Samuel and the Beginnings of the Prophetic Movement* (Cincinnati: Hebrew Union College Press, 1961); N. W. Porteous, "Prophecy," *Record and Revelation*, ed. H. Wheeler Robinson (Oxford: Clarendon Press, 1951), p. 230.

[7] J. M. P. Smith, *The Prophets and Their Times* (Chicago: The University of Chicago Press, 1925), p. 1963.

who openly responded without reservation to the spirit of Yahweh. Ezekiel dared to be receptive to the overtures of the Spirit. Such a heightened consciousness of the Spirit stands in stark contrast to other less sensitive Old Testament prophetic personalities. The real world of Ezekiel was one permeated with the Spirit of Yahweh. Such a quickened and heightened ecstatic frame of mind, produced by the Spirit, permitted Ezekiel to exceed the normal boundaries of time and place. While this facility is to be found in other religious personalities, none show such lengthy or repetitive experiences (cf. 2 Kings 5:26; Matt. 4:5–9).

If the accounts by Ezekiel were the products of a psychotic mind, one would expect them to be incoherent and devoid of reflective thought. The greatest argument for such behavior being normal is the fact that the messages of Ezekiel are cogent, unified, and filled with priestly logic. While it is true that the ecstatic experiences were mostly emotional and imaginative rather than intellectual, the messages emerging from the ecstatic experiences were a skillful blend of passionate Yahwism and deliberate thought.[8] Both the call vision (1:4—2:15) and the Temple vision (chs. 40—48) are excellent examples. These accounts reflect a lengthy process of contemplation upon the experience and its meaning prior to the time of writing. Each detail is agonizingly exact, and every effort is exerted to describe carefully each implication of the experience. Key words are "likeness" and "like": e.g., "the likeness of four living creatures" (1:5); "like burnished bronze" (1:7); "likeness of their faces" (1:10); "appearance was like" (1:16); "likeness of a firmament" (1:22); "likeness of a throne" (1:26); "likeness of the glory of the Lord" (1:28). It was only through the process of calm deliberation that Ezekiel ultimately arrived at an adequate description of the experiences.

The symbolic acts, or mimic messages, because of their repetitiveness in the book, have been taken by some to denote extreme irrational behavior.[9]

The enactment in miniature of the siege of Jerusalem (4:1–3), the cutting of the hair symbolizing the fate of Jerusalem's inhabitants (5:1–12), and the depiction of flight from the doomed city (12:1–7) are but little more picturesque than the acts of Ezekiel's contemporary, Jeremiah. It was Jeremiah before a throng who smashed an earthen flask to symbolize the destruction of Judah and Jerusalem (Jer. 19:1–13) and who buried stones at the entrance of the Egyptian Pharaoh's palace to indicate the place where Nebuchadnezzar would place his throne (Jer. 43:8–13). Certainly the acts of Ezekiel were less extreme than those of Isaiah who walked barefoot and naked for three years (Isa. 20:3)!

IV. Date of the Book

Although Isaiah, Jeremiah, Haggai, and Zechariah affixed dates to their prophetic ministry, Ezekiel was the first to place his prophetic utterances in a chronological sequence. One would almost suspect that Ezekiel maintained a diary of his oracles listing them by month and year. There is every indication that Ezekiel dated his messages according to the year of the deportation of Jehoiachin, king of Judah, about 598 or 599 B.C.[10]

Within the book there are affixed 12 specific dates and one uncertain date (cf. 26:1). Each of the dated oracles thus seems to have been proclaimed by Ezekiel prior to 573 B.C. or at the latest 571. If we accept the first of the dated prophecies as being in the year 592/593, then the dated span of the messages would be the

---

8 J. Lindblom, *Prophecy in Ancient Israel* (Philadelphia: Muhlenberg Press, 1962), p. 179.

9 Broome, *loc. cit.*

10 For various views, cf. C. G. Howie, *The Date and Composition of Ezekiel* (Philadelphia: Society of Biblical Literature, 1950), pp. 27–46; W. F. Albright, "The Seal of Eliakim and the Latest Pre-exilic History of Judah, with Some Observations on Ezekiel," JBL, LI (1932), 77–106; H. C. May, pp. 56–60; Walter Zimmerli, "The Message of the Prophet Ezekiel," *Interpretation*, 23.2 (1969), 131–157.

intervening years. Since the troublesome thirtieth year of 1:1 is considered to be the latest date in the book, then the period covered would extend to *ca.* 568–569. It could therefore be assumed that the call of the prophet occurred shortly before 592 and that Ezekiel had an active prophetic ministry of approximately 24 years.

Only a few major attempts have been made seriously to divorce Ezekiel from the period 592/593–573/567 B.C. Zunz places the prophetic work in the Persian period about 440–400; Torrey designates the book as a pseudepigraphon produced about 230; Messel places it about 400–350; while James Smith places the work during the days of Manasseh, king of Judah, about 684–642.[11]

As interesting and provocative as these theories may be, they have not seriously diminished the weight of scholarship in favor of Ezekiel's prophetic ministry falling within the limits previously mentioned.

V. Authorship of the Book

The book of Ezekiel was, until the twentieth century, considered to be by concensus of scholarship a unity produced by the hand of an historical Ezekiel. There were, however, those few among the rabbinical scholars, early church Fathers, and nineteenth-century investigators who had reservations about an Ezekelian authorship. It was not until the twentieth century that Ezekelian authorship was called into serious question.

Once the question of authorship was enjoined, major arguments centered as much on the location of the work and ministry as on whether or not Ezekiel composed the major portion of the work. The question was where did Ezekiel produce the work? In a Babylonian exile or in Palestine before and after the destruction of Jerusalem? Was part produced in the Babylonian exile and part in Judah? Scholarly

opinion is largely in agreement that the work, whether produced in Palestine or Babylonia, is distinctively Ezekelian in nature. Modern debate is more over the degree of the contribution of Ezekiel than it is over whether he wrote the work or not.

Rabbinical and early Christian scholars demonstrated little concern over the authorship of Ezekiel. Rabbinical debates were directed toward certain positions maintained in Ezekiel which were contrary to the Torah (e.g., Ezek. 46:6 vs. Num. 28:11) and the obscurity of such sections as the call vision and the temple vision (Ezek. 40—48). According to the Talmud it was Hannaniah ben Hezekiah who resolved these problems, thus paving the way for the acceptance of Ezekiel as authoritative in matters dealing with ceremonial cleanliness.[12]

Although the Talmud tends to indicate a solving of the problem, the writings of Jerome point to continuing reservations. We may infer from Jerome that the Jews of his day were prohibited from reading the obscure passages of Ezekiel (e.g., chs. 40—48) until they reached age 30. Thus the prohibition would have been in vogue as late as A.D. 385–420.

Only two initial notes regarding the actual authorship derive from the very early period. One is the Jewish tradition of the Babylonian Talmud (Baba bathra, folio 14b), which asserts that the men of the "Great Synagogue" wrote the book of Ezekiel. The other is that of Josephus, the Jewish historian, who states that Ezekiel wrote two books.[13]

During the nineteenth century the overwhelming position was that the book of Ezekiel was produced by one man, Ezekiel. Three major questions were raised by the scholars of this era. (1) When during

---

[11] Leopold Zunz, *Die Gottesdienstlichen Vortage der Juden* (Berlin: A. Asher, 1832); C. C. Torrey, *Pseudo-Ezekiel and the Original Prophecy* (New Haven: Yale University Press, 1930).

[12] Shabbath 136; Hagigah 13a; Menahoth 45a; Moed Qatan 5a.
[13] The words of the Babylonian Talmud do not intend to imply original writing of the work but a revision or reediting. For the Josephus passage, cf. *Antiq.*, X. 5.1. One of the earliest critical works on Ezekiel takes the key from the Josephus passage.

Ezekiel's lifetime was the work produced? (2) To whom specifically was it addressed? (3) How overcome the problem created by the very obscure and at times corrupt text?[14]

A notable exception was that of Leopold Zunz whose 1832 publication proposed that the book was first committed to writing during the Persian period and that its author was unknown. The twentieth century witnessed a dramatic change in Ezekiel scholarship with primary attention being focused upon the contribution of editors[15] and attempts to determine exactly the geographical setting of Ezekiel's ministry. The prime issue became not whether there was an Ezekiel but how much of the present book was from the mind and hand of Ezekiel. Obviously there were deviations from the main thrust of scholarship, and none is more striking than that of C. C. Torrey.[16]

Herrmann, Cooke, von Rad, Eissfeldt, and Kraetzschmar, among others, adhere to the position of extensive editorial expansion of the book yet maintaining that a significant portion was from the hand of Ezekiel.[17]

Among the severest critics as to the actual contribution of Ezekiel to the book are Holscher and Irwin.[18] Both authors act on the presupposition that Ezekiel was primarily a poet, and thus his contribution to the book is to be reduced severely. The analysis of Holscher leaves to Ezekiel approximately 12 percent of its content and that of Irwin but little more.

The other major thrust of twentieth-century studies, that of determining the immediate geographical location of Ezekiel's ministry, did not come into keen focus until the thirties. The major question was whether Ezekiel exercised the prophetic office in Palestine or in Babylonia or in both. Although previous works of the twentieth century alluded to the problem, it was Volkmar Herntrick[19] who produced the definitive work. Herntrick postulated a redactorship for the Babylonian materials and placed the entire ministry of the genuine Ezekiel in the Jerusalem area. Both I. G. Matthews and J. B. Harford were influenced in their works by the thought of Herntrick.[20] The three studies mentioned share a common view which virtually denies to Ezekiel any of the ecstaticism which permeates the book.

Major studies in this same period support the position of a dual ministry for Ezekiel: in Judah and in Babylonia.[21] On the other hand an additional number of commentators such as James Smith, Nils Messel, and D. N. Freedman have produced variations on the basic scheme presented. Only one major scholarly effort in the past two decades has been directed toward a reaffirmation of the traditional view, that of C. G. Howie.[22] Howie affirms the position that Ezekiel was the fundamental author of the work that bears his name and that his ministry was exercised solely in Babylonia.

Despite the number of varying positions, there is an undeniable Ezekelian character about the book. And additionally there ap-

---

14 Cf. C. H. Cornill, *Der Prophet Ezechiel*, (Heidelberg, 1882); S. R. Driver, *An Introduction to the Literature of the Old Testament* (New York: C. Scribner's Sons, 1891); H. Ewald, *The History of Israel* (London: Longmans, Green & Co., 1869).

15 For role of an editor, cf. John I. Durham, "Contemporary Approaches in Old Testament Study," *The Broadman Bible Commentary*, 1 (Nashville: Broadman Press, 1969), 91–92.

16 C. C. Torrey, *op. cit.*

17 J. Herrmann, *Ezekiel* (Leipzig: A. Deichert, 1924); G. A. Cooke, *Ezekiel*, ICC; Gerhard von Rad, *The Message of the Prophets* (London, SCM Press, 1968); Otto Eissfeldt, *The Old Testament, An Introduction* (New York: Harper and Row, 1965).

18 Gustav Holscher, *Hesekiel, Der Dichter and das Buch* (Giessen: A. Topelmann, 1924); W. A. Irwin, *The Problem of Ezekiel* (Chicago: The University of Chicago Press, 1943).

19 Volkmar Herntrick, *Ezechielprobleme* (Giessen: A. Topelmann, 1932).

20 I. G. Matthews, *Ezekiel* (Philadelphia: American Baptist Publication Society, 1939); J. B. Harford, *Studies in the Book of Ezekiel* (Cambridge: The University Press, 1935).

21 Cf. Alfred Bertholet and Kurt Galling, *Hesekiel* (Tübingen: J. C. B. Mohr, 1936); W. A. Irwin, *The Problem of Ezekiel* (Chicago: The University of Chicago Press, 1943); H. Wheeler Robinson, *Two Hebrew Prophets* (London: Lutterworth Press, 1948).

22 C. G. Howie, *op. cit.*

pears to be a genuine Ezekelian ministry related both to Judah and Babylonia.[23]

VI. Composition of the Book

Despite the position taken here that an historical Ezekiel was the primary contributor to the book which bears his name, the work in its present form shows some evidence of the hand of an editor or editors. One may well assume that Ezekiel was not only the originator of the book but the first of its editors. There is internal evidence of both oral and written transmission (cf. 2:4–7; 3:4–7,16–17; 8:1; 11:25; 14:1; 20:1; 20:49; 24:19–24; 35:30–33; and for a passage written by Ezekiel, cf. 3:16b–21).

Certain features of the book point to an editing process: for instance 7:2–4 and 7:5–9 have almost identical meaning. In 30:20–26 three oracles seem to have been telescoped into one; and 1:1–3,13–14; 3:4–9; 4:9–14; 7:1–9 contain doublets. All these are considered to point to an editorial process.

An example of a possible editing process by Ezekiel is to be found in 33:23–33. This is related to the question of rightful ownership of the land, with the remnant in Palestine claiming possession in opposition to the deportees. The three punishments upon the presumptuous claimants voiced in 33:27 are reaffirmations of 14:21 and 21:3–5. This lengthier and somewhat stronger indictment based on the contemporary reasoning of the remnant in the land (33:24) is an updating of the previous words of judgment.

The weightiest evidence for basic Ezekelian involvement in the composition of the book is to be found in three areas: (1) the general outline or framework for the book; (2) the sequence of the dated sections; and (3) the fact that practically all of the materials related to the first two are written in the first person. For the most part

23 Cf. Otto Eissfeldt, *The Old Testament, an Introduction* (New York: Harper and Row, 1965), pp. 372–381; H. H. Rowley, *Men of God* (London: Thomas Nelson and Sons Ltd., 1963), pp. 169–210.

the narratives in Ezekiel follow a logical sequence and are in a generally correct chronological order. The importance of this dated sequence of prophetic utterances cannot be stressed too much. They, above every other consideration, dictate the ultimate composition of the book.

It has long been affirmed that the first-person passages of Hosea, Isaiah, and Jeremiah attest to historical events. On this broad basis, therefore, the writer's position is that those materials subsequent to a date are from the hand of Ezekiel with but very few exceptions, and that these constituted the original prophetic writings of Ezekiel. That the book as we now have it passed through an extended period of compilation does not negate the impression that the extant book was largely formed by one man.

As to how the book arrived at its present form may be proposed in the following manner. Chapters 1—24 form a singular unit with a major theme, that of judgment on Israel. This is followed by chapters 25—32 containing a unitary thrust, judgment upon the nations. Chapters 34—37 and 38—39 form independent units, each unit being a combination of unrelated prophecies. Since there is abundant evidence of compilation in the production of chapters 1—39, yet with the vast majority of the material decidedly Ezekelian, we would assume that Ezekiel first compiled this material from among his prophetic utterances. This part of the work probably achieved distinctive form during Ezekiel's lifetime. Chapter 33 was later added by a disciple of Ezekiel to tie together and give unity to the work of the hands of his spiritual mentor.

Chapters 40—48 with the theme of a new age centered about a theocratic community in scope and originality is without an antecedent in prophetic literature. It is quite probable that this section of material, dated late in the career of the prophet, was first circulated independently and not attached to other prophecies. The emphases of the unit upon priestly functions, the centrality of the Temple, the restoration of the glory of the Lord, and the Zadokite priesthood as the only legitimate priesthood point to the fact that the prime content is definitely Ezekelian. Possibly no later than the fifth century B.C. the book was gathered into its extant form by those who were of the school of Ezekiel.

The weight of current scholarship is that a lengthy process was involved with numerous persons contributing editorially to the production of the book. Yet it was primarily the word of Ezekiel which was collated in the process. It is felt that Ezekiel's major prophetic utterances served as the basic framework into which was worked his numerous miscellaneous oracles, both minor sermons and poems. Thus the completed work became a compendium of every item of inspired Ezekelian material considered by the editors to be authentically from the hand of Ezekiel. Precisely how long the process of editing took is unknown, but the end result was the preservation of the dynamically inspired word of Yahweh to Ezekiel.[24]

VII. Text and Style of the Book

The problem of determining the correct Hebrew text for the book of Ezekiel is extremely difficult. One only has to note the brief but numerous references in the RSV notation system to recognize how much the text of Ezekiel has suffered in transmission. Repeatedly modern translators were forced to reconstruct on the basis of probability what the actual Hebrew construction happened to be. This occurs some 51 times, while very many variant readings from Greek, Syriac, Latin, and Hebrew manuscripts are referred to. That the text was corrupted at an early stage of its transmission is affirmed by the obvious attempts on the part of the translators of the LXX, i.e., the Septuagint, to rectify the mistakes.

Isolated papyri manuscripts do contain some Ezekiel passages, such as the Chester Beatty and the John H. Scheide. Of the two the Scheide papyri contain the greater portion of Ezekiel, i.e., 19:12—39:29, but omits 36:23b–38. Although the papyri are of significant import, they have not greatly aided in clearing up the obscure text of Ezekiel.

Attempts to evaluate the literary merit of the book of Ezekiel are varied. This is attributable to the fact that Ezekiel employed such a wide range of literary devices. Similitudes, parables, allegories, admonitions, invectives, and threats abound in the work. Both poetry and prose are employed, and frequently the poetry is in irregular form. The rhetorical device of employing questions to open arguments and the use of popular religious saying as a springboard for teachings set this book apart stylistically.

The symbolic acts which accompanied many of his messages were happily categorized by Moulton as "emblem prophecy." [25] Although symbolic acts were old and respectable media for conveying the prophetic message in Israel, the creative mind of Ezekiel seized upon the device and utilized it with extraordinary brilliance. In most instances the symbolic actions preceded the oral statement, and the pantomimes formed a prelude to the spoken word.

These acts, however, were more than flamboyant interest arrestors. To the people of the ancient Near East symbolic actions followed by oral declarations had powerful magical implications. The pantomime or mimic action followed by the spoken word sealed the certainty of those things portrayed.

In Ezekiel, Yahweh was the instigator not only of the word but the act. He, not the prophet, provided both message and method of presentation. The prophet thus enacted and spoke the intent of Yahweh. That which was proclaimed in word had

---

24 For differing views, cf. Eissfeldt, op. cit., pp. 372–381; May, op. cit., pp. 45–51; D. N. Freedman, "The Book of Ezekiel," Interpretation, VIII (1954), 446–472.

25 R. G. Moulton, Ezekiel (New York: The Macmillan Co., 1897), v.

previously been enacted as completed and thus it would be.[26]

VIII. The Message of the Book

The message of Ezekiel is largely unintelligible unless one deals with his priestly theology and his prophetic visionary insights. For Ezekiel stands as the major prophet-priest of Israel.

1. Concern for the Law

Influenced by the Deuteronomic and Priestly schools of religious reform both in theology and ritual, Ezekiel became the most articulate and demanding of all spokesmen of the sacral law (Cooke and von Rad).

This is clearly revealed when one contrasts the preexilic concerns over cultic religion with those of Ezekiel (cf. Amos 5:21–25; Hos. 6:6; Isa. 1:11–15; Mic. 6:6–8; Jer. 3:16,17). Preexilic prophets tended to deemphasize the role of religious ritual as an absolute of true religion, but the converse is normally the case with Ezekiel. Generally when Ezekiel takes an ethical stance on the religious life, there are undercurrents of legalism. Both the "new heart" and "new spirit" themes have legalistic connotations (cf. 11:19–20).

2. Yahweh, the God of History

Ezekiel felt that the very essence of Yahweh had been maligned by the people of Judah in particular and all Israel in general throughout her history. The honor and glory of Yahweh, the God of history, had been debased and sullied. Vindication of Yahweh's honor had to be effected.[27] Israel had rejected Yahweh as the God of history. Some 50 times in the book the formula is found—"that you may know that I am the Lord."

The impact of this part of the message is that within history Yahweh had performed mighty saving acts on behalf of Israel, but Israel from the initiation of her relationship had been an apostate (16:1–22; 20:1–44). The clearest evidence of this attitude on the part of Israel was failure to observe the laws of holiness. Israel became a defiled people who polluted even the land in which they lived (34:17–19).

To Ezekiel judgment upon Israel was absolutely deserved and with certainty unavoidable because the God of history had been denied. Jerusalem was more sinful than Samaria (16:47). Jerusalem was more corrupt than the surrounding nations (5:6–7). Sodom, in comparison, was less wicked than Jerusalem (16:48). Jerusalem's sin had impregnated the very heart of her being. And the city is likened to a caldron whose rust had spread into its inner core (24:6–14).

During an early phase of the message (chs. 1—24) there is a stern note of unconditioned judgment upon Judah and Jerusalem, as well as previous Israel, for presumptive sinfulness. Ezekiel utilizes every device to convince Israel that neither the people nor Jerusalem are inviolate or are to receive any immunity from judgment just because they were historically related to Yahweh. Ezekiel takes pains to lead the people into an understanding of the why of judgment and how to accept it.

The inflexibility of Yahweh's demand for judgment is harshly voiced in 5:13; 6:10; 7:1–27; 9:5–6, but in the death of the wicked Yahweh has no pleasure (18:23). It was not the physical death of the sinner which Yahweh sought but his repentance. For lack of repentance Jerusalem was to be devastated, the Temple demolished, and the people decimated.

3. Individual Responsibility

It is within the doom motif of chapters 1—24 that Ezekiel presents one of the loftiest of his insights: the concept of individual responsibility (cf. 3:17–21; 14:

26 Cf. William A. Irwin, *The Old Testament: Keystone of Human Culture* (New York: Henry Schuman, 1952), pp. 130–131; Harold Knight, *The Hebrew Prophetic Consciousness* (London: Lutterworth Press, 1947), pp. 48–51.
27 Simon J. DeVries, "Remembrance in Ezekiel," *Interpretation,* XVI (1962), 58–64.

12–23; 18:1–32; 33:1–20). Most scholars hold this to be a postexilic concept, a position with which this writer agrees. In this concept the individual is judged according to his state at the given moment of judgment. No clearer picture of the horribleness of sin and its consequences is to be found than in the passages on this theme (see comment on 18:1–32; 33:1–20). To know Yahweh was to know him in judgment. This is the central position of chapters 1—24.

4. Optimism and Hope

A change occurs in the second phase of the message which follows the destruction of Jerusalem (chs. 25—39). After the message of judgment has been actualized in the destruction of Judah, the message of Ezekiel changes to one of provisional optimism. There is redemption of life for the perserving faithful but retribution and death for the unrepentant. His message now begins to radiate hope to sustain the exiles who need direction in the midnight of a new helplessness. The oracles of hope (chs. 33—38) indicate that their effectual redemption was not being worked out in their immediate context but was consonant with the fate of Jerusalem.

Three major concepts evolve out of this section of the work: pastoral responsibility centered around concern for the individual (34:1–31); the new heart motif (36:26–27); and the renewed concept of the Spirit (37:1–14); (cf. comment on 34:1–31; 36:26,27; 37:1–14). Each of these is woven into the message of hope for the restructuring of a nation which would assure the intactness of the holiness of Yahweh (36:22–32).

The third phase of the message of Ezekiel centers around the promise of unconditional restoration and the absolute promise of deliverance (chs. 40—48), predicated upon a new heart and spirit within the people. This alone would assure, in Ezekiel's mind, the keeping of the statutes and ordinances of Yahweh. There is to be both religious and political restoration with the return of the glory of Yahweh to the rebuilt Temple.

It is within the context of the last section of the message that Ezekiel's concept of history becomes all important. All history was "salvation-history" (*heilsgeschichte*) with no distinction being made between that which was secular and that which was sacred. History was but that time segment of the whole of time within which Yahweh willed to elect and redeem his own. To Ezekiel history was a dynamic process infused, permeated, and acted upon by eternity.

History to Ezekiel had some kind of ultimate goal with definite meaning, and it moved inexorably forward to meet that goal. The goal in Ezekiel was a future idealistic kingdom. These visions of a theocratic community with its new Jerusalem would in time vastly influence a portion of New Testament thought.

Possibly of equal importance in Ezekiel's message are his breaks with cherished Israelite religious traditions. The confrontation of the prophet by Yahweh in Babylon shattered previous popular views that Yahweh was restricted in activity to the land of Canaan (3:22; 8:4). Another popular religious concept, that Yahweh would not permit the fall of Jerusalem, was completely rejected by Ezekiel and doubtless caused deep animosity toward his ministry.[28]

Israelite exclusivism, which had spawned among the people a blind confidence, was pronounced by Ezekiel as sheer nonsense.

Additionally the well-entrenched beliefs that the sins of a father were visited upon an innocent child and that individual sin produced corporate guilt were judged untenable by Ezekiel as valid religious doctrine.

The message of Ezekiel evidences that he was the most eminent priestly-prophetic organizer in Israelite history. The basic mandate he issued was directed toward the creation of a theocratic community based on definitive rules and basic prin-

28 Cf. John H. Hayes, "The Tradition of Zion's Inviolability," JBL, LXXXII (1963), 419–426.

ciples of religious legislation. His strong emphasis on the sabbath and cultic observance connected with statutes and ordinances may well have led to a great deal of deadening religious legislation which sapped the vitality and maimed the spirit of true prophetic religion.

It was, however, apparent that Ezekiel conceived of legislation as the only way to assure the intactness of Israel. For him national continuance could only be guaranteed so long as the glory of Yahweh resided in the Temple. This was predicated upon a people who would so faithfully keep the ordinances and statues that Yahweh would remain with them.

Outline

Selected Bibliography

COOKE, G. A. The Book of Ezekiel. ("The International Critical Commentary.") Edinburgh: T. & T. Clark, 1951.

EICHRODT, WALTHER. Ezekiel. Trans. C. Quin ("The Old Testament Library.") Philadelphia: The Westminster Press, 1970.

FISCH, S. Ezekiel. London: Soncino Press, 1950.

HARFORD, JOHN B. Studies in the Book of Ezekiel. Cambridge: Cambridge University Press, 1935.

HOWIE, CARL G. The Date and Composition of Ezekiel. Philadelphia: Society of Biblical Literature, 1950.

MATTHEWS, I. G. Ezekiel. Philadelphia: American Baptist Publication Society, 1939.

MAY, HERBERT G. "Ezekiel." The Interpreter's Bible. Nashville: Abingdon Press, 1956.

RITCHARD, JAMES A., ed. *Ancient Near Eastern Texts Relating to the Old Testament.* Princeton: Princeton University Press, 1950.

KINNER, JOHN. *The Book of Ezekiel.* London: Hodder & Stoughton, 1895.

TALKER, D. M. G. *Ezekiel.* ("Torch Bible Commentaries.") London: SCM Press, Ltd., 1968.

ON RAD, GERHARD. *Old Testament Theology.* Trans. E. W. Trueman Dicken. Edinburgh &

London: Oliver and Boyd, 1966.

WEVERS, JOHN W. *Ezekiel.* ("The New Century Bible," new series.) London: Thomas Nelson and Sons, 1969.

WHITLEY, C. F. *The Exilic Age.* Philadelphia: The Westminster Press, 1957.

ZIMMERLI, W. *Ezechiel. Biblischer Kommentar Altes Testament,* XIII. Neukirchen-Vluyn; Neukirchener Verlag, 1969.

Commentary on the Text

Part One: Judgment upon Judah and Jerusalem (1:1—24:27)

The Call (1:1—3:27)

Endowment with the divine word is but one of several equally indispensable and progressive features of the prophetic call. All the classical ingredients are to be observed in the call of Ezekiel: (1) confrontation by Yahweh; (2) commission to the task, (3) a message conveyed; (4) objection to the task due to inadequacy; (5) and empowering by Yahweh to carry out the commission.

Ezekiel's vision of the glory of Yahweh was an awesome experience, and he, just as Isaiah (cf. Isa. 6:1-13), was totally overwhelmed. Only the Spirit empowered him to withstand the impingement of Yahweh (2:2). The message which he received was to be consumed by him (2:2—3:3), literally implying the divine word was to permeate the whole of his being. As the inflexible hands of Yahweh were upon him (3:14,22), the frightening power of the Spirit from without dispossessed his being and dominated his will (3:14,15). And within the state of prophetic ecstasy the word of Yahweh was revealed and conveyed (2:8,9; 3:27).

From this point on Ezekiel exists within the perimeter of the Spirit's power. Sensitivity to customary patterns of life and reaction to the human condition through normal capacities are denied him. He be-

comes a radically liberated individual, one whose total being is quickened and enlivened.

Could it not be said, however, that Ezekiel was preconditioned by training, submersion in Israelite tradition, and natural disposition for such a call. Most frequently men see what their temperament and training have prepared them to see. In the call experience a new Ezekiel came into being. All restraints were shattered, and the enhancement of his personhood by the Spirit permitted fullest expression of his personality.[29]

Robinson, following A. Bertholet, sees in 1:1—3:27 the fusing of two separate calls.[30] The theophanic call of 1:1—2:2 may be looked upon as a commission to preach to the exiles in Babylon and 2:3—3:9 as a mandate to prophesy to Judah and Jerusalem. Of interest is the fact that the Targum of Jonathan alludes to this possibility: "On the fifth of the month, in the fifth year of the captivity of King Jehoiachin, the prophetic words came from the Lord to Ezekiel the son of Buzi, the priest, in the land of Israel; again a second time He spoke to him in the providence of the land of the Chaldees by the river Chebar."

29 Harold Knight, *The Hebrew Prophetic Consciousness* (London: Lutterworth Press, 1937), pp. 60–62.

30 H. Wheeler Robinson, *Two Hebrew Prophets* (London: Lutterworth Press, 1948), pp. 81–84.

1. Superscription (1:1–3)

¹ In the thirtieth year, in the fourth month, on the fifth day of the month, as I was among the exiles by the river Chebar, the heavens were opened, and I saw visions of God. ² On the fifth day of the month (it was the fifth year of the exile of King Jehoiachin), ³ the word of the LORD came to Ezekiel the priest, the son of Buzi, in the land of the Chaldeans by the river Chebar; and the hand of the LORD was upon him there.

The editorial superscription is written in both first and third person (i.e., v. 1, first person; vv. 2–3, third person) and specifically details, as is characteristic of Ezekiel, a precise date for the call. The **thirtieth year** possibly infers the length of time from his initial call which would place that call about 568/569 B.C. The **fifth day** is the same. The reckoning of time in v. 1 is simply based on the beginning of the exile of King Jehoiachin and thus dates the specific calls which are to follow (1:4 —3:27) about 593. The editorial expansion (vv. 2,3) doubtless was inserted to give clarification to the statement in v. 1. The phrase **land of the Chaldeans,** was an Assyrian designation for a portion of southern Babylonia (cf. IDB, pp. 549–550). **Chebar** defines the precise Chaldean location of the prophet. This is the nar Kabari, mentioned in Nippur business documents, a semicircular canal constructed so water from the Euphrates would flow through the city and then back into the river.

A recurrent expression of prophetic literature occurs in the superscription, **hand of the Lord** (cf. 3:14–22; 37:1). To the prophets this expression signified seizure by ecstatic experience. A salient feature of the superscription is the evidence of repeated calls to the prophet to his task. The first call occurred about 563 B.C. and some thirty years later the second. With each confrontation a message is given to be spoken to Israel in its contemporary condition.

2. The Theophanic Vision (1:4–28)

With descriptive language the prophet details what transpired on the day of his call to proclaim the word of Yahweh to the exiles. It appears that Ezekiel witnessed the gathering and climatic onrush of a storm (i.e., literally *a stormy wind*) over the flat plains of Babylon. With keenly intensified emotions he is caught up in an ecstatic visionary experience totally beyond himself. One may theorize that the approaching storm mirrored the mental state of the prophet. He was among a dejected people overwhelmed by religious and national disaster. They were cut off from their God and the city of Jerusalem with its sacred Temple precincts. Continuance of Israelite nationalism was at best tenuous. Knowledge of rampant apostasy within Judah and Jerusalem gnawed at the spirit of the prophet.

(1) The Storm and the Creatures (1:4–14)

⁴ As I looked, behold, a stormy wind came out of the north, and a great cloud, with brightness round about it, and fire flashing forth continually, and in the midst of the fire as it were gleaming bronze. ⁵ And from the midst of it came the likeness of four living creatures. And this was their appearance: they had the form of men, ⁶ but each had four faces and each of them had four wings. ⁷ Their legs were straight, and the soles of their feet were like the sole of a calf's foot; and they sparkled like burnished bronze. ⁸ Under their wings on their four sides they had human hands. And the four had their faces and their wings thus: ⁹ their wings touched one another; they went every one straight forward, without turning as they went. ¹⁰ As for the likeness of their faces, each had the face of a man in front; the four had the face of a lion on the right side, the four had the face of an ox on the left side, and the four had the face of an eagle at the back. ¹¹ Such were their faces. And their wings were spread out above; each creature had two wings, each of which touched the wing of another, while two covered their bodies. ¹² And each went straight forward; wherever the spirit would go, they went, without turning as they went. ¹³ In the midst of the living creatures there was something that looked like burning coals of fire, like torches moving to and fro among the living creatures; and the fire was bright, and out of the fire went forth lightning. ¹⁴ And the living creatures darted to and fro, like a flash of lightning.

Three terms (v. 4) normally used to signify such an experience *wind, cloud,* and *fire* (cf. Ex. 19:16; 1 Kings 19:11 ff.) point to a heavy electrical storm. Within he context of this setting the vision of the creatures first appears. Their description may infer seraphim (cf. Isa. 6:2) or cherubim (cf. Gen. 3:24; Ex. 37:9; Psalm 99:1; Ezek. 9:3; 10:1–20). In any case their importance lies in their association with the throne of Yahweh (cf. Ex. 25: 10–22; 1 Kings 6:23–28) and their function as guardians of or attendants to the throne. The form given here is that of the likeness of a winged man with a four-faceted head (v. 10).

(2) The Four Wheels (1:15–21)

15 Now as I looked at the living creatures, I saw a wheel upon the earth beside the living creatures, one for each of the four of them. 16 As for the appearance of the wheels and their construction: their appearance was like the gleaming of a chrysolite; and the four had the same likeness, their construction being as it were a wheel within a wheel. 17 When they went, they went in any of their four directions without turning as they went. 18 The four wheels had rims and they had spokes; and their rims were full of eyes round about. 19 And when the living creatures went, the wheels went beside them; and when the living creatures rose from the earth, the wheels rose. 20 Wherever the spirit would go, they went, and the wheels rose along with them; for the spirit of the living creatures was in the wheels. 21 When those went, these went; and when those stood, these stood; and when those rose from the earth, the wheels rose along with them; for the spirit of the living creatures was in the wheels.

The puzzle of the vehicle spoken of by Ezekiel has never been successfully solved. It appears that the prophet is alluding to a type of throne-chariot which, due to its unique construction, could move in any direction. Had the modern gyroscope been in existence in Ezekiel's day, his description of a *wheel within a wheel* (v. 16) would have been most apt. Ancient Near Eastern discoveries attest to the practice of depicting gods enthroned upon movable thrones and in sculpture as hovering over the backs of sacred animals.[31]

The four wheels of vv. 15–21 are associated with the winged creatures. It appeared to the prophet that each of the

creatures was beside a wheel. If it is the intent to show that the wheels were connected with the movement of the throne chariot, then the creatures may have been the elaborate ornamentation of the wheels themselves. As the wheels moved the creatures would move and in movement appear to be living. Verse 20 may offer additional insight in that the prophet implies that the spirit of the creature was within the wheel. We may surmise that this appeared to move the throne chariot.

(3) The Voice (1:22–25)

22 Over the heads of the living creatures there was the likeness of a firmament, shining like crystal, spread out above their heads. 23 And under the firmament their wings were stretched out straight, one toward another; and each creature had two wings covering its body. 24 And when they went, I heard the sound of their wings like the sound of many waters, like the thunder of the Almighty, a sound of tumult like the sound of a host; when they stood still, they let down their wings. 25 And there came a voice from above the firmament over their heads; when they stood still, they let down their wings.

From above the creatures there came a voice (v. 25) which was like the thunder of the Almighty with the obvious implication that the voice heard was that of Yahweh (cf. Isa. 13:6; Joel 1:15). This presence, from which eminated the voice, was like the firmament (v. 22), i.e., a canopy over the head of the creatures like the vault of the sky over the earth. The Hebrew term for presence is *kabod*. It implies some type of lustrous embodiment. In priestly circles this presence is associated with the tabernacle or the Temple (cf. Ex. 40:34; Lev. 9:6; 1 Kings 8:11; see Eichrodt, *Ezekiel,* p. 58).

Through this experience Yahweh is manifesting to Ezekiel that his presence knows no boundaries and that he freely moves throughout his creation.

(4) The Enthroned God (1:26–28)

26 And above the firmament over their heads there was the likeness of a throne, in appearance like sapphire; and seated above the likeness of a throne was a likeness as it were of a human form. 27 And upward from what had the

31 G. Ernest Wright, *Biblical Archaeology* (Philadelphia: The Westminster Press, 1957), pp. 147–148.

appearance of his loins I saw as it were gleaming bronze, like the appearance of fire enclosed round about; and downward from what had the appearance of his loins I saw as it were the appearance of fire, and there was brightness round about him. 28 Like the appearance of the bow that is in the cloud on the day of rain, so was the appearance of the brightness round about.

Such was the appearance of the likeness of the glory of the LORD. And when I saw it, I fell upon my face, and I heard the voice of one speaking.

The source then of the voice was Yahweh. In this theophany the *glory* mirrored the unapproachable nature of Yahweh (v. 28). In Old Testament thought there was that inner holiness of Yahweh which no man could confront; a manifestation of it was approachable, but its pure essence was not (cf. Gen. 32:30; Ex. 19:24; 33:21–33).[32]

Probably one of the most striking elements in the call theophany is the repeated use of the word "likeness" (Heb., *demuth*) and the preposition (Heb., *k*) for "like." This may have been an attempt on the part of the writer to avoid imputing to Yahweh physical characteristics (cf. Gen. 1:26–27). It seems, however, that a more important issue is at stake. The dispassionate description, minute in detail, indicates considerable reflective thought upon the experience and a grappling with a media of expression in order to describe the experience. Although traditional Israelite religion frequently portrayed Yahweh in a heightened or exalted human form (cf. Ex. 33:17–23; Amos 7:7; Isa. 6:1–2; Jer. 1:9; Dan. 7:9), Ezekiel made every effort to portray that which to him was real in symbolic language. Specifically, Ezekiel used similes to convey his impressions. What he saw in the spirit could not be accurately described in human language only likened to certain things. An identical effort on the part of a New Testament writer is found in Revelation 4.

[32] Cf. Walther Eichrodt, *Theology of the Old Testament* (Philadelphia: The Westminster Press, 1961), I 277.

3. The Mandates to the Prophet (2:1— 3:27)

The call account continues with a specifying of four mandates issued to the prophet by Yahweh.

(1) The Mandate to Proclaim the Given Word (2:1—3:3)

1 And he said to me, "Son of man, stand upon your feet, and I will speak with you." 2 And when he spoke to me, the Spirit entered into me and set me upon my feet; and I heard him speaking to me. 3 And he said to me, "Son of man, I send you to the people of Israel, to a nation of rebels, who have rebelled against me; they and their fathers have transgressed against me to this very day. 4 The people also are impudent and stubborn: I send you to them; and you shall say to them, 'Thus says the Lord GOD.' 5 And whether they hear or refuse to hear (for they are a rebellious house) they will know that there has been a prophet among them. 6 And you, son of man, be not afraid of them, nor be afraid of their words, though briers and thorns are with you and you sit upon scorpions; be not afraid of their words, nor be dismayed at their looks, for they are a rebellious house. 7 And you shall speak my words to them, whether they hear or refuse to hear; for they are a rebellious house.

8 "But you, son of man, hear what I say to you; be not rebellious like that rebellious house; open your mouth, and eat what I give you." 9 And when I looked, behold, a hand was stretched out to me, and, lo, a written scroll was in it; 10 and he spread it before me; and it had writing on the front and on the back, and there were written on it words of lamentation and mourning and woe.

1 And he said to me, "Son of man, eat what is offered to you; eat this scroll, and go, speak to the house of Israel." 2 So I opened my mouth, and he gave me the scroll to eat. 3 And he said to me, "Son of man, eat this scroll that I give you and fill your stomach with it." Then I ate it; and it was in my mouth as sweet as honey.

No more moving picture is presented in biblical literature of man's inadequacy and God's grace than is presented in the call experiences of Isaiah and especially Ezekiel. When Ezekiel experienced the glory of Yahweh and heard the voice, he not only recognized but acknowledged his sense of awe in that holy moment. When the vision broke upon him Ezekiel fell upon his face

1:28*b*). Literally he prostrated himself denoting subservience to Yahweh. Only when man volitionally and with true sincerity demonstrates abject humility can God raise him to the zenith of his designs for him. The gentle grace of God (2:1,2) in the awesome moment is evidenced in the command *stand upon your feet.* It is man's duty to be obeisant to God. It is God's prerogative to lift man.

Designation of the prophet as *son of man* (Heb. *ben adam*) is here used for the first of 87 times in the book (2:3). Although in later Old Testament interbiblical and New Testament literature it will bear a somewhat changed meaning, in Ezekiel it is used to distinguish between a heavenly and a divine being and has no messianic connotation. Since it appears in Ezekiel as the typical mode of address by Yahweh to Ezekiel, the emphasis is upon the humanness of the prophet. In this particular case it implies that Ezekiel was but a human being even though he witnessed the magnificent theophany.

Once the *Spirit entered* into the prophet a new condition existed. It is this which revealed the nature of Yahweh to Ezekiel and provided inspiration. With the incursion of the Spirit there came a state of ecstasy in which the prophet had auditions and visions revealing the mandates.

He is instructed to proclaim the message received to a rebellious people (2:4,5). His audience will express their hostility in the form of threats (2:6), and Ezekiel will be confronted by the same mentality that confronted Jeremiah (cf. Jer. 1:8,17). The prophet is not to be concerned with personal safety. His basic preoccupation is to be with the given word. This is both the peril and the privilege of the prophetic office. The true messenger of Yahweh will always be opposed due to the message he proclaims (cf. Isa. 6:10; Jer. 1:17–19).

Whereas Judah was a *rebellious house,* the one called by Yahweh could not afford that luxury of overt emotions (2:8). Above all, for the sake of his office the prophet must accede to the demands of Yahweh

upon him and accept the communication as given.

The message appeared in the form of a *scroll* written on both sides (2:10). This is quite unusual for a Chaldean setting since the Babylonian custom was that of inscribing cuneiform on clay tablets. Also scrolls of papyrus were generally inscribed on only one side. The words inscribed were words of lamentation, mourning, and woe, implying a message of judgment, stern and harsh.

This message was to be consumed in its entirety by Ezekiel. The metaphorical expression of eating the scroll implies digestion and assimilation of the entire content. Thus we have the implication of intellectual assent to and mental acknowledgement of the message. It is unlikely that the bitter message itself became sweet (3:3); but once the message was received, Ezekiel knew that Yahweh would sustain his spokesman.[33]

Disparate but meaningful insights leap forth in this section of the mandates to Ezekiel. One is that the force of the direct confrontation between Yahweh and man is that which produces the prophet, and it is within the context of the confrontation that the message to be proclaimed is imparted (cf. Ex. 3; Amos 7:15; Isa. 6; Jer. 1:4–10). Secondly, here there is an introduction to revelation by written word which becomes to Ezekiel a religion of written statutes and ordinances.

(2) The Mandate to Achieve Prophetic Endurance (3:4–15)

4 And he said to me, "Son of man, go, get you to the house of Israel, and speak with my words to them. 5 For you are not sent to a people of foreign speech and a hard language, but to the house of Israel—6 not to many peoples of foreign speech and a hard language, whose words you cannot understand. Surely, if I sent you to such, they would listen to you. 7 But the house of Israel will not listen to you; for they are not willing to listen to me; because all the house of Israel are of a hard forehead and of a stubborn heart. 8 Behold, I have made

33 Cf. Julius A. Bewer, *The Prophets* (New York: Harper and Brothers, 1955), p. 343; S. Fisch, p. 12.

your face hard against their faces, and your forehead hard against their foreheads. 9 Like adamant harder than flint have I made your forehead; fear them not, nor be dismayed at their looks, for they are a rebellious house." 10 Moreover he said to me, "Son of man, all my words that I shall speak to you receive in your heart, and hear with your ears. 11 And go, get you to the exiles, to your people, and say to them, 'Thus says the Lord God'; whether they hear or refuse to hear."

12 Then the Spirit lifted me up, and as the glory of the Lord arose from its place, I heard behind me the sound of a great earthquake; 13 it was the sound of the wings of the living creatures as they touched one another, and the sound of the wheels beside them, that sounded like a great earthquake. 14 The Spirit lifted me up and took me away, and I went in bitterness in the heat of my spirit, the hand of the Lord being strong upon me; 15 and I came to the exiles at Telabib, who dwelt by the river Chebar. And I sat there overwhelmed among them seven days.

Ezekiel is next admonished to avoid a natural prophetic pitfall. The prohpet may be inclined to believe that because he is called of Yahweh and given a message with a divine mandate to speak, the people will hear and heed. Yahweh attempts to lead Ezekiel away from such an assumption by informing him that Israel would be less responsive to the word than non-Israelites. The implication is that the heathen would believe when Israel would disbelieve (3:7). Israel had rejected Yahweh, and they would reject the prophet. The *hard forehead* and *stubborn heart* are typical examples of prophetic description to denote willful obstinacy (cf. Isa. 48:4).

In order to offset the resistance of the people to the message, Yahweh will imbue Ezekiel with a power to endure equal to their power to resist (v. 8). In effect, the thrust of the prophet for good must be more adamant than the bent of the people toward evil (v. 9). The term *adamant* is used for any substance of unusual hardness (cf. Jer. 17:1; Zech. 7:12) and implies in this context that Yahweh will make Ezekiel's determination to proclaim greater than their determination to reject. The prophetic injunction is to proclaim, whether Israel hears or refuses to hear.

Why then this lengthy passage detailing opposition? The very nature of the message of Yahweh will elicit such a response. Doubtless the *my words* (v. 4) refer back to the scroll written on both sides which by implication doubles the indictment containing lamentations, sorrow, and woe against Judah.

That force, however, which generates the will within the prophet to come face to face with rebellious Judah is the Spirit. Not only does the Spirit energize Ezekiel but transports him to the appointed place of task (v. 12). With Ezekiel the "hand of the Lord" implies control by a force from without, totally other than himself. It produces an acute ecstatic state in which the prophet is overwhelmed. At times there is dumbness (v. 15) or movement, but always there is revelation (cf. 3:22 ff.; 37: 1,2). Under the influence of the Spirit the prophet is emboldened to be what he could never be with natural abilities.

Even as Ezekiel was transported to his appointed task he went bitterly in the heat of his spirit (v. 14). Upon arriving at *Tel-abib* [34] he was overwhelmed (v. 15). What then created the trauma of the prophet? Was it the bitter message, the knowledge of an inordinately difficult task, awe as a result of the theophany, the suffering of the exiles, or the drastic change in the mode of life by the prophet? The condition of Ezekiel was not attributable to any one specific, rather the totality of them all. It was with Ezekiel as with Jesus in the Garden of Gethesemane. The awesome cup, which could not pass from him, contained all of the world's woe, sin, despair, hopelessness, and shame.

(3) The Mandate of Responsibility (3:16–21)

16 And at the end of seven days, the word of the Lord came to me: 17 "Son of man, I have made you a watchman for the house of Israel; whenever you hear a word from my mouth,

[34] Tel-abib literally means in Assyrian a sand heap, a typical designation for a mound containing a buried city. Its location seems to have been somewhere along the Chebar canal.

ou shall give them warning from me. [18] If I
ay to the wicked, 'You shall surely die,' and
ou give him no warning, nor speak to warn
he wicked from his wicked way, in order to
ave his life, that wicked man shall die in his
niquity; but his blood I will require at your
and. [19] But if you warn the wicked, and he
loes not turn from his wickedness, or from his
vicked way, he shall die in his iniquity; but
ou will have saved your life. [20] Again, if a
ighteous man turns from his righteousness and
ommits iniquity, and I lay a stumbling block
efore him, he shall die; because you have not
varned him, he shall die for his sin, and his
ighteous deeds which he has done shall not be
emembered; but his blood I will require at
our hand. [21] Nevertheless if you warn the
ighteous man not to sin, and he does not sin,
e shall surely live, because he took warning;
nd you will have saved your life."

Use of the simile *watchman* for prophet
eems to have been a favorite prophetic
nalogy (cf. Ezek. 33:2–6; Jer. 6:17; Hos.
):8; Hab. 2:1; Isa. 56:10). Doubtless the
magery arose from the security system of
ncient cities where watchmen or sentries
tood guard night and day to forewarn the
eople of an approaching enemy. Since the
welfare of the people was dependent upon
he vigilance of the watchmen, the slightest
lerelection of duty occassioned disaster.
The task of the watchman was to be alert
to danger and swift to warn the population
with a shout of alarm or a blast of the ram
horn trumpet, the *shofar*.

The point of fact in this passage, however, is that Yahweh actually is the watchman (i.e., *whenever you hear a word from
my mouth, you shall give them warning
from me* v. 17). Functionally, the prophet
is but the conveyer of the warning. In
prophetic literature the prophet is the servant, as it were, of the true watchman,
Yahweh. Failure on the part of the prophet
to act as transmitter of the message would
bring a disaster, for if prophetic silence
ensues the prophet by derelection of duty
will share the fate of those who were not
forewarned (v. 18). This results in nothing
less than spiritual catastrophe. The prophet
is not responsible for the effectiveness of
the message, its acceptance or rejection,
only proclamation of the message.

Perhaps the significant import of the
"watchman" passage and the seriousness
of its implied responsibility have to do with
the concept voiced in vv. 18–21. In this
passage Ezekiel sheds new light on the
nature of judgment, and the fresh insight
is expanded considerably in later portions
of the book (cf. 14:12–23; 18:1 ff.; 33:
1–20). The concept of individual responsibility and judgment becomes a hallmark
of Ezekiel. This personalizing of man's relationship to God stirs deeply the somewhat
fallow   ground   of   Israelite   religious
thought. Ezekiel interprets his prophetic
ministry as one to individuals who are
exiled.

(4) The Mandate of Faithfulness to Call-ing (3:22–27)

[22] And the hand of the LORD was there upon
me; and he said to me, "Arise, go forth into the
plain, and there I will speak with you." [23] So I
arose and went forth into the plain; and, lo, the
glory of the LORD stood there, like the glory
which I had seen by the river Chebar; and I
fell on my face. [24] But the Spirit entered into
me, and set me upon my feet; and he spoke
with me and said to me, "Go, shut yourself
within your house. [25] And you, O son of man,
behold, cords will be placed upon you, and you
shall be bound with them, so that you cannot
go out among the people; [26] and I will make
your tongue cleave to the roof of your mouth,
so that you shall be dumb and unable to
reprove them; for they are a rebellious house.
[27] But when I speak with you, I will open your
mouth, and you shall say to them, 'Thus says
the Lord GOD'; he that will hear, let him hear;
and he that will refuse to hear, let him refuse;
for they are a rebellious house.

Both the translation and interpretation
of this passage are fraught with difficulties.[35] Be that as it may, the following
scheme of interpretation may be used.
After Ezekiel had been transplanted among
the exiles, the Spirit moved upon him leading him to a place of solitude, *the plain*
(i.e., lit., the valley). The quietude of the

---

[35] May assigns vv. 25–27 to an editor. Holscher assigns the passage to a redactor, while Cooke sees v.
25 as a varient of 4:8 with v. 21 contradicting v. 27
and v. 27 related to 24:26,27 and 33:21,22. Eichrodt
points to the problem but with helpful suggestions for
solution.

solitary place, whether mountain or valley, has historically played a unique role in the communion of God with man. In a place apart, the *glory of the Lord* once again confronts Ezekiel, and as the Spirit enters into him (v. 24) he receives the divine mandate. It may be that the act of shutting himself in the house (v. 24) was symbolic of the *binding*. Ezekiel is warned that the people are intent upon their rebellion against Yahweh and rejection of his message. They will not hear (v. 27). One might well say at this point poor hearing makes poor preaching. Every entrance to their minds was locked against the prophetic word. They, by their refusal to listen, had bound the prophet. As the people had silenced the prophet by closing their minds, Yahweh would silence the prophet by withholding the message (v. 26).[36]

This seems to imply that to this point Ezekiel had been proclaiming the message of Yahweh to the exiles. That which ensues is the awesome silence of Yahweh. Thus there is the implication that when men refuse to hear, God will refuse to speak.

Such a period of silence will, however, have its effect, and when that silence is broken (v. 27) there is the possibility that some may hear. When the voice of the prophet is no longer heard in the land, the events of history, the natural disasters of life, and the yearnings of hope cry out for its return. Then and then only do the few become receptive to the wooing of God. But another implication here is of equal importance: It is God, not the prophet, who knows the time for fruitful proclamation (v. 27). The true prophet never speaks until the divinely appointed moment.

II. The Word of Judgment in Symbolic Acts (4:1—5:17)

Contained within this section is a major contribution of Ezekiel to the modes of presenting prophetic thought. The device

---

[36] The phrase, "tongue cleave to the roof of . . . mouth," is an OT figure of speech for one speechless (cf. Job 29:10; Psalm 137:6; Lam. 4:4).

---

utilized with consummate skill is that of pantomime or mimetic action. Although other Old Testament prophetic personalties employed the device in a minor form Ezekiel siezes upon it as a major method of enforcing his messages.

1. The Siege of Jerusalem (4:1–3)

[1] "And you, O son of man, take a brick and lay it before you, and portray upon it a city even Jerusalem; [2] and put siegeworks against it, and build a siege wall against it, and cast up a mound against it; set camps also against it and plant battering rams against it round about. [3] And take an iron plate, and place it as an iron wall between you and the city; and set your face toward it, and let it be in a state of siege, and press the siege against it. This is a sign for the house of Israel.

This is the first of a series of messages presented by Ezekiel in pantomime form Whereas spoken words are all too easily forgotten, when such words are reenforced by symbolic actions they are the more impressionable. As has been noted previously, Yahweh is the inspiration for both the mimic act and the words in v. 4.

Ezekiel is instructed to portray upon a *brick* the scene of a city besieged. The Babylonian brick was approximately $12'' \times 12'' \times 3''$, form pressed, and sun dried. Inscriptions were generally impressed upon them while the clay was in a leather hard condition. It may be assumed that the depiction was crudely etched on the brick with a sharp instrument. Possibly only the brick denoted the city. After it was incised and placed on the ground, a full scale attack was depicted by placing around it the siege machinery and walls of circumvallation (v. 2; for opposite view cf. Cooke, p. 50). Once the siege was depicted, Ezekiel was to place (v. 2) an *iron plate* (i.e., a small flat iron cooking griddle for baking bread) between himself and the city.

Symbolically the brick represented Jerusalem and the siege machinery the onslaught of the enemy. But the symbolism of the iron plate is devastatingly ironic. As Yahweh had fought for Israel in past time as an iron defense, now he shuts himself off

om them. In effect his hand will be
urned against them (cf. Jer. 21:5). This is
a sign to Jerusalem of the fate which will
befall it. Much has been made of the theory
that Yahweh never departs from man,
rather that man departs from Yahweh. A
passage from the Samson stories is quite
instructive at this point (cf. Judg. 16:20).

How awesome should have been the
initial impact of this upon those who witnessed the pantomime. Yet the foreboding
act on the part of Ezekiel, signifying ominous future events, seems to have had little
response. Ezekiel is being taught in the
crucible of human experience the incredible
resistance of man to the word of God.

The Duration of Punishment (4:4–17)

1) The Duration of Punishment upon Israel and Judah (4:4–8)

4 "Then lie upon your left side, and I will
lay the punishment of the house of Israel upon
you; for the number of the days that you lie
upon it, you shall bear their punishment. 5 For
I assign to you a number of days, three
hundred and ninety days, equal to the number
of the years of their punishment; so long shall
you bear the punishment of the house of Israel.
6 And when you have completed these, you
shall lie down a second time, but on your right
side, and bear the punishment of the house of
Judah; forty days I assign you, a day for each
year. 7 And you shall set your face toward the
siege of Jerusalem, with your arm bared; and
you shall prophesy against the city. 8 And,
behold, I will put cords upon you, so that you
cannot turn from one side to the other, till you
have completed the days of your siege.

Whereas in the first sign Ezekiel assumed the role of the enemy in the pantomime, in this case he assumes the role of
the rebellious people of Jerusalem. Here
Ezekiel dramatically depicts the years of
punishment which are to befall both the
Northern and Southern kingdoms. First,
Ezekiel is instructed to lie on his *left side*
for 390 days symbolizing a 390-year punishment for Israel (the LXX reads 190
rather than 390 as in the MT). Then he is
to lie on his right side for 40 days signifying a 40-year punishment for Judah.

One of the many unresolved enigmas in

the book of Ezekiel has to do with the
390-year period of punishment for Israel.
One may easily affirm the obvious and
assert that greater sin evoked the greater
punishment, yet this does not resolve the
question of the 390 years. If the 390 years
is computed from the fall of Samaria and
the Northern Kingdom in 721 B.C., it means
the punishment will continue until 231, a
date which has no especial significance. If
it is computed on the basis of the LXX,
then the punishment would end about 531,
another date without significant import (cf.
Stalker, pp. 62–64.)

There is in this passage the enlargement
and progression of a theme from the previous dramatic presentation. Formerly, Yahweh departed from Jerusalem, withdrew his
protective presence, but in vv. 7,8 the symbolic act of Ezekiel in setting his face
toward Jerusalem and having arms bared
signifies the stance of Yahweh. It is Yahweh
who will come against an erring people.
The intent of Yahweh and the certainty of
Jerusalem's disastrous fate is enforced by
Ezekiel's binding until the siege and destruction are complete (v. 8). Obviously
the cords with which the prophet were
bound were mental restraints or ecstatic
inhibitions.

(2) The Horror of Jerusalem's Punishment (4:9–17)

9 "And you, take wheat and barley, beans
and lentils, millet and spelt, and put them into
a single vessel, and make bread of them. During the number of days that you lie upon your
side, three hundred and ninety days, you shall
eat it. 10 And the food which you eat shall be
by weight, twenty shekels a day; once a day
you shall eat it. 11 And water you shall drink
by measure, the sixth part of a hin; once a day
you shall drink. 12 And you shall eat it as a
barley cake, baking it in their sight on human
dung." 13 And the LORD said, "Thus shall the
people of Israel eat their bread unclean, among
the nations whither I will drive them." 14 Then
I said, "Ah Lord GOD! behold, I have never
defiled myself; from my youth up till now I
have never eaten what died of itself or was
torn by beasts, nor has foul flesh come into my
mouth." 15 Then he said to me, "See, I will let
you have cow's dung instead of human dung,
on which you may prepare your bread."

16 Moreover he said to me, "Son of man, behold, I will break the staff of bread in Jerusalem; they shall eat bread by weight and with fearfulness; and they shall drink water by measure and in dismay. 17 I will do this that they may lack bread and water, and look at one another in dismay, and waste away under their punishment.

During the period of time while the prophet is lying on his side to symbolize the exile of Israel and Judah, he will eat and drink as well as prepare his food in the manner of one within a besieged city.

Little does modern man comprehend the sufferings endured by inhabitants of an ancient city under siege. In such warfare an aggressor would not unnecessarily commit his troops to frontal assaults upon heavily fortified city complexes until its defenders were weakened by starvation and perishing for lack of water. An ancient strategy was to encircle a city, cut off its food and water supply, and then wait for the inevitable. Once starvation, plague, sickness, death, and despair had withered the bodies of the defenders and broken their spirits, the walls would be breached while the hapless defenders made utterly futile attempts to resist the onslaught. The pantomime of Ezekiel (vv. 9–17) asserts that such would befall Jerusalem (cf. Jer. 37:21; Lam. 2:20; and similarly the siege of Samaria, 2 Kings 7:1–4).

The odd mixture of grains (v. 9) used in making bread indicates a severe siege. In order to survive one would be forced to scrape together a few grains of several different cereals in order to have enough flour to produce a single cake of bread. Such mixing of grains was objected to in priestly legislation and rendered the bread unclean (cf. Lev. 19:19; Deut. 22:9).

Allotted to the prophet per day was a specific amount of bread (i.e., *twenty shekels weight*) and water (i.e., *sixth part of a hin*). This constituted a starvation diet! It would amount to approximately one half pound of bread and one quart of water each 24 hours. That the amount of each is specified by precise weight points to stringent rationing (vv. 10,16).

The desperate plight of the besieged made more evident in the next command to the prophet. Ezekiel is commanded t bake his bread (v. 12) on a fire made wit human excretion. Customary fuels were n longer available due to the siege. Such fu added defilement to the already contami nated bread; such a command was loath some to Ezekiel (v. 14).

No clearer indication of Ezekiel's cor tinuing priestly stance is to be found tha his words of reply to Yahweh. His priestl defense is that he had been meticulous i keeping laws of ceremonial cleanliness. I is then that Yahweh grants Ezekiel th privilege of substituting *cow dung* for hu man *dung* (v. 15). Although the concessio was granted Ezekiel it would be denied t Jerusalem's citizens (v. 13).

Among the various laws of the book c Deuteronomy there is one which refers t human dung (cf., Deut. 23:12–14). It wa considered unclean and that which woul render the camp of Israel unholy. Leviticu 11:1–47 shows that that which is unclea is a ritual contaminant and as such is un holy. The basic religious principle bein voiced by Ezekiel was that he, as an Israel ite and a priest, was holy (cf. Ex. 22:31) If therefore he ate that which was unclean God, who was holy, could no longer be i his presence. This act to Ezekiel would i effect cut him off from Yahweh.

During the siege there would be added miseries for the inhabitants of Jerusalem (vv. 16,17). They would consume thei scant rations *with fearfulness and in dismay* and in the process see one another *waste away*. To eat and drink in this manner while watching one another grow weaker and weaker implies but one thing: they would watch one another starve to death.

3. The Fate of Jerusalem's Inhabitants (5: 1–17)

1 "And you, O son of man, take a sharp sword; use it as a barber's razor and pass it over your head and your beard; then take balances for weighing, and divide the hair. 2 A third part you shall burn in the fire in the midst of the city, when the days of the siege

are completed; and a third part you shall take and strike with the sword round about the city; and a third part you shall scatter to the wind, and I will unsheathe the sword after them. 3 And you shall take from these a small number, and bind them in the skirts of your robe. 4 And of these again you shall take some, and cast them into the fire, and burn them in the fire; from there a fire will come forth into all the house of Israel. 5 Thus says the Lord GOD: This is Jerusalem; I have set her in the center of the nations, with countries round about her. 6 And she has wickedly rebelled against my ordinances more than the nations, and against my statutes more than the countries round about her, by rejecting my ordinances and not walking in my statutes. 7 Therefore thus says the Lord GOD: Because you are more turbulent than the nations that are round about you, and have not walked in my statutes or kept my ordinances, but have acted according to the ordinances of the nations that are round about you; 8 therefore thus says the Lord GOD: Behold, I, even I, am against you; and I will execute judgments in the midst of you in the sight of the nations. 9 And because of all your abominations I will do with you what I have never yet done, and the like of which I will never do again. 10 Therefore fathers shall eat their sons in the midst of you, and sons shall eat their fathers; and I will execute judgments on you, and any of you who survive I will scatter to all the winds. 11 Wherefore, as I live, says the Lord GOD, surely, because you have defiled my sanctuary with all your detestable things and with all your abominations, therefore I will cut you down; my eye will not spare, and I will have no pity. 12 A third part of you shall die of pestilence and be consumed with famine in the midst of you; a third part shall fall by the sword round about you; and a third part I will scatter to all the winds and will unsheathe the sword after them. 13 "Thus shall my anger spend itself, and I will vent my fury upon them and satisfy myself; and they shall know that I, the LORD, have spoken in my jealousy, when I spend my fury upon them. 14 Moreover I will make you a desolation and an object of reproach among the nations round about you and in the sight of all that pass by. 15 You shall be a reproach and a taunt, a warning and a horror, to the nations round about you, when I execute judgments on you in anger and fury, and with furious chastisements—I, the LORD, have spoken—16 when I loose against you my deadly arrows of famine, arrows for destruction, which I will loose to destroy you, and when I bring more and more famine upon you, and break your staff of bread. 17 I will send famine and wild beasts against you, and they will rob you of your

children; pestilence and blood shall pass through you; and I will bring the sword upon you. I, the LORD, have spoken."

From chapter 5 to the end of the book the content bears an amazing affinity to the Holiness Code of the book of Leviticus (cf. Lev. 17–26). S. R. Driver has provided an excellent listing of the literary parallels between Leviticus 26 and Ezekiel. The list of parallels [37] in content and thought patterns between the Holiness Code and Ezekiel is so extensive some authorities have ventured to surmise that Ezekiel was the compiler of the Holiness Code. On the other hand, certain authorities insist that both Ezekiel and the compiler of the Holiness Code worked from the same original source. Suffice it to say that both Ezekiel and the Holiness Code came into existence during the same period of history and issued forth from an estranged religious community.[38]

Again the prophet is instructed to stage the message in symbolic act to depict the fate of Jerusalem's inhabitants due to their gross abominations. Ezekiel is instructed to take a *sword* and wielding it as a *barber's razor* to cut off his hair and beard. The sword symbolizes the invader who will decimate, with terrifying onslaught, the people who are represented by the hair and beard of Ezekiel. The impact of the imagery is intensified by the cropping of the hair, which in the Old Testament symbolically denotes mourning (cf. Isa. 22:12; Jer. 48:37; Amos 8:10; Mic. 1:16).

Once the hair had been removed it was to be divided into three equal parts (v. 2) with a few hairs from each third being secreted in the prophet's robe (v. 3). One third was to be burned in a small fire, symbolizing the third of the inhabitants who would meet death in the holocaust. Another third was to be scattered about the perimeter of the city by Ezekiel's

37 S. R. Driver, *An Introduction to the Literature of the Old Testament,* rev. ed. (New York: Charles Scribner's Sons, 1937), p. 147.
38 Otto Eissfeldt, *The Old Testament an Introduction,* trans. Peter R. Ackroyd (New York: Harper and Row, 1965), pp. 237,238.

sword, signifying those who would be slaughtered by the invaders' sword. The remaining third was to be cast up into the wind to be scattered, depicting those who were able to flee from the stricken city. These, however, would be cut down by the sword of Yahweh. Of those secreted in the robe (v. 4) some will be destroyed. This seemingly implies a few would be spared (on this very difficult point, cf. Cooke, pp. 57,58; May, pp. 90,91).

The reasons for such cataclysmic judgment are detailed (vv. 5-9). Basically Israel had become an abomination to Yahweh due to willful and perpetual rebellion. Jerusalem, the heart of Israel, and inhabited by an elect people was looked upon as the *center of the nations*. Because of her lofty elevation by Yahweh and her favored religious preeminence, Jerusalem was expected to accept responsibilities consonant with her privileges. But Jerusalem was more rebellious than other nations (v. 6). She betrayed her trust. The offense of Jerusalem was greater because the express will of Yahweh for her had been articulated in *ordinances* and *statutes*. Although Jerusalem should have acted in an enlightened manner, she was *more turbelent* than *other nations* and had adopted the alien *ways* of nations without the boundaries of centralized revelation. The specific issue at point is voiced in v. 11. Jerusalem had become a religious harlot. She had embraced the religious cults of surrounding nations and installed in *my sanctuary* (i.e., the Temple) pagan practices.

The act of Temple defilement was but symptomatic of the diseased spirit of the people. Such outward manifestations were but eminations of an inner corruption. It was this inner condition which caused the wrath of Yahweh to overflow.

In vv. 13-17 there appears a horrifying, literally awesome depiction of the nature of Yahweh. The relentless force of the message, the hammering repetition of words, such as *anger, fury, jealously, judgments, chastisements, destruction, destroy, famine, pestilence,* and *blood* evoke dread.

Through these the fury of Yahweh will be expended and his anger satiated. The and then only would Yahweh gain personal satisfaction (v. 13; Eichrodt, *Ezekiel,* p. 89). We must understand that this was one view or one aspect of the nature of God in the Old Testament and represents a pre-Christian evaluation. Even so this facet of God's nature cannot be taken lightly in Christian theology. There is a contemporary certainty of judgment, and the reality of God's presence is never to be forgotten.

This judgment upon Jerusalem is all the more certain since the passage concludes with the formula *I, the Lord, have spoken.* Since the spoken word of God is irrevocable in nature, its pronouncements are considered to be accomplished facts.

III. Oracles of Judgment (6:1—7:27)

1. Judgment upon Idolatrous High Places (6:1-7)

¹ The word of the Lord came to me: ² "Son of man, set your face toward the mountains of Israel, and prophesy against them, ³ and say, You mountains of Israel, hear the word of the Lord God! Thus says the Lord God to the mountains and the hills, to the ravines and the valleys: Behold, I, even I, will bring a sword upon you, and I will destroy your high places. ⁴ Your altars shall become desolate, and your incense altars shall be broken; and I will cast down your slain before your idols. ⁵ And I will lay the dead bodies of the people of Israel before their idols; and I will scatter your bones round about your altars. ⁶ Wherever you dwell your cities shall be waste and your high places ruined, so that your altars will be waste and ruined, your idols broken and destroyed, your incense altars cut down, and your works wiped out. ⁷ And the slain shall fall in the midst of you, and you shall know that I am the Lord.

Since the dawning awareness of the mystery of the gods to man, he has associated the high place or the mountain with the abode of deity. The gods either dwelt in the heights or the heights became access ways to the gods who dwelt in the heavens above.

One of the earliest traditions of Israel had to do with the construction of the tower of Babel (Gen. 11:9). The word Babel (Heb. *babel*) means "gate of god."

Literally in the account the people had erected a ziggurat (i.e., a terraced temple tower) with a sanctuary upon its crest. Thus on the plain of Shinar there arose an artificial mountain as a place of worship. Also in the Old Testament one of the appelations for God is *El-Shaddai,* which derives from the Akkadian term *sadu* meaning mountain. In addition Abraham was confronted by Yahweh on the mountaintop, possibly Mount Moriah (Gen. 22), and the Temple of Israel was erected during Solomonic days on that same gaunt mountain.

While there was complete legitimacy about the early mountain sanctuaries in Israel, once the central sanctuary was erected and the ark of the covenant installed, efforts were made to declare other sanctuaries illegitimate. In the early days, however, such mountain sanctuaries as Mizpah, Nob, Ramah, Gibeon, Shiloh, and Jerusalem were considered sacred and related to the true worship of Yahweh. The high places of worship which survived through the subsequent years of Israelite history were largely connected with Canaanite fertility rites, an orgiastic worship embodying drunkenness and cultic prostitution. Associated with such sanctuaries were idols, sacred stones and altars, sacred trees, and syncretistic rites.

During the reforms of Josiah centering around 621 B.C. these sanctuaries were destroyed, and efforts were directed toward restoring the centrality of worship in Jerusalem (2 Kings 23). In the intervening years, between Josiah's death and Ezekiel's ministry, there had been a resurgence of these pagan cults.[39] In the very late sections of the book of Isaiah there are references to the popularity of these forms of religious expression (cf. Isa. 57).

The reason for the stern judgment of Ezekiel upon these sanctuaries was not based on the fact that they were pagan centers of worship but that Israelite worship in these places combined facets of the

moral worship of Yahweh with natural worship characterized by every conceivable form of moral corruption and human indignity. The *high places* of v. 3 were, in Ezekiel's day, the center of idolatry.

No other Old Testament writer so frequently employs the term *idols* as does Ezekiel. The word used for idols is quite interesting and comes from a Hebrew root meaning "to roll"; and thus some commentators derive the concept that the term implies large blocks of stone which had to be rolled due to their size but in which it was believed a spirit resided (Cooke, p. 69). On the other hand, this imagery may have sprung from the activities of the dung beetle, which rolled balls of dung to encase the eggs and sustain its progeny in the larvae stage. If the second of these interpretations is correct, then Ezekiel by employment of the term implies that idols are nothing more than excrement.

An ultimate insult and devastating judgment upon the syncretistic high places occurs in v. 4. Dead bodies of worshipers will be cast before the idols implying their impotency and hopelessness in confrontation with Yahweh. Yahweh ironically demonstrates in this horrible manner that the idols are no gods because they cannot protect their own.

2. Yahweh's Warnings Not Empty Threats (6:8–10)

8 "Yet I will leave some of you alive. When you have among the nations some who escape the sword, and when you are scattered through the countries, 9 then those of you who escape will remember me among the nations where they are carried captive, when I have broken their wanton heart which has departed from me, and blinded their eyes which turn wantonly after their idols; and they will be loathsome in their own sight for the evils which they have committed, for all their abominations. 10 And they shall know that I am the LORD; I have not said in vain that I would do this evil to them."

The act of God's judgment reenforces his complete sovereignity and inflexible resolve (v. 10). Although some will escape (v. 8), they have been permitted to do so

39 Cf. W. F. Albright, *Yahweh and the Gods of Canaan* (London: The Athlone Press, 1968), pp. 181–229.

not because of their righteousness, goodness, or fidelity to Yahweh. They are to be a living testimony of the certainty of Yahweh's judgment (vv. 8,9).

Twice in this passage the term *wanton* is used. Basically it means here to commit fornication or to be a harlot. In both instances it refers to a harlotrous relationship with other gods. Wanton eyes and wanton hearts characterized the people (v. 9). How striking! The wanton eye brings to the wanton heart the visual objective. It is similar to the story of Lot who first "looked" toward Sodom and then went to dwell there (cf. Gen. 13:10). The wanton heart produced the inward desires which in turn produced the outward acts. How true it is that man sees what his mind conditions him to see.

3. Judgment upon Idolatry Wherever Found (6:11–14)

¹¹ Thus says the Lord God: "Clap your hands, and stamp your foot, and say, Alas! because of all the evil abominations of the house of Israel; for they shall fall by the sword, by famine, and by pestilence. ¹² He that is far off shall die of pestilence; and he that is near shall fall by the sword; and he that is left and is preserved shall die of famine. Thus I will spend my fury upon them. ¹³ And you shall know that I am the Lord, when their slain lie among their idols round about their altars, upon every high hill, on all the mountain tops, under every green tree, and under every leafy oak, wherever they offered pleasing odor to all their idols. ¹⁴ And I will stretch out my hand against them, and make the land desolate and waste, throughout all their habitations, from the wilderness to Riblah. Then they will know that I am the Lord."

As the word of Yahweh's judgment through the prophet continues, the inescapable nature of that judgment is revealed (v. 12). No matter where the idolater may be, *far off* or *near*, the *fury* of Yahweh will be unleashed upon him. Literally there will be no escape from the judgment to come. Almost sadistic pleasure in inevitable judgment is voiced in v. 11. The act of clapping hands and stamping feet may be jestures indicative of deep grief and mourning or heightened joy. Since the words are addressed to the prophet who acts and reacts as Yahweh, this seems to suggest an almost malevolent gratification on the part of God.[40]

The *green tree, oak,* and *pleasing odor* are terms associated with and indicative of primitive religious practices. Both types of trees were considered sacred and played an important role in Canaanite fertility worship. The odor was that of burnt offerings, animal or human flesh, to honor the gods.

4. The Execution of Judgment (7:1–27)

Chapter 7 contains one of the more corrupt textual divisions of the book of Ezekiel. The text, as it now exists, has undergone significant emendation. Eichrodt in his commentary on Ezekiel points to more than forty cases in the brief chapter where partial restoration of the Hebrew text is required.

(1) The Stored Wrath of Yahweh (7:1–9)

¹ The word of the Lord came to me: ² "And you, O son of man, thus says the Lord God to the land of Israel: An end! The end has come upon the four corners of the land. ³ Now the end is upon you, and I will let loose my anger upon you, and will judge you according to your ways; and I will punish you for all your abominations. ⁴ And my eye will not spare you, nor will I have pity; but I will punish you for your ways, while your abominations are in your midst. Then you will know that I am the Lord.

⁵ "Thus says the Lord God: Disaster after disaster! Behold, it comes. ⁶ An end has come, the end has come; it has awakened against you. Behold, it comes. ⁷ Your doom has come to you, O inhabitant of the land; the time has come, the day is near, a day of tumult, and not of joyful shouting upon the mountains. ⁸ Now I will soon pour out my wrath upon you, and spend my anger against you, and judge you according to your ways; and I will punish you for all your abominations. ⁹ And my eye will not spare, nor will I have pity; I will punish you according to your ways, while your abominations are in your midst. Then you will know that I am the Lord, who smite.

The initial section (vv. 1–4) introduces a chapter-long theme. In previous passages

---

[40] "Alas!" (Heb. *'ach*) of v. 11 is translated "Aha!" in 25:3; 26:2; 36:2; and should be rendered as such here.

the rebellion of Israel was exposed revealing its apostate character and abominable acts. Now the stored wrath of Yahweh will sweep over them in a cataclysmic inundation.

Judgment once pronounced by Yahweh is a certainty and is all inclusive (v. 2). The phrase *four corners of the land* implies complete desolation, an end to all the land. A sudden unleashing of the jealous anger of Yahweh constitutes a major Old Testament concept of the nature of God.[41] Yet the overpowering wrath of Yahweh does not constitute a permanent attribute; rather it is a sporadic activity triggered by obsessive stubbornness on the part of man and activated to purge and renew.

The word *anger* (v. 3) apparently means nostril or nose. The imagery is quite obvious for anger is quickly seen in the flaring of the nostrils and rapidity of heavy audible breathing. No quarter is to be given in this judgment—there will be no pity (v. 4)— for Judah and Jerusalem will receive repetitive blows (i.e., *Disaster after disaster!* or calamity upon calamity (Eichrodt, *Ezekiel*, p. 101).

Judgment, predicted by prophets from the eighth century on but which the people discounted, would be roused from its sleep and brought to jarring reality (v. 6). The day to come would be one of tumult. The Hebrew implies panic, literally "to rush to and fro madly." This is the reverse of their anticipations for the day as one of *joyful shouting upon the mountains.* This phrase implies either the joyous sounds of the grape harvesters on the mountain slopes or the revelry of idolaters at the high places. Here it is taken to mean the former (cf. Isa. 16:10; Jer. 48:33).

But for Judah it will be a day of panic because the wrath of Yahweh will be poured out upon the people. These ancients, as many moderns, simply did not believe that Yahweh would execute his judgment. The word *wrath* means burning anger or furious rage, one which erupts

41 Cf. Eichrodt, *Theology,* pp. 258–269.

with volcanic ferocity and then subsides. It is this which an apostate people will face.

(2) *The Day of the Lord* (7:10–23a)

10 "Behold, the day! Behold, it comes! Your doom has come, injustice has blossomed, pride has budded. 11 Violence has grown up into a rod of wickedness; none of them shall remain, nor their abundance, nor their wealth; neither shall there be pre-eminence among them. 12 The time has come, the day draws near. Let not the buyer rejoice, nor the seller mourn, for wrath is upon all their multitude. 13 For the seller shall not return to what he has sold, while they live. For wrath is upon all their multitude; it shall not turn back; and because of his iniquity, none can maintain his life.

14 "They have blown the trumpet and made all ready; but none goes to battle, for my wrath is upon all their multitude. 15 The sword is without, pestilence and famine are within; he that is in the field dies by the sword; and him that is in the city famine and pestilence devour. 16 And if any survivors escape, they will be on the mountains, like doves of the valleys, all of them moaning, every one over his iniquity. 17 All hands are feeble, and all knees weak as water. 18 They gird themselves with sackcloth, and horror covers them; shame is upon all faces, and baldness on all their heads. 19 They cast their silver into the streets, and their gold is like an unclean thing; their silver and gold are not able to deliver them in the day of the wrath of the LORD; they cannot satisfy their hunger or fill their stomachs with it. For it was the stumbling block of their iniquity. 20 Their beautiful ornament they used for vainglory, and they made their abominable images and their detestable things of it; therefore I will make it an unclean thing to them. 21 And I will give it into the hands of foreigners for a prey, and to the wicked of the earth for a spoil; and they shall profane it. 22 I will turn my face from them, that they may profane my precious place; robbers shall enter and profane it, 23 and make a desolation.

The day of the Lord motif is here used by Ezekiel not to denote some future eschatological event but the imminent destruction of Jerusalem (cf. Amos 5:18–20; Isa. 2:11–22; Mal. 4:1). On this day there is the full flowering of Judah and Jerusalem as protagonists of Yahweh, and at the moment their cup of rebellion overflows, the reservoir of Yahweh's wrath breaks upon them (i.e., injustice in full bloom and pride well budded). The violence of the people, their overwhelming bent to evil, has created the condition which requires their destruction. Simultaneously with the ripening of their evil, judgment blossomed full. The two, full grown, were ready for a confrontation of finality (vv. 10,11).

The meaning of the word (Heb., *noah*) translated *preeminence* is quite difficult to ascertain, being used only here in the Old Testament. The RSV translation is based on a cognate Arabic word. Many of the older commentators derived *noah* from *nehi*, meaning wailing. If interpreted in the latter sense, then the judgment would be so devastating that the people would not even be able to wail and express mourning. They would be totally overawed and dumbfounded.

A perpetual weakness of man is broached beginning with v. 11. It is the problem of man's misguided sense as to what constitutes security. Judah's abundance, wealth, and status (social, political, and religious), gave the people a sense of well-being. In these they felt secure. Their fatal mistake was to forget that temporal things never grant security since they are subject to the constantly shifting affairs of life. While it is true that socio-political and economic prestige favorably impress men they neither avert the judgment nor allay the punishment of God.

When the wealth of Jerusalem is stripped away by the avenging invader, there is panic. The commerce of Jerusalem, the heart of its financial structure, will be reduced to chaotic shambles (vv. 12,13). Those within the city will succumb to *famine* and *pestilence*, and those who escape to the surrounding fields will be savagely cut down by maruding bands of invaders (v. 15).

Imagery in vv. 14–18 is startling. The watchmen on the walls of Jerusalem had sounded the alarm, *blown the trumpet* (lit., blasted a blast) upon a wind instrument. This was a call to arms, a summons to the inhabitants to man the defenses. There is no response other than mourning. Ezekiel likens this mourning to that of the

doves who roosted among gaunt cliffs and filled the valleys below with their doleful plaintive call (v. 16).

The suddenness of the wrath of Yahweh leaves them with an uncontrollable weakness (v. 17).[42] Rather than preparing for battle with armor and weapons, they adorn themselves with the vesture of mourning and make themselves bald (v. 18). The act of shaving or plucking the hair as an act of mourning is expressly condemned in Israelite religious legislation (cf. Deut. 14:1).

That which had formerly constituted their source of pride and security becomes as nothing (vv. 19–23a). Wealth of *gold* and *silver* is cast aside as if it were an abhorrent unclean commodity. *Unclean* implies sexual offense and is thus a thing to be abhorred. (cf. Lev. 20:21; Ezra 9:11). The uselessness of wealth, in such an event, is boldly dramatized by Ezekiel. Money is useless for there is no food to buy! The incisive point, however, is that ill-used wealth was their downfall. They had utilized their gold and silver to produce images or idols which in turn were as powerless before the judgment of Yahweh as was their money (vv. 19,20).

Not only would an unclean people be delivered up but all sanctuaries where a corrupt religion had been practiced including *my precious place* (i.e., the Temple and the holy of holies). Yahweh will in no way attempt to protect the Temple for it had become as the people and through the people contaminated, defiled, and unclean (v. 22).

(3) The People Judged as They Have Judged (7:23b–27)

"Because the land is full of bloody crimes and the city is full of violence, 24 I will bring the worst of the nations to take possession of their houses; I will put an end to their proud might, and their holy places shall be profaned. 25 When anguish comes, they will seek peace, but there shall be none. 26 Disaster comes upon disaster, rumor follows rumor; they seek a vision from the prophet, but the law perishes

---

[42] The LXX reads "and all thighs shall be defiled with moisture," meaning their fright was so great they could not control their kidneys.

from the priest, and counsel from the elders. **27** The king mourns, the prince is wrapped in despair, and the hands of the people of the land are palsied by terror. According to their way I will do to them, and according to their own judgments I will judge them; and they shall know that I am the LORD."

When this horrible fate befalls Jerusalem, it will be at the hands of the *worst of nations*. The Hebrew word *ra'* is translated *worst* in the RSV but literally means worst in the sense of being evil or wicked; at times it implies ethical evil. Thus for the most evil or wicked offender Jerusalem, the most evil or wicked avenger is used. This does not compliment Nebuchadnezzar and Babylonia! And in the moment of their disaster there will be no hope, yet the people sue for peace (v. 25). As is characteristic of human beings, when it is too late for peace they pursue it.

The plight of the people comes not only from the horror of the siege but from the lack of leadership. There will be none to give them counsel, to distinguish truth from rumor, to speak the laws of Yahweh, or to provide prophetic vision (v. 26). Thus there is complete confusion.

Four groups of leaders are mentioned: prophets, priests, elders, and court officials. The vision of the *prophet*, the law from the *priest*, and wise counsel by the *elders* had traditionally been held in Israel as gifts of Yahweh. Even these had been cut off. Could it be that the prophet had so corrupted his office that he no longer could receive a vision! Could it be that the elder had lost interest in wisdom by devoting his energies to the pursuit of status! And the one above all who in a time of national crises was to maintain at least a semblance of stability, the *prince*, withdrew into despair. Such was the case. How awesome is the fate of a nation who in crises has no leadership. Possibly the despair of the prince [43] was heightened by the ineffective-

ness of the elders, who served in an advisory capacity to the king and governmental officials (cf. 2 Kings 23:1; Jer. 26:17; 27).

IV. The Temple Visions (8:1—11:25)

Previous to this point the prophet has been involved with relating his call as a spokesman of Yahweh and speaking the message received to the exiles in Babylon. Even as he speaks to his fellow exiles the Spirit of Yahweh descends upon him, and he is given insight into the abominations of the inhabitants of Jerusalem.

The inclusion of a date, coupled with a shift in locality (v. 3), implies a totally new section of the prophetic message. In this division (8:1—11:25) Ezekiel is transported in the spirit from the Chebar exilic community to the Jerusalem community. In Jerusalem the corrupt nature of Judahite worship is unveiled. The prophet witnesses the idolatrous practices and views the coming of the representatives of Yahweh who are to seal the fate of the inhabitants of Jerusalem. A divinely appointed scribe marks those to be spared, while divine executioners are sent out on a grisly task of spreading death. The city is subjected to the fire of destruction, and the glory of God departs from the Temple. After Ezekiel has witnessed these calamitous events he is transported in the spirit back to the Babylonian community.

1. The Vision of Temple Idolatry (8:1-18)

(1) Prelude to the Vision (8:1-4)

1 In the sixth year, in the sixth month, on the fifth day of the month, as I sat in my house, with the elders of Judah sitting before me, the hand of the Lord GOD fell there upon me. **2** Then I beheld, and, lo, a form that had the appearance of a man; below what appeared to be his loins it was fire, and above his loins it was like the appearance of brightness, like gleaming bronze. **3** He put forth the form of a hand, and took me by a lock of my head; and the Spirit lifted me up between earth and heaven, and brought me in visions of God to Jerusalem, to the entrance of the gateway of the inner court that faces north, where was the seat of the image of jealousy, which provokes

---

43 *Prince*—Heb., *nasi'*. Ezekiel favors the term "prince" rather than "king" for the chief political office in Israel. The designation of ruler as prince is a premonarchal motif. Cf. E. A. Spieser, *Oriental and Biblical Studies* (Philadelphia: University of Pennsylvania Press, 1967), pp. 113–122.

to jealousy. 4 And behold, the glory of the God of Israel was there, like the vision that I saw in the plain.

As Ezekiel sat in his own home in the exilic community on the Chebar canal, probably in the year 591 B.C., there came to him a deputation of the *elders of Judah.* Those who came were the leading men who represented the people of the exile, and this situation thus implies that by the sixth year of the exile the exilic community had developed an organizational pattern similar to that which had existed in their homeland. While the prophet was with the elders, Yahweh came to him in a vision, and in the resultant ecstatic state Ezekiel was transported *in visions* to the Temple in Jerusalem (v. 3).

Certain elements in the preface statement imply that Ezekiel did have a significant degree of prestige among the exilic group. We see him as the owner of his own home and one to whom the elders came for advice or counsel. The elders were esteemed men, literally "men of the full beard." Interestingly the book of Ezra employs similar imagery and uses a term meaning "grey headed" to signify one who was an elder. In both instances there is emphasis upon a correlation between age and wisdom.

Since the first sight seen by Ezekiel in the Temple was the *seat of the image of jealousy,* its meaning is quite important. May suggests an image of Tammuz, Albright suggests a wall slab depicting cultic scenes, and Fisch points to an image of Asherah.[44]

Jealousy is from the verb which means to acquire, such as land, cattle, etc. Basically the term implies possession. The major emphasis here is not precisely which image was installed but that the installation of any image indicated as a dispossession of Yahweh. Thus the ire of Yahweh was evoked because the image symbolized his dispossession.

___

[44] W. F. Albright, *Archaeology and the Religion of Israel* (Baltimore: The Johns Hopkins Press, 1946), pp. 165–166; S. Fisch, p. 42.

Regardless of the exact nature of the god or what god was involved, the import is devastating. Pagan emblems, signs or statues, had been installed by a corrupt people in the holy place of Yahweh. No greater blasphemy could have been perpetuated. In the words of the psalmist, "They set up their own signs for signs" (Psalm 74:4). Though we may view in horror with Ezekiel the displacement of the true God by man's fabricated concepts, we should sense no ease. Within twentieth-century society we find placed over against the brotherhood of man the depredation of racial and social injustice. Unity of the faith has been displaced by corrosive divisiveness. The dignity of man has been displaced by the indignity of warfare. And oneness in Christ has been marred by marks of class status within the community of faith. It could be said that pagan emblems are still emblazoned over God's altar.

(2) The Worship of Images and Idols (8:5-13)

5 Then he said to me, "Son of man, lift up your eyes now in the direction of the north." So I lifted up my eyes toward the north, and behold, north of the altar gate, in the entrance, was this image of jealousy. 6 And he said to me, "Son of man, do you see what they are doing, the great abominations that the house of Israel are committing here, to drive me far from my sanctuary? But you will see still greater abominations."

7 And he brought me to the door of the court; and when I looked, behold, there was a hole in the wall. 8 Then said he to me, "Son of man, dig in the wall"; and when I dug in the wall, lo, there was a door. 9 And he said to me, "Go in, and see the vile abominations that they are committing here." 10 So I went in and saw; and there, portrayed upon the wall round about, were all kinds of creeping things, and loathsome beasts, and all the idols of the house of Israel. 11 And before them stood seventy men of the elders of the house of Israel, with Jaazaniah the son of Shaphan standing among them. Each had his censer in his hand, and the smoke of the cloud of incense went up. 12 Then he said to me, "Son of man, have you seen what the elders of the house of Israel are doing in the dark, every man in his room of pictures? For they say, 'The LORD does not see us, the LORD has forsaken the land.'" 13 He said also

to me, "You will see still greater abominations which they commit."

As the visionary Temple experience unfolds it begins to expand the vista, but in so doing there is a focus upon the more blasphemous practices within the Temple. Ezekiel is commanded to uncover a hidden door through which he may enter and view secretive pagan rites (v. 7). It is not that the elders practiced such rites in secret in order not to be observed but that these were rites to be conducted in secret.

As to the exact religion involved in the rites there is debate. We may presume the rites to be connected with either Egyptian religion or certain Canaanite rituals.[45]

Indications are that these rites were considered to be most horrible and are referred to as *vile abominations*. Specifically the situation involved the pure worship of a pagan deity within Yahweh's Temple. The rites do not seem to be syncretistic in nature, i.e., a blending of heathen and Israelite religious acts to worship Yahweh. It was unalloyed idolatry practiced by defectors from the true faith of Yahweh.

The most appalling aspect was not that such would occur in the Temple, but that the worshipers were the *seventy men of the elders of the house of Israel, with Jaazaniah the son of Shaphan* (cf. 2 Kings 22:3 ff.).

The elders who were the leaders of the people and counselors to the court were themselves saying *The Lord does not see us, the Lord has forsaken the land*. The leadership of Judah had rationalized and justified their idolatry. If the zenith of religious expression and commitment on the part of the popular leaders was idolatry, would the common man rise higher? They who were to be the wise instructors of Judah to guide the people in the ways of Yahweh were leading the people by example into defection from Yahweh (cf. Isa. 3:12).

45 Cf. Albright, *op. cit.*, p. 66, who proposes that this was an Egyptian religious rite, and Theodore Gaster, "Ezekiel and the Mysteries," JBL, LX (1941), 289–310, who prefers a Canaanite origin for the rites.

Within this passage we see Ezekiel as the debater against popular Judahite religious shibboleths. In a number of instances the prophet picks up a popular religious catch-phrase or slogan and contests its validity (cf. 8:12; 9:9; 11:3,15; 12:22, 27: 18:2,25; 33:10,24,30; 35:12; 37:11). These are usually introduced with a formula (i.e., "for they say," "who say, or simply "saying"). Such popular slogans were to the prophet indicators of assumed societal positions on religion and, due to their very falseness, had to be challenged.

(3) The Worship of Tammuz and the Sun (8:14–18)

14 Then he brought me to the entrance of the north gate of the house of the LORD; and behold, there sat women weeping for Tammuz. 15 Then he said to me, "Have you seen this, O son of man? You will see still greater abominations than these."
16 And he brought me into the inner court of the house of the LORD; and behold, at the door of the temple of the LORD, between the porch and the altar, were about twenty-five men, with their backs to the temple of the LORD, and their faces toward the east, worshiping the sun toward the east. 17 Then he said to me, "Have you seen this, O son of man? Is it too slight a thing for the house of Judah to commit the abominations which they commit here, that they should fill the land with violence, and provoke me further to anger? Lo, they put the branch to their nose. 18 Therefore I will deal in wrath; my eye will not spare, nor will I have pity; and though they cry in my ears with a loud voice, I will not hear them."

Again the scene shifts. Attention is directed from the shrouded rites of the elders toward a group of women worshiping Tammuz (v. 14) and a body of men involved in sun worship (v. 16). Two charges are made: (1) the Temple had become the sanctuary for pagan cults; (2) the general population had adopted the false religious assumptions of the elders (cf. 8:12b).

The worship of Tammuz is hidden in the mysterious shadows of the ancient Near East, and this is the only direct Old Testament reference to the cult of Tammuz. Tammuz was a Sumerian fertility god related to the spring festival of renewal. In the Gilgamesh Epic he appears as the betrayed lover of Ishtar, the Sumerian goddess of love.[46] Such worship had at its center sexual rites symbolic of procreation. When the verdure of the plains wilted due to summer heat and lack of moisture, this symbolized the death of Tammuz. Elaborate rites were performed with choruses of weeping women (i.e., devotees of Tammuz) lamenting his death. In Babylonian worship Ishtar mourned for Dumuzi, the god of vegetation, who appeared to be overcome by the intense heat of the month of Tammuz (i.e., June–July). During this period when nature seemed to die rites were held. The female devotees of the god bewailed the dead Dumuzi in an effort to effect his return to life and with his return a revitalization of nature. The motifs of Tammuz worship are quite similar to those of the Adonis myth and the Osiris cult. It was this type of rite that was being performed in the Temple.

Much more ancient, however, was the worship of the sun (v. 16). Sun worship was rampant in Judah during the reign of Manasseh and was purged by Josiah during his reforms (cf. 2 Kings 23:5,11; Jer. 44:17; Deut. 4:19). Evidently Ezekiel was witnessing a resurgence of this cult.

The words of Ezekiel concerning these worshipers are fascinating. They were worshiping *between the porch and the altar, . . . with their backs to the temple of the Lord.* Literally, they had turned their backs on the true God and within his most hallowed place embraced a false religion. They had but to turn about to find that which was real. How ironic! This could have been nothing more than an act of defiant renunciation of Yahweh.

By these acts, that is the turning of the Temple into a "three-ring circus" of idolatry, *they put the branch to their nose.* All attempts both to translate and interpret this verse seem to fail.[47]

It is known, however, that gifts were proffered to the nose of the gods of Egypt, and this may be connected with solar worship. Others look upon this as a sign of contempt or mockery.[48]

The *branch to their nose* may be a ritual act of the pagan cults whose symbolism has been lost. The LXX saw it as a sign of contempt or mockery, while the Jewish commentators Kimchi and Rashi interpreted *branch* allegorically as *crepitus ventris* and see the whole as an abomination which created a stench in the nostrils of Yahweh.

The total thrust of chapter 8 points to the spiritual degeneracy of Judah and Jerusalem with cultic sins defiling the Temple and social evil impregnating the land (v. 17). The Temple, the abode of Yahweh, had been changed into a hall of infamy where people flaunted their pagan ideologies to the shame and rage of Yahweh.

2. The Vision of the Slain Idolaters (9: 1-11)

[1] Then he cried in my ears with a loud voice, saying, "Draw near, you executioners of the city, each with his destroying weapon in his hand." [2] And lo, six men came from the direction of the upper gate, which faces north, every man with his weapon for slaughter in his hand, and with them was a man clothed in linen, with a writing case at his side. And they went in and stood beside the bronze altar.

[3] Now the glory of the God of Israel had gone up from the cherubim on which it rested to the threshold of the house; and he called to the man clothed in linen, who had the writing case at his side. [4] And the LORD said to him, "Go through the city, through Jerusalem, and put a mark upon the foreheads of the men who sigh and groan over all the abominations that are committed in it." [5] And to the others he said in my hearing, "Pass through the city after him, and smite; your eye shall not spare, and you shall show no pity; [6] slay old men outright, young men and maidens, little children and women, but touch no one upon whom is the mark. And begin at my sanctuary." So they began with the elders who were before the house. [7] Then he said to them, "Defile the

[46] Pritchard, J. B. ed., Ancient Near Eastern Texts Relating to the Old Testament (Princeton: The Princeton Univesity Press, 1950).

[47] Cf. Shalom Spiegel, "Toward Certainty in Ezekiel," JBL, LIV (1935), 152–159.

[48] Cf. especially Nahum M. Sarna, "Ezekiel 8:17: A Fresh Examination," *Harvard Theological Review,* LVII (1964), 347–352, who resolves the problem by emending the text to read "and they provoke me still more, forsee, they send out the strong men to execute their anger/to anger me."

house, and fill the courts with the slain. Go forth." So they went forth, and smote in the city. 8 And while they were smiting, and I was left alone, I fell upon my face, and cried, "Ah Lord God! wilt thou destroy all that remains of Israel in the outpouring of thy wrath upon Jerusalem?"

9 Then he said to me, "The guilt of the house of Israel and Judah is exceedingly great; the land is full of blood, and the city full of injustice; for they say, 'The LORD has forsaken the land, and the LORD does not see.' 10 As for me, my eye will not spare, nor will I have pity, but I will requite their deeds upon their heads."

11 And lo, the man clothed in linen, with the writing case at his side, brought back word, saying, "I have done as thou didst command me."

When the caldron of Judah's religious corruption had overflowed, the divinely appointed executioners of God's judgment were sent against the people and city. As such the executioners (i.e., supernatural creatures in the form of men) were accompanied by a scribe (v. 2). The angelic scribe has parallels. In Egypt the god Thot and in Babylonia the god Nabu performed functions as divine scribes.

In the Talmud the divine scribe of Ezekiel is identified as Gabriel (cf. *Yoma,* 77a). Whereas the function of the *six men* was destruction and judgment, that of the scribe was grace. He was instructed to *mark* those who *sigh and groan over all the abominations* (v. 4). The *mark* constituted the last letter of the Hebrew alphabet executed in the old form like a T or cross (cf. Gen. 4:15; Ex. 12:22ff.). This expression and that of 5:3,4 are the only concrete allusions to the faithful among the inhabitants of Jerusalem.

Two major ideas are involved. One, in God's judgment there is justice. Two, there are always the choice few who maintain a sensitivity to true faith in spite of conditions. Seemingly the popular thing to do was to deny Yahweh's demands upon life. Yet there was a minority who had not lost their ability to feel, to care for the true faith, to be grieved over the sin of Judah and Jerusalem, and to bereave the corruption of the Temple. These the scribe would

mark, and thus, in the coming slaughter, they would be spared. This group alone had enough remaining sensitivity and potential responsiveness to be redemptive possibilities.

It is striking that Ezekiel sees destruction and slaughter initiating in the Temple (i.e., *sanctuary,* v. 6). This is the place where one would naturally expect the minority of the faithful to be. Doubtless the intent of the directive is to show that the destruction will begin at the place of greatest corruption, the Temple. Let this be an object lesson to all religious men in all ages!

The magnitude of the slaughter, merciless and unrelenting, crushes Ezekiel, and he cries out in utter anguish and despair saying *wilt thou destroy all the remains of Israel . . . ?* Obviously the number marked to be spared were so few in comparison to the number to be slaughtered it appeared to the prophet that all would be destroyed.

This verse and one other (11:13), in the early sections of the book, give an insight into the inner man of Ezekiel. It is this hidden heart of Ezekiel which will shatter the outward rigidity of his life and break forth with the tender blessing of pastoral care (ch. 34).

Yahweh answers the cry of Ezekiel and specifies why such a horrible judgment is required (vv. 9,10). Three major charges are leveled against the people of Jerusalem: (1) The land is *full of blood.* (2) The city of Jerusalem is *full of injustice.* (3) The people have accepted a false religious assumption: *the Lord has forsaken the land, and the Lord does not see.* The first of the three charges is specifically elaborated upon in a later section of Ezekiel (cf. comment on ch. 22).

Such an indictment is explicit only when we view the end result of the Judahites vile religious, social and economic practices. Operating upon a principle of expediency, all things became subservient to the end result. Human life was not sacred if it thwarted or diminished the goals toward which they strived. Men preyed upon men. The animal nature had risen above the elective nature in God's people.

The second charge, that of injustice, calls to remembrance the similar scathing indictments of Amos and Micah. Privation of the innocent, extortion from travelers, abuse of widows and orphans due to their disadvantaged status, assassination of character through premeditated slander, the taking of bribes for the purpose of perverting justice, the exacting of exorbitant interest rates, contempt for filial authority, adultery, and perversion only begin the list of offenses committed. They who were supposed to be the enlightened ones had become the children of darkness.

Of all charges, the third is the most devastating. These offenses were committed with the view that they would not be held accountable for them. But worse is the implication that it was really not their fault. They say, "The Lord has forsaken the land"—it was due to this that they sinned. Man has ever sought a scapegoat for his iniquity. Since they were without God, then they were left to develop their own norms for life and conduct without regard for Yahweh. In addition, since Yahweh had forsaken them and was, thus, no longer concerned with them, he did not see their sins, so they could do what they wished with impunity, and there would be no judgment. If Yahweh had forsaken them, how could he judge them?

The total invalidity of his position is pointed out by Ezekiel (vv. 10,11). The certainty of judgment is forcefully asserted when the scribe records the divine mandate. With the recording, the fate of the corrupt and rebellious is sealed.

3. The Vision of the Lord Forsaking the Temple (10:1–22)

[1] Then I looked, and behold, on the firmament that was over the heads of the cherubim there appeared above them something like a sapphire, in form resembling a throne. [2] And he said to the man clothed in linen, "Go in among the whirling wheels underneath the cherubim; fill your hands with burning coals from between the cherubim, and scatter them over the city."

And he went in before my eyes. [3] Now the cherubim were standing on the south side of the house, when the man went in; and a cloud filled the inner court. [4] And the glory of the LORD went up from the cherub to the threshold of the house; and the house was filled with the cloud, and the court was full of the brightness of the glory of the LORD. [5] And the sound of the wings of the cherubim was heard as far as the outer court, like the voice of God Almighty when he speaks.

[6] And when he commanded the man clothed in linen, "Take fire from between the whirling wheels, from between the cherubim," he went in and stood beside a wheel. [7] And a cherub stretched forth his hand from between the cherubim to the fire that was between the cherubim, and took some of it, and put it into the hands of the man clothed in linen, who took it and went out. [8] The cherubim appeared to have the form of a human hand under their wings.

[9] And I looked, and behold, there were four wheels beside the cherubim, one beside each cherub; and the appearance of the wheels was like sparkling chrysolite. [10] And as for their appearance, the four had the same likeness, as if a wheel were within a wheel. [11] When they went, they went in any of their four directions without turning as they went, but in whatever direction the front wheel faced the others followed without turning as they went. [12] And their rims, and their spokes, and the wheels were full of eyes round about—the wheels that the four of them had. [13] As for the wheels, they were called in my hearing the whirling wheels. [14] And every one had four faces: the first face was the face of the cherub, and the second face was the face of a man, and the third face of a lion, and the fourth the face of an eagle.

[15] And the cherubim mounted up. These were the living creatures that I saw by the river Chebar. [16] And when the cherubim went, the wheels went beside them; and when the cherubim lifted up their wings to mount up from the earth, the wheels did not turn from beside them. [17] When they stood still, these stood still, and when they mounted up, these mounted up with them; for the spirit of the living creatures was in them.

[18] Then the glory of the LORD went forth from the threshold of the house, and stood over the cherubim. [19] And the cherubim lifted up their wings and mounted up from the earth in my sight as they went forth, with the wheels beside them; and they stood at the door of the east gate of the house of the LORD; and the glory of the God of Israel was over them.

[20] These were the living creatures that I saw

underneath the God of Israel by the river Chebar; and I knew that they were cherubim. 21 Each had four faces, and each four wings, and underneath their wings the semblance of human hands. 22 And as for the likeness of their faces, they were the very faces whose appearance I had seen by the river Chebar. They went every one straight forward.

This passage's central facet is contained in vv. 18,19, for it is toward this one agonizing action and truth that the entire Temple vision is directed. These verses contain the climactically dramatic moment. Ezekiel experiences the identical theophanic vision which occurred in his call experience but with an added person, the scribe clothed in linen (v. 2).

A command is given by Yahweh to the scribe to initiate destruction of the holy city by holy fire (i.e., the distributing of *burning coals*). The gathering of coals from the lower section of the throne chariot (vv. 2,6) may imply some type of holy fire associated with the theophany. It could well be the case that the coals were gathered from the actual altar of the Temple above which the theophany was centered. Thus the destruction would originate from the Temple and not be initiated in the Temple.

Whereas in Isaiah (cf. Isa. 6:6 ff.) the coals were symbolic of purging and purifying, here they are symbolical of a judgmental destruction, which comes from a divine mandate. There can be no mistaking the implied meaning that Yahweh himself was executing judgment. The man clothed in linen (v. 1) is undoubtedly the same as the scribe in chapter 9. Literally, he who had previously moved about the city dispensing the grace of Yahweh, now spreads the judgment (v. 7). Doom and hope, judgment and grace are inseparable facets of God's activity toward man. Eichrodt says of this incident, "What is emphasized is that Yahweh himself turns the fire kindled in his honour into the fire of his wrath, in order to put an end to his own city" (Eichrodt, *Ezekiel*, p. 134). Once the command has been issued and the angelic figure initiates the destruction, Yahweh de-

parts from his Temple and people.

Indeed it is difficult for us to comprehend the full shock of the act of Yahweh in withdrawing his presence from the Temple. The reason for the departure of the glory of God had been made crystal clear; a corrupt people had monstrously fouled the holiness of the Temple, and therefore a holy God could neither abide with them nor within the Temple. Wickedness by its very presence repulses holiness.

This, the most extreme action on the part of a sovereign God, reveals the true extent of the sins of Judah and Jerusalem. Their sin had created such revulsion and loathing on the part of Yahweh that there was no recourse but to withdraw. When man becomes so offensive to God, there is little else left to do. From the moment of God's withdrawal and the resultant destruction there may still be religion, but it would be godless, ineffectual, and ultimately meaningless. This, however, was nothing new to Judah, for they had been practicing a godless religion. The difference is, now they will know!

Even in the harshness of stern divine judgment there is revealed, on the part of Yahweh, a twinge of godly bereavement. As the theophany departed from the Temple, there was a lingering for a moment over the *east gate* (v. 19). It is through this same gate that the glory of the Lord will return (cf. 43:4). The act imputes to Yahweh an emotion of overwhelming love for the Temple and for his people. How reluctant Yahweh was to depart from his people, knowing the inevitable consequences.

Here we stand in the very presence of the covenant love of God, a love which continues to radiate toward man in spite of what he is and what he becomes. This may well imply that Yahweh does not depart from man without suffering on Yahweh's part. How little do we know even now of the fathomless depths of God's love and concern for mankind! Would it do violence to the nature of God to say that with broken heart he gave up his own to their own devices and the natural causes which sealed their doom?

4. The Vision of Judgment upon Iniquitous Temple Leaders (11:1-21)

As the glory of God departs from the Temple there seems to be an interruption of the action which is continued in vv. 22–23 with the actual departure. The placing of the indictment against the leaders at this point interrupts the narrative and points to an editorial insertion.

(1) The Council of Infamy (11:1-4)

¹ The Spirit lifted me up, and brought me to the east gate of the house of the LORD, which faces east. And behold, at the door of the gateway there were twenty-five men; and I saw among them Jaazaniah the son of Azzur, and Pelatiah the son of Benaiah, princes of the people. ² And he said to me, "Son of man, these are the men who devise iniquity and who give wicked counsel in this city; ³ who say, 'The time is not near to build houses; this city is the caldron, and we are the flesh.' ⁴ Therefore prophesy against them, prophesy, O son of man."

The primary burden of guilt lies upon the leaders because they were the ones who *devised iniquity* and gave *wicked counsel.* It may well be that the account of the departure of the glory of the Lord was interrupted at this point in order specifically to condemn the leaders and their acts which were most responsible for the departure.

Specified offenses are twofold. To devise means to plan, to take into account, to scheme, or to devise procedures oftentimes with the connotation of evil intent. This word tends to imply a type of natural cunning or ingenuity in producing schemes. That which was devised was *iniquity.* Inherent in the usage of the word is the idea of trouble, travail, or sorrow. As applied to the leaders, here one may literally use the term troublemaker, but in this case such is not of sufficient force to connote their offense. Let us say that they had wicked, trouble-making, iniquitous imaginations, and out of their degenerate minds they produced sorrow for the people.

Wicked counsel implies evil in its most insidious form. That is the giving advice or counsel with full knowledge that it is untrue. The type of counsel here referred to has in several Old Testament usages the connotation of plans formulated with perception and wisdom that came from God. The charge could be that of perverting, contorting, or twisting, with full knowledge that they were so doing, the advice which issued from Yahweh (cf. Isa. 11:2; Prov. 8:14; 21:30; Jer. 32:19). The implication in v. 3 is that the intent and counsel of the leaders was directly contrary to the express desire of Yahweh.

Although the import of v. 7 is not at all certain, it could be construed to mean that the leaders clung tenaciously to the belief that Jerusalem was inviolate. It may even mean that they were willing to accede to a portion of Ezekiel's pronouncements, i.e., that which implied an attack upon the city; but they would not accept any word which spoke of the city's destruction. Jerusalem to them meant sanctuary though it boiled like a caldron and they like flesh in it. Since the leaders believed falsely that Yahweh would deliver them, they insisted *The time is not near to build houses.* For had not such judgment been long and loudly proclaimed by prophets, yet had never come to pass! Certainly this too would pass away, and they would be able to build. Had not the city previously faced aggressors without destruction? This is typical of the false sense of security provided by the corrupt and inept religious leaders to a people who wished to hear a mirroring of their own thoughts.[49]

(2) Charges Against Iniquitous Counselors (11:5-13)

⁵ And the Spirit of the LORD fell upon me, and he said to me, "Say, Thus says the LORD: So you think, O house of Israel; for I know the things that come into your mind. ⁶ You have multiplied your slain in this city, and have

---

49 KJV reads "It is not near; let us build houses." This implies a specific interpretation of the verse by the translator, who felt the words to imply total security.

filled its streets with the slain. 7 Therefore thus says the Lord God: Your slain whom you have laid in the midst of it, they are the flesh, and this city is the caldron; but you shall be brought forth out of the midst of it. 8 You have feared the sword; and I will bring the sword upon you, says the Lord God. 9 And I will bring you forth out of the midst of it, and give you into the hands of foreigners, and execute judgments upon you. 10 You shall fall by the sword; I will judge you at the border of Israel; and you shall know that I am the Lord. 11 This city shall not be your caldron, nor shall you be the flesh in the midst of it; I will judge you at the border of Israel; 12 and you shall know that I am the Lord; for you have not walked in my statutes, nor executed my ordinances, but have acted according to the ordinances of the nations that are round about you."

13 And it came to pass, while I was prophesying, that Pelatiah the son of Benaiah died. Then I fell down upon my face, and cried with a loud voice, and said, "Ah Lord God! wilt thou make a full end of the remnant of Israel?"

As Ezekiel continues the oracle against the leaders, the fact of Yahweh's knowledge of that which is within their minds (i.e., the motivations and intents which lie hidden behind the charge of v. 2) is made evident. That, however, which is hidden to man is known to Yahweh. The leaders took refuge in the concept that the thoughts of the mind were hidden from all, including Yahweh. Not only does Yahweh have knowledge of their ill counsel but of their deeds, which have made of them the instruments of decay.

Your slain (v. 7) may be connected with the charge of v. 3 and coupled with the depiction of the avengers in chapter 9. The slain refer to those whom the leaders had previously betrayed or sacrificed upon the altars of religious, political, or economic expediency (cf. 22:1–12). In addition it may well include their future victims, those who will be slain in the coming catastrophe. It was due to the complicity of the leaders in creating the conditions for judgment that judgment will be required of them. In a real sense those sacrificed in the judgment upon Judah and Jerusalem became those slain by the leaders.

An additional charge is leveled against them (v. 12). They had adopted as their norm of conduct *the ordinances of the nations . . . round about.* The leadership of Israel had premeditatively and with willful purpose lowered themselves to the standards of surrounding nations. They had substituted the highest standards of Yahweh for the lowest standards of men. So enamored had they become with their neighbors that they sought a level of compatibility with them. The standards of an alien people, rather than those of Yahweh, had become consistent with their desires.

The death of Pelatiah (v. 13) may be indicative of the power of the given prophetic word. The enormity of the charges of Ezekiel and the open indictment of the leaders may have so shocked Pelatiah that he died. Rare indeed is the leader, especially one under the mantle of religious leadership, who can survive the open revealing of his corruption without one of three events occurring: the onset of death swift or slow, the destruction of the one who exposed him, or genuine repentance.

Pelatiah's death produces a startling and unexpected response on the part of Ezekiel. The swiftness, sternness, and finality of the judgment would be, one may surmise, precisely what Ezekiel had anticipated. Yet he is shocked! The event probably sealed in the mind of Ezekiel the full import of his prophetic oracles. What had happened to Pelatiah was going to happen to all the leaders, all the people! Ezekiel now comes face to face with the immensity of Yahweh's displeasure with his people. They will be delivered up in the sternest of judgments. Thus the inner heart of Ezekiel breaks through the outer perimeter of firm discipline, and his agony is made clear.

(3) *The Inward Change (11:14–21)*

14 And the word of the Lord came to me: 15 "Son of man, your brethren, even your brethren, your fellow exiles, the whole house of Israel, all of them, are those of whom the inhabitants of Jerusalem have said, 'They have gone far from the Lord; to us this land is given for a possession.' 16 Therefore say, 'Thus says the Lord God: Though I removed them far off

among the nations, and though I scattered them among the countries, yet I have been a sanctuary to them for a while in the countries where they have gone.' [17] Therefore say, 'Thus says the Lord God: I will gather you from the peoples, and assemble you out of the countries where you have been scattered, and I will give you the land of Israel.' [18] And when they come there, they will remove from it all its detestable things and all its abominations. [19] And I will give them one heart, and put a new spirit within them; I will take the stony heart out of their flesh and give them a heart of flesh, [20] that they may walk in my statutes and keep my ordinances and obey them; and they shall be my people, and I will be their God. [21] But as for those whose heart goes after their detestable things and their abominations, I will require their deeds upon their own heads, says the Lord God."

Again the word comes to Ezekiel, but this time it is fused with hope and doubtless speaks to the agony of the prophet reflected in v. 13. This hope radiates from the concept of Yahweh as sanctuary (v. 16) and Yahweh as re-creator of Israel (v. 19).

A statement of incredible insight and force initiates one of the two primary features of this passage: *yet I have been a sanctuary to them . . . in the countries where they have gone.* This is the beginning of a major breakthrough in the understanding of the nature of Yahweh. Late in Israelite theological development the concept came that Yahweh had power and exercised dominion outside the geographical boundaries of Israel. Twice in the book of Ezekiel there is the phrase, "I will judge you at the border of Israel," but strikingly enough they are in this same general section (cf. 11:10,11). It seems we have here two ideas side by side, that of God's exercising judgment within the borders of the land and also the exercising of his presence in other nations. The somewhat traditional stance of Israel was to provide a sanctuary for Yahweh or to seek sanctuary within the Temple of Yahweh but not to look upon Yahweh himself as sanctuary.

Exilic conditions did not permit a temple, and thus sacrificial worship and full ritual could not be practiced. It may well imply that the exiles felt absolute religious futility, since traditionally Israelite worship was an act of ritual connected with a sanctuary. That which is here implied in rudimentary form is an idea certainly not typical of hard core priestly thought. Yahweh as sanctuary ultimately means that temple and cult, structure and forms which tradition had produced to embellish the worship of Yahweh were, in the final analysis, of secondary importance.

The second major idea of the passage has to do with Yahweh as the re-creator of Israel, of the *one heart* (note the marg., "a new" rather than "one") and *new spirit* (v. 19). Both extreme judgment and change were absolute necessities for Israel. As always, initiative is on the part of Yahweh, for it is not within the power of man to perform such radical surgery upon himself. Specifically the "heart change" has to do with a oneness of inner will among the people. The new spirit is divine energy imparted to generate the reviviscent heart.

One can scarcely avoid comparing this with the new covenant of Jeremiah 31:31–34 since the wording (v. 21) is reminiscent of the covenant language of Genesis 12:2. The one heart given will preclude the possibility of divided allegiance on the part of the people between Yahweh and images (cf. Jer. 32:39).

Restoration and reformation will go hand in hand. The newly restored community will be a community of the redeemed, they will cleanse the land, and this will assure their continuance (v. 18). Thus the final outcome is the keeping of *statutes* and *ordinances* (v. 20), the typical priestly position. It is quite unique in the same general passage to find a disclaimer of the absolute necessity for keeping the cultus of religion operating and at the same time to find a firm assertion of the finality of legalism.

(4) The Exodus of the Glory of the Lord (11:22-25)

[22] Then the cherubim lifted up their wings, with the wheels beside them; and the glory of

the God of Israel was over them. 23 And the glory of the LORD went up from the midst of the city, and stood upon the mountain which is on the east side of the city. 24 And the Spirit lifted me up and brought me in the vision by the Spirit of God into Chaldea, to the exiles. Then the vision that I had seen went up from me. 25 And I told the exiles all the things that the LORD had showed me.

The culminating event of the Temple vision is the departure of the glory of the Lord. This withdrawal would permit time and circumstance to take their full and devastating effect. Israel had been confronted on one other occasion with a similar blow to religious optimism, the capture of Shiloh about 1050 B.C. and the spiriting away of the ark of the covenant, which symbolized Yahweh's presence (1 Sam. 4: 1–22).

The fateful circumstances of the situation in Ezekiel's day are exemplified in the life situation of Samson. After a short lifetime of rebellion against Yahweh and gross neglect of Nazirite vows, Samson went out to do battle with the Philistines as previously, but *he did not know that the Lord had left him* (cf. Judg. 16:20). Whereas Samson was merely left alone, not only would Jerusalem be without the presence of Yahweh, but Yahweh would send the adversary against the people. Quite like Samson, they would be forced to do battle without their God. This tragic circumstance was primarily due to a group of leaders who lacked sufficient moral fiber to hold them ethically faithful before a sovereign God.

The ecstatic seizure is lifted from the prophet (v. 24), i.e., that which had initiated the oracles in 8:1, and now he relates to the exiles what has occurred. This reenforces the objective nature of ecstatic experience as an experience to be shared intelligently and coherently.

V. The Word of Exile in Symbolic Action (12:1–20)

1. The Baggage and the Wall (12:1–16)

1 The word of the LORD came to me: 2 "Son of man, you dwell in the midst of a rebellious house, who have eyes to see, but see not, who

have ears to hear, but hear not; 3 for they are a rebellious house. Therefore, son of man, prepare for yourself an exile's baggage, and go into exile by day in their sight; you shall go like an exile from your place to another place in their sight. Perhaps they will understand, though they are a rebellious house. 4 You shall bring out your baggage by day in their sight, as baggage for exile; and you shall go forth yourself at evening in their sight, as men do who must go into exile. 5 Dig through the wall in their sight, and go out through it. 6 In their sight you shall lift the baggage upon your shoulder, and carry it out in the dark; you shall cover your face, that you may not see the land, for I have made you a sign for the house of Israel."

7 And I did as I was commanded. I brought out my baggage by day, as baggage for exile, and in the evening I dug through the wall with my own hands; I went forth in the dark, carrying my outfit upon my shoulder in their sight.

8 In the morning the word of the LORD came to me: 9 "Son of man, has not the house of Israel, the rebellious house, said to you, 'What are you doing?' 10 Say to them, 'Thus says the Lord GOD: This oracle concerns the prince in Jerusalem and all the house of Israel who are in it.' 11 Say, 'I am a sign for you: as I have done, so shall it be done to them; they shall go into exile, into captivity.' 12 And the prince who is among them shall lift his baggage upon his shoulder in the dark, and shall go forth; he shall dig through the wall and go out through it; he shall cover his face, that he may not see the land with his eyes. 13 And I will spread my net over him, and he shall be taken in my snare; and I will bring him to Babylon in the land of the Chaldeans, yet he shall not see it; and he shall die there. 14 And I will scatter toward every wind all who are round about him, his helpers and all his troops; and I will unsheath the sword after them. 15 And they shall know that I am the LORD, when I disperse them among the nations and scatter them through the countries. 16 But I will let a few of them escape from the sword, from famine and pestilence, that they may confess all their abominations among the nations where they go, and may know that I am the LORD."

The unusual methods for presenting the oracles of Yahweh have been the object of considerable attention.[50] Here the reason for such presentation is made clear. The people have eyes to see and ears to hear,

---

[50] Cf. M. Pierce Matheney, Jr., "Interpretation of Hebrew Prophetic Symbolic Act," *Encounter*, 3 (1968), 256–267.

but they neither see nor hear. The inference is that perhaps they will understand (v. 3) when the oracles of Yahweh are presented to them in symbolic action.

Ezekiel is instructed to portray the typical city dweller caught up in the activities of a besieged and doomed city. He is to gather a minimum of personal possessions, i.e., *an exile's baggage*. The Hebrew literally reads "make you vessels of exile" and probably implies containers for provisions which could be carried in the hand or upon the back. The prophet was to gather together these items and place them outside his house in the full sight of all passersby during the day. Such an act would draw considerable attention and result in a number of inquisitive persons gathering about to see what would happen next. Then in the evening (v. 4) or at dark, probably meaning first darkness after the setting of the sun (v. 6) which was the most advantageous time for escape and flight, he was to dig through the wall, lift his pitiful handful of provisions, cover his face, and imitate a dejected refugee as he departed.

The act of digging through the wall implies that the prophet dug through the wall of his own home as he enacted the scene. *Wall* (Heb., *bagir*) normally means house wall in contradistinction to *chomah* meaning city wall (vv. 5,7). Since Babylonian houses were constructed of sun-dried brick, the act of digging through with his own hands was not an extremely arduous task for the prophet and does not necessarily imply an act of utter desperation.

Witnesses to these strange actions on the part of the prophet were intrigued by what they saw and responded with a hoped-for inquiry *What are you doing?* (v. 9). It is now possible for Ezekiel to explain the meaning of his message. What they have seen depicted by him will become a reality to the Judahites and the *prince in Jerusalem*. The prince referred to (v. 13) appears to be Jehoiachin, who was sent blinded into exile and there died (Cooke, pp. 128–129, prefers to have this passage apply to Zedekiah).

Verses 14–16 seem to refer to 5:2,10,12 where in the symbols of the siege the scattered inhabitants of Jerusalem are subjected to relentless pursuit and slaughter. The new note reflected in vv. 14–16 is one of keen distinction. Whereas it may be interpreted that 5:2,4 does indicate a glimmer of hope for a few, vv. 14–16 affirms flatly that some will be spared.

Immunity was granted to a few for the honor of the name of Yahweh; not as an act of mercy. It was done for the sake of God's personal integrity. As they were dispersed among the nations they would testify that Yahweh was indeed Lord (v. 15) and be living confessions to his sovereignty (v. 16). We cannot escape the repeated rapier-like thrusts of the words of Ezekiel evidencing his concern to vindicate the actions of Yahweh.

2. The Dread of Invasion (12:17–20)

17 Moreover the word of the LORD came to me: 18 "Son of man, eat your bread with quaking, and drink water with trembling and with fearfulness; 19 and say of the people of the land, Thus says the Lord GOD concerning the inhabitants of Jerusalem in the land of Israel: They shall eat their bread with fearfulness, and drink water in dismay, because their land will be stripped of all it contains, on account of the violence of all those who dwell in it. 20 And the inhabited cities shall be laid waste, and the land shall become a desolation; and you shall know that I am the LORD."

Bread and water, in ancient times, constituted the only nourishment for a people besieged any appreciable length of time. Previous sections in Ezekiel treating the subject of the siege of Jerusalem (cf. ch. 4) placed primary emphasis upon the physical sufferings occasioned by starvation diets. In this section, however, the emphasis is upon the psychological hardships of a siege.

The words of vv. 17–19 (i.e., *quaking, trembling, fearfulness, dismay*) are those which indicate mental trauma. To illustrate, the Hebrew for quaking literally means an earthquake, that which turns the countryside upside down. It denotes a tumultuous mental state evidenced by palsied hands, unstable knees, halting steps, choked voices, and facial twitches. To eat bread and drink water in poverty and in peace is one thing, but to partake of the slightest of diets when hope is gone and destruction is imminent is meaningless. The most sumptuous of banquets would have had little meaning under such conditions.

VI. The Prophetic Proclamation and Popular Response (12:21—14:23)
1. The Popular Attitude Toward Prophecy (12:21-28)

21 And the word of the LORD came to me: 22 "Son of man, what is this proverb that you have about the land of Israel, saying, 'The days grow long, and every vision comes to nought'? 23 Tell them therefore, 'Thus says the Lord GOD: I will put an end to this proverb, and they shall no more use it as a proverb in Israel.' But say to them, The days are at hand, and the fulfilment of every vision. 24 For there shall be no more any false vision or flattering divination within the house of Israel. 25 But I the LORD will speak the word which I will speak, and it will be performed. It will no longer be delayed, but in your days, O rebellious house, I will speak the word and perform it, says the Lord GOD."
26 Again the word of the LORD came to me: 27 "Son of man, behold, they of the house of Israel say, 'The vision that he sees is for many days hence, and he prophesies of times far off.' 28 Therefore say to them, Thus says the Lord GOD: None of my words will be delayed any longer, but the word which I speak will be performed, says the Lord GOD."

Ezekiel next deals with what had become the popular skeptical attitude toward prophetic utterance, especially those oracles on retribution and judgment. A popular proverb connected with this attitude is reflected in the words: *The days grow long, and every vision comes to naught.* This reveals the inner attitudes of people toward such oracles. If day after day passed without the prophecy being fulfilled, the people considered it nullified.

The voicing of stern prophetic judgment had reached a crescendo during the days of the eighth-century ethical prophets— Amos, Hosea, Micah, and Isaiah. Since the judgments pronounced by the eighth-century prophets did not come into effect

historically, and since the day of Ezekiel was some 150 years removed from them, the people had begun to say *the days grow long!* Obviously, the people were saying, since it has been so long and judgment has not descended, it will not come. Thus every *vision* (i.e., prophetic word) *comes to naught,* which is to say, has not been fulfilled.

Therefore why should they listen to, heed, and respond to the words of Ezekiel. He was just another man babbling judgment which would no more be fulfilled than those utterances of 150 years previous. As far as Ezekiel was concerned, he was to them like other prophetic figures. *The vision that he sees is for many days hence, and he prophesies of times far off* (v. 27). Thus the words of Ezekiel, even if true, would not affect them. Ezekiel admits to a delay in the culmination of previous prophecies but not his own. Three replies to this attitude are given.

(1) Prophetic utterance does not fail, i.e., *the days are at hand, and the fulfilment of every vision* (v. 23). In this day, in this time, the prophet says, all previous prophetic utterance will be validated. Prophecy had not failed; the people had failed. With the introduction of ethical monotheism by the eighth-century prophets, there had developed the twin motif of doom and hope in prophetic proclamation. Consistently the prophets asserted that judgment could be averted by return to God, but when judgment came because of refusal to repent some would be spared. The tragedy of Israel was the fact that they did not understand that such delay in the execution of prophetic pronouncements was not due to the ineffectiveness of Yahweh but the love of Yahweh for Israel. God had granted to Israel a period of grace. They had wrongly interpreted the grace of God to be the ineffectual power of God. But now, Ezekiel asserts, the period of grace has finally lapsed.

(2) There will be no more *false vision* (false prophecy) or *flattering divination* (v. 24). Admittedly, the prophet is affirm-

ing that Israel has been misled, duped by pseudo-prophets and diviners. The diviner, in contrast with the true prophet, was one who sought to foretell the future through use of artificial devices such as casting lots, reading signs, or giving meaning to omens. They are like the false prophets and are legislated against (cf. Lev. 19:26; Deut. 18:14–15; Jer. 8:11; 14:14; 28:1ff). Both the false prophet and the diviner played to the audience. The false prophet tickled the ears of the hearers by speaking what they wished to hear, while the diviner invariably gave a favorable reading of the omens.

(3) In Ezekiel's case Yahweh not only speaks the word of judgment through the prophet but he, himself, *will . . . perform it* (vv. 25,28). The word of judgment will become flesh, sword, pestilence, famine, holocaust, catastrophe, and exile.

2. Rebuke of the False Prophets (13:1–16)

¹ The word of the LORD came to me: ² "Son of man, prophesy against the prophets of Israel, prophesy and say to those who prophesy out of their own minds: 'Hear the word of the LORD!' ² Thus says the Lord GOD, Woe to the foolish prophets who follow their own spirit, and have seen nothing! ⁴ Your prophets have been like foxes among ruins, O Israel. ⁵ You have not gone up into the breaches, or built up a wall for the house of Israel, that it might stand in battle in the day of the LORD. ⁶ They have spoken falsehood and divined a lie; they say, 'Says the LORD,' when the LORD has not sent them, and yet they expect him to fulfil their word. ⁷ Have you not seen a delusive vision, and uttered a lying divination, whenever you have said, 'Says the LORD,' although I have not spoken?"

⁸ Therefore thus says the Lord GOD: "Because you have uttered delusions and seen lies, therefore behold, I am against you, says the Lord GOD. ⁹ My hand will be against the prophets who see delusive visions and who give lying divinations; they shall not be in the council of my people, nor be enrolled in the register of the house of Israel, nor shall they enter the land of Israel; and you shall know that I am the Lord GOD. ¹⁰ Because, yea, because they have misled my people, saying, 'Peace,' when there is no peace; and because, when the people build a wall, these prophets daub it with whitewash; ¹¹ say to those who

daub it with whitewash that it shall fall! There will be a deluge of rain, great hailstones will fall, and a stormy wind break out; ¹² and when the wall falls, will it not be said to you, 'Where is the daubing with which you daubed it?' ¹³ Therefore thus says the Lord GOD: I will make a stormy wind break out in my wrath; and there shall be a deluge of rain in my anger, and great hailstones in wrath to destroy it. ¹⁴ And I will break down the wall that you have daubed with whitewash, and bring it down to the ground, so that its foundation will be laid bare; when it falls, you shall perish in the midst of it; and you shall know that I am the LORD. ¹⁵ Thus will I spend my wrath upon the wall, and upon those who have daubed it with whitewash; and I will say to you, The wall is no more, nor those who daubed it, ¹⁶ the prophets of Israel who prophesied concerning Jerusalem and saw visions of peace for her, when there was no peace, says the Lord GOD.

With Israel, as with every nation modern or ancient, there was the problem of false prophets and prophecy. While it may be true that some of these were self-realized frauds, by far the larger segment were those who could not distinguish between the voice of self and the voice of Yahweh. Doubtless the majority of false prophets felt that they uttered the words of Yahweh when in actuality they were the words of man. Possibly many of them had convinced themselves that they were so centered in God that no matter what they spoke it would be a true message.

The false prophets assailed by Ezekiel, however, had so abused, dissipated, corrupted, and compromised their prophetic gifts that they were no longer a viable religious force. Six specific charges are leveled against these prophets by Ezekiel, with the first being an all-inclusive indictment of their major offense.

(1) They *prophesy out of their own minds.* This is the primary charge, and from it springs additional accusations. This has to do with the originator of the prophetic message and the very nature of the role of the prophet. Throughout the Old Testament the conflict between the false and true prophet centered in this issue (cf. 1 Kings 22; Isa. 9:15; Jer. 2:8–23; Amos 7:14; Mic. 2:11; 3:5,11). In effect, the

source of the oracle of a true prophet is Yahweh, and the specific function of the prophet is to convey that oracle bound only by his own personal limitations. The false prophet, on the other hand, is one self-deceived who thinks rather than knows that his message issues from Yahweh.

Further, with the false prophet the message in transition is infused with unique limitations imposed on the proclamation by the theological inadequacy of the individual. It is the mind of the false prophet which becomes the contaminant. Even pure water entering a polluted stream is rendered impure. If such prophets did receive an oracle of Yahweh, it was transmitted as the word of man.

(2) The false prophets *follow their own spirit.* This implies a following of the spirit of man rather than the Spirit of Yahweh. Thus it might be construed to mean the following of the natural inner spirit or promptings of man rather than the external impinging Spirit of Yahweh which would energize and make effective the message. Knight would have it mean that the dead structure of religious experience remains when the vitalizing spirit which filled it has fled.[51] Since the term *foolish* is utilized to define more clearly this type of prophet, it may imply one without perception, meaning that they prophesied out of their own spirits which were devoid of religious perception.

Since Ezekiel, however, placed such great importance on seizure by the Spirit, (i.e., ecstatic experience) as the context for revelation, he may well be implying that they were false prophets because their messages came from without the boundaries of ecstatic experience.

(3) The false prophets *have seen nothing* (v. 3). Not only does this imply that they had no specific revelations but that they were men devoid of vision. Though they believed true vision was theirs, they were deluded. This may well be a play on words. *Seen* (Heb., *rucham*) is from the

same root word that lies behind the term seer (Heb., *roeh*) and implies one who sees a vision given of Yahweh. First Samuel 9:9 equates seer with prophet. Ezekiel may well be saying, they think themselves to be seers but they see nothing.

Ezekiel designates these prophets, your *prophets* (v. 4). This defines them as the prophets of men rather than prophets of Yahweh. As the prophets of men the source of their message would be the will of the people rather than that of Yahweh. They but mirrored or reflected what the people wanted to hear.

As a result of their lack of definitive vision from Yahweh they were like young *foxes* playing in *ruins,* without true sense of direction or bearing (v. 4). When a man listens to Yahweh there is only one voice; when a man listens to the people there is a multitude of voices. They were little more than an echo chamber for the people.

(4) The prophets of the people offered no crisis ministry (v. 5). This may be a charge directed at the reaction of the popular prophet in the time of crisis, or directed toward their lack of insight in preparing the people for a crisis. They had not *built up a wall* (lit., thrown up a fence) or instilled in the people through prophetic proclamation that which would fortify, sustain, and nourish their spirits. True prophetic ministry is an undergirding ministry. Due to their defection from this role prior to the catastrophe (i.e., the fall of Judah), they would be denied a crisis ministry. Prophetic self-delusion prevented them from proclaiming the word of Yahweh in crisis, just when they were most needed by the people.

(5) The prophets had *spoken falsehood and divined a lie* (v. 6). As to the future these men knew nothing. Theirs was not a message from Yahweh. They voiced their own vain imaginations and expected vindication by Yahweh. Such an affront was unthinkable to Ezekiel. It appears that this charge was directed not only to prophets in Jerusalem but certain prophets who like Ezekiel were among the exilic community

51 Knight, *op. cit.,* p. 77

in Babylon (v. 9).[52]

(6) The prophets had *misled* the people of Yahweh (v. 10); (cf. Jer. 6:14; 8:11; Mic. 3:5). This section (vv. 10–16) depicts the popular prophet as having led the people down a path of delusion by crying *Peace* when there was no peace (vv. 10,16). In effect they had led the people like lambs to the altar of Yahweh's judgment. The *wall* of v. 10 is interpreted in the Mishna (i.e., Shebi 3,8) to be a wall of stone without cement of mud. The depiction appears to be that of a wall built weakly without a bonding agent and then plastered over in a way to make it appear to have strength.

Evidently Ezekiel is referring to the ill-constructed belief system of the people. The false prophets accepted the false assumptions of the people without question and assured them that they believed correctly (v. 10). The spiritual and moral defenses of Judah and Jerusalem were haphazard affairs erected with the stones of haughty exclusivism, arrogant self-sufficiency, and smug complacency. Jammed together with these were boulders of political expediency, economic opportunism, religious apostasy, and ethical relativity. Such falsely erected positions crumble before Yahweh (v. 11).

The hideousness of the situation was that these grotesque symbols of security were caulked and plastered over by the approbation of the prophets. They covered over the insidious inner corruption causing the outer façade to appear perfect. The whole structure by its very nature is preconditioned to crumble (vv. 13,14). Yahweh's judgment will strip away the superficial façade erected by the prophets and reveal the total worthlessness of their belief structures. The popular prophet had hidden the weakness through false prophecies and delusive encouragement. But in the crumbling of the walls the false prophets are revealed for what they truly are and they are destroyed by their own idle

words (v. 14).

Ironically the people will assume the attitude of innocence and disclaim any responsibility for their complicity in the matter. They lay the blame at the feet of the prophets (v. 12). He who was the popular prophet becomes the people's scapegoat.

3. Rebuke of the Dealers in Magic (13: 17–23)

[17] "And you, son of man, set your face against the daughters of your people, who prophesy out of their own minds; prophesy against them [18] and say, Thus says the Lord God: Woe to the women who sew magic bands upon all wrists, and make veils for the heads of persons of every stature, in the hunt for souls! Will you hunt down souls belonging to my people, and keep other souls alive for your profit? [19] You have profaned me among my people for handfuls of barley and for pieces of bread, putting to death persons who should not die and keeping alive persons who should not live, by your lies to my people, who listen to lies.

[20] "Wherefore thus says the Lord God: Behold, I am against your magic bands with which you hunt the souls, and I will tear them from your arms; and I will let the souls that you hunt go free like birds. [21] Your veils also will tear off, and deliver my people out of your hand, and they shall be no more in your hand as prey; and you shall know that I am the Lord. [22] Because you have disheartened the righteous falsely, although I have not disheartened him, and you have encouraged the wicked, that he should not turn from his wicked way to save his life; [23] therefore you shall no more see delusive visions nor practice divination; I will deliver my people out of your hand. Then you will know that I am the Lord."

The dealers in magic were prophetesses but by Ezekiel's description appear to be more in the role of sorceresses. An identical charge previously directed toward the popular prophets is here leveled against these women (v. 17), that of prophesying out of their own minds. Implied are acts of sorcery utilizing *magic bands and veils* (v. 18), words which appear only here in the Old Testament.

It seems that this is a similar type of control over individuals as one sees in

---

[52] The register of the house of Israel may be a census of the exilic community (cf. Ezra 2; Neh. 7).

oodoo cults. It was an art practiced heerly from the profit motive (v. 19). The ndisious part of the trade in human fear vas to associate Yahweh with it. When ahweh was connected with such dark and vil designs it profaned him.

Whereas Bewer [53] describes the sin involved to be that of falsely declaring the vill and purpose of Yahweh, i.e., that ighteous men die and unrighteous men ive, Cooke (p. 144) interprets it to be an ct to injure the good and bless the evil.

What is of significant issue is the preyng upon a shared human weakness, the lesire to know the unknown. The prophetsses preyed upon the fears, superstition, nd ignorance of human beings. Such pracices have always found ready victims mong those of the low credulity threshold. rom this victimizing of the less intelligent and perceptive they made a living as eligious leeches gorging themselves upon he fears of simple folk. Their primary inent was not to be truly of help to the people but to gain and maintain an unatural hold on their adherents in order to btain wealth and power.

. Rebuke of the Idolatrous (14:1–11)

1 Then came certain of the elders of Israel to e, and sat before me. 2 And the word of the ORD came to me: 3 "Son of man, these men ave taken their idols into their hearts, and set 1e stumbling block of their iniquity before 1eir faces; should I let myself be inquired of t all by them? 4 Therefore speak to them, and y to them, Thus says the Lord GOD: Any man f the house of Israel who takes his idols into is heart and sets the stumbling block of his niquity before his face, and yet comes to the rophet, I the LORD will answer him myself ecause of the multitude of his idols, 5 that I 1ay lay hold of the hearts of the house of rael, who are all estranged from me through 1eir idols.

6 "Therefore say to the house of Israel, Thus ys the Lord GOD: Repent and turn away from our idols; and turn away your faces from all our abominations. 7 For any one of the house f Israel, or of the strangers that sojourn in

Israel, who separates himself from me, taking his idols into his heart and putting the stumbling block of his iniquity before his face, and yet comes to a prophet to inquire for himself of me, I the LORD will answer him myself; 8 and I will set my face against that man, I will make him a sign and a byword and cut him off from the midst of my people; and you shall know that I am the LORD. 9 And if the prophet be deceived and speak a word, I, the LORD, have deceived that prophet, and I will stretch out my hand against him, and will destroy him from the midst of my people Israel. 10 And they shall bear their punishment—the punishment of the prophet and the punishment of the inquirer shall be alike—11 that the house of Israel may go no more astray from me, nor defile themselves any more with all their transgressions, but that they may be my people and I may be their God, says the Lord GOD."

This scene is strikingly similar to that of chapter 8, but here the *elders of Israel* rather than the elders of Judah (8:1) approach the prophet. The exact purpose of their visit and the precise nature of the inquiry is not known, for when the words of Yahweh came to the prophet they were not what the elders wished to hear. They are condemned because they have *taken idols into their hearts* (v. 3) and as a result had neither the right nor the privilege of making inquiries of Yahweh.

No graver religious condition or distasteful effrontery could have been involved. They came to inquire not in sincere devotion to Yahweh but with inner commitments to their own idols. Such a one could not be permitted to believe that he might receive an oracle from God— forgiveness yes, blessings no! Every indicator points to an inner commitment, a secret allegiance, to idols rather than the open idolatry.

The act of inquiring of Yahweh while at the same time holding idols before their faces (v. 4) constituted undiluted mockery. For this affront, this insult of insults, Yahweh will *lay hold of the hearts* (v. 5). Since the heart was the throne room of their idolatry it means that Yahweh will lay hold of their idols. In addition, *I will set my face* (v. 8) against them, Yahweh warns.

To "set the face" indicates firm resolve when used of man (cf. Gen. 31:21; Num. 24:1; 2 Kings 12:17; Isa. 50:7; Ezek. 4:3,7; 6:2; 20:46; 21:2; 25:2; 28:21; 29:2; 35:2; 38:2); but when used of God it implies the sternest of displeasure (cf. Lev. 17:10; 20:3,5,6; 26:17; Jer. 21:10; 44:11; Ezek. 14:8; 15:7; Dan. 11:17). The preponderant usage of the term is to be found in the late canonical writings such as the Holiness Code (Lev. 17–26), Ezekiel, and Jeremiah. It appears that this phrase came to be a favorite of the late canonical writers, and especially Ezekiel, to denote the epitome of Yahweh's anger.

This set of the face of Yahweh against the elders will have disastrous results. Should a prophet be so bold as to deliver an oracle to an idolatrous inquirer, that inquirer may be assured that the only words he receives will be misleading, damaging, and disastrous (v. 9). Such a condition will exist because both prophet and inquirer are guilty of a grievous offense. No man may convey an oracle of Yahweh, without penalty, to anyone other than a true believer. It is not that Yahweh would deliberately mislead the prophet. A prophet presumptuous enough to deliver such an oracle has deluded himself. And under the delusion that it was a true oracle he would inevitably deceive his listeners.

5. Righteousness Imputed Only to the Righteous (14:12–23)

12 And the word of the Lord came to me: 13 "Son of man, when a land sins against me by acting faithlessly, and I stretch out my hand against it, and break its staff of bread and send famine upon it, and cut off from it man and beast, 14 even if these three men, Noah, Daniel, and Job, were in it, they would deliver but their own lives by their righteousness, says the Lord God. 15 If I cause wild beasts to pass through the land, and they ravage it, and it be made desolate, so that no man may pass through because of the beasts; 16 even if these three men were in it, as I live, says the Lord God, they would deliver neither sons nor daughters; they alone would be delivered, but the land would be desolate. 17 Or if I bring a sword upon that land, and say, Let a sword go

through the land; and I cut off from it man an beast; 18 though these three men were in it, as live, says the Lord God, they would delive neither sons nor daughters, but they alon would be delivered. 19 Or if I send a pestilenc into that land, and pour out my wrath upon with blood, to cut off from it man and beast 20 even if Noah, Daniel, and Job were in it, as live, says the Lord God, they would delive neither son nor daughter; they would delive but their own lives by their righteousness.

21 "For thus says the Lord God: How muc more when I send upon Jerusalem my four so acts of judgment, sword, famine, evil beast and pestilence, to cut off from it man an beast! 22 Yet, if there should be left in it an survivors to lead out sons and daughters, whe they come forth to you, and you see their way and their doings, you will be consoled for th evil that I have brought upon Jerusalem, for a that I have brought upon it. 23 They will con sole you, when you see their ways and thei doings; and you shall know that I have no done without cause all that I have done in i says the Lord God."

In this oracle of judgment a hypothetica case is set before the mind of Ezekiel. I in the act of judgment God sent as th instruments of retribution *famine* (v. 13) *wild beasts* (v. 15), *sword* (v. 17) an *pestilence* (v. 19), and if in that lan there dwelled three of the most righteou of men, **Noah, Daniel, and Job** (vv. 14,20) who wished to have their children spared along with them because of the father' righteousness, would they be spared? [54]

The basic principle articulated here i that righteousness is an individual, not corporate affair, that righteousness is nei ther negotiable nor transferable, and tha the unrighteous cannot be immune t judgment due to any kind of human rela tionship. Righteousness is a personal re lationship between God and man. No im munity can be obtained by birth, friend ship, acquaintanceship, or physical prox imity. The three—Noah, Daniel, and Jol —could only escape themselves (vv. 14

---

[54] Daniel in this passage may refer to the Dan-el c the Canaanite religious literature. Dan-el was a righ eous judge who pled the cause of social justice fc widows and orphans. Because of this the Ugariti literature of the fifteenth century B.C depicts him a the most righteous of all judges. Cf. ANET, pp. 149 155.

16,18,20). This is quite different from the account of Abraham, who, in characteristic Semitic fashion, "bargained" with God over the fate of the inhabitants of Sodom (cf. Gen. 18:20–33).

One must keep in mind a central fact. Ezekiel feels compelled to defend the position that the annihilation of Jerusalem was a just act on the part of God. It was thoroughly bad, so bad in fact that the most righteous of the righteous could not avert its destruction. Yahweh had to be vindicated. And the righteous had to suffer with the wicked.

The full impact of the entire hypothetical situation comes with shocking effect (v. 22,23). That the people of Jerusalem and Judah justly deserved punishment was a belief held in common by Ezekiel and Jeremiah (cf. Jer. 24:8–10). Ezekiel by employing the figure *four* (v. 21) is utilizing a "formula word" indicating completeness. Amos, in the eighth century B.C., used the expression eight times in its most classic form: "for three transgressions . . . and for four." Their cup of rebellion was filled to the brim, in fact it was running over. Judgment by *sword, famine, evil beasts, and pestilence* (v. 21) would befall them. It is the severity that is shocking. There is no hope, only deepest gloom.

Verses 22,23 contain a consoling word from Yahweh to Ezekiel. When the destruction occurs and Ezekiel sees the actions of the survivors, he will fully realize that the judgment was just. The survivors would surmise that their escape was due to their righteousness. Ezekiel, however, would know this to be untrue. He would finally understand that the very best of Judah and Jerusalem were bad. Comparatively speaking, some were not quite so evil as others but they were all evil.

VII. Allegories on God's Major Concerns (15:1—17:24)

1. The Worthless Vine (15:1–8)

¹ And the word of the LORD came to me: ² "Son of man, how does the wood of the vine surpass any wood, the vine branch which is among the trees of the forest? ³ Is wood taken from it to make anything? Do men take a peg from it to hang any vessel on? ⁴ Lo, it is given to the fire for fuel: when the fire has consumed both ends of it, and the middle of it is charred, is it useful for anything? ⁵ Behold, when it was whole, it was used for nothing; how much less, when the fire has consumed it and it is charred, can it ever be used for anything! ⁶ Therefore thus says the Lord GOD: Like the wood of the vine among the trees of the forest, which I have given to the fire for fuel, so will I give up the inhabitants of Jerusalem. ⁷ And I will set my face against them; though they escape from the fire, the fire shall yet consume them; and you will know that I am the LORD, when I set my face against them. ⁸ And I will make the land desolate, because they have acted faithlessly, says the Lord GOD."

Frequently in the Old Testament *vine* is used as a metaphor for Israel. Normally the metaphor indicated a vine tended, nourished, protected, and cultivated by Yahweh (cf. Psalm 80:8–16; Isa. 5:17; Jer. 2:21; Ezek. 17:6–7; Hos. 10:1). These references to Israel as a cultivated vine anticipated that with such careful husbandry it should produce excellent fruit. Ezekiel shatters the general pattern and with incredible reversal of thought introduces Israel as a wild vine.

Vine branch (v. 2) literally means "trees of tendrils" or creeping branches, thus a vine growing wild. Thus the people of Jerusalem are depicted as a vine uncultivated and one which produces no fruit and has no value other than fuel for fire (v. 4). On the one hand it is so thin and pliable when green and on the other hand so stiff and brittle when dried it has no utilitarian use—not even for pegs to hang a vessel (v. 3).

Unerringly and devastatingly Ezekiel pursues his analogy. Not only is it useless in natural form, but even when charred its residue is worthless. Literally it does not even make decent charcoal (v. 4). It was no good to begin with, and that state is constant (v. 5). Thus are *the inhabitants of Jerusalem!* As the wild vine was useless, the people of Jerusalem were useless— which was exactly opposite of their appraisal of themselves (cf. Deut. 32:32; Isa.

5:1 ff.; Hos. 10:1; Jer. 2:21). Due to its utter uselessness the population of Jerusalem will be given up to a holocaust of destruction (v. 6). But even the harsh judgment will not make of the inhabitants a thing of value. If they survived they would be as worthless after the destruction as before.

This is a reaffirmation of 14:21–23. Should there be escapees from the doomed city their life style would not be altered by the event. Both of these passages point to a cardinal facility of man—the ability to maintain his delusions. How awesome are the words of Yahweh: I will *give up the inhabitants of Jerusalem* (v. 6). There is no loneliness to be compared with that occasioned by the departure of God.

2. The Adulterous Wife: Jerusalem (16: 1–59)

This division extends certain of the concepts that are merely hinted at in the analogy of the worthless vine.

Within the passage is a unique strangeness. Generally speaking, late Old Testament thought expresses the relationship between Yahweh and Israel in a servant motif (cf. Isa. 41:8–9; 42:1; 43:10; Jer. 20:10; 46:27–28). Here we have a consort motif, so familiar in other ancient Near Eastern religions. Ezekiel projects the hypothetical picture of Yahweh with an unfaithful consort, Israel. The gods were conceived of and depicted in "pair" categories with each god accorded a goddess. Both Isaiah and Jeremiah, by inference, allude to the consort concept by using the word harlot as descriptive of the unfaithfulness practiced by Israel (cf. Isa. 1:21; Jer. 3:1,8). Israel the consort had played the harlot.[55]

No clearer evidence is to be found of Ezekiel's innovative thinking. There is a drastic break with traditional interpretation of Israel's history at this point. Prophetic tradition had generally looked upon Israel's infant years as years of innocent purity. Normally Israel's corruption was thought to have occurred during the conquest when Canaanite religious practices worked their insidious designs. The book of Hosea, Isaiah, and Jeremiah reflect this position.

Ezekiel argues the case differently, affirming that Israel was corrupt from her nativity. This evidences one of the most fascinating aspects of the outlook of Ezekiel. In one moment he embraces and fiercely protects tradition, in the next he radically departs from it. Ezekiel moves far beyond the thinking of other prophets, asserting that from birth Jerusalem had the genes of depravity with her being!

It is likely that the extreme thought of Ezekiel in the passage led to the elimination of it from the synagogue services.[56]

(1) Jerusalem the Outcast Infant (16:1–7)

[1] Again the word of the LORD came to me [2] "Son of man, make known to Jerusalem her abominations [3] and say, Thus says the Lord GOD to Jerusalem: Your origin and your birth are of the land of the Canaanites; your father was an Amorite, and your mother a Hittite. [4] And as for your birth, on the day you were born your navel string was not cut, nor were you washed with water to cleanse you, nor rubbed with salt, nor swathed with bands. [5] No eye pitied you, to do any of these things to you out of compassion for you; but you were cast out on the open field, for you were abhorred on the day that you were born.

[6] "And when I passed by you, and saw you weltering in your blood, I said to you in your blood, 'Live, [7] and grow up like a plant of the field.' And you grew up and became tall and arrived at full maidenhood; your breasts were formed, and your hair had grown; yet you were naked and bare.

The command of Yahweh is that the prophet *make known to Jerusalem her abominations*. Contextually the term abomination implies not only religious apostasy but political apostasy which produced a perfect climate for religious defection.

Ezekiel viewed the problem of foreign alliances from the standpoint of the religious implications. To him the danger

---

[55] For detailed discussions, cf. Raphael Patai, *The Hebrew Goddess* (New York: Ktav Publishing House, 1967).

[56] Mishna, Meg. 5.10: Tosephta 4:34.

eologically were graver than they were olitically. Ezekiel, as an astute observer nd student of Israelite history, saw that olitical alliances resulted in religious syn- retism. In addition the mainstream of rophetic thought viewed political alli- nces, especially those executed during rises, as an affront to Yahweh. They evi- lenced a lack of confidence in Yahweh nd dependence upon men.

No more sordid picture leaps from the ages of the Old Testament than that of olomon's personal defection from belief n Yahweh brought about by commercial lliances sealed with marriages to foreign rincesses who imported their religions nto Jerusalem (cf. 1 Kings 11:1–13).

To expose Jerusalem's abominations Ezekiel first likens her to an outcast in- ant (v. 5), who was rejected by both arents and left exposed to the elements nd beasts of prey—with not one sign of ompassion demonstrated by her parents.

A keen knowledge of Jerusalem's history tarting with the period of the conquest is rojected in the passage. When Joshua ought for control of the southern hill ountry, Jerusalem was the leading city f an Amorite coalition (cf. Josh. 10:1–5); nd, in Joshua 24:15, the hill country of Palestine is referred to as the land of the Amorites. As to the Hittites, before David's ime Jerusalem had a Hittite governing lass over the indigenous Canaanite and Amorite population. Thus Ezekiel speaks of he parentage of Jerusalem as being Amorite-Hittite (v. 3).

Ezekiel may well be implying that Jeru- salem was abandoned as a bastard child, or the Amorites were Semitic peoples nd the Hittites non-Semitic. So little did he parents care for the offspring it was ast out with the afterbirth and lay *welter- ng* (v. 6), literally "kicking out in all lirections." The imagery implies that Yah- veh came upon the infant struggling to separate itself from the afterbirth.

At this point Ezekiel sees Yahweh as one who came to the forsaken infant and proffered the words of life: *Live, and*

grow up like a plant of the field (v. 7). The RSV reads with the LXX and Syriac, rather than the Masoretic Text, and by thus reading implies that the infant Jeru- salem would grow like a wild plant unat- tended but flourishing. The word of Yah- weh, in the mind of Ezekiel, assured the life of the infant Jerusalem. They were words expressing compassion, love, and concern on the part of God. Yahweh thus gave to the infant Jerusalem what had been denied by the parents. Resultantly the infant flourished as a wild creature and arrived at the age of puberty, yet she was in all of her wild beauty still *naked and bare* (v. 7). Literally she was still ex- posed and unattended.

(2) *Jerusalem the Beloved of Yahweh (16:8–14)*

⁸ "When I passed by you again and looked upon you, behold, you were at the age for love; and I spread my skirt over you, and covered your nakedness: yea, I plighted my troth to you and entered into a covenant with you, says the Lord Gᴏᴅ, and you became mine. ⁹ Then I bathed you with water and washed off your blood from you, and anointed you with oil. ¹⁰ I clothed you also with embroidered cloth and shod you with leather, I swathed you in fine linen and covered you with silk. ¹¹ And I decked you with ornaments, and put bracelets on your arms, and a chain on your neck. ¹² And I put a ring on your nose, and earrings in your ears, and a beautiful crown upon your head. ¹³ Thus you were decked with gold and silver; and your raiment was of fine linen, and silk, and embroidered cloth; you ate fine flour and honey and oil. You grew exceedingly beautiful, and came to regal estate. ¹⁴ And your renown went forth among the nations because of your beauty, for it was perfect through the splendor which I had bestowed upon you, says the Lord Gᴏᴅ.

As the history of the relationship be- tween Yahweh and Jerusalem unfolds, the abandoned one is elevated from desti- tution to royalty, from one devoid of luxury to one lavishly accorded every desire. This comes to pass the third time Yahweh views Jerusalem. Previously he has seen her as an abandoned infant and as one who has arrived at the *age for love*, i.e., the bearing of children (v. 8). Symbolically the act of marriage between Yahweh and Jerusalem is referred to (v. 8) with the spread *skirt* simile and the *covenant* affirmation.

Helpful in understanding the skirt ritual is the account of Boaz and Ruth where the spreading of the skirt symbolized Boaz's marriage intent (cf. Ruth 3:6–13). The covenant of marriage is referred to in Malachi 2:14. Once Jerusalem had become the bride of Yahweh, he lavishes upon her every luxury (vv. 9–12). Reference to a *crown* (v. 12) reenforces the hypothetical consort idea, i.e., a goddess enthroned reigning regally. As a result of Yahweh's care the consort, Jerusalem, achieves international fame (v. 14: cf. Eichrodt, *Ezekiel*, pp. 201–206).

(3) Jerusalem the Idolatrous Wife (16: 15–22)

15 "But you trusted in your beauty, and played the harlot because of your renown, and lavished your harlotries on any passer-by. 16 You took some of your garments, and made for yourself gaily decked shrines, and on them played the harlot; the like has never been, nor ever shall be. 17 You also took your fair jewels of my gold and of my silver, which I had given you, and made for yourself images of men, and with them played the harlot; 18 and you took your embroidered garments to cover them, and set my oil and my incense before them. 19 Also my bread which I gave you—I fed you with fine flour and oil and honey—you set before them for a pleasing odor, says the Lord God. 20 And you took your sons and your daughters, whom you had borne to me, and these you sacrificed to them to be devoured. Were your harlotries so small a matter 21 that you slaughtered my children and delivered them up as an offering by fire to them? 22 And in all your abominations and your harlotries you did not remember the days of your youth, when you were naked and bare, weltering in your blood.

The covenant relationship is, however, betrayed by Yahweh's consort, Jerusalem. She disregards her vows as binding, and perverts the loveliest gifts of Yahweh through grotesque usage in her ungodly pursuits. Once Yahweh has made her a thing of beauty, she relies upon the thing given rather than the one who was the giver. Since she had come to her new

state, she now felt no need for the original lover who had lifted her to preeminence. Now she turns to other lovers.

Jerusalem, the former outcast transformed into one eminently desirable, begins to play the role of the *harlot* (v. 15). This picture of wanton unfaithfulness denotes a type of religious harlotry produced by foreign alliances and entanglements. The basic idea is that Jerusalem broke the covenant with Yahweh and entered into covenants with other nations. Ezekiel likens this to the act of temple prostitution inherent in foreign religions. Much the same picture develops in the book of Hosea with Gomer, the wife of the prophet, defecting to temple prostitution.

As Ezekiel expands the imagery, the details indicate how gross the defection became. The gifts of love, i.e., the *garments* (v. 16), were used to make pallets or cushions upon which she gave herself to the pagan gods. The gifts of jewelry were melted down and cast into phallic forms and then grossly and sickeningly used for stimulation (v. 17), while gifts of finest *embroidered garments* were turned into wall tapestries either to gaily decorate the rooms of her temple brothel or as coverlets for the phallic symbols (v. 18). Even the choicest of foods given in love by Yahweh to his consort, Jerusalem, were used by her as offerings to her new lover gods. As if this was not enough, Jerusalem went a step farther. The children born of the union of love between Yahweh and the consort were offered up by her as human sacrifices, burnt offerings to her pagan lover deities. Apparently the children were first ritually sacrificed and then their bodies offered up as burnt offering (for the practice of human sacrifice, cf. Ex. 22:29; Judg. 11:39; Mic. 6:7; 2 Kings 16:3; Jer. 7:31).

Of all the offenses committed by harlotrous and idolatrous Jerusalem, the crowning sin was that of ingratitude—Jerusalem did *not remember* (v. 22). Not only did she not remember the acts of Yahweh's love, but she in fact repudiated the memory

ry and its concurrent responsibilities. This
rings us to the cardinal idea in the pas-
age. The sin of Jerusalem is exposed as
hat of a thankless attitude.

In human relationship there is no more
devastating offense than that of un-
ppreciation. The ungrateful are those
who tear the heart, lacerate the spirit, and
hame the goodness of the love relation-
hip. Nothing so quickly turns the dreams
f parents to dust than a child's ingratitude.
But how much greater the damage in the
relationship between Yahweh and the
bjects of his love!

4) *Jerusalem the Apostate (16:23–29)*

23 "And after all your wickedness (woe, woe
o you! says the Lord GoD), 24 you built your-
elf a vaulted chamber, and made yourself a
ofty place in every square; 25 at the head of
very street you built your lofty place and
rostituted your beauty, offering yourself to any
asser-by, and multiplying your harlotry. 26 You
lso played the harlot with the Egyptians, your
ustful neighbors, multiplying your harlotry, to
rovoke me to anger. 27 Behold, therefore, I
tretched out my hand against you, and dimin-
shed your allotted portion, and delivered you
o the greed of your enemies, the daughters of
he Philistines, who were ashamed of your
ewd behavior. 28 You played the harlot also
with the Assyrians, because you were insatia-
le; yea, you played the harlot with them, and
till you were not satisfied. 29 You multiplied
our harlotry also with the trading land of
Chaldea; and even with this you were not
atisfied.

Ezekiel pursues the analogy specifying
he three nations with whom Jerusalem
as prostituted herself through alliances:
Egypt (v. 26), Assyria (v. 28), and Chal-
lea, i.e., Babylonia (v. 29). Jerusalem is
lepicted as a harlot who established pagan
hrines at every street intersection (vv.
3,24) and in these places played the
ole of a temple prostitute to any foreign
leity who chanced to pass by.[57] Jerusalem
vas *insatiable* (v. 28) in her desires to
rostitute herself through foreign alliances,
nd her *lewd behavior* was looked upon
with shame even by her enemies (v. 27).

57 "Offering yourself" (v. 25), lit., "you spread your
egs apart to any passerby," implying the wantonness
f Jerusalem.

Essentially, lewd means unchaste. But its
meaning here implies willing acceptance of
base sensual responses. Only the most
monstrous of sexual behavior would be
viewed by the Philistines as lewd, for their
sexual mores left a great deal to be desired.[58] Literally, Ezekiel is indicating that
the behavior of Jerusalem in running after
other nations was viewed by them with
disgust.

There is no way to escape the inevitable
import of this passage. Israel had been
warned repeatedly to avoid foreign alliances because they involved the danger of
pagan religious philosophies being transplanted into Israel. The city of Jerusalem
was of critical importance. Not only was it
the seat of government but the center of
Israel's religion. In a sense, as Jerusalem
went so went the nation (cf. Ex. 20:3;
32:1–9; Josh. 24:14–15; 2 Chron. 7:19–22,
etc.).

The Solomonic era witnessed an exact
working out of this very fact (cf. 1 Kings
11:1–13). The importation of foreign religious influences ultimately resulted in the
defection of Solomon to the worship of
Chemosh and Molech.

(5) *Jerusalem the Degenerate (16:30–43)*

30 "How lovesick is your heart, says the Lord
GoD, seeing you did all these things, the deeds
of a brazen harlot; 31 building your vaulted
chamber at the head of every street, and making your lofty place in every square. Yet you
were not like a harlot, because you scorned
hire. 32 Adulterous wife, who receives strangers
instead of her husband! 33 Men give gifts to all
harlots; but you gave your gifts to all your
lovers, bribing them to come to you from every
side for your harlotries. 34 So you were different from other women in your harlotries: none
solicited you to play the harlot; and you gave
hire, while no hire was given to you; therefore
you were different.

The venom of bitterness spews from the
prophet as he continues to depict Jeru-

58 This may have some connection with the Assyrian crises of 701 B.C., when Sennacherib of Assyria captured a group of Judahite cities during the
reign of Hezekiah and gave them to the Philistine
Kings of Ashdod, Ekron, and Gaza. Cf. ANET, pp.
287–288.

salem. She was far more depraved than the ordinary sacred or secular prostitute; she was a *brazen harlot* (v. 30) not restrained by any moral principle not even the morality current among that class.

It was not for financial gain that she plied the trade, it was due to uncontrollable lust. The key to Jerusalem's condition lies in the word *lovesick,* translated "weak" in the KJV. In ordinary usage it means to be weak or feeble or to languish. Thus we could interpret the condition to be one of weak resolves, a person susceptible to or who easily succumbs to such a temptation —thus one of weak, pliable, persuadable moral fiber. This, however, does not fit the context. Jerusalem's illness may better be categorized as spiritual and political nymphomania.

Jerusalem, the beloved and the consort of Yahweh, made an open and flagrant display of herself (v. 31), paraded her lewdness, and gave herself freely, never requesting payment as demanded by the code of the profession (v. 31). Ultimately she sank so low she solicited lovers and paid for their services rather than being paid by them (vv. 33,34). One cannot help but conclude that Jerusalem had completely prostituted herself. She had become so offensive that her only way to obtain lovers was to purchase them.

The consort of Yahweh had sold herself upon the auction block of international alliances, disgusting not only those with whom she made the alliances, but Yahweh who loved her. The overwhelming disgust of Yahweh is forcefully worded in Bewer's interpretation of v. 30. What shall I call you? I have no name for you because of your unheard-of depravity!

(6) Jerusalem the Exposed (16:35–43)

35 "Wherefore, O harlot, hear the word of the LORD: 36 Thus says the Lord GOD, Because your shame was laid bare and your nakedness uncovered in your harlotries with your lovers, and because of all your idols, and because of the blood of your children that you gave to them, 37 therefore, behold, I will gather all your lovers, with whom you took pleasure, all those you loved and all those you loathed; will gather them against you from every side and will uncover your nakedness to them, that they may see all your nakedness. 38 And I will judge you as women who break wedlock and shed blood are judged, and bring upon you the blood of wrath and jealousy. 39 And I will give you into the hand of your lovers, and they shall throw down your vaulted chamber and break down your lofty places; they shall strip you of your clothes and take your fair jewels, and leave you naked and bare. 40 They shall bring up a host against you, and they shall stone you and cut you to pieces with their swords. 41 And they shall burn your houses and execute judgments upon you in the sight of many women; will make you stop playing the harlot, and you shall also give hire no more. 42 So will I satisfy my fury on you, and my jealousy shall depart from you; I will be calm, and will no more be angry. 43 Because you have not remembered the days of your youth, but have enraged me with all these things; therefore, behold, I will requite your deeds upon your head, says the Lord GOD.

"Have you not committed lewdness in addition to all your abominations?"

Because Jerusalem had, with insatiable appetite for foreign alliances, forsaken Yahweh and prostituted herself to other nations and gods, she will once again be exposed (vv. 36,37). The prophet draws his analogy of punishment from Israelite law (cf. Lev. 20:10 ff.; more likely Deut. 17:2–7). The offense of Jerusalem was in a sense twofold, adultery and apostasy. It may well have been that a woman guilty of such an offense was stripped before the assembly and the eyes of her lover before they both were stoned to death (cf. Eichrodt, *Ezekiel,* p. 209).

Ironically, her former lovers will be the instrument of Yahweh's punishment. Those to whom once she had given herself will ravage her with sword and fire (vv. 37,40,41). Then and then only will the fury of Yahweh be satisfied and his jealousy abated (v. 42). This was the "blood wrath" (v. 38) which had to be appeased (v. 42). Such wrath could only be assuaged by the spilling of blood and is graphically depicted by the use of *cut . . . to pieces* (v. 40). The Hebrew word here is used only here in the Old Testa-

ent. The RSV translation is derived from
a Assyrian cognate which means to hack
chop into small pieces. The harlotrous
rusalem will be hacked into a bloody
utilated corpse. Such wrath was oc-
sioned, in the mind of the prophet, by
e ingratitude of Jerusalem who had not
membered the days of abandonment in
r infancy and *youth* (v. 43).

As the execution of judgment was made
ublic, it was to serve as an object lesson
all who saw it and later heard of it (cf.
41, *in the sight of many women*). This
ppears to be a moralizing of the account
y the editor directed as an object lesson
the women.

7) *Jerusalem the Gross Offender*
(16:44–52)

Behold, everyone who uses proverbs will use
is proverb about you, 'Like mother, like
aughter.' 45 You are the daughter of your
other, who loathed her husband and her chil-
ren; and you are the sister of your sisters, who
athed their husbands and their children.
our mother was a Hittite and your father an
morite. 46 And your elder sister is Samaria,
ho lived with her daughters to the north of
ou; and your younger sister, who lived to the
uth of you, is Sodom with her daughters.
7 Yet you were not content to walk in their
ays, or do according to their abominations;
ithin a very little time you were more cor-
upt than they in all your ways. 48 As I live,
ays the Lord GOD, your sister Sodom and her
aughters have not done as you and your
aughters have done. 49 Behold, this was the
uilt of your sister Sodom: she and her daugh-
ers had pride, surfeit of food, and prosperous
ase, but did not aid the poor and needy.
0 They were haughty, and did abominable
hings before me; therefore I removed them,
when I saw it. 51 Samaria has not committed
alf your sins; you have committed more abom-
nations than they, and have made your sisters
ppear righteous by all the abominations which
ou have committed. 52 Bear your disgrace, you
lso, for you have made judgment favorable to
our sisters; because of your sins in which you
cted more abominably than they, they are
nore in the right than you. So be ashamed, you
lso, and bear your disgrace, for you have
nade your sisters appear righteous.

Again Ezekiel seeks to make plain why
uch a horrible penalty would be exacted
f Jerusalem. Since Samaria and Sodom

were destroyed for their wickedness and
since Jerusalem's wickedness far surpassed
theirs, should it not also be destroyed?

Allegorically Jerusalem is depicted as the
zenith of sordidness. The dramatic impact
of the account is heightened by extending
the family background of Jerusalem (cf.
16:2). Of the union between the Amorite
father and Hittite mother there were other
children, an elder sister Samaria and a
younger sister Sodom (v. 46). Each of
these sisters had progeny (v. 48), i.e., the
surrounding cities over whom they exercised influence.

In addition each of the sisters was corrupt in her own way. Sodom and her
daughters were guilty of *pride* and economic abundance (i.e., *Surfeit of food*).
Its prosperity was so great it created idle-
ness. Experimentation with and quest for
gross immorality marked its sordid existence. But the greater sin was neglect of
the *poor and needy* (vv. 49,50).[59] Sodom's
infamy, so specifically detailed in Genesis
19, has provided modern language with
one of its most graphic words to describe
homosexual activity and carnal copulation:
sodomy.

Samaria, the elder sister, on the other
hand had committed abominations (v. 51).
She was guilty of an abhorrent offense.
Samaria had involved herself in foreign
religious-political alliances. Entanglement
in foreign alliances resulted in pagan religious incursions.

Doubtless the historically-oriented
prophet was conscious of the early apostasy
in the Northern Kingdom connected with
the acts of Jeroboam I (*ca.* 922–901 B.C.).
It was Jeroboam who had installed golden
bulls in the twin sanctuaries of Bethel and
Dan to denote the invisible presence of
Yahweh (cf. 1 Kings 12,13). More specifically, Ezekiel may have had in mind the
episode of the Omride Dynasty when
Jezebel, wife of Ahab (*ca.* 869–850), vir-

---

59 Cf. Amos 6:4–7 where the idle rich eat of the
best, lavishly entertain themselves, consume staggering
amounts of wine, but are not grieved over the ruin
of Joseph.

tually succeeded in displacing the worship of Yahweh with the worship of Baal-Melkart, the national deity of Phoenicia.

By contrast, however, the offense of Jerusalem was twice as bad as that of Samaria, i.e., *Samaria has not committed half your sins* (v. 51). In fact the transgression of Jerusalem was worse than the offenses of Sodom. Jerusalem was the exact image of her wanton Hittite mother (vv. 44,45). A part of Jerusalem's detestable nature was that she felt by comparison haughtily superior to both elder and younger sisters (v. 52).

In the pure white heat of Yahweh's judgment, however, the sins of Sodom and Samaria seem righteous in comparison to the sin of Jerusalem (v. 51b). Why then was this the case? Simply put, to whom much has been given much will be required. Jerusalem had been the favored of Yahweh. It was Jerusalem which Yahweh found abandoned and unloved. It was Jerusalem whom Yahweh had elected of the three daughters to be his consort. Opportunities for and avenues to greatness had been provided her by divine sanction and approval. Therefore the appraisal of her offenses take into account all mitigating circumstances and privileges. Thus Jerusalem will be horribly humiliated and the revelation of her sin will uncover a shocking fact. Jerusalem was the worst offender of the three (v. 52)!

A point not to be overlooked in this passage has to do with social wrong. The lengthiest discussion deals with the sins of Sodom and concludes not with a denunciation of prosperity but a denunciation of those who with abundance have no concern for the poor and needy. Wealth is not proscribed; rather the inability to feel and to care is condemned.

(8) Jerusalem the Recipient of Covenant and Promise (16:53–63)

53 "I will restore their fortunes, both the fortunes of Sodom and her daughters, and the fortunes of Samaria and her daughters, and I will restore your own fortunes in the midst of them, 54 that you may bear your disgrace and

be ashamed of all that you have done, becom ing a consolation to them. 55 As for your sister Sodom and her daughters shall return to the former estate, and Samaria and her daughte shall return to their former estate; and you ar your daughters shall return to your forme estate. 56 Was not your sister Sodom a bywor in your mouth in the day of your prid 57 before your wickedness was uncovered? No you have become like her an object of reproac for the daughters of Edom and all her neig bors, and for the daughters of the Philistine those round about who despise you. 58 Y bear the penalty of your lewdness and yo abominations, says the LORD.

59 "Yea, thus says the Lord GOD: I will de with you as you have done, who have despise the oath in breaking the covenant, 60 yet I wi remember my covenant with you in the days your youth, and I will establish with you a everlasting covenant. 61 Then you will remer ber your ways, and be ashamed when I tak your sisters, both your elder and your younge and give them to you as daughters, but not o account of the covenant with you. 62 I wi establish my covenant with you, and you sha know that I am the LORD, 63 that you ma remember and be confounded, and never ope your mouth again because of your sham when I forgive you all that you have done, say the Lord GOD."

As devastating as were the charge against Jerusalem in the previous section of this chapter, Yahweh will extend hope Not only Jerusalem but Sodom and Samari will share in a restoration.

Samaria and Sodom had previously re ceived punishment for their offenses, an in the face of this, Judah, who bore th greater guilt, could not expect to go un disciplined (v. 53). In fact the excesse of Jerusalem and Judah should be of com fort to Samaria and Sodom because thei sin was the greater (v. 54).

Judah had looked upon Sodom's sin an then assumed an attitude of superior right eousness. Any nation may appear in favorable light, though corrupt, if com pared with another who is less upright When judgment falls, however, Judah true state will be revealed (v. 57).

The exceeding pains which Ezekiel tak to justify the condemnation of Jerusalem is amazing. Much of this passage reads a a polemic and tends to indicate that Ezek el is offering rebuttal to an attack on his position related to the justice of Yahweh in such a horrible outpouring of wrath.

To reenforce his position Ezekiel refers to the ancient curse *oath* (v. 59) which was attached to a *covenant* agreement. In the Old Testament, on certain occasions, the lesser party in a covenant agreement bound himself by oath to a curse which would become operable if he broke the covenant (cf. Deut. 28:15 ff.; 29:12,14; Lev. 26:14–23). If for no other reason, judgment would come due to the curse oath.

Restoration is here connected with a new covenant, an *everlasting covenant* (v. 60). No covenant with Yahweh is ever consummated without its attending responsibilities (cf. Gen. 9:5,6; 12:2; Ex. 24:1–8). Whenever there is a covenant with Yahweh, ethical response and moral commitment are paramount.[60]

3. The Story of the Eagles (17:1–21)

Chapter 17 falls into two natural categories, each containing an allegory. The first of the two allegories has a natural division, with the first part being a presentation of the allegory and the second part an interpretation. The second allegory is extremely brief. The passage reflects the relations between Judah, Babylonia, and Egypt during the period about 597–588 B.C. Specifically it is concerned with the Jehoiachin exile (*ca.* 594) and the coming of Zedekiah to the throne of Judah as a vassal of Babylonia. The Egyptian phase has to do with the revolt of Zedekiah against Nebuchadnezzar (*ca.* 588).

(1) The Two Eagles (17:1–10)

¹ The word of the LORD came to me: ² "Son of man, propound a riddle, and speak an allegory to the house of Israel; ³ say, Thus says the Lord GOD: A great eagle with great wings and long pinions, rich in plumage of many colors, came to Lebanon and took the top of the cedar; ⁴ he broke off the topmost of its young

60 For full discussion cf. George E. Mendenhall, *Law and Covenant in Israel and the Ancient Near East* (Pittsburgh: The Biblical Colloquium, 1955).

twigs and carried it to a land of trade, and set it in a city of merchants. ⁵ Then he took of the seed of the land and planted it in fertile soil; he placed it beside abundant waters. He set it like a willow twig, ⁶ and it sprouted and became a low spreading vine, and its branches turned toward him, and its roots remained where it stood. So it became a vine, and brought forth branches and put forth foliage.

⁷ "But there was another great eagle with great wings and much plumage; and behold, this vine bent its roots toward him, and shot forth its branches toward him that he might water it. From the bed where it was planted ⁸ he transplanted it to good soil by abundant waters, that it might bring forth branches, and bear fruit, and become a noble vine. ⁹ Say, Thus says the Lord GOD: Will it thrive? Will he not pull up its roots and cut off its branches, so that all its fresh sprouting leaves wither? It will not take a strong arm or many people to pull it from its roots. ¹⁰ Behold, when it is transplanted, will it thrive? Will it not utterly wither when the east wind strikes it—wither away on the bed where it grew?

The *riddle* (*chidah;* cf. Judg. 14:12; I Kings 10:1; Psalm 49:4; Prov. 1:6) or the *allegory* (*m°shol*), which may equally as well be translated "parable" as in the KJV, has to do with two eagles, the first of which was the king of Babylon. It was Nebuchadnezzar who broke off the *topmost of its young twigs* (i.e., the young king, Jehoiachin, v. 4). Once captured, Jehoiachin was carried into Babylonian captivity. The *land of trade* would have been the country, Babylonia; and the *city of merchants*, the capital city, Babylon (v. 4). Next, the eagle (i.e., Nebuchadnezzar) took the *seed* of the land, i.e., Zedekiah, who was placed upon the throne of Judah following the deportation of Jehoiachin (v. 5). Zedekiah, as a vassal of his Babylonian overlord, is accorded privilege and status. The prophet likens Zedekiah to a vine nourished from a seedling which looked toward his suzerain, Nebuchadnezzar (i.e., *its branches turned toward him,* v. 6).

Ezekiel introduces another eagle into the allegory or similitude (vv. 7–10). This eagle contends with the first eagle for the allegiance of Zedekiah. As a result of the initial care by the first eagle, the vine, Zedekiah, had become a noble or majestic plant. But it begins to send out tender feelers toward the second eagle, who would be Psammetichus II, Pharoah of Egypt (v. 7).[61] The opinion of the prophet is that a defection from the obligation to Babylonia and political alliance with Egypt will only result in the destruction of the vine (i.e., literally kingship in Judah; cf. v. 10).

(2) The Interpretation (17:11–21)

11 Then the word of the Lord came to me: 12 "Say now to the rebellious house, Do you not know what these things mean? Tell them, Behold, the king of Babylon came to Jerusalem, and took her king and her princes and brought them to him to Babylon. 13 And he took one of the seed royal and made a covenant with him, putting him under oath. (The chief men of the land he had taken away, 14 that the kingdom might be humble and not lift itself up, and that by keeping his covenant it might stand.) 15 But he rebelled against him by sending ambassadors to Egypt, that they might give him horses and a large army. Will he succeed? Can a man escape who does such things? Can he break the covenant and yet escape? 16 As I live, says the Lord God, surely in the place where the king dwells who made him king, whose oath he despised, and whose covenant with him he broke, in Babylon he shall die. 17 Pharoah with his mighty army and great company will not help him in war, when mounds are cast up and siege walls built to cut off many lives. 18 Because he despised the oath and broke the covenant, because he gave his hand and yet did all these things, he shall not escape. 19 Therefore thus says the Lord God: As I live, surely my oath which he despised, and my covenant which he broke, I will requite upon his head. 20 I will spread my net over him, and he shall be taken in my snare, and I will bring him to Babylon and enter into judgment with him there for the treason he has committed against me. 21 And all the pick of his troops shall fall by the sword, and the survivors shall be scattered to every wind; and you shall know that I, the Lord, have spoken."

As interpreted by Ezekiel the allegory becomes a blistering denunciation of surreptitious political maneuvering which involved the breaking of firm commitments already consummated between Nebuchad-

nezzar and Zedekiah.

The king of Babylon had elevate Zedekiah, a member of the royal Judahit ruling house, to kingship after deportin Jehoiachin. A covenant had been entere into, and oaths involving sacred affirma tions had been executed by Zedekial Zedekiah may well have sworn by Yahwe his fidelity to the covenant (cf. 2 Chror 36:13). To the prophet it was incompre hensible that one would take lightly such an oath.[62]

Implied in v. 19 is the fact that an oath involving the name of Yahweh become Yahweh's oath. The mere fact of lightl regarding the oath was not the onl offense of Zedekiah.

Predicated upon the keeping of the oath was the continued existence of the nation Judah (v. 14). Zedekiah's overtures to Egypt for an alliance not only broke the sacred oath but placed the future of Judal in jeopardy. Ezekiel is convinced tha Egypt, who historically had defected from her alliances with the people of Israel would continue to do so (v. 15). The previous experience of Judah bore vivid testimony to this fact of history (cf. Isa 36:6; Ezek. 29:6,7).

Therefore because of Zedekiah's com plicity in bringing destruction upon Judal and building false hopes for a successfu alliance with Egypt, he will receive a jus and full retribution (vv. 17,18). Most ar resting, however, is the charge agains Zedekiah in v. 21. The acts of the king o Judah are looked upon not as treasonou in relationship to Nebuchadnezzar but i relationship to Yahweh. Ezekiel takes the same position as Jeremiah but gives ar unusual reason for so doing (cf. Jer 27:1 ff.

4. The Story of the Cedar Sprig (17 22–24)

22 Thus says the Lord God: "I myself wil take a sprig from the lofty top of the ceda

---

61 Cf. Jer. 44:30. Zedekiah conspired with both Psammetichus II and his son Apries. Also Moshe Greenberg, "Ezekiel 17 and the Policy of Psammetichus II," JBL, LXXVI (1957), 304–309.

62 Matitiahu Tserat, "The Neo-Assyrian and Neo Babylonian Vassal Oaths and the Prophet Ezekiel," JBL LXXVIII (1959), 199–204.

and will set it out; I will break off from the topmost of its young twigs a tender one, and I myself will plant it upon a high and lofty mountain; 23 on the mountain height of Israel will I plant it, that it may bring forth boughs and bear fruit, and become a noble cedar; and under it will dwell all kinds of beasts; in the shade of its branches birds of every sort will nest. 24 And all the trees of the field shall know that I the LORD bring low the high tree, and make high the low tree, dry up the green tree, and make the dry tree flourish. I the LORD have spoken, and I will do it."

This passage, employing highly figurative imagery, may be a messianic allegory. The language of v. 23 superficially points in that direction. As with most of the possible messianic allusions in Ezekiel, the images are highly guarded and definitely obscure (cf. 21:32,37; 34:23 ff.; 37:24 ff.; 40—48).

Inevitably when allegory is presented, the possibilities of interpretation are almost unlimited. This passage implies that beasts and birds, which may be interpreted as various types of people, dwell securely under the protective canopy of a king or nation appointed by Yahweh. In addition it would seem that they all acknowledge the legitimacy of Yahweh. On the other hand, it should be pointed out that the passage does not imply a universal kingdom or an incorporation of the diverse kingdoms into a kingdom of Yahweh. Certainly there is no evidence of conversion to the rulership of Yahweh. If indeed this is a messianic passage, it is primitive in form.

VIII. The Principle of Individual Responsibility (18:1–32)

Articulation of the doctrine of individual responsibility is one of the more advanced theological concepts in the Old Testament. Although prime consideration was given to the individual throughout Israel's history, this incredibly encompassing and forcefully stated position on individual responsibility for sin clearly constituted a watershed in the prophetic understanding of the nature of Yahweh and man. Previously, the concept of corporateness with aggregate responsibility for acts of sin characterized

Israelite religion. (cf. Ex. 20:4; 34:7; Num. 14:18; Deut. 5:9; Lam. 5:7).

Let us not be presumptuous and require of Ezekiel the presentation of a full Christian view of responsibility of sin. We must understand that Ezekiel gave added impetus to a thought which ultimately, in the words of Jesus, produced the Christian view of individual responsibility and personal salvation. This is, however, the first lengthy and well defined attempt in Israelite religious history to present the concept that every man's ultimate fate is inexorably related to his own actions (cf. Jer. 31).

Heredity, environment, and associations are totally discounted. Ezekiel's disregard for an environmental factor influencing the life, for good or evil, is predicated upon the way he saw Israel historically. To him environment could be discounted as a corruptive influence. Israel of all nations, due to its relationship with Yahweh, its law, its priesthood, its cultus, its Temple and its prophets, had the better environment to produce the righteous individual. To Ezekiel, Israel sinned in spite of its cultural environment, not because of it.

The position held by Ezekiel's listener's and fellow exiles is made quite plain. They felt their suffering was not due to their sin but to that of their forefathers. It was the forebearers who had eaten the sour grapes (i.e., committed the sin) and their teeth were set on edge (i.e., they were paying the penalty; cf. 18:2). Their forefathers were the sinners. But they had to pay the penalty. From this basic position new avenues of thought are pursued. If the forefathers had sinned and they were judged for that sin, where was the justice of Yahweh? The exiles assumed they were without sin; and if they were sinless, then Yahweh's justice was called into open question. In fatalistic despair, looking upon themselves as nothing more than pawns of previous offenses, they questioned Yahweh's judgment.

The reply of Ezekiel, which constitutes chapter 18, is a simple one, their plight was due to their own sin. Ezekiel also affirms with equal force that neither penalty for sin nor the fruits of righteousness is transferable from one generation to another.

Within the context of chapter 18 there is a standard list of morals evidencing an influence upon the prophet by both the Deuteronomic writer and the Holiness Code. The righteous life is determined by a norm of certain prohibitions with emphasis upon negative actions which constituted righteousness. In the mind of Ezekiel, righteousness is what one does, not what one does not do. The positive action of the righteous life has to do with the keeping of statutes and ordinances.[63] Here Ezekiel stands in the mainstream of legalism, which will ultimately create staggering problems within Judaism and hamper the ministry of Jesus.

1. Retribution for Sin Falls upon the Sinner (18:1-4)

¹ The word of the LORD came to me again: ² "What do you mean by repeating this proverb concerning the land of Israel, 'The fathers have eaten sour grapes, and the children's teeth are set on edge'? ³ As I live, says the Lord GOD, this proverb shall no more be used by you in Israel. ⁴ Behold, all souls are mine; the soul of the father as well as the soul of the son is mine: the soul that sins shall die.

In setting forth the concept of individual responsibility Ezekiel clearly states the premise upon which his position is based. Opposing the traditional Israelite position that the sin of the fathers will be visited upon the children to the third and fourth generations (cf. Ex. 20:5; 34:7; Jer. 31: 28) the prophet says, *all souls are mine* (referring to Yahweh) . . . *the soul that sins shall die*.

Soul, here and elsewhere in the Old Testament, does not imply some nebulous abstract facet of man. In the Old Testament, man is a soul, and perhaps from the Old Testament standpoint we may best define soul as "person."[64]

63 J. N. Schofield, "Righteousness in the Old Testament," *Bible Translator*, 1965, 112–116.
64 S. H. Hooke, "Life After Death: V. Israel and the After-Life," *The Expository Times*, 1965, pp. 236–239.

Since all souls (i.e., persons) are the unique possession of Yahweh, it is his judgment of that "person" in opposition to any other which has a sense of finality. The soul (i.e., person) who sins will die. He will not die for the sins of another but for his own sin. Yahweh thus declares there can be no transferral of guilt and its consequences in the same way as there can be no transferral of righteousness (see comment on 14: 12–20).

2. Proofs of Righteousness Are Discernible (18:5-29)

As a method for setting forth this new idea Ezekiel uses three illustrations: that of the righteous man (vv. 5–9), that of the sinful son of the righteous man (vv. 10–13), and that of the righteous son of the wicked father (vv. 14–18). This is caste in the guise of hypothetical succeeding generations in the same family in order to combat the concept of Exodus 20:5 and 34:7. It is the intent of this teaching to eradicate forever an erroneous belief historically perpetuated in Israel (v. 3).

(1) The First Generation (18:5-9)

⁵ "If a man is righteous and does what is lawful and right—⁶ if he does not eat upon the mountains or lift up his eyes to the idols of the house of Israel, does not defile his neighbor's wife or approach a woman in her time of impurity, ⁷ does not oppress any one, but restores to the debtor his pledge, commits no robbery, gives his bread to the hungry and covers the naked with a garment, ⁸ does not lend at interest or take any increase, withholds his hand from iniquity, executes true justice between man and man, ⁹ walks in my statutes, and is careful to observe my ordinances—he is righteous, he shall surely live, says the Lord GOD.

Ezekiel does not specifically relate contemporary Judah to one of the three generations. The specific application of the teaching is to be found in vv. 21–24. Judah was the wicked man who should turn from his sin and keep the statutes.

Ezekiel, as priest, is more in evidence in the initial section on individual responsibility. This deals with the first generation, the righteous father, whose righteousness is synonymous with the keeping of the legal statutes. To keep the statutes and observe the ordinances is to be righteous (v. 9). Because this first father figure in the hypothetical family has adhered to the prohibitions of the law, especially those contained in Leviticus 17—26 and Deuteronomy 20—24, he will live (v. 9).

Associations with Israelite religious legislation is inescapable. Restoring of the pledge (v. 7) is prominent in Exodus 22: 25 ff. As to the matter of exacting interest (v. 8) there are almost countless references (cf. Ex. 22:24,25; 23:1–3, 6–8; Lev. 19:15,35; 25:35–37; Deut. 16:18–20; 23: 19,20; 24:17; 25:1; 27:19, etc.). Concern for the unfortunate who are hungry and naked (v. 7) is voiced in Deuteronomy 15:7–11, picked up by Isaiah (58:7), and reaffirmed in the teachings of Jesus (Matt. 25:35 ff.). Topically the prohibitions cover both social and religious offenses, but the avoidance of such offenses constitutes righteousness.

Significant in understanding the priestly point of view of the prophet is v. 9 with the stern admonition to observe and keep the legal system. Only when one is meticulous or careful, with the Hebrew reading "to deal truly," can he be righteous. No halfhearted partial allegiance to the law will avail; it involves full commitment to the law.[65]

(2) The Second Generation (18:10–13)

10 "If he begets a son who is a robber, a shedder of blood, 11 who does none of these duties, but eats upon the mountains, defiles his neighbor's wife, 12 oppresses the poor and needy, commits robbery, does not restore the pledge, lifts up his eyes to the idols, commits abomination, 13 lends at interest, and takes increase; shall he then live? He shall not live. He has done all these abominable things; he shall surely die; his blood shall be upon himself.

[65] Cf. G. von Rad, "Righteousness and Life in the Cultic Language of the Psalms," *The Problem of the Hexateuch and Other Essays* (New York: McGraw-Hill, 1966), pp. 243–266. Von Rad connects this section with Temple liturgy, and Eichrodt looks upon the section as being directly related to liturgical declaratory formulas.

Next the prophet supposes that the father, who kept the law and thereby was righteous, had a son who did not keep the law and was therefore unrighteous. Could the righteousness of the father be imputed to the son? This is the first major question posed in this series.

In this case that which the father embraced was rejected by the son. He was guilty of all the offenses from which the father abstained, and in fact he added offenses. In effect the son's degree of wickedness exceeded the father's degree of righteousness, for he was a *robber* (Heb.: *parits*), which means one of violence, i.e., a shedder of blood (v. 10). This is the same as saying he was a thief and a murderer, one who did physical violence to the victim, and it may even imply sadism. The oppression of the poor and needy (v. 12) connotes exploitation of such groups within society since they had neither prestige, power, nor money to aid their just cause.

What then is to be the fate of this individual? He will die. But the key is in the words, his blood shall be upon himself (v. 13). He and he alone must pay the penalty for his sinfulness. His life condition was not created by his father but by himself.

(3) The Third Generation (18:14–20)

14 "But if this man begets a son who sees all the sins which his father has done, and fears, and does not do likewise, 15 who does not eat upon the mountains or lift up his eyes to the idols of the house of Israel, does not defile his neighbor's wife, 16 does not wrong any one, exacts no pledge, commits no robbery, but gives his bread to the hungry and covers the naked with a garment, 17 withholds his hand from iniquity, takes no interest or increase, observes my ordinances, and walks in my statutes; he shall not die for his father's iniquity; he shall surely live. 18 As for his father, because he practiced extortion, robbed his brother, and did what is not good among his people, behold, he shall die for his iniquity.

19 "Yet you say, 'Why should not the son suffer for the iniquity of the father?' When the son has done what is lawful and right, and has been careful to observe all my statutes, he shall surely live. 20 The soul that sins shall die. The son shall not suffer for the iniquity of the

father, nor the father suffer for the iniquity of the son; the righteousness of the righteous shall be upon himself, and the wickedness of the wicked shall be upon himself.

Ezekiel focuses upon the third generation, the son of the unrighteous father (v. 14). Let us say that this son was revolted by the actions of his father and saw in the grandfather a better example of life. Therefore he kept the law and embraced the norms of Israelite religious legalistic morality. Through the keeping of the law he avoided sin and thus is to *live* (v. 17). This does not mean eternal life in the New Testament sense; it means to continue physical existence and achieve the longevity intended by Yahweh for mankind.

Basic to Israelite theology was the concept that sin shortens life. As a result of acts of sin, the death principle would set in, and physical life would be severely curtailed.

The prophet then enters the crucial point of his argument directed against the popular saying, "The fathers have eaten sour grapes, and the children's teeth are set on edge." Folk religion would require the righteous son to suffer for the iniquity of his father (v. 19). Ezekiel, however, argues to the contrary. The son is to live because he has kept the law. But the father will die because he has broken the law (vv. 17,18.)

A lucid statement of Ezekiel's theological position is to be found in vv. 19,20. It combines priestly legalism with individual retribution. We must point out, however, that both Deuteronomy 24:16 and 2 Kings 14:6 call the problem of guilt, as interpreted popularly in Israel, into question. But it is Ezekiel who fully works out the principle of individual responsibility along legalistic lines. To Ezekiel there was no universality implied in his new doctrine. The redemptive possibility of righteousness was restricted totally to Israel because it involved the law. To Ezekiel the saving grace of the law was to save Israel and Israel alone.

(4) The Principle of Individual Redemption (18:21–32)

21 "But if a wicked man turns away from all his sins which he has committed and keeps all my statutes and does what is lawful and right, he shall surely live; he shall not die. 22 None of the transgressions which he has committed shall be remembered against him; for the righteousness which he has done he shall live. 23 Have I any pleasure in the death of the wicked, says the Lord God, and not rather that he should turn from his way and live? 24 But when a righteous man turns away from his righteousness and commits iniquity and does the same abominable things that the wicked man does, shall he live? None of the righteous deeds which he has done shall be remembered; for the treachery of which he is guilty and the sin he has committed, he shall die.

25 "Yet you say, 'The way of the Lord is not just.' Hear now, O house of Israel: Is my way not just? Is it not your ways that are not just? 26 When a righteous man turns away from his righteousness and commits iniquity, he shall die for it; for the iniquity which he has committed he shall die. 27 Again, when a wicked man turns away from the wickedness he has committed and does what is lawful and right, he shall save his life. 28 Because he considered and turned away from all the transgressions which he had committed, he shall surely live, he shall not die. 29 Yet the house of Israel says, 'The way of the Lord is not just.' O house of Israel, are my ways not just? Is it not your ways that are not just?

30 "Therefore I will judge you, O house of Israel, every one according to his ways, says the Lord God. Repent and turn from all your transgressions, lest iniquity be your ruin. 31 Cast away from you all the transgressions which you have committed against me, and get yourselves a new heart and a new spirit! Why will you die, O house of Israel? 32 For I have no pleasure in the death of any one, says the Lord God; so turn, and live."

Ezekiel now applies the principle of non-negotiability within the context of an individual life. As there may be righteous and unrighteous generations succeeding one another, there may be succeeding phases of righteousness and unrighteousness with an individual's life-span. How does Yahweh judge such an individual? Ezekiel uses a deadly logic reflected in the previous sections of chapter 18.

The prophet contends that the wicked man who embraces righteousness will have none of his previous transgression remembered against him (v. 22). Similarly should a righteous man defect to wickedness none of his righteous deeds will be remembered (v. 24). Precisely given is the reason for the righteous acts having no efficacy, the man is guilty of treachery (Heb.: *ma'al*). The word is unusual and is generally associated with the priestly group. It is found chiefly in late works connected with priestly theology (i.e., D document, Chronicles and Ezekiel). It is used in two other instances in Ezekiel to denote an offense connected with the laws related to holy objects (cf. 14:3; 15:8; also Lev. 5:15; 26:40; Num. 5:6,12,27; 1 Chron. 10:13; 2 Chron. 28:19; 36:14).

To Ezekiel there is complete justice in the position taken (vv. 25–29). Each individual would be judged on the basis of his inherent condition (v. 30). Yet key concepts pertaining to the opposing conditions, righteousness and treacherousness, are found in vv. 21,30*b*. It is the keeping of the statutes and ordinances which is equated with righteousness and the defection from them that is equated with treacherous iniquity. To Ezekiel a religion not divorced from morality provided the basis for intimate relationship with Yahweh. But the context of that morality was circumscribed by a legal structure, the statutes and ordinances.

Nor can the fact be circumvented that the new heart and new spirit (v. 31) come only after repentance and a return to the law. Be that as it may, Ezekiel subsequently delivers a somewhat surprising concept. It requires both Yahweh's grace and man's earnest endeavors to effect the new condition of the everlasting covenant. At a glance we might feel that more is being demanded of man than he is capable of accomplishing (i.e., *get yourselves*, v. 31). Certainly man does not have the innate power to save himself, to reclaim life, to radically restructure inner commitments and motives. Possibly the implication of Ezekiel is that man must face himself, acknowledge his inner condition

and the fact that he cannot change easily the power structures of his inner drives. The new condition is achieved through repentance (v. 30), and the beginning of repentance is the self-acknowledgment of personal inadequacy.

Yahweh has no desire to see even one of Israel condemned. Therefore a call to legalistic repentance, promise, and hope is extended (vv. 30,32). The condition which had created the inevitability of judgment was an attitude of rebellion against the law. Only repentance and return to the law would save life (v. 32).

IX. The Story of the Lioness and the Vine (19:1–14)

These twin laments are in a perfectly executed Hebrew meter designated *kinah*, which is the dirge meter of Hebrew poetry (cf. 2 Sam. 1:17–27; 3:33,34; Amos 5:1–2). The simile for Judah in the first lament is that of a lioness (vv. 1–9), and in the second lament the vine personifies either Jehoiachin or Zedekiah. Upon the mind of the prophet there bears the crushing weight of his sure knowledge of coming events, not far in the future but immediate. Thus Ezekiel gives vent to his inner grief over the imminent and horrifying fate of Judah, for judgment will bring to a tragic end the Davidic lineage of kings of Judah and the last remaining semblance of Israelite nationalism.

1. The Lament over the Whelps of the Lioness (19:1–9)

¹ And you, take up a lamentation for the princes of Israel, and say:
> What a lioness was your mother
>   among lions!
> She couched in the midst of young lions,
>   rearing her whelps.
> ³ And she brought up one of her whelps;
>   he became a young lion,
> and he learned to catch prey;
>   he devoured men.
> ⁴ The nations sounded an alarm against him;
>   he was taken in their pit;
> and they brought him with hooks
>   to the land of Egypt.
> ⁵ When she saw that she was baffled,
>   that her hope was lost,

she took another of her whelps
   and made him a young lion.
6 He prowled among the lions;
   he became a young lion,
and he learned to catch prey;
   he devoured men.
7 And he ravaged their strongholds,
   and laid waste their cities;
and the land was appalled and all who were
   in it
at the sound of his roaring.
8 Then the nations set against him
   snares on every side;
they spread their net over him;
   he was taken in their pit.
9 With hooks they put him in a cage,
   and brought him to the king of Babylon;
they brought him into custody,
   that his voice should no more be heard
upon the mountains of Israel.

Jehoahaz II (i.e., Shallum), the first of the whelps, was carried into captivity at the end of a three-month reign during the year 609 B.C. by Neco, the Egyptian pharaoh (cf. 2 Kings 23:37 ff.; Jer. 22: 10–12). Jehoiachin (i.e., Jeconiah) was deported to Babylon by Nebuchadnezzar after a reign of approximately three months during the year 598. Jehoahaz II is listed as being the son of Josiah and Hamutal (cf. 2 Kings 23:31), being born during the reign of his father about 640–609. Jehoiachin was the son of Jehoiakim (i.e., ruler of Judah about 609–598) and his wife Nehushta (cf. 2 Kings 24:8; also Eichrodt, *Ezekiel*, pp. 252–256).

Implications are that each of the whelps was of sufficient stature to create international problems resulting in their subjugation. Jehoiachin supposedly *prowled* (v. 6). The term literally means "to go up and down," possibly implying vacillation in alliances between Babylon and Egypt. Jehoahaz II is imputed to have been an aggressor whose actions were duplicated by his son (vv. 4,6,7). So troublesome were the whelps it became necessary for the powers of Egypt and Babylonia to contain them. The imagery of ensnaring the young lions with net and pit (vv. 4,8) denotes familiarity with early Mesopotamian hunting practices depicted in art and described in literature. And the practice of

caging an enemy (v. 9) is attested to in ancient Near Eastern documents.

Biblical documents furnish sparse information on the reigns of the two kings referred to in this passage. And the context of such passages point to little activity of import on their part. In the lament, however, the surface impression given is that both kings, who ruled only three months each, were of significant stature.

The lament of vv. 1–9 contains a judgmental commentary on kingship. Kingship which exists in order to obtain power and to wield that power ruthlessly without restraint makes subjects less than men and destroys all possibilities for true justice. Whenever a ruler of Israel acted in this manner, his rule accomplished little but to insure Yahweh's judgment.

It is at this point that the nature of a formal lament be taken into consideration. As such the lament normally aggrandizes the individual involved and causes him to loom large historically.

2. The Lament over the Fruit of the Vine (19:10–14)

10 Your mother was like a vine in a vineyard
   transplanted by the water,
fruitful and full of branches
   by reason of abundant water.
11 Its strongest stem became
   a ruler's scepter;
it towered aloft
   among the thick boughs;
it was seen in its height
   with the mass of its branches.
12 But the vine was plucked up in fury,
   cast down to the ground;
the east wind dried it up;
   its fruit was stripped off,
its strong stem was withered;
   the fire consumed it.
13 Now it is transplanted in the wilderness,
   in a dry and thirsty land.
14 And fire has gone out from its stem,
   has consumed its branches and fruit,
so that there remains in it no strong stem,
   no scepter for a ruler.

This is a lamentation, and has become a lamentation.

A continuation of the lament seems to personify Zedekiah (i.e., Mattaniah), ruler of Judah around 598–587 B.C. as the *strongest stem* of the vine (v. 11). Imagery in v. 12 indicates that the vine (i.e., Judah) was snatched from its well-watered bed and thrown down to wither, to be despoiled of its fruit and consumed in fire.

A probable interpretation of the allegory is that the Davidic line would end with Zedekiah and his sons and that a remnant, being transplanted in exile, would be left to wither and die in a strange new habitat. As the people ponder how this has come to pass, Ezekiel cuts through their argumentation, speculation, pretense, and pride. He asserts that the reason for the downfall of the Davidic line and Judah was not due to any external condition but rather due to Judah's own folly and the disastrous leadership given it by her kings. From its (own) *stem* (i.e., from within) had come those forces which led to destruction (v. 14).

X. *The Apostate History of Israel (20:1–45)*

This dated prophecy would fall around July–August 591 B.C.

Previously two sections (cf. comment on 14:1–11; 16) have given insights into the apostate history of Israel. This division, however, clarifies the history of Israel's rebellion. Events are telescoped in such a way to cover the history of that insubordination from election in Egypt to the day of Ezekiel. In bold, broad sweeps the prophet paints upon the canvas of time the grotesque figure of an apostate people bent upon mutiny against Yahweh. Because of their rebellion Yahweh will return them to a wilderness. They will be judged and purged in order to enter a new era of promise, hope, reclamation, and restoration. Plainly revealed is the attitude of God toward those whom he has elected and who have elected him.[66]

Two recurring phrases set the tempo of chapter 20: "sake of my name" and "my

ordinances, by whose observance man shall live." Central in the thought of Ezekiel is concern that the name of Yahweh be restored to preeminence along with the law.

The name of Yahweh in Old Testament thought involves the honor, renown, position, and essential prestige of the God of Israel. God's mighty acts on behalf of Israel in the Exodus event had maintained the integrity of his name. To have permitted Egypt to thwart deliverance of his people would have brought shame to his name.

Deeply embedded within these thought patterns is the covenant concept. Yahweh had elected Israel. This election was attested to by covenant and sealed with the word and name of Yahweh. God bound himself to this covenant with such rigidity that he could not break it. Thus the act of delivery from Egypt was not because of the worth of Israel but in spite of Israel's worthlessness, a known fact at the time of the covenant execution.

1. *Israel, an Apostate in Egypt (20:1–8)*

¹ In the seventh year, in the fifth month, on the tenth day of the month, certain of the elders of Israel came to inquire of the LORD, and sat before me. ² And the word of the LORD came to me: ³ "Son of man, speak to the elders of Israel, and say to them, Thus says the Lord GOD, Is it to inquire of me that you come? As I live, says the Lord GOD, I will not be inquired of by you. ⁴ Will you judge them, son of man, will you judge them? Then let them know the abominations of their fathers, ⁵ and say to them, Thus says the Lord GOD: On the day when I chose Israel, I swore to the seed of the house of Jacob, making myself known to them in the land of Egypt, I swore to them, saying, I am the LORD your God. ⁶ On that day I swore to them that I would bring them out of the land of Egypt into a land that I had searched out for them, a land flowing with milk and honey, the most glorious of all lands. ⁷ And I said to them, Cast away the detestable things your eyes feast on, every one of you, and do not defile yourselves with the idols of Egypt; I am the LORD your God. ⁸ But they rebelled against me and would not listen to me; they did not every man cast away the detestable things their eyes feasted on, nor did they forsake the idols of Egypt.

"Then I thought I would pour out my wrath

66 On chapter 20, cf. Walther Zimmerli, "The Word of God in the Book of Ezekiel," *History and Hermeneutic* (New York: Harper and Row, 1967), pp. 1–13.

upon them and spend my anger against them in the midst of the land of Egypt.

As on previous occasions, the elders came to Ezekiel to request of him the oracles of Yahweh. Again Yahweh refuses to be inquired of by less than adequate leaders who represent a thoroughly renegade people. Such a privilege was reserved for the sincere of life and pure of relationship. Certainly the elders had no anticipation of what would ensue, and, as on previous occasions, the exact nature of the inquiry of the people through the elders is not detailed. The completed message, included in 20:1–44, was one of stern judgment ameliorated only by a slight tempering with hope. The witness against Israel will be her own history (v. 4).

On the very *day* of Israel's election in Egypt Yahweh had enunciated his stance of brooking no rival for Israel's allegiance. Even though he had set before them the land of promise as an inheritance and clearly defined their responsibility to cast aside all idolatry, they rebelled (vv. 7,8). Concrete evidence of this apostasy on the part of Israel in Egypt is echoed in Joshua 24:14 and Leviticus 18:3. Joshua urged the people of the tribes following the conquest to "put away the gods which your fathers served beyond the River, and in Egypt." On the basis of Israel's election she was to be attendantly obedient to Yahweh.[67]

While it is true no act of rebellion in Egypt is alluded to, the wilderness legislation prohibiting any other gods before the face of Yahweh (ex. 20:3) and the act of Aaron in fabricating an object of veneration (Ex. 32) forcefully assert that such was in some way connected with Israelite-Egyptian religious practices.

From the content it is evident that judgment is not being leveled against the elders per se. What follows is a picture of national guilt. Judgment upon the elders was in actuality judgment upon the people

whom they represented. As the continuing story unfolds a point is dramatically made: The Israelites of Ezekiel's day were equally as rebellious as their forefathers. Therefore judgment upon them was to be all the more certain. They possessed the identical inner attitudes of their ancestors. The contemporary descendants of Ezekiel's day were indeed their fathers' progeny not only by blood but by attitude of rebellion.

2. Israel, an Apostate in the Wilderness (20:9–26)

9 But I acted for the sake of my name, that it should not be profaned in the sight of the nations among whom they dwelt, in whose sight I made myself known to them in bringing them out of the land of Egypt. 10 So I led them out of the land of Egypt and brought them into the wilderness. 11 I gave them my statutes and showed them my ordinances, by whose observance man shall live. 12 Moreover I gave them my sabbaths, as a sign between me and them, that they might know that I the LORD sanctify. 13 But the house of Israel rebelled against me in the wilderness; they did not walk in my statutes but rejected my ordinances, by whose observance man shall live; and my sabbaths they greatly profaned.

"Then I thought I would pour out my wrath upon them in the wilderness, to make a full end of them. 14 But I acted for the sake of my name, that it should not be profaned in the sight of the nations, in whose sight I had brought them out. 15 Moreover I swore to them in the wilderness that I would not bring them into the land which I had given them, a land flowing with milk and honey, the most glorious of all lands, 16 because they rejected my ordinances and did not walk in my statutes, and profaned my sabbaths; for their heart went after their idols. 17 Nevertheless my eye spared them, and I did not destroy them or make a full end of them in the wilderness.

18 "And I said to their children in the wilderness, Do not walk in the statutes of your fathers, nor observe their ordinances, nor defile yourselves with their idols. 19 I the LORD am your God; walk in my statutes, and be careful to observe my ordinances, 20 and hallow my sabbaths that they may be a sign between me and you, that you may know that I the LORD am your God. 21 But the children rebelled against me; they did not walk in my statutes, and were not careful to observe my ordinances, by whose observance man shall live; they profaned my sabbaths.

"Then I thought I would pour out my wrath

---

[67] For complete discussion, cf. H. H. Rowley, *The Biblical Doctrine of Election* (London: Lutterworth Press, 1958), pp. 15–44.

upon them and spend my anger against them in the wilderness. 22 But I withheld my hand, and acted for the sake of my name, that it should not be profaned in the sight of the nations, in whose sight I had brought them out. 23 Moreover I swore to them in the wilderness that I would scatter them among the nations and disperse them through the countries, 24 because they had not executed my ordinances, but had rejected my statutes and profaned my sabbaths, and their eyes were set on their fathers' idols. 25 Moreover I gave them statutes that were not good and ordinances by which they could not have life; 26 and I defiled them through their very gifts in making them offer by fire all their first-born, that I might horrify them; I did it that they might know that I am the LORD.

Rebellion as an inner attitude of Israel did not cease after the mighty act of Yahweh's deliverance from Egypt. Since this was an inherent weakness, Israel bore her apostate heart into the wilderness and added to rejection of the statutes and ordinances denial of the sabbath. It is within this section that the prophet adds the offense of profaning the sabbath day (vv. 13,16,21,24). If man's problem is an inner weakness, he carries it with him wherever he goes.

In the wilderness the *sabbaths* (v. 12) were added to the statutes and ordinances to affirm the Yahweh-Israel relationship and to denote Israel's sacredness. In profaning the sabbaths, that which symbolized their consecration, the Israelites denied their elect station. As a sign of the covenant between Yahweh and Israel (cf. Ex. 31:13) the sabbath became a hallmark of exilic religion and as such was a visible, distinguishing act for them (Ex. 21: 12 ff.). Two blasphemous sabbath corruptions during the wilderness period are referred to: that of an attempt to gather manna on the holy day (Ex. 16:27) and that of the man who gathered sticks on the sabbath (Num. 15:32 ff.). Yet it appears that Ezekiel conceived of far more flagrant and repeated abuses of the sabbath than those recorded in the wilderness narratives. We may assume that the charge of idolatry—*their heart went after their idols*

(v. 16)—which appears in the middle of this passage on sabbath profanation was the primary offense. There were two images fabricated during the wilderness period, the golden calf and the bronze serpent-staff (cf. Ex. 32; Num. 21:8,9). Both in later periods of Israelite history received fame as being objects of veneration and worship (cf. 2 Kings 18:4; 1 Kings 13:28). First Kings 13:28 implies that the calf-image concept was brought out of Egypt.[68] Seemingly during the very act of election and in those moments of protective blessing in the wilderness while receiving Yahweh's grace and love, Israel was unfaithful in intent and purpose. It is, however, quite true that frequently in moments of highest religious reflection and endeavor the most insidious of temptations occur.

Verses 25,26 constitute one of the more difficult problems in the book of Ezekiel, and were of major concern to Jewish commentators (Fisch, *Ezekiel*, p. 25). Rashi explains that when Israel rejected the exactitudes of the law, Yahweh permitted their own inner evil to have complete control over them. Kimchi interprets the passage differently implying that since Israel had refused the statutes of Yahweh, Yahweh delivered them to an enemy whose laws were not good.

One cannot, however, escape the inevitable import of the words which imply that Yahweh gave laws and placed requirements upon the will of Israel which were contrary to specific prohibitions and the very nature of the character of Yahweh (cf. Lev. 18:21; 20:2 ff.; Deut. 12:31; 18:9 ff.). Possibly in this instance we have the basic problem created in religion by traditionalism. Statutes and ordinances, which tradition had fabricated, were justified as actually being given by God. Religion frequently seeks to justify man-made religious traditions by imputing their origin to God. Ezekiel, as a priest, looked upon religion in the traditionalist mould and

---

68 The calf was probably an Apis bull statue, one of the major deities of Egypt, along with its consort Hathor, the cow-goddess.

considered the act which tradition had made sacred both valid and authoritative.

3. Israel, a Presumptuous Apostate in the Land of Promise (20:27–32)

27 "Therefore, son of man, speak to the house of Israel and say to them, Thus says the Lord God: In this again your fathers blasphemed me, by dealing treacherously with me. 28 For when I had brought them into the land which I swore to give them, then wherever they saw any high hill or any leafy tree, there they offered their sacrifices and presented the provocation of their offering; there they sent up their soothing odors, and there they poured out their drink offerings. 29 (I said to them, What is the high place to which you go? So its name is called Bamah to this day.) 30 Wherefore say to the house of Israel, Thus says the Lord God: Will you defile yourselves after the manner of your fathers and go astray after their detestable things? 31 When you offer your gifts and sacrifice your sons by fire, you defile yourselves with all your idols to this day. And shall I be inquired of by you, O house of Israel? As I live, says the Lord God, I will not be inquired of by you.
32 "What is in your mind shall never happen —the thought, 'Let us be like the nations, like the tribes of the countries, and worship wood and stone.'

Once Israel was in Canaan she continued her apostate way. Even after Yahweh had elected Israel in Egypt, extricated her from bondage with powerful acts, protected her in the wilderness, fought on her behalf in the conquest, and brought her into nationhood, she, with continuing ingratitude, maintained her waywardness. *To this day,* says Ezekiel, Israel has continued her rebellious ways (v. 31).

The specific acts of apostasy in Canaan (vv. 28,29,31) had to do with defection to Canaanite fertility cults, primarily the worship of the local baals (i.e., those of the woods and fields) as well as participation in the ritual acts connected with the worship of the great Baal or Lord Baal and his consort Anath. Direct reference is made to worship at the high places (v. 29) which involved highly erotic and lewd rites (cf. comment on 6:1–7; 16:15–22).

One key is given here as to the nature of the elders' inquiry on behalf of the people to the prophet Ezekiel. *What is in your*

mind (v. 32) rather literally translated is, "What is gone up upon your spirit or heart."

Since these words fall within the context of a section on idolatry it is both implied and stated that the exiles wished to embrace idolatry fully. Since the nation had been destroyed, the Temple had been ravished, and their traditional religious practices were no longer viable due to life in a strange land, they considered Yahweh to be no more. He was no longer their God; therefore they wished to seek and embrace another deity. As their forefathers had sought a king like other nations (1 Sam. 8:5), they in the exile wished to have a god as other nations (v. 32). They in essence wished to embrace idolatry.

With such thoughts captivating the minds of those on whose behalf the elders inquired, an oracle is denied. Again Ezekiel enunciates the principle that a people who have defiled themselves, literally polluted and saturated themselves with a continual process of apostasy, can neither expect nor command any intimate relationship with Yahweh (v. 31). Had the inner attitudinal posture been one of penitence, doubtless all avenues of communion would have been opened.

4. The Purging of Apostate Israel (20:33–44)

A stern affirmation is given that the intent of the people to embrace a strange god will be denied. Rather than giving the exiles over to full idolatry, Yahweh will judge, purge, and refine the people. Their intent to become pure idolaters will be dispelled by the very act of Yahweh himself. He will exercise his sovereignty over them, deliver them, and restore their unique status among the nations (vv. 33, 34). This will be accomplished through a new wilderness and a new exodus experience.

(1) The New Wilderness (20:33–39)

33 "As I live, says the Lord God, surely with a mighty hand and an outstretched arm, and with wrath poured out, I will be king over you. 34 I will bring you out from the peoples and

gather you out of the countries where you are scattered, with a mighty hand and an outstretched arm, and with wrath poured out; 35 and I will bring you into the wilderness of the peoples, and there I will enter into judgment with you face to face. 36 As I entered into judgment with your fathers in the wilderness of the land of Egypt, so I will enter into judgment with you, says the Lord GOD. 37 I will make you pass under the rod, and I will let you go in by number. 38 I will purge out the rebels from among you, and those who transgress against me; I will bring them out of the land where they sojourn, but they shall not enter the land of Israel. Then you will know that I am the LORD.
39 "As for you, O house of Israel, thus says the Lord GOD: Go serve every one of you his idols, now and hereafter, if you will not listen to me; but my holy name you shall no more profane with your gifts and your idols.

In order to reclaim a remnant of his people Yahweh will once again place them in a wilderness, that of exile (v. 35). Whereas Yahweh had previously judged Israel in the geographical wilderness of Egypt and Sinai (v. 36), he will now judge them in their new wilderness of strange people, unusual social customs, and unfamiliar scenes.

The people will be caused to *pass under the rod* (v. 37). This bit of pastoral imagery is taken from the familiar scene of a shepherd holding his staff over the sheep as they entered the foal. As each sheep passed it was counted and thus the shepherd could tell if all his sheep were accounted for.[69]

A strengthening of the imagery is provided (v. 38). At times during the process of the count, a shepherd would find animals which did not belong to his flock. These, when found, would be separated and denied entrance.

Thus the purpose in causing the people of Judah to pass under the rod of Yahweh's judgmental scrutiny and exile was to determine who among the people would become fit subjects for a return to the homeland (v. 38). Through the new wilderness experience Yahweh's people will be refined,

69 The RSV of v. 37b follows the LXX. The MT reads as the footnote given in RSV. The imagery of passing under the rod may denote a covenant ceremony (cf. Lev. 27:32; Jer. 33:13).

purged, and reclaimed. Those who will not hearken to the voice of Yahweh through the judgment of the exile will be delivered over to their own idolatrous way (v. 39). They must choose whom they will serve even as they are chosen.

(2) *The New Exodus (20:40–44)*

40 "For on my holy mountain, the mountain height of Israel, says the Lord GOD, there all the house of Israel, all of them, shall serve me in the land; there I will accept them, and there I will require your contributions and the choicest of your gifts, with all your sacred offerings. 41 As a pleasing odor I will accept you, when I bring you out from the peoples, and gather you out of the countries where you have been scattered; and I will manifest my holiness among you in the sight of the nations. 42 And you shall know that I am the LORD, when I bring you into the land of Israel, the country which I swore to give to your fathers. 43 And there you shall remember your ways and all the doings with which you have polluted yourselves; and you shall loathe yourselves for all the evils that you have committed. 44 And you shall know that I am the LORD, when I deal with you for my name's sake, not according to your evil ways, nor according to your corrupt doings, O house of Israel, says the Lord GOD."

Once the people have been renewed through judgment and their own inner resolves, they will return to Palestine where their worship will be acceptable to Yahweh. The inner change which has occurred will make their gifts and sacrifices not only acceptable but the object of Yahweh's solicitation (vv. 40,41); cf. Ex. 13:2, 12 ff.; Num. 15:20 ff.; Deut. 26:2 ff.).

The term *I will inquire* (v. 40), literally meaning "I will seek," is remarkable in that only Ezekiel and Micah (cf. Mic. 6:8) employ such an idea. Both imply that Yahweh will not just accept the gifts of a regenerate people but will actively seek them out. Another unique concept is also projected in v. 41 concerning the nature of Yahweh. *My holiness* is here used for the first time in the book of Ezekiel (cf. 28:22, 25; 36:23; 38:16,23; 29:27). This specifically applies to the holiness of Yahweh, an important concept especially to those of the priestly or prophetic class.

In Ezekiel the holiness of God was

God's very person; it is associated with the Ezekelian phrase "my holy name." To Ezekiel God's holiness was both his power (36:20–24) and his promise (20:41 ff.). To Ezekiel, the priest, things might or might not be holy (i.e., the Temple once holy, rendered unholy), but Yahweh was always holy. It was his pure nature. Thus to Ezekiel the activities or the manifested characteristics of Yahweh were also holy.[70]

Yahweh's act of grace in reclaiming his people will not, however, eradicate from their memories what they have been. The scars of apostasy will remain, not to condemn them but to serve as a warning against future offenses (v. 43). That which will amaze the people in their reclaimed state is how Yahweh could continue to abide them after they had been so utterly corrupt.

It is here that Ezekiel again scales the mountain of understanding Yahweh's true nature. He had judged them not *according to your evil ways, nor according to your corrupt doings* (v. 44). To have done so would have brought about total rejection and annihilation.

Ezekiel sees far more operating here than the justice of Yahweh. Justice would have called for unrelenting, unrestrained, and ruthless judgment. Here we see both covenant and election love as viable instruments of Yahweh's relationship to man. Tempered judgment in the sense of v. 44 implies the consideration of love and enforces the concept that Yahweh both judged and loved his people in spite of what they had become.

XI. The Irrevocable Judgment of Yahweh Against Judah and Jerusalem (20: 45—24:27)

1. General Judgment Against the South (20:45–49)

[45] And the word of the Lord came to me: [46] "Son of man, set your face toward the south, preach against the south, and prophesy against the forest land in the Negeb; [47] say to the forest of the Negeb, Hear the word of the Lord: Thus says the Lord God, Behold, I will kindle a fire in you, and it shall devour every green tree in you and every dry tree; the blazing flame shall not be quenched, and all faces from south to north shall be scorched by it. [48] All flesh shall see that I the Lord have kindled it; it shall not be quenched." [49] Then I said, "Ah Lord God! they are saying of me, 'Is he not a maker of allegories?' "

Although this brief excursus is considered by most modern commentators to come from the hand of an editor (cf. May, p. 176), it contains genuine difficulties in the RSV translation and intriguing avenues for homiletical thought. The RSV translation of vv. 46,47 is misleading by use of the word *Negeb* to denote a forested area. The Negeb, in biblical times, was neither a forested area nor a completely barren waste.[71] The word Negeb would best be translated "south" implying the forested areas of Judah.

Judgment upon the south (v. 46) will come in a catastrophic manner. It will come as a forest *fire* which rages completely out of control. Such a motif was already in evidence in the writings of Isaiah (cf. 9:18; 10:17 ff.). Whereas in Isaiah briars and thorns will be consumed, implying a brushfire, in Ezekiel all trees, dry and green, will be devoured (v. 47). Man, as well as nature, will suffer from the onslaught. The word *scorched* (v. 47) means an actual burning of the skin. In effect the intense heat from the raging fire will be felt in every quarter of the land, from *north* to *south* (v. 47). And all exposed flesh, such as the faces of men, will be burned enough to change the color and texture of the skin surface. A fire of such magnitude, one unquenchable that supercharges the entire atmosphere of the nation with intolerable heat, could only be the handiwork of Yahweh (v. 48).

The reply of Ezekiel, when commanded by Yahweh to speak such a highly figurative allegory, indicates that if he speaks thus he will be considered a *maker of*

---

[70] Cf. Helmer Ringgren, *The Prophetical Conception of Holiness* (Uppsala: Sweden, 1948).

[71] Cf. Nelson Glueck, *Rivers in the Desert* (New York: Farrar, Straus and Cudahy, 1959), pp. 14–18.

allegories (v. 49). The thought is conveyed that the people will consider him just a good storyteller. The people probably delighted in the imaginative parables yet never took them or the prophet seriously. It may well be that the people understood the allegories but refused to apply the message in any personal way to themselves.

2. Slain by the Sword (21:1-32)

Chapter 21 falls into five natural divisions with oracles of judgment being centered about a central theme, the sword-slain. Considerable debate has developed over the Ezekelian originality of certain of these oracles.[72] Along with the various critical problems involved is the contrast between the approach and execution of judgment in chapter 21 and the concept of individual responsibility with its resultant hope in chapters 14, 18, and 33.

Depicted in chapter 21 is total annihilation. Such ruthless slaughter implies that there was not a single individual to be found who would be the recipient of tempered judgment, much less one to whom righteousness could be imputed.

(1) The Unsheathed Sword (21:1-7)

1 The word of the LORD came to me: **2** "Son of man, set your face toward Jerusalem and preach against the sanctuaries; prophesy against the land of Israel **3** and say to the land of Israel, Thus says the LORD: Behold, I am against you, and will draw forth my sword out of its sheath, and will cut off from you both righteous and wicked. **4** Because I will cut off from you both righteous and wicked, therefore my sword shall go out of its sheath against all flesh from south to north; **5** and all flesh shall know that I the LORD have drawn my sword out of its sheath; it shall not be sheathed again. **6** Sigh therefore, son of man; sigh with breaking heart and bitter grief before their eyes. **7** And when they say to you, 'Why do you sigh?' you shall say, 'Because of the tidings. When it comes, every heart will melt and all hands will be feeble, every spirit will faint and all knees will be weak as water. Behold, it comes and it will be fulfilled,'" says the Lord GOD.

The prophet is commanded to *set* his *face* toward Jerusalem and proclaim oracles of judgment (v. 2). To preach is literally to "drop words." The same word is used of water poured from a vessel. The word of Ezekiel is that Yahweh is *against* the people and will exact grim recompense for their sin with both the *righteous* and the *wicked* falling to an avenging sword (v. 4). Exacting of punishment upon both groups is contrary to certain Old Testament positions (cf. Gen. 18:23,25) and conflicts with chapter 18.

Several alternate possibilities of interpretation are present. Judgment, since it was to be executed through an instrument, Babylon, which was at its best imperfect, would inevitably create some inequities. On the other hand, one might suggest that righteousness here constitutes a relative condition, which is to say because most were so wicked the less wicked appeared righteous by comparison. These by no means resolve the issue. At point in this passage, regardless of the way it is stated and in whose mouth the words are placed, are both a simple fact of existence and a need among men. The fact is that the righteous often do suffer, even death, with the wicked. But more important, is there not a definite need for the righteous to enter into the suffering of the wicked? Who should be the more likely candidate to endure suffering and to experience the woe of the world than the righteous?

All flesh (v. 5) will participate in the agony of this judgment. The unsheathed sword of judgment, which is Babylon, will not be stayed or sheathed until its purposes have been completed (v. 5); cf. Jer. 5:6; 14:13).

Ezekiel is commanded to pantomime the terrifying import of the oracle by feigning lamentations. He is to express the deepest pathos and sorrow by sighing as one with a *breaking heart* demonstrative of the bitterest of grief (v. 6). Such actions were to evoke questions by those who had heard

---

[72] Cf. Otto Eissfeldt, "Schwertschlagene bei Hesekiel," *Studies in Old Testament Prophecy* (Edinburgh: T. and T. Clark, 1950), pp. 73-81; May, IB, p. 177.

the oracle but who either did not understand its import or did not accept its
validity. This would entice them to inquire
(v. 7) and with their attention thus ar-
rested would afford Ezekiel an opportunity
to elaborate on the theme.

This but rivets attention upon a perpetual problem with the oracles of God in
both ancient and modern times—the extreme reluctance on the part of people
genuinely to hear a prophetic message.
Yahweh had been reduced to the most
childlike methods in order to gain a hearing for his word. Proclamation in depth is
futile without hearing in depth.

(2) The Psalm of the Sword (21:8–17)

⁸ And the word of the Lord came to me;
⁹ "Son of man, prophesy and say, Thus says the
Lord, Say:
A sword, a sword is sharpened
    and also polished,
¹⁰ sharpened for slaughter,
    polished to flash like lightning!
Or do we make mirth? You have despised the
rod, my son, with everything of wood. ¹¹ So the
sword is given to be polished, that it may be
handled; it is sharpened and polished to be
given into the hand of the slayer. ¹² Cry and
wail, son of man, for it is against my people; it
is against all the princes of Israel; they are
delivered over to the sword with my people.
Smite therefore upon your thigh. ¹³ For it will
not be a testing—what could it do if you
despise the rod?" says the Lord God.
¹⁴ "Prophesy therefore, son of man; clap your
hands and let the sword come down twice, yea
thrice, the sword for those to be slain; it is the
sword for the great slaughter, which encompas-
ses them, ¹⁵ that their hearts may melt, and
many fall at all their gates. I have given the
glittering sword; ah! it is made like lightning,
it is polished for slaughter. ¹⁶ Cut sharply to
right and left where your edge is directed. ¹⁷ I
also will clap my hands, and I will satisfy my
fury; I the Lord have spoken."

Seldom does one find in all prophetic
literature a more shocking or awesome passage than this. Its words almost depict
Yahweh as a sadistic, scheming, venal
deity, who with deadly passion and sullen
cruelty prepares for the total ravaging of
his enemies.

We can envision Ezekiel sharpening and
polishing a sword and suddenly like an

apparition of death wielding the glittering
sword, slashing with lightning strokes right
and left while at the same time crying and
wailing lamentations—and then slapping
his thigh exultantly or clapping the sword-
filled hands in joyous glee over the death
of the opponents of Yahweh. All these acts
by the prophet (vv. 14,16) will be accompanied by Yahweh, who also will clap
his hands as his fury is satisfied (v. 17).

Previously Ezekiel had been concerned
that the people regarded his oracles as
nothing more than delightful pleasantries
(20:49). In this passage there is additional
insight into the response of the people to
the prophetic oracles of judgment (v. 10b;
21:10 is 21:15 in Heb. text). *Mirth* (Heb.:
nasis) means to exult or to display joy and
may imply to leap or to spring with joy as
with a similar Hebrew word *sus*. The implication is that the people looked upon
such a strange pantomime of the prophetic message as sport or jest on the part
of Ezekiel. To them it was a comic act.

Not only did the people see the mimic
actions as a laughing matter, but scorned
all attempts at discipline, even the less
stern instrument of punishment, the *rod*
(v. 10). The discipline of Yahweh was
held in open contempt (v. 13). Since the
rod, which implied authority, had been
despised, the sword would take its place,
not to test, but to destroy (cf. Isa. 10:24;
30:31; Lam. 3:1; Mic. 5:1).

Two acts, those of smiting the thigh (v.
12) and clapping the hands (vv. 14,17),
possess varied interpretive possibilities.
Nominally the act of smiting the thigh was
indicative of hopelessness, despair, and
mourning (cf. Jer. 31:19). The act of hand
clapping may either denote an action of
sorrow or an action of exultation. On other
occasions it served as a summons. In this
general context, with both Yahweh and the
prophet clapping their hands, it would denote either a summons of the agent of
destruction (i.e., the *slayer* of v. 11) or
exultation over the gratification of Yahweh's anger. The former of the two seems
to fit better the context.

(3) The Sword of Babylon (21:18-23)

18 The word of the LORD came to me again: 19 "Son of man, mark two ways for the sword of the king of Babylon to come; both of them shall come forth from the same land. And make a signpost, make it at the head of the way to a city; 20 mark a way for the sword to come to Rabbah of the Ammonites and to Judah and to Jerusalem the fortified. 21 For the king of Babylon stands at the parting of the way, at the head of the two ways, to use divination; he shakes the arrows, he consults the teraphim, he looks at the liver. 22 Into his right hand comes the lot for Jerusalem, to open the mouth with a cry, to lift up the voice with shouting, to set battering rams against the gates, to cast up mounds, to build siege towers. 23 But to them it will seem like a false divination; they have sworn solemn oaths; but he brings their guilt to remembrance, that they may be captured.

Once the summons has been given, Ezekiel enacts dramatically the coming of the sword of Babylon, the slayer (v. 11). Ezekiel may have drawn a map on the ground before the people indicating the primary artery of travel from Babylon into Palestine. At a fork in the road he erected a signpost indicating the way the king of Babylon would travel with his armies to attack either Rabbah (Rabbath-Ammon, modern Amman, in Ezekiel's day the capital of the Ammonite kingdom) or Jerusalem (vv. 19,20). The reason for including Rabbah of the Ammonites as an alternate objective is supported by Jeremiah 27: 1-3, where evidence is given that the Ammonites were fomenting revolt against Babylonia. Judah, due to her secret alliances, and Ammon, due to her rebellion, were both legitimate objectives for Nebuchadnezzar. Attack on either would be justifiable.

Apparently Ezekiel assumed the role of Nebuchadnezzar who stood at the crossroads trying to determine which nation to assault (v. 21). The decision of the king is to obtain divine instruction. Ezekiel, portraying Nebuchadnezzar, performs three acts of divination.

The use of sacred lots, a type of divination designated formally as "belomancy," was one in which arrows or sticks were in-

scribed with individual names. These were then placed in a container and shaken. That which fell from the container was considered the choice of the gods. Ezekiel had probably marked each stick with the name Jerusalem or Rabbah. The second consultation was that of the teraphim. These were small god-images somewhat larger than an ordinary piece of writing chalk or crayon (cf. Gen. 31:19; 1 Sam. 15:23; 19:13; 2 Kings 23:24; Hos. 3:4). The third method employed was that of reading the omens by inspection of the configuration of the outer surface of a sheep's liver. The practice of hepatoscopy utilized clay representations of the sheep liver when it was impractical to use the liver from a freshly slaughtered animal. The answer given pointed toward Jerusalem. Yahweh had decreed destruction by Babylon.

But the response of the people to the dramatic enactment will be identical to that of previous pantomimes. They will look upon it as a false thing (v. 23). Again, the presumptiveness of Jerusalem's inhabtants and Judah's people is made plain. They considered the oracle false for they believed Jerusalem to be inviolate and they themselves righteous. To them such an event was an impossibility.

(4) The Sword and Zedekiah (21:24-27)

24 "Therefore thus says the Lord GOD: Because you have made your guilt to be remembered, in that your transgressions are uncovered, so that in all your doings your sins appear—because you have come to remembrance, you shall be taken in them. 25 And you, O unhallowed wicked one, prince of Israel, whose day has come, the time of your final punishment, 26 thus says the LORD GOD: Remove the turban, and take off the crown; things shall not remain as they are; exalt that which is low, and abase that which is high. 27 A ruin, ruin, ruin I will make it; there shall not be even a trace of it until he comes whose right it is; and to him I will give it.

Scarcely could one frame a more devastating indictment than that of v. 25 where the *prince* (i.e., Zedekiah) is defined as *unhallowed wicked*. The nature of the full and final judgment upon the prince is a cataclysmic event which will reverse totally (v. 26) all social, economic, and political order. The implication of v. 26b is that of everything being turned upside down like the effects of an earthquake (cf. Gen. 9:24,25 where "overthrew" means to turn upside down like turning a pancake). Royal succession through the Davidic bloodline will vanish without a solitary reminder of its existence until the true successor comes (v. 27b), and to him the crown will be given by Yahweh. Verse 27 may however refer to the city of Jerusalem which will be destroyed without any trace; literally, not to be found until he who is the rightful and righteous ruler comes. There may be some connection here with Genesis 49:10, where Shiloh may mean "to whom it belongs." [73]

That which is certain, however, is the completeness of the destruction. The threefold repetition of *ruin* (v. 27) is a prophetic formula and denotes completeness. *Ruin,* upon *ruin,* upon *ruin* is the fate awaiting both Jerusalem and the royal family.

(5) The Sword and Ammon (21:28–32)

28 "And you, son of man, prophesy, and say, Thus says the Lord GOD concerning the Ammonites, and concerning their reproach; say, A sword, a sword is drawn for the slaughter, it is polished to glitter and to flash like lightning— 29 while they see for you false visions, while they divine lies for you—to be laid on the necks of the unhallowed wicked, whose day has come, the time of their final punishment. 30 Return it to its sheath. In the place where you were created, in the land of your origin, I will judge you. 31 And I will pour out my indignation upon you; I will blow upon you with the fire of my wrath; and I will deliver you into the hands of brutal men, skilful to destroy. 32 You shall be fuel for the fire; your blood shall be in the midst of the land; you shall be no more remembered; for I the LORD have spoken."

An episode which occurred after the fall of Jerusalem may be the point at issue

in this brief division. In the book of Jeremiah (cf. Jer. 40:13 ff.) there is an account of Ammon's interference in the affairs of the ravaged Southern Kingdom. The importunate condition of Judah, as a result of the Babylonian assault, provided Ammon an opportunity to extend her borders by assuming control over Judahite territory. Also in the same account Ammon is implicated in the conspiracy which led to the death of Gedaliah, the Babylonian appointed governor of the province of Judah (cf. Jer. 40:14). Because of this Ammon, too, will succumb to the sword and enter into a similar fate to that of Judah.[74]

3. Indictment Against the Bloody City (22:1–31)

This is the most detailed indictment of Ezekiel against Jerusalem. Specified offenses fall into broad categories, such as individual rebellion and corporate social and religious corruption. All segments of Jerusalem's societal structure receive a withering denunciation. The city is shown as being corrupt from the palace of the ruler to the hovel of the common man. Ezekiel is specifically instructed to deliver a bill of particulars (v. 2). Once again we note Ezekiel utilizing every procedure to make plain that Yahweh's judgment was justifiable.

(1) The First Indictment (22:1–16)

1 Moreover the word of the LORD came to me, saying, 2 "And you, son of man, will you judge, will you judge the bloody city? Then declare to her all her abominable deeds. 3 You shall say, Thus says the Lord GOD: A city that sheds blood in the midst of her, that her time may come, and that makes idols to defile herself! 4 You have become guilty by the blood which you have shed, and defiled by the idols which you have made; and you have brought your day near, the appointed time of your years has come. Therefore I have made you a reproach to the nations, and a mocking to all the countries. 5 Those who are near and those who are far from you will mock you, you infamous one, full of tumult.

---

73 Cf. Henri Cazelles, "Shiloh, The Customary Laws and the Return of the Ancient Kings," *Proclamation and Presence,* ed. Durham and Porter (London: SCM Press, 1970), pp. 239–251.

74 Cf. Bewer, *op. cit.* p. 387, who sees 21:30–32 as being out of context and an oracle of judgment against Nebuchadnezzar.

6 "Behold, the princes of Israel in you, every one according to his power, have been bent on shedding blood. 7 Father and mother are treated with contempt in you; the sojourner suffers extortion in your midst; the fatherless and the widow are wronged in you. 8 You have despised my holy things, and profaned my sabbaths. 9 There are men in you who slander to shed blood, and men in you who eat upon the mountains; men commit lewdness in your midst. 10 In you men uncover their fathers' nakedness; in you they humble women who are unclean in their impurity. 11 One commits abomination with his neighbor's wife; another lewdly defiles his daughter-in-law; another in you defiles his sister, his father's daughter. 12 In you men take bribes to shed blood; you take interest and increase and make gain of your neighbors by extortion; and you have forgotten me, says the Lord God.

13 "Behold, therefore, I strike my hands together at the dishonest gain which you have made, and at the blood which has been in the midst of you. 14 Can your courage endure, or can your hands be strong, in the days that I shall deal with you? I the Lord have spoken, and I will do it. 15 I will scatter you among the nations and disperse you through the countries, and I will consume your filthiness out of you. 16 And I shall be profaned through you in the sight of the nations; and you shall know that I am the Lord."

Ezekiel initially charges Jerusalem with being a city of blood (vv. 1–5), an inevitable result of embracing idolatry. Doubtless the indictment is connected with the giving of human sacrifices to foreign gods. Such an accusation had previously been delivered (cf. comment on 20:31).

A second accusation deals with the matter of Jerusalem being a bloody city as the result of social and personal corruption (vv. 6–16). This specification has to do with open bloodshed without any moral compunction. Ethical relativity was rampant among the ruling class for to them position and power constituted right (v. 6). But for all other classes there was the same offense. Each preyed on the other according to the opportunities afforded by rank. Among all classes ethical filial relationships were scorned and the role of parental authority denied. Even the *sojourner*—a visitor in the city who may or may not be a convert to Israelite religion—

became the target of corrupt schemes, and illegal force was used to strip him of his possessions (v. 7). If the sojourner was a proselyte then the offense is the more insidious. For he who had embraced the religion of Israel had become the prime prey of those who should have exemplified the best in ethical religion.

A low ebb in social justice is brought to light by the denunciation of unjust treatment of orphans and widows (v. 7b). The defenseless, helpless, and powerless, those who could not defend themselves due to their importunity, were the objects of evil designs.

If v. 8 is an indictment of the priesthood, which it may well be, then the corruption had worked its foul will where greatest damage could be accomplished. Ingrained sin was not only to be found among the upper echelons of Jerusalem's society. Men told lies, *slander* (v. 9), which resulted in tragic death for the innocent and economic gain or political advantage for the slanderer (cf. Lev. 19:16, but especially the Naboth incident in 1 Kings 21).

Stygian depths of gross immorality are imputed to the people by Ezekiel (vv. 10, 11). The enormity of the charge dealing with sexual offenses is almost incomprehensible. Perversion, adultery, and incestuous relationships are referred to as if they were common and repeated occurrences, even a way of life. The act of humbling a woman (v. 10) implies rape at a time when the woman was unclean due to menstrual flow (cf. Lev. 18:19; 20:18). Such offenses were committed with the half-sister (i.e., one's father's daughter, v. 11b; cf. Lev. 18:9,11,15,19; 20:10,12, 17; Deut. 27:22). The uncovering of the father's nakedness (v. 10) may imply an unnatural relationship with a stepmother (cf. Lev. 18:7 ff.; Deut. 22:30).

Positioned next are the concerns equally shared by Ezekiel and the great eighth-century ethical prophets—Amos, Isaiah, and Micah (cf. Isa. 1:23; 5:23; 33:15; Amos 5:12; Mic. 3:11; 7:3). Bribes were taken which corrupted the judicial system.

And for a bribe to be taken, it must not be overlooked that one offered the bribe (v. 12). Israelite laws dealt clearly with bribery (cf. Ex. 23:8; Deut. 16:19; 27: 25). Bribes, when taken, generally led to false testimony against innocent defendants. The pleading of a just cause led directly to a verdict of death when there were situations involving monetary gain, political expediency, or personal vendetta.

In like manner, the inequities of economic power come under attack, especially those dealing with exorbitant rates of interest. The people had resorted to outright extortion in order to reap financial dividends. Extortion is not always by force but may be an act of wrongful acquisition by illegal power or cunning. *Extortion* means to oppress or to wrong especially by overcharge. Many Old Testament writers use the term in reference to preying upon the poor or the helpless (cf. Amos 4:1; Deut. 24:14; Jer. 7:6; Zech. 7:10; Prov. 14:31). The act is the more offensive because one Jerusalemite preyed upon his fellow Jerusalemite by force, intimidation, and cunning. The victims were not strangers, but friends, neighbors, and kinsmen (v. 12b).

Such acts, on the part of the people, provided eloquent evidence for Yahweh. They were proof positive that the people had forgotten him (v. 12). With the dissipation of and defection from the true religion of Israel there had occurred personal moral corruption. The ethical fiber of Israel, which was to hold it morally erect in the eyes of Yahweh, had rotted within. When a nation has lost its morality it cannot stand. Its courage and the by-product of that courage, endurance, come to an end (v. 14). It is inescapable that Ezekiel viewed public immorality as an evidence of the neglect of Yahweh.

As a result of such grievous offenses Yahweh will demand retribution (vv. 13, 15,16). The striking together of the hands of Yahweh (v. 13) specifically implies the epitome of Yahweh's anger and disgust. It evidences his extreme displeasure with the

sinfulness of Jerusalem. For Jerusalem, which was meant to be the crown jewel of Yahweh's people, the city which was to have been the example par excellence of true religion, was nothing more than a cankering, festering eruption of evil: its filthiness could not go unpurged.

(2) The Refining of Jerusalem (22:17–22)

17 And the word of the Lord came to me: 18 "Son of man, the house of Israel has become dross to me; all of them, silver and bronze and tin and iron and lead in the furnace, have become dross. 19 Therefore thus says the Lord God: Because you have all become dross, therefore, behold, I will gather you into the midst of Jerusalem. 20 As men gather silver and bronze and iron and lead and tin into a furnace, to blow the fire upon it in order to melt it; so I will gather you in my anger and in my wrath, and I will put you in and melt you. 21 I will gather you and blow upon you with the fire of my wrath, and you shall be melted in the midst of it. 22 As silver is melted in a furnace, so you shall be melted in the midst of it; and you shall know that I the Lord have poured out my wrath upon you."

Ezekiel depicts the judgment upon Jerusalem in a "smelterer" simile. There is no indication in the allegory that the act of refining was to produce a pure metal or to reclaim metal. Jerusalem is simply to be cast into the crucible of Yahweh's heated judgment. Israel (v. 18) means Judah and its people. They are to Yahweh nothing more than dross (vv. 17,18). The imagery is telling. Dross is either a raw metal still retaining its impurities or unusable sludge (i.e., slag), a by-product of smelting. Jerusalem is to be the crucible, and Yahweh is to be the smelterer (vv. 20,21) who subjects the metal to the blast of the furnace in order to destroy it, not to refine it.

The import of the passage is unique. In an aggregate sense Yahweh's intent for Jerusalem and Judah was that they be of unalloyed allegiance to the true faith. But Jerusalem had become one of alloyed allegiance embracing diverse pagan religious elements. Singular allegiance to Yahweh had been diffused by multitudinous idolatries (i.e., symbolized by the different metals, v. 18). And it had thus become dross, a totally useless commodity.

None of the inhabitants of Jerusalem will escape. When the instrument of Yahweh's destruction comes upon the city, Jerusalem will be turned into a raging blast furnace (v. 22).

(3) The Second Indictment (22:23–31)

23 And the word of the LORD came to me: **24** "Son of man, say to her, You are a land that is not cleansed, or rained upon in the day of indignation. **25** Her princes in the midst of her are like a roaring lion tearing the prey; they have devoured human lives; they have taken treasure and precious things; they have made many widows in the midst of her. **26** Her priests have done violence to my law and have profaned my holy things; they have made no distinction between the holy and the common, neither have they taught the difference between the unclean and the clean, and they have disregarded my sabbaths, so that I am profaned among them. **27** Her princes in the midst of her are like wolves tearing the prey, shedding blood, destroying lives to get dishonest gain. **28** And her prophets have daubed for them with whitewash, seeing false visions and divining lies for them, saying, 'Thus says the Lord GOD,' when the LORD has not spoken. **29** The people of the land have practiced extortion and committed robbery; they have oppressed the poor and needy, and have extorted from the sojourner without redress. **30** And I sought for a man among them who should build up the wall and stand in the breach before me for the land, that I should not destroy it; but I found none. **31** Therefore I have poured out my indignation upon them; I have consumed them with the fire of my wrath; their way have I requited upon their heads, says the Lord GOD."

A second specification of the sins of Jerusalem stands in stylistic contrast to the first indictment of 22:1–16. In a well-ordered progression each socio-religious class in the city from highest to lowest is specified in a bill of particulars. Although no analogy should be pressed toward an argument to absurdity, the implication is, as the leadership goes, so go the people.

In any institutional structure the gravest danger does not lie in the lowest levels of leadership but in the highest, from which point corruption spreads contagion like the deadly rays of atomic fallout.

Three broad categories of leadership are detailed: (1) political, the *princes* of v. 25; (2) education, the *priests* of v. 26, who were obligated to teach the law (cf. Lev. 10:10 ff.); and (3) the religious, the *prophets* of v. 28, whose task it was to proclaim the true word of Yahweh. Each group in turn had betrayed their obligation of trust. By their acts, along with those of the common man whom they had assisted in corrupting, the land itself had become defiled (v. 24; cf. Num. 35:34; Deut. 21:23; and comment on Ezek. 36:17 ff.).

The *princes*, who were commissioned to protect and guide their people, to render justice, and to express righteousness concretely, were destroying their subjects. They who were to be servants used weapons of violence and devices of extortion on their people. They were like *a roaring lion* (v. 25) and *wolves* (v. 27). What strong imagery! Upon launching his attack the lion roars in order to paralyze his prey with fear and continues to roar as he mauls his victims. Only then does the beast become quiet. Thus the princes attacked, tore to shreds, and devoured their subjects like beasts of prey for gain.[75]

As for the *priests*, they perverted the law for personal gain. Obviously they refused to teach the law (v. 26) because in so doing they would expose themselves and be condemned by their own teaching. Since moral offenses seem to be the burden of this section, *law* (lit., instruction) may refer either to civil or religious legislation. It may well be the case that the priests who were experts in civil law, since it like religious law was considered to be of Yahweh, rendered those decisions which would give them personal advantage.

Specifically the failure in teaching the laws of cleanliness and of "hiding their eyes," i.e., the literal meaning of the term

---

75 Cf. the alternate RSV (marg.) reading taken from the MT, "a conspiracy of her prophets." According to this translation, rather than the LXX reading, the passage would imply that these were false prophets.

disregarded, led the common people into rebellion (v. 29). Failure to teach the law and the act of looking the other way at the flaunting of sabbath regulations gave the people a "carte blanche" for sin.

While the priests refused involvement, the *prophets* (v. 28) were actively engaged in erecting false facades over the events of history by placing in the mouth of Yahweh words produced by their own minds. Literally they were playing God for the people; they abused their prophetic privilege in order to enrich themselves. The phrase *have daubed for them* (v. 28) means the prophets aided and abetted the corruption of the priests and princes. They had covered up, i.e., whitewashed, their sins rather than exposing them.

The population of Jerusalem—preyed upon by the princes, forsaken by the priests, lied to by the prophets, and victimized by their leadership—in turn found a victim: the *poor,* the *needy,* and the *sojourner* (v. 29). The ecology of nature was at work. The prey turned predator, and Jerusalem and Judah reverted to a jungle.

Among all the inhabitants (i.e., princes, priests, prophets, and people) Yahweh sought just one who would hear and heed, just one who would stand against the overwhelming tide of iniquity; but none was found. It was all corruption (v. 30), and this therefore concretely sealed the fate of the city (v. 31).

An extraordinary verse (v. 30) has posed several searching questions. Is it not implied that the city would have been spared if a righteous one were found? Is it not strange that Ezekiel makes no mention of Jeremiah? Also what of Ezekiel himself? Would Jeremiah, or for that matter Ezekiel be of sufficient righteousness? Did not both of these prophets expose the sin and stand in the breach as instruments of Yahweh?

Are not these questions, however, somewhat extraneous? Is it not the implication that no one was really capable of averting the disaster—neither a Jeremiah nor an Ezekiel? That even if one supremely righteous were found and if he did stand in the breach, the rebellion of Jerusalem was so great it would be of no avail? They were thoroughly corrupt!

4. The Allegory of Two Women (23:1-49)

In the allegorical account Yahweh is depicted as having two wives who are sisters, Oholah and Oholibah. The imagery may have come from the story of Jacob's marriage to Rachel and Leah. Each of the wives proved to be unfaithful with Oholah (v. 4) representing Samaria, capital of the Northern Kingdom, and Oholibah (v. 4) representing Jerusalem, capital of the Southern Kingdom. Oholah prostituted herself in an adulterous and idolatrous relationship with Assyria; and Oholibah in like manner with two lovers, Assyria and Babylonia.

The unfaithful wife motif may have been evoked by Ezekiel's familiarity with the book of Hosea (cf. Hos. 2:1–20). Although the wives are symbols for the cities of Samaria and Jerusalem, they are in turn symbolical of the two nations and their people. This is similar in import to chapter 16 where religious apostasy was the destructive agent. Here the corrupting instrument is the foreign alliance which occasions idolatry.

(1) Preface to the Story (23:1-4)

[1] The word of the LORD came to me: [2] "Son of man, there were two women, the daughters of one mother; [3] they played the harlot in Egypt; they played the harlot in their youth; there their breasts were pressed and their virgin bosoms handled. [4] Oholah was the name of the elder and Oholibah the name of her sister. They became mine, and they bore sons and daughters. As for their names, Oholah is Samaria, and Oholibah is Jerusalem.

Employing the same geographical setting as is found in chapter 16, Ezekiel poses a hypothetical situation. The sisters *Oholah* (Samaria) and *Oholibah* (Jerusalem), who also signify the two nations Israel and Judah, were the offspring of *one mother.* They were the chosen of the seed of Abraham. In Egypt the two maidens were initiated into the rites of sexual experience (v. 31), which signifies an introduction to Egyptian idolatry. That such was the case is clearly identifiable in Exodus 32 and Joshua 24:14. Ezekiel is asserting that from their youth in Egypt the two nations had inbred and cultivated habits of infidelity (v. 2). The two daughters became the wives of Yahweh and bore him children, (i.e., *became mine* implies the covenant of marriage, v. 4). They were both alike in name (i.e., "tent") with slightly different emphasis, as well as in character and disposition. Each was depraved and wayward.

(2) *The Harlotry of Samaria* (23:5–10)

5 "Oholah played the harlot while she was mine; and she doted on her lovers the Assyrians, 6 warriors clothed in purple, governors and commanders, all of them desirable young men, horsemen riding on horses. 7 She bestowed her harlotries upon them, the choicest men of Assyria all of them; and she defiled herself with all the idols of every one on whom she doted. 8 She did not give up her harlotry which she had practiced since her days in Egypt; for in her youth men had lain with her and handled her virgin bosom and poured out their lust upon her. 9 Therefore I delivered her into the hands of her lovers, into the hands of the Assyrians, upon whom she doted. 10 These uncovered her nakedness; they seized her sons and her daughters; and her they slew with the sword; and she became a byword among women, when judgment had been executed upon her.

Throughout the passage the phrase "to play the harlot" is used to denote foreign alliances which resulted in religious defection. Overt acts on the part of Yahweh's people to make alliances were considered to be a denial of Yahweh. Historically Israel's first line of defense was to be faith in and dependence upon Yahweh. Since the national faith was so irretrievably connected to the political policy, any act which adversely affected one affected the other. Israel as a chosen people were not to be as other people in their national and international affairs. Ideally Israel was not

to establish a monarchy but retain the theocracy (cf. 1 Sam. 8:4–22). Subsequently all kings were judged according to their support of traditional religion and their rejection of alliances which would result in apostasy.

Samaria, true to her heritage of being the fondling of Egypt in past times (v. 8), defected from moral ties with Yahweh and gave herself in an alliance to Assyraia (v. 5. As she had in past times played the harlot with Egypt, now she embraced a new lover. In the new relationship Oholah (Samaria) gave herself to Assyrian officers (v. 6). This indicates symbolically the intimate embracing of the gods of Assyria. Oholah (Samaria), true to her corrupt self, had superimposed upon the anciently embraced Egyptian cults the Assyrian religious rites thereby producing a syncretistic religion. She who was Yahweh's (i.e., *she was mine*, lit., under me) has become the one upon whom the Assyrian lovers have *poured out* their lust.

(3) *The Harlotry of Jerusalem* (23:11–21)

11 "Her sister Oholibah saw this, yet she was more corrupt than she in her doting and in her harlotry, which was worse than that of her sister. 12 She doted upon the Assyrians, governors and commanders, warriors clothed in full armor, horsemen riding on horses, all of them desirable young men. 13 And I saw that she was defiled; they both took the same way. 14 But she carried her harlotry further; she saw men portrayed upon the wall, the images of the Chaldeans portrayed in vermilion, 15 girded with belts on their loins, with flowing turbans on their heads, all of them looking like officers, a picture of Babylonians whose native land was Chaldea. 16 When she saw them she doted upon them, and sent messengers to them in Chaldea. 17 And the Babylonians came to her into the bed of love, and they defiled her with their lust; and after she was polluted by them, she turned from them in disgust. 18 When she carried on her harlotry so openly and flaunted her nakedness, I turned in disgust from her, as I had turned from her sister. 19 Yet she increased her harlotry, remembering the days of her youth, when she played the harlot in the land of Egypt 20 and doted upon her paramours there, whose members were like those of asses, and whose issue was like that of horses. 21 Thus you longed for the lewdness of your

youth, when the Egyptians handled your bosom and pressed your young breasts."

Jerusalem and Judah (Obolibah) exceeded by far the infidelity of Oholah (Samaria). They both chose the same course of seeking foreign alliances, and to both nations it brought national corruption and religious decadence (v. 13). Not only did Oholibah defile herself with whoring after Assyria, but she compounded the guilt by embracing an even more disgusting lover, Babylonia.

The actions of both Oholah and Oholibah toward their lovers are defined as a doting love (23:5,7,9,11,12,16,20). Basically *doted* means inordinate love, literally a lustful love in its most sensual sense. This desire so emboldened her that she sought out Babylonia rather than being sought by Babylonia (v. 16). She was no naïve and artless maiden seduced by an opportunist. She was a lustfully mature seductress. The Babylonians responded to the invitation so mightily that she was repulsed (vv. 17,20).[76] Judah was so brazen and wanton in the affair (v. 18), Yahweh could only turn away from her *in disgust*. The utter depravity is revealed by the term *openly*, implying that the acts of lustful Judah were openly committed for all to see—thus emphasizing the openness and brazenness with which she embraced the idolatry of the Babylonians.

Judah's inordinate excesses are listed in vv. 14,15. While married to Yahweh, Oholibah became the plaything of Assyria and then abandoned Assyria for the Chaldeans (i.e., Babylonians), whom she knew not personally but only by pictures portrayed upon the wall. The appearance of their bearing was enough to kindle the desire of the wayward Oholibah to enter into a relationship with them.

The *officers* whose images were portrayed were likely the third man who occupied

the chariot along with the king and charioteer. Thus, it implies an official of high rank (cf. Ex. 14:7).

Therefore while Judah (Oholibah) played the apostate with Assyrian entanglements she compounded her capricious unfaithfulness by another act of infidelity. The pattern of infidelity breeding infidelity had reached its climax. Oholibah (Judah) showed herself to be not the equal of Oholah (Israel) in political and religious disloyalty but the superior offender.

(4) The Judgment Against Jerusalem (23:22-35)

22 Therefore, O Oholibah, thus says the Lord GOD: "Behold, I will rouse against you your lovers from whom you turned in disgust, and I will bring them against you from every side: 23 the Babylonians and all the Chaldeans, Pekod and Shoa and Koa, and all the Assyrians with them, desirable young men, governors and commanders all of them, officers and warriors, all of them riding on horses. 24 And they shall come against you from the north with chariots and wagons and a host of peoples; they shall set themselves against you on every side with buckler, shield, and helmet, and I will commit the judgment to them, and they shall judge you according to their judgments. 25 And I will direct my indignation against you, that they may deal with you in fury. They shall cut off your nose and your ears, and your survivors shall fall by the sword. They shall seize your sons and your daughters, and your survivors shall be devoured by fire. 26 They shall also strip you of your clothes and take away your fine jewels. 27 Thus I will put an end to your lewdness and your harlotry brought from the land of Egypt; so that you shall not lift up your eyes to the Egyptians or remember them any more. 28 For thus says the Lord GOD: Behold, I will deliver you into the hands of those whom you hate, into the hands of those from whom you turned in disgust; 29 and they shall deal with you in hatred, and take away all the fruit of your labor, and leave you naked and bare, and the nakedness of your harlotry shall be uncovered. Your lewdness and your harlotry 30 have brought this upon you, because you played the harlot with the nations, and polluted yourself with their idols. 31 You have gone the way of your sister; therefore I will give her cup into your hand. 32 Thus says the Lord GOD:

"You shall drink your sister's cup
    which is deep and large;

---

[76] Frequently the words and imagery employed by Ezekiel are quite explicit. Translators have sought to express these in more delicate terms, e.g., "whose members" or private parts instead of terms for sex organs or references to sexual activity.

you shall be laughed at and held in derision,
    for it contains much;
33 you will be filled with drunkenness and
    sorrow.
A cup of horror and desolation,
    is the cup of your sister Samaria;
34 you shall drink it and drain it out,
    and pluck out your hair,
    and tear your breasts;
for I have spoken, says the Lord God.
35 Therefore thus says the Lord God: Because
you have forgotten me and cast me behind
your back, therefore bear the consequences of
your lewdness and harlotry."

A prophetic formula *thus says the Lord
God* is used four times in this division (vv.
22,28,32,35). Following each usage is a
terse indictment of the people of Judah
and Jerusalem personified by the wife figure Oholibah. Use of such a formula intensifies the certainty of the judgments
given and reenforces the surety of the punishment.

Ezekiel proclaims with irony how the
very lovers to whom Oholibah had given
herself, those who had debased her with
every untoward indecency, will be the instrument of her final humiliation. Babylonia and her allies (v. 23) [77] will completely ravish and destroy Oholibah without mercy (vv. 24–27). The inclusion here
of Aramaean tribesmen implies Judah's additional defilement by involvement with
such groups.

Boldly striking is that part of v. 24
which depicts Yahweh permitting Judah's
lovers to judge her, not according to Yahweh's methods of judgment, but according
to their ways. A precedent for such an act
is set in 16:37 ff. where the lover Jerusalem
is "set bare" before her lovers and executed.
It may well be that Yahweh is permitting
Judah to be judged by the standards of
alien nations whose ways she has chosen.
This absolutely negates any possibility of
Yahweh's intervening grace.

Yahweh had excluded himself and de-
ferred judgment to the most vicious of

men. Nowhere is there such overwhelming
evidence of the indignation of Yahweh toward the wanton wife. There are at least
two very possible and plausible interpretations: (1) that judgment was assigned to
the former lovers because Yahweh's judgment might be the more devastating; or (2)
that judgment was yielded to others because
the overwhelming compassion of Yahweh
for the people of the covenant would have
lessened the penalty. The latter of the two
interpretations would seem preferable.

The penalties exacted for foreign judgment will be horrifying (v. 25). Mutilation
evidently was not a practice in Israelite
warfare, but both Babylonians and Egyptians severed portions of the bodies of victims as sure evidence of their prowess and
ruthlessness in battle. Eichrodt sees in v.
26 the depiction of the ravaging of Oholiah
(Jerusalem) by any warrior who wished to
satisfy his lustful desires.

The *cup* of Oholah (Samaria) which is
passed to Oholibah (Judah) poses intriguing interpretive possibilities (vv. 31–34).
What does the cup symbolize? It is described as being *deep* and *large* with the
one drinking of its content being subjected
to boisterous derision (v. 31). Ingredients
within the cup are *horror and desolation*
which when consumed will produce a
foreboding, awesome, unconsolable, and
uncontrollable bereavement (v. 34). This
horrifying cup will be Judah's lot, for she ·
will consume the last minute particle of its
content.

The cup symbolism is a major motif not
only in Old and New Testament literature
but is found in other ancient Near Eastern
literature. Inherent in "cup symbolism" is
the idea of destiny—that of a god, an individual, a tribe, or a nation. In biblical
literature it symbolizes the lot which falls
to a man whether it be good or evil.
Eichrodt points out the fact that Jeremiah
(cf. Jer. 25) uses such symbolism for the
destiny of heathen nations while Ezekiel
utilizes the cup to signal Judah's destiny.

The phrase *pluck out your hair* (v. 34)
is taken from the Syriac manuscript with

---

[77] Pekod, Shoa, and Koa were Aramaean mercenaries (cf. Jer. 50:21) from semi-nomadic tribes. The
Assyrians were also mercenaries.

the Masoretic Text reading literally "crunch or gnaw its shred." The Masoretic Text rendering may be preferable here. Once Judah has drained the contents, the cup will be broken into pieces (i.e., shreds). Then the shreds will be gnawed forcing Judah to consume even the woe which has permeated the core of the vessel. Even those minute drops which had impregnated the walls of the vessel will be swallowed. All the lot of bitterness will be the fate of Judah.

May points to Yahweh's cup of wrath and the Ugaritic passages referring to the disgraceful or scornful cup. But the overall symbolism is a direct reference to the bitterness of total national destruction and exile.

(5) Adulterated Worship Intolerable to Yahweh (23:36-45)

36 The Lord said to me: "Son of man, will you judge Oholah and Oholibah? Then declare to them their abominable deeds. 37 For they have committed adultery, and blood is upon their hands; with their idols they have committed adultery; and they have even offered up to them for food the sons whom they had borne to me. 38 Moreover this they have done to me: they have defiled my sanctuary on the same day and profaned my sabbaths. 39 For when they had slaughtered their children in sacrifice to their idols, on the same day they came into my sanctuary to profane it. And lo, this is what they did in my house. 40 They even sent for men to come from far, to whom a messenger was sent, and lo, they came. For them you bathed yourself, painted your eyes, and decked yourself with ornaments; 41 you sat upon a stately couch, with a table spread before it on which you had placed my incense and my oil. 42 The sound of a carefree multitude was with her; and with men of the common sort drunkards were brought from the wilderness; and they put bracelets upon the hands of the women, and beautiful crowns upon their heads. 43 "Then I said, Do not men now commit adultery when they practice harlotry with her? 44 For they have gone in to her, as men go in to a harlot. Thus they went in to Oholah and to Oholibah to commit lewdness. 45 But righteous men shall pass judgment on them with the sentence of adulteresses, and with the sentence of women that shed blood; because they are adulteresses, and blood is upon their hands."

Attention is divided in this section between religious offenses (vv. 37-39) and political offenses (vv. 40-44). Apostasy on the part of the Oholah and Oholibah was within itself a grievous offense, but this was compounded when their children of union with Yahweh were corrupted and given as sacrifices to pagan dieties. Those who were possessions of Yahweh, and therefore holy, were taken from him and committed to gods to whom they did not belong (v. 37). This, coupled with their complete indifference toward Yahweh's holy places of worship, produced utter religious insensitivity.

On the sabbaths the people would participate in the horrifying rites of human sacrifice and come straight from the sanctuaries of idolatry to the Temple (v. 39). So corrupt had they become, there was in their minds no inconsistency between offering human sacrifice in pagan cultic rites and on the same day presenting themselves in the Temple as devotees of Yahweh.

There is the condition when worship becomes sin. Amos sarcastically refers to just such a condition when he says to the people of Israel, come to worship in your impurity and thus multiply your sin (cf. Amos 4:4,5). The presence of such individuals in worship is desecration.

As those who solicited lovers (i.e., solicited alliances), both Oholah and Oholibah made themselves as enticing as possible in order to lure attention (vv. 40-44). They perfumed and bathed themselves, even painted your eyes. *Paint* (Heb., *kachalte*) is used only here in the Old Testament. It may refer to the use of antimony as a cosmetic (cf. 2 Kings 9:30; Jer. 4:30). The effect of the cosmetic application, which was likely silver in hue, served to enlarge the eyes and make them more lustrous.

The deepening of the debauchery of the two is evidenced by v. 42. Not only did the two depraved wives give themselves to great and powerful lovers, but they consorted with *drunkards . . . from the wilderness*—the roving nomadic groups who dwelt on the fringes of society. Judah, in

her degradation, sank lower and lower
until she as a nation frolicked with the
basest of men in unholy alliances. From
the darling of great nations she sank to the
level of embracing the lowest of ethnic
subgroups.

(6) In Judgment Yahweh Is Known (23:46–49)

46 For thus says the Lord GOD: "Bring up a
host against them, and make them an object of
terror and a spoil. 47 And the host shall stone
them and despatch them with their swords;
they shall slay their sons and their daughters,
and burn up their houses. 48 Thus will I put an
end to lewdness in the land, that all women
may take warning and not commit lewdness as
you have done. 49 And your lewdness shall be
requited upon you, and you shall bear the
penalty for your sinful idolatry; and you shall
know that I am the Lord GOD."

There is an abrupt transition within the
text which points to the assumption that
the verses are textual additions. Rather
than having a continued focus upon
Oholah and Oholibah, the verses constitute a general warning for women. They
are not to emulate the example of Oholah
and Oholibah! Thus it gives every indication of being a general social injunction
against sexual wantoness added to the
prophecy by a later hand.

5. The End Is Accomplished (24:1–27)

The prophecies of this chapter are dated
on the day of the beginning of the siege of
Jerusalem, probably January 15, 588 B.C.
(v. 1; cf. 2 Kings 25:1; Jer. 52:4). In two
moving scenes Ezekiel depicts the attack
upon the city and its fall (24:1–4; 24:
15–27). In the first of the two oracles both
the people and the city are depicted as
drastically purged. Ezekiel again utilizes
the theme of the caldron (cf. comment. on
11:3). The symbolism employed is self-
explanatory: "caldron" (Jerusalem), "flesh"
(the inhabitants), and "rust" (ingrained
wickedness). (cf. Eichrodt, *Ezekiel*, pp.
337–339 for varying opinions.) The theme
of the second oracle is that of overwhelming grief as exemplified by the death of the
prophet's wife.

(1) The Allegory of the Rusted Pot (24:1–14)

1 In the ninth year, in the tenth month, on
the tenth day of the month, the word of the
LORD came to me: 2 "Son of man, write down
the name of this day, this very day. The king
of Babylon has laid siege to Jerusalem this
very day. 3 And utter an allegory to the rebellious house and say to them, Thus says the
Lord GOD:
Set on the pot, set it on,
    pour in water also;
4 put in it the pieces of flesh,
    all the good pieces, the thigh and the
        shoulder;
fill it with choice bones.
5 Take the choicest one of the flock,
    pile the logs under it;
boil its pieces,
    seethe also its bones in it.
6 "Therefore thus says the Lord GOD: Woe to
the bloody city, to the pot whose rust is in it,
and whose rust has not gone out of it! Take out
of it piece after piece, without making any
choice. 7 For the blood she has shed is still in
the midst of her; she put it on the bare rock,
she did not pour it upon the ground to cover it
with dust. 8 To rouse my wrath, to take vengeance, I have set on the bare rock the blood she
has shed, that it may not be covered.
9 Therefore thus says the Lord GOD: Woe to
the bloody city! I also will make the pile great.
10 Heap on the logs, kindle the fire, boil well
the flesh, and empty out the broth, and let the
bones be burned up. 11 Then set it empty upon
the coals, that it may become hot, and its
copper may burn, that its filthiness may be
melted in it, its rust consumed. 12 In vain I
have wearied myself; its thick rust does not go
out of it by fire. 13 Its rust is your filthy lewdness. Because I would have cleansed you and
you were not cleansed from your filthiness, you
shall not be cleansed any more till I have
satisfied my fury upon you. 14 I the LORD have
spoken; it shall come to pass, I will do it; I will
not go back, I will not spare, I will not repent;
according to your ways and your doings I will
judge you, says the Lord GOD."

Whether this is another enacted vignette
portrayed by Ezekiel is debatable, yet the
imagery suggests the possibility of symbolic prophetic enactment. Since it is defined as an allegory or a parable (v. 3),
one must seek out not only the symbolism
of the caldron (i.e., *pot*, cf. 11:3 ff.) but
also its content (i.e., *pieces of flesh*, v. 4).
If the caldron is taken to be Jerusalem and

flesh, the people, it may provide a simple solution. Thus it would imply that under siege the inhabitants of Jerusalem would be like pieces of meat stewing in a bubbling pot. The simple solution, however, frequently creates problems of its own.[78]

Two basic problems are involved, one having to do with "blood guilt" and the other with "holiness." Jerusalem was a flagrant example of a *bloody city*. The moral insensitivity of the people was so great, they made no attempt to cover their corruption. As the blood of innocents spilled into the streets and on the altars of pagan rites, it pled for vengeance, it demanded requittal (vv. 6–8; cf. Gen. 4:10; Lev. 17:13; Deut. 12:24; Isa. 26:21; Job 16:18). The uncovered blood (v. 8) was a bold testimony against the people and a reminder to Yahweh of their wanton ways.

Further, there is a general principle operable in this section. Jerusalem as well as the people were holy. This holiness had, however, been negated by the unholy acts of the people. They had desecrated the very city itself. Both had to be cleansed or destroyed; they could not continue as affronts to Yahweh.

Thus the city of Jerusalem would be the vessel in which a corrupt people would be consumed without any respect of persons. No discrimination will be shown, for in judgment position power and prestige make no difference (v. 6, note the phrasing *without . . . choice*). Once Jerusalem itself has served as the vehicle of judgment for the people, it too will be destroyed because a corrupt people have thoroughly contaminated the city with innocent blood (v. 11). So great has the pollution been that no device other than destruction will suffice. The caldron, i.e., Jerusalem, will be smelted, totally destroyed, in order to eradicate its impregnated taint. The sins of the people have eaten into the city's core as rust eats into metal (v. 13).

Only the stubborn excesses of the peo-

ple have prompted such an onslaught. Every effort of Yahweh to purify Jerusalem has been in vain (v. 13), and at no place in the book of Ezekiel do we find any effort on the part of Jerusalem to attempt reform. Literally Yahweh had worn himself out attempting to purify the people (v. 12). The people were cleansed but not clean. This rather devastating word by Ezekiel reinforces an unassailable impression that the judgment upon Jerusalem was not a reclamation project.

(2) The Double Tragedy (24:15–27)

15 Also the word of the LORD came to me: 16 "Son of man, behold, I am about to take the delight of your eyes away from you at a stroke; yet you shall not mourn or weep nor shall your tears run down. 17 Sigh, but not aloud; make no mourning for the dead. Bind on your turban, and put your shoes on your feet; do not cover your lips, nor eat the bread of mourners." 18 So I spoke to the people in the morning, and at evening my wife died. And on the next morning I did as I was commanded.

19 And the people said to me, "Will you not tell us what these things mean for us, that you are acting thus?" 20 Then I said to them, "The word of the LORD came to me: 21 'Say to the house of Israel, Thus says the Lord GOD: Behold, I will profane my sanctuary, the pride of your power, the delight of your eyes, and the desire of your soul; and your sons and your daughters whom you left behind shall fall by the sword. 22 And you shall do as I have done; you shall not cover your lips, nor eat the bread of mourners. 23 Your turbans shall be on your heads and your shoes on your feet; you shall not mourn or weep, but you shall pine away in your iniquities and groan to one another. 24 Thus shall Ezekiel be to you a sign; according to all that he has done you shall do. When this comes, then you will know that I am the Lord GOD.'

25 "And you, son of man, on the day when I take from them their stronghold, their joy and glory, the delight of their eyes and their heart's desire, and also their sons and daughters, 26 on that day a fugitive will come to you to report to you the news. 27 On that day your mouth will be opened to the fugitive, and you shall speak and be no longer dumb. So you will be a sign to them; and they will know that I am the LORD."

Ezekiel is here using his personal loss as an object lesson for all the people. It is to become their manner of response in na-

---

[78] Cf. Stalker, pp. 195–199. Eichrodt and Zimmerli place emphasis on the preparations and see this as descriptive of cooking arrangements for a feast.

ional bereavement. Yahweh announces that the prophet's grief will be intensified by the death of his wife (v. 16). Ezekiel will not be permitted to express his grief in traditional ways (v. 17)—he is to sigh in silence. This is contrary to the customary act of wailing with a loud voice.

Socially accepted expressions of bereavement were exclamatory lamentations, wearing of sack cloth, and the powdering of body and head with ashes or dust (cf. Jer. 4:8; 49:3; Joel 1:13; Mic. 1:8; Esther 4:1,3; Job 2:8). The prohibition against removing the shoes was given, for it also was a sign of mourning (cf. 2 Sam. 15:30).

The use of the idiomatic expression *delight of your eyes* (vv. 15,21) is telling. The phrase implies a thing for which one has singular fondness or attraction (cf. Gen. 3:6). The people are to bear their loss of Jerusalem and the Temple (i.e., the delight of their eyes) with the same aplomb that Ezekiel bears the loss of the delight of his eyes (i.e., his wife, vv. 22 f.).

In somewhat the same fashion prohibitions against mourning were issued by Yahweh to Jeremiah, although personal loss was not involved. Ezekiel could only sigh in silence (v. 17) while the people would express their grief to one another in barely audible moans (v. 23). The overall impression, to an observor of the people, would be that they were too overcome by the shock of what had occurred for their grief to be expressed. No outward act of bereavement could possibly reflect the inner conditions.

The awesomeness of the situation is reflected by v. 25. It indicates that the two most favored objects of adoration by the people, *the stronghold* (i.e., the Temple as the dwelling place of Yahweh) and their *children,* would be destroyed. In effect national and family continuance would come to an abrupt halt.

However, we see within the passage the plight of both prophet and people. Although the delight of Ezekiel's eyes will die and the prophet thereby be plunged into the abyss of acute bereavement, there will occur a total reorientation of his ministry. His *mouth will be opened* (v. 24), and a new message will spring forth. Ezekiel will become the watchman rather than the bearer of stern unalterable judgment.

It may well be that this is the watershed of Ezekiel's prophetic ministry, that moment of release permitting Ezekiel to become the type of prophetic personality he truly wished to be. It is apparent that beneath the granite facade of his life there was an inner core of tenderness which ached for expression. In crises and despair there came the liberating call. It was a new ministry which would point the way out of Ezekiel's personal suffering and give direction for an entire people who had lost their reason for existence.

Part Two: Judgment Against the Nations (25:1—32:32)

This point initiates a distinctively different subject approach within the book of Ezekiel. Such a series of oracles seems to be a traditional part of most major prophetic works (cf. Isa. 13:27; Jer. 46—51; Amos 1:1—2:3).

From the time of Amos until the latest of the prophetic sections of the book of Daniel, words of judgment were directed toward foreign nations. It is justifiable to point out that in Ezekiel there is no threatened punishment of Babylon or of its ruler Nebuchadnezzar. This may have been omitted for any one of several reasons: (1) because Ezekiel saw Babylon as the instrument of Yahweh's judgment; (2) because Babylon was not a traditional enemy of Israel; or (3) because Ezekiel feared retaliation against the exiled peoples if he was outspoken against their overlord.

Generally speaking we have two primary reasons for the singling out of the specific nations: (1) these were the nations which saw Yahweh's judgment upon his own people but did not interpret the event as one which spoke to them; (2) these were the nations which exulted with malicious glee over the downfall of Israel and Judah.

Their taunts and deadly sarcasm cast

disparagement upon the elect of Yahweh and the person of Yahweh. This constituted an affront to the name and covenant promise of the God of Israel. Only the downfall of such nations could, in the mind of Ezekiel, vindicate the name of Yahweh and validate his purpose in history. Additionally, there may be the implication that before the ideal nation (i.e., a recreated Israel) could be effected it would be necessary to reduce to ineffectiveness those who had been its traditional enemies.

I. Judgment Against Ammon, Moab, Edom, and Philistia (25:1–17)

1. Ammon (25:1–7)

[1] The word of the LORD came to me: [2] "Son of man, set your face toward the Ammonites, and prophesy against them. [3] Say to the Ammonites, Hear the word of the Lord GOD: Thus says the Lord GOD, Because you said, 'Aha!' over my sanctuary when it was profaned, and over the land of Israel when it was made desolate, and over the house of Judah when it went into exile; [4] therefore I am handing you over to the people of the East for a possession, and they shall set their encampments among you and make their dwellings in your midst; they shall eat your fruit, and they shall drink your milk. [5] I will make Rabbah a pasture for camels and the cities of the Ammonites a fold for flocks. Then you will know that I am the LORD. [6] For thus says the Lord GOD: Because you have clapped your hands and stamped your feet and rejoiced with all the malice within you against the land of Israel, [7] therefore, behold, I have stretched out my hand against you, and will hand you over as spoil to the nations; and I will cut you off from the peoples and will make you perish out of the countries; I will destroy you. Then you will know that I am the LORD.

An Israelite tradition traces the origin of the Ammonites to the family of Lot (Gen. 19:38). Although it is now established that they were an indigenous people of Northern Syria at least as early as the middle of the second millenium B.C., it was accepted by the Israelites that they were kindred.[79] The Israelite-Ammonite struggle probably had its origin with the incursion

[79] Cf. especially George M. Landes, "The Material Civilization of the Ammonites," *Biblical Archaeologist*, 24.3 (1961), 65–86.

of the Israelites into the Transjordan under Moses; it continued through the period of the judges (Judg. 10:8; 11:11–33) and the united kingdom (1 Sam. 11:1–11; 2 Sam. 10,11). Antagonism continued (2 Chron. 20:23—27:5) during the divided kingdom rising to a zenith in the Omrid dynastic period of Israel (2 Kings 3). There was continuing animosity down to the Ezekelian period. Subsequent to the fall of Samaria around 721 B.C., the Ammonites took possession of Israelite land (Jer. 49:1); and, according to Jeremiah they were involved in the assassination of Gedaliah (Jer. 40:14). In addition, a late source (Neh. 4:1) indicates that the Ammonites attempted to thwart resettlement of the returning exiles.

To Ezekiel the offense of Ammon was not so much their historical hostility as it was their exultation over the destruction of Israel and Judah. It was a malignant joy on their part, and they reveled in the hardships and sufferings of their enemies (vv. 3,6).

Joy over the misfortune of another, even if it is an enemy, is a base emotion worthy of strongest condemnation. Involved, however, is a more profound theological reason for judgment upon Ammon. Twice in the oracle the phrase *then you will know* (vv. 5,7) is used. Only in such judgment would Ammon come to know the power and authority of Yahweh. This does not imply the acceptance of Yahweh as God by the Ammonites but an acknowledgment of his sovereignty over the affairs of men.

Ammon will become subject to the *peoples of the East* (v. 4)—the nomadic tribes who roved the fringes of the great Arabian Desert where it bordered the Transjordan. Thus the character and being of Yahweh, maligned by Ammonite taunts and attitudes, will be vindicated.

2. Moab (25:8–11)

[8] "Thus says the Lord GOD: Because Moab said, Behold, the house of Judah is like all the other nations, [9] therefore I will lay open the flank of Moab from the cities on its frontier, the glory of the country, Bethjeshimoth, Baalmeon, and Kiriathaim. [10] I will give it along

ith the Ammonites to the people of the East
s a possession, that it may be remembered no
tore among the nations, [11] and I will execute
idgments upon Moab. Then they will know
hat I am the LORD.

Moab, as Ammon, was considered to
tave issued from the family of Lot (Gen.
;0:30–38). The first direct conflict be-
ween Israel and Moab occurred during
he Exodus event (cf. Deut. 2:9; Judg.
1:17). Hostilities errupted between the
wo nations during the conquest (Josh.
:4:9) and quickened during the period of
he judges (Judg. 3:12–20).
Saul subjected the Moabites to Israel's
:ontrol, and David found it necessary to
eassert his authority over them (2 Sam.
3:2; 1 Chron. 18:2). Moab was a constant
hreat and source of disquiet for Israel
ind Judah during the period of the divided
cingdom. Moab's fortunes as an independ-
:nt state ended about 600 B.C. with their
erritory largely occupied by roving no-
nadic tribes. There is the indication, how-
:ver, that Moabite contingents joined with
Nebuchadnezzar in the attack upon Jerusalem and Judah (2 Kings 24:2).
Specifically the charge of Ezekiel against
Moab was that they adjudged Judah to be
is other nations (v. 8). One can only surmise that this had to do with Judah's fate.
Evidently the Moabites derived great satisfaction from the destruction. This they
interpreted as demonstrating that Judah,
although claiming inviolability as an elect
people of Yahweh, was like other nations,
which is to say that the God of Israel was
no more than the gods of other nations.
From this destruction Moab derived
tremendous self-satisfaction. There is an
evil delight when one is able to say that
others are as low, corrupt, contemptable,
and debased as oneself. Again the rationale for judgment is given (v. 11). In their
judgment Moab will come to know that
the God of Judah is more than other gods.

3. Edom (25:12–14)

12 "Thus says the Lord GOD: Because Edom
acted revengefully against the house of Judah
and has grievously offended in taking vengeance upon them, 13 therefore thus says the

Lord GOD, I will stretch out my hand against
Edom, and cut off from it man and beast; and I
will make it desolate; from Teman even to
Dedan they shall fall by the sword. [14] And I
will lay my vengeance upon Edom by the hand
of my people Israel; and they shall do in Edom
according to my anger and according to my
wrath; and they shall know my vengeance, says
the Lord GOD.

Tradition connects the Edomites [80] with
Israel through Esau, the twin brother of
Jacob (Gen. 25:30; 32:3). An initial point
of conflict between Israel and Edom occurred during the Exodus (Num. 20:14–
21). In the time of Saul there was additional conflict (1 Sam. 14:47). David
found it necessary to launch a major campaign against Edom 1 Kings 11:15 ff.).
Sporadic hostilities occurred in the period
of the divided kingdom. Jehoshaphat and
Joram weathered Edomitic belligerence
(2 Kings 3; 8:20–22), and later Amaziah
and Uzziah launched successful attacks
upon them (2 Kings 14).
About 600 B.C. the Edomites became the
vassals of Babylonia and apparently joined
with the Babylonians in their assault upon
Jerusalem about 586. In the chaotic period
following the fall of Jerusalem, elements of
the Edomites moved into the Hebron district of Judah and ultimately became the
Idumeans, whose most famous figure was
Herod. Amos, Jeremiah, Ezekiel, and
Obadiah are vehement in their denunciation of Edom. This may largely be attributable to the close family relationship (cf.
Gen. 36:43).
Edom is charged with acting *revengefully* toward Judah (v. 12). As the vengeance of Edom has been directed toward
Judah, the Edomites will experience the
vengeance of Judah's God being directed
against them.[81] Placing of this execution of
judgment in the *hand of . . . Israel* poses
a problem. Certainly the possibility of such
was not current and would have to be
delayed until some future time, i.e., during
the ideal age yet to come (chaps. 40—48).

[80] Cf. Nelson Glueck, "The Civilization of the Edomites," *Biblical Archaeologist* x.4 (1947), 77–84.
[81] M. H. Woudstra, "Edom and Israel in Ezekiel,"
Calvin Theological Journal, 3.1 (1968), 21–35.

This may come from the hand of a later editor since it reflects a much later historical period.

4. Philistia (25:15-17)

15 "Thus says the Lord GOD: Because the Philistines acted revengefully and took vengeance with malice of heart to destroy in never-ending enmity; 16 therefore thus says the Lord GOD, Behold, I will stretch out my hand against the Philistines, and I will cut off the Cherethites, and destroy the rest of the seacoast. 17 I will execute great vengeance upon them with wrathful chastisements. Then they will know that I am the LORD, when I lay my vengeance upon them."

The Philistines, a mortal antagonist of the Israelites during the period of the judges and the early monarchy, settled along the coastline of Palestine shortly after 1190 B.C. This settlement took place following their expulsion from Egypt by the forces of Ramses III. The Philistines were the remnant of a tribe of the "sea peoples," the Pelast. They occupied coastal areas in Palestine and developed a strong coalition of cities basing their economy on the smelting and working of iron.

By developing a monopoly in iron, the Philistines gained an economic and military stranglehold on Palestine. With the coming of the Israelites under Joshua and the subsequent settlement of the tribes in Canaan, Philistine authority was challenged. Shamgar, a minor judge, fought limited and local actions against the Philistines (Judg. 4:31). The Samson stories, however, point to heightening conflict between the diverse Israelite tribal units and the Philistines (Judg. 14-16). The first account of major hostile Philistine action deals with the attack upon Shiloh around 1050 B.C. This resulted in the capture and spiriting away of the ark of the covenant. The fall of Shiloh was an excessively harsh blow to the infant attempts of Israel to achieve nationhood.

The Philistine defeat of Israel and the death of Saul and his sons in the battle at Mount Gilboa plunged Israel into a period of harsh oppression at the hands of the victors. It was not until the reign of David that the Philistines were contained and subdued (2 Sam. 8:1). Although the Philistines dropped from the major stage of events in Palestine after Davidic times, Joel refers to some Philistine strength when he relates the inhumanities suffered by the defeated Judahites at the hands of the Philistines following 586 B.C. (cf. Joel 3. 4-8).

Ezekiel's charge is that the Philistines executed their vengeance with deliberate malice, for they possessed an historically undiminished enmity toward Judah (v. 15). Here Ezekiel is charging the Philistines with attitudes of hate passed to each succeeding generation. The words may reflect the national historical animosity of Philistia against Israel. Israel had destroyed Philistine nationalistic dreams hundreds of years prior to Ezekiel's day. To the mind of Ezekiel dire judgment was necessary to vindicate the name of Yahweh (v. 17).

II. Judgment Against Tyre (26:1—28:19)

These three chapters deal with the fate of the maritime nation of Phoenicia. Historically the relationship between Tyre and Israel had been erratic, yet the quality of association had been one of rewarding interdependence more often than not. Problems had arisen as a result of the commercial alliance between Solomon and Hiram I of Tyre especially in connection with the services rendered in the erection of the Temple (2 Kings 9:10-14).

The purging of the worship of Baal-Melkart by Elijah (cf. 2 Kings 18:1-40) and the sanguinary assaults of Jehu (cf. 2 Kings 9,10) upon the royal family (i.e., those related to Ittobaal the Sidonian king of Tyre through Jezebel his daughter) must have created national Phoenician animosity. Yet the two nations did enjoy a type of reciprocity in economic and military ventures which was far better than most. We cannot therefore cast Phoenicia into the role of a traditional enemy of Israel. The offense of Tyre must be grounded elsewhere.

Perhaps the sin of Tyre was her lust for national acclaim through commercial exploits. Overt commercialization had created within Phoenicia an arrogant pride, and all things were relative to the production of material wealth. She brazenly asserted her commercial prowess and looked upon herself as the greatest of maritime trade nations.

A revealing of Phoenicia's inner character is evident when she exults over the fall of Judah (26:2). Judah's demise meant that Phoenicia would be the richer for another competitor had fallen. Phoenicia personifies the ignoble position of "never enough." She wanted complete monopoly, total control, over trade. Her driving obsession reflects that of many business cartels which are not satisfied with being financial giants; they wish to be the only giant. This validates the elusive dream of totally cornering a market or exercising absolute monopoly. When such conditions exist within individuals or nations, all human conditions are disregarded.

1. Destruction Decreed (26:1–21)

(1) Judgment Announced (26:1–6)

¹ In the eleventh year, on the first day of the month, the word of the LORD came to me: ² "Son of man, because Tyre said concerning Jerusalem, 'Aha, the gate of the peoples is broken, it has swung open to me; I shall be replenished, now that she is laid waste,' ³ therefore thus says the Lord GOD: Behold, I am against you, O Tyre, and will bring up many nations against you, as the sea brings up its waves. ⁴ They shall destroy the walls of Tyre, and break down her towers; and I will scrape her soil from her, and make her a bare rock. ⁵ She shall be in the midst of the sea a place for the spreading of nets; for I have spoken, says the Lord GOD; and she shall become a spoil to the nations; ⁶ and her daughters on the mainland shall be slain by the sword. Then they will know that I am the LORD.

Charged initially with glee over the fate of Jerusalem, Tyre is to be delivered into the hands of the Babylonians. The reaction of the Phoenicians over the destruction of Jerusalem may best be interpreted in the light of commercial rivalry between the two nations. Possibly this had to do not only with Jerusalem as the major center of land trade in Palestine, but also with the Judahite practice of controlling movement of caravan goods across its borders. As early as the time of Solomon the strategic economic nature of Palestine as a land bridge connecting the continents of Africa and Asia was recognized (1 Kings 10:1–20).[82] Control of the land bridge meant control of caravan trade. The demise of Jerusalem would thus eliminate tolls on caravan goods and provide unlimited caravan access to Phoenician shipping points. No longer would Jerusalem vie with Tyre. Tyre would be supreme in commerce.

Aptly described is the location of Tyre and its ultimate fate (vv. 3–6). Tyre, like early Crete, ruled the mainland coastal area and its towns and villages (i.e., the *daughters* of v. 6.; cf. Num. 21:25) from an island fortress. Located little more than one-quarter mile off shore, the citadel was virtually impregnable in its day. Alexander the Great around 332 B.C. was forced to erect a causeway from the mainland to the offshore citadel in order successfully to conquer the Tyrians.

Ezekiel envisions the final fate of Tyre and expresses it in graphic imagery. The island fortress will be leveled leaving only the rock foundation jutting from the sea. Its only use would be a place for fishermen to spread their nets to dry. (v. 5).

(2) The Instrument of Destruction (26:7–14)

⁷ "For thus says the Lord GOD: Behold, I will bring upon Tyre from the north Nebuchadrezzar king of Babylon, king of kings, with horses and chariots, and with horsemen and a host of many soldiers. ⁸ He will slay with the sword your daughters on the mainland; he will set up a siege wall against you, and throw up a mound against you, and raise a roof of shields against you. ⁹ He will direct the shock of his battering rams against your walls, and with his axes he will break down your towers. ¹⁰ His

---

[82] Cf. complete discussion in Wendell Phillips, *Qataban* and *Sheba* (New York: Harcourt, Brace and Company, 1955).

horses will be so many that their dust will cover you; your walls will shake at the noise of the horsemen and wagons and chariots, when he enters your gates as one enters a city which has been breached. 11 With the hoofs of his horses he will trample all your streets; he will slay your people with the sword; and your mighty pillars will fall to the ground. 12 They will make a spoil of your riches and a prey of your merchandise; they will break down your walls and destroy your pleasant houses; your stones and timber and soil they will cast into the midst of the waters. 13 And I will stop the music of your songs, and the sound of your lyres shall be heard no more. 14 I will make you a bare rock; you shall be a place for the spreading of nets; you shall never be rebuilt; for I the LORD have spoken, says the Lord GOD.

The agent of Yahweh who will ravage Tyre is Nebuchadnezzar, king of Babylon (v. 7).[83] The siege description (vv. 8–11) is that of a typical land assault similar to that portrayed of Sennacherib's attack upon the city of Lachish around 701 B.C. (cf. comment. on 29:17–21).

Verses 7–14 indicate an accurate knowledge, on the part of the prophet, of Babylonian siege strategy. In fact Ezekiel is predicting the battle plans for subjugation of Tyre. First the *daughters* (i.e., coastal towns and suburbs controlled from the island fortress) will be overrun with foot soliders and swift chariot assaults (v. 8). Once all lines of supply and support for the island citadel have been reduced, the stronghold, which lay approximately one-half mile offshore, would be subjected to siege. The *mound* and *roof of shields* (v. 8) would constitute the earthen ramp erected like a causeway leading to the island and the towers of timbers covered with metal shields to protect the assault force. Once the battering rams (v. 9) have breached the walls, cavalry (v. 11) will enter the city, pillaging, plundering, and putting its inhabitants to the sword (v. 12). The entire citadel will be de-

spoiled and cast into the surrounding water (v. 12), and mute silence will ensue (v. 13). Thus Tyre will be no more!

(3) Lament of the Allies of Tyre (26:15–18)

15 "Thus says the Lord GOD to Tyre: Will not the coastlands shake at the sound of your fall, when the wounded groan, when slaughter is made in the midst of you? 16 Then all the princes of the sea will step down from their thrones, and remove their robes, and strip off their embroidered garments; they will clothe themselves with trembling; they will sit upon the ground and tremble every moment, and be appalled at you. 17 And they will raise a lamentation over you, and say to you,
'How you have vanished from the seas,
    O city renowned,
that was mighty on the sea,
    you and your inhabitants,
who imposed your terror
    on all the mainland!
18 Now the isles tremble
    on the day of your fall;
yea, the isles that are in the sea
    are dismayed at your passing.'

Terrible indeed is the fall of the mighty, for the fortunes of others are all too frequently tied to such powers. The alarm of *the princes of the sea* (v. 16) who ruled coastal cities involved in maritime trade was not only occasioned by the severe disruption of commercial arrangements and therefore financial solvency but by the fact that the destruction of Tyre was potentially a portent of the future for them. It prefigured their own domination by another power. If Tyre the strongest of the strong had fallen, what hope did they the lesser and weaker powers have against the identical adversary? (cf. May, p. 208; Cooke, p. 292).

The first lamentation is typical *kinah* meter and is an introduction to the more extensive dirge of chapter 27. This lament meter is an unequal stress form for writing poetry. It is the dominant meter of the book of Lamentations and is to be observed in the laments of the prophets and psalmists. A line of such poetry has three accents in the first half-line and two

---

83 Note the spelling of the king's name by both Jeremiah and Ezekiel—Nebuchadrezzar. The name means "Nebo protect my work" or "Nabu protect my boundary."

in the last half of the line. When read in Hebrew there is an undulation in sound resembling the rise and fall of the voice of an individual under intense emotional pressure. It may, however, express joy equally as well. A smooth and free flow process of thought is observable when one reads the poetical sections (26:17–18; 27:3–9,25–36; 28:2–19,22–23) as one continuous unit avoiding the prose interruptions. Originally this may have been one single dirge in kinah meter which was divided by editorial prose explanations.

(4) Descent into Sheol (26:19–21)

19 "For thus says the Lord GOD: When I make you a city laid waste, like the cities that are not inhabited, when I bring up the deep over you, and the great waters cover you, 20 then I will thrust you down with those who descend into the Pit, to the people of old, and I will make you to dwell in the nether world, among primeval ruins, with those who go down to the Pit, so that you will not be inhabited or have a place in the land of the living. 21 I will bring you to a dreadful end, and you shall be no more; though you be sought for, you will never be found again, says the Lord GOD."

Vain Tyre's fate is to be consigned to the subterranean abyss, the *Pit* (i.e., Sheol, v. 20), the abode of the shades of the dead.[84]

Whereas in 26:3 the depiction is that of a storm of warfare which would sweep the island citadel as a tidal wave, v. 19 intensifies the imagery depicting total inundation, i.e., *the great waters cover you.* The word for waters (Heb., *techom*) is not that of v. 3. *Techom* constitutes the waters, indicative of chaos, in the creation story. Therefore we may interpret this in the sense of a cosmic catastrophe.

One may feel surprise with the realization that Ezekiel is not speaking of the people of Phoenicia (v. 20) but the city of Tyre. The city itself will be *thrust . . . down* into Sheol, the *Pit.* Tyre will be no more—a city sought for but never to be found. Literally Tyre is to become the Atlantis of the Palestinian coastline (v. 21).

84 Cf. comment. on Isa. 14:4–20, BBC, 5.

2. *The Proud Splendor of Tyre (27:1–24)*

This passage initiates a skillful survey of the offenses of Tyre, the center of which was the development of a deadly attitude of self-sufficiency. Tyre's assumption of divine prerogatives resulted in the deification of self.

Ezekiel with magnificent imagery depicts Tyre as a sumptuous merchant ship constructed and adorned with choicest materials. Its crew was select and its cargo not only valuable but representative of the far-flung network of Phoenician maritime stations.

As the ship of Tyre, a symbol of national pride, plowed the seas, she was struck by a disastrous storm with total loss of ship, cargo, and crew. This disaster was a catastrophe of cataclysmic proportions to the commercial world of the day and created havoc among the trade nations. This points to the interdependency of allied interests and caused the gigantic question mark of survival to loom above every trade nation. "If this can happen to Tyre, what hope for us?" How many nations asked the identical type of question following the 1929 collapse of the American economy. Near panic ensued among the other industrial nations of the world.

(1) The Ship of Tyre (27:1–11)

1 The word of the LORD came to me: 2 "Now you, son of man, raise a lamentation over Tyre, 3 and say to Tyre, who dwells at the entrance to the sea, merchant of the peoples on many coastlands, thus says the Lord GOD:
"O Tyre, you have said,
   'I am perfect in beauty.'
4 Your borders are in the heart of the seas;
   your builders made perfect your beauty.
5 They made all your planks
   of fir trees from Senir;
they took a cedar from Lebanon
   to make a mast for you.
6 Of oaks of Bashan
   they made your oars;
they made your deck of pines
   from the coasts of Cyprus,
   inlaid with ivory.
7 Of fine embroidered linen from Egypt
   was your sail,
   serving as your ensign;

blue and purple from the coasts of Elishah
was your awning.
8 The inhabitants of Sidon and Arvad
were your rowers;
skilled men of Zemer were in you,
they were your pilots.
9 The elders of Gebal and her skilled men
were in you,
caulking your seams;
all the ships of the sea with their mariners
were in you,
to barter for your wares.
10 "Persia and Lud and Put were in your
army as your men of war; they hung the shield
and helmet in you; they gave you splendor.
11 The men of Arvad and Helech were upon
your walls round about, and men of Gamad
were in your towers; they hung their shields
upon your walls round about; they made perfect your beauty.

Tyre is depicted as a lavishly adorned
merchant ship [85] befitting her rank as the
most prestigious of all maritime nations.
In fact when Tyre viewed herself she appeared as the epitome of grandeur. (v. 3).
Simply put, her pride and self-adulation
knew no bounds, and she was inordinately arrogant.

Only the finest and costliest materials
went into the construction. Her hull was
planked with *fir* from Senir (v. 5), or
timbers hewn from the trees of the Lebanon mountain range.[86] One gigantic
cedar of Lebanon, the most majestic coni-
fer of the ancient Near East, served as a
mast; while oak oars from trees of Bashan
and decks of pine from Cyprus were utilized (v. 6).

A curious problem develops in v. 6 with
the reference to ivory inlay. Some authorities feel that the word *ivory* entered the
text either by mistake or dittography. The
Hebrew word translated *deck* literally
means "boards." There is a use of the same
word in Exodus 26:15-16 and Numbers
3:36; 4:31 with reference to the framing
of the tabernacle. This framing of the
sanctuary was to be overlaid with gold
and serve as highly decorative fascia

boards.

Certainly Ezekiel was not implying that
the deck, upon which there was constant
foot traffic and abuse by cargo movement,
was inlaid with ivory. The reference is
more likely to the rails or gunwales of the
ship which rose above the deck. The
bows, gunwales, and sterns of boats from
most primitive times bore the elaborate
decorative motifs of their builders.

Taut above the deck were Egyptian
linen sails of the finest quality (v. 7). Nor
were the sails without their decorative designs. Hand embroidered patterns upon
the sails identified the ship for all mariners
as the ship of Tyre. The sails with their
distinctive pattern served the same purpose as the identifying flags of nations in
the modern merchant marine.

Awnings, literally "coverings," of brilliant hue served as deck canopies to
shield the mariners from the sun. Ship's
crews were the finest. *Pilots* (v. 8) literally means "pullers of rope," inferring not
pilot in the sense of navigator but rather
those seaman skilled in the setting of sails
and operation of tiller. Equally skilled
were the craftsmen who maintained repair
(v. 9).

As a result, from every quarter of the
Mediterranean came those who lived by
sea trade thronging to Tyre to barter and
trade for her wares (v. 9).

Since Tyre was geographically small as
a nation and limited in population, her defenses were vested in mercenary soldiers
(vv. 10,11). Only the excessive wealth of
Tyre could afford such luxury—that of a
paid professional army.

(2) The Commercial Allies of Tyre
(27:12-24)

12 "Tarshish trafficked with you because of
your great wealth of every kind; silver, iron,
tin, and lead they exchanged for your wares.
13 Javan, Tubal, and Meshech traded with you;
they exchanged the persons of men and vessels
of bronze for your merchandise.
14 Bethtogarmah exchanged for your wares
horses, war horses, and mules. 15 The men of
Rhodes traded with you; many coastlands were

---

[85] Cf. Sidney Smith, "The Ship Tyre," *Palestine Exploration Quarterly* (May–October, 1953), pp. 97–110.
[86] *Senir* in Amoritic literally means "snow," and the
direct reference may well be to trees felled on Mount
Hermon, which has a perineal sonwcap.

your own special markets, they brought you in payment ivory tusks and ebony. [16] Edom trafficked with you because of your abundant goods; they exchanged for your wares emeralds, purple, embroidered work, fine linen, coral, and agate. [17] Judah and the land of Israel traded with you; they exchanged for your merchandise wheat, olives and early figs, honey, oil, and balm. [18] Damascus trafficked with you for your abundant goods, because of your great wealth of every kind; wine of Helbon, and white wool, [19] and wine from Uzal they exchanged for your wares; wrought iron, cassia, and calamus were bartered for your merchandise. [20] Dedan traded with you in saddlecloths for riding. [21] Arabia and all the princes of Kedar were your favored dealers in lambs, rams, and goats; in these they trafficked with you. [22] The traders of Sheba and Raamah traded with you; they exchanged for your wares the best of all kinds of spices, and all precious stones, and gold. [23] Haran, Canneh, Eden, Asshur, and Chilmad traded with you. [24] These traded with you in choice garments, in clothes of blue and embroidered work, and in carpets of colored stuff, bound with cords and made secure; in these they traded with you.

Knowledge of Tyre's immense maritime trade empire was well known among the informed of the ancient world due to its economic prestige. Amazing, however, is the scope of Ezekiel's knowledge not only of major trade centers but of various trade items. The listing in this section is a veritable catalogue of trade goods linked with the primary source of supply.

If the identification of Tarshish (v. 12) with Sardinia or Tartessus of Spain is accurate [87] Ezekiel describes a trade network from Spain to Greece (i.e., *Javan* (v. 13), northern Assyria (i.e., *Tubal, Meshech, Beth-togarmah*, vv. 13,14), the Mediterranean island of *Rhodes* (v. 15), throughout Palestine (i.e., *Israel, Judah, Edom*, vv. 16,17), Syria (i.e., *Damascus, Helbon*), *Arabia* (i.e., Uzal, Dedan, Sheba, v. 22), and Mesopotamia (i.e., Haran, Canneh, Eden, Asshur, Chilmad, v. 23).[88]

[87] Cf. W. F. Albright, "New Light on the Early History of Phoenician Colonization," *Bulletin of the American Schools of Oriental Research*, LXXXIII (1941), 21.

[88] Cf. Howie *Date and Composition of Ezekiel*, p. 60; R. LeBaron Bowen and Frank P. Albright, *Archaeological Discoveries in South Arabia* (Baltimore: The Johns Hopkins Press, 1958), III. No. 33, 42.

One particular reference to a trade commodity may have veiled implications. Javan, Tubal, and Meshech dealt in the *persons of men,* literally slave traffic. If indeed Javan is Greece, and possibly a reference to the group designated as Ionians, then the historical validity of the oracle is strengthened. Amos 1:9 and Joel 3:6 both refer to a slave traffic conducted by the Phoenicians. Amos refers to the Tyrians selling Israelites to Edom. Joel and Ezekiel both refer to the selling of Israelite slaves to the Greeks. Phoenicia is accused in this passage of selling the people of Judah and Jerusalem to the Greeks as slaves. Thus a commercial venture of the Phoenicians initiated many years before Joel's time was continued to his day.

3. The Fate of the Ship of Tyre (27:25–36)

[25] The ships of Tarshish traveled for you with your merchandise.
  "So you were filled and heavily laden
    in the heart of the seas.
[26] Your rowers have brought you out
    into the high seas.
  The east wind has wrecked you
    in the heart of the seas.
[27] Your riches, your wares, your merchandise,
    your mariners and your pilots,
  your caulkers, your dealers in merchandise,
    and all your men of war who are in you,
  with all your company
    that is in your midst,
  sink into the heart of the seas
    on the day of your ruin.
[28] At the sound of the cry of your pilots
    the countryside shakes,
[29] and down from their ships
    come all that handle the oar.
  The mariners and all the pilots of the sea
    stand on the shore
[30] and wail aloud over you,
    and cry bitterly.
  They cast dust on their heads
    and wallow in ashes;
[31] they make themselves bald for you,
    and gird themselves with sackcloth,
  and they weep over you in bitterness of soul,
    with bitter mourning.
[32] In their wailing they raise a lamentation for you,
    and lament over you:
  'Who was ever destroyed like Tyre

in the midst of the sea?
33 When your wares came from the seas,
     you satisfied many peoples;
     with your abundant wealth and merchandise
     you enriched the kings of the earth.
34 Now you are wrecked by the seas,
     in the depths of the waters;
     your merchandise and all your crew
     have sunk with you.
35 All the inhabitants of the coastlands
     are appalled at you;
     and their kings are horribly afraid,
     their faces are convulsed.
36 The merchants among the peoples hiss at
        you;
     you have come to a dreadful end
     and shall be no more for ever.' "

The end of Tyre is depicted as the sinking of the ship so elaborately wrought (27:27–36), so well protected (27:10,11), and so eminently successful in world trade (27:12–24). This vessel heavily laden with the merchandise of many nations plied the sea lanes riding dangerously low in the water. In the open sea it encountered a storm (i.e., *east wind*) and was ravaged by the furious onslaught (vv. 25,26).

A wind from the east is often referred to in the Old Testament as an instrument of Yahweh (cf. Ex. 10:13; Job 27:21; Psalms 48:7; Isa. 27:8; Jer. 18:17; Hos. 13:15; Jon. 4:8). An east wind upon the Mediterranean was particularly disastrous, and it is described in the Talmud as creating furrows in the water like a plow in the field (Git. 31b). In this particular instance the east wind is a figure of speech for Babylon whose attack upon Phoenicia brought to an end its strength as a major maritime power (v. 27).

As a result of the reduction of Tyre, the entire maritime trade empire of the ancient Near East is reduced to mourning and lamentation (vv. 29b–32). When the death cries of the sailors upon the ship of Tyre were heard (v. 28), other ships' crews left their vessels and assembled on the shore lining the beaches (v. 29). So great was the storm they could render no assistance. Their only recourse was to prostrate themselves in agonized disbelief that

such had occurred (vv. 29–32). Their lament *Who was ever destroyed like Tyre in the midst of the sea?* only makes more poignant their feelings (v. 32).

The RSV utilizes the reading of the Targum and Vulgate manuscripts in rendering the wording *destroyed* (v. 32b), while the Masoretic Text would read "brought to silence." The implications of Tyre's fate are the more clearly described by the Masoretic Text. Tyre, the bustling, noisy, merchantman, becomes mute in the calm after the storm. Tyre has been brought to silent death, and only the funeral sounds of gently lapping waves are to be heard upon the desolate shores.[89]

Its effect upon other coastal maritime nations was overpowering (v. 35). Their kings were *horribly afraid* and *covered their faces* (i.e., the result of their uncontrollable inner fears that similar fate awaited them). The people, merchants, and rulers (vv. 34–36) were all caught up in the destruction of Tyre for their future was interwoven with Tyre's commercial solidarity. The great never fall alone.

4. The Reason for Judgment (28:1–19)

This chapter specifies more exactly the reasons for judgment upon Tyre and its rulers. The addition of an oracle against Sidon (28:20–23) seems to be out of character, breaking the movement of thought in relating the connection between Tyre's judgment and her relationship with Israel (28:24–26).

Generally a nation is led in its national policies by its chief officer be it monarch, president, dictator, or hireling. The prince of Tyre was the one who had forged the will of the people into a mad pursuit for commercial gain. King after king had adopted the same policy, and ultimately the whole people were gripped by an obsessive mania for commercial genius. It was their manifest destiny, so they thought, to rule the maritime world of their day.

[89] For a different view, cf. Frederick Moriarty, "The Lament over Tyre (Ez. 27)," *Gregorianum*, 46 (1965), 83–88.

Tyre thus deified herself, and her genius for gaining wealth was her life's purpose.

Ezekiel devotes an entire chapter to this national image projected by the ruler. He was the epitomy of the nation's spirit, the personification of its character.

(1) Oracle Against Tyre (28:1–10)

¹ The word of the Lord came to me: ² "Son of man, say to the prince of Tyre, Thus says the Lord God:

"Because your heart is proud,
   and you have said, 'I am a god,
I sit in the seat of the gods,
   in the heart of the seas,'
yet you are but a man, and no god,
   though you consider yourself as wise as
      a god—
³ you are indeed wiser than Daniel;
   no secret is hidden from you;
⁴ by your wisdom and your understanding
   you have gotten wealth for yourself,
and have gathered gold and silver
   into your treasuries;
⁵ by your great wisdom in trade
   you have increased your wealth,
   and your heart has become proud in
      your wealth—
⁶ therefore thus says the Lord God:
"Because you consider yourself
   as wise as a god,
⁷ therefore, behold, I will bring strangers
      upon you,
   the most terrible of the nations;
and they shall draw their swords against
      the beauty of your wisdom
   and defile your splendor.
⁸ They shall thrust you down into the Pit,
   and you shall die the death of the slain
   in the heart of the seas.
⁹ Will you still say, 'I am a god,'
   in the presence of those who slay you,
though you are but a man, and no god,
   in the hands of those who wound you?
¹⁰ You shall die the death of the uncircum-
      cised
   by the hand of foreigners;
for I have spoken, says the Lord God."

Tyre's offense is embodied in the person of her ruler (v. 2), who typifies the national attitude. National business acumen (i.e., wisdom), which should be viewed here as shrewdness, cunning, or craftiness in trade, had brought unrestricted prosperity and fame to the nation. Its people basked in the accolades of other trade nations. They were satiated with grandiose waves of self-adulation. Since there seemed to be no limit to their ability to amass wealth, they rationalized that they were *as wise as a god* (vv. 2,6). They were their own god. In fact they considered themselves to be superior to Dan-el, thought by many to be the legendary figure of Canaanite wisdom.

Tyrian pride, which knew no bounds, created the demand for a humbling punishment. The basic problem with their wisdom was that it lay in one direction, trade, and as a result their *heart* (i.e., mind) was obsessed. They had made the disastrous mistake in assuming that only a segment of wisdom, commercial acumen, constituted the whole of wisdom. It was this which inexorably led them to cry *I am a god.*

With cold logic Ezekiel points to their self-delusion. Will they still say "I am a god" when destruction falls and they suffer an ignoble death, that of the uncircumcised (v. 10)? When they are dealt a death blow by the most terrible of nations, Babylonia (v. 7), can they still claim godly status? There is the ironic question, Can a god fall? Ezekiel drives home a cardinal truth. The greater one's self-aggrandizement becomes, the higher one's presumptive pride rises, the more expansive becomes one's self-esteem, the more ignominious is the end.

(2) Lamentation over the King of Tyre (28:11–19)

¹¹ Moreover the word of the Lord came to me: ¹² "Son of man, raise a lamentation over the king of Tyre, and say to him, Thus says the Lord God:

"You were the signet of perfection,
   full of wisdom
   and perfect in beauty.
¹³ You were in Eden, the garden of God;
   every precious stone was your covering,
carnelian, topaz, and jasper,
   chrysolite, beryl, and onyx,
sapphire, carbuncle, and emerald;
   and wrought in gold were your settings
   and your engravings.
On the day that you were created
   they were prepared.
¹⁴ With an anointed guardian cherub I
      placed you;

you were on the holy mountain of God;
in the midst of the stones of fire you
walked.
15 You were blameless in your ways
from the day you were created,
till iniquity was found in you.
16 In the abundance of your trade
you were filled with violence, and you
sinned;
so I cast you as a profane thing from the
mountain of God,
and the guardian cherub drove you out
from the midst of the stones of fire.
17 Your heart was proud because of your
beauty;
you corrupted your wisdom for the sake of
your splendor.
I cast you to the ground;
I exposed you before kings,
to feast their eyes on you.
18 By the multitude of your iniquities,
in the unrighteousness of your trade
you profaned your sanctuaries;
so I brought forth fire from the midst of
you;
it consumed you,
and I turned you to ashes upon the earth
in the sight of all who saw you.
19 All who know you among the peoples
are appalled at you;
you have come to a dreadful end
and shall be no more for ever."

A universalistic viewpoint is clearly
definable in the lament over the king of
Tyre and, as such, creates genuine theological puzzles. In flowing imagery Ezekiel
depicts the king of Tyre as if he were
Adam occupying a less than primordial
Eden.

The fact that he is depicted as being in
Eden, the garden of God (v. 13), and
upon the holy mountain of God (v. 14)
intimates a close and protective relationship between Yahweh and the Tyrian
king.[90] As a protégé of Yahweh, every
splendor was prepared on the day of
Tyre's creation (v. 13), and the relationship between the two was perfection until
rebellion occurred (v. 15). As a result
Tyre became corrupt and was excluded
from the original relationship created by
Yahweh (v. 16).

The sin of misdirected wisdom was the
sin of Tyre (v. 17). The wisdom, will, and
mind of the king were perverted. All wisdom was expended toward one end, the
aggrandizement of self. True wisdom and
arrogance are mutually exclusive agents.
One will either destroy or transform the
other. In Tyre's case her willful pride
perverted and polarized her wisdom.

Different interpretations are feasible and
acceptable for the somewhat perplexing
passage.[91] (1) Ezekiel may have employed
a primitive prototype of a paradise myth,
one of the popular myths of his day concerning Tyre's origin. (2) The entire story
may be taken symbolically in that Tyre
with all her wealth was like an earthly
paradise, like Eden which was corrupted.
(3) On the other hand, Ezekiel may simply have been comparing Tyre's fall to
that of Adam's fall, seeing the sin of Tyre
as being similar to that of Adam and Eve
but with Tyre far surpassing the pair, who
wanted to be *like* God, by claiming to *be* a
god.

III. Judgment Against Sidon and Restoration for Israel (28:20-26)

1. Judgment Against Sidon (28:20-23)

20 The word of the LORD came to me: 21 Son
of man, set your face toward Sidon, and
prophesy against her 22 and say, Thus says the
Lord GOD:
"Behold, I am against you, O Sidon,
and I will manifest my glory in the midst
of you.
And they shall know that I am the LORD
when I execute judgments in her,
and manifest my holiness in her;
23 for I will send pestilence into her,
and blood into her streets;
and the slain shall fall in the midst of her,
by the sword that is against her on every
side.
Then they will know that I am the LORD.

Tyre and Sidon were the two major
cities of Phoenicia but with Tyre generally
in political ascendancy. There are
evidences, however, that at times Sidon
was of considerable prominence. During

---

90 Norman C. Habel, "Ezekiel 28 and the Fall of
the First Man," *Concordia Theological Monthly*, 38.8
(1967), 516–524.

91 Cf. John L. McKenzie, "Mythological Allusions
in Ezekiel 28:12–18," JBL, LXXV (1956), 332–337.

the Omride dynasty (*ca.* 876–842 B.C.), Itto-baal, the father of Jezebel and ruler of Phoenicia, was a Sidonian (1 Kings 16:31).[92]

Although the passage may be an editorial insertion, its implication is quite evident. Sidon will share in the fate of Tyre as she had shared in her fame, wealth, and pride. Historically the two cities worked in concert and were coconspirators in monopolizing sea trade. Of the cities of the mainland group controlled by Tyre, Sidon was preeminent. Sidon was not guilty by virtue of association but by active participation in the vanity of Tyre.

2. Restoration of Israel (28:24–26)

24 "And for the house of Israel there shall be no more a brier to prick or a thorn to hurt them among all their neighbors who have treated them with contempt. Then they will know that I am the Lord GOD. 25 "Thus says the Lord GOD: When I gather the house of Israel from the peoples among whom they are scattered, and manifest my holiness in them in the sight of the nations, then they shall dwell in their own land which I gave to my servant Jacob. 26 And they shall dwell securely in it, and they shall build houses and plant vineyards. They shall dwell securely, when I execute judgments upon all their neighbors who have treated them with contempt. Then they will know that I am the LORD their God."

Again Ezekiel reveals the inner intensity of feeling that the name of Yahweh should be vindicated. Contempt shown for Yahweh's people was looked upon by the prophet as an affront to Yahweh (v. 24). The reference to the scattered remnants (v. 25) obviously refers to all the exiles; those of the Northern as well as the Southern Kingdom.

The phrase *my servant Jacob* is a synonym for the entire house of Israel (cf. 37:25; Jer. 30:10; 46:27,28; Isa. 41:8; 44:1; 45:4), thus enforcing the concept of a general return. The security of the returnees to the Land of Promise will be assured through the reduction of all enemies by the judgment of Yahweh (v. 26). Both the return of the exiles and the devastating judgment upon the enemies of Israel will conclusively demonstrate that Yahweh is God.

IV. Judgment Against Egypt (29:1— 32:32)

Within this division there are seven specific utterances of judgment against one of Israel's oldest and most deceptive enemies. Any oracle against Egypt carried the historical venom of an ignominious oppression. Thus the passages are pregnant with Exodus terminology (i.e., wilderness, Migdol, forty years, Zoan, cover the sun with a cloud, darkness upon your land, etc.) These lengthy oracles against Egypt are indicative of the smarting wounds and smoldering hatred created by Egypt's repeated offenses against Israel. One cannot help but feel that this Israelite animosity toward Egypt was due, at least in part, to the Egyptian attitude toward Asiatics in general. Ancient Egyptian literature quite clearly reveals as anti-Asiatic stance (cf. ANET, p. 440).

In addition Egypt had lured the rulers of Israel and Judah down the pathways of deceptive alliances. Without exception these had been destructive to Israelite nationalism. Israel's history is replete with instances of the detrimental effects of such associations. Solomon's marriage to an Egyptian princess, to seal a commercial alliance, helped speed him toward religious apostasy (1 Kings 11:1–13). An alliance between Jeroboam I of Israel and Shishak of Egypt ended with an Egyptian attack not only on Judah but Israel (cf. 1 Kings 14:25–28; 2 Chron. 12:1–8).[93] Hosea refers to Ephraim as a "silly dove" calling to Egypt for assistance while being taken into captivity by the Assyrians (Hos. 7:11), the very enemy who had warned them of Egypt's ineffectiveness (cf. 2 Kings 18:19–25). Egypt's influence upon Israel

---

92 Cf. John Bright, *A History of Israel* (Philadelphia: The Westminster Press, 1959), pp 222–226.

93 Cf. ANET, p. 242; G. E. Wright, *Biblical Archaeology* (Philadelphia: The Westminster Press, 1957), pp. 148–149.

was traditionally viewed as being evil and particularly disastrous. Clear evidence of this is to be found in the narratives relating the pathetic rebellion of Hoshea of Israel (*ca.* 732–724 B.C.) against Assyria on the promise of Egyptian military aid (cf. 2 Kings 17).

1. Judgment Against Pharaoh (29:1–16)

¹ In the tenth year, in the tenth month, on the twelfth day of the month, the word of the LORD came to me: ² "Son of man, set your face against Pharaoh king of Egypt, and prophesy against him and against all Egypt; ³ speak, and say, Thus says the Lord GOD:
"Behold, I am against you,
    Pharaoh king of Egypt,
the great dragon that lies
    in the midst of his streams,
that says, 'My Nile is my own;
    I made it.'
⁴ I will put hooks in your jaws,
    and make the fish of your streams stick to your scales;
and I will draw you up out of the midst of your streams,
    with all the fish of your streams which stick to your scales.
⁵ And I will cast you forth into the wilderness,
    you and all the fish of your streams;
you shall fall upon the open field,
    and not be gathered and buried.
To the beasts of the earth and to the birds of the air
    I have given you as food.
⁶ "Then all the inhabitants of Egypt shall know that I am the LORD. Because you have been a staff of reed to the house of Israel; ⁷ when they grasped you with the hand, you broke, and tore all their shoulders; and when they leaned upon you, you broke, and made all their loins to shake; ⁸ therefore thus says the Lord GOD: Behold, I will bring a sword upon you, and will cut off from you man and beast; ⁹ and the land of Egypt shall be a desolation and a waste. Then they will know that I am the LORD.

"Because you said, 'The Nile is mine, and I made it,' ¹⁰ therefore, behold, I am against you, and against your streams, and I will make the land of Egypt an utter waste and desolation, from Migdol to Syene, as far as the border of Ethiopia. ¹¹ No foot of man shall pass through it, and no foot of beast shall pass through it; it shall be uninhabited forty years. ¹² And I will make the land of Egypt a desolation in the midst of desolated countries; and her cities shall be a desolation forty years among cities that are laid waste. I will scatter the Egyptians

among the nations, and disperse them among the countries.
¹³ "For thus says the Lord GOD: At the end of forty years I will gather the Egyptians from the peoples among whom they were scattered; ¹⁴ and I will restore the fortunes of Egypt, and bring them back to the land of Pathros, the land of their origin; and there they shall be a lowly kingdom. ¹⁵ It shall be the most lowly of the kingdoms, and never again exalt itself above the nations; and I will make them so small that they will never again rule over the nations. ¹⁶ And it shall never again be the reliance of the house of Israel, recalling their iniquity, when they turn to them for aid. Then they will know that I am the Lord GOD."

The Pharaoh, Hophra or Apries (cf. Jer. 44:30), reigned around 589–570 B.C. (v. 2). Identification of the Pharaoh is not the big question of vv. 3–5; rather it is the identification of the symbolical dragon. Does the dragon symbolism stand for Hophra or Apries, or does it refer to the primordial monster of chaos, Apep or Apophis, who inhabited the Nile in Egyptian mythology?

More simply, "dragon" could imply crocodile or even the serpentine Nile itself which gave life to all of Egypt. A Roman emperor, Augustus, must have had some such imagery in mind when he had Egypt symbolized as a crocodile on certain coinage.[94] The line *My Nile is my own; I made it,* the last half of which literally reads in Hebrew "I have made myself," serves as a key for understanding. The RSV follows the reading of the LXX and the Syriac manuscripts. If we take the Masoretic Text rendering, then we have in Ezekiel an echoing of a basic Egyptian religious concept in which the sun god Re was considered to have begotten himself. Additionally, the pharaoh was considered by the Egyptians to be Re incarnate upon the throne of Egypt. Thus symbolic reference to the pharaoh as a *dragon* (v. 3) was traditionally Egyptian (cf. ANET, pp. 6–7, 11–12 for sections on the primordial monster, pp. 12–14 for self-creation of Re,

---

[94] The *Aegypto capta* memorial coins. Cf. Michael Grant, *Roman Imperial Coinage* (London: Thomas Nelson and Sons, Ltd., 1954), p. 60.

and pp. 368–369 for self-creation of Amon).

It is then the pharaoh himself who will be contemptuously snatched from his life-giving source, the Nile (v. 4). He will be cast upon the desert sands, a meal for jackals and vultures (v. 5). No more dishonorable death could possibly occur. To those who so carefully attended the bodies of the dead, especially the pharaohs, such exposure would be a gross abomination; not to mention the fact that such an end jeopardized the possibility of entrance into afterlife. The fate of the pharaoh reminds one of the modern Bedouin curse, "May the sands drink your blood and the vultures consume your flesh."

Two reasons are given for such a fate befalling Egypt. Egypt had betrayed Judah (vv. 7–9a), and she possessed a grotesquely exaggerated sense of self-sufficiency (vv. 9b–16).

Appropriate imagery is used in the first charge against Egypt. Egypt was like a staff made from a reed (v. 6; cf. 2 Kings 18:21; Isa. 36:6). This refers to the political gambits, deadly and destructive, employed by Egypt in her relationships with Judah. Isaiah bitterly denounced Egypt for defaulting in alliance with Ashdod and used the occasion to protest any kind of Judahite alliance with Egypt (cf. Isa. 20). Zedekiah, king of Judah (ca. 598–587 B.C.) and a contemporary of Ezekiel, became involved in conspiracies with Psammetichus II and his son Apries against Nebuchadnezzar and was left without their major assistance. These events as well as those referred to in the introduction to this section make quite plain the implication of Ezekiel's words.

Whenever the people of Yahweh had joined with Egypt, grasped the reed so to speak, the reed snapped and injury resulted. Ezekiel is maintaining a position that Egypt had no national integrity. She looked upon other nations as pawns to be used and discarded at will.

Pharaoh was one of the prototypes in history of that individual who would promise much and deliver little or the government which leads others to commitments and risks which it will not take. Egypt represents the strong nation which uses other less powerful nations as pawns upon the chess board of international power politics and then discards them when their political usefulness is ended. For such offenses Egypt would feel the sword.

Not only did Egypt lack national integrity, but she felt inordinately proud of her self-sufficiency (vv. 9b–16). A typical Egyptian position is given: *The Nile is mine, and I made it* (v. 9b). Ezekiel had in mind not only the Egyptian sense of self-sufficiency but the fact that this frame of mind was an affront to Yahweh. It was Yahweh who had called all things into being. Yahweh had created the earth, not the Egyptian gods. For this offense the land would become totally desolate, ravaged by the sword of Nebuchadnezzar (v. 11). As Egypt had forced Israel to be a wilderness people for forty years (v. 13), Egypt would be a wilderness for forty years. The destruction heaped upon Egypt would extend from its northernmost Mediterranean coastal area (i.e., Migdol) to its southernmost border (i.e., Syene) at the first cataract of the Nile (v. 11).

Thus exalted Egypt, which once ruled the entirety of the Near East, would become inferior to all nations. Of the lowly she would become the lowliest (v. 15). Never again would Egypt either become strong enough to entice the people of Yahweh into faulty alliances or be of sufficient stature to remind God's people of their stupidity in trusting her (v. 16).

2. Egypt, the Wages of Babylon (29: 17–21)

17 In the twenty-seventh year, in the first month, on the first day of the month, the word of the LORD came to me: 18 "Son of man, Nebuchadrezzar king of Babylon made his army labor hard against Tyre; every head was made bald and every shoulder was rubbed bare; yet neither he nor his army got anything from Tyre to pay for the labor that he had performed against it. 19 Therefore thus says the

Lord God: Behold, I will give the land of Egypt to Nebuchadrezzar king of Babylon; and he shall carry off its wealth and despoil it and plunder it; and it shall be the wages for his army. [20] I have given him the land of Egypt as his recompense for which he labored, because they worked for me, says the Lord God.

[21] "On that day I will cause a horn to spring forth to the house of Israel, and I will open your lips among them. Then they will know that I am the Lord."

Implications within this section suggest Nebuchadnezzar either failed to reduce Tyre or that after the destruction he did not receive spoil commensurate to the energies, hardships, and labors connected with the siege (v. 18). Certainly the effort poured into the assault upon such a stronghold was considerable. Historical evidences indicate that the siege of the stronghold, the island citadel of Tyre, failed. Therefore the treasury of Tyre never fell into the hands of Nebuchadnezzar.

Ezekiel graphically describes the hardships of the attack; *every head was made bald and every shoulder was rubbed bare* (v. 18). The abused shoulders were possibly occasioned by the transporting of materials to erect siege towers and then pulling them into place by rope slings over the shoulders. Even the hair was worn from the heads by the head straps used for assistance in carrying heavy loads upon the back.

As striking as the imagery of v. 18 may be, the thought of vv. 19,20 is truly amazing. Egypt will be given to Babylonia as *wages.* Ezekiel depicts Nebuchadnezzar as a workman of Yahweh, a laborer employed on a percentage basis. Yahweh will compensate him for his loss in Phoenicia by delivering up to him the riches of Egypt. Here Yahweh, in the mind of Ezekiel, is using one heathen nation as a vehicle of judgment upon another heathen nation, and his hire as the executioner of Yahweh will be the wealth of his victim.

Doubtless Ezekiel reflects here in a rudimentary form the concept of a movement within history through which Yahweh is judging all nations in order to affirm his universal sovereignty. The process is one which would not ultimately end with the redeeming of Israel alone, but the firm establishment of God's kingdom among men. In effect, history and its events constitute the arena in which God is seeking to fulfill his plan of redemption.

The *horn* (v. 21) has been taken to imply the Messiah by some commentators;[95] but most Jewish commentators follow Kimchi and interpret this as having to do with the return from exile. Allusions to the *horn* are found elsewhere in the Old Testament and at times with possible Messianic implications (cf. Luke 1:69). It implies here a return of the power of Israel but not in a final messianic sense. In most Old Testament passages the term horn is used as a symbol of strength or power. This is uniquely the case in the Psalms and Daniel.

3. Egypt and the Day of the Lord (30: 1–26)

The day of the Lord is defined in classic terms in these oracles against Egypt. Imagery used is indicative of a major Old Testament prophetic motif which appears at least as early as the time of Amos (cf. Amos 5:18–20). In Old Testament theology the day of the Lord was associated not just with judgment but with Israel's restored fortunes, politically and militarily. This day would occasion the rejuvenation not only of Israel but of nature itself. It is significant to note that in Ezekiel the term does not imply an eschatological cosmic event but a day of historical judgment close at hand (May, p. 229).

(1) The Imminent Fall of Egypt (30:1–9)

[1] The word of the Lord came to me: [2] "Son of man, prophesy, and say, Thus says the Lord God:

"Wail, 'Alas for the day!'
[3]   For the day is near,
    the day of the Lord is near;
  it will be a day of clouds,
    a time of doom for the nations.

---

[95] Cf. especially Kraeling, *op. cit.* p. 491; Cooke, p. 330.

4   A sword shall come upon Egypt,
> and anguish shall be in Ethiopia,
> when the slain fall in Egypt,
> > and her wealth is carried away,
> > and her foundations are torn down.

5 Ethiopia, and Put, and Lud, and all Arabia, and Libya, and the people of the land that is in league, shall fall with them by the sword.

6 "Thus says the LORD:
> Those who support Egypt shall fall,
> > and her proud might shall come down;
> from Migdol to Syene
> they shall fall within her by the sword,
> says the Lord GOD.

7   And she shall be desolated in the midst of desolated countries
> and her cities shall be in the midst of cities that are laid waste.

8   Then they will know that I am the LORD,
> when I have set fire to Egypt,
> and all her helpers are broken.

9 "On that day swift messengers shall go forth from me to terrify the unsuspecting Ethiopians; and anguish shall come upon them on the day of Egypt's doom; for, lo, it comes!

When the *day of the Lord* (i.e., Yahweh's judgment) falls upon Egypt, it will be in the form of the sword (i.e., Nebuchadnezzar) who will annihilate her armies, plunder her wealth, and level her towns (vv. 3,4). And as Egypt falls so will her allies, those in league with her. *In league* literally means "the land of covenant," and pertains to all with whom Egypt had formerly allied herself. Egypt and her allies will share a mutual fate (v. 5).

Previously (27:10,11) *Put* and *Lud* are referred to as providing mercenary soldiers for Tyre. The identical areas are mentioned in v. 5, and there follows an oracle of destruction for them as allies. Thus this judgment may have a twofold implication. (1) Put and Lud may also have provided mercenary soldiers for Egypt and thus were to come under condemnation. (2) Put and Lud were to be judged for their association not only with Egypt but with Tyre. Even Egypt's southernmost neighbor, the *Ethiopians* (v. 9), will be caught up in the holocaust of destruction.

(2) *The Instrument of Destruction* (30:10–12)

10 "Thus says the Lord GOD:
> I will put an end to the wealth of Egypt,
> by the hand of Nebuchadrezzar king of Babylon.

11   He and his people with him, the most terrible of the nations,
> shall be brought in to destroy the land;
> and they shall draw their swords against Egypt,
> and fill the land with the slain.

12   And I will dry up the Nile,
> and will sell the land into the hand of evil men;
> I will bring desolation upon the land and everything in it,
> by the hand of foreigners;
> I, the LORD, have spoken.

Babylon is again identified as the *most terrible of nations,* whose men are evil and who are foreigners (v. 12). Terrible is here to be taken in the sense of ruthless, merciless, remorseless. The question which looms large is one of the ethical nature of Yahweh. Described is an instrument, ostensibly that of Yahweh, which was the epitome of all an ethical God would abhor. Would Yahweh use Babylon as the instrument of his will? This extremely delicate question can be answered only on the basis of assurance of the righteousness and sovereignty of God. Included among the disasters confronting Egypt was that of drying up the waters of the Nile which would cause the fertile land to return to desert. It was this act which would bring the desolation to the land (v. 12b).

(3) *The Initial Attack upon Egypt* (30:13–19)

13 "Thus says the Lord GOD:
> I will destroy the idols,
> and put an end to the images, in Memphis;
> there shall no longer be a prince in the land of Egypt;
> so I will put fear in the land of Egypt.

14   I will make Pathros a desolation,
> and will set fire to Zoan,
> and will execute acts of judgment upon Thebes.

15   And I will pour my wrath upon Pelusium,
> the stronghold of Egypt,

and cut off the multitude of Thebes.
16 And I will set fire to Egypt;
   Pelusium shall be in great agony;
   Thebes shall be breached,
   and its walls broken down.
17 The young man of On and of Pibeseth shall
   fall by the sword;
   and the women shall go into captivity.
18 At Tehaphnehes the day shall be dark,
   when I break there the dominion of
   Egypt,
   and her proud might shall come to an end;
   she shall be covered by a cloud,
   and her daughters shall go into captivity.
19 Thus I will execute acts of judgment upon
   Egypt.
   Then they will know that I am the
   LORD."

The city lists of vv. 13–19 have been
verified and each city located with reasonable certainty. As such the listing indicates
an exact knowledge of the chief cities of
Egypt for the period. Memphis (v. 13), as
an ancient capital of Egypt, had associated
with it the multitudes of religious cults
which tended to centralize in political centers. Pathros (v. 14), although not designated in the documents as a city, seems to
be a general geographical designation for
the Theban area (cf. Jer. 44:1,15 and
Ezek. 29:14, which allude to this area as
the homeland of the Egyptians, their place
of origin). Zoan was Tanis, and Thebes,
the present Karnak (v. 14). Thebes was
the venerable capital of upper Egypt.
Nahum 3:8 (marg.) uses the name No-
amon for Thebes (see also Jer. 46:25).
Pelusium (v. 15) was a stronghold on the
northern Egyptian border with On (i.e.,
Heliopolis) and Pibeseth (i.e., Bubastis)
located in the Delta area (v. 17).
Tehaphnehes (v. 18) is modern Tel el-
Defneh. Both Jeremiah and Ezekiel considered the destruction of Tehaphnehes
(i.e., Tahpanhes) to be crucial in the attack upon Egypt (cf. Jer. 43:7), since it
was considered to be the official residency
of the pharaoh. There the *dominion* of
Egypt would be broken. In common usage
the Hebrew word meant bars or pegs used
to hold together the crossbeams of animal
yokes.

To Ezekiel the destruction of Egypt
meant the releasing of Israel from the
clutches of a nation which time and again
had been the betrayer. Literally Israel
would be "un-yoked" from Egypt.

(4) The Final Devastation of Egypt (30:20-26)

20 In the eleventh year, in the first month, on
the seventh day of the month, the word of the
LORD came to me: 21 "Son of man, I have
broken the arm of Pharaoh king of Egypt; and
lo, it has not been bound up, to heal it by
binding it with a bandage, so that it may
become strong to wield the sword. 22 Therefore
thus says the Lord GOD: Behold, I am against
Pharaoh king of Egypt, and will break his
arms, both the strong arm and the one that was
broken; and I will make the sword fall from his
hand. 23 I will scatter the Egyptians among the
nations, and disperse them throughout the
lands. 24 And I will strengthen the arms of the
king of Babylon, and put my sword in his
hand: but I will break the arms of Pharaoh,
and he will groan before him like a man
mortally wounded. 25 I will strengthen the arms
of the king of Babylon, but the arms of Pharaoh shall fall; and they shall know that I am
the LORD. When I put my sword into the hand
of the king of Babylon, he shall stretch it out
against the land of Egypt; 26 and I will scatter
the Egyptians among the nations and disperse
them throughout the countries. Then they will
know that I am the LORD."

The date of v. 20 would be April 587
B.C. Egypt is depicted as a man with an
arm broken and healing (v. 21). Subsequently another injury is inflicted upon
the unhealed arm as well as the whole arm
(v. 22). This asserts Egypt received two
judgmental blows by Yahweh's instrument,
Nebuchadnezzar (v. 24). It is known from
biblical records that, at the beginning of
the siege of Jerusalem, Hophra (i.e.,
Apries), the Egyptian pharaoh, led Egyptian relief columns to the Jerusalem area
where he was soundly defeated (Jer. 37:
1-10; 34:21).

This may be Ezekiel's allusion to the
arm broken and healing. Yet on that occasion the back of Egypt's power was not
broken (cf. Eichrodt, *Ezekiel*, pp. 419 ff.,
for the difficult textual problems involved).

Ezekiel then asserts that Yahweh will strengthen the power of Babylon (v. 24) so that in the near future, before the wound can be bound and complete healing effected (v. 21), Babylonia will reduce Egypt to total subjugation. This ultimate defeat is recorded in 2 Kings 24:7 (cf. ANET, p. 308).

Central in the imagery employed is the "broken arm" motif (vv. 21,22,24) and the "strengthened arm" motif (vv. 24, 25). Similar imagery is employed elsewhere in the Old Testament (cf. Psalms 10:15; 37:17; Jer. 48:25). Usage of the symbol is, however, more characteristic of the Exodus experience of Israel and the conquest of Canaan. The phrase "outstretched arm" is particularly noticeable in the Deuteronomic accounts. The outstretched arm in warfare signifies victory or signals attack. Egyptian art depicts the triumphant pharaoh with outstretched arm. By divine intervention the arms of the pharaoh will be crippled (v. 22) and the arm of Babylon strengthened in order to assure victory.

4. The Allegory of the Great Cedar (31:1–18)

Ezekiel, in a continuation of the oracles against Egypt, employs the allegorical method of presentation. It is quite similar to the ship allegory on Tyre. This allegory presents Egypt historically as a world power, but it does not imply that Ezekiel considered it to be a first-rate power in his own day.

Egypt historically had stood head-and-shoulders above all other nations (cf. vv. 5a,6,8a,10a). But due to its lofty status as a nation it had become excessively proud (v. 10b) and grossly wicked (v. 11b). Therefore it was to be delivered up in judgment. We have noticed how carefully Ezekiel spells out the charges against nations to make certain in the mind of his hearers that Yahweh's judgment is valid. Previously Ezekiel has noted Egypt's offenses. Now he expands and reinforces them.

(1) The Incomparable Greatness of Egypt (31:1–9)

1 In the eleventh year, in the third month, on the first day of the month, the word of the LORD came to me: 2 "Son of man, say to Pharaoh king of Egypt and to his multitude:
"Whom are you like in your greatness?
3   Behold, I will liken you to a cedar in Lebanon,
with fair branches and forest shade,
and of great height,
its top among the clouds.
4 The waters nourished it,
the deep made it grow tall,
making its rivers flow
round the place of its planting,
sending forth its streams
to all the trees of the forest.
5 So it towered high
above all the trees of the forest;
its boughs grew large
and its branches long,
from abundant water in its shoots.
6 All the birds of the air
made their nests in its boughs;
under its branches all the beasts of the field
brought forth their young;
and under its shadow
dwelt all great nations.
7 It was beautiful in its greatness,
in the length of its branches;
for its roots went down
to abundant waters.
8 The cedars in the garden of God could not rival it,
nor the fir trees equal its boughs;
the plane trees were as nothing
compared with its branches;
no tree in the garden of God
was like it in beauty.
9 I made it beautiful
in the mass of its branches,
and all the trees of Eden envied it,
that were in the garden of God.

Egypt, who had in past history eclipsed all other nations, is likened to a majestic *cedar of Lebanon*. This was the one tree of the forest without peer (v. 3). The reason for the gigantic stature of the tree was the source of its nourishment. Its sustenance came not from rainfall as most trees, but from *the deep*, the primordial waters beneath the earth (vv. 4,5). Since "the deep" figures so largely in Babylonian mythology and has direct connection with the religious cult, especially in the creation accounts, the implications are of divine nourishment of this particular tree (cf. Psalm 1 for the tree attended and nourished).

The strength and extension of its branches (v. 5) imply expansion of Egypt's authority over other nations and the rise of Egypt to preeminence in the Near East. Thus the Nilotic empire eventually overshadowed all other nations (v. 6). We would take this to mean overshadow in the sense not only of economic prosperity but political and military might. Egypt's reputation as a world empire is difficult to deny or underrate. Its magnificence, grandeur, pageantry, and authority (vv. 7,8) made it one of the great nations of history. All this, however, (i.e., the lofty status of Egypt) was attributed by Ezekiel to Yahweh: *I made it beautiful* (v. 9a). Not only does this again strike the universalistic note, but it also combats Egypt's contentions that she had lifted herself to such prominence (cf. 29:3–9).

(2) The Fallen Proud (31:10–18)

10 "Therefore thus says the Lord God: Because it towered high and set its top among the clouds, and its heart was proud of its height, 11 I will give it into the hand of a mighty one of the nations; he shall surely deal with it as its wickedness deserves. I have cast it out. 12 Foreigners, the most terrible of the nations, will cut it down and leave it. On the mountains and in all the valleys its branches will fall, and its boughs will lie broken in all the watercourses of the land; and all the peoples of the earth will go from its shadow and leave it. 13 Upon its ruin will dwell all the birds of the air, and upon its branches will be all the beasts of the field. 14 All this is in order that no trees by the waters may grow to lofty height or set their tops among the clouds, and that no trees that drink water may reach up to them in height; for they are all given over to death, to the nether world among mortal men, with those who go down to the Pit. 15 "Thus says the Lord God: When it goes down to Sheol I will make the deep mourn for it, and restrain its rivers, and many waters shall be stopped; I will clothe Lebanon in gloom for it, and all the trees of the field shall faint because of it. 16 I will make the nations quake at the sound of its fall, when I cast it down to Sheol with those who go down to the Pit; and all the trees of Eden, the choice and best of Lebanon, all that drink water, will be comforted in the nether world. 17 They also shall go down to Sheol with it, to those who are slain by the sword; yea, those who dwelt under its shadow among the nations shall perish. 18 Whom are you thus like in glory and in greatness among the trees of Eden? You shall be brought down with the trees of Eden to the nether world; you shall lie among the uncircumcised, with those who are slain by the sword.

"This is Pharaoh and all his multitude, says the Lord God."

Regardless of its lofty status or the causative agent of that status, Egypt had fallen into the besetting sin of all world powers. It had succumbed to pride (v. 10b)—the most damaging of all national offenses. Pride tends to place nation above and beyond commitment to deity and makes the cause of the state the cause of right. Such presumption created a lack of tension with the historic past and a decay of those historic forces which gave it birth. Inevitably such a nation moves into the role of one prone to consider itself the norm of all things. The state becomes an end within itself and is therefore accountable, in its own mind, to no other power.

As extensive as was the power and influence of Egypt for wickedness, so will its judgment be (vv. 11,12). The scope, intensity, and sternness of judgment will be as great as was its capacity for wickedness. Such a judgmental principle is not to be lightly overlooked and could not be dismissed by those nations surrounding Egypt. Egypt's fall, as an unforgettable object lesson, will have universal impact (vv. (15–16). Those nations once under the authority of Egypt will be able to wander about in its desolation (v. 13).

Ezekiel sees in this judgment a finality for Egypt as a nation. The fallen proud will not revive but will be relegated to Sheol as any other mortal man (v. 14). In this there is cutting irony. Egypt who considered itself not to be like other nations will share the judgment of every nation. As there is no immunity for the ordinary or lesser nation, there is no immunity for the great. Nations are not just equal at times before

God but are equal at all times before God.

As with the allies of Tyre, the allies and national associates of Egypt will share its fate (v. 17). Likely this refers to those nations who historically had cast their lot with Egypt; it may include Judah. The final lot which they share is a common one, the abode of Sheol (v. 18).

As a people the Egyptians scorned circumcision and placed emphasis upon meticulous care of the bodies of the dead. No more ignoble fate could descend upon the Egyptians than this. They would be forced to share common graves with their bodies unattended for burial. They will lie in death not with the honored dead but with the unhonored. No greater affront could be possible—the proud Egyptian in death beside the hated Asiatic (v. 18).[96]

5. The Snared Dragon (32:1-8)

¹ In the twelfth year, in the twelfth month, on the first day of the month, the word of the Lord came to me: ² "Son of man, raise a lamentation over Pharaoh king of Egypt, and say to him:
"You consider yourself a lion among the nations,
but you are like a dragon in the seas;
you burst forth in your rivers,
trouble the waters with your feet,
and foul their rivers.
³ Thus says the Lord God:
I will throw my net over you
with a host of many peoples;
and I will haul you up in my dragnet.
⁴ And I will cast you on the ground,
on the open field I will fling you,
and will cause all the birds of the air to
settle on you,
and I will gorge the beasts of the whole
earth with you.
⁵ I will strew your flesh upon the mountains,
and fill the valleys with your carcass.
⁶ I will drench the land even to the mountains
with your flowing blood;
and the watercourses will be full of you.
⁷ When I blot you out, I will cover the heavens,
and make their stars dark;
I will cover the sun with a cloud,
and the moon shall not give its light.

⁸ All the bright lights of heaven
will I make dark over you,
and put darkness upon your land,
says the Lord God.

Crucial to the interpretation of this section is the play on the two words *lion* and *dragon* (v. 2) and their symbolical implications. While Pharaoh looked upon himself as a lion among the nations (i.e., powerful, dominating, and regal), he was nothing more than an inhabiter of the waters which he fouls.

The critical issue is the symbolism of the dragon and meaning of its actions. "Dragon" may stand for the great dragon like Tiamat in Babylonian cosmic mythology (cf. ANET, pp. 60-72). Or it might pertain to Apep or Apophis, the primordial god of chaos in Egyptian mythology. The reference, on the other hand, may simply be to the crocodile or sacred hippopotamus which inhabit the Nile stirring and polluting its waters.

More likely the reference is to the primordial dragon which personified disorder, for the imagery points to the chaotic effect that Egypt had on international relations. It befouled, stirred, and polluted the calm of international peace by its intrigues and deceitful alliances. Because Egypt had created such stress, disquieted and corrupted the history of its day, it would come to a horrible end (vv. 4-6).

Of keen interest is the assertion in vv. 7,8. Egypt is depicted as shrouded by a canopy of mourning. The entire land is dark. Blotted from it are all the heavenly luminaries. A similar darkness is implied in 30:18. Darkness over Egypt had profound religious meaning. During the course of the plagues in the Exodus event one of the more telling miracles was that of deep darkness (cf. Ex. 10:21,22). Darkness during normal daylight hours in Egypt was an awesome event since it implied the blotting out of the face of their major deity Re, the sun-god. If this is the intimation of Ezekiel, then indeed the name of Yahweh will be known as the Lord!

---

[96] Georg Fohrer, "Das Geschick des Menschen nach dem Tode in Alten Testament," *Kerygma und Dogma*, 14.4 (1968), 249-262.

6. The Sword of Yahweh's Terror (32: 9–16)

9 "I will trouble the hearts of many peoples, when I carry you captive among the nations, into the countries which you have not known. 10 I will make many peoples appalled at you, and their kings shall shudder because of you, when I brandish my sword before them; they shall tremble every moment, every one for his own life, on the day of your downfall. 11 For thus says the Lord God: The sword of the king of Babylon shall come upon you. 12 I will cause your multitude to fall by the swords of mighty ones, all of them most terrible among the nations.

"They shall bring to nought the pride of Egypt,
and all its multitude shall perish.
13 I will destroy all its beasts
from beside many waters;
and no foot of man shall trouble them any more,
nor shall the hoofs of beasts trouble them.
14 Then I will make their waters clear,
and cause their rivers to run like oil,
says the Lord God.
15 When I make the land of Egypt desolate
and when the land is stripped of all that fills it,
when I smite all who dwell in it,
then they will know that I am the Lord.
16 This is a lamentation which shall be chanted; the daughters of the nations shall chant it; over Egypt, and over all her multitude, shall they chant it, says the Lord God."

When the dragon is overcome it will be by the sword of Babylon (v. 11), and the destruction will reduce the grandeur of Egypt to utter desolation (vv. 12–15). As with the fate of Tyre, which brought dismay to the maritime nations, the end of Egypt's existence will create widespread international dismay (v. 10). Egypt, who in her past conquests had made displaced persons of other nations, would in turn become a remnant scattered in captivity among the nations, and the lamentation of the daughters of nations will go up for Egypt (v. 16). This may imply professional mourners, women engaged to lament the dead (cf. Jer. 9:16).

7. The Citizens of Sheol (32:17–32)

17 In the twelfth year, in the first month, on the fifteenth day of the month, the word of the Lord came to me: 18 "Son of man, wail over the multitude of Egypt, and send them down, her and the daughters of majestic nations, to the nether world, to those who have gone down to the Pit:
19 'Whom do you surpass in beauty?
Go down, and be laid with the uncircumcised.'
20 They shall fall amid those who are slain by the sword, and with her shall lie all her multitudes. 21 The mighty chiefs shall speak of them, with their helpers, out of the midst of Sheol: 'They have come down, they lie still, the uncircumcised, slain by the sword.'

22 "Assyria is there, and all her company, their graves round about her, all of them slain, fallen by the sword; 23 whose graves are set in the uttermost parts of the Pit, and her company is round about her grave; all of them slain, fallen by the sword, who spread terror in the land of the living.

24 "Elam is there, and all her multitude about her grave; all of them slain, fallen by the sword, who went down uncircumcised into the nether world, who spread terror in the land of the living, and they bear their shame with those who go down to the Pit. 25 They have made her a bed among the slain with all her multitude, their graves round about her, all of them uncircumcised, slain by the sword; for terror of them was spread in the land of the living, and they bear their shame with those who go down to the Pit; they are placed among the slain.

26 "Meshech and Tubal are there, and all their multitude, their graves round about them, all of them uncircumcised, slain by the sword; for they spread terror in the land of the living. 27 And they do not lie with the fallen mighty men of old who went down to Sheol with their weapons of war, whose swords were laid under their heads, and whose shields are upon their bones; for the terror of the mighty men was in the land of the living. 28 So you shall be broken and lie among the uncircumcised, with those who are slain by the sword.

29 "Edom is there, her kings and all her princes, who for all their might are laid with those who are slain by the sword; they lie with the uncircumcised, with those who go down to the Pit.

30 "The princes of the north are there, all of them, and all the Sidonians, who have gone down in shame with the slain, for all the terror which they caused by their might; they lie uncircumcised with those who are slain by the sword, and bear their shame with those who go down to the Pit.

31 "When Pharaoh sees them, he will comfort himself for all his multitude, Pharaoh and all his army, slain by the sword, says the Lord

GOD. [32] For he spread terror in the land of the living; therefore he shall be laid among the uncircumcised, with those who are slain by the sword, Pharaoh and all his multitude, says the Lord GOD."

Prophetic utterance perhaps contains no more biting satire than this overwhelmingly caustic passage. Ezekiel here depicts the descent of Egypt into the *nether world* (i.e., Sheol or *Pit*). In this view of Sheol there is compartmentalization or groupings of shades according to the way of previous human conduct. In Sheol Egypt will share the ultimate fate and occupy that part of the pit designated for the vain world powers which have lived and died by the sword (vv. 19,20). Each of the occupants, other than Edom, are described as those which during their national existence had spread terror in the land of the living (vv. 23,24,25,30,32). These nations, the conquerors, the purveyors of terror, share a common fate. For example, Assyria had conquered Elam about 650 B.C., but then Assyria fell to Babylonia in 612 B.C. Each had considered itself invincible, a law unto itself and beyond Yahweh's workings; yet ultimately the slow workings of Yahweh's judgment had conquered the conquerors.

An especial case is made of Egypt, however (v. 19). She is greeted with mockery by Yahweh. No boastful pretention, no expression of power, no earthly renown, no inexpressive beauty can allay the judgment of Yahweh. Egypt shares the common fate in judgment. Nations, as men, die as they have lived, and what their lives have been given for is what their existences were worth.

Two recurring expressions fall in this section with the violent force of a triphammer, *slain . . . by the sword* and *uncircumcised*, both having the apparent connotation of special infamy or dishonor. To be "sword-slain" implies violent death precluding ordinary burial customs (i.e., preparation of body, religious ritual, etc.). In the case of the Egyptians, with immediate descent into Sheol, it preempted the appearance of the dead before Osiris, judge of the dead, in the hall of eternal justice. Only in this manner could one secure eternal happiness according to Egyptian religious belief (cf. ANET, pp. 34–36; Eichrodt, *Theology*, p. 212). An Egyptian could not conceive of a more dishonorable or awesome destiny.

It is quite another matter, however, to deal with the problem of uncircumcision. While it is affirmed that the Egyptians from an early period practiced the rite of circumcision, why should grouping with the uncircumcised be so overtly debilitating? In fact it is most difficult to obtain from Egyptian sources a clear view of their beliefs as related to circumcision and the extent to which it was practiced.[97]

The act may have been a puberty rite of cultic significance as related to procreation. Or it may have been an initiatory rite into marriageable status. In the passage, however, those from the Mesopotamian area (i.e., Assyrians, Elamites, Mesheck, Tubal), those from the north, and the Sidonians were considered uncircumcised. Edom (v. 29) is apparently a circumcised people.

The indignity of an ultimate fate consonant with that of the uncircumcised is difficult to fathom. Zimmerli has pointed out that the Ezekelian references to the uncircumcised dead implies something of a dishonorable death. We cannot overlook, however, that death in battle by those who live by the sword is the most honorable of all deaths. Perhaps we should attempt an approach to this problem from the Israelite priestly point of view. To the priestly mind uncircumcision put one beyond all laws of ritual cleanliness, cut one off from covenant blessings, and estranged one from all holy things. To be uncircumcised was to be unclean. Perhaps Ezekiel is postulating the concept of compartmentalization in Sheol with clean and unclean segregation, and suggesting that this and this alone will ultimately convince the nations that the level

[97] Cf. Roland de Vaux, *Ancient Israel Its Life and Institutions*, trans. John McHugh (New York: McGraw-Hill, 1961), pp. 46–47.

of existence in death was their true level of national existence in life.

Part Three: Oracles of Hope
33:1—48:35

The major transition in the ministry of Ezekiel came with the destruction of Jerusalem, which snuffed out even the faintest spark of hope among the remnant of Israel. It is at this point that Ezekiel becomes the affirming voice of Yahweh, not to condemn, but to proffer hope. With vigor equal to that given to the proclamation of judgment, the prophet proclaims the attentiveness of Yahweh to the needs of a broken people.

I. The Prophecies of Restoration (33: 1—39:29)

With this division there is a decided change in both tone and mood of the prophetic message. Yahweh's judgment had been fully effected in the painful experience of the destruction of Judah, the ravaging of Jerusalem and the Temple, and the exile of the Judahite remnant. Abruptly the message changes from one of doom to one of hope, from destruction to restoration. Even the prophet himself is cast in a new role. Within him the heart of a pastor begins to beat, transforming the unyielding man of stern oracular pronouncement into one of warmth, compassion, and concerned caring.

To sustain, to comfort, to inculcate hope is the new prophetic task. Yet there remains the stern disciplinarian. Ezekiel places incredible stress upon rigorous forms to maintain and perpetuate holiness. Strictly adhered-to ritual, with religious power centered in a Zadokite priesthood, was demanded. Popular religion, the new religion of hope, was to be worked out in conformity with new modes.

Marking this division is a new prophetic device, the use of popular religious sayings as the springboard for discourses. Utilization of streetcorner religious shibboleths adds an interesting dimension to the dialogues of Ezekiel with the people.

1. The Principle of Individual Responsibility (33:1–20)

The doctrine of individual responsibility is here reaffirmed. At this point, however, attention is directed toward prophetic responsibility (vv. 1–9) and the responsibility of the individual exile (vv. 10–20). Previously the ministry of the prophet was directed toward the nation. In this division of the book attention is focused upon the individual.

(1) The Peril and Privilege of the Prophetic Office (33:1–9)

[1] The word of the LORD came to me: [2] "Son of man, speak to your people and say to them, If I bring the sword upon a land, and the people of the land take a man from among them, and make him their watchman; [3] and if he sees the sword coming upon the land and blows the trumpet and warns the people; [4] then if any one who hears the sound of the trumpet does not take warning, and the sword comes and takes him away, his blood shall be upon his own head. [5] He heard the sound of the trumpet, and did not take warning; his blood shall be upon himself. But if he had taken warning, he would have saved his life. [6] But if the watchman sees the sword coming and does not blow the trumpet, so that the people are not warned, and the sword comes, and takes any one of them; that man is taken away in his iniquity, but his blood I will require at the watchman's hand.
[7] "So you, son of man, I have made a watchman for the house of Israel; whenever you hear a word from my mouth, you shall give them warning from me. [8] If I say to the wicked, O wicked man, you shall surely die, and you do not speak to warn the wicked to turn from his way, that wicked man shall die in his iniquity, but his blood I will require at your hand. [9] But if you warn the wicked to turn from his way, and he does not turn from his way; he shall die in his iniquity, but you will have saved your life.

Ezekiel 33:1–9 deals with the very essence of the prophetic office—the responsibility of the prophet to proclaim faithfully the message of Yahweh to the people. It is the prerogative of the people either to accept or to reject the message. The prophet as well as the people may exercise free will in the matter.

A prophet may refuse to convey the message as given but in so doing he will incur judgment. Judgment upon the prophet, however, will be more exacting than that upon the people, for his responsibility is greater. All would-be prophets stand in double jeopardy according to Ezekiel, for theirs is a dual responsibility, to man and to God.

Ezekiel forcefully presents the case by first defining the function of a watchman appointed during warfare (v. 2). In times of crisis additional watchmen would be conscripted from the populace to serve as additional wall sentries. Immediately upon observing the approach of an enemy, or any hostile activity, it was the task of the watchman to alert the citizens and defenders (v. 3). Once the sentry had sounded the alarm his appointed task had been accomplished. It was then the responsibility of the citizen to react as he chose (v. 4). If the citizens heeded the warning, well and good; but if they heard but refused to respond and then died by the enemy's sword, the watchman was blameless (v. 5).

If, however, the watchman saw the danger but refused or failed to warn the citizens and if just one citizen (i.e., *any one of them*, v. 6) was killed, the watchman was guilty of that man's death. Although no such law is to be found in Old Testament legal sections, the passage is so legally stated one wonders if Ezekiel was not quoting a civil law.

Ezekiel applies this case to himself as a prophet. Yahweh had set him as a watchman among the exiles (v. 7); not to proclaim judgment but to give warning (vv. 7–9). His task was to speak to the *wicked* (v. 8), warn them of the danger of their ways, and call them to repentance. If Ezekiel failed to warn the wicked, their deaths would be upon his hands. If he warned the wicked and they refused to heed, then the prophet would save his own life (v. 9).

Life, as referred to throughout this passage, literally means "soul." This is not "soul" in the Greek sense of that which is separate from the body, but soul in the Hebraic sense of soul and body as a living unity. Ezekiel's theology has a simple application: sin shortens life, righteousness effects longevity.

(2) The Doctrine of Individual Responsibility (33:10–20)

10 "And you, son of man, say to the house of Israel, Thus have you said: 'Our transgressions and our sins are upon us, and we waste away because of them; how then can we live?' 11 Say to them, As I live, says the Lord GOD, I have no pleasure in the death of the wicked, but that the wicked turn from his way and live; turn back, turn back from your evil ways; for why will you die, O house of Israel? 12 And you, son of man, say to your people, The righteousness of the righteous shall not deliver him when he transgresses; and as for the wickedness of the wicked, he shall not fall by it when he turns from his wickedness; and the righteous shall not be able to live by his righteousness when he sins. 13 Though I say to the righteous that he shall surely live, yet if he trusts in his righteousness and commits iniquity, none of his righteous deeds shall be remembered; but in the iniquity that he has committed he shall die. 14 Again, though I say to the wicked, 'You shall surely die,' yet if he turns from his sin and does what is lawful and right, 15 if the wicked restores the pledge, gives back what he has taken by robbery, and walks in the statutes of life, committing no iniquity; he shall surely live, he shall not die. 16 None of the sins that he has committed shall be remembered against him; he has done what is lawful and right, he shall surely live.

17 "Yet your people say, 'The way of the Lord is not just'; when it is their own way that is not just. 18 When the righteous turns from his righteousness, and commits iniquity, he shall die for it. 19 And when the wicked turns from his wickedness, and does what is lawful and right, he shall live by it. 20 Yet you say, 'The way of the Lord is not just.' O house of Israel, I will judge each of you according to his ways."

Within the context of 33:10–20 one should make no attempt to read the New Testament concept of God's abundant mercy. Although there is revealed an advance in understanding the nature of Yahweh and his dealings with man, there is an unequivocal and legalistic assertion of divine justice. The significant development is that which moves from a concept of corporate guilt to the concept of individual guilt.

That corporate guilt was felt by the exiles is made plain (v. 10). As a result of the sins of Judah both nation and Temple had fallen. Upon the exiles there bore down an overwhelming sense of guilt for their aggregate sin. The awesomeness of Yahweh's judgment had finally caused them to realize their national excesses. Due to their composite guilt, which they now acknowledged, they were wasting *away* (v. 10) literally rotting, decaying, or decomposing. They could not hope for forgiveness by Yahweh or restoration to his favor. Thus they cried to their prophet, *How then can we live* (v. 10)?

There is but one prophetic answer to the query—Repent (v. 11). That is to *turn back*, to move away from, to depart from those precise rebellious attitudes and iniquitous postures which had been their lifestyle prior to the judgment. It is the repentance of the sinful, not their death, which pleases Yahweh. Ezekiel here affirms that Yahweh took no pleasure in the execution of judgment; it was a necessity created by the utter lack of repentance.

This is followed by a legally defined plan of Yahweh's justice as shown to individuals. If a righteous man sins, feeling there is a sufficient reservoir of righteousness within him to drown the effects of that sin, he deludes himself (vv. 12,13). On the other hand if the wicked man repents (i.e., *turns from his sin and does what is lawful and right*), he will live, and previous offenses will not be held against him (vv. 14–16).

Thus the justice of Yahweh is that he condemns the righteous when he sins and forgives the sinful when he repents. Inescapable legalism is, however, involved. Doing what is *lawful* and *right* constitutes both the state of righteousness and the fruit of repentance.

The charge of the people is that this system of justice is unjust (v. 17a); for with rigid legalism both the wicked man's acts of rebellion and the righteous man's previous goodness are equally negated.

An expanded development of the doctrine of individual responsibility was initiated by Ezekiel to meet the changed condition of the people. It was no longer viable to think of the nation in a corporate sense, for there was no nation. Thus under exilic condition the individual became of prime importance.

Yet the basic overall religious problem on their part had to do with priorities. They emphasized their corporate guilt complex, and deemphasized or neglected their need for deep individual repentance, a characteristic failing of humankind.

2. Prophetic Popularity (33:21–33)

21 In the twelfth year of our exile, in the tenth month, on the fifth day of the month, a man who had escaped from Jerusalem came to me and said, "The city has fallen." 22 Now the hand of the LORD had been upon me the evening before the fugitive came; and he had opened my mouth by the time the man came to me in the morning; so my mouth was opened, and I was no longer dumb.

23 The word of the LORD came to me: 24 "Son of man, the inhabitants of these waste places in the land of Israel keep saying, 'Abraham was only one man, yet he got possession of the land; but we are many; the land is surely given us to possess.' 25 Therefore say to them, Thus says the Lord GOD: You eat flesh with the blood, and lift up your eyes to your idols, and shed blood; shall you then possess the land? 26 You resort to the sword, you commit abominations and each of you defiles his neighbor's wife; shall you then possess the land? 27 Say this to them, Thus says the Lord GOD: As I live, surely those who are in the waste places shall fall by the sword; and him that is in the open field I will give to the beasts to be devoured; and those who are in strongholds and in caves shall die by pestilence. 28 And I will make the land a desolation and a waste; and her proud might shall come to an end; and the mountains of Israel shall be so desolate that none will pass through. 29 Then they will know that I am the LORD, when I have made the land a desolation and a waste because of all their abominations which they have committed.

30 "As for you, son of man, your people who talk together about you by the walls and at the doors of the houses, say to one another, each to his brother, 'Come, and hear what the word is that comes forth from the LORD.' 31 And they come to you as people come, and they sit before you as my people, and they hear what you say but they will not do it; for with their

ips they show much love, but their heart is set on their gain. ³² And, lo, you are to them like one who sings love songs with a beautiful voice and plays well on an instrument, for they hear what you say, but they will not do it. ³³ When this comes—and come it will!—then they will know that a prophet has been among them."

The dating of 33:21–33 is problematical. Unless one accepts the variant reading "eleventh year" as found in numerous manuscripts instead of *twelfth year* (v. 21), the date would fall one and one-half years following the destruction of Jerusalem (cf. Howie, pp. 35,39,50; Cooke, p. 366; May, p. 248).

If the events in vv. 21,22 refer back to 24:26,27, then the implication is that the escapee from the city of Jerusalem (v. 21) came to Ezekiel in the exilic community on the very day of the fall of Jerusalem. During the evening before the arrival of the fugitive the dumbness of the prophet was being lifted by Yahweh (v. 22). Direct reference to this precise state is made in chapter 24, and only after the fall of Judah and the arrival of news of that event would the prophetic message return to Ezekiel.

Once the inability to proclaim the word of Yahweh has been broken, the message is one of denunciation of the remnant remaining in Judah after its destruction (vv. 23–29). An assumption, on the part of the remnant, was that since they were spared it demonstrated Yahweh's will and therefore they were the divinely ordained successors to the land of promise (v. 24). Such presumptuousness, on their part, staggered Ezekiel because judgment had produced no change in their lives. In utterly false confidence and with foolish logic, they presumed to be the true elect of Yahweh. They imputed to themselves the promises of Abraham (v. 24) while continuing to commit the offenses which had brought about the retribution of Yahweh (vv. 25,26).

Specifically Ezekiel charges them with "eating with blood." This act was an abhorrence to the true religion of Israel (cf. Lev. 3:17; 17:10–14; 19:26; Deut. 12:23). It may imply (1) a prohibition against eat-

ing flesh in the presence of its blood; (2) a prohibition against eating flesh not thoroughly drained of its blood; or (3) simply eating bloody flesh.

The Canaanites were considered to have contaminated the land by such an offense (Lev. 18:24 ff.). Possibly the basic premise behind the prohibition had to do with the Israelite view that the life principle resided in the blood (cf. 1 Sam. 14:33).

Chapter 18 details the offenses which had demanded the judgmental attention of Yahweh. The same ones will of necessity be judged again, for they have not responded to Yahweh (vv. 27–29).

Ezekiel next focuses attention upon the remnant in exile (vv. 30–33) and in so doing reveals a basic problem with his newfound ministry. Ezekiel suddenly finds himself in a truly unique prophetic situation. He, as well as the people to whom he has spoken, had lived to see his message authenticated by historical event. Upon the exiles the impact was incredible.

Ezekiel was elevated to the status of a public idol. He became, as it were, a legend in his own day. The exiles massed themselves flocking to hear his words. He was the topic of conversation as men sat exchanging small talk in the shade of a wall or about the entrances to homes (v. 30).

There comes to Ezekiel, however, a stern warning from Yahweh (v. 31). Popularity, throngs, words of commendation, apparent attentiveness, and seeming acceptance of the prophetic word did not mean genuine understanding or true acceptance of the message. Self-interest permitted the people to be only hearers. They could not actualize the message, for their hearts were set on *gain.* The Hebrew implies gain by violence or dishonesty associated with greed, especially greed in profits. Two reasonable conclusions are to be drawn: (1) the people were continuing their ways as before the exile (cf. comment on ch. 22); and (2) the exiles by this time had already become involved in Babylonian business affairs. Thus their exilic conditions were not so harsh as one might surmise.

To the exiles Ezekiel was little more than a popular entertainer whose voice was excellent and instrumental skill delightful (v. 32). The people saw the prophet as they wished to see him, not as he was. To them, his was a popular word about national revival, restoration of political fortunes, and return to their homeland. But the religious regulations, the keeping of the laws of righteousness which would make this possible, were totally rejected. They heard the commandments but would not heed them.

Yahweh informs Ezekiel that an event of judgment will come to pass, and herein lies the quandry (v. 33). Precisely what event is referred to? Does it mean the fall of Jerusalem? If so we would interpret the verse to imply that proof of prophetic prediction is in its occurrence. If a major function of the prophet is to speak to the contemporary condition, and if it implies the declaring of history with a Yahweh world view, then vindication of the message comes in Yahweh's historical involvement. On the other hand, the verse may refer to the negative response of the people to the prophetic message. It would imply that rejection of the demands of the prophetic message proves the validity of the message. The first of the two positions seems to be the intentional thrust of Ezekiel.

Regardless of varied approaches to 33:21–33, one salient feature stands boldly etched for all who would proclaim the words of Yahweh: prophetic popularity more often than not denotes response to personality not assent to and acceptance of the message. It is approval and reception of the messenger, not the message.

3. The Shepherds and the Shepherd (34:1–31) [98]

Employed in chapter 34 is the shepherd motif for deity familiar not only in Israelite religious literature (cf. Psalms 23; 74:1; Jer. 23:1–4; Mic. 5:5; Zech. 10:2–3; Isa. 40:11) but also in other ancient Near East-

ern literature. Also quite evident is messianic (cf. ANET, pp. 368,443), terminology and act (i.e., a leader of David's descent, feeding of sheep, healing of sick, binding up of the crippled, and seeking out the strayed or lost). One entire section (vv. 13–16) employs the imagery of a typical messianic era. In this chapter, however, all of the messianism deals with the concept of ideal rulership rather than traditional apocalyptic messianism.

Central in the chapter is a rigid hypothesis. For Israel to be restored, certain basic national reforms had to be effected. First, there had to come into existence a new kind of national leader who would be both just and righteous. Secondly, in order for this to be accomplished there had to be a new ruler whose role and purpose was clearly defined.

Ezekiel draws upon the concept of an ideal theocracy, whose leader would be a prince rather than a king. Divine approval, popular acceptance, and strict covenant agreement were all involved. In this we find Ezekiel once again returning to earliest Israelite religious tradition (cf. Judg. 8:23; 1 Sam. 8:7; 10:19; 12:12; Hos. 8:4,10; and later Zeph. 3:15 ff.).

(1) The Evil Shepherds (34:1–10)

[1] The word of the LORD came to me: [2] "Son of man, prophesy against the shepherds of Israel, prophesy, and say to them, even to the shepherds, Thus says the Lord GOD: Ho, shepherds of Israel who have been feeding yourselves! Should not shepherds feed the sheep? [3] You eat the fat, you clothe yourselves with the wool, you slaughter the fatlings; but you do not feed the sheep. [4] The weak you have not strengthened, the sick you have not healed, the crippled you have not bound up, the strayed you have not brought back, the lost you have not sought, and with force and harshness you have ruled them. [5] So they were scattered, because there was no shepherd; and they became food for all the wild beasts. [6] My sheep were scattered, they wandered over all the mountains and on every high hill; my sheep were scattered over all the face of the earth, with none to search or seek for them.

[7] "Therefore, you shepherds, hear the word of the LORD: [8] As I live, says the Lord GOD, because my sheep have become a prey, and my

---

[98] For a critical text analysis, cf. William H. Brownlee, "Ezekiel's Poetic Indictment of the Shepherds," *Harvard Theological Review* (1958), LI. 4, 191–213.

sheep have become food for all the wild beasts, since there was no shepherd; and because my shepherds have not searched for my sheep, but the shepherds have fed themselves, and have not fed my sheep; 9 therefore, you shepherds, hear the word of the LORD: 10 Thus says the Lord GOD, Behold, I am against the shepherds; and I will require my sheep at their hand, and put a stop to their feeding the sheep; no longer shall the shepherds feed themselves. I will rescue my sheep from their mouths, that they may not be food for them.

Israel's political leaders, to Ezekiel, had been evil shepherds, who rather than feeding the sheep fed upon them (vv. 2,3). Their station in life afforded a perfect base of power utilized to abuse and betray their own people. They enriched themselves at the expense of their subjects rather than promoting the common good. Prime consideration was directed not toward the needs of the general populace but their own selfish appetites and vested interests— *feeding yourselves!*

Thus the evil shepherd thought not of the condition of the flock but how that flock could contribute to his own personal wealth and aggrandizement (v. 4). Consideration was given neither to the plight nor the condition of the flock. To the contrary, with force and harshness, the leaders dealt cruelly with the indefensible: the *weak,* the *sick,* the *crippled,* the *strayed,* and the *lost.* This grave breach of religious ethic was betrayal of trust and invested responsibility. The weak and defenseless easily fall when not protected. To protect them was a task specifically assigned to those in high office. Under such conditions there was no redress of grievances and no one to champion the cause of the lowly. They were left defenseless before the onslaught of those whose sacred task was to protect them. It was as if Amos spoke once again (cf. Amos 6:4-6).

For the want of leadership the people *wandered* aimlessly (v. 6), literally to go "to and fro" as if in a drunken stupor. They were caught up in a wilderness of futility and, as sheep lost in the wilderness fell to predators, they fell victim to their own

leaders. Even more revealing is the fact that the leaders evidenced no concern; they did not search out the dispersed people, possibly inferring that they sought them only to feed upon them rather than feed them (v. 8).

This total lack of humaneness speaks eloquently to the condition of the rulers. So voracious and depraved were they, the people are depicted as being snatched from their ravenous mouths by Yahweh himself as a shepherd would snatch a sheep from the devouring jaws of a lion (v. 10).

As the watchman who betrays his trust is held accountable (cf. 33:1-9) so is the leader of the people. *I will require my sheep at their hand* says Yahweh (v. 10).

The grounds upon which the major political figure is castigated was one of long standing in Israel. The theory of kingship was that Israelite kings, bad as they were, ruled by the prior sanction of Yahweh over his people and on his behalf. They were directly accountable to Yahweh!

(2) The Role of the Good Shepherd (34: 11-16)

11 "For thus says the Lord GOD: Behold, I, I myself will search for my sheep, and will seek them out. 12 As a shepherd seeks out his flock when some of his sheep have been scattered abroad, so will I seek out my sheep; and I will rescue them from all places where they have been scattered on a day of clouds and thick darkness. 13 And I will bring them out from the peoples, and gather them from the countries, and will bring them into their own land; and I will feed them on the mountains of Israel, by the fountains, and in all the inhabited places of the country. 14 I will feed them with good pasture, and upon the mountain heights of Israel shall be their pasture; there they shall lie down in good grazing land, and on fat pasture they shall feed on the mountains of Israel. 15 I myself will be the shepherd of my sheep, and I will make them lie down, says the Lord GOD. 16 I will seek the lost, and I will bring back the strayed, and I will bind up the crippled, and I will strengthen the weak, and the fat and the strong I will watch over; I will feed them in justice.

Personal intervention on the part of Yahweh is a striking and bold thought and connotes more than just a simple return to a theocracy. Characteristically in the Old Testament Yahweh acted on behalf of his people through an intermediary force, being, or individual (i.e., the east wind at the crossing of the Red Sea, Ex. 14:21; the three men of Gen. 18 and the two angels of Gen. 19:1; Moses, Saul, or David and the prophets in general). In this passage there is an intermediary produced by new conceptual patterns.

Here we also find unique emphasis upon the personal pronoun "I" used 15 times as Yahweh speaks in first person. In addition, within the span of six verses *my* and *myself* are used three times. With keen anticipatory insight Ezekiel affirms and reaffirms that Yahweh himself will assume the role of the good shepherd: one who will gather the people together (vv. 12,13), reestablish them in their own land, and initiate an age marked by economic plenty and peace (vv. 14,15). Such strong messianic imagery has to do, however, with an idealized or restructured theocracy. The essential ingredient added is the ethical dimension of caring for those in need of care and justice (v. 16). This ideal leader will be the exact opposite of the former theocratic leaders.

(3) The Good Shepherd as Judge (34: 17-24)

[17] "As for you, my flock, thus says the Lord Gov: Behold, I judge between sheep and sheep, rams and he-goats. [18] Is it not enough for you to feed on the good pasture, that you must tread down with your feet the rest of your pasture; and to drink of clear water, that you must foul the rest with your feet? [19] And must my sheep eat what you have trodden with your feet, and drink what you have fouled with your feet?
[20] "Therefore, thus says the Lord Gov to them: Behold, I, I myself will judge between the fat sheep and the lean sheep. [21] Because you push with side and shoulder, and thrust at all the weak with your horns, till you have scattered them abroad, [22] I will save my flock, they shall no longer be a prey; and I will judge between sheep and sheep. [23] And I will set up over them one shepherd, my servant David, and he shall feed them: he shall feed them and be their shepherd. [24] And I, the Lord, will be their God, and my servant David shall be

prince among them; I, the Lord, have spoken.

Not only will Yahweh intervene through the good shepherd in order to displace the evil shepherds, but he will also deal with the evil sheep among the flock. Both this and the following imagery is taken from simple observation of a flock of sheep.

Sheep graze hungrily cropping the choicest grass, and in so doing trample down much of the good pasturage. Also the first of the flock to a stream always muddy and stir the water which the remainder of the flock are forced to drink.

Verses 17 and 18 expose that facet of gross human nature which offends even those of insensitive nature. There are those who with malice despoil that which they neither want nor need in order to deny it to other human beings. This is the act of a truly evil individual. For he well knows there is that degree in the human condition when need is so great and desperation so acute one is forced to accept that which is despoiled. The impact of v. 19 is that Yahweh's true people must be recipients of the inhumanity of Yahweh's untrue people (v. 19). This is like the gross and offensive act of a well-fed man who after eating his fill with much left over would mix offal with the food to prevent the starving from eating. But the unfortunate man in order to survive was reduced to eating the offensive mass.

Intervention must also occur on the part of the good shepherd because the *fat sheep* exploit and take advantage of the weakness of the *lean sheep* (v. 20). This may apply either to the upper strata of society, the economically advantaged who oppressed the weak, or to strong aggressor nations who overpowered lesser nations (vv. 20–22).

Among grazing sheep the stronger will shoulder aside the weaker in a chain reaction until the weakest sheep, who need the best pasturage, have inadequate pasturage. The use of brute force is certainly implied (v. 21).

Often such acts are seen indelibly etched upon the scarred face of history—exploiation of minority groups, child labor, loan sharking, intimidation of lesser nations by more powerful nations, and business cartels voraciously consuming small independent businesses. Such ethical relativity, with might constituting right, completely dehumanizes man.

Correction of these conditions will come with new leadership. The one shepherd concept (cf. comment on 20:40) implies that they either had in past times several shepherds or anticipated more than one shepherd. More likely this refers to the concept that Israel had had a succession of evil shepherds (i.e., the kings) but that from this new point of beginning there would be but one from the lineage of David (v. 23). He would not be a messianic king but a prince designate under Yahweh through whom Yahweh would directly rule (v. 24).[99]

(4) The Good Shepherd and the Covenant of Peace (34:25–31)

25 "I will make with them a covenant of peace and banish wild beasts from the land, so that they may dwell securely in the wilderness and sleep in the woods. 26 And I will make them and the places round about my hill a blessing; and I will send down the showers in their season; they shall be showers of blessing. 27 And the trees of the field shall yield their fruit, and the earth shall yield its increase, and they shall be secure in their land; and they shall know that I am the LORD, when I break the bars of their yoke, and deliver them from the hand of those who enslaved them. 28 They shall no more be a prey to the nations, nor shall the beasts of the land devour them; they shall dwell securely, and none shall make them afraid. 29 And I will provide for them prosperous plantations so that they shall no more be consumed with hunger in the land, and no longer suffer the reproach of the nations. 30 And they shall know that I, the LORD their God, am with them, and that they, the house of Israel, are my people, says the Lord GOD. 31 And you are my sheep, the sheep of my pasture, and I am your God, says the Lord GOD."

With the coming of the Davidic prince a new covenant will be executed. This *covenant of peace* (Heb., *berit shalom*), while employing an extremely old word for covenant, is pregnant with new meaning. This is a covenant quite different from those of the patriarchal days.[100] The sign of this covenant is the peace associated with ascent of a Davidic ruler.

Noticeably the terminology is of the messianic type and is closely associated with the thought of other Old Testament prophets (cf. principally Isa. 11:6–8; Jer. 31:31 ff.; Hos. 2:18). The idyllic age, which is to be instituted, will be characterized by peace between man and animal (vv. 25, 28), rain in season without fail (v. 26), productivity of fields, vineyards, and trees (v. 27), alleviation of hunger (v. 29), and a knowledge on the part of the people as to who they are and whose they are (vv. 30,31).

While the sublimity of the age is not quite so lavish as that projected by other Old Testament prophets (cf. especially Isa. 55:12,13; 60:1–18; 65:17–25), it is infused with a spirit of extreme nationalism. To Ezekiel this was an age to be characterized by Israelite exclusivism and a restoration of economic and political fortunes (vv. 29,30). Such an age was for the returned exilic nation and for none other.

4. Judgment Against Edom (35:1–15)

1 The word of the LORD came to me: 2 "Son of man, set your face against Mount Seir, and prophesy against it, 3 and say to it, Thus says the Lord GOD: Behold, I am against you, Mount Seir, and I will stretch out my hand against you, and I will make you a desolation and a waste. 4 I will lay your cities waste, and you shall become a desolation; and you shall know that I am the LORD. 5 Because you cherished perpetual enmity, and gave over the people of Israel to the power of the sword at the time of their calamity, at the time of their final punishment; 6 therefore, as I live, says the Lord GOD, I will prepare you for blood, and blood shall pursue you; because you are guilty of blood, therefore blood shall pursue you. 7 I

99 The ruler is designated "prince" (Heb. *nasi'*) here and in 37:25; 44:3; 46:2; etc., yet in 37:22,24 the same idealized ruler is designated "king" (Heb. *melek*). Only 37:22,24 refers to the idealized ruler as king. The LXX changes 37:22,24 to read "prince."

100 Cf. Gen. 9:1–17; 12:1–3; 17:1–14; 26:24; 28: 13–15 or even that of Moses and the Exodus (Ex. 6:2–8; 29:43–45; 31:22–17).

will make Mount Seir a waste and a desolation; and I will cut off from it all who come and go. ⁸ And I will fill your mountains with the slain; on your hills and in your valleys and in all your ravines those slain with the sword shall fall. ⁹ I will make you a perpetual desolation, and your cities shall not be inhabited. Then you will know that I am the Lord.

¹⁰ "Because you said, 'These two nations and these two countries shall be mine, and we will take possession of them,'—although the Lord was there—¹¹ therefore, as I live, says the Lord God, I will deal with you according to the anger and envy which you showed because of your hatred against them; and I will make myself known among you, when I judge you. ¹² And you shall know that I, the Lord, have heard all the revilings which you uttered against the mountains of Israel, saying, 'They are laid desolate, they are given us to devour.' ¹³ And you magnified yourselves against me with your mouth, and multiplied your words against me; I heard it. ¹⁴ Thus says the Lord God: For the rejoicing of the whole earth I will make you desolate. ¹⁵ As you rejoiced over the inheritance of the house of Israel, because it was desolate, so I will deal with you; you shall be desolate, Mount Seir, and all Edom, all of it. Then they will know that I am the Lord.

Once the ideal prince has replaced the evil and inadequate monarchy, another condition had to be met in order to usher in the era of Israel's restored fortunes. Those nations who had throughout history attempted to thwart Israel, and thus in the mind of the prophet the purposes of Yahweh in history, had to be eliminated. This seems to be the only plausible reason for inclusion of a second oracle against Edom, unless one wishes to take the position that the section is non-Ezekelian (cf. May, p. 256). Edom had already been castigated by Ezekiel for its historical animosity toward Israel (cf. comment on 25:12–14). This second denunciation must have been due to additional offenses. This would be the hostile acts of Edom against Judah following the destruction around 586 B.C.

Seir (Heb., *se'ir*) literally means "hairy" and implies a brushy geographical area. As a synonym for Edom this is quite understandable, since the peak is the most prominent of the Seir mountain range which dominated the area of ancient Edom (v. 2). The offense of Edom is outrageous to the

prophet. The Edomites, of close blood relation to the Israelites (cf. Gen. 25), had not only been a *perpetual* enemy of Israel (v. 5) and involved in a vendetta (v. 6) but had attacked her kinsmen when they were defenseless *at the time of their calamity.*

Edom's attack was evidence of her long desire to displace both Judah and Israel and gain political ascendancy in spite of Yahweh's intent to perpetuate his people, i.e., *although the Lord was there* (v. 10). The depth of Edom's hatred toward Israel is clearly revealed in the way she gloated over Judah's fall and celebrated her misfortune (vv. 12,13). An insight into the national character of Edom is given in v. 14. If the whole earth would rejoice over the destruction of Edom, then it follows that Edom is the object of dislike by all nations. It is strange but true that the worst of humanity is revolted by those who prey upon the helpless. Edom's fate is to become like that of Judah—a desolation (v. 15).

5. The Restoration of Israel (36:1—39:29)

Once a change in leadership had been effected and the major antagonist in the land of promise destroyed, conditions were fulfilled for a restored people to occupy a renewed land. The renewal concept involves not only spiritual rehabilitation but material recovery. Both were essential to the new age. Transformation of the land itself would accompany the restoration of the people.

(1) The Renewal of the Land (36:1-15)

¹ "And you, son of man, prophesy to the mountains of Israel, and say, O mountains of Israel, hear the word of the Lord. ² Thus says the Lord God: Because the enemy said of you, 'Aha!' and, 'The ancient heights have become our possession,' ³ therefore prophesy, and say, Thus says the Lord God: Because, yea, because they made you desolate, and crushed you from all sides, so that you became the possession of the rest of the nations, and you became the talk and evil gossip of the people; ⁴ therefore, O mountains of Israel, hear the word of the Lord God: Thus says the Lord God to the

mountains and the hills, the ravines and the valleys, the desolate wastes and the deserted cities, which have become a prey and derision to the rest of the nations round about; 5 therefore thus says the Lord God: I speak in my hot jealousy against the rest of the nations, and against all Edom, who gave my land to themselves as a possession with wholehearted joy and utter contempt, that they might possess it and plunder it. 6 Therefore prophesy concerning the land of Israel, and say to the mountains and hills, to the ravines and valleys, Thus says the Lord God: Behold, I speak in my jealous wrath, because you have suffered the reproach of the nations; 7 therefore thus says the Lord God: I swear that the nations that are round about you shall themselves suffer reproach.

8 "But you, O mountains of Israel, shall shoot forth your branches, and yield your fruit to my people Israel; for they will soon come home. 9 For, behold, I am for you, and I will turn to you, and you shall be tilled and sown; 10 and I will multiply men upon you, the whole house of Israel, all of it; the cities shall be inhabited and the waste places rebuilt; 11 and I will multiply upon you man and beast; and they shall increase and be fruitful; and I will cause you to be inhabited as in your former times, and will do more good to you than ever before. Then you will know that I am the Lord. 12 Yea, I will let men walk upon you, even my people Israel; and they shall possess you, and you shall be their inheritance, and you shall no longer bereave them of children. 13 Thus says the Lord God: Because men say to you, 'You devour men, and you bereave your nation of children,' 14 therefore you shall no longer devour men and no longer bereave your nation of children, says the Lord God; 15 and I will not let you hear any more the reproach of the nations, and you shall no longer bear the disgrace of the peoples and no longer cause your nation to stumble, says the Lord God."

If ever the love of a man for his native soil has been articulated in words and conveyed meaningfully to others, it is here. In the mind of the prophet the land takes on form, character, personality, and feeling. The very land has been impuned by the sarcasm of surrounding nations (vv. 2–4) and its very body violated (v. 5).

Its joy had been turned to mourning and its beautiful adornments stripped away leaving it derelict and silent. Ravaging of the land aroused the jealous concern of

Yahweh for his land. Enemy nations, including Edom, had infringed upon Yahweh's domain and had caused the land to be shamed before other lands. As such the actions were an affront to the sovereignty of Yahweh over the land, and his name had to be vindicated (vv. 6–7). Those nations which had treated the land of Yahweh so shamefully will find their lands so treated.

Productivity far exceeding its former limits will be granted to the land, i.e., *will do more good to you than ever before* (v. 11), and the land as an individual will know that Yahweh is the Lord (cf. Hos. 11:1–4; Jer. 2:1–3). Nor will the land commit aggravated offenses against Yahweh (v. 13). The image of the land devouring men and children probably is a reference to human sacrifices proffered the gods of fertility associated with the land and its productivity. The renewal of the land with its fruitful increase will be so great that such acts will cease (vv. 13,14). Could this not suggest that false gods will not be worshiped?

The very act of the restoration of the land will take away its shame and reproach. Because of its renewal the land will no longer be an object of derision, and its fertility will no longer offend by enticing its inhabitants to sin through offering human sacrifice (v. 15).

(2) The Uncleanness of Israel (36:16–21)

16 The word of the Lord came to me: 17 "Son of man, when the house of Israel dwelt in their own land, they defiled it by their ways and their doings; their conduct before me was like the uncleanness of a woman in her impurity. 18 So I poured out my wrath upon them for the blood which they had shed in the land, for the idols with which they had defiled it. 19 I scattered them among the nations, and they were dispersed through the countries; in accordance with their conduct and their deeds I judged them. 20 But when they came to the nations, wherever they came, they profaned my holy name, in that men said of them, 'These are the people of the Lord, and yet they had to go out of his land.' 21 But I had concern for my holy name, which the house of Israel caused to be profaned among the nations to which they came.

The central idea in this passage is that the people of Israel defiled the land on which they lived through the worship of pagan gods, whose human sacrifices were an abomination to Yahweh. Thus man was the defiler, perverter, and contaminator of Canaan. The land, holy because it was a possession of Yahweh and occupied by Yahweh through his abiding presence, was rendered unclean as a woman was unclean due to menstrual flow (v. 17; cf. (Lev. 18:25,27 ff.). Because of the conditions due to the worship of idols (cf. comment on 6:4), the judgment of Yahweh fell upon the people and the land. Once again we find Ezekiel seeking to vindicate the name of Yahweh and to justify the ways of Yahweh with Israel in punishment.

The presence of those who claimed to be of Yahweh in exile continued to be an object of concern to Yahweh in that they provided the foreign nations with an opportunity to deride him. The fact of the exile seemed proof to the enemy nations that Yahweh was incapable of protecting his own possessions—both people and land (v. 20). Underlying this is a false implication, that history and its events were beyond Yahweh's control. Ezekiel is attempting to point out a misreading of historical event on the part of heathen nations and to disprove their false assumptions.

(3) The Renewal of the People of Israel (36:22–32)

22 "Therefore say to the house of Israel, Thus says the Lord GOD: It is not for your sake, O house of Israel, that I am about to act, but for the sake of my holy name, which you have profaned among the nations to which you came. 23 And I will vindicate the holiness of my great name, which has been profaned among the nations, and which you have profaned among them; and the nations will know that I am the LORD, says the Lord GOD, when through you I vindicate my holiness before their eyes. 24 For I will take you from the nations, and gather you from all the countries, and bring you into your own land. 25 I will sprinkle clean water upon you, and you shall be clean from all your uncleannesses, and from all your idols I will cleanse you. 26 A new heart I will give you, and a new spirit I will put within you; and I will take out of your flesh the heart of stone and give you a heart of flesh 27 And I will put my spirit within you, and cause you to walk in my statutes and be careful to observe my ordinances. 28 You shall dwell in the land which I gave to your fathers; and you shall be my people, and I will be your God 29 And I will deliver you from all your uncleannesses; and I will summon the grain and make it abundant and lay no famine upon you. 30 I will make the fruit of the tree and the increase of the field abundant, that you may never again suffer the disgrace of famine among the nations. 31 Then you will remember your evil ways, and your deeds that were not good; and you will loathe yourselves for your iniquities and your abominable deeds. 32 It is not for your sake that I will act, says the Lord GOD; let that be known to you. Be ashamed and confounded for your ways, O house of Israel.

Only restoration will show the taunting nations that they have wrongly interpreted the events of destruction and exile. Again we have the key phrase, *for my namesake* (v. 22). Restoration will not occur because Israel is deserving or even worth rescuing. Israel will be used as an instrument. She will become the medium through which the message of Yahweh's sovereignty is delivered. The *holiness* of Yahweh's name (v. 23) will be manifested in the regeneration of Israel and restoration of the land. Such an accomplishment could not possibly be interpreted as the singular efforts of man. Only Yahweh could effect such a change.

As such, the restored land will be occupied by a renewed people. Only a *new heart* and a *new spirit* within Israel will vindicate Yahweh and his holiness before the eyes of the nations (v. 26).

In typical priestly fashion Ezekiel utilizes the sprinkling motif (v. 25) which personifies cultic purification or ritual cleansing. The *new spirit* engendered in the people (v. 26) is defined as *my spirit* (i.e., Yahweh's spirit) in v. 27. The age to come, as described in vv. 29,30, will be effected through a chain of events. First, there will be the new heart and spirit. *Heart* and *spirit* take on specific connotations in this context. Heart implies more than just the will of man; it denotes the whole person. Spirit in this context has to lo with the ethical posture. In essence Ezekiel is projecting the concept of new persons with new ethical determinations created by the power of Yahweh. Second, the new heart and spirit will result in ritual cleanliness and the keeping of the law. Third, the new age will come.

It is implied that under the Sinai Covenant Israel never learned the true role of an elect people (i.e., to keep the law which safeguarded the covenant). Additionally it may be assumed that even the cataclysmic destruction of Jerusalem, a perfect object lesson, had failed to penetrate their minds to the level of genuine understanding. Thus only a thoroughgoing change of the whole man brought about by Yahweh on an individual basis would create the desired results. This act on the part of Yahweh was one of his undeserved goodness (v. 32).

Regardless of the strong note of grace in the passage, Ezekiel stresses the law as the norm of righteousness (v. 27). Only a divine act by God can cause men to live in godliness. But to Ezekiel godliness and the observance of the law were inseparable.

(4) The Renewal of Israel's Image (36: 33–38)

33 "Thus says the Lord GOD: On the day that I cleanse you from all your iniquities, I will cause the cities to be inhabited, and the waste places shall be rebuilt. 34 And the land that was desolate shall be tilled, instead of being the desolation that it was in the sight of all who passed by. 35 And they will say, 'This land that was desolate has become like the garden of Eden; and the waste and desolate and ruined cities are now inhabited and fortified.' 36 Then the nations that are left round about you shall know that I, the LORD, have rebuilt the ruined places, and replanted that which was desolate; I, the LORD, have spoken, and I will do it. 37 "Thus says the Lord GOD: This also I will let the house of Israel ask me to do for them: to increase their men like a flock. 38 Like the flock for sacrifices, like the flock at Jerusalem during her appointed feasts, so shall the waste cities be filled with flocks of men. Then they will know that I am the LORD."

As Ezekiel speaks of renewal, one may discern a strong pulse of nationalism. Ezekiel firmly believed in a universal God but not a universal community of faith. Other nations might come to see the universal implications of Yahweh, but they would not be assimilated into the celebrating community of believers. Yahweh and Israel were to constitute an exclusive religious community—at least, as here described by the prophet.

Restoration of Israel's nationalism within history was to be an object lesson to the surrounding nations. As they viewed the land of promise, the vista was one of ruin —total devastation. Here and there among the nations was an exiled people decimated by conquest. When, however, from the exile the deportees began to trickle back (v. 33), *towns emerged from ruins* (vv. 33,35) [101] and fields returned to productivity. The surrounding nations would question, How can this be? When they see emerging from chaos a veritable Eden (v. 35), there can be but one answer, Yahweh.

Yet the reminder of Ezekiel is that access to the benevolent grace of Yahweh occurs only after a restored relationship (vv. 37,38). He affirms that such blessings as release from exile and increased population in the land are subsequent to cleansing (cf. v. 33). This refers directly back to the previous passage in which cleansing is attested to by keeping of statutes and ordinances.

6. The Valley of Dry Bones (37:1–14)

1 The hand of the LORD was upon me, and he brought me out by the Spirit of the LORD, and set me down in the midst of the valley; it was full of bones. 2 And he led me round among them; and behold, there were very many upon the valley; and lo, they were very dry. 3 And he said to me, "Son of man, can these bones live?" And I answered, "O Lord GOD, thou knowest." 4 Again he said to me, "Prophesy to these bones, and say to them, O dry bones, hear the word of the LORD. 5 Thus says the Lord GOD to these bones: Behold, I will cause breath to enter you, and you shall live. 6 And I will lay sinews upon you, and will cause flesh to come upon you, and cover you with skin, and put breath in you, and you shall

---

101 In v. 35 the villages are described as being "fortified," i.e., walled. In 38:11, which is of a more apocalyptic tone, the cities are not walled.

live; and you shall know that I am the
Lord."

⁷ So I prophesied as I was commanded; and
as I prophesied, there was a noise, and behold,
a rattling; and the bones came together, bone
to its bone. ⁸ And as I looked, there were
sinews on them, and flesh had come upon
them, and skin had covered them; but there
was no breath in them. ⁹ Then he said to me,
"Prophesy to the breath, prophesy, son of man,
and say to the breath, Thus says the Lord God:
Come from the four winds, O breath, and
breathe upon these slain, that they may live."
¹⁰ So I prophesied as he commanded me, and
the breath came into them, and they lived, and
stood upon their feet, an exceedingly great
host.
¹¹ Then he said to me, "Son of man, these
bones are the whole house of Israel. Behold,
they say, 'Our bones are dried up, and our
hope is lost; we are clean cut off.' ¹² Therefore
prophesy, and say to them, Thus says the Lord
God: Behold, I will open your graves, and raise
you from your graves, O my people; and I will
bring you home into the land of Israel. ¹³ And
you shall know that I am the Lord, when I
open your graves, and raise you from your
graves, O my people. ¹⁴ And I will put my
Spirit within you, and you shall live, and I will
place you in your own land; then you shall
know that I, the Lord, have spoken, and I
have done it, says the Lord."

This passage, possibly the best known in
the book of Ezekiel, readdresses a previous
question (cf. 33:10) and elaborates most
eloquently the answer. Chapter 36 has
affirmed restoration, yet 37:1–14 placed at
just this position may intimate that Ezekiel
either had reservations about such a possibility or needed to be cautioned that
such could transpire only as an act of
Yahweh's creative grace. The theme of hope
revived is central in the passage.[102]

As on previous occasions the *Spirit* of
Yahweh moved Ezekiel to a *valley;* (lit.
in Heb., upon the face of a plain). Associated with the call experience was a plain
where the Spirit entered into Ezekiel (v.
3:23 f.). Though it cannot be known with
certainty, both references may be to the
same location. Scattered over the surface
of the plain were bones *very dry* and brittle

—bleached by the sun. It was as if Ezekiel
had been set down upon a former field of
battle where thousands had been slain and
their bodies left unburied. Viewing the
ghastly scene Ezekiel becomes the object of
Yahweh's question, *can these bones live?*
The immediate response of natural man
would be an unequivocal no. But the reply
of Ezekiel, conditioned by previous experience, was *thou knowest* (v. 3). The
prophet had learned a lesson which few
learn. Situations such as this are matters
better left to Yahweh's providence and
knowledge.

Next, Ezekiel is commanded to proclaim
the *word of the Lord* to the inanimate
bones (v. 4). As the words are spoken actions occur. This is the spoken word of
Yahweh. In the prophetic office preeminence is given to the spoken word which
derives from Yahweh. The word carries
inherently its own power to call into being.
Thus you have in Israelite thought the
creative word such as that which is used
in the Genesis creation narratives. The
word was spoken, and, as voiced, creation
transpired (cf. Eichrodt, *Theology*, pp. 69–
80). Skeletal units reform (v. 7) as sinews
knit them together. Then flesh covers
sinew and skin covers flesh (v. 8). At this
point upon the plain there was nothing
more than an extensive army of fresh
cadavers.

At a second command from Yahweh
Ezekiel is instructed to call forth *breath,*
meaning wind or spirit. It is this which
reanimates the dead. *Ruach* (spirit) in
Ezekiel is a supernatural power which not
only energizes the prophet and induces
states of ecstasy but is that force which revitalizes Israel (cf. 11:19; 36:26; 39:29).
The term is used some 52 times in the book
with less than one-fourth applying to the
"wind." Yet even when used in this connotation it is associated with divine power or
activity.[103] However, when *ruach* is connected with *adonai* (i.e., *the Spirit of the*

102 J. Grassi, "Ezekiel 37:1–14 and the New Testament," *New Testament Studies* (1965), 11.2, 162–
164.

103 Norman Snaith, *Distinctive Ideas of the Old
Testament* (London: The Epworth Press, 1950), pp.
152, 153.

Lord) it is a supra-human, dominating, controlling, overwhelming, and energizing power.

An explanation of the event is given to the prophet (vv. 11–14). The bones scattered upon the plain symbolized the *whole house of Israel,* both Israel, the Northern Kingdom which fell around 721 B.C., and Judah, the Southern Kingdom, whose demise had but recently come to pass. The full implication was that Israel as Yahweh's people and a nation was no more, and v. 11*b* indicates just this feeling on the part of the people. The hope which they felt was lost can only mean hope for national continuance within the land of Canaan. For them the exile had become not only their physical but national burial site. Their hopes, dreams, glories, and nationalism (i.e., their reason for existence) had been entombed in an alien land.

Now, however, hope for national survival would be revived by the *Spirit* of Yahweh within them (v. 14). They would be freed from the graveyard of the exile, restored to favor, and returned to their homeland. Human power could not effect this, only the power of Yahweh (i.e., *my Spirit*).

7. The Oracle of the Sticks (37:15–28)

Restoration will effect the reunification of Israel and Judah. Thus Ezekiel interprets the event in a religio-political sense. Repeatedly the Old Testament motif of the age to come, being more political than spiritual in character, is reinforced in Ezekiel. The epitome of the state to come, as well as the restoration of religious law, is involved with the cult and its rites. Those forces which will unify Israel and Judah are covenant and sanctuary, the same factors involved in the Exodus experience.

(1) Political Reunification (37:15–23)

15 The word of the LORD came to me: 16 "Son of man, take a stick and write on it, 'For Judah, and the children of Israel associated with him'; then take another stick and write upon it, 'For Joseph (the stick of Ephraim) and all the house of Israel associated with

him'; 17 and join them together into one stick, that they may become one in your hand. 18 And when your people say to you, 'Will you not show us what you mean by these?' 19 say to them, Thus says the Lord GOD: Behold, I am about to take the stick of Joseph (which is in the hand of Ephraim) and the tribes of Israel associated with him; and I will join with it the stick of Judah, and make them one stick, that they may be one in my hand. 20 When the sticks on which you write are in your hand before their eyes, 21 then say to them, Thus says the Lord GOD: Behold, I will take the people of Israel from the nations among which they have gone, and will gather them from all sides, and bring them to their own land; 22 and I will make them one nation in the land, upon the mountains of Israel; and one king shall be king over them all; and they shall be no longer two nations, and no longer divided into two kingdoms. 23 They shall not defile themselves any more with their idols and their detestable things, or with any of their transgressions; but I will save them from all the backslidings in which they have sinned, and will cleanse them; and they shall be my people, and I will be their God.

Hope for political realignment of the two nations was commonly held by a few prophets (cf. Isa. 11:13; Jer. 3:18; Hos. 1:11). Yet none so dramatically portrayed their hopes as did Ezekiel. Again the prophet presents the prophetic message in symbolic action utilizing two sticks inscribed with the names Judah and Israel (v. 16); cf. Zech. 11:7, which employs somewhat similar symbolism).

By placing these sticks end to end in his hand they appeared to be one stick signifying one kingdom (vv. 19,22): *I will make them one nation.* As Ezekiel conducted his pantomime before the exiles it elicited their questions and with attention intensified he explained the meaning of his acts (v. 18).

(2) Covenant of Peace (37:24–28)

24 "My servant David shall be king over them; and they shall all have one shepherd. They shall follow my ordinances and be careful to observe my statutes. 25 They shall dwell in the land where your fathers dwelt that I gave to my servant Jacob; they and their children and their children's children shall dwell there for ever; and David my servant shall be their prince for ever. 26 I will make a covenant

of peace with them; it shall be an everlasting covenant with them; and I will bless them and multiply them, and will set my sanctuary in the midst of them for evermore. [27] My dwelling place shall be with them; and I will be their God, and they shall be my people. [28] Then the nations will know that I the Lord sanctify Israel, when my sanctuary is is in the midst of them for evermore."

Reunification, however, will proceed along certain predetermined lines and produce specific results. The sole leader will be both political (i.e., king) and religious (i.e., shepherd) because a major obligation will be the keeping of ordinances and statutes implying cultic and social regulations (v. 24). Existence of the state in perpetuity (v. 25) governed by one of Davidic descent infers national continuance as one people.

The everlasting *covenant of peace* (v. 26) will be safeguarded by Yahweh's *sanctuary in the midst of them* (cf. 5:27,28; 43:9). This seems to point to the return of Yahweh's glory to a reconstructed temple in a renewed land occupied by a regenerated people. We understand it best in terms of emphasizing the presence of Yahweh in their midst.

The concept of Yahweh in the midst of Israel is central to covenant theology (cf. Ex. 25:8; 29:45; Lev. 15:31, 26:11; Num. 5:3). In chapters 40—48 the execution of this promise is seen as fulfilled.

Only the restoration of the sanctuary would indicate to the nations that Israel was holy (i.e., v. 28). *Sanctify Israel* means to set it apart. The return of Yahweh's presence and glory (v. 27) would signify his approval of Israel and protection over Israel as a revived nation. Only then would the nations know that Yahweh was God. It is to this promise that Ezekiel has been leading. For the nations to know Yahweh they must know him not only in judgment but in acts of grace and renewal.

8. The Invincibility of Yahweh (38:1— 39:29)

Chapters 38 and 39 have been the object of unusual speculation and not infrequently have been abused by affirmation of absolute certainty of interpretation. Attempts to identify Gog or Magog with any degree of finality have failed.

Previously Ezekiel had spoken of the promised restoration with the glory of Yahweh abiding once again with his people in the renewed land. These two promises, when actualized, would not go unnoticed nor unchallenged by other nations. Yahweh's presence would not preclude aggression against the reborn state. The critical difference would lie in Yahweh being with them rather than withdrawing as had been the case in 586 B.C. As in the days of the Exodus and the conquest of Canaan, Yahweh will fight on their behalf and perform mighty acts for them.

The simplicity of the account is striking. Seemingly just before, or during, the process of the building of the new state by the returnees (i.e., ch. 37), an invader from the north (38:15) designated as "Gog of the land of Magog" (38:2) launches an attack upon the foundling nation. This becomes at once a despicable act to Yahweh and arouses his ire, for his people are particularly defenseless (38:11). Such an assault would seek to thwart Yahweh's purposes and thus evoke incredible wrath, even the marshaling of cosmic forces against Gog (38:20-22). Gog's forces will be caught up on a catastrophic upheaval and annihilated (39:4,9,10,12,14,17-20). Not only will the attackers in the land be consumed, but their homeland Magog will be ravaged (39:6).

A large issue revolves about the question of a literal interpretation of Gog of Magog. Does this stand for an actual nation? And, if so, what nation? Or is this an apocalyptic vision dealing with an eschatalogical battle at the end of the days? To identify the nation would also demand identification of its ruler Gog.

Numerous interpretations have been advanced associating Gog of Magog with Babylon, Alexander the Great and Greece, Gyges and Lydia, and an unidentified ruler of the Scythians, even Antiochus Eupator.

In rabbinic sources Gog and Magog are both considered to be individuals, leaders of enemy forces, who would attack Israel prior to the coming of the Messiah.[104]

On the other hand, equally as many interpreters prefer not to take the chapters in a literal or historical sense and characteristically date the section late designating it as non-Ezekelian. Because of the similarity between chapters 38—39 and certain other passages (notably Isa. 29:5 ff.; 63:1 ff.; 66:15 ff.; Joel 2:28 ff.; 3:15 ff.; Zech. 12:1—14:21; Obad. 15–16; Rev. 20:7–10) which imply a cosmic conflict between apposing forces of good and evil or light and darkness, the Ezekiel passage has been designated as pure eschatology. Two phrases in 38:8 are marshalled as being strongest evidence for this position (i.e., "after many days" and "the latter years"). Both are often interpreted to apply to the distant or indefinite future and thus connote the messianic era.[105]

(1) The Divine Oracle Against Gog's Invading Host (38:1–9)

[1] The word of the Lord came to me: [2] "Son of man, set your face toward Gog, of the land of Magog, the chief prince of Meshech and Tubal, and prophesy against him [3] and say, Thus says the Lord God: Behold, I am against you, O Gog, chief prince of Meshech and Tubal; [4] and I will turn you about, and put hooks into your jaws, and I will bring you forth, and all your army, horses and horsemen, all of them clothed in full armor, a great company, all of them with buckler and shield, wielding swords; [5] Persia, Cush, and Put are with them, all of them with shield and helmet; [6] Gomer and all his hordes; Bethtogarmah from the uttermost parts of the north with all his hordes—many peoples are with you. [7] "Be ready and keep ready, you and all the hosts that are assembled about you, and be a guard for them. [8] After many days you will be mustered; in the latter years you will go against the land that is restored from war, the land where people are gathered from many nations upon the mountains of Israel, which had been a continual waste; its people were

brought out from the nations and now dwell securely, all of them. [9] You will advance, coming on like a storm, you will be like a cloud covering the land, you and all your hordes, and many peoples with you.

Gog is depicted as the leader of a coalition of attacking forces bent upon destroying the newly emergent state of Israel. Ezekiel carefully specifies the confederates of Gog, of the land of Magog.[106]

Other allies from the same general geographical location are Gomer, the eldest son of Japheth (cf. Gen. 10:2), and his son Beth-togarmah (cf. Gen. 10:3; 1 Chron. 1:6), an Indo-European horde which swept into Asia Minor under pressure from nomadic tribesmen, principally the Scythians.

Beth-togarmah may relate to the people of the city-state of Til-Garimmu in Asia Minor. Beth-togarmah is associated with trade in horses (cf. Ezek. 27:14), and Ezekiel implies calvary as the main force of the invaders (38:4). In Solomonic passages Kue of Asia Minor is considered to be the source of supply for chariot horses (1 Kings 10:28; 2 Chron. 1:16). Both passages relating to Kue and Beth-togarmah have in common trade in horses and both are located in Asia Minor.

Thus we have depicted a coalition from the north composed of barbaric elements in Asia Minor which constituted the major force, but with two southern allies Cush, modern Ethiopia, and Put—located by Ezekiel in the same general area (cf. 30:5) —along with Persia (v. 5).

(2) The Evil Scheme of Gog (38:10–16)

[10] "Thus says the Lord God: On that day thoughts will come into your mind, and you will devise an evil scheme [11] and say, 'I will go up against the land of unwalled villages; I will fall upon the quiet people who dwell securely,

---

104 Cf. *Talmud*, Meg. 71*b*; Yoma 10*a*; Josephus, *Antiq.* I.6.1; Midrash Tanchuma.

105 Cf. Charles de Santo, "Gog and Gog," *Religion in Life*, XXX, 112–117, for the concept of a "double eschaton" in this section of Ezekiel.

106 Cf. Gen. 10:2; 1 Chron. 1:5 which designate Magog as a people and defines explicitly the office of Gog as prince of Meshech and Tubal. Both Meshech and Tubal were sons of Japheth (cf. Gen. 16:2; 1 Chron. 1:5) and were closely associated in the mind of Ezekiel (cf. Ezek. 27:13; 32:26; 39:1). As a land Meshech should likely be connected with Mushki of Asia Minor, and Tubal should be connected with Tabal in the same area (Cf. Isa. 66:19).

all of them dwelling without walls, and having no bars or gates'; [12] to seize spoil and carry off plunder; to assail the waste places which are now inhabited, and the people who were gathered from the nations, who have gotten cattle and goods, who dwell at the center of the earth. [13] Sheba and Dedan and the merchants of Tarshish and all its villages will say to you, 'Have you come to seize spoil? Have you assembled your hosts to carry off plunder, to carry away silver and gold, to take away cattle and goods, to seize great spoil?'

[14] "Therefore, son of man, prophesy, and say to Gog, Thus says the Lord GOD: On that day when my people Israel are dwelling securely, you will bestir yourself [15] and come from your place out of the uttermost parts of the north, you and many peoples with you, all of them riding on horses, a great host, a mighty army; [16] you will come up against my people Israel, like a cloud covering the land. In the latter days I will bring you against my land, that the nations may know me, when through you, O Gog, I vindicate my holiness before their eyes.

Gog's strategy is to attack the reforming nation of exiles before they are able to raise defensive walls (v. 11). In 36:35 the intent is that the cities be walled in the new state. The fact that they lived under a sense of security (38:8,11,14), without fortifications, does not imply the messianic age of peace. Yahweh constituted their security. He was with them in the rebuilding. Once defenses were erected, there would be double protection, that of Yahweh and that of man.

Ezekiel's words reveal the nature of the attack. These invaders were nothing more than barbaric hordes intent upon the swift raid against less heavily defended cities and villages. They struck wherever opportunity and cavalry mobility permitted.

No evidence is presented to show them as a world power or a coalition of strong armies. No siege machinery is mentioned, nor do we find a desire for territorial control. They were marauders, all horsemen (v. 15), who attacked only to gain booty (vv. 12,13).

The reference (v. 12) to Palestine as the center of the earth is a recognizable theme from comparative religious literature and is similar to the reference in 5:5. That other religious cultures considered the most important sanctuary to be the center of the earth is an established fact.[107]

(3) Yahweh Protects His Own (38:17-23)

[17] "Thus says the Lord GOD: Are you he of whom I spoke in former days by my servants the prophets of Israel, who in those days prophesied for years that I would bring you against them? [18] But on that day, when Gog shall come against the land of Israel, says the Lord GOD, my wrath will be roused. [19] For in my jealousy and in my blazing wrath I declare, On that day there shall be a great shaking in the land of Israel; [20] the fish of the sea, and the birds of the air, and the beasts of the field, and all creeping things that creep on the ground, and all the men that are upon the face of the earth, shall quake at my presence, and the mountains shall be thrown down, and the cliffs shall fall, and every wall shall tumble to the ground. [21] I will summon every kind of terror against Gog, says the Lord GOD; every man's sword will be against his brother. [22] With pestilence and bloodshed I will enter into judgment with him; and I will rain upon him and his hordes and the many peoples that are with him, torrential rains and hailstones, fire and brimstone. [23] So I will show my greatness and my holiness and make myself known in the eyes of many nations. Then they will know that I am the LORD.

Ezekiel views the conflict to come as the day of the Lord spoken of by previous prophets (v. 17; cf. Jer. 4:5; Zeph. 1) and as such will involve cosmic forces. Terminology is typical of prophetic utterance connected with the day. It will be a day of Yahweh's overflowing wrath (vv. 18,19). Nature in the form of earthquakes, rain, hailstorms, fire, and brimstone (i.e., volcanic activity) will contend with the enemy in a holy alliance with Israel (vv. 20,22).

Joshua, while engaging the Amorite coalition in battle, was aided by a hailstorm (Josh. 10:11); while in the Song of Deborah reference is made to the forces of nature aiding the cause of Deborah and Barak as they fought the Canaanites (Judg. 5:20,21). The plagues of Egypt (Ex. 7-12), the crossing of the marshland after the

[107] A. J. Wensinck, "The Ideas of the Western Semites Concerning the Navel of the Earth," Afdeeling Letterkunde, Deel 17.1 (Amsterdam: Johannes, 1916), pp. 1-65.

water had been driven back by a strong east wind (Ex. 14:21), water from rock (Ex. 17), and manna and quail (Ex. 16:13–21) were all interpreted as Yahweh's mighty acts as he commandeered the forces of nature on behalf of his people (Cf. Isa. 28:18; Joel 3:3).

The Lord of Israel as Yahweh of hosts, who leads his people into battle and fights on their behalf using the forces of nature, was indicative of the Exodus and Conquest period. Ezekiel again turns to the early relationships between Yahweh and Israel to draw his imagery.

So chaotic will be the situation that the forces of Gog will turn their swords against each other in absolute confusion (v. 21).

(4) The Defeat of Gog (39:1-20)

1 "And you, son of man, prophesy against Gog, and say, Thus says the Lord God: Behold, I am against you, O Gog, chief prince of Meshech and Tubal; 2 and I will turn you about and drive you forward, and bring you up from the uttermost parts of the north, and lead you against the mountains of Israel; 3 then I will strike your bow from your left hand, and will make your arrows drop out of your right hand. 4 You shall fall upon the mountains of Israel, you and all your hordes and the peoples that are with you; I will give you to birds of prey of every sort and to the wild beasts to be devoured. 5 You shall fall in the open field; for I have spoken, says the Lord God. 6 I will send fire on Magog and on those who dwell securely in the coastlands; and they shall know that I am the Lord.

7 "And my holy name I will make known in the midst of my people Israel; and I will not let my holy name be profaned any more; and the nations shall know that I am the Lord, the Holy One in Israel. 8 Behold, it is coming and it will be brought about, says the Lord God. That is the day of which I have spoken.

9 "Then those who dwell in the cities of Israel will go forth and make fires of the weapons and burn them, shields and bucklers, bows and arrows, handpikes and spears, and they will make fires of them for seven years; 10 so that they will not need to take wood out of the field or cut down any out of the forests, for they will make their fires of the weapons; they will despoil those who despoiled them, and plunder those who plundered them, says the Lord God.

11 "On that day I will give to Gog a place for burial in Israel, the Valley of the Travelers east of the sea; it will block the travelers, for there Gog and all his multitude will be buried; it will be called the Valley of Hamongog. 12 For seven months the house of Israel will be burying them, in order to cleanse the land. 13 All the people of the land will bury them; and it will redound to their honor on the day that I show my glory, says the Lord God. 14 They will set apart men to pass through the land continually and bury those remaining upon the face of the land, so as to cleanse it; at the end of seven months they will make their search. 15 And when these pass through the land and any one sees a man's bone, then he shall set up a sign by it, till the buriers have buried it in the Valley of Hamongog. 16 (A city Hamonah is there also.) Thus shall they cleanse the land.

17 "As for you, son of man, thus says the Lord God: Speak to the birds of every sort and to all beasts of the field, 'Assemble and come, gather from all sides to the sacrificial feast which I am preparing for you, a great sacrificial feast upon the mountains of Israel, and you shall eat flesh and drink blood. 18 You shall eat the flesh of the mighty, and drink the blood of the princes of the earth—of rams, of lambs, and of goats, of bulls, all of them fatlings of Bashan. 19 And you shall eat fat till you are filled, and drink blood till you are drunk, at the sacrificial feast which I am preparing for you. 20 And you shall be filled at my table with horses and riders, with mighty men and all kinds of warriors,' says the Lord God.

A problem of significant proportions is raised by chapter 38. The hordes will be brought against a practically defenseless people through the instrumentality of Yahweh (38:16). In the ensuing conflict the unleashing of cosmic forces will be devastating both to invader and defender. Their cities, homes, fields, vineyards, and defenses (38:20,22) could not escape the cosmic onslaught. Nor does chapter 39 answer this problem to any significant degree of satisfaction. Assuredly chapter 39 does denote the purpose in calling up the hordes of the north with their allies. It was to affirm Yahweh's role as the *Holy One in Israel* (39:7). Basically Ezekiel considered the defeat of Gog as an affirmation of the authority of Yahweh in history. Yet there is the lingering question of penetrating force. Would this not also be particularly destructive to the wards of Yahweh with whom the covenant of peace had been made?

The Old Testament has many incomplete understandings of Yahweh's nature. Yahweh takes no joy in the death of a wicked Israelite according to 18:23,32; yet he devotes to sacrificial slaughter the foes from the north (39:17–20). Let us understand that we are not to expect the full light of New Testament insight into the true nature of God to appear at this point. Accepting honestly that the revelation to Ezekiel leaves us with an unresolved problem, we leave it in the context of the prophet's situation, assured that we find in Christ the full truth for understanding and faith.

Chapter 39:1–20 emphasizes two cardinal points: (1) the overwhelming victory of Yahweh over the foe, and (2) the priestly concerns of Ezekiel. As in chapter 38, the conflict is depicted as a personal encounter of Yahweh with those who would thwart his purposes. *I am against you,* says Yahweh (v. 1). Slaughter of the swarms of invaders upon mountains and in the valleys will ensue (vv. 4,5). Not only will destruction fall upon the invaders in the land, but a holocaust will descend upon their homeland (v. 6). It is this act which will reveal Yahweh's sovereignty (v. 7). The import of the words *it is coming . . . will be brought about* (v. 8) signifies a thing certain to happen.

The numerical strength of the invaders is emphasized and heightens the significance of their defeat (vv. 9–16). Staggering quantities of weapons are abandoned (vv. 9,10), and the time required to bury the dead adds to the overall theme of an incredible victory. The dead would be so numerous that their place of interment, *the Valley of the Travelers,* would be completely filled and blocked. The KJV translation implies that the valley would be filled with corpses whose stench would block the valley (v. 11). So abundant would be the useless weapons of the enemy that they would serve for fuel for seven years, precluding the necessity of cutting fire wood (vv. 9,10). So multitudinous

would the corpses be it would take seven months to bury the dead (vv. 12,14,15). The entire house of Israel, all the people (v. 13), would assist in the endeavor with some appointed to the task of traveling about the land to search out and bury every corpse, even collecting the bones of the fallen for burial (vv. 14,15).

Ezekiel is here following the strict cult procedure for cleansing the land (v. 12). This was to avoid contamination and provide ritual purification (cf. Deut. 21:23; Lev. 5:2; 21:1–4; 22:4–7; Num. 5:2; 6:6–12). Ezekiel does not command ritual purification for the people of the land who had defiled themselves in the process of burying the slain enemy (cf. Num. 31:19). Possibly this should be taken for granted.

The great sacrificial feast passage (vv. 17–20) is but an expansion, possibly by an editor, of 39:4b. Here the enemy is portrayed as a sacrificial meal prepared by Yahweh for the birds and beasts, i.e., the carrion eaters, vulture and jackal (v. 17). At the summons of Yahweh they gather at his table (v. 20) to gorge themselves on the bodies and blood of the slain (cf. Rev. 19:19 for the same idea but with different imagery).

(5) The Restoration of Israel's Fortunes (39:21–29)

21 "And I will set my glory among the nations; and all the nations shall see my judgment which I have executed, and my hand which I have laid on them. 22 The house of Israel shall know that I am the LORD their God, from that day forward. 23 And the nations shall know that the house of Israel went into captivity for their iniquity, because they dealt so treacherously with me that I hid my face from them and gave them into the hand of their adversaries, and they all fell by the sword. 24 I dealt with them according to their uncleanness and their transgressions, and hid my face from them.

25 "Therefore thus says the Lord GOD: Now I will restore the fortunes of Jacob, and have mercy upon the whole house of Israel; and I will be jealous for my holy name. 26 They shall forget their shame, and all the treachery they have practiced against me, when they dwell securely in their land with none to make them afraid, 27 when I have brought them back from

the peoples and gathered them from their enemies' lands, and through them have vindicated my holiness in the sight of many nations. 28 Then they shall know that I am the LORD their God because I sent them into exile among the nations, and then gathered them into their own land. I will leave none of them remaining among the nations any more; 29 and I will not hide my face any more from them, when I pour out my Spirit upon the house of Israel, says the Lord GOD."

This brief section which concludes the oracles of Ezekiel is marked by a reaffirmation of the theme of restoration (cf. 5:8; 28:26; 34:30). It is through this victory that *all nations will see* the judgment of Yahweh. More importantly, however, Israel will *know* that he is God (vv. 21,22). A clever distinction is made. While the nations will see that Yahweh is the God of Israel, Israel will know he is their God. It does not imply any kind of universal acceptance or acknowledgment. It does, on the other hand, indicate Israelite acceptance and acknowledgment.

Yahweh's previous delivering up of Israel into the hands of Babylon and their subsequent sufferings and exile (vv. 23,24), when viewed in the light of this deliverance from Gog of Magog, will convince them that the previous judgment was truly justifiable (vv. 25-28). Thus with all opposition crushed the fortunes of Israel may be restored. The affirmations of v. 29 provide the point of departure for the following vision related to the restored nation in unique form.

II. *The Restored Nation (40:1—48:35)*

In chapters 40—48 we find depicted a new and unique Temple community made possible by the defeat of Gog and the ushering in of the new era. Centrality of position is given to the Temple as the abode of Yahweh and the Zadokite priests as his servants. Here one may find a direct relation to chapters 33—39, for only after the conditions of those chapters have been brought to a successful conclusion could there be an Israelite religio-political utopian state.

For the new estate to arise certain stipulative situations, in the mind of Ezekiel, had to be effected: (1) the acknowledgment on the part of the nations of Yahweh's role in history; (2) a general respect for the holiness of Yahweh; (3) the reclamation of Israel; (4) the ritual purification of the people of Israel and of the land. All these were but preludes to and conditions for the return of the glory of Yahweh to the new Temple.

Throughout this section there is woven the strongest of priestly concepts of the holiness of Yahweh. This holiness had to be guarded and protected at all costs, for it and it alone assured the continuance of the new state. It is not possible to escape the inevitable possibility that Ezekiel had, during his period of priestly activity and service in the former Temple, actually dreamed of the thoroughgoing changes in ritualism and legalism here presented.

Ezekiel's elevation of Temple and cult would appear particularistic, exclusivistic, and legalistic. Ezekiel considered his divine imperative to be the creation of a totally reoriented priestly cult built upon a foundation of somewhat rigid religious norms.

Some persons with Eiselen [108] would interpret this to mean that Ezekiel felt the common man could not comprehend the abstract ethical principles of previous prophets and make them applicable to the life situation, thus creating the need for a legalistic formula. Ezekiel's concern is more comprehensive. Duhm moves to the other extreme by insisting that Ezekiel transformed the ideals of the prophets into laws and dogmas and as a result destroyed spiritually free and moral religion.[109]

Indeed it is accurate to affirm that Ezekiel is here seen as an ecclesiastical organizer who centered and then anchored the Temple in the nation's life. Additionally it was he, more than any other, who estab-

---

108 F. C. Eiselen, *Prophecy and the Prophet in Their Historical Relations* (New York: The Methodist Book Concern, 1909), p. 217.
109 B. Duhm, *Die Theologie der Propheten* (Bonn: Germany, 1875), p. 263.

lished the sabbath as the fundamental expression of institutionalized postexilic worship. Furthermore he exerted crucial influence in the origin of an ecclesiastical state perpetuated by ritualism. Yet all of this must be viewed in the light of two positions, here assumed on the part of Ezekiel.

The initial assumption is that Ezekiel strongly believed that only a thoroughgoing ritualism could keep the holiness of Yahweh intact, protect the new state, and prevent Israel's defection from Yahweh. Ezekiel's life had spanned a watershed in Israel's history. His ministry occurred during the most traumatic episode in Israel's journey with God. Foundations of older religious positions had been washed away upon the ravaging waves of historical events. So much that was revered in Israelite religious thought had been smashed in the flux of time.

Ezekiel, though a prophet, had priestly love for venerable institutions. To preserve the Temple institution Ezekiel felt that new forms had to come into being. Thus we find the institution of the Temple, the priesthood, the sabbath, and the law all intact but with different modes of expression. They are neither decidedly Deuteronomic nor priestly, in the traditional sense and approach, but do somewhat coincide with the Holiness Code (cf. Lev. 17—26). What we find are new modes for expressing traditional religion in a nontraditional era.

A second assumption is that the extreme priestly position taken in chapters 40—48 implies that Ezekiel saw little or no need for the prophetic figure in the new era. To Ezekiel there were only two viable options: popular prophetic religion or prophetic-priestly cult religion. Since prevailing Israelite prophetic thought centered on a twin motif of doom and hope with a call to ethical expression of religious belief, such proclamation would no longer be of prime necessity. Instead, the prophetic call to ethical life would find special motivation in the cult. Doom had occurred. Hope had been vindicated in the restoration.

Ethical living would now have a new imperative from the law. True religion would be restored, but it would require priestly instruction and administration. Thus Ezekiel shifts from a prophetic-priestly role to a priestly-prophetic stance. This major shift in emphasis to priestly concerns to the exclusion of others produces a definitive pattern in chapters 40—48. The whole constitutes a fantastic vision of an era yet to come.

It was this unreserved and epoch-making espousal of innovative priestly religion that nearly caused the book of Ezekiel to be excluded from the canon.[110] Ezekiel's break with tradition, so revered by the rabbis, may be seen by comparing the following concepts: a Zadokite versus a Levitical priesthood and a prince versus king as the chief of state. Or compare the following verses in Ezekiel with those in Leviticus and Numbers (44:27 vs. Lev. 6:13; 45:24 vs. Num. 28:4 ff.). These variations and modifications in Ezekiel's religious thought were enough to give the rabbinical schools pause and concern (cf. Cooke, pp. 427–429 for an analysis of critical problems).

Yet with all the intricate problems of language and concept in chapters 40—48, the ideals of the age to come are brought to a forceful and logical conclusion. A divine messenger, not Yahweh himself, gives to Ezekiel certain instructions for delivery to the people. In the vision sequence the new Temple is depicted as the most grandiose edifice ever to grace Jerusalem. In grandeur, size, and importance it would eclipse that of Solomon. As such it would become not only the perpetual abiding place of Yahweh, but the geographical and religio-political center of the new state. From this Temple there would emanate those forces which would bless the people and their land.

1. The Vision of the New Temple (40: 1—43:27)

Debate on the nature of the Temple depicted will probably never cease. Ezekiel

---

110 Cf. "Authorship" in the Introduction.

ostensibly knew only one Israelite Temple—that of Solomon. Yet in captivity he doubtless was exposed to Babylonian centers of worship. That which compounds the difficulty is the combining in Ezekiel 40—48 of most unusual visionary elements with those which are intensely practical: agonizingly exact rules for worship; elements related to sacrifices, worshipers, and priests bracketed with visions of supernatural waters, the return of the glory of Yahweh, and a miraculously rejuvenated land. Although it seems the Solomonic Temple constituted something of a point of departure for the Temple vision, the total result is an idealized Temple. Such a Temple would be the epitome of the dreams of a priest or priestly group. One issue must be kept central: only an ideal Temple would suffice as a center of worship for an ideal people.

(1) The East Processional Gate (40:1–16)

¹ In the twenty-fifth year of our exile, at the beginning of the year, on the tenth day of the month, in the fourteenth year after the city was conquered, on that very day, the hand of the Lord was upon me, ² and brought me in the visions of God into the land of Israel, and set me down upon a very high mountain, on which was a structure like a city opposite me. ³ When he brought me there, behold, there was a man, whose appearance was like bronze, with a line of flax and a measuring reed in his hand; and he was standing in the gateway. ⁴ And the man said to me, "Son of man, look with your eyes, and hear with your ears, and set your mind upon all that I shall show you, for you were brought here in order that I might show it to you; declare all that you see to the house of Israel."

⁵ And behold, there was a wall all around the outside of the temple area, and the length of the measuring reed in the man's hand was six long cubits, each being a cubit and a handbreadth in length; so he measured the thickness of the wall, one reed; and the height, one reed. ⁶ Then he went into the gateway facing east, going up its steps, and measured the threshold of the gate, one reed deep; ⁷ and the side rooms, one reed long, and one reed broad; and the space between the side rooms, five cubits; and the threshold of the gate by the vestibule of the gate at the inner end, one reed. ⁸ Then he measured the vestibule of the gateway, eight cubits; ⁹ and its jambs, two cubits; and the vestibule of the gate was at the inner end. ¹⁰ And there were three side rooms on either side of the east gate; the three were of the same size; and the jambs on either side were of the same size. ¹¹ Then he measured the breadth of the opening of the gateway, ten cubits; and the breadth of the gateway, thirteen cubits. ¹² There was a barrier before the side rooms, one cubit on either side; and the side rooms were six cubits on either side. ¹³ Then he measured the gate from the back of the one side room to the back of the other, a breadth of five and twenty cubits, from door to door. ¹⁴ He measured also the vestibule, twenty cubits; and round about the vestibule of the gateway was the court. ¹⁵ From the front of the gate at the entrance to the end of the inner vestibule of the gate was fifty cubits. ¹⁶ And the gateway had windows round about, narrowing inward into their jambs in the side rooms, and likewise the vestibule had windows round about inside, and on the jambs were palm trees.

Ezekiel in *visions of God* (v. 2) was transported from his location among the exiles to Jerusalem (thus v. 1 would date the event *ca.* 572 B.C.). Upon arrival he was greeted by a heavenly messenger who acted as his guide on a tour of the hypothetically reconstructed Jerusalem area, specifically the Temple complex (vv. 3,4). Though the guide may have been the otherworldly architect of the city and Temple, he appears more in the role of one who explains that which was already designed (cf. ANET, pp. 268–269 for the so-called "dream of Gudea" on Temple construction.)

Attention is initially directed toward the eastern gateway flanked by six rooms (v. 6). There were three rooms on each side along the passageway leading into the Temple complex (v. 10). The description of the gateway through the massive wall (i.e., *narrowing inwards*, v. 16) which served as ports for crossfire into the passageway indicates a gate plan rather well known from archaeological findings at Megiddo, Hazor, and Gezer.[111] All dimensions from this point on are given in well-known terms other than the *line of flax* and *measuring reed* of v. 3. These two instruments of measure may be likened to a measuring

111 Cf. C. G. Howie, "The East Gate of Ezekiel's Temple Enclosure and the Solomonic Gateway of Megiddo," *Bulletin of the American Schools of Oriental Research,* 117 (1950), 13–19.

tape and a meter rod. The reed as a unit of measure according to the Mishnah was approximately ten and one half feet.[112] We may postulate that the line of flax was knotted at one-reed intervals to permit measuring of greater distances with facility.

An overall impression is that the east or processional gateway was designed to withstand effectively assault as were the other two gates, north and south, indicating the felt concern for such protection in the new state. Though the heavenly guide charged the prophet to concentrate on the purpose of the vision (v. 4), we are left to wonder exactly what that purpose was.

(2) The Outer Court, Northern and Southern Gates (40:17-27)

17 Then he brought me into the outer court; and behold, there were chambers and a pavement, round about the court; thirty chambers fronted on the pavement. 18 And the pavement ran along the side of the gates, corresponding to the length of the gates; this was the lower pavement. 19 Then he measured the distance from the inner front of the lower gate to the outer front of the inner court, a hundred cubits.

Then he went before me to the north, 20 and behold, there was a gate which faced toward the north, belonging to the outer court. He measured its length and its breadth. 21 Its side rooms, three on either side, and its jambs and its vestibule were of the same size as those of the first gate; its length was fifty cubits, and its breadth twenty-five cubits. 22 And its windows, its vestibule, and its palm trees were of the same size as those of the gate which faced toward the east; and seven steps led up to it; and its vestibule was on the inside. 23 And opposite the gate on the north, as on the east, was a gate to the inner court; and he measured from gate to gate, a hundred cubits.

24 And he led me toward the south, and behold, there was a gate on the south; and he measured its jambs and its vestibule; they had the same size as the others. 25 And there were windows round about in it and in its vestibule, like the windows of the others; its length was fifty cubits, and its breadth twenty-five cubits. 26 And there were seven steps leading up to it, and its vestibule was on the inside; and it had palm trees on its jambs, one on either side. 27 And there was a gate on the south of the inner court; and he measured from gate to gate toward the south, a hundred cubits.

112 Cf. Mishnah Kelim 17.10.

Once, in visions, the prophet had passed through the eastern gateway which led to an elevated platform or fill upon which the Temple complex was constructed, he entered the outer court surrounded on its perimeter by *thirty chambers* (v. 17). It is this outer court area that the Talmud designates as "the court of women."

It is generally surmised that these chambers were utilized by worshipers restricted from the inner court. This could be construed to mean the non-Korahite Levitical priests, Gentiles, proselytes (?), and women.

Since the outer court is referred to as the *lower pavement* (v. 18), and since entrance to the east gate was attained by ascending a series of steps (40:6), the overall plan of the complex begins to take shape. The entire structure was conceived of as being erected on a series of platforms or fills, each rising above the other in the form of terraces. This architectural device was used in Babylonian temple structures.

Two other gateways led into the outer court, north and south, each with seven ascending steps (vv. 22,26). Descriptions of the two gates are quite similar to that of the east gate. In a sense the outer court proper had three practically identical gateways.

(3) The Inner Court and Gates (40:28-37)

28 Then he brought me to the inner court by the south gate, and he measured the south gate; it was of the same size as the others. 29 Its side rooms, its jambs, and its vestibule were of the same size as the others; and there were windows round about in it and in its vestibule; its length was fifty cubits, and its breadth twenty-five cubits. 30 And there were vestibules round about, twenty-five cubits long and five cubits broad. 31 Its vestibule faced the outer court, and palm trees were on its jambs, and its stairway had eight steps.

32 Then he brought me to the inner court on the east side, and he measured the gate; it was of the same size as the others. 33 Its side rooms, its jambs, and its vestibule were of the same size as the others; and there were windows round about in it and in its vestibule; its length was fifty cubits, and its breadth twenty-five

cubits. 34 Its vestibule faced the outer court, and it had palm trees on its jambs, one on either side; and its stairway had eight steps. 35 Then he brought me to the north gate, and he measured it; it had the same size as the others. 36 Its side rooms, its jambs, and its vestibule were of the same size as the others; and it had windows round about; its length was fifty cubits, and its breadth twenty-five cubits. 37 Its vestibule faced the outer court, and it had palm trees on its jambs, one on either side; and its stairway had eight steps.

Three gateways—south, east, and north —provided access from the outer to the inner court but with each having eight steps leading up to the passageways. A description of the architectural features indicated that these gates were identical to those in the lower court and served as additional defense for the heart of the sanctuary and citadel.

(4) The Tables of Sacrifice (40:38–43)

38 There was a chamber with its door in the vestibule of the gate, where the burnt offering was to be washed. 39 And in the vestibule of the gate were two tables on either side, on which the burnt offering and the sin offering and the guilt offering were to be slaughtered. 40 And on the outside of the vestibule at the entrance of the north gate were two tables; and on the other side of the vestibule of the gate were two tables. 41 Four tables were on the inside, and four tables on the outside of the side of the gate, eight tables, on which the sacrifices were to be slaughtered. 42 And there were also four tables of hewn stone for the burnt offering, a cubit and a half long, and a cubit and a half broad, and one cubit high, on which the instruments were to be laid with which the burnt offerings and the sacrifices were slaughtered. 43 And hooks, a handbreadth long, were fastened round about within. And on the tables the flesh of the offering was to be laid.

Connected with one of the gates, the precise one is not known, (i.e., RSV translation assumes north gate) there was a preparation center for sacrificial offerings. Animals for burnt, sin, and guilt offerings were prepared within the vestibule or passage of the gateway, where there were four tables. Outside, in the inner court, there were four additional tables (v. 41).

The question of four tables within and

four without is somewhat perplexing. As such the tables in v. 41 were to be used for slaughtering purposes, but in v. 43 the tables were to be used for storing the flesh. In addition there were four tables of hewn stone to hold the instruments used in slaughtering the sacrifices.

One can only hypothetically structure a solution. The arrangement follows certain logical steps. First the animals for the burnt offering were carried to a chamber just inside the gate where they were washed (v. 38). From this point the animals were taken to the slaughterers' stations at four tables, two on either side within the gateway (v. 39), each of the slaughtering tables having an additional stone table (v. 42) to hold the instruments. Once the flesh was prepared it was taken to four tables in the outer court (v. 41).

Three specific sacrificial offerings are mentioned: *burnt, sin,* and *guilt.* Dominant, however, is the burnt offering, that which is wholly burnt upon the altar. The Hebrew *'ola* means literally "that which goes up," implying that sacrifice which is conveyed upward in the form of smoke.

(5) The Priests' Chambers (40:44–49)

44 Then he brought me from without into the inner court, and behold, there were two chambers in the inner court, one at the side of the north gate facing south, the other at the side of the south gate facing north. 45 And he said to me, This chamber which faces south is for the priests who have charge of the temple, 46 and the chamber which faces north is for the priests who have charge of the altar; these are the sons of Zadok, who alone among the sons of Levi may come near to the LORD to minister to him. 47 And he measured the court, a hundred cubits long, and a hundred cubits broad, foursquare; and the altar was in front of the temple. 48 Then he brought me to the vestibule of the temple and measured the jambs of the vestibule, five cubits on either side; and the breadth of the gate was fourteen cubits; and the sidewalls of the gate were three cubits on either side. 49 The length of the vestibule was twenty cubits, and the breadth twelve cubits; and ten steps led up to it; and there were pillars beside the jambs on either side.

A description of the inner court reveals that it was a perfect square (v. 47) flanked on the northern and southern sides by the priests' chambers (v. 46).[113] The altar of sacrifice stood before the front entrance to the temple proper. (v. 47).

Behind the altar was the porch entranceway to the Temple (vv. 48,49). The porch was elevated above the court with ten ascending steps flanked by pillars on either side (v. 49). Thus the Temple proper was on a third and higher level dominating the courts and gates. The pillars flanking the entrance are generally interpreted to be similar to the Jachin and Boaz pillars of the Temple of Solomon.[114]

(6) The General Temple Structure (41: 1-26)

[1] Then he brought me to the nave, and measured the jambs; on each side six cubits was the breadth of the jambs. [2] And the breadth of the entrance was ten cubits; and the sidewalls of the entrance were five cubits on either side; and he measured the length of the nave forty cubits, and its breadth, twenty cubits. [3] Then he went into the inner room and measured the jambs of the entrance, two cubits; and the breadth of the entrance, six cubits; and the sidewalls of the entrance, seven cubits. [4] And he measured the length of the room, twenty cubits, and its breadth, twenty cubits, beyond the nave. And he said to me, This is the most holy place. [5] Then he measured the wall of the temple, six cubits thick; and the breadth of the side chambers, four cubits, round about the temple. [6] And the side chambers were in three stories, one over another, thirty in each story. There were offsets all around the wall of the temple to serve as supports for the side chambers, so that they should not be supported by the wall of the temple. [7] And the side chambers became broader as they rose from story to story, corresponding to the enlargement of the offset from story to story round about the temple; on the side of the temple a stairway led upward, and thus one went up from the lowest story to the top story through the middle story. [8] I saw also that the temple had a raised platform round about; the foundations of the side chambers measured a full reed of six long cubits. [9] The thickness of the outer wall of the side chambers was five cubits; and the part of the plat-

form which was left free was five cubits. Between the platform of the temple and the [10] chambers of the court was a breadth of twenty cubits round about the temple on every side. [11] And the doors of the side chambers opened on the part of the platform that was left free, one door toward the north, and another door toward the south; and the breadth of the part that was left free was five cubits round about.

[12] The building that was facing the temple yard on the west side was seventy cubits broad; and the wall of the building was five cubits thick round about, and its length ninety cubits.

[13] Then he measured the temple, a hundred cubits long; and the yard and the building with its walls, a hundred cubits long; [14] also the breadth of the east front of the temple and the yard, a hundred cubits.

[15] Then he measured the length of the building facing the yard which was at the west and its walls on either side, a hundred cubits. The nave of the temple and the inner room and the outer vestibule [16] were paneled and round about all three had windows with recessed frames. Over against the threshold the temple was paneled with wood round about, from the floor up to the windows (now the windows were covered), [17] to the space above the door, even to the inner room, and on the outside. And on all the walls round about in the inner room and the nave were carved likenesses [18] of cherubim and palm trees, a palm tree between cherub and cherub. Every cherub had two faces: [19] the face of a man toward the palm tree on the one side, and the face of a young lion toward the palm tree on the other side. They were carved on the whole temple round about; [20] from the floor to above the door cherubim and palm trees were carved on the wall.

[21] The doorposts of the nave were squared; and in front of the holy place was something resembling [22] an altar of wood, three cubits high, two cubits long, and two cubits broad; its corners, its base, and its walls were of wood. He said to me, "This is the table which is before the LORD." [23] The nave and the holy place had each a double door. [24] The doors had two leaves apiece, two swinging leaves for each door. [25] And on the doors of the nave were carved cherubim and palm trees, such as were carved on the walls; and there was a canopy of wood in front of the vestibule outside. [26] And there were recessed windows and palm trees on either side, on the sidewalls of the vestibule.

In overall design the Temple contained three compartmentalized areas: the entrance hall or vestibule (40:48), the main

---

[113] MT implies the chambers were used by Temple singers rather than priests. RSV text follows LXX and uses priests.

[114] Cf. 1 Kings 7:21; 2 Chronicles 3:17; also R. B. Y. Scott, "The Pillars Jackin and Boaz," JBL, LXVIII (1939), 143–149.

sanctuary or *nave* (v. 1), and the inner room (v. 3), which was the holy of holies—*the most holy place.*[115]

A raised platform (v. 8) served as a base structure for the main sanctuary. This area, approximately 35 x 70 feet (v. 2a), apparently contained only one item of furniture, a *table* (v. 22) which in design resembled an altar. Undoubtedly this was the table of the bread of presence located before the dual swinging doors (v. 24) of the holy of holies (cf. Ex. 25:23 ff.; Lev. 24:5 ff.; 1 Kings 6:1 ff.; 2 Chron. 3:1 ff.).

Three-story chambers rose above three sides of the nave, and it is quite surprising that the express utilization of the chambers is not given (vv. 5–11). One may only surmise their purpose on the basis of location. Such chambers may have served as storage areas holding the paraphernalia related to cultic worship, or they could have found use as depositories for temple treasures (cf. 1 Kings 14:26; 15:15; 2 Kings 14:14).[116]

A primary decorative motif is specified (vv. 15a–20). It consisted of alternating two-faced cherubim, one face that of a man and the other that of a lion, between palm trees also carved into the panels of the interior walls. This decorative scheme was not unlike that of the Temple of Solomon in which palms were used (cf. 1 Kings 6:8,29; 7:29,36). The change made was that of alternating a cherubim and palm in a repetitive pattern. The two-faced cherubim (i.e., man and lion) may have had its origin in the call vision (cf. 1:10). The presence of the cherubim may have been symbolical of their protective presence over the abiding place of Yahweh, the holy of holies.

(7) The Chambers of the Priests (42: 1–20)

¹ Then he led me out into the inner court, toward the north, and he brought me to the

chambers which were opposite the temple yard and opposite the building on the north. ² The length of the building which was on the north side was a hundred cubits, and the breadth fifty cubits. ³ Adjoining the twenty cubits which belonged to the inner court, and facing the pavement which belonged to the outer court, was gallery against gallery in three stories. ⁴ And before the chambers was a passage inward, ten cubits wide and a hundred cubits long, and their doors were on the north. ⁵ Now the upper chambers were narrower, for the galleries took more away from them than from the lower and middle chambers in the building. ⁶ For they were in three stories, and they had no pillars like the pillars of the outer court; hence the upper chambers were set back from the ground more than the lower and the middle ones. ⁷ And there was a wall outside parallel to the chambers, toward the outer court, opposite the chambers, fifty cubits long. ⁸ For the chambers on the outer court were fifty cubits long, while those opposite the temple were a hundred cubits long. ⁹ Below these chambers was an entrance on the east side, as one enters them from the outer court, ¹⁰ where the outside wall begins.

On the south also, opposite the yard and opposite the building, there were chambers ¹¹ with a passage in front of them; they were similar to the chambers on the north, of the same length and breadth, with the same exits and arrangements and doors. ¹² And below the south chambers was an entrance on the east side, where one enters the passage, and opposite them was a dividing wall.

¹³ Then he said to me, "The north chambers and the south chambers opposite the yard are the holy chambers, where the priests who approach the LORD shall eat the most holy offerings; there they shall put the the most holy offerings—the cereal offering, the sin offering, and the guilt offering, for the place is holy. ¹⁴ When the priests enter the holy place, they shall not go out of it into the outer court without laying there the garments in which they minister, for these are holy; they shall put on other garments before they go near to that which is for the people."

¹⁵ Now when he had finished measuring the interior of the temple area, he led me out by the gate which faced east, and measured the temple area round about. ¹⁶ He measured the east side with the measuring reed, five hundred cubits by the measuring reed. ¹⁷ Then he turned and measured the north side, five hundred cubits by the measuring reed. ¹⁸ Then he turned and measured the south side, five hundred cubits by the measuring reed. ¹⁹ Then he turned to the west side and measured, five hundred cubits by the measuring reed. ²⁰ He measured it on the four sides. It had a wall

---

[115] Cf. Paul L. Garber, "Reconstruction of Solomon's Temple," *Biblical Archaeologist*, XIV (1951), 2–24; G. E. Wright, "Solomon's Temple Resurrected," *Biblical Archaeologist*, VII (1944), 65–77.

[116] Leroy Waterman, "The Treasuries of Solomon's Private Chapel," *Journal of Near Eastern Studies*, VI (1947), 161–163.

around it, five hundred cubits long and five hundred cubits broad, to make a separation between the holy and the common.

This section on accommodations for the priests is exceedingly difficult to translate and interpret due to a seriously corrupt Hebrew text. There are at least 12 major items of inordinate difficulty with the Masoretic Text requiring emendation and/ or substitution of the LXX or Syriac renderings in order to achieve a semblance of clarity.

There appear to have been two areas, possibly between the outer and inner courts one to the north and another to the south, where rooms were constructed for the priests. These served both the Temple and those who worshiped in the outer court. Arranged in three-story complexes (v. 3), they functioned as dining accommodations for the priests when they consumed their portion of the sacrificial gifts (v. 13) and as decontamination chambers for changing of clothing which had been rendered ritually unclean (v. 14). These vestry chambers were considered to be holy (vv. 13,14) because they housed holy objects.

It is evident that the chambers served as protective barriers to avoid defilement of the most sacred areas by movement directly from the outer to the inner court, and to prohibit the reverse movement of that which was holy from the inner court to a ritually unclean outer court.

The concluding section of the chapter (vv. 15–20) records the dimension of the total Temple complex. It was a square, some 860 feet on each side or 500 cubits on each side.

(8) The Vision of Yahweh's Return to the Temple (43:1–12)

¹ Afterward he brought me to the gate, the gate facing east. ² And behold, the glory of the God of Israel came from the east; and the sound of his coming was like the sound of many waters; and the earth shone with his glory. ³ And the vision I saw was like the vision which I had seen when he came to destroy the city, and like the vision which I had seen by the river Chebar; and I fell upon my face. ⁴ As the glory of the LORD entered the temple by

the gate facing east, ⁵ the Spirit lifted me up, and brought me into the inner court; and behold, the glory of the LORD filled the temple.

⁶ While the man was standing beside me, I heard one speaking to me out of the temple; ⁷ and he said to me, "Son of man, this is the place of my throne and the place of the soles of my feet, where I will dwell in the midst of the people of Israel for ever. And the house of Israel shall no more defile my holy name, neither they, nor their kings, by their harlotry, and by the dead bodies of their kings, ⁸ by setting their threshold by my threshold and their doorposts beside my doorposts, with only a wall between me and them. They have defiled my holy name by their abominations which they have committed, so I have consumed them in my anger. ⁹ Now let them put away their idolatry and the dead bodies of their kings far from me, and I will dwell in their midst for ever.

¹⁰ "And you, son of man, describe to the house of Israel the temple and its appearance and plan, that they may be ashamed of their iniquities. ¹¹ And if they are ashamed of all that they have done, portray the temple, its arrangement, its exits and its entrances, and its whole form; and make known to them all its ordinances and all its laws; and write down in their sight, so that they may observe all its laws and all its ordinances. ¹² This is the law of the temple: the whole territory round about upon the top of the mountain shall be most holy. Behold, this is the law of the temple.

Ezekiel in a visionary moment of ecstasy sees the glory of the Lord (i.e., *his glory* v. 2), referred to by the rabbis as the face of the Shekinah, returning to the Temple (v. 4). As the prophet had seen previously a vision of Yahweh's departing glory (cf. 10:1–19), now he witnessed its return. The theophany, as before, created an audio-visual experience (v. 2). Employment of such imagery forcefully asserts that it is Yahweh himself who returned, not some divine messenger or representative force.

Doubtless the phrase *the earth shone with his glory* (v. 3) and the advance of Yahweh *from the east* (v. 2) had its origin in the cosmic symbolism of the sun rising in the east. Also the coming is likened to the Chebar theophany (1: 4–28), where the glory of Yahweh came in the vision of a throne chariot. It was this glory of the reenthroned Yahweh which filled the Temple (cf. Ex. 40:34 ff.; Lev. 9:23; 1 Kings 8:11; Isa. 6:1 ff.).

Although the glory of the Lord filled the entire Temple complex, it resided in the holy of holies. It is noticeable that Ezekiel makes no attempt to infringe upon that most sacred of places but from a position without observes the emanating glory and voice from within (v. 6). The entire enthronement proceeding may have had as its background the proceedings of an Oriental monarch as he was installed upon his throne yet inaccessible to his subjects.

A charge heretofore unmentioned, but which figured in the judgment of Israel, is now voiced (vv. 7–9). In times past the bodies of the kings, actually some fourteen in number, were buried in Jerusalem on the southeast hill (i.e., area of the palace-Temple complex). This establishment of tombs contingent to the Temple and separated from it only by a wall was considered an impingement upon Yahweh's holy place and an act of ritual difilement (cf. 1 Sam. 25:1; 1 Kings 2: 34; 2 Kings 21:18, 26).

Once it is established that such a practice would no longer be permitted, Ezekiel is instructed to reveal to the people not only the plans for the Temple but those laws and ordinances related to it (vv. 10–12). Although there were many laws to be enacted (v. 11), one would be paramount: the entire Temple complex was to be considered most holy (v. 12). There was to be no fetish over the structure itself; the holiness lay entirely in the abiding presence of Yahweh.

There are those things which are not inherently sacred but are sacred because they symbolize something of inestimable worth. The burning, bombing, and vandalizing of sanctuaries become the more insidious crimes for places of worship, even in their insufficiency, symbolize God's presence among men.

(9) The Altar of Burnt Offerings and Its Ordinances (43:13–27)

13 "These are the dimensions of the altar by cubits (the cubit being a cubit and a hand-breadth): its base shall be one cubit high, and one cubit broad, with a rim of one span around its edge. And this shall be the height of the altar: 14 from the base on the ground to the lower ledge, two cubits, with a breadth of one cubit; and from the smaller ledge to the larger ledge, four cubits, with a breadth of one cubit; 15 and the altar hearth, four cubits; and from the altar hearth projecting upward, four horns, one cubit high. 16 The altar hearth shall be square, twelve cubits long by twelve broad. 17 The ledge also shall be square, fourteen cubits long by fourteen broad, with a rim around it half a cubit broad, and its base one cubit round about. The steps of the altar shall face east."

18 And he said to me, "Son of man, thus says the Lord God: These are the ordinances for the altar: On the day when it is erected for offering burnt offerings upon it and for throwing blood against it, 19 you shall give to the Levitical priests of the family of Zadok, who draw near to me to minister to me, says the Lord God, a bull for a sin offering. 20 And you shall take some of its blood, and put it on the four horns of the altar, and on the four corners of the ledge, and upon the rim round about; thus you shall cleanse the altar and make atonement for it. 21 You shall also take the bull of the sin offering, and it shall be burnt in the appointed place belonging to the temple, outside the sacred area. 22 And on the second day you shall offer a he-goat without blemish for a sin offering; and the altar shall be cleansed, as it was cleansed with the bull. 23 When you have finished cleansing it, you shall offer a bull without blemish and a ram from the flock without blemish. 24 You shall present them before the Lord, and the priests shall sprinkle salt upon them and offer them up as a burnt offering to the Lord. 25 For seven days you shall provide daily a goat for a sin offering; also a bull and a ram from the flock, without blemish, shall be provided. 26 Seven days shall they make atonement for the altar and purify it, and so consecrate it. 27 And when they have completed these days, then from the eighth day onward the priests shall offer upon the altar your burnt offerings and your peace offerings; and I will accept you, says the Lord God."

Certain of the features of the altar construction elicit general comment. The terraced design of the Temple with its superimposed levels and the tiered construction of the altar point to Mesopotamian influences.[117]

[117] A. Leo Oppenheim, "The Mesopotamian Temple, Part II," *Biblical Archaeologist* (1944), 7.3,4, 41–83.

The more unusual of the forms, that of the altar, creates certain difficulties. Precise dimensions, such as were given for its construction, precluded the possibility of construction with unhewn stone. The base was to be one cubit in height (i.e., about 18 inches) with a rim of one *hand breadth* (v. 13), while the altar hearth was to be 12 by 12 cubits. Such precise dimensions would only be possible with hewn stone construction.

In addition steps would traverse the east side of the altar from bottom to top (v. 17). Both hewn stones and altar steps are expressly forbidden (cf. Ex. 20:24-26). Yet both here and in the Solomonic narratives the mandate is avoided (cf. 1 Kings 8:64; 2 Kings 16:14; 2 Chron. 4:1). Voiding of the mandate maybe linked to the total renewal of the land and the lifting of the stigma attached to hewn stones. More likely, however, the explanation is that this represents a known breach of the law, but with the anticipation that a ritual cleansing of the altar would remove all uncleanness. The horns of the altar (v. 15) are well known not only from Old Testament references but archaeological findings (cf. Ex. 27:2; 29:12; 30:10; Lev. 4:25; 1 Kings 1:50; Amos 3:14; Jer. 17:1).

Once instructions had been given for erection of the altar, specifics are detailed for its ritual cleansing (vv. 18-27). Such a cleansing imparted holiness and removed contamination (v. 20). Those who were to consecrate the altar had to be of the Zadokite priestly line (v. 19).

Only the descendants of Zadok, first high priest under Solomon in the original Temple, were to be permitted in the sacred environs of the new complex. Specific reasons for proscription of the Levites is given in 44:10-16. One cannot help sensing Ezekiel's tendency to exclusivism at this point.

First, the Zadokite priests would cleanse the altar by offering a burnt offering *outside the sacred area* (v. 21). The blood of the sacrificial bull would be taken to the altar and sprinkled or smeared upon it. This constituted day one of the rites. On the second day a *he-goat* would be used

following the identical procedure (v. 23), and then a goat, bull, and ram were to be offered but sprinkled with salt (v. 23; cf. Lev. 2:13). By the eighth day the altar would be sanctified, and the priest could offer up sacrifices for the people.

All of the ritual was conducted in order to *cleanse* the altar and to make *atonement* for it. The first term literally implies the removal of offense by applications of sacrificial blood (cf. Lev. 8:15; 14:49, 52), while the latter means to spread over, to cover, or to wipe away, hence to expiate offense (cf. Ex. 32:20; 2 Sam. 21:3; Isa. 6:7; 22: 14; 29:9; Prov. 16:6).

Emphasis upon such lengthy procedures to cleanse the altar are highly idealistic, yet not beyond the bounds of reason. It should not be forgotten that a contaminated altar would make sacrifice ineffectual. Emphasis is upon the priestly concept that expiation of sin was dependent upon acceptable sacrifice.

2. Ordinances of the Restored Temple (44: 1-31)

After Ezekiel has heard the voice of commandment from the holy of holies, his divine guide takes him to the outer court where he is shown the closed east gate for through it the glory of the Lord had returned. Only the prince was permitted to sit in it and eat (vv. 1-3). From this point the prophet is again escorted before the place of holiness where instructions are given concerning regulations for the selection and government of Temple personnel (vv. 4-31).

(1) The Sealed Gate (44:1-3)

¹ Then he brought me back to the outer gate of the sanctuary, which faces east; and it was shut. ² And he said to me, "This gate shall remain shut; it shall not be opened, and no one shall enter by it; for the LORD, the God of Israel, has entered by it; therefore it shall remain shut. ³ Only the prince may sit in it to eat bread before the LORD; he shall enter by way of the vestibule of the gate, and shall go out by the same way."

Sealing of the east gate through which the glory of the Lord returned may have divergent interpretations. Since the presence of the Holy One had entered and departed from this gate, it could have become taboo for man, the gate being a thing holy and set apart. On the other hand, the sealing may signify, since it was the processional gate, not only the return of the glory of the Lord but with that return installation of an idealized prince-ruler. Thus the gate, as a ceremonial entrance, would no longer be necessary.

It is evident from Ezekiel's viewpoint that the gateway was not totally taboo for special privileges were accorded the prince who ate within the gateway in order to participate in sacrificial meals (v. 3). This follows an established pattern in Israelite religious history but with restrictions. Rulers in the past had been granted special priestly Temple privileges, but Ezekiel modifies the traditional position (cf. 1 Kings 8:22,54; 9:25; 2 Kings 16:12; 2 Chron. 26:16).

The real prohibition here described legislates against usage of the east gate for normal travel, both secular and priestly. As such the closed gate stood as a symbol of Yahweh's presence. It was no longer of value as a cultic passageway associated with enthronement ceremonies, for Yahweh had ascended the throne forever. That which symbolized Yahweh's return would soon lose its symbolic impact upon the people were it used for ordinary traffic. Thus the sealed gate stood ever before the people—a constant reminder of Yahweh's eternal presence.

(2) Prohibitions on Temple Personnel (44:4–14)

4 Then he brought me by way of the north gate to the front of the temple; and I looked, and behold, the glory of the Lord filled the temple of the Lord; and I fell upon my face. 5 And the Lord said to me, "Son of man, mark well, see with your eyes, and hear with your ears all that I shall tell you concerning all the ordinances of the temple of the Lord and all its laws; and mark well those who may be admitted to the temple and all those who are to be excluded from the sanctuary. 6 And say to the rebellious house, to the house of Israel, Thus says the Lord God: O house of Israel, let there be an end to all your abominations, 7 in admitting foreigners, uncircumcised in heart and flesh, to be in my sanctuary, profaning it, when you offer to me my food, the fat and the blood. You have broken my covenant, in addition to all your abominations. 8 And you have not kept charge of my holy things; but you have set foreigners to keep my charge in my sanctuary.

9 "Therefore thus says the Lord God: No foreigner, uncircumcised in heart and flesh, of all the foreigners who are among the people of Israel, shall enter my sanctuary. 10 But the Levites who went far from me, going astray from me after their idols when Israel went astray, shall bear their punishment. 11 They shall be ministers in my sanctuary, having oversight at the gates of the temple, and serving in the temple; they shall slay the burnt offering and the sacrifice for the people, and they shall attend on the people, to serve them. 12 Because they ministered to them before their idols and became a stumbling block of iniquity to the house of Israel, therefore I have sworn concerning them, says the Lord God, that they shall bear their punishment. 13 They shall not come near to me, to serve me as priest, nor come near any of my sacred things and the things that are most sacred; but they shall bear their shame, because of the abominations which they have committed. 14 Yet I will appoint them to keep charge of the temple, to do all its service and all that is to be done in it.

Under the power of the Spirit, Ezekiel moves to the north gate before the Temple where the theophany recurs, and the prophet prostrates himself (v. 4). He does not, however, rise to his feet as on previous occasions (cf. 2:1,2; 3:24).

At this point specific injunctions are delivered to exclude foreigners from the sacred precincts because they were unclean, being circumcised neither in heart nor in flesh (v. 7). As such they were unfit as Temple servants and attendants (cf. Lev. 26:41; Jer. 9:25). These injunctions are marked well (v. 5), which literally implies "to grasp thoroughly" and "remember."

The uncircumcised of heart and flesh and foreigners (lit., heathen persons) were restricted from the inner court even if they had embraced Yahwism (vv. 7,9). They were by lineage alien both in race and character. That such a prohibition was in effect at a later date is attested to by a warning inscribed upon stone and placed at the entrance to the inner court of the Temple of Herod. Such an inscription, discovered by Clermont-Ganneau and recovered about A.D. 1870, is on display at the Istanbul Museum. It forbade a Gentile to enter, under the pain of death, the inner Temple area.

Sufficient evidence is at hand to show that Israel once permitted foreigners to perform menial domestic and military tasks about the Temple (cf. Deut. 29:10; Josh. 9:23,27; 1 Chron. 9:2; Ezra 2:43–54; 8:20; Neh. 7:46,73; Zech. 14:21). If, however, we understand Ezekiel correctly, the prohibition was made not only to prohibit the entrance of unclean persons but to preclude the possibility of corrupt practices being transmitted to the sacred precincts (cf. 8: 5 ff.).

Not only were aliens legislated against but also certain Levites (v. 10). Those functions once carried out by non-Israelite devotees of Yahweh (i.e., guards, gate keepers, slaughterers of sacrificial animals, and performers of menial services to assist worshipers other than in religious ritual) were assigned to these Levites (v. 11). In the view of Ezekiel the Levites were a degraded priestly group who had directly attributed to the corruption and fall of Jerusalem and Judah.

This restrictive attitude on Ezekiel's part is articulated in both Ezra and Nehemiah and may have had great influence upon Jewish exclusivism found in Palestine following 398 B.C. (cf. Ezra 4:3; Neh. 13: 7–9). Aliens were excluded because they came neither under the old covenant signified by circumcision nor the new covenant of peace typified by the changed or circumcised heart. The Levites were restricted and reduced to humiliating tasks for breaking the covenant and its restrictions (v. 12).

(3) Elevation of the Zadokite Priesthood (44:15-31)

15 "But the Levitical priests, the sons of Zadok, who kept the charge of my sanctuary when the people of Israel went astray from me,

shall come near to me to minister to me; and they shall attend on me to offer me the fat and the blood, says the Lord God; 16 they shall enter my sanctuary, and they shall approach my table, to minister to me, and they shall keep my charge. 17 When they enter the gates of the inner court, they shall wear linen garments; they shall have nothing of wool on them, while they minister at the gates of the inner court, and within. 18 They shall have linen turbans upon their heads, and linen breeches upon their loins; they shall not gird themselves with anything that causes sweat. 19 And when they go out into the outer court to the people, they shall put off the garments in which they have been ministering, and lay them in the holy chambers; and they shall put on other garments, lest they communicate holiness to the people with their garments. 20 They shall not shave their heads or let their locks grow long; they shall only trim the hair of their heads. 21 No priest shall drink wine, when he enters the inner court. 22 They shall not marry a widow, or a divorced woman, but only a virgin of the stock of the house of Israel, or a widow who is the widow of a priest. 23 They shall teach my people the difference between the holy and the common, and show them how to distinguish between the unclean and the clean. 24 In a controversy they shall act as judges, and they shall judge it according to my judgments. They shall keep my laws and my statutes in all my appointed feasts, and they shall keep my sabbaths holy. 25 They shall not defile themselves by going near to a dead person; however, for father or mother, for son or daughter, for brother or unmarried sister they may defile themselves. 26 After he is defiled, he shall count for himself seven days, and then he shall be clean. 27 And on the day that he goes into the holy place, into the inner court, to minister in the holy place, he shall offer his sin offering, says the Lord God.

28 "They shall have no inheritance; I am their inheritance: and you shall give them no possession in Israel; I am their possession. 29 They shall eat the cereal offering, the sin offering, and the guilt offering; and every devoted thing in Israel shall be theirs. 30 And the first of all the first fruits of all kinds, and every offering of all kinds from all your offerings, shall belong to the priests; you shall also give to the priests the first of your coarse meal, that a blessing may rest on your house. 31 The priests shall not eat of anything, whether bird or beast, that has died of itself or is torn.

Deuteronomic tradition considered the mutual sharing of priestly duties between Levites and Zadokites to be a legitimate and accepted practice (cf. Deut. 12:2–18; 14:27; 16:11; 18:6–8). Ezekiel, however, now understands the purpose of Yahweh to supersede the Deuteronomic pattern and elevates the Zadokite priesthood to pre-eminence.

Zadok appears during the Davidic period when Zadok and Abiathar represented the leading priestly families. Under Solomon, around 961–922 B.C., Zadok became the primary priest (cf. 1 Kings 2:27,35). Generally Israelite tradition associated the Zadokite lineage with Eleazar, Aaron's son (cf. Ex. 6:23; Lev. 10:6; Num. 4:28).

A thorny issue thus arises. Since Zadokites and Levites shared in the priestly duties, both may have defected from the reform Deuteronomic faith subsequent to around 621 B.C. If this is the case, Ezekiel may have favored the Zadokite priesthood because he was a Zadokite and desired ascendancy for his group. It is of course possible that only the Levites defected, with the Zadokites remaining faithful.

Ezekiel's appraisal of the Jerusalem situation (cf. chaps. 8, 9, 11, 12, 16, 22, 23) tends to assert forcefully that all the priesthood was corrupt. If the priesthood at the time included both Zadokites and Levites, then both parties contributed to the apostasy which brought about judgment. Now only the sons of Zadok could enter the Temple and approach the table of presence (v. 16).

There follows a series of prohibitions to be meticulously kept by the Zadokites as they ministered in the sanctuary. Use of linen clothing instead of woolen, as was normal, is based on a rather unique rationale. No clothing was to be worn which caused the person to perspire (v. 18). In two other Old Testament books linen clothing is prescribed for the priests (Ex. 28:6; 39:27,29; Lev. 6:10; 16:4), while both Leviticus and Deuteronomy specify no blended fabrics (cf. Lev. 19:19; Deut. 22:11). The weaving of two dissimilar yarns was considered unclean. But the question of linen to avoid perspiration or *sweat* is somewhat puzzling. One may only surmise

that the prohibition of woolen clothing has to do with secretions from the body which were considered to be ritually unclean.

Extreme caution was to be exercised by the Zadokites as they moved from the inner to the outer courts. Clothing was to be removed in their chambers lest holiness be transferred to the people by the garments themselves (v. 19). This concept of the contagious nature of holiness radiates priestly separateness—for function and responsibility. Only the Zadokites were to be partakers of Yahweh's pure holiness. The restriction, or prohibitive legislation related to the clothing, may be taken as a protective measure. This presupposes that all were potential sharers of the holiness of Yahweh, and at times an encounter with holiness could have disastrous results. An element in Old Testament thought is that man could not stand in the presence of Yahweh's pure essence without dire results (cf. Gen. 32:30; Ex. 33:20; 2 Sam. 6:7) and that holiness was transferable even to clothing (cf. 2 Kings 2:13,14 where the mantle of Elijah is infused with power and Lev. 16:4,23 where the clothing of Aaron is considered holy). Interestingly enough the insight of Haggai seems to have advanced to a higher level (cf. Hag. 2:12). It seems apparent throughout this section that the effort is made to subordinate the Levitical priesthood and to reserve the privilege of direct access to the glory of the Lord for the Zadokites (cf. Eichrodt, *Ezekiel*, pp. 565–566).

Additionally the Zadokites were to observe certain personal denials (vv. 20–22) and entertain specific obligations (vv. 23–31). Neither hair could be long nor heads shaven, and no wine was to be consumed in the inner court (v. 21).

The act of shaving the head was forbidden by general Levitical law (cf. Num. 6:5), while unrestricted growth of hair was symbolical of two groups in Israelite tradition, the warrior (cf. Judg. 5:2) and the Nazirite (cf. Num. 6:5). Several Old Testament books affirm the restriction on drinking wine in the inner court (cf. Lev.

10:9; Hos. 4:11; Prov. 20:1; Psalm 104: 15).

Marriage was restricted to a virgin of pure Israelite ancestry or the widow of another Zadokite who before her marriage had been in the former category (v. 23). In addition, the Zadokites were strictly to avoid personal defilement (vv. 25–27) and shun certain foods, especially the flesh of an animal which had died of itself (v. 31; (cf. Lev. 7:24).

Responsibilities to the people were two-fold. In the first instance, they were to be teachers of ceremonial law, literally, that law which would keep the people ritually clean (v. 23). In effect they were to instruct the people on the difference between clean and unclean according to the teaching of the Torah or law (cf. Lev. 10:11; 13:59; 14:57; Num. 5:29; Deut. 33:10; Hag. 2:1–13). Secondly, they were to execute judgments on the basis of the laws of ritual purity (v. 24).

This implies control and administration of the courts—both civil and religious (cf. Deut. 33:10; 1 Sam. 4:18; 7:15; Hos. 4:6). Such legislation decidedly increased the power previously held by the priesthood (cf. Deut. 17:8 ff.; 19:17; 21:1–5); it also gave the priestly group a greater degree of power for good or evil over the citizens.

Possession of real and personal property by the Zadokite priesthood is denied (v. 28), yet legislation is effected to care for their every need. They received a share not only of the sacrificial offerings (v. 29) but of every *devoted thing in Israel* (cf. Lev. 2:3 ff.; 7:1–38; Num. 18:8–32). The scope of their share might be quite munificent (cf. Lev. 27:28; Num. 18:14). Since all *first* fruits and offerings were designated as a priestly portion (v. 30), they indeed faired well.

3. Miscellaneous Ordinances (45:1–17)

(1) The Sacred and the Princely Allocations (45:1–9)

1 "When you allot the land as a possession, you shall set apart for the LORD a portion of the land as a holy district, twenty-five thousand cubits long and twenty thousand cubits broad; it shall be holy throughout its whole extent. 2 Of this a square plot of five hundred by five hundred cubits shall be for the sanctuary, with fifty cubits for an open space around it. 3 And in the holy district you shall measure off a section twenty-five thousand cubits long and ten thousand broad, in which shall be the sanctuary, the most holy place. 4 It shall be the holy portion of the land; it shall be for the priests, who minister in the sanctuary and approach the LORD to minister to him; and it shall be a place for their houses and a holy place for the sanctuary. 5 Another section, twenty-five thousand cubits long and ten thousand cubits broad, shall be for the Levites who minister at the temple, as their possession for cities to live in.

6 "Alongside the portion set apart as the holy district you shall assign for the possession of the city an area five thousand cubits broad, and twenty-five thousand cubits long; it shall belong to the whole house of Israel.

7 "And to the prince shall belong the land on both sides of the holy district and the property of the city, alongside the holy district and the property of the city, on the west and on the east, corresponding in length to one of the tribal portions, and extending from the western to the eastern boundary of the land. 8 It is to be his property in Israel. And my princes shall no more oppress my people; but they shall let the house of Israel have the land according to their tribes.

9 "Thus says the Lord GOD: Enough, O princes of Israel! Put away violence and oppression, and execute justice and righteousness; cease your evictions of my people, says the Lord GOD.

The presence of a passage on allocation of lands as a holy district (v. 1) with subdivisions for both Zadokites (v. 4) and Levites (v. 5), as well as the general populace, should be seen in the light of the statements in 48:8–22.

It may be postulated that 48:8–22 is but the continuation of a single passage which in transmission was affected by editorial additions. On the other hand it may be surmised that 48:8–22 constituted an additional allocation. Such measures would have been necessary when sufficient exiles had returned to the land. The increased numbers of returnees created the need for larger allocations.

A matter of initial concern for the first

returnees from exile would be that of establishing allocations of land for the Temple and prince, plus smaller holdings for the people. As time passed and the influx of the diverse tribal elements grew, the situation would necessitate tribal allocations. A third avenue of approach would be to consider the duplication as a simple editorial repetition which is characteristic of the latter portions of Ezekiel.

This passage, as well as 48:8–22 (see comment on this passage), replaces all traditional tribal boundaries which were in themselves quite unrealistic and haphazard in distribution. Not only were the venerable and revered tribal territories totally dispensed with in the Ezekelian restoration, but the Levitical cities were relegated to the exigencies of the new order. These cities, 48 in number, were formally introduced into Israelite life by David about 1000–961 B.C. They were accorded, however, an earlier existence by late developers of certain narratives (cf. Josh. 21; Lev. 25: 33, 34; Num. 35:1–8). The cities had doubtless become strong centers of priestly political influence and as genuine institutions of religious life caused no little concern to Levitical priestly interests when treated so lightly by the Ezekiel. We see in the abandoning of the Levitical cities a step toward reducing the power of this particular party. The reestablishment of the cities would have provided the Levites a power structure throughout the country.

Allocations of land to the prince equaled that of a tribe (v. 7) because its revenues were to sustain the royal household. This was an overt attempt in the new state to avoid abuse of the people by the ruling house (vv. 8, 9). Historically certain kings of Israel had oppressed the people by excessive taxation, nullification of human rights, and confiscation of personal property. Two cases serve to illustrate the point: one, the actions of Solomon, who became vainglorious, corrupt, and oppressive (cf. 1 Kings 4:7; 5:13; 9:11–15; 11:28; 2 Chron. 2:17, 18; 10:4, etc.), and the other the position of Ahab in the vineyard of Naboth

affair (cf. 1 Kings 21:1–15).

A specific injunction to put away violence and oppression and to institute justice and righteousness (v. 9) was directed to all subsequent rulers. This merely echoes the thoughts of the eighth-century ethical prophets, Amos and Micah (cf. Amos 3:10; Mic. 2:9). Ezekiel intended to thwart, in the new era, any tyrannical acts on the part of the ruling class.

(2) Weights and Measures (45:10–12)

10 "You shall have just balances, a just ephah, and a just bath. 11 The ephah and the bath shall be of the same measure, the bath containing one tenth of a homer, and the ephah one tenth of a homer; the homer shall be the standard measure. 12 The shekel shall be twenty gerahs; five shekels shall be five shekels, and ten shekels shall be ten shekels, and your mina shall be fifty shekels.

Few passages among the Old Testament exilic or postexilic writers more clearly reflect the ethical standards set by the eighth-century prophets for business relationships than this. The use in business of short weights and standards of measure was of intense prophetic concern (cf. Amos 8:5; Mic. 6:10,11; Hos. 12:8; also Lev. 19:35 ff.; Deut. 25:13 ff.; Prov. 11:1; 16:11; 20:10).

Here standards are set for scales (i.e., *balances*), dry measure (i.e., *bath*), and monetary units (i.e., *shekel*, a weight of metal). The *epah*, given as one-tenth of an *homer* (v. 11), may be estimated as approximately two-thirds of a bushel, while the *bath*, a liquid measure, would be approximately five and one-half gallons.[118]

(3) Offerings to the Prince (45:13–17)

13 "This is the offering which you shall make: one sixth of an ephah from each homer of wheat, and one sixth of an ephah from each homer of barley, 14 and as the fixed portion of oil, one tenth of a bath from each cor (the cor, like the homer, contains ten baths); 15 and one sheep from every flock of two hundred, from the families of Israel. This is the offering for cereal offerings, burnt offerings, and peace offerings, to make atonement for them, says the Lord God. 16 All the people of the land shall

118 Cf. O. R. Sellers, "Weights and Measures," IDB, IV, 828–839.

give this offering to the prince in Israel. [17] It shall be the prince's duty to furnish the burnt offerings, cereal offerings, and drink offerings, at the feasts, the new moons, and the sabbaths, all the appointed feasts of the house of Israel: he shall provide the sin offerings, cereal offerings, burnt offerings, and peace offerings, to make atonement for the house of Israel.

Although this section supports taxation in kind as an offering to the prince (v. 16), the gifts were to be used on behalf of the people in cultic rites. This is quite different from the levy of Solomon demanded from each of the twelve administrative districts of Israel (cf. 1 Kings 4:7–23). The requirement here is to provide only that which would be utilized in the religious ceremonies of the major religious festivals and days of cult observance (v. 17).

Offerings were simply channeled through the prince who acted as an intermediary (i.e., used to make reconciliation for the house of Israel). Designation of the prince as intermediary would assure the prompt delivery of offerings, for without them the religious ceremonies could not be observed. There was a historical precedent for this legislation, and it may have occasioned the adoption of such a procedure by Ezekiel (cf. 2 Chron., 30:24; 35:7).

4. Ordinances for Festivals and Offerings (45:18—46:15)

This division is a continuation of the regulations associated with the Temple ceremonial acts but with greater detail of specifics. Regulations for the feasts of the first and seventh months (vv. 18–20)—such as the Passover and Tabernacles (vv. 21–24), sabbaths and new moons (46:1–8), and festal processions (46:9–10)—are given in exact terms. But here we see definite signs of either modification or supplementation of previous Old Testament patterns of observance.

Two rather surprising situations develop in the section. First, there is no mention of the feast of the first-fruits (cf. Ex. 23:14–

17; Deut. 16:1–16) or of the feast of atonement (cf. Lev. 16). Secondly, there is an unusually prominent connection of the prince with cultic affairs (cf. 45:22; 46:2–12). In 45:18–24; 46:6–10, address or reference is directly to the prince. The strength of the statements and the unusual involvement of the prince in cultic acts casts this figure somewhat in the role of a priest-prince.

We may see in this emphasis upon the priest figure a modification of Old Testament thought which connects messiah with priest (cf. Jer. 30:9,21; Zech. 6:12 ff.; Dan. 9:25 ff.). Certainly the theme is more apparent in late Israelite thought, but it is Ezekiel who gives it the greater emphasis. One may venture to interpret the priest figure in the light of the restored community. The kingdom image was a theocratic community, a community of God. Such a community could only have at its head one who was both religious and secular. Since the community was to be centered about the Temple and priesthood, the new figure was a necessity.

(1) Feasts of the First and Seventh Months (45:18–25)

[18] "Thus says the Lord GOD: In the first month, on the first day of the month, you shall take a young bull without blemish, and cleanse the sanctuary. [19] The priest shall take some of the blood of the sin offering and put it on the doorposts of the temple, the four corners of the ledge of the altar, and the posts of the gate of the inner court. [20] You shall do the same on the seventh day of the month for any one who has sinned through error or ignorance; so you shall make atonement for the temple.

[21] "In the first month, on the fourteenth day of the month, you shall celebrate the feast of the passover, and for seven days unleavened bread shall be eaten. [22] On that day the prince shall provide for himself and all the people of the land a young bull for a sin offering. [23] And on the seven days of the festival he shall provide as a burnt offering to the LORD seven young bulls and seven rams without blemish, on each of the seven days; and a he-goat daily for a sin offering. [24] And he shall provide as a cereal offering an ephah for each bull, an ephah for each ram, and a hin of oil to each

phah. 25 In the seventh month, on the fifteenth day of the month and for the seven days of the feast, he shall make the same provision for sin offerings, burnt offerings, and cereal offerings, and for the oil.

Since the first and seventh months were the beginning months of either half of the ritual calendar year, purification of the central sanctuary was necessary. Such ritual cleansings were effected by beginning each half of the liturgical year with a sin offering to avoid the possibility of conducting any religious rite which might be negated by sin of error or ignorance (v. 20). Precisely detailed are the instructions for the cleansing, which initiated each half of the religious year. These rites actually made atonement for the Temple and rendered it ritually clean.

Festival regulations for the Passover and Unleavened Bread follow (vv. 21–25). According to Leviticus these two festivals compose a unit (cf. Lev. 23:5 ff.). The Passover was celebrated on the evening of the first day (i.e., the fourteenth day of the month), at which time the sacrificial lamb was slaughtered. Then for seven consecutive days, beginning on the morning of the fifteenth day, unleavened bread would be eaten (cf. Ex. 23:15; Deut. 16:16).

There are evidences, which cannot be discussed in detail here, that these festivals had roots prior to the time of the Exodus— at least that more ancient rites provided formative influences in their development.

(2) Regulations for Sabbaths and New Moons (46:1–8)

1 "Thus says the Lord God: The gate of the inner court that faces east shall be shut on the six working days; but on the sabbath day it shall be opened and on the day of the new moon it shall be opened. 2 The prince shall enter by the vestibule of the gate from without, and shall take his stand by the post of the gate. The priests shall offer his burnt offering and his peace offerings, and he shall worship at the threshold of the gate. Then he shall go out, but the gate shall not be shut until evening. 3 The people of the land shall worship at the entrance of that gate before the LORD on the

sabbaths and on the new moons. 4 The burnt offering that the prince offers to the LORD on the sabbath day shall be six lambs without blemish and a ram without blemish; 5 and the cereal offering with the ram shall be an ephah, and the cereal offering with the lambs shall be as much as he is able, together with a hin of oil to each ephah. 6 On the day of the new moon he shall offer a young bull without blemish, and six lambs and a ram, which shall be without blemish; 7 as a cereal offering he shall provide an ephah with the bull and an ephah with the ram, and with the lambs as much as he is able, together with a hin of oil to each ephah. 8 When the prince enters, he shall go in by the vestibule of the gate, and he shall go out by the same way.

Restrictions described in this section and the emphasis placed upon sabbath and/or new moon festivals give strong testimony both to priestly exclusivism and sabbath importance in postexilic times. During the six secular days of the week the east gate of the inner court which led to the altar and Temple were closed. This does not mean, however, that within the court and Temple there were no cultic acts (cf. 46: 13,14; 2 Kings 18:29; 2 Kings 16:15; Dan. 8:11–13). It simply means that on the sabbath and/or new moon public worship was observed (v. 1).

On the seventh day the prince was permitted to enter the gateway of the east gate, traverse he vestibule, and stand at the threshold of the inner court but was not permitted actually to enter the court. From that vantage point he could worship observing the priestly ritual in the inner court (v. 2). The people, however, were restricted to the outer court from which point they could neither observe nor participate in the ritual (v. 3). Thus the general worshiper was completely cut off from any direct involvement in the acts of cultic worship.

The prescribed observance of new moons and sabbaths points to long-established traditions in Israel's life. Much research suggests that the Israelites earlier borrowed from and adapted religious rites of surrounding cultures. This likely applies also to new moons and sabbaths, as the Israelites made these observances the vehicle of their own religious expression.[119]

(3) Regulations for Festal Processions (46:9-10)

9 "When the people of the land come before the LORD at the appointed feasts, he who enters by the north gate to worship shall go out by the south gate; and he who enters by the south gate shall go out by the north gate: no one shall return by way of the gate by which he entered, but each shall go out straight ahead. 10 When they go in, the prince shall go in with them; and when they go out, he shall go out.

Since the *appointed feasts* (v. 9) were the great festivals for the entire nation (cf. Ex. 23:17; 34:23; Deut. 16:16), it was necessary to establish some orderly procedure for handling the throngs entering and leaving the outer court of the Temple complex. One may surmise from the passage that some type of procession led by the prince was structured.

The people would gather at one of the gates, either north or south, from which point the prince would lead them into the outer court, move to his appointed place at the threshold of the east gate, observe the rites, and then lead the people from the outer court through the gate opposite from the one by which they entered. In this event it appears that the prince observes the ritual not as a personal act but on behalf of the total community of worshipers.

(4) Regulations for Sacrifices (46:11-15)

11 "At the feasts and the appointed seasons the cereal offering with a young bull shall be an ephah, and with a ram an ephah, and with the lambs as much as one is able to give, together with a hin of oil to an ephah. 12 When the prince provides a freewill offering, either a burnt offering or peace offerings as a freewill offering to the LORD, the gate facing east shall be opened for him; and he shall offer his burnt offering or his peace offerings as he does on the sabbath day. Then he shall go out, and after he has gone out the gate shall be shut.

119 Cf. Kraus, *op. cit.*, pp. 78-87; H. H. Rowley, *Worship in Ancient Israel* (Philadelphia: Fortress Press, 1967), pp. 91-92; A. T. Clay, *The Origin of Biblical Traditions* (New Haven: Yale University Press, 1923), pp. 117-123.

13 "He shall provide a lamb a year old without blemish for a burnt offering to the LORD daily; morning by morning he shall provide it. 14 And he shall provide a cereal offering with it morning by morning, one sixth of an ephah, and one third of a hin of oil to moisten the flour, as a cereal offering to the LORD; this is the ordinance for the continual burnt offering. 15 Thus the lamb and the meal offering and the oil shall be provided, morning by morning, for a continual burnt offering.

Whereas 46:1 required the east gate to the inner court be closed on all secular days, one exception is made (v. 12). Whenever the prince desired to make a freewill offering the east gate was to be opened. Yet he, as on other occasions, was prohibited from actually entering the inner court. This points to the fact that the prince occupied a cultic position higher than that of a Levite but less than that of a Zadokite.

There follows a listing of the daily sacrifices and offerings to be provided by the prince (vv. 13-15), which would obviously come from his own personal holdings equal to that of a tribe (cf. 45:7-8). Such a precedent for the daily offering is found in 1 Kings 18:29,26; 1 Kings 16:15.

5. Regulations on Crown Property (46:16-18)

16 "Thus says the Lord GOD: If the prince makes a gift to any of his sons out of his inheritance, it shall belong to his sons, it is their property by inheritance. 17 But if he makes a gift out of his inheritance to one of his servants, it shall be his to the year of liberty; then it shall revert to the prince; only his sons may keep a gift from his inheritance. 18 The prince shall not take any of the inheritance of the people, thrusting them out of their property; he shall give his sons their inheritance out of his own property, so that none of my people shall be dispossessed of his property."

The section 45:7-9 refers to an allocation of crown property from which the throne would derive personal revenues. Strict procedures were to be followed in conveying either the property or its revenues. The prince could convey to his sons only that real and personal property which was his by original allocation or income from that allocation. Additionally the *prince* s prohibited from conveying any of his property in perpetuity to anyone other than a member of the royal family (v. 17). Additionally he is prohibited from confiscating public property in order to convey it to his sons (v. 18). Should he grant property rights to one other than a member of the family (e.g., a servant), it would revert to the crown in the *year of liberty*. This year of liberty may imply the Jubilee Year. These restrictions are but safeguards related to the concerns voiced in 45:9.

6. Temple Kitchens (46:19-24)

19 Then he brought me through the entrance, which was at the side of the gate, to the north row of the holy chambers for the priests; and there I saw a place at the extreme western end of them. 20 And he said to me, "This is the place where the priests shall boil the guilt offering and the sin offering, and where they shall bake the cereal offering, in order not to bring them out into the outer court and so communicate holiness to the people." 21 Then he brought me forth to the outer court, and led me to the four corners of the court; and in each corner of the court there was a court—22 in the four corners of the court were small courts, forty cubits long and thirty broad; the four were of the same size. 23 On the inside, around each of the four courts was a row of masonry, with hearths made at the bottom of the rows round about. 24 Then he said to me, "These are the kitchens where those who minister at the temple shall boil the sacrifices of the people."

This abrupt transition back to the Temple tour, which was interrupted at 44:4, suggests that the entire section (44:5—46:18) involves a major editorial revision or handling of the text.

The prophet is here shown the two cooking areas within the Temple complex. One was the kitchen in which the meat of the guilt and sin offerings, allocated to the priests, was prepared for their tables (vv. 19-20). This kitchen was located between the outer and inner courts. Another kitchen was located in the outer court where the portions of the sacrifices on behalf of the people were prepared for them by *those who minister* (i.e., the Levites, v. 24)

7. Allegory of the Sacred River (47:1-12)

1 Then he brought me back to the door of the temple; and behold, water was issuing from below the threshold of the temple toward the east (for the temple faced east); and the water was flowing down from below the south end of the threshold of the temple, south of the altar. 2 Then he brought me out by way of the north gate, and led me round on the outside to the outer gate, that faces toward the east; and the water was coming out on the south side.

3 Going on eastward with a line in his hand, the man measured a thousand cubits, and then led me through the water, and it was ankle-deep. 4 Again he measured a thousand, and led me through the water; and it was knee-deep. Again he measured a thousand, and led me through the water; and it was up to the loins. 5 Again he measured a thousand, and it was a river that I could not pass through, for the water had risen; it was deep enough to swim in, a river that could not be passed through. 6 And he said to me, "Son of man, have you seen this?"

Then he led me back along the bank of the river. 7 As I went back, I saw upon the bank of the river very many trees on the one side and on the other. 8 And he said to me, "This water flows toward the eastern region and goes down into the Arabah; and when it enters the stagnant waters of the sea, the water will become fresh. 9 And wherever the river goes every living creature which swarms will live, and there will be very many fish; for this water goes there, that the waters of the sea may become fresh; so everything will live where the river goes. 10 Fishermen will stand beside the sea; from Engedi to Eneglaim it will be a place for the spreading of nets; its fish will be of very many kinds, like the fish of the Great Sea. 11 But its swamps and marshes will not become fresh; they are to be left for salt. 12 And on the banks, on both sides of the river, there will grow all kinds of trees for food. Their leaves will not wither nor their fruit fail, but they will bear fresh fruit every month, because the water for them flows from the sanctuary. Their fruit will be for food, and their leaves for healing."

Climaxing the Temple vision is the allegory of the sacred river. Ezekiel's guide points to an issue of water coming from the threshold of the Temple (v. 1). The fact that the water flowed south of the altar (v. 1), past the east gate (v. 2), and toward the wilderness of Judah, implicates the holy of holies as being the original source.

The farther the flow the greater was the volume of the flow (vv. 3–5). At its point of origin, it was merely a trickle (vv. 1,2). In v. 2 the Hebrew *m°pakim* is translated *coming out;* but it is rendered "trickling" in the NEB. The word, found nowhere else in the Old Testament, is the root from which the term "jar" is derived. It implies most likely a jar with a narrow mouth. We may infer from its usage here that in origin the issue of water was like the gurgling trickle of liquid from a small-mouth jar.

It is this ever intensifying stream of water which imparts life to the dead wilderness (v. 7). It purges, makes clean and pure, the saline reservoir of the Dead Sea (vv. 9, 10) and reclaims the Arabah (v. 12).[120]

Thus the central meaning of the allegory is that with the return of the glory of the Lord to the restored Temple that glory functions as the source of renewal for the entire nation. Yahweh's glory is that which renews, restores, rejuvenates, and revitalizes both land and people. Similar imagery is used in other biblical books (cf. Zech. 13:1; 14:8; Joel 3:18; Eccl. 24:30 ff.; John 4:14; 7:37,38; Rev. 22:1,2).

The symbolism in this passage is most striking when we consider the geography of the area. The movement of the water is directed toward a most desolate region, the wilderness of Judah which contained only two oases, Ziph and En-gedi. These wastelands had historically been the haunt of outlaw bands (cf. 1 Sam. 25).

The *Arabah* (v. 8) is the southern extension of the Jordan Valley which provides a burial plot for the interment of the Jordan River in the Dead Sea. The translation in v. 8 of *stagnant waters* is not quite so accurate as "bitter waters" or "stinking waters." This is an obvious reference to the waters of the sulphurous hot springs along the Dead Sea whose smell and taste is putrid although highly prized for its medicinal qualities in antiquity. It is this offensive water that will be made *fresh.* Literally it will be healed, made sweet and

pallatable by the glory of Yahweh.

The continuation of the valley from the the Dead Sea toward the Gulf of Akaba is called Wadi-el-Arabah. This gigantic depression in the earth's crust is both awesome and appealing, lovely in its deadliness. It has no mercy upon its intruder with intense daytime heat, devastatingly cold nights, and precipitously dangerous ridges and canyons. This is a sea so contaminated by mineral salt pollutants that it supports no living organism.

This entire area of the dead and the dying was to become one of life and living Trees would sprout; the Dead Sea would be transformed into a living sea. Fruit trees would not only grow in the area but be superabundantly productive. It would be a land transformed from death to life. There was only one exclusion—the *swamps* and *marshes* (v. 11). They would be preserved as a perpetual source of salt.

Of considerable import is the general religious outlook of the prophet: specifically the material blessings of Yahweh are only for his chosen people. Ezekiel typifies the traditional position that faithfulness to Yahweh will be rewarded by material prosperity. The Israelite religious logic which implied if one was righteous he would be prosperous and if sinful be bereft of possessions, or the position that wealth was a proof of righteousness and poverty and suffering a proof of unrighteousness, of course lacks the full truth of the New Testament—and it is challenged by the book of Job and Psalm 73.

8. Israel's Tribal Boundaries (47:13–23)

13 Thus says the Lord God: "These are the boundaries by which you shall divide the land for inheritance among the twelve tribes of Israel. Joseph shall have two portions. 14 And you shall divide it equally; I swore to give it to your fathers, and this land shall fall to you as your inheritance.

15 "This shall be the boundary of the land: On the north side, from the Great Sea by way of Hethlon to the entrance of Hamath, and on to Zedad, 16 Berothah, Sibraim (which lies on the border between Damascus and of Hamath), as far as Hazer hatticon, which is on the

120 William R. Farmer, "The Geography of Ezekiel's River of Life," BA XIX.1 (1956), 17–22.

order of Hauran. 17 So the boundary shall run
from the sea to Hazarenon, which is on the
northern border of Damascus, with the border
of Hamath to the north. This shall be the north
side.
18 "On the east side, the boundary shall run
from Hazarenon between Hauran and Damascus; along the Jordan between Gilead and the
land of Israel; to the eastern sea and as far as
Tamar. This shall be the east side.
19 "On the south side, it shall run from
Tamar as far as the waters of Meribath kadesh,
thence along the Brook of Egypt to the Great
Sea. This shall be the south side.
20 "On the west side, the Great Sea shall be
the boundary to a point opposite the entrance
of Hamath. This shall be the west side.
21 "So you shall divide this land among you
according to the tribes of Israel. 22 You shall
allot it as an inheritance for yourselves and for
the aliens who reside among you and have
begotten children among you. They shall be to
you as native-born sons of Israel; with you they
shall be allotted an inheritance among the
tribes of Israel. 23 In whatever tribe the alien
resides, there you shall assign him his inheritance, says the Lord GOD.

We find in this division three specific
items: (1) an affirmation of the tribal rights
of Ephraim and Manasseh, the sons of
Joseph, who are to share and share alike in
the allocations of tribal territories (vv.
13, 14); (2) the overall boundaries of the
land to be subdivided among the tribes
(vv. 15-20); (3) the rights of the alien
within the new state (vv. 21-23).

The equality of the divisions among the
tribes (v. 14) was assured by the previous
sworn commitment of Yahweh. *I swore*
implies the taking of an oath with upraised
hand (cf. Ex. 20:5). Yahweh had committed himself in a formal and sacred way
to assure the equity of tribal land grants.

The rights of aliens are worked out on
the basis of precise status. These were to
be considered *native-born sons* of Israel
(v. 22). This is a provision for those aliens
who had embraced the religion of the restored community and thus would be considered religious proselytes. Certain late
sources such as the Holiness and Priestly
codes affirm this distinction (cf. Lev. 16:
29; 17:15; 19:34; 24:16; Num. 15:29,30).
As such the proselytes would only share in

the tribal allocation granted to the tribe to
which they were attached. (v. 23).

There seems to be inconsistency here
when we recall restrictions about entrance
into the Temple (cf. 44:9). The proselytes
were fully acceptable socially and politically
but stigmatized religiously by being restricted when it came to certain aspects of
Temple worship.

9. Allocation of Tribal Lands (48:1-29)

This section details the tribal subdivisions, the holy portion, and the prince's
allocation within the general boundaries
specified previously (cf. 47:15-20). Allocations for the seven tribes, north of the
prince's holdings, are given first (vv. 1-7).
Then attention is directed to the *holy portion* (v. 10), that set apart for the Temple,
the Zadokites, the Levites, the city complex,
and the prince (vv. 8-23). The book concludes with the allocation of the territory
south of the holy portion, divided equally
among the remaining five tribes (vv. 23-
29).

(1) Tribal Allocations in the North (48: 1-7)

1 "These are the names of the tribes: Beginning at the northern border, from the sea by
way of Hethlon to the entrance of Hamath, as
far as Hazarenon (which is on the northern
border of Damascus over against Hamath),
and extending from the east side to the west,
Dan, one portion. 2 Adjoining the territory of
Dan, from the east side to the west, Asher, one
portion. 3 Adjoining the territory of Asher, from
the east side to the west, Naphtali, one portion.
4 Adjoining the territory of Naphtali, from the
east side to the west, Manasseh, one portion.
5 Adjoining the territory of Manasseh, from the
east side to the west, Ephraim, one portion.
6 Adjoining the territory of Ephraim, from the
east side to the west, Reuben, one portion.
7 Adjoining the territory of Reuben, from the
east side to the west, Judah, one portion.

The northernmost boundary is defined as
being the area of Riblah and Kadesh, i.e.,
entrance of Hamath (v. 1), along the
Orontes River. Seven tribes—Dan, Asher,
Naphtali, Manasseh, Ephraim, Reuben, and
Judah—are allocated east-west strips of territory extending from the Mediterranean

Ocean to the Jordan Valley. Judah is granted that section just north of the holy portion containing the Temple complex. Five of the tribes were normally associated with the northern part of the land; while tradition connected Judah with the south and Reuben with the Transjordan. Implications of the repositioning of Judah can only be surmised (cf. comment on 48:30–35).

(2) The Holy Allocations (48:8-22)

8 "Adjoining the territory of Judah, from the east side to the west, shall be the portion which you shall set apart, twenty-five thousand cubits in breadth, and in length equal to one of the tribal portions, from the east side to the west, with the sanctuary in the midst of it. 9 The portion which you shall set apart for the LORD shall be twenty-five thousand cubits in length, and twenty thousand in breadth. 10 These shall be the allotments of the holy portion: the priests shall have an allotment measuring twenty-five thousand cubits on the northern side, ten thousand cubits in breadth on the western side, ten thousand in breadth on the eastern side, and twenty-five thousand in length on the southern side, with the sanctuary of the LORD in the midst of it. 11 This shall be for the consecrated priests, the sons of Zadok, who kept my charge, who did not go astray when the people of Israel went astray, as the Levites did. 12 And it shall belong to them as a special portion from the holy portion of the land, a most holy place, adjoining the territory of the Levites. 13 And alongside the territory of the priests, the Levites shall have an allotment twenty-five thousand cubits in length and ten thousand in breadth. The whole length shall be twenty-five thousand cubits and the breadth twenty thousand. 14 They shall not sell or exchange any of it; they shall not alienate this choice portion of the land, for it is holy to the LORD.

15 "The remainder, five thousand cubits in breadth and twenty-five thousand in length, shall be for ordinary use for the city, for dwellings and for open country. In the midst of it shall be the city; 16 and these shall be its dimensions: the north side four thousand five hundred cubits, the south side four thousand five hundred, the east side four thousand five hundred, and the west side four thousand five hundred. 17 And the city shall have open land: on the north two hundred and fifty cubits, on the south two hundred and fifty, on the east two hundred and fifty, and on the west two hundred and fifty. 18 The remainder of the length alongside the holy portion shall be ten thousand cubits to the east, and ten thousand to the west, and it shall be alongside the holy portion. Its produce shall be food for the workers of the city. 19 And the workers of the city from all the tribes of Israel, shall till it. 20 The whole portion which you shall set apart shall be twenty-five thousand cubits square, that is the holy portion together with the property of the city.

21 "What remains on both sides of the holy portion and of the property of the city shall belong to the prince. Extending from the twenty-five thousand cubits of the holy portion to the east border, and westward from the twenty-five thousand cubits to the west border parallel to the tribal portions, it shall belong to the prince. The holy portion with the sanctuary of the temple in its midst, 22 and the property of the Levites and the property of the city shall be in the midst of that which belongs to the prince. The portion of the prince shall lie between the territory of Judah and the territory of Benjamin.

Much the same restrictions were placed upon the Zadokite and Levite allocations as were levied against the prince (cf. 45:1–9). Details on the holy allotment specify three parallel east-west zones with the holdings of the Zadokites north of the prince's holdings and city complex and that of the Levites south of the prince's area and the city complex (vv. 8–14). These lands lying on either side of the holy portion, like the holy portion itself, were to be held in perpetuity. Neither the whole nor portions of it could be sold or exchanged (v. 14). Doubtless this was an effort to assure the greatest degree of ritual security for the holy portion. With priestly territory completely surrounding the holy portion the possibility of contamination by uncleanliness was kept at a minimum.

The open section (vv. 15–22) was that of the city itself with its contingent lands. The size of the portion is exactly ten times that of the Temple complex in its center. This was actually the prince's allocation with the exception of the Temple complex (cf. v. 21).

(3) Tribal Allocations in the South (48: 23-29)

23 "As for the rest of the tribes: from the east side to the west, Benjamin, one portion

⁴ Adjoining the territory of Benjamin, from the east side to the west, Simeon, one portion. ⁵ Adjoining the territory of Simeon, from the east side to the west, Issachar, one portion. ⁶ Adjoining the territory of Issachar, from the east side to the west, Zebulun, one portion. ⁷ Adjoining the territory of Zebulun, from the east side to the west, Gad, one portion. ²⁸ And adjoining the territory of Gad to the south, the boundary shall run from Tamar to the waters of Meribath-kadesh, thence along the Brook of Egypt to the Great Sea. ²⁹ This is the land which you shall allot as an inheritance among the tribes of Israel, and these are their several portions, says the Lord GOD.

Tribal allocations for five tribes; Benjamin, Simeon, Issachar, Zebulun, and Dan constituted the land south of Jerusalem to the *Brook of Egypt* (v. 28). It is at once noticeable that Ezekiel has given preeminence in the tribal allocations to Judah and Benjamin, with one being north of the heart of the land and the other south.

The two sections, 48:1–7 and 48:23–29, present a seemingly idealized distribution of the land. It totally disregarded natural boundaries, geographical disparities, inhabitableness, potential productivity, and access to water, an important consideration especially in Palestine. Also no reference is made to inclusion of the Transjordan, that territory beyond the Jordan Valley formerly granted to one-half Manasseh, Gad, and Reuben following the conquest. Kraeling feels that here we see the doctrinal mind at work in order to fulfill its own concepts and ideals.[121]

Greenberg feels that the allocation is not only reasonable but rather ingenious, overcoming many of the shortcomings evident in former tribal allocations.[122]

Most questions about the Ezekelian division center around total disregard for geographical inequities related to soil fertility and water supply. What one must not overlook is that Ezekiel does project a highly idealized division, but it is predicated upon the concept of a totally re-

juvenated land, one superabundant in all things and in its entirety something of a restored Eden.

10. *The Holy City* (*48:30–35*)

³⁰ "These shall be the exits of the city: On the north side, which is to be four thousand five hundred cubits by measure, ³¹ three gates, the gate of Reuben, the gate of Judah, and the gate of Levi, the gates of the city being named after the tribes of Israel. ³² On the east side, which is to be four thousand five hundred cubits, three gates, the gate of Joseph, the gate of Benjamin, and the gate of Dan. ³³ On the south side, which is to be four thousand five hundred cubits by measure, three gates, the gate of Simeon, the gate of Issachar, and the gate of Zebulun. ³⁴ On the west side, which is to be four thousand five hundred cubits, three gates, the gate of Gad, the gate of Asher, and the gate of Naphtali. ³⁵ The circumference of the city shall be eighteen thousand cubits. And the name of the city henceforth shall be, The LORD is there."

The city, a perfect square, is to have twelve gates. Three gates are to be situated on each side of the square and one named for each of the tribes. Of prime interest is the east side of the city which had unusual connections with the religious cult, since it was through the east gate that the glory of the Lord returned. In addition, just south of the east gate, there issued forth the unique and rejuvenating river. Gates on the east are connected with the tribes of Joseph, Benjamin, and Dan. Joseph and Benjamin were the sons of Rachel, the most beloved of Jacob, while Dan was the last son of Rachel's handmaiden Bilhah. Preference given in this case is similar to that shown in the tribal allocations where the sons of Rachel and Leah, rather than those of their handmaidens, were shown decided favor.

Most striking of all is the new city-name, *the Lord is there* (v. 35). The new name denotes change in character and conditions, a classic Old Testament way of indicating a radical change.

Thus the circle was completed, perfectly executed by Yahweh on behalf of his own. To Ezekiel and his prophetic sons this constituted the epitome of true religion.

---

121 Kraeling, *op. cit.*, p. 541.
122 Moshe Greenberg, "Idealism and Practicality in Numbers 35:4–5 and Ezekiel 48," *Journal of the American Oriental Society*, LXXXVIII (1968), 59–66.

Daniel

JOHN JOSEPH OWENS

Introduction

The book of Daniel is unique in the biblical canon. It serves as the vital link between various developing aspects of Hebrew religion. The prophetic movement uniquely interacts with both apocalyptic and wisdom thought. This book has the most highly developed appearances of angels in the Old Testament. There is the clearest statement of the doctrine of a resurrection in the Old Testament which capitalizes on the thoughts of Job and Isaiah and peers into the future of the soul.

The despair and disenchantment which suffering and persecution bring are tempered by the reality of hope. Facts of past historical experiences are viewed in the context of future possibilities. The sovereignty of God is balanced by the necessity of individual reactivity and also by the deterministic policy of God.

I. Place in the Canon

The earlier Hebrew order, preserved at the Council of Jamnia, included Daniel among the Writings between Esther and Ezra-Nehemiah. The English order places Daniel between Ezekiel and the twelve minor prophets. The Greek-speaking Jews placed Daniel as one of the major prophets. This change reflects a reaction against apocalyptic, an emphasis on the prophetic portion, and also a tendency toward chronological arrangements of content.

Daniel is not mentioned in Ecclesiasticus (chs. 44—50) among Isaiah, Jeremiah, Ezekiel, and the Twelve (ca. 180 B.C.).

Evidence in other literature indicates that the book was not quoted before the middle of the second century B.C. However, it was known and revered from the middle of the second century B.C. (ca. 135). The Dead Sea Scrolls, 1 Enoch, and 1 Maccabees have clear references to Daniel.

Josephus (Antiq. XI.8.4–5) relates that Daniel was shown to Alexander the Great (ca. 336–323 B.C.). This was probably not the book of Daniel in its present form but was the Daniel corpus. This Danielic material could have been the basic Aramaic portion.

The latest historical focus of the book of Daniel is within the second century B.C. If this is the time that the book was finally compiled, it would account for the book being placed in the Writings.

II. Language

Daniel is preserved with part in Hebrew and part in Aramaic. Chapters 1:1—2:4a and 8:1—12:13 (157½ verses) are in the Hebrew language. Chapters 2:4b—7:28 (199½ verses) are in Aramaic. Different explanations are proposed for the language problem. Montgomery, Torrey, and Dalman hold that the stories (chs. 1—6) were written in Aramaic and circulated as a complete work. The visions (chs. 7—12) were written later in Hebrew. In an appropriate time these two were brought together. A translation into Hebrew of 1:1—2:4a and an Aramaic translation of chapter 7 were made to unify the two

373

sections.

Bevan and others hold that the entire book was written originally in Hebrew and that chapters 2—7 were subsequently lost. These chapters were recovered from an existent Aramaic translation. R. H. Charles builds upon the principle that Aramaic was the language of common conversation and court use, whereas Hebrew was the language of piety and of cultic usage. H. H. Rowley varied the view slightly in suggesting that the stories (chs. 2—6) circulated as separate Aramaic pieces.

The Hebrew is not of the classical variety found in Isaiah, Jeremiah, or Ezekiel. The Hebrew sections have a distinct Aramaic character. The state of the Hebrew leads to a conclusion that either that portion was translated from the Aramaic into Hebrew or that it was written by one who knew Aramaic better and was not as familiar with classical Hebrew.

There are also remnants of at least two other languages. The fifteen Persian expressions suggest a date during or after the Persian period accentuating the historicity of the background events. The presence of Greek terms point no earlier than 336 B.C.

III. Versions

Sources available to assist in the evaluation of the Hebrew-Aramaic text are: the Chester Beatty Papyri (2nd cent. A.D.), which has around five chapters from the heart of the book; the Dead Sea Scrolls, which have excerpts from five chapters.

The version known as the Septuagint is known only from Codex Chisianus in the Vatican, generally dated from the eleventh century A.D. (no earlier than the ninth). It contains an expanded text in many places and is more of a paraphrase than a translation. Most Septuagint editors rely on the Theodotion text and print it alongside the LXX of Codex Chisianus. The Theodotion text is more literal and closer to the Hebrew-Aramaic. It was the text used mainly by the early Christian communities when the LXX text was banned.

IV. The Man

Nothing is known of the man Daniel outside of the book itself. According to rabbinic tradition, Daniel was of royal descent, probably akin to King Zedekiah. Within the book he was a young Jew who was taken captive by the forces of Nebuchadnezzar in 605 B.C. He and three other Jewish lads were among the trainees at the foreign court. He served as a governmental official until the third year of Cyrus (536 B.C.; 1:21; 10:1) under both Babylonian and Persian potentates. The record about him is clearly set in wisdom terms (Heaton, pp. 19–24). He is shown to be superior to the wise men, magicians, and counselors of both kingdoms.

The name Daniel is recorded also as a son of David (1 Chron. 3:1) and as a priest of the line of Ithamar (Ezra 8:2; Neh. 10:6). No biblical record indicates that Daniel ever returned to Palestine. However, there is a tradition that he returned under the command of Cyrus. Within that tradition Daniel is identified with the one named in Ezra-Nehemiah.

A Daniel is recorded three times in Ezekiel (14:14,20; 28:3). This is not the youth in the book of Daniel. The names are spelled differently. The Daniel of Ezekiel 14 is a revered saint of antiquity as Noah and Job. Ezekiel and Daniel were contemporaries.

The Tale of Aqhat of the Ras Shamra Tablets (J. B. Pritchard, pp. 149 ff.) contains the name Danel (spelled as in Ezekiel). These tablets date from the fourteenth century B.C. The literary tradition of wisdom and judgment makes Daniel the ideal person to convey the message the author intended to portray.

V. Historical Focus

Daniel concentrates on two widely separated periods. The first chronological focus is the time, pictured in the first six chapters, during which Daniel was active in the Babylonian and Persian governments. The first four chapters are set in the reign of Nebuchadnezzar, king of Babylonia, 604–

61 B.C. Chapter 5 is set in the time of Belshazzar, the son of Nabonidus, king of Babylonia, 556–539. Chapter 6 is set in the time of Darius. This was probably the Darius, king of Persia, 522–486.

The second focal point of chronology is the period of the Ptolemies and Seleucids, beginning ca. 323 B.C. after the death of Alexander the Great. The account connects with the Babylonian period but moves quickly to the primary interest of the author, i.e., 175–164. More specific detail and record is given to the exploits of Antiochus Epiphanes than to any other single character in the book.

Between these two general eras the book of Daniel operates. The Semitic thought pattern is crystal clear in the manner in which the author parallels these two segments of the history of the Hebrew people.

V. Book Divisions

It is very apparent that a change occurs between chapters 6 and 7. The first six chapters are individual stories from the Babylonian and Persian periods. The last six chapters are not historical narratives but are visions. The first six chapters are marked by clarity and simplicity, but the last six are complicated and obscure. The first six chapters are marked by human interest, but the last six are apocalyptic. In the first six chapters, Daniel is spoken of in the third person, but the last six chapters have Daniel speaking in the first person (with the exception of the superscription of 7:1 and 10:1). Chapters 1—6 read as a biography and 7—12 read as an autobiography.

In chapters 1—6 the dreams or phenomena come to the heathen kings, but in 7—12 it is Daniel who has dreams. In 1—6 it is Daniel who interprets the dreams, but in 7—12 it is "someone" who interprets the dreams and visions to Daniel.

One would expect the language and style change to be at the end of chapter 6. But linguistic changes are very abrupt in the midst of both the story section and the vision section. The book introduction and the first story and the first verses of the second story are in Hebrew. The remainder of the second story and stories three to six are in Palestinian Aramaic. One would expect the shift back to the Hebrew to occur at the end of the stories if at all. But the first vision (ch. 7) is also in Palestinian Aramaic. Chapters 8—12 are in Hebrew. No real answer to the language problems has been agreed upon by scholars. The direction of fruitful investigation lies in the source and genre of the materials and in the audience for which the author wrote the total book.

Many writers argue concerning the unity of the book. It is important to identify with accuracy the scope under investigation when using the term unity. Linguistic unity, unity of date, unity of authorship, and literary unity are separate problems.

The traditional view has been that Daniel wrote the entire book from the Babylonian and Persian setting (605–536 B.C.). This view of authorship has been argued on the basis that if Daniel did not write it, the book of Daniel is not the word of God, a conclusion completely unjustified.

The grounds for this view of the sixth century B.C. authorship by Daniel are as follows: the name Daniel is prominent; Daniel speaks in the first person in chapters 7—12; the dates within the book are in that period; the sealing up of the scroll for a later period; Daniel's acceptance as a prophet; the long-standing tradition that Daniel was the author was unquestioned until the seventeenth century A.D. (except for Porphyry, 3rd cent. A.D.). These are valid evidences which must be incorporated into any conclusion as to the unity of authorship. However, there are many other facts which must be examined.

The historical setting of the first six chapters is Mesopotamia from Nebuchadnezzar, the Babylonian king, to Darius, the king of Persia. Practically all scholars agree that the historical setting of the last section of Daniel is in the Seleucid-Ptolemaic struggle over Palestine in the second century B.C. The traditional view holds that Daniel from his vantage in Mesopotamia wrote in advance of all these events.

Most scholars see many sources in the development of the book. The stories of the first six chapters are the most ancient and are based upon historical personages, events, and situations. Bentzen argued that these stories existed as individual oral records for a long time before they were fixed in literary form. If so, the stories could have been formed by individual authors originally. These accounts were probably collected and written at least by the third century B.C.

H. H. Rowley, the late British Baptist scholar, has argued vigorously for the unity of the book's thought and purpose. He said that the book was constructed on these ancient records by one man for a second-century use. The crisis situation of that century called forth this expression of hope. The inspired writer was led to proclaim the imminence of God's intervention and the reaffirmation of the sovereignty of God over the land of God's people.

It would have been dangerous to spell out with equal clarity the application of these ancient records to such a crisis. The prophetic-apocalyptic proclamation through visions was authoritative and understood by the worshiping community to whom the book was addressed. The difference in forms and contents of the various visions can be explained by the possibility that the prophetic-apocalyptic voices were preserved accurately as proclaimed. The amazing unanimity and hoped for climax of that segment of history bound these proclamations together and provided through faith in the imminent God the courage and hope which the endangered community needed to resist the abominating desolator.

Since it was to the worshiping community to which the author was providing hope, he wrote the first chapter in the language of worship (Hebrew) to explain the real crux of the situation in the light of the ancient record of Daniel and the three youths. The six chapters in Aramaic are records from the vast store of conversational historical information as preserved by the

patriarchs' telling and retelling of the events. The final chapters of the book were written and preserved in Hebrew for therein lies the real message of hope in the dangerous times under the "little horn."

It is to be expected that serious student of the book of Daniel will have varying approaches to the historical background and focus of the book, also about the nature of its contents, the purpose of the book as a whole, and the symbolic phenomena recorded and portrayed. Each person has the right to arrive at his own conclusion in the light of all the discoverable facts that should provide a clue to the interpretation of the book and that provide for him a meaningful understanding of the revelation of the Lord through this book. The viewpoint set forth in this treatment of the book reflects the author's conviction that the book of Daniel spoke, first of all, to the people of God in the contemporary situation of persecution and despair, but that it speaks, also, to the people of God through the ages to declare the sovereignty of God and to encourage them in hope of his intervention for their deliverance.

VII. Relation to Other Literature

When the comparison with the books of Jeremiah and Ezekiel is made there are some similarities but also some glaring dissimilarities. In Daniel, Jeremiah, and Ezekiel an introduction establishes the theological focus for the entire work. These three books make a proclamation concerning future events based on an interpretation of contemporaneous events.

Daniel does not use the "word of the Lord came unto me" or "thus says the Lord" which are so frequent in the classical prophets. There can be no question that the prophetic element is important in Daniel (cf. Matt. 24:15; Mark 13:14). However, in style and language there is a great variance between Daniel and the canonical prophets.

Daniel is the epitome of wisdom (cf. Ezek. 28:3). A very close parallel can be seen in the biblical record of Joseph in that both were recorded as superior to the wise men of their day and locale and both were instruments of God in working out his purpose for the world (Gen. 40—41; cf. Heaton, pp. 39, 122–123). The book of Job relates wisdom with the proper conduct of man in knowing and following God's purpose. Proverbs personifies wisdom. Ecclesiastes makes clear that wisdom resides in Israel and was identical with Yahweh's law. All these figures of wisdom are reflected in Daniel.

The book of Daniel is regularly interpreted in the light of the book of Revelation as apocalyptic literature. Martin Rist (IDB, A-D, pp. 157–161) explains that the basic patterns of apocalypticism are dualism and eschatology. He lists as secondary elements of apocalyptic literature visions, pseudonymity, messianism, angelology, animal symbolism, numerology, predicted woes, and astral influence. These are clearly seen in Daniel. For a study of apocalyptic see the works by Welch, Russell, and Rowley.

The predominant literature during the later historical setting of the book of Daniel is strikingly similar to Daniel. Particularly significant are some books in the Apocrypha. Tobit is the account of a man of the tribe of Naphtali who was taken into captivity in the eighth century B.C. by the Assyrian Shalmaneser. The book of Judith has a setting of the twelfth year of Nebuchadnezzar. The book of 1 Esdras begins in the time of Josiah (ca. 621 B.C.) and ends abruptly about 398 B.C. It contains a record of three young men as bodyguards (3:4) of King Darius.

The Apocrypha contains three additions to the book of Daniel which appear in many Greek and Latin versions. These additions were composed in the second and first centuries B.C. The Prayer of Azariah and the Song of the Three Young Men (68 verses) was inserted between Daniel 3:23 and 3:24. Susanna (64 verses) is listed as chapter 13 of Daniel in the LXX and the Vulgate. In Theodotion and many other versions, it is prefixed to the first chapter of Daniel. It relates how a young lad Daniel saved Susanna from being a victim of an evil plot by two evil elders. Bel and the Dragon (42 verses) is an addition to the twelfth chapter of Daniel in Greek manuscripts. In the Vulgate it is chapter 14. It contains a pair of stories about Daniel. The first story shows how Daniel in his service of God uncovered the evil hypocrisy of the priests of Bel. The second story shows Daniel's refusal to worship a dragon god. When Daniel slew the dragon god, the Babylonians angrily threw Daniel into the lions' den. He was fed by Habakkuk and on the seventh day was liberated. His enemies were thrown into the den and were devoured immediately.

Among the books of the Pseudepigrapha are works bearing names of ancient saints. Among them are the books of Enoch, the Testament of the Twelve Patriarchs, Apocalypse of Moses, the Testament of Job, the Martyrdom of Isaiah, and Psalms of Solomon. These Jewish writings were known and used beginning with the second century B.C. Their abundance establishes the validity in which pseudonymous literature was viewed.

VIII. Theological Position

1. God Is Sovereign

In both historical segments, God is shown as ultimately in control. The people are not acting like mechanical robots with no personal choice either as to their own actions and reactions or as to their effect on the existence or outcome of an event. God's sovereignty is ultimate, but it does not remove a man, such as Nebuchadnezzar, Daniel, or Antiochus, from making his own decisions. A tension exists between the choice of man and the determinism of God. God, in his sovereignty, did not determine each element of each minute event. He permitted events in the free choice of man, but he did not surrender his sovereign control. For God to permit man to exercise his own free choice does not mean that God does not possess or that he surrenders any of his sovereignty. He did not so much determine the course of history as to determine the climax of it. No event was out of the survey of God's power.

2. Determinism

Among all the possible avenues there was a determinism that evil could not go unpunished indefinitely. Man as a creature of freedom was given ample opportunity to show his faith both in innocence and in situations where he was backed against a wall. God's sovereign will involves man in the business of building character and fulfilling a mission as much as in breaking out of a crisis.

This faith or lack of it was a distinct factor in their fate. The determinism of the book of Daniel is not a determinism of each separate event, but a determined end was a fact of faith. Determinism must be seen in the light of the prophets who preceded. Apocalyptic was not antiprophetic. It is a developing stage of the concept that God was working out his plan in history. It was clear that God was about to break into the world in manifestation, judgment, and determinism.

3. View of Time

The author of the book of Daniel joined the end of all time and the end of the fourth segment of his specific world view. The book does not encompass all time from the beginning. The first half begins in the period beginning with Nebuchadnezzar and focuses on the fourth segment of the time, i.e., the second century B.C. For him the determined end of the fourth power marked the end of unfettered evil activity. The kingdom of God was to come in at the destruction of Antiochus Epiphanes. The inbreaking of God into the world, in which evil had become so rampant, was imminent. God was about to bring his intense presence with all its sovereignty to free the oppressed, to punish the evil, and to resurrect the wise departed.

The author's choice of the four-segmented world view was evidence that God was not only transcendent but also

imminent. In the common literary form of the second century B.C. the author could authentically revitalize the experiences of the ancient hero in different symbols.

A close examination of the various accounts clearly unveils the author's stance in time. In the early period the details and specific nuances are rather vague and obscure. The events during the time of Antiochus Epiphanes are very accurate and detailed. The events which were after Antiochus are again very general and lacking in sharp outline. The focus of his knowledge was in the second century B.C. The twentieth-century reader has a responsibility to interpret the literature of the second century B.C. as precisely that. It is not proper to posit either the language, literary style, or theological historical interpretation of the twentieth century A.D. as the criterion for understanding something written in an ancient period or milieu.

4. Angels

The view of angels was that of the interbiblical period. Michael and Gabriel are named in Daniel. No other book in the Old Testament names angels. Michael (10:13; 12:1) and Gabriel (8:16) are seen as also in Enoch (9:1; 10:11; 20:7; 40:9). Angels are much more than conveyors of messages. In the late literature they are seen as beings which control natural phenomena such as celestial bodies, winds, and seasons. Consequently, in Daniel they affect nations (10:19–21). There is an apparent hierarchy among angels. They act as intercessors and guardians of the righteous.

5. Resurrection

The clearest and most positive reference to resurrection in the Old Testament is in Daniel (12:1–2). It builds on the hope as seen in Isaiah 26, Job 19, and Psalm 17. Death was pictured as sleep (12:2) and thus resurrection as being awake, the natural and normal sequel. This doctrine arose during religious persecution and even martyrdom. It established an assurance to the wise and faithful that God would reward them. On the other hand, the evil ones would be given to everlasting contempt. The parallel figures (12:3) are those of the shining out of darkness and of continuous light in the figure of a star.

The fusing of the rewards and punishment in judgment with the doctrine of resurrection is clearly seen in the second and first centuries B.C. literature. In these books it is generally only the righteous who are to be resurrected.

IX. Practical Truths

Many similarities are apparent between the experiences of Daniel (*ca.* 605–520 B.C.) and those of the Jewish people (during the 2nd century). Such similarities do not indicate a necessary and cyclic repetition, but when seen in history they do show a definite pattern, though not an absolute duplication. In this fact lies one great value in the fuller knowledge of historical events. By the investigation of an event, including the factors involving its cause, situation in life, the conditioning factors, and related persons and events, it is possible to change outcomes and directions. With the knowledge that a particular set of circumstances caused or were related to a specific outcome, we can be warned about that possible outcome in a parallel and similar set of events. When we know what God did to one man or group of men in a specific situation, we can recognize how God will act in the same situation later. One of the deepest tragedies of human sinfulness is man's refusal or inability to learn from history.

1. There is an inevitable confrontation between righteousness and unrighteousness. Consequently, individuals, communities, and societies are going to find themselves at the point of decision as to whether to live by the principles of biblical faith or by any conflicting legal directions of a nonbelieving power.

2. It is inevitable that the church should suffer. Her nature, purpose, and divine commission bring her into conflict with selfishness, greed, and evil.

3. If man is going to be true to God and himself, he must not judge issues in the face of personal danger, risk, or advantage.

4. The men who fear God and serve him faithfully prove in the long run to be more useful to their day and generation than do those who renounce him for any form of godless culture.

5. As important as stubbornness may be in its place, there is a place for statesmanship in the life of an imperiled saint.

6. There is another alternative beyond obedience or rejection of the human laws. The obedience to God is always a viable imperative.

7. In any emergency God is able to make a way of escape for his people. That escape may or may not occur at the time a man desires it, but God has that escape possible in every situation—according to his wisdom and grace.

8. God does not abandon his people to pass through the fiery furnace or the lions' den alone.

9. The kingdom of God is certain to triumph over all attempts to destroy or eradicate it. Man must be faithful; God's timetable is not the same as man's desire.

10. It is possible for an evil man in a good place to ruin an entire empire.

11. God sends his angels to comfort, admonish, and instruct his distressed saints.

12. God cherishes his valiant saints. He will not permit even death to rob him of their presence in his kingdom.

The book of Daniel is a resource book of hope, faith, and fortitude for men in perilous times. The unifying theme of the book is encouragement of the Jews who had endured the Babylonian captivity yet were freed by the sovereignty of God. Now they were being persecuted mercilessly by the heathen Seleucid king. He was attempting to eradicate every trace of Yahweh worship. But God was about to bring judgment on evil. Therein lies the hope of the book of Daniel.

Outline

Introduction to the book (1:1–7)
I. Six records of conflict (1:8—6:28)

Selected Bibliography

BENTZEN, AAGE. *Daniel.* Handbuch zum Alten Testament. Tübingen: J. C. B. Mohr, 1952.

BRIGHT, JOHN. *A History of Israel.* Philadelphia: The Westminster Press, 1959.

CHARLES, R. H. *A Critical and Exegetical Commentary on the Book of Daniel.* Oxford: Clarendon Press, 1929.

GINSBERG, H. LOUIS. *Studies in Daniel.* New York: The Jewish Theological Seminary of America, 1948.

HEATON, E. W. *The Book of Daniel.* ("The Torch Bible Commentaries.") London: SCM Press Ltd., 1956.

JEFFERY, ARTHUR. "The Book of Daniel," *The Interpreter's Bible,* Vol. VI. Nashville: Abingdon Press, 1956.

MONTGOMERY, JAMES A. *A Critical and Exegetical Commentary on the Book of Daniel.* ("The International Critical Commentary.") New York: Charles Scribner's Sons, 1927.

Plöger, Otto. *Theocracy and Eschatology.* Richmond: John Knox Press, 1968.

Porteous, Norman W. *Daniel.* ("The Old Testament Library.") Philadelphia: The Westminster Press, 1965.

Rowley, H. H. *Darius the Mede and the Four World Empires in the Book of Daniel.* Cardiff: University of Wales Press Board, 1959.

———. *The Relevance of Apocalyptic.* Rev. ed. New York: Harper & Brothers, 1963.

Russell, D. S. The Method and Message of Jewish Apocalyptic. ("The Old Testament Library.") Philadelphia: The Westminster

Press, 1964.

Welch, Adam C. *Visions of the End.* London: James Clarke, 1958.

Whitcomb, John C., Jr. *Darius the Mede.* Grand Rapids: Wm. B. Eerdmans Publishing Co., 1959.

Wiseman, D. J. *Notes on Some Problems in the Book of Daniel.* Wheaton, Ill.: Tyndale House, 1965.

Young, Edward J. *The Prophecy of Daniel.* Grand Rapids: Wm. B. Eerdmans Publishing Co., 1957.

Commentary on the Text

The first paragraph of the text is of utmost importance in understanding the remainder of the material inasmuch as it sets the stage historically and theologically. This introduction shows the attempt by a heathen power to remove all evidences of the authority and worship of the Hebrew God.

Introduction to the Book (1:1–7)

¹ In the third year of the reign of Jehoiakim king of Judah, Nebuchadnezzar king of Babylon came to Jerusalem and besieged it. ² And the Lord gave Jehoiakim king of Judah into his hand, with some of the vessels of the house of God; and he brought them to the land of Shinar, to the house of his god, and placed the vessels in the treasury of his god. ³ Then the king commanded Ashpenaz, his chief eunuch, to bring some of the people of Israel, both of the royal family and of the nobility, ⁴ youths without blemish, handsome and skilful in all wisdom, endowed with knowledge, understanding learning, and competent to serve in the king's palace, and to teach them the letters and language of the Chaldeans. ⁵ The king assigned them a daily portion of the rich food which the king ate, and of the wine which he drank. They were to be educated for three years, and at the end of that time they were to stand before the king. ⁶ Among these were Daniel, Hananiah, Mishael, and Azariah of the tribe of Judah. ⁷ And the chief of the eunuchs gave them names: Daniel he called Belteshazzar, Hananiah he called Shadrach, Mishael he called Meshach, and Azariah he called Abednego.

Verse 1 has reference to the battle of Carchemish (May or June, 605 b.c.), in which Nebuchadnezzar defeated Pharaoh Neco II of Egypt (Jer. 46:2; 25:1; the fourth year of Jehoiakim). Jehoiakim reigned 609–598. However, the third year of Jehoiakim would have been in 606. Nebuchadnezzar was the crown prince and chief of the army. He did not become king until 604.

The problem of the specific chronology indicates that the author wrote at some time distant from the event. All the bits of information are individually true. They are put together in a general sense, in that the man who later became the king of Babylon did lay siege to Jerusalem.

The word Nebuchadnezzar is found with various spellings in the Old Testament. The correct spelling according to Babylonian records is Nebuchadrezzar (cf. Ezek. and 29 times in Jeremiah). Nebuchadnezzar, which is listed as incorrect by most scholars and lexicons, is found in 2 Kings, a few times in Jeremiah, 2 Chronicles, Ezra, and Nehemiah as well as the book of Daniel.

The name Nebuchadnezzar is spelled in 1:1 (Heb.) different from the other 31 occurrences in the book. An 'aleph is inserted in 1:1. Without the 'aleph it appears only in Daniel (31 times) and Ezra-Nehemiah (5 times). This variation clearly indicates that the superscription (1:1) is different from the body of the book.

Verse 2 took place eight years after the time mentioned in v. 1. Pharaoh Neco had carried Jehoahaz (a son of Josiah) into Egypt (2 Kings 23:31–34) and had made an older son of Josiah, Eliakim, king and changed his name to Jehoiakim. Judah was under Egyptian control. At the battle of Carchemish (605 B.C.), Nebuchadnezzar took control of Judah by defeating the Egyptians and Assyrians. Later Jehoiakim revolted against the Babylonians (2 Kings 24:1) but died (598) before Nebuchadnezzar inflicted any punishment upon him.

Jehoiachin, an 18-year-old son of Jehoiakim (2 Kings 24:8; called Jeconiah in 1 Chron. 3:16 or Coniah in Jer. 22:24), reigned only three months (2 Kings 24:8). He quickly surrendered to Nebuchadnezzar on March 16, 597 B.C. in the seventh year of Nebuchadnezzar (cf. Jer. 52:28).[1]

Since Jehoiachin reigned only three months and surrendered to Nebuchadnezzar, though the revolt was actually that of his father Jehoiakim, the writer did not expand the story with exacting details in order to meet the future standards of historical details. In a strict historical sense there is imprecision here.

The king of Judah was taken prisoner and carried into Babylonian captivity (2 Kings 24:12,15). Nebuchadnezzar also took *the vessels of the house of God* (2 Kings 24:13; 2 Chron. 36:7) . . . *to the land of Shinar.* Shinar is an ancient name for the territory which came to be known as Babylon (cf. Gen. 10:10; 11:2; Isa. 11:11). *The vessels of the house of God* were of great value as objects of precious metals which were used in the Temple services. Invading armies searched immediately for such objects. Attention is drawn to the attempt to divert these vessels from the worship of the God of the Hebrews into the treasure of the Babylonian god.

[1] Cf. Wiseman in D. Winton Thomas, *Documents from Old Testament Times* (New York: Harper & Row).

Verses 3–7 demonstrate additional elements hostile to true faith as applied to the captives. As some of the vessels were converted to the use of Marduk, the king commanded that *some of the people of Israel* be brought. Choice young men who had the potential for serving in *the king's palace* were selected to *stand before the king.* It is impossible to determine the age of the youths. The description was of young men who gave evidence of the best in appearance, intelligence, and ability.

Of the rich food which the king ate is literally "of *patbag* of the king." *Patbag* (only in 1:5,8,13,15,16; 11:26) is a Persian loan-word (Charles, p. 17) and means portion or delicacies.

Daniel appears first in v. 6 with the three friends (cf. Neh. 8:4; 10:2,23); for identifications of Daniel, see Int. The four young men of the tribe of Judah are Daniel, Hananiah, Mishael, and Azariah. How many other youths were selected cannot be ascertained. There were others for they were *among* (v. 6) those chosen.

The chief officer, Ashpenaz, changed the names of the four Jewish youths. Among reasons for changing one's name are: a change in status, commemoration of some specific event, or an honor to a person's king or god. When a king conquered an enemy, he could change the name of the vanquished to demonstrate his superiority. In the case of servants, the renaming would also provide a name easier to pronounce.

The specific reason for changing the names of these four youths is unclear. An element which is common to all names indicate a hostility to the faith of the Jews. The Hebrew names contain the name of the Hebrew God (either El or Yah-weh). The Babylonian names contained a title of Babylonian deity. Daniel was translated "El is my judge." Daniel's new name was Belteshazzar, which is an Akkadian word meaning "may he protect his life." Nebuchadnezzar *named Belteshazzar after the name of my god* (4:8). The author saw the name Bel in this title (note the similarity to Ba'al). Bel was the chief god of Babylon, Bel-Marduk (cf. Isa. 46:1).

Hananiah meant "Yahweh has been gracious." His new name was *Shadrach,* which can be translated "command of Aku." Aku is the moon-god. The author was intentionally indicating by these name changes that the Babylonian was attempting to eradicate the evidences of the Hebrew God and religion and to replace such with heathen deities and worship.

Mishael was translated "who is what El is." He was named *Meshach,* "who is what Aku is." Basically the only change in this name is the change of the Hebrew word El (God) to Aku (the Sumerian moon-god).

Azariah meant "Yahweh has helped." He was renamed *Abednego.* This name is a corruption of the words meaning "servant of Nebo." Nebo was the Babylonian god Nabu, son of Marduk (cf. Isa. 46:1).

The historical and theological setting is made clear in vv. 1–7. The vessels which were valuable to the Hebrews in the worship of their God were made treasures dedicated to a heathen deity. The youths who were choice as *without blemish, . . . skilful,* and *competent* were assigned to be reeducated into the *king's palace* (temple). Even the vestiges of Hebrew worship, represented by the names, were to be replaced by names of Babylonian gods. The conflict is in clear perspective.

I. Six Records of Conflict (1:8—6:28)

1. The Youths Resist Idolatry (1:8–21)

(1) Physical Appearance (1:8–16)

⁸ But Daniel resolved that he would not defile himself with the king's rich food, or with the wine which he drank; therefore he asked the chief of the eunuchs to allow him not to defile himself. ⁹ And God gave Daniel favor and compassion in the sight of the chief of the eunuchs; ¹⁰ and the chief of the eunuchs said to Daniel, "I fear lest my lord the king, who appointed your food and your drink, should see that you were in poorer condition than the youths who are of your own age. So you would endanger my head with the king." ¹¹ Then Daniel said to the steward whom the chief of the eunuchs had appointed over Daniel, Hananiah, Mishael, and Azariah; ¹² "Test your servants for ten days; let us be given vegeta-bles to eat and water to drink. ¹³ Then let our appearance and the appearance of the youths who eat the king's rich food be observed by you, and according to what you see deal with your servants." ¹⁴ So he hearkened to them in this matter, and tested them for ten days. ¹⁵ At the end of ten days it was seen that they were better in appearance and fatter in flesh than all the youths who ate the king's rich food. ¹⁶ So the steward took away their rich food and the wine they were to drink, and gave them vegetables.

Daniel resolved is literally "proceeded to put upon his heart." The heart is considered in Hebrew thought as the controlling organ in man. It is represented today as the will or inner man. Daniel's character is evidenced by an action from his heart.

Defile himself is from a word found in late Hebrew literature. *The king's rich food* was prepared for the royal table and would be the best in the kingdom. The wine was from the king's wine cellar and would be the best vintage. Both the food and wine would be tasty and exotic. The king's food would not have been prepared according to Jewish priestly rules and would include some animals which were regarded as unclean under Hebrew law (Deut. 14). These foods and wines "had doubtless been associated in some way with idolatrous worship" (Porteous, p. 29). Daniel considered the eating of such food as the breaking of the law and thus as uncleanness. Abstinence from unclean foods was by no means an isolated occurrence in Jewish literature. Tobit 1:10 f. reads, "all my brethren and my relatives ate the food of the Gentiles; but I kept myself from eating it, because I remembered God with all my heart" (cf. 1 Macc. 1:62 f.; Judith 10:5; Jubilees 22:16).

The chief of the eunuchs was Ashpenaz (v. 3). The term eunuch is used of a high Assyrian official (2 Kings 18:17, Rabsaris—chief eunuch) and a Babylonian officer (Jer. 39:3,13—the Rabsaris). Eunuch etymologically designated the harem attendant, but it came to be used of a high officer of state in Oriental courts. Potiphar is called "officer" (Gen. 37:36; 39:1), but literally is eunuch, and was married

(39:7). There is no evidence that Daniel and the three Jewish trainees were ever castrated as eunuchs.

God gave . . . favor. Daniel made his request of the eunuch on the basis of religious principles. The eunuch respected the request, but v. 10 indicates hesitation and no final answer. "Jewish romance always represents its heroes as on good terms with officialdom, cf. Esther, . . . the cases of Zerubbabel, Ezra and Nehemiah" (Montgomery, p. 131).

In poorer condition is used elsewhere in the sense of mental condition (Gen. 40:6— "were troubled" in the sense of fret against or be out of humor; Prov. 19:3—"rages"; 2 Chron. 26:19—"was angry"). In the concrete expression of Hebrew thought, the external appearance would indicate the internal condition. The physical features (v. 15) demonstrate health. The root **endanger** does not occur elsewhere in the Old Testament. It is an Aramaic word which emphasizes responsibility (LXX, "I will run the risk of my head").

Daniel turned to **the steward**. Evidently he had failed to gain a favorable answer to his request and therefore he turned to another official. The steward (*meltsar*) is Melzar in the KJV and occurs only in 1:11, 16. Friedrich Delitzsch related steward to the Assyrian "Massaru"—guardian.

The confusion of the translations and versions raises the question of the original text. The LXX continues the same relationship between Daniel and the prince of the eunuchs. But the Hebrew text suggests that Daniel turned to a subordinate official in order to gain his request even though v. 9 stated that Daniel had gained favor in the eyes of the chief eunuch. There may have been different traditions used by the Masoretic Text and the LXX. On the other hand, the LXX may have attempted to smooth out a difficult text.

Ten days are requested. This is a round number (cf. Young, p. 46; Charles, p. 21; 1:20; Amos 5:3). The most frequently used numbers in Daniel are four and seven. **Vegetables** (KJV and ASV—"pulse") are requested. The term (*zero'im*) is used only here. A similar word is used in v. 16 (*zero'nim*). The root consonants should be translated "something sown." No doubt these sown things included parched grain which was common in their diet.

Daniel staked his life on the outcome of the request. In a stated amount of time with a stated treatment and a stated result he had only his faith as support. The judgment would be in the hands of the steward (or the chief eunuch if the LXX is followed). **Deal with** could describe either favorable or unfavorable action according to the steward's decision. The result of the trial experience was that the youths attained a better physical appearance than the other youths who were in training. They were **fatter in flesh** (same terms as used of the fat cows in Pharaoh's dream, Gen. 41:2,18).

The faith which prompted Daniel to submit himself to the dangerous proposition was rewarded by God with an appearance which was evident to the objective official. Verse 16 indicates the victory for which Daniel struggled. The period of danger was comparatively brief. The wisdom of Daniel was acknowledged.

This does not mean that adherence to a principle will in every situation be rewarded by visible success. The victory in the contest is a major point in ascertaining the historical situation which dictated the selection of the events in the first six chapters of the book. The *Sitz im Leben* must be a time in which adherence to ceremonial laws and dietary principles was important. Such a story would bring definite encouragement in spite of danger.

One such period would be the time of persecution under Antiochus Epiphanes. Antiochus commanded that Jews should partake of "unlawful swine's flesh" (2 Macc. 7:1; 1 Macc. 1:47–63). The account of the martyrdom of the seven brothers and their mother in 2 Maccabees 7:1–42 illustrates the test under investigation here. "Many in Israel stood firm and were resolved in their hearts not to eat unclean

food. They chose to die rather than to be
defiled by food or to profane the holy
covenant" (1 Macc. 1:62–63). The story
of Daniel and the three friends is a parallel
experience which evokes courage and ad-
miration in the lives of inquisitive readers.

(2) Letters and Wisdom (1:17–21)

17 As for these four youths, God gave them
learning and skill in all letters and wisdom;
and Daniel had understanding in all visions
and dreams. 18 At the end of the time, when
the king had commanded that they should be
brought in, the chief of the eunuchs brought
them in before Nebuchadnezzar. 19 And the
king spoke with them, and among them all
none was found like Daniel, Hananiah, Mishael, and Azariah; therefore they stood before
the king. 20 And in every matter of wisdom and
understanding concerning which the king inquired of them, he found them ten times better
than all the magicians and enchanters that
were in all his kingdom. 21 And Daniel continued until the first year of King Cyrus.

Another facet of the Chaldeans (1:4) is
added. In matters of wisdom, Daniel demonstrated superiority. *At the end of the
time* is probably at the end of the three
years' training. The four young men, with
the many other youths, were taught *letters*
(literature and all kinds of books) and
wisdom. Wisdom is used in the sense of
systematized information and opinion. It
included science and superstition.

The four Hebrew youths are the only
trainees whose names are recorded here.
The fact that the Hebrew names are kept
instead of the Babylonian indicates that the
record is preserved by Hebrew tradition
rather than Babylonian court records. They
stood before the king is equivalent to receiving the commission or appointment in
the court to serve as personal attendants to
the king. The conclusion to this pericope is
v. 20. It is a sweeping generalization.
These young men were *found . . . ten
times better* (round figures) than *all* the
skilled men in *all* the kingdom in all matters. Verse 21 is comparable to a "happy
ending note."

The first year of King Cyrus as king over
Babylon was 538 B.C. which was slightly

less than 70 years after Daniel was taken
to Babylon. The meaning of *continued* is
not certain. It has been interpreted to
mean "in honor" (Ibn Ezra), "in the king's
gate or court" (Ewald, Hitzig), "in Babylon" (Michaelis), or "and beyond"
(Young). The comparison with 10:1 (in
the third year of Cyrus) would indicate
that these chapters were composed and
preserved as individual records and have
not been changed to correlate or remove
any apparent contradiction. Verse 20 had
indicated that they were better than all
the magicians in every place. Verse 21
indicated that this condition was true
through all the period under consideration.

2. The Realm of Wisdom (2:1–49)

(1) Chaldeans Unable to Interpret Dreams (2:1–11)

1 In the second year of the reign of Nebuchadnezzar, Nebuchadnezzar had dreams; and
his spirit was troubled, and his sleep left him.
2 Then the king commanded that the magicians, the enchanters, the sorcerers, and the
Chaldeans be summoned, to tell the king his
dreams. So they came in and stood before the
king. 3 And the king said to them, "I had a
dream, and my spirit is troubled to know the
dream." 4 Then the Chaldeans said to the king,
"O king, live for ever! Tell your servants the
dream, and we will show the interpretation."
5 The king answered the Chaldeans, "The word
from me is sure: if you do not make known to
me the dream and its interpretation, you shall
be torn limb from limb, and your houses shall
be laid in ruins. 6 But if you show the dream
and its interpretation, you shall receive from
me gifts and rewards and great honor. Therefore show me the dream and its interpretation."
7 They answered a second time, "Let the king
tell his servants the dream, and we will show
its interpretation." 8 The king answered, "I
know with certainty that you are trying to gain
time, because you see that the word from me is
sure 9 that if you do not make the dream
known to me, there is but one sentence for you.
You have agreed to speak lying and corrupt
words before me till the times change. Therefore tell me the dream, and I shall know that
you can show me its interpretations." 10 The
Chaldeans answered the king, "There is not a
man on earth who can meet the king's demand;
for no great and powerful king has asked such
a thing of any magician or enchanter or Chaldean. 11 The thing that the king asks is difficult,

and none can show it to the king except the gods, whose dwelling is not with flesh."

Each of the first six chapters has a didactic purpose. The record of events, dates, and names is the instrument whereby the teaching may be applied directly to the situation of the one using the record. The first chapter emphasized the personal victory of the Hebrews as they demonstrated fidelity to the laws of their God. Chapter 2 is of a more public and national nature. Bentzen interprets it as directed against polytheism. The wisdom of the Jews is shown to be superior to that of the other nations. This wisdom is not inherent in the Hebrew people but comes to them as a direct revelation of their God. God is the source of all their victories.

The position of Daniel in the interpretation of the dreams resembles in some respects the experiences of Joseph in Genesis 41. There are points of similarities both in content and expression, reflecting a common wisdom theme. In each story, a foreign king was troubled by a dream; the king's wise men were unable to interpret the dream; an inexperienced Hebrew lad proved capable of making the interpretation; the lad revealed that his God enabled him to do what the professional wise men could not; the youth is rewarded with high position.

Dreams were understood as a means by which God communicated with mankind (cf. Job 33:14–17). They had a spiritually inferior character. Dreams were, however, another element common with all of Israel's neighbors. Dreams could be so easily fabricated and were so unauthenticable that it was simple for insecure leaders and false prophets to misuse them. Jeremiah (23: 23–32; cf. Deut. 13:1–3; Zech. 10:2) warns against the misuse of dreams as the authenticating element in revelation.

The second year of . . . Nebuchadnezzar reverses the chronological sequence. Chapter 1 established a three-year period of training for the youths. The Hebrew text (KJV, ASV) opens chapter 2 with "and." The conjunction necessitates an explana-

tion of the chronology. Interpreters have attempted to bring these two accounts into agreement by various theories. Some call it a contradiction (Prince, Haller). Driver and Young defend the accuracy of the text by counting portions of years as full years. In this way, the three years of training could have been only portions of three years and thus could have ended during the second year of Nebuchadnezzar. With this reckoning, one system of time is found in chapter 1 but a different method in chapter 2.

Had dreams is literally dreamed dreams. But only one dream is recorded in chapter 2. The introduction to the dream account uses the plural "dreams" in distinction to the singular in the remainder of the chapter. Whether the plural indicates a recurrence of dreams, the recurrence of the same dream, or one dream with separate parts is uncertain.

Nebuchadnezzar summoned all of the dream interpreters. Four classes are named, indicating the entire fraternity. These titles are apparently used as synonymous terms. Four classes are noted five times (2:2,27; 4:7; 5:7,11). The presence of professional interpreters in the king's court was universal (Montgomery, pp. 142–143). Daniel is called the chief of the magicians (5:11).

Sorcerers is a Babylonian loan-word. Robertson-Smith suggests that this class of omen seekers are ones who cut and prepare herbs.[2] Prince relates the term to a well-known Babylonian root word "to bewitch," and translates sorcerers to be "reciters of incantations" (Young, p. 57; Charles, p. 27).

Chaldeans does not refer here to a nationality. It is a technical word for wise man. Originally, it had an ethnic sense but developed to refer to a class of practitioners in magic and esoteric wisdom. All four classes are called "wise men of Babylon" (2:12).

The wise men ask "in Aramaic" (Marg.) language that he tell them the dream. The

2 *Journ. Phil.* XIV, 125–126.

RSV omits the term "in Aramaic" from the text but adds in a footnote that the text from that point to the end of chapter 7 is in the Aramaic language (KJV has "in Syriac").

The king tells *the Chaldeans. The word from me is sure.* The KJV translates it, "The thing is gone from me." The king had not forgotten the dream. The word means sure or certain. He had locked the dream within himself and would not tell them. If the wise men could learn the dream they could secure an interpretation from their dream books. The problem of proving their skill by revealing the dream itself was unique in the experience of professional wise men. This dream was so important to the king's peace of mind that he dared not risk missing the message from the gods.

The message of the king to the Chaldeans (v. 3) is recorded in Hebrew. The conversation between the king and the Chaldeans was in Aramaic.

Aramaic supplanted Akkadian as the *lingua franca* of Mesopotamia by the end of the eighth century B.C. Aramaic was the main language of the people of Palestine in the second century B.C. During this period the language of religion was Hebrew. The erroneous designation of biblical Aramaic as Chaldean continued until the latter part of the nineteenth century A.D. The materials of Daniel which are in Hebrew were preserved within the religious context, and those in Aramaic have been preserved in and by the vernacular use.

Laid in ruins (v. 5) reads the word *newali* as an Akkadian loan-word. The KJV relates the word to the Targum and translates it "made a dunghill." Since the historical setting of the book is Mesopotamian, the RSV rendering is preferred. There is no question that the Eastern world was often subjected to such ruthless and cruel treatment by powerful and barbarous despots (Montgomery, p. 146; Young, p. 60). The bodies of the frustrated wise men were to be torn *limb from limb* and their houses destroyed if both the dream and the interpretation were not related.

The king accuses the wise men of stalling *till the times change* (v. 9). The decree of the king made judgment upon them inevitable. The wise men knew they did not have any connection with the source of revelation.

This story involving a warning dream of a king is one of many. Nabonidus was the last great king of Babylon and reigned 556–539 B.C. Dreams which terrified him are recounted in the Istanbul Stele (Pritchard, pp. 308 ff.). The controversy between Nebuchadnezzar and the wise men is very reminiscent of the quarrel which Nabonidus had with the priests of Babylon. That quarrel was so bitter that the priests of Nabonidus were able to transfer their loyalties readily to Cyrus the conqueror of Babylon.

It has been suggested that the actual dream is a record from Nabonidus which has been transferred in later time to the most famous of all the kings of Babylon. The main record of the dream refers to the dreamer as "the king" or "king" forty times. The name Nebuchadnezzar actually appears only four times (vv. 1,28,46). These occurrences may have been inserted as scribal notes in later transmission.

(2) Death Decree Includes Daniel (2:12–16)

12 Because of this the king was angry and very furious, and commanded that all the wise men of Babylon be destroyed. 13 So the decree went forth that the wise men were to be slain, and they sought Daniel and his companions, to slay them. 14 Then Daniel replied with prudence and discretion to Arioch, the captain of the king's guard, who had gone out to slay the wise men of Babylon; 15 he said to Arioch, the king's captain, "Why is the decree of the king so severe?" Then Arioch made the matter known to Daniel. 16 And Daniel went in and besought the king to appoint him a time, that he might show to the king the interpretation.

Daniel and his companions were among the wise men who *were to be slain.* There is no indication that Daniel had been inaugurated into the guild of wise men beyond his having been trained for services in the king's court. Some suggest that Daniel was in training to become a heathen priest and to perform religious duties. But this reads too much into the text. The general terms used previously for wise men could include the wise men and those in training as well.

Daniel answered with *prudence and discretion* (cf. Prov. 26:16*b*). He displayed good sense, a characteristic of Hebrew heroes, by taking the matter to *Arioch.* Arioch is an ancient Babylonian name (cf. Gen. 14:1). It is a transliteration of *Eriaku,* servant of Aku (the moon-god). Arioch is *the captain of the king's guard* (v. 14, lit., chief of the slaughterers, i.e., of animals for food). This is the same title held by Potiphar (Gen. 37:36; 39:1).

(3) Mystery Revealed to Daniel (2:17–23)

¹⁷ Then Daniel went to his house and made the matter known to Hananiah, Mishael, and Azariah, his companions, ¹⁸ and told them to seek mercy of the God of heaven concerning this mystery, so that Daniel and his companions might not perish with the rest of the wise men of Babylon. ¹⁹ Then the mystery was revealed to Daniel in a vision of the night. Then Daniel blessed the God of heaven. ²⁰ Daniel said:

"Blessed be the name of God for ever and ever,
  to whom belong wisdom and might.
²¹ He changes times and seasons;
  he removes kings and sets up kings;
he gives wisdom to the wise
  and knowledge to those who have understanding;
²² he reveals deep and mysterious things;
  he knows what is in the darkness,
  and the light dwells with him.
²³ To thee, O God of my fathers,
  I give thanks and praise,
for thou hast given me wisdom and strength,
  and hast now made known to me what we asked of thee,
  for thou hast made known to us the king's matter."

Daniel asks for an appointment in order to reveal the interpretation. It could appear that Daniel was egotistical and brash. Particularly so in light of the fact that he asks his companions *to seek mercy of the God of*

heaven concerning this mystery. Since the story is told by one who knew the outcome this fact is only a skill of the ancient preserver of history.

Daniel confers with his three companions (their Hebrew names are preserved in v. 17). To *seek mercy* is a synonym of pray. The LXX adds the idea of fasting. Faith is a central element in the practice of Daniel and his three friends. They seek the mercy of the *God of heaven.* The term was used in Genesis 24:7 and "was revived after the Exile, when it became the title by which the Persian government recognized the Jewish God" (Montgomery, p. 158; cf. Ezra, Nehemiah, Psalms, Tobit, 1 Enoch).

The term *mystery* is a Persian loan-word meaning secret. Nebuchadnezzar was a Babylonian. Persia's influence and authority became evident among the Hebrews only with and after Cyrus, who became king of Persia about 547 B.C. and became ruler over Babylon in 538. The term secret attains special significance in the New Testament and the Qumran records. It is one of the many evidences of apocalyptic writings.

By prayer Daniel expresses his firm faith that God can reveal the mystery through His wisdom. Verses 20–23 are a wisdom hymn. The verse is in free liturgical style. The wisdom and power of God are the themes of his praise and gratitude for the uncovering of the secret *in a vision of the night.* This does not mean necessarily that it was a dream for a vision could come to the wise man when awake.

Verse 20 contains phrases which are similar to Psalm 41:14 (*for ever and ever*) and Job 12:13 (*wisdom and might*). The name of God is equivalent to the being of God himself. The word *name* means sign or designation. Thus, it embodies reputation, fame, and character, especially as embodied in his dealings with man.

Verse 21*a* and *b* are references to the might of God and vv. 21*c*–22 refer to his wisdom. *He changes times and seasons.* God is contrasted with the little horn (7:25) who "shall think to change the times and the law." Antiochus sought to take the place of God in image and fact but could not effect the change of times or law. Verse 21 makes the contrast more vivid in exalting the one who *removes kings and sets up kings.* Even before the dream of the king is told, Daniel expresses his dependence upon the God of time, seasons, wisdom, and strength. Note the careful intermixture of references to Daniel himself and the three friends (cf. v. 23, *known to me . . . to us*).

Verse 16 has Daniel before the king, while vv. 24–25 have him before Arioch. E. W. Heaton (p. 128) suggests that vv. 14–23 "develop the theme of wisdom beyond the immediate needs of the story." It is true that the wisdom emphasis reveals the type of literature and the emphasis of the writer. But it is not necessarily an inordinate emphasis.

(4) The Dream Told (2:24–35)

24 Therefore Daniel went in to Arioch, whom the king had appointed to destroy the wise men of Babylon; he went and said thus to him, "Do not destroy the wise men of Babylon; bring me in before the king, and I will show the king the interpretation." 25 Then Arioch brought in Daniel before the king in haste, and said thus to him: "I have found among the exiles from Judah a man who can make known to the king the interpretation." 26 The king said to Daniel, whose name was Belteshazzar, "Are you able to make known to me the dream that I have seen and its interpretation?" 27 Daniel answered the king, "No wise men, enchanters, magicians, or astrologers can show to the king the mystery which the king has asked, 28 but there is a God in heaven who reveals mysteries, and he has made known to King Nebuchadnezzar what will be in the latter days. Your dream and the visions of your head as you lay in bed are these: 29 To you, O king, as you lay in bed came thoughts of what would be hereafter, and he who reveals mysteries made known to you what is to be. 30 But as for me, not because of any wisdom that I have more than all the living has this mystery been revealed to me, but in order that the interpretation may be made known to the king, and that you may know the thoughts of your mind. 31 "You saw, O king, and behold, a great image. This image, mighty and of exceeding brightness, stood before you, and its appear-

ance was frightening. 32 The head of this image was of fine gold, its breast and arms of silver, its belly and thighs of bronze, 33 its legs of iron, its feet partly of iron and partly of clay. 34 As you looked, a stone was cut out by no human hand, and it smote the image on its feet of iron and clay, and broke them in pieces; 35 then the iron, the clay, the bronze, the silver, and the gold, all together were broken in pieces, and became like the chaff of the summer threshing floors; and the wind carried them away, so that not a trace of them could be found. But the stone that struck the image became a great mountain and filled the whole earth.

Daniel contacts Arioch (v. 24) and asks for an audience with the king for the expressed purpose of revealing the dream and the interpretation. Arioch seizes the opportunity of escaping the undesirable duty of slaying all of the wise men. He brings Daniel *before the king in haste.* Arioch tells the king that one from *among the exiles from Judah* will tell him the interpretation. The low estate of Daniel is contrasted to the authoritative position of the king.

Both the Hebrew and Babylonian names of Daniel are used. The writer records *Daniel, whose name was Belteshazzar* as a reminder of the theme, "the God of the Hebrews *vs.* the Babylonian gods."

Arioch had drawn the king's attention to *a man,* but Daniel quickly exalts his God. No man, regardless of his office or talents, could unfold the *mystery.* But *there is a God in heaven who reveals.* Man cannot reveal; he can only relate. It is God only who can reveal. The two main characters of the story now are Daniel and Nebuchadnezzar (cf. v. 29, *To you, O King;* v. 30, *But as for me*). What a contrast is made between these two men! Nebuchadnezzar had received a message from God of *what will be in the latter days* but could not comprehend. It was the lowly exile by the name of Daniel who was used by God to make known the revelation, not *because of any wisdom* that he possessed.

In the latter days is a phrase occurring only 14 times in the Old Testament. Variations of it appear as "the time of the end" (12:4) or "the end" (7:26). Different meanings are given to this term in different contexts. Each occurrence, however, has an eschatological impact. It refers to the end of one segment of history, whether the final one or not. The specific definition of time must be ascertained from each context itself. It refers here to the closing days of history when God will bring in his kingdom. Nebuchadnezzar is told that events are rushing toward decisive confrontations.

The order of the phrase "King Nebuchadnezzar" (v. 28) shows this context to be unquestionably late. The classical order would read "Nebuchadnezzar the king." Fifth-century Aramaic papyri and Ezra have the classical order. The appearance in Daniel is the earliest occurrence of this order.

Visions of *your head* (v. 28) shows a non-Hebraic influence (cf. 4:5,10,13; 7: 1,15 for other biblical occurrences). The Hebrew expression would be "your heart" (v. 30, *your mind*).

The dream was of *a great image* (v. 31). The image was not pictured as an idol. This statue may have had the huge statues of Babylonian art or even the famous Egyptian colossi as its prototype. The huge image had four parts, each with distinct composition. The descending position matches the degrading value of the metals, i.e., gold, silver, bronze, and the mixture of iron and clay.

The number four is very prominent throughout this book. There were four Hebrew children, four metals representing four kingdoms, four classes of wise men, etc. The number is more symbolic than historic. These four kingdoms are connected vitally to the coming kingdom of God and thus this view of history is eschatological.

The purest of metals is the head. The weakest part of the image is that of the lower legs and feet. The meaning of *clay* is difficult to determine. The word usually refers to pottery objects both complete and fragmentary. So Montgomery (pp. 167, 189) suggests that the leg work was potsherds, tile work, or ceramic. Bel and the Dragon, in the Apocrypha is an addition

in the Greek manuscripts of Daniel at the close of chapter 12. It explains (v. 7) "clay inside and brass outside." In such construction, the weakness would not be evident to the naked eye since the internal framework would not be known. Much use of tile work was made in ancient Babylonian architecture. It is apparent that the lower legs, i.e., the last kingdom of the four, had a greatly enhanced decoration without structural strength. Iron itself is stronger than the other metals and so any appearance of strength was illusory.

The weakness was not apparent until a stone, usually more crushable than metal, smote the image. All elements are involved in the cataclysm and are *broken in pieces*.

The writer's historical view involved all four kingdoms and the "stone." The image was of humanly shaped materials, but the stone was *cut out by no human hand* (v. 34). The stone increased *and filled the whole earth*. The humanly shaped kingdoms are displaced by the "earthly type of eternity" (Montgomery, p. 191).

(5) *The Interpretation* (2:36-45)

36 "This was the dream; now we will tell the king its interpretation. 37 You, O king, the king of kings, to whom the God of heaven has given the kingdom, the power, and the might, and the glory, 38 and into whose hand he has given, wherever they dwell, the sons of men, the beasts of the field, and the birds of the air, making you rule over them all—you are the head of gold. 39 After you shall arise another kingdom inferior to you, and yet a third kingdom of bronze, which shall rule over all the earth. 40 And there shall be a fourth kingdom, strong as iron, because iron breaks to pieces and shatters all things; and like iron which crushes, it shall break and crush all these. 41 And as you saw the feet and toes partly of potter's clay and partly of iron, it shall be a divided kingdom; but some of the firmness of iron shall be in it, just as you saw iron mixed with the miry clay. 42 And as the toes of the feet were partly iron and partly clay, so the kingdom shall be partly strong and partly brittle. 43 As you saw the iron mixed with miry clay, so they will mix with one another in marriage, but they will not hold together, just as iron does not mix with clay. 44 And in the days of those kings the God of heaven will set up a kingdom which shall never be destroyed,

nor shall its sovereignty be left to another people. It shall break in pieces all these kingdoms and bring them to an end, and it shall stand for ever; [45] just as you saw that a stone was cut from a mountain by no human hand, and that it broke in pieces the iron, the bronze, the clay, the silver, and the gold. A great God has made known to the king what shall be hereafter. The dream is certain, and its interpretation sure."

When Daniel said *we will tell the king its interpretation,* he involved the three other Hebrew youths as he involved them in the prayer (2:17–18). In his prayer of gratitude he acknowledged that God had made the king's matter known to them (2:23). The "we" may be a plural of majesty or authority. Montgomery (p. 171) and Young (p. 72) say that the use of "we" is with humility (cf. 1 Cor. 1:6).

Daniel addresses Nebuchadnezzar as *the king of kings* (the Persian title; cf. Ezra 7:12; Ezek. 26:7) instead of "the great king" which was the accustomed Assyrian title (cf. Isa. 36:4).

The effusive compliments (*to whom . . . over them all*) form a parenthesis in vv. 37–38. They are taken by Heaton (p. 131) and Bentzen (Porteous, p. 48) to reflect elements of the Babylonian New Year Festival. The king in Babylon was reenthroned annually as God's representative, at which time the Creation Epic was recited (Heaton, pp. 168–172). The king is told that he was *given* the authority and that the animals had been *given* into his hand. In the Babylonian festival the god Marduk was so praised. Nebuchadnezzar's sovereignty is only a derived one, and therefore it could be removed by the same one who had given it to him.

The mention of human beings, the wild animals, and the birds gives an absoluteness to the extent of Nebuchadnezzar's power. The LXX adds also "and the fishes of the sea."

The four metals of the image are clearly interpeted as kingdoms. Nebuchadnezzar is identified as *the head of gold* (v. 38). In Hebrew thought there is not the distinction between king and kingdom (cf. Isa.

7:1–9). There is no question as to the identification of regimes instead of persons. It was not Nebuchadnezzar as a person but rather as the Babylonian era. The second and third kingdoms are relatively unimportant to the writer, being described in a single verse. They serve mainly as a historical connection between the head of gold and the fourth kingdom. The writer began his segment of history with the exile (under Nebuchadnezzar). The central focus of his attention is in the fourth kingdom.

The second kingdom was named as *inferior* (lit., lower than thou) to Nebuchadnezzar. The measure or area of inferiority is not suggested. No identification is made of the second kingdom.

The third kingdom is said to *rule over all the earth* (the word *inferior* and the word *earth* have the same consonants). Ezra 1:2 says that "all the kingdoms of the earth" had been given to "Cyrus king of Persia." The identification of the second and third kingdoms is closely related to that of the fourth kingdom. The interest of the writer of Daniel lies clearly in the fourth kingdom (see chs. 7 and 8).

This fourth kingdom was described as *strong as iron* (v. 40). Later the empire was a *divided kingdom,* i.e., at first iron and then iron mixed with clay. This fact has led many to see the Greek kingdom as divided after the death of Alexander. As far as Palestine was concerned there were two main stems known as the Seleucids and the Ptolemies (see ch. 11).

The mixture of iron and clay is further described as *they will mix with one another in marriage* (v. 43, lit., by the seed of man). Daniel 11:6,17 refer to a marriage union between the Ptolemies and the Seleucids as temporary: but *they will not hold together* (2:43). Montgomery (p.190) takes the reference to marriage in a more general sense. Alexander the Great took a Persian wife and encouraged his soldiers to do so also. This amalgamation of racial stock was repulsive to the Jews.

A view which has been widely argued is

that the fourth kingdom is the Roman Empire. It was first advanced in the apocryphal book 2 Esdras. The author clearly states that it is a view different from the view of Daniel. "But it was not explained to him as I now explain or have explained it to you" (2 Esdras 12:12). This apocryphal interpretation came after the rise and expansion of the Roman Empire.

The time of the writer (ch. 2) was centered in the Ptolemy-Seleucid period. The powerful and dreaded ruler was Antiochus Epiphanes. The kingdom which destroyed the four kingdoms was interpreted as an eternal and divine one. Care must be exercised in the interpretation of the kingdom of God.

One must come to grips with the problem as to whether the eschatology of chapter 2 is referring exclusively to the absolutely final days of time or to the final segment of that established period. There is a sense in which the imminent future is directly related to the end. The principle of this revelation is valid in all successive generations. Through the passing of time and of powers, does the truth within the interpretation of the fourth kingdom (as applied to the twentieth century) move from Greece to Rome and to other forms of dominion? *In the days of those kings* (v. 44) must refer to the kings involved in the marriage bonds (cf. the king of the south and of the king of the north in 11:5–6,14–15). This interpretation is consistent in the various chapters.

However, there are other views which have been proposed. It may be that "those kings" refer to the kings of all four kingdoms (see Montgomery, pp. 177–178; Young, p. 78) with no distinctions necessarily drawn as to the identification of which kingdoms are intended. As the interest of the writer moved from the time of the great exile under Nebuchadnezzar to his own time, foreign domination may be viewed as a unit (cf. vv. 44–45).

The great stone was *cut from a mountian by no human hand* (v. 45). This contrasts the kingdom of God with the kingdom of

men. This kingdom destroys the previously noted kingdoms. This kingdom *shall stand for ever* (v. 44). The emphasis is seen in the comparison of the human and the divine; temporal and eternal; the image and the stone. Barr sees that the "stone is the eschatological kingdom of God, and breaks the succession of foreign dominations which has lasted since the exile began."[3]

(6) Conclusion (2:46–49)

46 Then King Nebuchadnezzar **fell upon his face, and did homage to Daniel, and commanded that an offering and incense be offered up to him.** 47 The king said to Daniel, **"Truly, your God is God of gods and Lord of kings, and a revealer of mysteries, for you have been able to reveal this mystery."** 48 Then the king gave Daniel high honors and many great gifts, and made him ruler over the whole province of Babylon, and chief prefect over all the wise men of Babylon. 49 Daniel made request of the king, and he appointed Shadrach, Meshach, and Abednego over the affairs of the province of Babylon; but Daniel remained at the king's court.

Each segment ends in the pattern of a victorious note (cf. 3:30; 5:29; 6:28). The dream, interpretation, and revelation cause a change in Nebuchadnezzar. He ordered an offering to be made to Daniel; proclaimed that Daniel's God was supreme; honored Daniel with high position and gifts; and granted Daniel's request to give the three Hebrew men high positions. A record such as this would encourage an oppressed people to look hopefully for God to change the oppressor.

3. Test of Fidelity (3:1–30)

(1) King Erects the Image (3:1–7)

1 King Nebuchadnezzar made an image of gold, whose height was sixty cubits and its breadth six cubits. He set it up on the plain of Dura, in the province of Babylon. 2 Then King Nebuchadnezzar sent to assemble the satraps, the prefects, and the governors, the counselors, the treasurers, the justices, the magistrates, and all the officials of the provinces to come to the dedication of the image which King Nebuchad-

3 Matthew Black and H. H. Rowley, *Peake's Commentary on the Bible* (Camden, N. J.: Thomas Nelson and Sons, 1962), p. 594.

nezzar had set up. ³ Then the satraps, the prefects, and the governors, the counselors, the treasurers, the justices, the magistrates, and all the officials of the provinces, were assembled for the dedication of the image that King Nebuchadnezzar had set up; and they stood before the image that Nebuchadnezzar had set up. ⁴ And the herald proclaimed aloud, "You are commanded, O peoples, nations, and languages, ⁵ that when you hear the sound of the horn, pipe, lyre, trigon, harp, bagpipe, and every kind of music, you are to fall down and worship the golden image that King Nebuchadnezzar has set up; ⁶ and whoever does not fall down and worship shall immediately be cast into a burning fiery furnace." ⁷ Therefore, as soon as all the peoples heard the sound of the horn, pipe, lyre, trigon, harp, bagpipe, and every kind of music, all the peoples, nations, and languages fell down and worshiped the golden image which King Nebuchadnezzar had set up.

Mighty conquering rulers often erected colossal images to mark special occasions. The images were at times of the king himself or at other times of the deity who had led the king and his army to victory. The dream (ch. 2) may have prompted Nebuchadnezzar to create this huge image. The LXX adds to the superscription of this chapter, "in the eighteenth year of his reign" (587 B.C.) when his forces destroyed Jerusalem. The image was approximately 90 feet high and 9 feet wide (*sixty* and *six* cubits). These dimensions emphasize the immensity and grandeur of the erected image. This would be important if the image was to be of the god who was victor. Verse 12 relates the gods with the worship of *the golden image*. Probably it was not of solid gold but a wooden statue with gold overlay. Herodotus (i, 183) records two huge statues of gold in Babylon, one of Zeus and another of a man in the time of Cyrus. No other record of such an image being erected by Nebuchadnezzar exists. There is, however, a record that Nabonidus erected a statue of the moon god Sin in the temple of Ehulhul.

Antiochus Epiphanes erected a huge image at Daphne (Jeffery, p. 395; Porteous, p. 57). The narration about the Nebuchadnezzar image would no doubt bring the Antiochus image into clear focus in the minds of the second century B.C. Jews. The figure of Nebuchadnezzar loomed large in the memory of the Jews for he sought to "destroy all the gods of the land so that all nations should worship Nebuchadnezzar only, and all their tongues and tribes should call upon him as god" (Judith 3:8).

Dura was not an uncommon name. There was a Dura near the Euphrates River, but would this be *in the province of Babylon?* It could be near Hillah at Tolul Dura (mounds of Dura) as suggested by Oppert. For the dedication (hanukkah) ceremony the king assembled all the officials of his government. *Satraps* is a Persian title (cf. Ezra 8:36; Esther 3:12; 8:9; 9:3) meaning "protectors of the realm." As Persian it would be after Nebuchadnezzar. The empire was first divided into satraps by Darius I (522–486 B.C.).

The *governors* were "lord of a district," (a loan-word from Assyrian). *Counselors* (a Persian loan-word) occurs in the Old Testament only in vv. 2 and 3. It may be a military position.

Treasurers is not known from other sources (only in vv. 2 and 3). It may be another spelling of treasurer (as in Ezra 7:21). Since the LXX has only seven titles in this verse and the Aramaic has eight, it has been proposed that this word should be omitted as an example of dittography. The word *justices* is very similar (*gdbry'*, treasurer; *dtbry'*, justice). It means judge or law-bearer and is not found elsewhere in the Old Testament.

Magistrates is "sheriffs" in the KJV. In the Old Testament it is found only here and v. 3. This entire list must be the list of officials in their rank as invited to the "hanukkah" ceremony. The list is repeated in v. 3 of the Aramaic, but the LXX omits the second list.

All the officials *stood before the image.* The *herald* addressed them, *O peoples, nations, and languages* (cf. 3:7,29; 4:1; 5:19; 6:25; 7:14). In a kingdom which spread "from India to Ethiopia," there would be many nationalities and languages.

The author of Daniel is fond of long lists. The horn and the pipe are of Semitic origin. The lyre, harp, and bagpipe are Greek in origin. The *trigon* (*sabbeka'*, Greek *sambuke*) is of Oriental origin and is a triangular instrument of four strings with high notes. It was used particularly for music at banquets.[4]

The *harp* is the word psaltery, a triangular shaped stringed instrument. The *bagpipe* (*sumponyah*, cf. Greek word symphony) is "dulcimer" in the KJV. It is omitted in the list of v. 7. The use of this word as a musical instrument is a late Greek usage (Charles, p. 64). There is no record of the word being used to refer to an instrument prior to Polybius (204–122 B.C.) who cites the "symphony" as the favorite instrument of Antiochus Epiphanes (xxvi, 10 and xxxi, 4).

If this passage were used to urge the fidelity of believers during the threats of Antiochus, the use of the name symphony would have a direct application.

Kind is a loan-word from Persia. At the sound of music *all the peoples, nations, and languages fell down* (v. 7). The punishment for failing to fall down before the image was to be cast *into a burning fiery furnace*. The punishment was immediate, i.e., in a small period of time (later the term came to mean hour).

The *furnace* was a "beehive kiln" fed through a perpendicular shaft from the top. There was a side opening near the bottom for extracting the fused lime.

This type of punishment is well attested among the records of the Near East (cf. Gen. 38:24; Lev. 21:9; Josh. 7:15,25; Jer. 29:22). It can be documented from the Code of Hammurabi (25,110,157). It was used by Cyrus, the Scythians, and the Egyptians. For reference to burning with fire in the time of Antiochus see 2 Maccabees 7:3 ff. and 4 Maccabees 18:20 (cf. Jubilees 20:4; 30:7; 41:19,25).

(2) Accusation of the Chaldeans (3:8–12)

8 Therefore at that time certain Chaldeans came forward and maliciously accused the

4 A. Sendry, *Music in Ancient Israel.*

Jews. 9 They said to King Nebuchadnezzar, "O king, live for ever! 10 You, O king, have made a decree, that every man who hears the sound of the horn, pipe, lyre, trigon, harp, bagpipe, and every kind of music, shall fall down and worship the golden image; 11 and whoever does not fall down and worship shall be cast into a burning fiery furnace. 12 There are certain Jews whom you have appointed over the affairs of the province of Babylon: Shadrach, Meshach, and Abednego. These men, O king, pay no heed to you; they do not serve your gods or worship the golden image which you have set up."

They *maliciously accused* is literally "ate their pieces." The presence of the informer at the court is characteristic of Oriental stories. The repetition of the king's full statement word for word is a part of the literary style. The accusation was true since the Hebrews had not fallen down before the image. The Jews were singled out as Shadrach, Meshach, and Abednego.

These three had been exalted by the king. But when an order is given which would cause them to violate their religion they refuse to comply. The fidelity which demonstrated their differences from the other youths (ch. 1) is under another test.

(3) Confrontation with the King (3:13–15)

13 Then Nebuchadnezzar in furious rage commanded that Shadrach, Meshach, and Abednego be brought. Then they brought these men before the king. 14 Nebuchadnezzar said to them, "Is it true, O Shadrach, Meshach, and Abednego, that you do not serve my gods or worship the golden image which I have set up? 15 Now if you are ready when you hear the sound of the horn, pipe, lyre, trigon, harp, bagpipe, and every kind of music, to fall down and worship the image which I have made, well and good; but if you do not worship, you shall immediately be cast into a burning fiery furnace; and who is the god that will deliver you out of my hands?"

Nebuchadnezzar reacted to the news *in furious rage* (lit., in rage and burning anger). He did not act without personal investigation. He gave them an opportunity to accede to his command. A characteristic of the martyr legends is the permission for participants to make a statement or confession in person.

Who is the god (v. 15) is actually "what kind of a god can deliver you out of my hand?" The king in his wrath flaunts his power (cf. Sennacherib and Rabshakeh in Isa. 36:19–20; 37:11–12). This challenge has a direct bearing upon the sphere in which the image is to be interpreted. The relation of the king and his god is very close. Whether the image is of the king or of the god, the god was involved.

(4) The Hebrews' Answer (3:16–18)

16 Shadrach, Meshach, and Abednego answered the king, "O Nebuchadnezzar, we have no need to answer you in this matter. 17 If it be so, our God whom we serve is able to deliver us from the burning fiery furnace; and he will deliver us out of your hand, O king. 18 But if not, be it known to you, O king, that we will not serve your gods or worship the golden image which you have set up."

The three Hebrews *have no need to answer.* This type of answer is typical of the martyr stories. There was no reason for them to answer a man for God is now involved. *In this matter* is literally "a word concerning this." Human words would only confuse the issue. Divine actions are needed. The young men did not act in arrogance but in vitality of faith. They were not positive that God would deliver them from punishment, but they were sure that they would continue to refuse to bow down to the image. They had no doubt that their God could deliver them but they did not know that he would. The answer of the three youths is similar to that of the seven brothers in 2 Maccabees 7. They compared the God whom they served to the god of the king.

(5) The Three Cast into the Furnace (3:19–23)

19 Then Nebuchadnezzar was full of fury, and the expression of his face was changed against Shadrach, Meshach, and Abednego. He ordered the furnace heated seven times more than it was wont to be heated. 20 And he ordered certain mighty men of his army to bind Shadrach, Meshach, and Abednego, and to cast them into the burning fiery furnace. 21 Then these men were bound in their mantles, their tunics, their hats, and their other gar-ments, and they were cast into the burning fiery furnace. 22 Because the king's order was strict and the furnace very hot, the flame of the fire slew those men who took up Shadrach, Meshach, and Abednego. 23 And these three men, Shadrach, Meshach, and Abednego, fell bound into the burning fiery furnace.

The king had agreed in condescension and generosity to meet the three accused face to face. When his magnanimous gesture was so flatly repulsed, he became furious. *The expression of his face* (the image of his face) *was changed.* His face was distorted. He reacted in fury and *ordered the furnace heated seven times more . . .* The number is not to be taken literally. Seven is often the picture of completeness. He commanded that the furnace be heated more than necessary.

The men were bound in their clothes. The meaning of the terms is not certain. Customarily the condemned would be stripped of clothing. The inclusion of the garments heightens the miracle. The three men had attended the ceremony in their official robes. The king may have been showing the young men that they could not hide behind his official appointment.

The orders of the king were so *strict* ("severe" in 2:15). It means in this case was overbearing or exaggerated. Since the three condemned men were bound securely in their clothes they were carried bodily to the top edge of the furnace. The fuel was so heaped up that the flames were spilling over on every side. The flames spread in such a way that the *mighty men,* ordered to cast them into the furnace, were burned to death. A characteristic of the martyr legends is that the accusers of the righteous are exposed to the same fate decreed for their enemies (cf. Haman's fate, Esther 7:10; or the accusers being cast into the lions' den, Dan. 6:24).

Following v. 23 in some ancient Greek and Latin versions 68 additional verses known as The Prayer of Azariah and the Song of the Three Young Men are inserted. The interpolation has three parts. The first 22 verses are a prayer of Abednego (Hebrew name—Azariah) as he walked in the furnace "singing hymns to God and blessing the Lord." The next five verses give various details about the furnace. The fuel used was "naphtha, pitch, tow, and brush." It was so hot that the flames extended 49 cubits (*ca.* 73½ feet) above the top of the furnace. "The angel of the Lord" came into the furnace and created an area "like a moist whistling wind" in the midst of the flame in such a manner that the three Hebrews were not touched by the fire. The following 40 verses are the "Song of the Three Young Men." In this song the three praise and glorify God and exhort all creation to praise the Lord.

(6) The Miracle Discovered (3:24-25)

24 Then King Nebuchadnezzar was astonished and rose up in haste. He said to his counselors, "Did we not cast three men bound into the fire?" They answered the king, "True, O king." 25 He answered, "But I see four men loose, walking in the midst of the fire, and they are not hurt; and the appearance of the fourth is like a son of the gods."

The astonishment and haste of the king accentuate the idea of the unusual. The king calls for his *counselors* (cf. v. 27 and 4:36, the only other two uses of this Aramaic word in the OT). It was probably a Persian title. He verifies that three had been thrown into the furnace. The king saw *four men.* The fourth figure attracted the king's attention first. *The appearance of the fourth is like a son of the gods.* He resembled a divine being. The KJV has "Son of God." But this translation "is not grammatically defensible." In Aramaic the plural *'elahin* (gods) is always a true plural. This godly being is called *his angel* (v. 28). Early Christian commentators thought the fourth being to be "the second person of the Trinity." Montgomery (p. 215) says, "This view has been generally given up by modern Christian commentaries." Nebuchadnezzar was not knowledgeable enough of the power and resources of the true and living God to be able to discern the identity of the fourth image. Since no specification is added, it is improper to read too much into the text.

(7) Nebuchadnezzar's Reaction (3:26-30)

26 Then Nebuchadnezzar came near to the door of the burning fiery furnace and said, "Shadrach, Meshach, and Abednego, servants of the Most High God, come forth, and come here!" Then Shadrach, Meshach, and Abednego came out from the fire. 27 And the satraps, the prefects, the governors, and the king's counselors gathered together and saw that the fire had not had any power over the bodies of those men; the hair of their heads was not singed, their mantles were not harmed, and no smell of fire had come upon them. 28 Nebuchadnezzar said, "Blessed be the God of Shadrach, Meshach, and Abednego, who has sent his angel and delivered his servants, who trusted in him, and set at nought the king's command, and yielded up their bodies rather than serve and worship any god except their own God. 29 Therefore I make a decree: Any people, nation, or language that speaks anything against the God of Shadrach, Meshach, and Abednego shall be torn limb from limb, and their houses laid in ruins; for there is no other god who is able to deliver in this way." 30 Then the king promoted Shadrach, Meshach, and Abednego in the province of Babylon.

The king approaches the side door of the furnace and calls Shadrach, Meshach, and Abednego to come out. He addressed them as *servants of the Most High God* (the Aramaic equivalent of *'El 'Elyon*). This is not a confession that the God of the Hebrews was the only God. The term "Most High" was used by both Hebrews and non-Hebrews (cf. Gen. 14:18,19,22; Num. 24:16; Isa. 14:14; Tobit 1:13; 1 Esdras 2:3).

Four groups of officers are mentioned as verifying the miracle. Seven groups were listed in v. 2. One group, *the counselors* (also in v. 24), is not listed in v. 2.

The fire, which had been so strong that the mighty Chaldeans who tended the furnace were killed, was not strong enough to touch the bodies of the three or even to singe their hair. The cords binding the men were burned away by the fire, but their garments were not affected at all. The fire was so remote from them that there was no *smell of fire* clinging to them. These elements are indications of the martyr legend style. The writer exercised great skill as he developed with mounting intensity the account of the danger and miraculous deliverance of the three Yahweh worshipers. The men had no assurance or spiritual revelation which made them know that God would produce an angel or a miracle on their behalf. They were remaining faithful in their worship experiences regardless of the cost.

The writer of Daniel is not teaching that God will always work a miracle to reward fidelity, even though the vehicle is a victorious story. This record, being told and retold in Hebrew history, would bolster the courage of all those who would suffer for their fidelity to God's law. Such events were preserved as legends since they have demonstrated great validity as a repository of truth and revelation.

Verse 28 is the king's doxology. Verse 29 contains the king's decrees. Verse 30 has the promotion of the three. These three verses form the happy ending to the account of danger. One of the main concessions which Nebuchadnezzar made was that he established the religion of Shadrach, Meshach, and Abednego as lawful in Babylon.

4. Contest for Sovereignty (4:1-37)

Throughout history, some individuals have attained positions of authority and honor only to take themselves more seriously than they should. It is only natural that a man in a respected and honored position should take great pride in his work, his accomplishments, and even the ceremonial activities. At times, some of these individuals get such a hold on positions, committees, institutions, and governments that they wield an inordinate amount of power with little regard for other human beings or for any higher power. Nebuchadnezzar is pictured in the book of Daniel as being the sovereign of "the whole earth." He is portrayed as exalting himself as "lord" over the kingdoms and even mankind itself, with no thought that another power could bring him into subjection.

(1) An Imperial Pronouncement (4:1-3)

¹ King Nebuchadnezzar to all peoples, nations, and languages, that dwell in all the earth: Peace be multiplied to you! ² It has seemed good to me to show the signs and wonders that the Most High God has wrought toward me.
³ How great are his signs,
  how mighty his wonders!
His kingdom is an everlasting kingdom,
  and his dominion is from generation to
  generation.

These verses are marked as the opening of the fourth chapter in the English versions but in reality are the final verses of chapter three. The pronouncement which is the kingly confession of the sovereignty of the Most High God is the happy ending of chapter three. This paragraph may have been retained to show the effect that the experience has upon Nebuchadnezzar himself. But if this is intended, the submissiveness of Nebuchadnezzar seems to have been short-lived for the dream (ch. 4) pictures him as unrelated to God.

It is true that the identification of the ones being addressed, i.e., all peoples, nations, and languages, is also in 3:4,7,29. God is also called "the Most High God" in 3:26; 4:2. In chapters 2 and 4 the dreams are interpreted to the king, but the account of the fiery furnace (ch. 3) does not speak directly to the king. These relationships may be the reason that the Aramaic text includes these verses in the third chapter.

The omission of the LXX shows that there was a version of these records which did not contain the pronouncement. The problem as to whether these verses are very ancient or have been added cannot be settled on the basis of existing evidence. They may very well have been placed here as the transition from chapter three to chapter four when these two independent stories were placed together in the formation of the book.

(2) The Dream of a Tree (4:4-18)

⁴ I, Nebuchadnezzar, was at ease in my house and prospering in my palace. ⁵ I had a dream which made me afraid; as I lay in bed the fancies and the visions of my head alarmed

me. [6] Therefore I made a decree that all the wise men of Babylon should be brought before me, that they might make known to me the interpretation of the dream. [7] Then the magicians, the enchanters, the Chaldeans, and the astrologers came in; and I told them the dream, but they could not make known to me its interpretation. [8] At last Daniel came in before me—he who was named Belteshazzar after the name of my god, and in whom is the spirit of the holy gods—and I told him the dream, saying, [9] "O Belteshazzar, chief of the magicians, because I know that the spirit of the holy gods is in you and that no mystery is difficult for you, here is the dream which I saw; tell me its interpretation. [10] The visions of my head as I lay in bed were these: I saw, and behold, a tree in the midst of the earth; and its height was great. [11] The tree grew and became strong, and its top reached to heaven, and it was visible to the end of the whole earth. [12] Its leaves were fair and its fruit abundant, and in it was food for all. The beasts of the field found shade under it, and the birds of the air dwelt in its branches, and all flesh was fed from it.

[13] "I saw in the visions of my head as I lay in bed, and behold, a watcher, a holy one, came down from heaven. [14] He cried aloud and said thus, 'Hew down the tree and cut off its branches, strip off its leaves and scatter its fruit; let the beasts flee from under it and the birds from its branches. [15] But leave the stump of its roots in the earth, bound with a band of iron and bronze, amid the tender grass of the field. Let him be wet with the dew of heaven; let his lot be with the beasts in the grass of the earth; [16] let his mind be changed from a man's, and let a beast's mind be given to him; and let seven times pass over him. [17] The sentence is by the decree of the watchers, the decision by the word of the holy ones, to the end that the living may know that the Most High rules the kingdom of men, and gives it to whom he will, and sets over it the lowliest of men.' [18] This dream I, King Nebuchadnezzar, saw. And you, O Belteshazzar, declare the interpretation, because all the wise men of my kingdom are not able to make known to me the interpretation, but you are able, for the spirit of the holy gods is in you."

This is the beginning of chapter four in the Aramaic text. The LXX notes that this took place in "the eighteenth year of his reign," i.e., the same time as chapter 3, 587 B.C. Nebuchadnezzar was riding the crest of success. He was *at ease* (secure) at home and *prospering* in business. *Prospering* is literally luxuriant or fresh. This word

is used of the flourishing tree and no doubt is selected on the basis of the dream itself being of a tree. The dream made him *afraid*, i.e., shrink away, as crawling into the earth to hide (BDB, pp. 267, 1087).

Fancies appears nowhere else in the Old Testament. In later Aramaic it means evil imaginations. *Visions of my head* was probably included to add color and parallel to the term "fancies." These two terms probably are a hendiadys (two terms conveying a single idea). Montgomery (p. 227) explains it to be "impure dreams," recalling a suggestion of Margolis of "pruriency." Nebuchadnezzar called for the wise men who by position and reputation were thought to possess uncanny ability in deciphering a meaning for dreams. Four classes of *wise men of Babylon* are noted in v. 7. This is not a routine list. *Magicians* and *enchanters* are also in 2:2,7,10. *Chaldeans* is also in 2:2,10. *Astrologers* is also in 2:27 but not in 2:2,10.

No reason is given for consulting the other wise men without calling first the *chief of the magicians* (v. 9). The LXX omits (vv. 6–10) the reference to the calling of the other wise men and thus removes the problem.

The meaning of *at least* (v. 8) is obscure. Young, Jeffery, and Montgomery read "until at last" or finally. Montgomery (p. 225) adds the extra note that the reason for bringing Daniel in last is that "a higher dramatic end is gained."

Verse 8 makes a direct connection between Daniel's name and the name of Nebuchadnezzar's god. Linguistically this is not supportable unless a contraction has taken place. The name Belteshazzar means "protect his life" (*Balatsu usur*). The writer may have understood a contraction from *Bel Balatsu usur*. Montgomery (p. 123) says, "If the writer meant to include 'Bel,' then he did not know how to analyze Bab. names." The later compiler who did not know Babylonian may have seen the name reflected therein and included the added interpretative touch, in what Jeffery calls "folk etymology" (p. 409).

The spirit of the holy gods is not a surprising expression from the mouth of a foreign monarch who believed in many gods. Polytheism was a fact in Babylonian thought. When the king tells Daniel that *no mystery is difficult* for him, he may be recalling Daniel's past or merely making an expression of his confidence.

Here is the dream. In Aramaic and the KJV this is read "tell me the visions of my dream." Verse 8 explicitly states *I told him the dream.* Most commentaries agree that something has been omitted or was misunderstood. The term "visions of my dream" is not used elsewhere in the Old Testament.

The tree (vv. 10–12) reflects a figure in Ezekiel 31:3–14 (the glory of the Assyrian is compared to a cedar of Lebanon). Verses 10b–12a are clearly in poetic form. However, there is no explanation given for the shift from prose to poetry to prose. The author may have quoted the poetry to heighten the impact for the reader. The tree was often the figure representing men (Psalms 1:3; 37:35; Jer. 17:8; Ezek. 17: 3–24). This picture is remarkably similar to the Oriental view of the "world tree" (see Jeffery, p. 410; Porteous, p. 67). The earth was pictured as a flat disk and the heavens as an overturned saucer. The tree was thought of as being on the navel of the earth (cf. *in the midst of the earth*, v. 10). It *grew* and extended upward touching the vault of heaven (*its top reached to heaven*). It was thus open to the sight of anyone even to the edge (*it was visible to the end of the whole earth*).

The dream emphasized the superiority of the tree. It was in the center and reached both to the top and to the edge. All beasts and birds were under its protection. All flesh depended on it. The verbal usage describes habitual occurrences.

A watcher, a holy one (lit., a watcher and a holy one, as in KJV) refers to one instead of two figures. The term *watcher* (also 4:17) is not found elsewhere in the Old Testament. It is found often in the pseudepigraphical books. In 1 Enoch it is used of both archangels and fallen angels.

The word "holy one" is connected with watcher (cf. 4:17,23) to denote a supernatural being. This mysterious, vague, celestial figure cries out to his attendants. Orders are given for the calamitous dismemberment of the tree and the concomitant disengaging of the animals.

It is not a complete destruction of the tree. The stump is to be left *bound with a band of iron and bronze.* The idea that this band was to keep the tree trunk from splitting is a modern application. Such practice is unknown in that period of history. Charles (p. 92) says it adds sternness and crushing qualities to the king's fate (cf. Deut. 28:48; Jer. 1:18).

The phrase *amid the tender grass* raises some question. Is the presence of the bound stump a figure of utter futility in the midst of luxurious growth? G. R. Driver suggests that *bronze* (*nehash*) may actually contain a verb, and so he reads "let it luxuriate in the meadow grass" (Porteous, p. 68). The figure is shifted from the tree to the man with the second half of v. 15. Driver's proposed reading would be a synonymous parallel with the figure of the king in v. 15b.

His mind is literally his heart. "His intelligence is to be dehumanized, made like that of a beast; the distinctive glory of man is to be taken away from him" (Montgomery, p. 233; cf. Young, p. 105).

Seven times is translated in the LXX "seven years." Time may be any period of time and thus may be a conventional number of years (Charles, p. 92). Since the word times is any unit of time, a variety of meanings is possible. It could be that "time" would be one of the four seasons of the year, i.e., a total of one and three-fourths years, or perhaps only two seasons as reckoned in Persia (i.e., 3½ years). History does not help in determining the meaning of "seven times." It should be noted that the modern obsession with time and accuracy was unknown to the Hebrew way of life and thought. The idea of every detail of "prophecy" having to be fulfilled in the minutest detail is a postbiblical imposition. "Seven times" carries the general meaning of an indeterminable period.

By the decree of the watchers. The Babylonian background of Nebuchadnezzar is clearly seen in the concept that there was a group of celestial beings who comprised a sort of heavenly council between the divine and human realms. Such figures were an attempt on man's part to explain many phenomena. When Daniel interprets the dream (v. 24) he calls it *a decree of the Most High.* There were many things which called for explanation and which, according to ancient philosophy and theology, should not be related directly to God. So a structure of "above human" and "below divine" beings was used.

Verse 18 is the basic truth of the entire dream which was given to the king without any interpretation at all. "That God can set up in a position of power the lowliest of men is a commonplace of Scripture" (Porteous, p. 69; cf. Job 5:11; 1 Sam. 2:7–8). Nebuchadnezzar could relate the dream but was blinded to the fact that he was one of the *lowliest of men* who acted at the consent of the Most High.

Daniel and Joseph were examples of men who rose to a high place of authority yet continued with proper balance to give the glory to God. Daniel was known as one in whom there was the *spirit of the holy gods.*

(3) Daniel's Interpretation (4:19–27)

¹⁹ Then Daniel whose name was Belteshazzar, was dismayed for a moment, and his thoughts alarmed him. The king said, "Belteshazzar, let not the dream or the interpretation alarm you." Belteshazzar answered, "My lord, may the dream be for those who hate you and its interpretation for your enemies! ²⁰ The tree you saw, which grew and became strong, so that its top reached to heaven, and it was visible to the end of the whole earth; ²¹ whose leaves were fair and its fruit abundant, and in which was food for all; under which beasts of the field found shade, and in whose branches the birds of the air dwelt—²² it is you, O king, who have grown and become strong. Your greatness has grown and reaches to heaven, and your dominion to the ends of the earth. ²³ And whereas the king saw a watcher, a holy

one, coming down from heaven and saying, 'Hew down the tree and destroy it, but leave the stump of its roots in the earth, bound with a band of iron and bronze, in the tender grass of the field; and let him be wet with the dew of heaven; and let his lot be with the beasts of the field, till seven times pass over him'; ²⁴ this is the interpretation, O king: It is a decree of the Most High, which has come upon my lord the king, ²⁵ that you shall be driven from among men, and your dwelling shall be with the beasts of the field; you shall be made to eat grass like an ox, and you shall be wet with the dew of heaven, and seven times shall pass over you, till you know that the Most High rules the kingdom of men, and gives it to whom he will. ²⁶ And as it was commanded to leave the stump of the roots of the tree, your kingdom shall be sure for you from the time that you know that Heaven rules. ²⁷ Therefore, O king, let my counsel be acceptable to you; break off your sins by practicing righteousness, and your iniquities by showing mercy to the oppressed, that there may perhaps be a lengthening of your tranquillity.'

Heaton (p. 151) calls attention to the dismay of Daniel and the courtesy of the king as being "nice touches" of the artist. These are a part of the great accumulation of evidence that this story, as the others of the first six chapters, is one which has been preserved in the repeated telling around the campfires and home circles.

Daniel *was dismayed* at the terrifying task of telling the fearful truth to the self-exalted ruler. *For a moment* is an expression which came to be translated in later times "for an hour" (KJV). The idiomatic force is, as in RSV and ASV, for a brief time or moment. Daniel's *thoughts alarmed him* because of the devastating contents of the dream. The king sensed his perplexity and courteously urged that neither the dream nor the interpretation give undue concern.

Daniel opened his interpretation with a statement softening the impact upon the king. He wished that the interpretation would apply to the king's *enemies.* Daniel may have used a formula familiar throughout the Eastern world for averting evil. Underlying this wish is a possibility that the king could take heed so that his doom would be postponed and consequently the enemies would be confounded.

The interpretation proper begins in v. 22 with *it is you, O king*. This is the same clear presentation made in the dream of chapter 2 (2:36–37). The recounting of the descriptive elements of the tree does not condemn the king or even veil the rightness or the wrongness of the king's greatness. Verse 23 recounts the *decree of the watchers* (v. 17) and the coming *down from heaven* (v. 13). The watcher's presence demonstrates vividly that there is a power above the king even though the king's greatness *reaches to heaven* and his *dominion to the ends of the earth* (v. 22). In Daniel's interpretation (v. 24) he points out the source of real authority and power. It is not a decree of the watchers, as understood in the limited understanding of the Babylonian king. It was *a decree of the Most High . . . upon . . . the king*. The LXX adds a section between vv. 22 and 23 and relates this chapter to Maccabean times and Antiochus Epiphanes.

Human sovereignty is not wrong in itself, but when it so exalts any human being that it ignores the Person of creation and providence it is incorrect. The God of creation and reality cannot permit such an usurpation without eventual confrontation. "The king's outward form and actions are adapted to his inward transformation" (Charles, p. 99).

Nebuchadnezzar is told that he will be given the form and existence of an animal. The writer resorts to zoomorphic expressions to explain that the man who had sought a position higher than God will be forced into the subhuman position of an animal. He may be describing *insania zoanthropia*, i.e., insanity in which a man acts curiously like a wild animal.

The stump of the tree was left. The king will not be completely destroyed. *From the time that you know* shows a conditionality of the endurance of the kingdom. Young interprets that expression in the dream to mean that it was certain that the king would make a change. This overdraws the evidence. The emphasis should be in the possibility that a change may be made.

The expression *Heaven rules* is found nowhere else in the Old Testament. This is a way of avoiding the word God, as often in rabbinic and apocryphal literature (e.g., 1 Macc. 3:18,19; 4:10,24,55; 9:46; 2 Macc. 9:20; Susanna 1:9).

Daniel counsels the king to change his way of life. He urges him to start *practicing righteousness* and *showing mercy to the oppressed*. It is important that *righteousness* be understood properly. King Nebuchadnezzar is urged to practice righteousness, but he does not know the only true God. In such condition he could not be righteous. In this context righteousness is practically equivalent to almsgiving. This use of righteousness is clear in late Hebrew, Aramaic, Syriac, the Targums, and the Talmud. Ecclesiasticus 3:30*b* reads "almsgiving atones for sin." In this teaching the giving of alms is the highest form of righteousness (cf. Ecclus. 29:11; Tobit 4:7–11).

Hebrew thought packs into a single word the total concept of righteousness, i.e., the being right, the performance of rightness, and the fruit of this rightness. When any element of the term is omitted, there is a danger of the violation or obviation of righteousness. If righteousness is merely almsgiving or charity it is not biblical righteousness. Likewise, if the righteousness is only a thought and does not result in actions of doing for others, it is improperly called righteousness. Righteousness will become deeds because of the reality of a vital relationship of a man and his God.

(4) Nebuchadnezzar's Madness (4:28–33)

28 All this came upon King Nebuchadnezzar. 29 At the end of twelve months he was walking on the roof of the royal palace of Babylon, 30 and the king said, "Is not this great Babylon, which I have built by my mighty power as a royal residence and for the glory of my majesty?" 31 While the words were still in the king's mouth, there fell a voice from heaven, "O King Nebuchadnezzar, to you it is spoken: The kingdom has departed from you, 32 and you shall be driven from among men, and your dwelling shall be with the beasts of the field; and you shall be made to eat grass like an ox;

and seven times shall pass over you, until you have learned that the Most High rules the kingdom of men and gives it to whom he will." [33] Immediately the word was fulfilled upon Nebuchadnezzar. He was driven from among men, and ate grass like an ox, and his body was wet with the dew of heaven till his hair grew as long as eagles' feathers, and his nails were like birds' claws.

All this came is typical of Hebrew thought in that it is a summary statement of what is about to be described. It has the force of "this is what actually took place upon Nebuchadnezzar."

One year had passed after the king received a warning. The time of his tranquility expired *at the end of twelve months.* The king had refused the advice whereby the impending catastrophe could be postponed. *He was walking on the roof of the royal palace of Babylon.* Buildings were generally constructed with a flat roof. His palace was erected on one of the high points of Babylon. From this vantage point he could admire a great portion of his walled city.

The historical records of this period indicate that Nebuchadnezzar was not like his predecessors. They had been occupied with warring conquest. But Nebuchadnezzar is recorded as building or restoring the walls, temples, and palaces. In Babylon alone [5] Nebuchadnezzar renovated the two temples of Marduk, 15 other temples, and the two great walls. He rebuilt the palace of Nabopolassar. He also constructed a palace with the hanging gardens, known as one of the wonders of the world. It was probably this palace upon which he was walking. All of the grandeur of these magnificent achievements stirred within him a great sense of pride. Success had gone to his head. A king customarily gave credit to his god, but Nebuchadnezzar boasted that Babylon and its grandeur was *for the glory of my majesty.*

Even while the king was claiming the kingdom as his own and as built by his own power *there fell a voice from heaven*

which said, *the kingdom has departed from you* (cf. v. 32). Verse 25 is a more complete itemization of the dream. The successive rehearsals, characteristic of apocalyptic writers, are clear remnants of the larger account. Verse 25 contains five events within the interpretation. The king would be (1) *driven from among men;* (2) his *dwelling shall be with the beasts of the field;* (3) he would be *made to eat grass like an ox;* (4) *be wet with the dew of heaven;* (5) *seven times shall pass over* him. Verse 32 is the same list except it omits the fourth statement. Verse 33 gives a recital of the events which took place on king Nebuchadnezzar immediately after the voice from heaven had spoken. This list includes three of the five segments of v. 25 (1,3,4) but adds a lengthy explanation that *his hair grew as long as eagles' feathers, and his nails were like birds' claws.*

The actions of the king could be described as boanthropy. This is a form of a madness which is known technically as lycanthropy. It is a kind of insanity in which a person imagines that he is a wolf or some other beast. The biblical record indicated the king was driven out and made to eat grass like an ox.

In recent years, the Prayer of Nabonidus has come to light from among the Dead Sea Scrolls.[6] There are some very precise parallels between this document from Cave Four and chapters four and five of Daniel. A king has a serious malady which lasted seven years (4:25-32); it was at the decree of the "Most High" (4:17,25,32); there was a Jewish diviner; the king had a dream; the "calm of my repose" parallels the "lengthening of your tranquility" (4:27); the Scroll mentions "gods of silver, gold (copper, iron), wood, stone, clay" (cf. 5:4,23); in both, the narrative style goes from the first person to the third and back to the first person again.

The one striking difference is that the

5 Cf. East India House Inscription vii, 34; KB, Grotefend Cylinder, iii, 2, pp. 25, 39.

6 See Burrows, *More Light on the Dead Sea Scrolls,* p. 400; J. T. Milik, *Revue Biblique* 63, 1956, 407–415.

king is called Nebuchadnezzar in Daniel
but Nabonidus in the Qumran Scroll. There
is no historical corroboration of any such
sickness on the part of Nebuchadnezzar.

The events in the Qumran Scroll are substantiated by historical records. Nabonidus
was absent from Babylon for nearly ten
years. He did fall sick. He made his headquarters in Teima in northwest Arabia.

This apparent contradiction has aroused
in practically every commentator one of
two views. Some have reacted vigorously
to defend the historical accuracy of the
Scripture in every detail and have insisted that Nebuchadnezzar had an experience precisely as in the book of Daniel. They expect that records eventually
will be found which will authenticate in
every detail the accuracy of this chapter
in the life of Nebuchadnezzar. Indeed, so
it may occur. But until such happens there
will remain the haunting question which is
often settled only by preexisting theories.

Other interpreters have sought a logical
conclusion using only the existing historical
evidence. Their attempt is to square all
known facts with the record of the Scripture and vice versa. On the one hand,
it may be that such occurrence was not in
the life of Nebuchadnezzar. Some would
even say that Daniel 4 confused the names
of the two kings.

An overadherence to one aspect may
fail to uncover the deepest truths of a
passage. Nabonidus was the last king of
Babylon. Only three relatively unimportant
kings reigned in Babylon between Nebuchadnezzar (604–561 B.C.) and Nabonidus (556–539). These three kings were
Nebuchadnezzar's son, his son-in-law,
and his grandson. Also, it should be noted
that the man left in charge of the Babylonian kingdom during the long absence
of Nabonidus was Belshazzar who is listed
as of the Nebuchadnezzar dynasty. The
Babylonian kingdom was remembered as
the era of Nebuchadnezzar, the "king par
excellence." In a period during which the
specific details of Babylonian events had
faded, the events themselves were basically

true. As time passes, the central figure of
a regime is the one who is remembered.

(5) Nebuchadnezzar's Recovery (4:34–37)

34 At the end of the days I, Nebuchadnezzar,
lifted my eyes to heaven, and my reason returned to me, and I blessed the Most High,
and praised and honored him who lives for
ever;
> for his dominion is an everlasting dominion,
>> and his kingdom endures from generation
>> to generation;
35 all the inhabitants of the earth are accounted
as nothing;
>> and he does according to his will in the
>> host of heaven
> and among the inhabitants of the earth;
> and none can stay his hand
> or say to him, "What doest thou?"
36 At the same time my reason returned to me;
and for the glory of my kingdom, my majesty
and splendor returned to me. My counselors
and my lords sought me, and I was established
in my kingdom, and still more greatness was
added to me. 37 Now I, Nebuchadnezzar, praise
and extol and honor the King of heaven; for all
his works are right and his ways are just; and
those who walk in pride he is able to abase.

The conclusion to the chapter gives the
happy answer which is typical of the first
chapters of the book. *At the end of the
days* changes the time unit which had
been used in the previous part of the chapter. It may refer to the phrase *seven times
shall pass* (vv. 25,32).

When the king came to his "right mind"
(NEB) *he blessed . . . praised and honored* the eternal God. It is pressing the text
too far to say that the regaining of his
sanity was the result of the praise of God.
However, in the context the two ideas may
be closely connected. The format of the
first six chapters contains the final note of
victory. It is noted (1) the king's *reason
returned;* (2) the kingdom was restored in
all of its *glory* and *splendor;* (3) the ministers of state and the royal courtiers
rallied to his side; (4) the king extols *the
King of heaven;* and (5) he confesses
that God is able to abase any who walk in
inordinate pride.

The central figure of this chapter is the
king with his overexalted opinion of him-

self, his demented actions, and his turn to the true God. Such a historicized account could be used during the threat or dominance of any tyrannical ruler to bring encouragement and direction to a downtrodden defeated people. Antiochus Epiphanes was an egotistical political figure who sought to exalt himself above the accepted law and the ancient religion of the Jews. His actions were so reminiscent of the acts of the king of chapter 4 that the Jews called him Antiochus Epimanes rather than Epiphanes. This was an obvious play on his name. Epimanes meant "madman." Chapter 4 would show that God could debase any self-exalting tyrant (v. 37b).

5. Belshazzar's Insolence Thwarted (5:1–31)

A unity of purpose, throughout the first six chapters, centers around the theme that ill-founded human authority will be thwarted by divine intervention. In chapter 4 the madness of the king sprang from his inordinate pride. Chapter 5 goes deeper into the problem of pride and looks at the result of insolence. This insolence is not arrogant rudeness but is an expression of bold disrespect of a subordinate human official for the omnipotent Deity.

(1) Belshazzar's Sacrilegious Feast (5:1–4)

¹ King Belshazzar made a great feast for a thousand of his lords, and drank wine in front of the thousand.
² Belshazzar, when he tasted the wine, commanded that the vessels of gold and of silver which Nebuchadnezzar his father had taken out of the temple in Jerusalem be brought, that the king and his lords, his wives, and his concubines might drink from them. ³ Then they brought in the golden and silver vessels which had been taken out of the temple, the house of God in Jerusalem; and the king and his lords, his wives, and his concubines drank from them. ⁴ They drank wine, and praised the gods of gold and silver, bronze, iron, wood, and stone.

The feast is interpreted as an impious flaunting of Belshazzar's authority and position and as sacrilegious control over the sacred vessels.

This chapter has been a battleground among commentators of recent centuries. One of the points of contention is the kingship of Belshazzar (ca. 552–545 B.C.). He is called king repeatedly in chapter 5 but in the full secular records he is never called king. Historical records show that Nabonidus (556–539) was the only crowned king of Babylon of that period.

The royal succession can be ascertained from biblical and secular records. Nebuchadnezzar (604–561 B.C.) was succeeded by his son Evil-Merodach (561–560). Nebuchadnezzar's son-in-law Neriglissar reigned 560–556. Nebuchadnezzar's grandson, the son of Neriglissar, Labashi-Marduk reigned only a few months in 556. He was succeeded by Nabonidus (556–539) who reigned until Cyrus captured Babylon.

Belshazzar was the son of Nabonidus. Even though Belshazzar was never technically invested with the full crown of kingship, he performed many of the duties of directing the kingdom of Babylon. Belshazzar assumed the position of king and asserted himself as the only one of importance. The fact that the text of Daniel makes no reference to his father, the enthroned monarch, but rather puts great emphasis on the term "King Belshazzar" adds support to the understanding of the total episode that Belshazzar insolently and arrogantly took to himself a higher position and authority than was rightfully his. Technically he was acting under the authority of the crowned monarch. Many elected officials of church and state have arrogantly seized authority and power. They strut physically and in public announcements as though they were deserving of exclusive honor and praise. The author was skillfully using the figure to indicate Belshazzar's pompous egocentricity.

A great feast for a thousand. Twice in v. 1 a point is made of the size of the banquet. Records of many such feasts have been preserved.

Nebuchadnezzar his father refers to Nebuchadnezzar as Belshazzar's predecessor. There were three kings who reigned between Nebuchadnezzar and Nabonidus. The relationship of Belshazzar and Nebuchadnezzar is referred to in vv. 2,11,13,18, 22 (Nebuchadnezzar is called father; Belshazzar is called his son). The most natural interpretation is that Belshazzar was the natural son of Nebuchadnezzar. There was no physical kinship between the two. This has caused some interpreters [7] to produce all kinds of unsupportable possibilities. The Semitic terms father and son are used in various ways in addition to that of physical lineage. Since the reputation of Nebuchadnezzar was so much greater than that of Nabonidus, the viceroy (Belshazzar) kept emphasizing that he was of the "class" of Nebuchadnezzar.

Josephus, Herodotus, and Xenophon record that this banquet was on the same eve of Babylon's capitulation. Athenaeus (cf. Porteous, p. 78) indicates that later Persian monarchs dined in a rather exclusive surrounding. But on the occasion of a high holiday the entire company dined in a single large banquet room with the king. There is no established custom in regard to the attendance of wives and/or concubines. The size of the company, the inclusion of the wives and concubines, and the use of vessels of silver and gold add to the magnitude of the occasion.

When he tasted the wine was a technical term for banquet. It may be equivalent of saying the wine flowed after the meal or that the king was under such influence. If so, it would add to the portrayal of a self-indulgent despot.

The readers of this canonical record were worshipers with high respect for the worship of the Hebrew God. The vessels which Nebuchadnezzar *had taken out of the temple in Jerusalem* had been consecrated in the worship of Yahweh. They would have been reserved for use in the temple and would never have been used in a secular banquet or in pagan revelry. It is impossible to determine whether the banquet was secular or sacred. Bentzen interprets it as orgiastic and cultic. There

[7] Cf. Leupold, pp. 211–212.

was some religious character since these vessels were used as they *praised the gods of gold and silver.* The main force of this account is that a self-exalted ruler in a very highhanded manner desecrated the sacred vessels. The desecration of the sacred vessels was made doubly repulsive to the Yahweh worshipers who would read that libations were poured out to pagan gods.

(2) Handwriting on the Wall (5:5–9)

[5] Immediately the fingers of a man's hand appeared and wrote on the plaster of the wall of the king's palace, opposite the lampstand; and the king saw the hand as it wrote. [6] Then the king's color changed, and his thoughts alarmed him; his limbs gave way, and his knees knocked together. [7] The king cried aloud to bring in the enchanters, the Chaldeans, and the astrologers. The king said to the wise men of Babylon, "Whoever reads this writing, and shows me its interpretation, shall be clothed with purple, and have a chain of gold about his neck, and shall be the third ruler in the kingdom." [8] Then all the king's wise men came in, but they could not read the writing or make known to the king the interpretation. [9] Then King Belshazzar was greatly alarmed, and his color changed; and his lords were perplexed.

In the very moment of praising the heathen deities and the misusing of the sacred Jewish vessels, a human hand was seen writing on the wall. As the king was eating and drinking on a raised dais at the front of the large banquet hall, there was a *lampstand* nearby illuminating that section of the banquet hall. The *lampstand* is a foreign word and is used only here in the Old Testament. No unusual significance can be given to the presence of a light source. Excavations at Babylon have uncovered a great hall more than 50 feet wide and 160 feet long.

The king saw the hand. It is literally the palm of the hand to distinguish from the arm above the wrist. Whether the hand was disembodied or was the hand of a supernatural being is to fill in details which are not specified in the text.

Even though no indication is given to the contents or nature of the written message, the king reacted immediately. The disturbed reaction of the one seeing the vision is a characteristic of symbolic dream reports (cf. ch. 2). His *color* was translated splendor in 4:36. The word is used of the human countenance. Whereas he had been eating and drinking with total attention being fixed on himself, the appearance of the hand disrupted his peace of mind and ego-building banquet.

The king gives a loud command to bring in *the wise men of Babylon.* Four classes are noted (cf. 2:2,10,27). They are charged with reading and interpreting the writing. The reward for a successful fulfillment of the task would be elevation to the position of third in command with all of the rights and privileges appertaining thereto. He would *be clothed with purple,* indicating a royal prerogative and would be known as the friend of the king (cf. 1 Macc. 10:20,62,64; Esther 8:5).

The precise meaning of *the third ruler* is not known since it is not an established position. It may mean third after Nabonidus the king and Belshazzar.

Daniel is recorded in 6:2 as one of the *three* presidents during the time of Darius. The Aramaic words are the same in both chapters. H. H. Rowley has pointed out that such a position in the kingdom of Belshazzar would not be a very great honor since the kingdom was decadent and tottering. To give such an honor would be to place a man in great danger. In light of this fact, the teaching of chapters 5 and 6 would be very important. A self-exalted egotist could bestow honors but would pass from the scene quickly. But the lowly follower of the God worshiped in Jerusalem would be honored, protected, and sustained.

All the king's wise men came in. Daniel was not in this group. These men were called the king's, and so there may have been a wider circle of wise men. The ones called in may have been the board of professional court wise men. The fact that his personal wise men were not able to read the writing or translate it alarmed the king exceedingly. *His lords were perplexed.* The role of the lords is not indicated.

(3) The Queen Recommends Daniel (5: 10–12)

¹⁰ The queen, because of the words of the king and his lords, came into the banqueting hall; and the queen said, "O king, live for ever! Let not your thoughts alarm you or your color change. ¹¹ There is in your kingdom a man in whom is the spirit of the holy gods. In the days of your father light and understanding and wisdom, like the wisdom of the gods, were found in him, and King Nebuchadnezzar, your father, made him chief of the magicians, enchanters, Chaldeans, and astrologers, ¹² because an excellent spirit, knowledge, and understanding to interpret dreams, explain riddles, and solve problems were found in this Daniel, whom the king named Belteshazzar. Now let Daniel be called, and he will show the interpretation."

In spite of all the confusion, word of the disturbing events spread. *The queen* heard that none of the wise men had been able to interpret. She was probably the queen mother since the king's wives had been at the banquet. When the queen mother heard, perhaps from the scurrying servants, she came to the banquet hall. The LXX indicates that the king sent for the queen. She was highly esteemed for she entered the presence of the king on her own initiative (unless the LXX is accepted as authentic). Her advice was accepted readily. She showed a knowledge of historical events which were either unknown to or forgotten by Belshazzar.

The queen informs the king of the presence in his kingdom of a man who had been made *chief of the magicians, enchanters, Chaldeans, and astrologers* by Nebuchadnezzar. He was identified by his Babylonian name. Evidently she knew of the historical situation in which Nebuchadnezzar elevated Daniel. Daniel would have been an elderly gentleman who by his age would have the respect of the young king and lords. The record gives no indication where Daniel was, or how the queen knew where he was, why Daniel was not counted among Belshazzar's wise men, or why Belshazzar or the other wise men knew nothing of him. The queen also added other qualifications to that of age and position. She told the king that Daniel possessed (1) *the spirit of the holy gods,* (2) *light and understanding and wisdom,* (3) an *excellent spirit,* (4) *knowledge.* He was described as a man possessing the light, knowledge, and wisdom which could only come from God. In v. 12 there are three needed skills listed for Daniel. The first was that of an *understanding to interpret dreams.* The vision of the handwriting on the white plaster wall was not recorded as a dream. But the record has the form and outline of other symbolic dream reports.

The second skill of Daniel was the explanation of *riddles.* The Hebrew equivalent of riddle is in Judges 14:12f. (the riddle—sweeter than honey and stronger than a lion), in 1 Kings 10:1 (the questions to Solomon from the queen of Sheba), in Psalm 49:4 (a perplexing moral problem), and in Habakkuk 2:6 (an enigmatic comparison).

The third skill was to *solve problems.* Literally it reads "to loosen knots." The same word was used in 5:6, "his limbs gave way." The solving of problems has been found to refer to "magic knots" (cf. Charles, p. 130; Porteous, p. 80), which were tied by a sorcerer symbolically binding a victim. These knots could be untied by a loosening of the knot, a type of counter-magic.

(4) Daniel Is Briefed (5:13–16)

13 Then Daniel was brought in before the king. The king said to Daniel, "You are that Daniel, one of the exiles of Judah, whom the king my father brought from Judah. 14 I have heard of you that the spirit of the holy gods is in you, and that light and understanding and excellent wisdom are found in you. 15 Now the wise men, the enchanters, have been brought in before me to read this writing and make known to me its interpretation; but they could not show the interpretation of the matter. 16 But I have heard that you can give interpretations and solve problems. Now if you can read the writing and make known to me its interpretation, you shall be clothed with purple, and have a chain of gold about your neck, and shall be the third ruler in the kingdom."

One important theme of the first half of Daniel is the confrontation of a heathen king and a Jewish subject. Daniel is identified as *one of the exiles of Judah* taken by Nebuchadnezzar. The contrast between the captor and the captive (v. 16) accentuates the lowly Jew as the victor.

Belshazzar repeats the credentials which had been given by the queen. He said, *I have heard of you.* The king did not know Daniel. He appeals to him by telling him of the failure of the wise men to interpret the writing and by offering him the same reward. No mention had been made either to the wise men or to Daniel of any threat of punishment in case of failure. This may be an underlying reason for the perplexity of the lords (5:9) when the wise men were not able to enlighten the king.

(5) Daniel Reads and Interprets the Writing (5:17–28)

17 Then Daniel answered before the king, "Let your gifts be for yourself, and give your rewards to another; nevertheless I will read the writing to the king and make known to him the interpretation. 18 O king, the Most High God gave Nebuchadnezzar your father kingship and greatness and glory and majesty; 19 and because of the greatness that he gave him, all peoples, nations, and languages trembled and feared before him; whom he would he slew, and whom he would he kept alive; whom he would he raised up, and whom he would he put down. 20 But when his heart was lifted up and his spirit was hardened so that he dealt proudly, he was deposed from his kingly throne, and his glory was taken from him; 21 he was driven from among men, and his mind was made like that of a beast, and his dwelling was with the wild asses; he was fed grass like an ox, and his body was wet with the dew of heaven, until he knew that the Most High God rules the kingdom of men, and sets over it whom he will. 22 And you his son, Belshazzar, have not humbled your heart, though you knew all this, 23 but you have lifted up yourself against the Lord of heaven; and the vessels of his house have been brought in before you, and you and your lords, your wives, and your concubines have drunk wine from them; and you have praised the gods of silver and gold, of bronze, iron, wood, and stone, which do not see or hear or know, but the God in whose hand is your breath, and whose are all your ways, you have not honored.

[24] "Then from his presence the hand was sent, and this writing was inscribed. [25] And this is the writing that was inscribed: MENE, MENE, TEKEL, and PARSIN. [26] This is the interpretation of the matter: MENE, God has numbered the days of your kingdom and brought it to an end; [27] TEKEL, you have been weighed in the balances and found wanting; [28] PERES, your kingdom is divided and given to the Medes and Persians."

Daniel disavows himself of the rewards. He bluntly rules out any profit motive. In keeping with his reputation of divinely given wisdom, he offers to read and interpret the writing.

Daniel rehearses (vv. 18–19) elements which were a part of Nebuchadnezzar's being the "king par excellence" of the Babylonian dynasty. He had been in reality the possessor of *greatness and glory* because *the Most High God* had given it to him. An absolute monarch, feared by all humanity, Nebuchadnezzar was deposed because he exalted himself inordinately (v. 20). When the king acted as though he were superhuman, God dethroned him and sentenced him to act as subhuman. This debasement is described in many of the same terms as in chapter 4. It is verification that though the nations feared the king it was necessary that the king realize (know) that the *kingdom of men* is under the rule of God.

The contrast between Nebuchadnezzar and Belshazzar is very great. Nebuchadnezzar had been exalted by God, but Belshazzar exalted himself (v. 23). Belshazzar brought the sacred vessels and used them in a rite of self-aggrandizement. He *praised* powerless gods which could not see or hear, an act which was clearly against the God who gave to Nebuchadnezzar power and to Belshazzar breath.

The occasion of the display of Belshazzar's utter disregard for the vessels from Jerusalem and the God of Israel's Temple may have been a miscalculation on his part. The Jewish Talmud (Megillah 11*b*) recounts that Belshazzar figured on the basis of Jeremiah's statement concerning 70 years of captivity. Belshazzar had been

in the kingdom 23 years, Evil-Merodach for two years, and Nebuchadnezzar for 45 years. Since the Jews were in his power now after the passing of 70 years, he surmised that the God of the Jews was powerless to act in their behalf. Therefore, he exalted himself and the silver, gold, bronze, iron, wood, and stone which had reality for him.

Daniel (v. 23) contrasts the impotency of material gods with the vitality of the God of the Jews. Belshazzar had been guilty of sacrilege in the perversion of the Temple vessels and was also guilty of idolatry in worshiping images. The description of the images is very similar to Deuteronomy 4:28; 28:36,64; Psalm 115: 4–6; and the Prayer of Nabonidus in the Dead Sea Scrolls.

From his (God's) *presence* (v. 24) specifies that, even though Belshazzar had perverted the vessels of Yahweh and had worshiped idols, the true God was reaching to him in judgment. This message is not one of warning but a pronouncement of guilt and sentence. Daniel interprets that the hand was not that of a ghost or apparition. Belshazzar praised gods which had no power. But the God of Daniel showed his power (note the use of hand in vv. 23,24).

Daniel read (v. 17) the signs which appeared on the wall. As was the custom the consonants only were written. The reader supplied the vowels in his pronunciation. It was strange that the Babylonian wise men could not even pronounce the words. No doubt, some of the wise men were knowledgeable in Aramaic. Commentators have made many suggestions to explain the failure of the Babylonians: (1) it was in some strange script (Grotius); (2) it was an Athbash system of cryptograph (Jewish commentators); (3) it may have been ideograms (Charles, p. 133); (4) the characters were written vertically instead of horizontally (rabbis, cf. Young, p. 126). The answer may lie in the interpretation of the word *read* to mean to intone or pronounce correctly in contradistinction to read with meaning.

The specific text of the writing is reported in basically two different forms. The RSV and *The Jerusalem Bible* have *Mene, Mene, Tekel, and Parsin.* The ASV, NEB, and KJV have "Mene, Mene, Tekel, Upharsin." The difference here is only a translation of the Semitic conjunction *u* as "and." However, there are other problems presented by the versions. Was the word *Mene* written once or twice? The LXX, Theodotion, Vulgate, Josephus, and Jerome record it only once. The explanation (v. 26) makes note of only one *Mene.*

One problem lies in the fact that *Parsin* is a plural word whereas in the interpretation (v. 28) it is considered only as singular. The preservation of the more complex and difficult forms would indicate that the actual text has been retained. Many commentators, basing their views on the three word interpretation and the difficulty of the text, take the shorter text as original.

The interpretation found in vv. 26–28 is not absolutely literal. *Mene* is *M°ne'*, but the word numbered is *m°nah. Tekel* is an Aramaic noun equated with the Hebrew shekel. Thus, it is interpreted as meaning weigh. The word brings forth readily the idea *weighed in the balances* (pass. perf. 2nd mas. sing.).

Peres probably is a weight of a half mina from the root verb which means to break in two. The consonants of the singular noun could also reflect Persia. Consequently, the plural noun could include both the idea of weights of half mina and that of the Persians.

The complex writing (v. 25) coupled with the comparatively simplex interpretation has given rise to the idea that the writing was a well-known proverb which the wise men could not relate to the historical situation.

One of the most fantastic applications is that which makes this passage refer to the twentieth century A.D. return of the Jews to Palestine. This view equates each *mene* with a mina which is a Babylonian weight measure of about 1,000 gerahs. Applying this scale to the writing in Daniel the following figures can be amassed: two minas would be 2,000 gerahs; a shekel was equal to 20 gerahs; *parsin* (a dividing of a mina) equal to 500 gerahs; a total of 2,520 gerahs. If a gerah represents a year, one could get the figure of 2,520 years. Now if the Jewish captivity occurred in 603 B.C. and this figure is used as a starting point, the end date would be A.D. 1917. This is the date on which the Jews started back to Jerusalem since General Allenby and forces captured Jerusalem on December 8, 1917. There is no indication whatsoever in the biblical text that such an interpretation is remotely applicable. Such theories are pure fantasy and mathematical juggling. The captivity was not 603 B.C. There are no bases for transferring the application from the Medes and Persians to a General Allenby, or of making a condemnation become a victory.

The interpretation which is directly applicable to the historical situation of the Babylonians, Medes, and Persians is in line with the text and context. The ease with which Daniel could move from one word to a closely related word or idea clearly is a factor in Hebrew thought.[8] The thorough examination of the manner in which the New Testament and early church writers used Scriptural quotations and interpretations will reveal a much greater emphasis on the spiritual, theological, and contextual direction than on specific philological, verbal, numerical literalness.

In the Talmud (Ta'anith 21*b*) weights were used to designate the relative weight of individuals. A man, designated as more important than his father, would be referred to as "a mina son of a half-mina." Using this principle that weights referred to individual kings, an interpretation which would be directly applicable to the time of Daniel could be easily understood.[9] If there were three words (*Mene, Tekel,*

[8] Cf. the interpretation found in the Dead Sea Scrolls; Eissfeldt, ZAW, 63, 1951, 105–114.

[9] Cf. Clermont-Ganneau, *Journal Asiatique,* 1886, pp. 36 ff.

Peres), there would be three kings. If there were two *menes*, one tekel, and one *peres*, there would be four kings. However, if the plural of *peres* as *parsin* indicates two *peres* words then there would be five kings in the writing. In the Aramaic text there are four or five terms.

Kraeling (JBL, 1944, pp. 11–18) takes the inscription to refer to the successors of Nebuchadnezzar, i.e., *Mene*—Evil-Mero-dach; *Mene*—Neriglissar; *Tekel*—Labashi-Marduk, who reigned only eight months and so valued only a shekel; dual *Parsin*—Nabonidus and Belshazzar (each valued lightly as a half-mina).

Jeffery (p. 432) says that the "usual interpretation" would have Nebuchadnez-zar as worth a mina, Belshazzar valued as no more than a shekel (1/60 of a mina, Ezek. 45:12, Heb. text), and the Medes and Persians (v. 28) estimated as only a divided measure each. This view would be clear from the interpretation which Daniel gave to the inscription (vv. 26–28). The meaning ascribed to *Mene* refers to *the days of your kingdom.* The days of the Nebuchadnezzar dynasty are to be brought to *an end. Tekel* is seen to mean *you have been . . . found wanting.* Belshazzar had seen the writing on the wall and is specifically singled out for condemnation. The writing on the wall was intended for him. *Peres* is explained to indicate that the Babylonian kingdom would be *given to the Medes and Persians.* The Medes and Persians are noted as combined also in 6:8,12, 15.

(6) Daniel Honored (5:29–31)

²⁹ Then Belshazzar commanded, and Daniel was clothed with purple, a chain of gold was put about his neck, and proclamation was made concerning him, that he should be the third ruler in the kingdom.
³⁰ That very night Belshazzar the Chaldean king was slain. ³¹ And Darius the Mede received the kingdom, being about sixty-two years old.

The promise of the king to the wise men (5:7) is fulfilled now to Daniel. The hero is rewarded and is victorious over all foreign powers. Each of the individual episodes in chapters 1—6 has a victorious conclusion. The word to Belshazzar was carried out in the promotion of Daniel to the position of *the third ruler* in the kingdom. The word of God was carried out *that very night* when Belshazzar *was slain* and the kingdom was given to *the Mede.*

"The Medes and Persians" (5:28) are referred to as a single unit in 6:8,12,15. In the Greek period they were often referred to indiscriminately either as the Medes or the Persians. A specific designation of the kingdom of the Medes as distinguished from the Persian kingdom is not found characteristically in or after the Greek domination except in later historical works (cf. Charles, p. 137). The writing indicates that the Babylonian kingdom would be turned over to the Medes "and" Persians. In 5:28 the Medes and Persians are taken to be a single unit.

The meaning and accuracy of v. 31 has been one of the most debated areas of Daniel. Each portion when compared with known facts of secular historical records has raised much question.

The existence of a political figure by the name of Darius is not a problem. There were three rulers who bore the name of Darius. Darius I, Hystaspes, was monarch of the Persian (Achaemenian) Empire 522–486 B.C. Darius II, Nothus, reigned 423–404. Darius III, Codomannus, ruled 336–331. Each of these kings was Persian (Bright, pp. 469–470). To call Darius the Mede does call for some explanation in view of the fact that all of the rulers by the name of Darius were technically Persian and not Medes.

The greatest difficulty in this verse revolves around the insertion of a Darius at this juncture of history. Belshazzar was a political figure who dominated the scene in chapter 5. He was second in command to Nabonidus. The end of the Babylonian regime occurred in 539 B.C. The impression is left that Darius conquered Babylon if vv. 30 and 31 are historically consecutive. The succession of events during the time of the fall of Babylon are clear. Cyrus, a Persian, conquered the Median kingdom when he overthrew Astyages in 550. At this time the Median Empire ceased. This took place during the reign of Nabonidus over the Babylonian Empire. Babylon capitulated without resistance to the Persians, Cyrus the king (550–530 B.C.), on October 13, 539.[10] No secular record includes anyone by the name of Darius in this transfer of power.

Dougherty[11] records two separate Babylonian records which overlap two months right at this juncture. These show no lapse of time or reign between Belshazzar and Cyrus. General Gobryas entered Babylon and took Nabonidus prisoner. Two weeks later, October 27, Cyrus the Persian king entered Babylon with Gobryas; November 4, Gobryas slew the king's son; November 6, Gobryas died.

Working within the framework of these dates and names, attempts have been made to identify *Darius the Mede* (5:31) with various figures whose name and existence are substantiated in secular records (Whitcomb, pp. 10–16). A thorough refutation of these various theories is given by H. H. Rowley (*Darius the Mede*).

Rowley (pp. 57,150 f.) and Porteous (p. 83) show that a tradition that Babylon would fall to the Medians actually existed (Isa. 13:17–22; 21:5; Jer. 51:11,39,57).

However, v. 31 of chapter 5 is actually not a part of chapter 5 but is the first verse of chapter 6 in the Aramaic original. There is thus an entirely different set of problems. No longer is there the problem of Babylon being taken over by Darius the Mede.

The first six chapters are not consecutive accounts. Each is a record which stands to itself and must be interpreted individually even though the contents may be related. The book in its total impact will be understood when these separate accounts form an interpretative unit.

Darius is called a *Mede* in 5:31 (6:1 in the Aramaic text) and 11:1. In 9:1 Darius is said to be "the son of Ahasuerus, by birth a Mede." The three kings by the name of Darius were not Medes but were technically Persians. Years ago conjecture was possible for there was a lack of much historical evidence. Relying upon the possibility of future discovery (cf. Whitcomb, p. 67; Young, p. 131) is dangerous in light of substantiated information. Rowley states, "No Median king succeeded to the control of the Babylonian kingdom, and no person answering to this Darius is known, or can be fitted into the known history of the period" (*Darius the Mede*, p. 59).

A source of the problem may be the methodology of an interpreter. Whitcomb demands twentieth century methodology and understanding of history instead of viewing the book of Daniel in the light of ancient literature, its date, and the purpose of the writer. It is important that an interpreter interpret a work from the same standpoint of its writing and not from the presupposition and training of the interpreter. No Darius is referred to elsewhere as a Mede. Consequently, twentieth-century literality demands that the literalist conjecture that one of the known kings of Media was the Darius referred to in the book of Daniel. The criterion of literalism has given rise to much argument and writing which obscure the context and full message of the book. Many have emphasized these arguments and objections and have not been swept along by the mighty message of the book. Many a truth has overshadowed the form in which it was placed.

In the day in which Daniel was written, the author did not possess historical sources by which all matters could be checked. He used the knowledge and traditions that he had.

Writers, in demonstrating a deep message, could compress history. A fall of Babylon in 539 B.C. would not stand out, some centuries later, as absolutely separate from the fall of Babylon in 520. The fact that Darius I Hystaspes conquered Baby-

---

[10] Cyrus Cylinder, ANET 315b; Nabonidus Chronicle in Barton, *Archaeology and the Bible*, 1937, p. 482.

[11] *Nabonidus and Belshazzar*, 1929, p. 180.

lon in 520 B.C., after the death of his predecessor Cambyses, may have led the versions to connect v. 31 with the fall of Babylon (v. 30; 539).

If the writer of chapter 6 were viewing the material after some centuries he would know the Medo-Persian kingdom as historically more important than the Median kingdom. He could loosely write of the "Medes and Persians." So the King Darius of chapter 6 would refer to Darius I. Chapter 6 refers to "the law of the Medes and the Persians" (vv. 8,12,15). Cyrus, a Persian, overthrew Astyages in 550 B.C. and absorbed the Median Empire into that of the Persian Empire. Together they became the Medo-Persian Empire. Cyrus (550–530) was succeeded by his son Cambyses (530–522 B.C.). Following Cambyses as king of Medo-Persia was Darius I (522–486). So even though Darius was genealogically a Persian, as a ruler of the Medo-Persian empire he could be referred to generally, though not technically, as a Mede.

This account was used in a situation of tension involving sacred temple objects. Such a time could be when Antiochus Epiphanes removed the sacred objects from the Temple in 169 (see 1 Macc. 1: 21–23 for this record). Such an occasion could also be the attempt of Heliodorus to violate the sanctity of the Temple and to confiscate it for the king's treasury (2 Macc. 3:9–30; prior to 175). Chapter 5 would bolster the Jews during such threats. They needed to be reminded that God would bring punishment on one who committed such sacrilege. Antiochus would receive the same end as Belshazzar for the same heinous deed.

6. Daniel in the Lions' Den (6:1–28)

(1) Daniel Caught in Power Struggle (6: 1–5)

[1] It pleased Darius to set over the kingdom a hundred and twenty satraps, to be throughout the whole kingdom; [2] and over them three presidents, of whom Daniel was one, to whom these satraps should give account, so that the king might suffer no loss. [3] Then this Daniel became distinguished above all the other presidents and satraps, because an excellent spirit was in him; and the king planned to set him over the whole kingdom. [4] Then the presidents and the satraps sought to find a ground for complaint against Daniel with regard to the kingdom; but they could find no ground for complaint or any fault, because he was faithful, and no error or fault was found in him. [5] Then these men said, "We shall not find any ground for complaint against this Daniel unless we find it in connection with the law of his God."

The historical situation is begun in 5:31 (Aramaic, 6:1). Verse 31 records that Darius was *about sixty-two years old* when he assumed the kingship. This is the only reference to the age of a Gentile's accession to a throne contained in all canonical records (Rowley, *Darius the Mede*, p. 14). This was probably the age of Cyrus' general, Gobryas, when the Babylonian kingdom was taken in 539 B.C.[12] The age reference is probably concerning the conqueror of Babylon. The king who received the kingdom was Cyrus. He was about 62 years old at the time of the fall of Babylon to his forces (Rowley, *Darius the Mede*, p. 55).[13]

Darius became king in a period of revolts and catastrophes. When Cambyses was king, he succeeded in bringing Egypt under Persian rule (525 B.C.). As Cambyses was journeying from Egypt through Syria, bad news reached him. Gaumata, claiming to be Cambyses' brother Bardiya, had seized control over most of the eastern part of the Persian Empire. Whereupon Cambyses committed suicide. This provided the background for Darius, the son of Hystaspes, to take the army eastward to Media and to slay Gaumata the usurper. Revolts also broke out in Elam, Parsa, and Armenia.

A rebellion in Babylon was led by Nidintubel under the name of Nebuchadnezzar III, claiming to be the son of Nabonidus. After a few months Darius

[12] Cf. *Oxford Annotated Bible*, note on 5:31, p. 1076.

[13] Cicero, *De divinatione* in Loeb edition I. xxiii (46), p. 274.

executed him and thus squelched the revolt. Soon thereafter another rebel, calling himself Nebuchadnezzar and a son of Nabonidus, led a revolt for several months before Darius eradicated him. During the first two years of Darius I there were various attempts to seize control.[14] The power struggle within the Persian ruling class was probably the reason that Darius set up a single line of command involving his *whole kingdom* (v. 1).

In order to bring some solidarity to the kingdom Darius I appointed *a hundred and twenty satraps.* Satrap in an Old Persian term which means "protector of the realm" (cf. in Heb. Ezra 8:36; Esther 3:12; 8:9; 9:3; in Aramaic only in Daniel 3 and 6). The appointment of satraps was not initiated by Darius for the first time in history. Herodotus (iii. 89 ff.) states that Darius divided his whole empire into 20 satrapies. The LXX (cf. Esther 1:1; 8:9; 1 Esdras 3:2; Additions to Esther 13:1; 16:1) gives the number of provinces or satrapies as 127. Darius' own inscriptions indicate at various times an organization into 21,23, or 29 satrapies.

The line of command used by Darius was that directly beneath the king there were *three presidents.* The precise meaning of the title presidents is not clear. There is no other record of having three subrulers under the king. It is not exactly a third ruler as in 5:7. The word president is generally taken to be a Persian word for chief, head, or overseer. Herodotus (iii. 128; cf. *The Oxford Annotated Bible* p. 1076) indicates that each satrap had three officials with some degree of independence, i.e., the satrap, his military chief, and his secretary. Since the presidents and satraps are mentioned individually (vv. 3,4,6,7), it would suggest that the three presidents were the three men who comprised the second level of authority, *to whom these satraps should give account.* The satraps formed the next level of authority. The *prefects* (v. 7) were the members of the entourage surrounding

the presidents or the satraps.

If the historical situation of this passage is actually that of the early years of Darius Hystaspes, it would be no surprise that the king should take measures to *suffer no loss.* In the wake of rebellions during which certain territories sought to pull out from under the Persian control, the ruler would attempt to hold *the whole kingdom* (vv. 1, 3) securely. The usual interpretation is that the satraps watched over the finances of the empire. Bentzen suggests the arrangement was such that the king would not be bothered with the burden of state affairs.

In the succeeding months Daniel's preeminence and reliability became evident to the king (v. 3). The other presidents and satraps felt threatened, as to their own positions, for *the king planned to set him over the whole kingdom.*

In order to hold their positions in government, the other presidents and satraps *sought to find a ground for complaint.* Since the entire basis of this power struggle was political they sought for a flaw *in regard to the kingdom.* There was no hint of divided loyalties or lack of ability in the performance of the political office.

They sought vainly for a complaint (vv. 4,5), i.e., a ground for legal indictment, so they turned to *the law of his God.* The law (*dath*) is a Persian word translating *torah* as a law-code of religious rules (cf. 7:25; Ezra 7:12,14). These men knew that Daniel observed the law as a rule of life decreed by his God.

(2) Daniel Forced to Make a Choice (6: 6–18)

6 Then these presidents and satraps came by agreement to the king and said to him, "O King Darius, live for ever! 7 All the presidents of the kingdom, the prefects and the satraps, the counselors and the governors are agreed that the king should establish an ordinance and enforce an interdict, that whoever makes petition to any god or man for thirty days, except to you, O king, shall be cast into the den of lions. 8 Now, O king, establish the interdict and sign the document, so that it cannot be changed, according to the law of the Medes and the Persians, which cannot be revoked."

---

[14] Cf. *Behistun Inscription;* Cowley, *Aramaic Papyri,* pp. 248 ff.

9 Therefore King Darius signed the document and interdict.

10 When Daniel knew that the document had been signed, he went to his house where he had windows in his upper chamber open toward Jerusalem; and he got down upon his knees three times a day and prayed and gave thanks before his God, as he had done previously. 11 Then these men came by agreement and found Daniel making petition and supplication before his God. 12 Then they came near and said before the king, concerning the interdict, "O king! Did you not sign an interdict, that any man who makes petition to any god or man within thirty days except to you, O king, shall be cast into the den of lions?" The king answered, "The thing stands fast, according to the law of the Medes and Persians, which cannot be revoked." 13 Then they answered before the king, "That Daniel, who is one of the exiles from Judah, pays no heed to you, O king, or the interdict you have signed, but makes his petition three times a day."

14 Then the king, when he heard these words, was much distressed, and set his mind to deliver Daniel; and he labored till the sun went down to rescue him. 15 Then these men came by agreement to the king, and said to the king, "Know, O king, that it is a law of the Medes and Persians that no interdict or ordinance which the king establishes can be changed."

16 Then the king commanded, and Daniel was brought and cast into the den of lions. The king said to Daniel, "May your God, whom you serve continually, deliver you!" 17 And a stone was brought and laid upon the mouth of the den, and the king sealed it with his own signet and with the signet of his lords, that nothing might be changed concerning Daniel. 18 Then the king went to his palace, and spent the night fasting; no diversions were brought to him, and sleep fled from him.

The officials *came by agreement*. This expression is not clear at all. The Aramaic word is found only in this chapter (6:6,11, 15; in Heb. it is only in Psalm 2:1; cf. noun in Psalms 55:14; 64:2). Some interpreters translate it "came tumultuously." This type of precipitant action on the part of a group of appointed officials would not be in keeping with the dignity of the king's court. That translation does not fit the use in v. 15. Following the use in Psalms 55 and 64 with its parallel idea of confidential conversation, the force here also may be consensus as "in concert or collusion." The late

use came to be *came by agreement* or acted in concert (Montgomery, pp. 272–273; Jeffery, p. 440; Young, p. 133).

The Aramaic text does not indicate how many came into the presence of the king. The LXX indicates that only the other two presidents were involved. Likewise then only these two with their families were punished (cf. v. 24). They presented themselves as representatives of *all* the officials. Verse 7 gives an order slightly different from that in 3:2–3. This was not intended to refer to an order of rank but merely to show the king the unanimity of their request. They attempt to secure a decree from the king. This *interdict* was in regard to a godly law (cf. v. 5). It could have been viewed as an additional measure of governmental unification. In keeping with the efforts to bring all aspects of government under the control of Darius, they instituted a loyalty campaign. They sought a law to make it evident that for a period of *thirty days* Darius would be sole representative of Deity. All *petitions* must be mediated through the king.

The idea of Darius being the sole representative of deity is not in keeping with the history of Persian kings and Darius unless it is the use of religion as a cohesive factor in the kingdom. Such a figure of the king possessing such a relation to God would be in keeping with the Hellenistic period or later when kings exalted themselves to the position of gods.

The *interdict* would prohibit anyone making a religious request *to any god or man* except to Darius (LXX omits "or man"). The punishment was to be thrust *into the den of lions*. The den was a cistern or pit instead of a cage. Verse 17 indicates that the top of the den could be covered by a stone and v. 23 shows that Daniel was taken up out of the den. Animals could not live long in such an enclosure. It is strange that the writer did not use the word cages (if such it was; cf. Ezek. 19:9). Lions were captured to be placed in the Assyrian zoos. Assyrian kings were known to participate in lion hunts. It may have been (cf. Porteous, p. 90) that lions were captured only to be released at the bidding of the king for his sport. Jeffery (p. 441) suggests that the idea of keeping a lion in a pit would only be used by "a writer unfamiliar with lions outside the pages of literature."

The stringency of the law is absolute in that it was a *law of the Medes and the Persians, which cannot be revoked*. Esther 1:19 gives the proper evaluation of the rank in "Persians and Medes" instead of the later view as in Daniel. A distinct point of the irrevocability of the law is made. The presidents repeat the idea to the king so that he will recognize the fact that he cannot vary the decree at any time.

The king signed the *document and interdict*. It was only one law. The two words are hendiadys.

Daniel was forced to make a decision. Daniel was confronted with a dilemma upon the knowledge that the legally binding decree *had been signed*. He continued to live by the same law and principles even after the law of Darius was publicized. He went to the same place, i.e., *his upper chamber;* he did not change his attitude, i.e., *he got down upon his knees;* the time was the same, i.e., the regular *three times a day;* he did the same things, i.e., he *prayed and gave thanks;* he did not let anything or anyone intervene between him and his God, i.e., he prayed directly to *his God (toward Jerusalem)*.

The *upper chamber* was the place especially prepared for prayer, mourning, and other acts of religious devotion. *Toward Jerusalem* indicates a custom after the exile. Such a direction can be seen in 1 Kings 8:44 (cf. Psalms 5:7; 28:2; Tobit 3:11; 1 Esdras 4:58).

As he had done previously makes it clear that the God who controlled Daniel's life before the interdict was not pushed aside by a human legal decree (regardless of threatened punishment).

The second planned step in the conspiracy was (v. 11) to find Daniel *making petition* (same word in vv. 7,15). Daniel made *supplication before his God*. He was seeking the favor of God while the officials were appearing to seek the favor of the king. Continuing their collusion they find Daniel, as they knew they would, praying to his God even though it was now contrary to the religious moratorium. Armed now with the evidence that they had so carefully prepared, they go to the king. They remind the king of the interdict, of the time stipulations, and of the punishment for failure to obey by asking him a question. The king affirms that he had signed such an order and that the law could not be revoked.

The presidents felt a sense of exhilaration at being able to outwit the innocent king. Adroitly they proceed to reveal the identity of the disloyal lawbreaker. Young (p. 136) accuses the presidents of the trickery of corrupt politicians in presenting Daniel in as bad a light as possible. They did not refer to him as one of the presidents but rather as *one of the exiles from Judah.* Instead of putting the emphasis on the broken decree they stress Daniel's disloyalty to the king.

The king's recognition of the excellence of Daniel was based on his own observation and evaluation of the man. When he heard the report of the treacherous politicians he *was much distressed*, literally it was evil (displeasing) to him. The KJV adds "with himself," but this addition is not in the Aramaic text. The king *set his mind* (cf. the similar expression in 1 Sam. 9:20). The word mind (*bal*) is used in biblical Aramaic only here. We are not told what measures the king took to rescue Daniel.

The third step in the collusion is the forcing of the hand of the king. The reply which they make to the king borders on insolence, but this is the author's manner of emphasizing the essential elements and of dramatizing the event in good literary style.

The king accedes to their scheme for he has no other choice. Daniel is *cast into the den of lions*. Bentzen suggests that the meaning here is related to the use that the

Psalms make of a cistern as a picture of the underworld. Thus, Daniel's being thrust into the den (cistern) would have the force of plunging our hero into the realm of death. The king expresses the hope that the God whom Daniel served *continually* would deliver him, i.e., do for Daniel what he had tried to do but failed.

The mouth of the den was an opening at the top of the cistern. All arguments as to whether there was also an opening lower at the side are arguments from silence based on a modicum of knowledge of the actual cistern.

The mouth was *sealed* with the *signet* of both the king and *his lords.* This is the climax in the legal maneuvering of the opposing presidents. These presidents are the real culprits in the record for they had not done anything illegal, but everything they did was destructive, selfish, and unrighteous. There is a vast difference between being lawful and being right. Those presidents were upholders of the law to the extreme but they were not supporters of state, civil, or personal rights. Just as the enemies of Daniel had involved the law and the king in their devious activities, they made sure that the final act was carried out legally and with no possibility of circumvention.

Nothing might be changed concerning Daniel. The details of the law had been observed so meticulously that the culprits had the king and the law working for them. The real aim of these culprits was the eradication of Daniel in such a way that they would not be responsible. If the animals killed Daniel, legally the presidents would not have blood on their hands.

Antiochus Epiphanes' attempt at gaining personal power and aggrandizement serves as a parallel to this event. This account would encourage the Jews of that time to continue to live by the laws of God as Daniel had. Since Daniel survived his accusers' chicanery, so those who live by God's laws could expect relief.

Daniel's accusers were very thorough. The seal of both the king and of his lords

was *upon the mouth of the den.* Herodotus (iii. 128) mentions the seal of Darius which represents the king as engaged in a lion hunt.[15] This seal was so fixed that the stone could not be moved clandestinely. With this seal on the only opening of the den, it would be impossible for any of Daniel's friends to rescue him. They could not throw any food to the lions in an attempt to lure the lions into eating that food instead of eating Daniel. They could not pass any weapon to Daniel with which to defend himself from the ferocious beasts. Daniel was defenseless from law and lions.

Verse 18 shows that the prayer of the king (v. 16) was a matter of deep sincerity and concern. The king *spent the night fasting.* This is not the word fast which is common for remaining foodless as a religious act (*tsom* is that word; cf. Dan. 9:3; Neh. 9:1; Esther 4:3). This word (*t^ewath*) means foodlessly or hungrily.

The meaning of *no diversions* is uncertain. The word is not known elsewhere. *Dah^ewan* is similar to the word meaning thrust. So it is interpreted by Ibn Ezra and Calvin as strike strings in music or instruments of song. Theodotion and the Peshitta related it to the preceding phrase and took it to mean food. The RSV and Luther follow the idea of diversion or pleasure. *The Jerusalem Bible,* Berthold, Bevan, and Prince translate as concubines.

His *sleep fled from him.* The text does not say that he stayed awake as a religious action. He could not sleep for the entire matter troubled him to the point of worry.

(3) Daniel Delivered from the Den (6: 19-24)

19 Then, at break of day, the king arose and went in haste to the den of lions. 20 When he came near to the den where Daniel was, he cried out in a tone of anguish and said to Daniel, "O Daniel, servant of the living God, has your God, whom you serve continually, been able to deliver you from the lions?" 21 Then Daniel said to the king, "O king, live for ever! 22 My God sent his angel and shut the lions' mouths, and they have not hurt me,

15 Soncino, p. 52.

because I was found blameless before him; and also before you, O king, I have done no wrong." 23 Then the king was exceedingly glad, and commanded that Daniel be taken up out of the den. So Daniel was taken up out of the den, and no kind of hurt was found upon him, because he had trusted in his God. 24 And the king commanded, and those men who had accused Daniel were brought and cast into the den of lions—they, their children, and their wives; and before they reached the bottom of the den the lions overpowered them and broke all their bones in pieces.

The sincerity of the king's wish (6:16*b*) is shown to be genuine in several ways: he could not sleep through the night; he went to the den at the first appearance of enough light with which to see (*at break of day*); he *went in haste;* he *cried out in . . . anguish* to Daniel.

The *angel* (v. 22) was a messenger of God. The same word is used in 3:28 of the angel who was the servant of God delivering the three youths from the fiery furnace. There is a great similarity in this story and that of the three men who were delivered from certain fiery destruction for failing to live by the orders of Nebuchadnezzar. The two stories are connected in 1 Maccabees 2:59–60.

The mouths of the lions were shut. This experience is a familiar motif in the ancient martyr histories (Jeffery, p. 446). It is obviously referred to in Hebrews 11:33 and 1 Maccabees 2:60.

In the mouth of Daniel, his relationship to God comes first. He says that the reason that the lions did not touch him was that he *was found blameless* before God. Daniel vows that he had *done no wrong* in regard to the king.

When Daniel was *taken up* from the den he was unharmed *because he had trusted in his God.* Daniel's accusers received the punishment which they had so cunningly devised for Daniel. Royal retribution was heaped upon those who accused Daniel (lit., ate the pieces of Daniel; cf. 3:8). Family solidarity is evident in the condemnation of the wives and the children of the guilty ones to the same fate (cf. Esther 9:10–13; Herodotus iii. 119). The artistry

of the writer is evident in the quick summary of the results. The entire families were hurled from the opening at the top of the lions' den. They were slain *before they reached the* bottom. The word *overpowered* is used also in 3:27. The apparent voraciousness of the animals shows that Daniel had not been spared for the lack of an appetite. The power and presence of the living God is emphasized.

(4) The Decree of Darius (6:25–28)

25 Then King Darius wrote to all the peoples, nations, and languages that dwell in all the earth: "Peace be multiplied to you. 26 I make a decree, that in all my royal dominion men tremble and fear before the God of Daniel,

for he is the living God,
  enduring for ever;
his kingdom shall never be destroyed,
  and his dominion shall be to the end.
27 He delivers and rescues,
  he works signs and wonders
  in heaven and on earth,
he who has saved Daniel
  from the power of the lions."
28 So this Daniel prospered during the reign of Darius and the reign of Cyrus the Persian.

Verses 25–27 have a striking similarity to the decree of Nebuchadnezzar (4:1–3) which formed the climax of the parallel story of chapter 3. The poetic exaggeration concerning *all the peoples, nations, and languages . . . in all the earth* probably is flowery royal language exaggerating the vast extent of his royal dominion (v. 26).

The living God (cf. 6:20) comes from speeches of Darius. It is an idea used repeatedly in Hebrew literature. The idea *enduring* is found in relation to God in the Targum, in rabbinical and Samaritan literature.

Darius decrees that men *tremble and fear before the God of Daniel.* He does not claim that this God is the only God. He elevates Daniel's God to the position of highest honor. He was the *living* God; an *enduring* God; and everlasting God whose *dominion shall be to the end;* he was a miracle-working God on earth and above; he saved Daniel from the *power* of the wild beast. The elevation and inclusion of the worship of the God of Daniel agrees with the religious policy of toleration instituted by Cyrus and continued in the reign of Cambyses (Bright, pp. 342–343).[16]

Most interpreters see v. 28 as having been written as a historical reference. But such a reference, if history, is chronologically reversed since Cyrus the Persian preceded Darius. The confusing order of the two kings may have been caused by the final clause having been added as a scribal note to call attention to the similarity in Daniel's position under Darius with that of the earlier kingdom.

II. The Imminent Intervention of God (7: 1–28)

The first six chapters are individual historical accounts which when combined express great encouragement to any who have been backed against a wall and forced to make life-shattering decisions. Chapter 7 begins another section of the book. The dreams and visions of Daniel form the framework within which the author now works. The style, content, and outline have led many interpreters to separate the first six chapters into one unit and the second six chapters into another unit.

Chapters 1—6 have conveyed hope and encouragement to a threatened community. This hope was strengthened in that Daniel and his three friends had endured the same problems and had come through victoriously. The hope in chapters 7–12 stems from the reality of God's presence and the imminence of his taking a direct hand in their affairs.

1. The Superscription (7:1)

¹ In the first year of Belshazzar king of Babylon, Daniel had a dream and visions of his head as he lay in his bed. Then he wrote down the dream, and told the sum of the matter.

The superscription joins the other chronological notes and establishes the fact that the contents of Daniel are not chronologically arranged. There are two ideas inher-

---

ent in this fact. (1) The book is not a history of the man Daniel *per se*. (2) There is an essential purpose of the arrangement which has nothing directly to do with a chronological arrangement. The book is theological in its framework and outlook. This superscription ascribes this dream to the *first year of Belshazzar* (probably 555 B.C. when he began to function as coruler with his father).

The sum of the matter has been given different meanings by writers. It has been explained as Daniel giving the essence or recapitulation of the dream without the secondary elements (LXX, Jeffery, Young, Charles, and Montgomery). It has been read as the "beginning of the story" (Aquila, Theodotion, and Soncino). Some have taken it to refer to a chapter heading.

Verse 1 and 10:1 (also a superscription) are the only locations in the last half of the book in which Daniel is spoken of in the third person. This verse is a typical literary instrument in postexilic, apocalyptic, and apocryphal literature. This superscription, as well as 10:1, may be an introduction in the form of a division heading.

2. The Vision of the Four Beasts (7:2–8)

² Daniel said, "I saw in my vision by night, and behold, the four winds of heaven were stirring up the great sea. ³ And four great beasts came up out of the sea, different from one another. ⁴ The first was like a lion and had eagles' wings. Then as I looked its wings were plucked off, and it was lifted up from the ground and made to stand upon two feet like a man; and the mind of a man was given to it. ⁵ And behold, another beast, a second one, like a bear. It was raised up on one side; it had three ribs in its mouth between its teeth; and it was told, 'Arise, devour much flesh.' ⁶ After this I looked, and lo, another, like a leopard, with four wings of a bird on its back; and the beast had four heads; and dominion was given to it. ⁷ After this I saw in the night visions, and behold, a fourth beast, terrible and dreadful and exceedingly strong; and it had great iron teeth; it devoured and broke in pieces, and stamped the residue with its feet. It was different from all the beasts that were before it; and it had ten horns. ⁸ I considered the horns, and behold, there came up among them another horn, a little one, before which three of the first horns were plucked up by the roots; and

behold, in this horn were eyes like the eyes of a man, and a mouth speaking great things.

Practically all interpreters agree that there is a very striking pattern in chapter 2 which is adhered to also in this chapter. In both chapters there are four images which represent four kingdoms. The writer is not expressing a world view which incorporates all time from the beginning to the end of time. He is taking a specific look from the time of Daniel in Babylonian captivity to the time of his very minute interests. The dominance of the figure four is very intriguing, i.e., four winds, four great beasts, four wings, and four heads.

The *four winds* (cf. 8:8; 11:4; Zech. 2:6; 6:5; Ezek. 37:9) are known as from each direction.[17] They are not references to heavenly forces such as angels (Jerome, Keil). They are elements of a literary type well known in the postexilic literature (cf. Zech., 2 Esdras, and Enoch).

This section shows a relation to the prophets, though Daniel is not referred to as a prophet in the Old Testament. The superscription dating the vision has prophetic overtones. The vision is a literary type rather than an oral message. In this type of writing, composite figures of beastly nature are very common as seen in the artistic picturizations.

The *great sea* is not the Mediterranean Sea. It is a vast expanse of water in turmoil. It also has reference to the "great deep" of Isaiah 51:10; Amos 7:4; Psalms 36:6; 74:13 f.; 78:15; 89:9–12; Genesis 1:2. These figures were common in ancient cosmogonies. As figures, they produced a message of expanse and practical universality. The Hebrews had received the knowledge of watery chaos, the monsters, the winds from the four corners, etc., from Babylonia, Ugarit, and Egypt.

Out of the vast turbulent world, there *came up* four important kingdoms to affect the life of the author and the people for whom he was writing. The symbolism of the *four . . . beasts* arising from the great

17 Cf. Babylonian Creation Tablets IV, 42, 43.

sea, the seat of evil and the home of terrifying monsters, is closely related to the presentation in ancient mythologies. These were common vocabulary in postexilic times (1 Enoch 60:7; Rev. 13:1; 2 Esdras 6:49–50).

They were *different from one another* (lit., changed). The KJV translates it "diverse." Compare the different metals of 2:32. Each of these beasts is more destructive than the former. The term does not determine different dynasties or even nationalities.

The first was a grotesque figure of a *lion* with *eagles' wings*. The symbolizing of enemy nations as terrifying beasts or mythological monsters is seen in Ezekiel 29:3 and Isaiah 27:1. Jeremiah (4:7; 49:19; 50:17) compared Nebuchadnezzar to a lion. Nebuchadnezzar's armies were described as eagles (Jer. 49:22; Hab. 1:8; Ezek. 17:3). The winged lions from Nimrud and Babylon were probably the sources of these symbols as applicable to Babylon.

The lion was king of the beasts and the eagle was the greatest of birds. This feature agrees with chapter 2 in which Nebuchadnezzar is the head of gold, the most precious of metals. Nebuchadnezzar as the king of Babylon was the figure of the kingdom (see Rowley's *Darius the Mede*, pp. 67–186, for thorough study of the four beasts).

The *wings were plucked off* so it could not fly. It was *made to stand* on two legs instead of bounding along on four. It was given *the mind* of a man instead of the fierce nature of a wild beast. There are similarities to the figure in chapter 2, but there are also irreconcilable dissimilarities. It is erroneous to attempt a harmonization of all the details in these two chapters. It is noteworthy that all the kings of the powerful Babylonian kingdom are not listed. In reality, reference to Nebuchadnezzar is to the Babylonian kingdom under the figure of the dominant person, the king par excellence. It is apparent that Nebuchadnezzar is the one king to whom reference is made. A single verse is given to the description of this kingdom. The three descriptions of the king have been taken to mean that the kingdom was so weak it could be conquered easily.

The second beast was *like a bear.* The bear is often used with the lion (cf. Hos. 13:8; Amos 5:19; Prov. 28:15). The bear is second only to the lion in size or in fierceness of all the animals which were known in Palestine. The remainder of v. 5 is difficult and has not been interpreted with any unanimity. Attempts have been made to show that all of it conveys one single concept. The being *raised up on one side* is interpreted to mean rearing up in preparation for attack. Having *three ribs in its mouth* is a figure of ferocity and the voracious nature of the bear. The interpretation of these portions will affect the interpreter's conclusion as to the identity of the kingdom represented by the bear. The kingdom could be the kingdom of the Medes (cf. Charles, Jeffery, and Porteous). This view has been put forth with some strength and historical insight. *Raised up on one side* has been explained to mean unbalanced or shaky when compared to Babylon. It has been explained also as referring to the Medes being set to one side so as not to play any part in the main stream of history.

There is a connection between chapters 2 and 7 and also between chapters 7 and 8. Daniel 8:3 has another animal, i.e., a ram with two horns, one higher than the other. This animal is explained to be Medo-Persia (8:20). If there is a parallelism in this regard, being raised on one side would be a synonym for one horn of the ram being higher than the other. The *three ribs in its mouth* would have to be of a very small animal unless the mouth of the bear were exceptionally large. If we follow the identification of chapter 8 in interpreting the bear as the kingdom of Medo-Persia, the three ribs would be naturally Babylon, Lydia, and Egypt. It states in 8:4 that the ram was pushing west, i.e., Babylon; north, i.e., Lydia; and south, i.e., Egypt. Lydia and Babylon were conquered by Cyrus, and Egypt was taken by Cambyses.

The third beast was *like a leopard,* with four wings and four heads. The leopard is used with the lion in Jeremiah 5:6; Isaiah 11:6 and with both the lion and bear in Hosea 13:7. The *four wings* have reference to the swiftness and agility of the kingdom. The Persian army was noted for mobility (cf. Isa. 41:2–3). This attribute may be seen also in the rapidity of the Alexandrian forces of the Greek Empire. If the bear (v. 5) was Media, it would be logical that the following beast (kingdom) would be Persia. But if the bear was Medo-Persia, the leopard would be the kingdom following Medo-Persia, i.e., the Greek Empire.

It is important to incorporate all of the biblical evidence into one's interpretation. What is the meaning of the four heads? If the third beast is Persia, they are taken to be a part of a hendiadys, i.e., the four heads and the four wings refer to the same idea of swiftness. However, the figure of a head does not relate to swiftness in fact or in poetic literature. It is suggested that the four heads represent the Persian claim to rule over the four corners of the earth. Others take the four heads to represent the four kings of the Persian Empire (cf. 11:2).

If the third beast is the Greek kingdom, the four wings could represent the four directions (or the four winds of 8:8 and 11:4) and the four heads could represent the four generals (four conspicuous horns of 8:8 or the four kingdoms of 8:22) who were parts of the Greek Empire (namely, Egypt with Ptolemy; Macedonia with Philip; Syria-Babylonia with Seleucus; Thrace with Lysimachus).

The main focus of the author's purpose is on the fourth beast inasmuch as each of the first three beasts were accorded attention in one verse only. These three kingdoms served as historical background for the important message.

The fourth beast is not given a name as the first three. It was *terrible and dreadful and exceedingly strong* with *great iron teeth.* This beast was so terrifying and fierce that it could not even be likened to any earthly animals at all. It may be that the writer used an historical background to identify the preceding kingdoms. Since he was writing in a time of persecution and danger he could not call names for fear of being prevented from getting his message of courage and hope to those in need. Just as in chapter 2 the details are very evident, here in chapter 7 the details are brought out in striking clarity. Three terms of destruction are used to describe the beast's activities, i.e., *devoured and broke in pieces, and stamped* with its feet. This beast was the worst of all. It was different (vv. 3,19, 23,24; "change" is the same word in vv. 25,28). The *iron teeth* of the fourth beast adds to the parallelism between chapters 2 and 7.

The *ten horns* are ten kings which are successive instead of simultaneous. The identity of these kings is difficult. It is closely interwoven with the identification of the fourth power. This power has been variously identified: Greeks, Seleucids, Romans, Edom, Ishmael and the Saracens, the Turks, or the power before the antichrist.

If the ten horns are of the Roman Empire, the number is explained as only being used in a symbolic sense such as an indefinitely large number of kings. It is also taken to indicate that the power of the kingdom was in full force.

Generally the ten horns bring to mind the ten toes of 2:41–42. They are explained as being members of the Seleucid line by those interpreters who understand the fourth kingdom to be Greece and by those who see the successors of the kingdom of Alexander, i.e., the Seleucids.

Alexander made an amazingly swift task at conquering the vast reaches of the Greek Empire. In the brief span of 13 years he expanded control to the four corners of the biblical world and took complete control over Asia Minor, Persia, Syria, and Egypt. At the age of 33 after such a blitzkrieg career, he became ill in Babylon and died in 323 B.C. His death was a signal for a long struggle between his generals for control of various portions of the old Greek

Empire. At the battle of Ipsus (301) Ptolemy I, Soter or Lagi, defeated Antigonus. This left four heads of the old Greek Empire in existence for a brief period of time before it shrank to three distinct branches. Only two of these are of great concern to the book of Daniel.

Palestine was under the control of the Ptolemies following Ptolemy I's victory. It remained under their control for approximately 100 years. Palestine was sought after by the Seleucids (who controlled Syria and Babylonia) on various occasions, but they were not strong enough to defeat the Ptolemies until the Seleucid ruler Antiochus III the Great (223–187 B.C.) shattered the Egyptian army of Ptolemy V Epiphanes (203–181) at Paneas, southwest of Mount Hermon, in 198. The change of rule from the king of the south to the rule of the king of the north was a welcomed transfer to the Jews.[18]

If the fourth beast is the Seleucid Empire there is a distinct possibility of identifying the horns (cf. Rowley, *Darius the Mede*, pp. 98–115). Bleek, Davidson, and Venema seek to find the ten horns as ten divisions or commanders of Alexander's empire. This would make the little horn Seleucus Nicator the founder of the Seleucid Empire. The three horns would be Antigonus, Ptolemy Lagi, and Lysimachus. Seleucus Nicator was the founder of the Seleucid Empire which included Antiochus Epiphanes.

Just as Bleek has sought to find ten divisions of the Greek Empire, some who hold that the fourth beast is Rome have sought to identify ten divisions of the Roman Empire. Failing in this attempt, they insist that there is no need to hold to the specific number (Montgomery, p. 293n). Rosenmüller and Cowles agree on the basic principle that these ten horns were kings who had come into direct relationship with Palestine. Cowles included five kings of the south and five kings of the north.

The earliest written source outside of the

---

[18] Josephus, *Antiq.* XII, III. 3 f.

book of Daniel relating to the ten horns, the Sibylline Oracles (III, 381–400; probably dating 140–124 B.C.), points to the view that all the kings were of the Seleucid line. This leads to the principle that the horns were understood in their relation to Palestine *per se* and in their relation to the little horn, Antiochus.

The Seleucid line was established by Seleucus Nicator (312–280 B.C.). He was followed by Antiochus I Soter, 279–261; Antiochus II Theos, 261–247; Seleucus II Callinicus, 247–226; Seleucus III Ceraunus, 226–223; Antiochus III the Great, 223–187; Seleucus IV Philopator, 187–175. These are the first seven Seleucid kings. The next Seleucid ruler was Antiochus IV Epiphanes (175–164). It has been suggested that these seven were preceded by Alexander, Antigonus, and Demetrius in order to name ten kings.

One problem which first must be faced is the total number of horns included in vv. 7,8,20. Ten horns were followed by another horn (v. 8) or the other horn (v. 20) totaling 11 horns. The three horns are noted as *three of the first horns* (v. 8) and thus would be among the group of ten. If the three are part of the ten, the seven predecessors of Antiochus Epiphanes are logical selections for the first seven of the ten horns. Who are the three who *were plucked up by the roots?*

It is not possible to assert with any certainty the identity of the three horns mentioned by our author. No doubt, he had a meaning in mind, but the details have not been preserved. The little horn occupied a major portion of his attention. This little horn was so powerful that he became victorious in various attempted coups. He *uprooted* three of the royal line.

Antiochus Epiphanes succeeded his brother Seleucus IV Philopator (187–175 B.C.). Seleucus was murdered by Heliodorus. Since Antiochus took the place of Seleucus, some have taken the position that Philopator was one of the three horns set aside (Cowles, Grotius). If, however, Alexander the Great is one of the ten horns,

Seleucus IV would be number eight and thus one of the three horns.

Another possible horn uprooted by the little horn could be Demetrius. He was a rightful heir, son of Seleucus IV Philopator and thus a nephew of Antiochus Epiphanes. Demetrius was a hostage in Rome during the time of Antiochus Epiphanes. According to 7:24 there were three kings. Demetrius was not king when he was shunted aside. But he was of the kingly family and thus a king-elect.

Heliodorus has been suggested (Prince, Charles, Bewer) as one of the three horns. Heliodorus assassinated Seleucus IV and thus put himself into contention for the kingship. Actually he made it possible for Antiochus Epiphanes to take control of the kingdom. Heliodorus was never king or even seriously considered as such.

Also, an heir apparent to the throne would be a brother of Demetrius. Events are uncertain but he may have been actually proclaimed king after the assassination of Seleucus. For a time he and Antiochus may have occupied the throne jointly. Bevan thinks that the Antiochus in whose name coins were struck at this time was this brother of Demetrius.

Another contender for the throne after the death of Seleucus IV was Ptolemy Philometor. He was king of the south (182–170 B.C.) at the time of Seleucus' death. It would not have been surprising for an attempt to have been made at that juncture for the two kingdoms to be brought together under Egyptian control. He was the son of Cleopatra, who was sister of Seleucus Philopator. Therefore, Philometor was one-half Seleucid.

Of these suggestions the three who fit the records best are Demetrius, Antiochus the brother of Demetrius, and Ptolemy Philometor.

The little horn is very prominent in this chapter. Those who interpret the fourth beast to be Rome are as indefinite at this point as in the explanation of the ten horns. Among their ranks the little horn is said to be Julius Caesar, Nero, Vespasian, Trajan, the Papacy, the Khalifate, or an antichrist.

Those who interpret the fourth beast as the Greeks or the Seleucids are specific in their agreement that the little horn refers to Antiochus Epiphanes. When the entire book is considered there is an amazing consistency in that all the records focus on the Antiochus Epiphanes period. The figure of the little horn of chapter 7 fits with the facts of the activity of Antiochus known from secular records. The little horn's character and activities are singled out in chapters 7 and 8 (8:9–26). He is described as having *eyes like the eyes of a man.* The period of this little horn is no doubt the period in which great encouragement and hope were called forth. The author provides an evaluative overall historical view to show his people both the past and the future as a setting of the fierce persecution which they were enduring. The little horn is insignificant when compared to a lion with eagles' wings, a devouring bear, or a dominating leopard. This king, even though a king, is only a man with human eyes and a big mouth. He had a *mouth speaking great things.* He is described as speaking "against the Most High" (7:25). The little horn had a human propensity for self-exaltation against the divine Being. The LXX adds "he made war against the saints" (cf. 7: 21,25).

3. *Three Interpretations of the Vision* (7: 9–28)

(1) *Interpretation of Coming Judgment* (7:9–10)

⁹ As I looked,
    thrones were placed
        and one that was ancient of days took his
            seat;
    his raiment was white as snow,
        and the hair of his head like pure wool;
    his throne was fiery flames,
        its wheels were burning fire.
¹⁰ A stream of fire issued
        and came forth from before him;
    a thousand thousands served him,
        and ten thousand times ten thousand stood
            before him;
    the court sat in judgment,
        and the books were opened.

From the confusion of the vision of four beasts we are now in an organized courtroom. *Thrones were placed* sets the scene as a judicial bench. The identity of those who may occupy these thrones is not made. These associated judges are not a point of the vision. It is pointless to argue as to whether it would be the Son of Man (1 Enoch 37—71), or the elders of Israel (some Jewish commentators), or angels (Keil, Young, Charles, Montgomery). The common view is that this is an angelic or heavenly court. The mention of the placement of the thrones sets the proper scene. In this case the plural of thrones would be considered a "majestic plural" (a plural which is used to emphasize the majestic nature of the thing mentioned).

One that was ancient of days is the only one who actually *took his seat.* The KJV translates it "the Ancient of days," but the RSV, the NEB, and *The Jerusalem Bible* are more accurate (7:13,22 have the article in Aramaic but it is not in 7:9). This one ancient of days or "advanced of days" is a being (not a human being) in contrast to the little horn (7:8). In Ugaritic material God is called "the king, father of years." The origin of this figure is unknown. It may have relation to the Persian figure of a great judge. The figure of Yahweh sitting on a throne was well known in Jewish Scripture (Ezek. 1:26; 43:7; Isa. 6:1; Psalm 55:19). This figure is clearly Yahweh.

These anthropomorphic expressions concerning an infinite God are not intended to describe God. They are but concrete figures to illustrate particular attributes concerning him. He was *ancient of days.* In the Near East advanced age is an attainment of honor, wisdom, and respect. He *took his seat* represents his exalted position of judge/king. *His raiment was white as snow* reflects the figure of notables always having white vesture indicating majesty and purity. *The hair of his head like pure wool* means "spotless as white wool" as the LXX reads it. It does not suggest the gray hair of old age but the purity and venerableness of a unique king figure. The symbolic parallelism of wool and snow is clear in Isaiah 1:18.

The *fiery flames* which served as his throne indicate the specific element of Deity (cf. Ex. 3:2; 19:18; Deut. 4:24; Ezek. 1:4 f.; 1 Enoch 14:22). Fire was an element in many theophanies (cf. Psalm 50:3; Deut. 9:3). The *wheels* used in conjunction with the fire are figures as seen in Ezekiel 1. Gods of many religions are thought to have their blazing chariots (cf. Apollo, Helios). The flaming chariot-throne indicates a vital, flowing, moving, spectacular reality of purity instead of a static capturable concept.

The *stream of fire* marks the boundary of the king's throne which may not be traversed. The river emanating from the throne illustrates vividly the undammable power of God's throne. The million servants are the ministering angels who carry out the decisions of the God as judge. The myriad myriads who stand *before him* suggest the limitless number of celestial beings who are gathered to await God's bidding.

The description of the judge/God is finished. The scene is the court of judgment. The *books were opened.* The record of man's deeds is no doubt related to the fact that the kings had chronicles and histories. This is not the "book of life" as found in Exodus 32:32. It is the "book of remembrance" (cf. Mal. 3:16; Isa. 65:6).

(2) *Interpretation of Judgment and Victory (7:11-20)*

11 I looked then because of the sound of the great words which the horn was speaking. And as I looked, the beast was slain, and its body destroyed and given over to be burned with fire. 12 As for the rest of the beasts, their dominion was taken away, but their lives were prolonged for a season and a time. 13 I saw in the night visions,

and behold, with the clouds of heaven
there came one like a son of man,
and he came to the Ancient of Days
and was presented before him.
14 And to him was given dominion
and glory and kingdom,
that all peoples, nations, and languages
should serve him;

his dominion is an everlasting dominion,
which shall not pass away,
and his kingdom one
that shall not be destroyed.
15 "As for me, Daniel, my spirit within me was anxious and the visions of my head alarmed me. 16 I approached one of those who stood there and asked him the truth concerning all this. So he told me, and made known to me the interpretation of the things. 17 'These four great beasts are four kings who shall arise out of the earth. 18 But the saints of the Most High shall receive the kingdom, and possess the kingdom for ever, for ever and ever.'

19 "Then I desired to know the truth concerning the fourth beast, which was different from all the rest, exceedingly terrible, with its teeth of iron and claws of bronze; and which devoured and broke in pieces, and stamped the residue with its feet; 20 and concerning the ten horns that were on its head, and the other horn which came up and before which three of them fell, the horn which had eyes and a mouth that spoke great things, and which seemed greater than its fellows.

The reason that the judge looked is stated as being the *sound of the great words* of the little horn. What a contrast is shown between the purity of the *Ancient of Days* and the blasphemous megalomania of the little horn!

Note the parallel of contrast between the self-exalting great words of the little horn and the destruction of the beast. Anthropomorphic expressions concerning the destruction of the beast are not to be pressed to literal ends any more than those of the vision of the ancient of days. The reference to the consummation by fire within the context of the "fiery flames . . . burning fire" (7:9) shows that whereas the little horn had sought to exalt himself above every power he would be completely destroyed by the power of Deity (the symbol of fire). The whole continuity of the vision (vv. 9-14) involves the presence, power, and purity of the "Ancient of Days." Likewise, the other beasts would have their power thwarted by the power of God. Rowley may be correct in his suggestion that the author saw the destruction of this little horn and thus saw the end of his empire. The other beasts, i.e., Babylon, Media, Persia, and

Greece, would continue to exist as separate states (independent, i.e., without dominion) temporarily until they were absorbed into the kingdom of the saints.

Under the threatening persecution of Antiochus Epiphanes, another encouragement to the Jews is added to that of the announcement of the presence of God and his power over the little horn. The vision is carried forward over a period of time (vv. 9,11,13). The oppression which the Jews had been enduring would not only come to an end but the impudent king would be catastrophically destroyed.

In the night visions is singular in the LXX, the Vulgate, and Peshitta texts. This vision is a sequel to that of vv. 9–10. There is a division of opinion as to whether it is *with* the clouds of heaven or "upon" (LXX, Peshitta, Charles) the clouds. Insignificant details may be pressed too far and thus blur the focus of the interpretation. *The clouds* were known as a method of transportation in passages involving celestial beings (cf. Psalms 18:10–12; 104:3; Isa. 19:1; 2 Esdras 13:3). A striking contrast can be seen between the floating gentleness of a cloud and the turbulent tossing of the great sea (ch. 2).

One like a son of man (*keʹbar ʹeʹnosh*) is the literal translation. The KJV is incorrect in reading "the Son of man" and thus making it a formal title. Later development and use of the term made it a formal title. This figure was *like* a human being. In 7:4 (lit., upon feet like a man and a heart of a man) and 7:8 (lit., like the eyes of the man) the word for man (*ʹeʹnosh*) is the term for man as weak, being susceptible to illness. It is not the same word for man as found in Psalms 8, 10, and Ezekiel (*ʹadam*). Chapter 7 uses the word man as a term of humanity as opposed to the divine. If *son of man* refers to one formally titled individual, there would be a problem with the correlation of v. 13 with vv. 18,22,27. Since the figure of "son of man" means a human who was, as Heaton suggests (p. 184), the embodiment of the principle of corporate personality, the two

applications of the vision are in complete agreement. There is no reason why this figure could not be used to refer both to saints as a whole and to a saint as an individual. C. H. Dodd points out three passages of the Old Testament which are background in the development of the term son of man as a title of Christ in the New Testament (Psalms 8, 80, and Dan. 7; see Heaton, pp. 184–185).[19] First Enoch 37—71 is important in the history of "son of man."

When the term is restricted to chapter 7 of Daniel and is confined to the historical situation of the book of Daniel, the term would probably be identified with *the saints of the Most High* and would embody the principle of "triumph after suffering," which could be applied to a later and successive situation. Later uses may be used to show the direction in which history carried the interpretation, but it does not prove what the original author had in mind. Son of man came to refer to Jesus formally, spiritually, and messianically. In fact, some early written sources which use the "son of man" image use it to refer to an individual Messiah (cf. 1 Enoch 37—71, which uses the term 14 times; Mark 14:62; 2 Esdras 13:1–3,32,37). These passages adopted this term from the earlier Daniel 7 passage, but they did not adopt the seventh chapter of Daniel. The term underwent a development apart from the historical context of Daniel 7 (for a wider examination of the term, see Russell, pp. 324–352).

The passage in Daniel 7 has the context of persecution of God's chosen people. God, the Ancient of Days, intervenes and destroys the little horn which is the persecutor. The exaltation of the oppressed is promised. In fact, their humiliation is the beginning of their victory (cf. the principle seen in Isa. 53 as exaltation through humiliation). Just as the early messianic figure of the people of God developed from the corporate figure of the whole to an in-

[19] Dodd, *According to the Scriptures*, pp. 117 f.

dividual Messiah, so did the figure of son of man develop: son of man as saints of the Most High seems to have developed to "the" Son of man as in the New Testament.

This figure may reflect the annual kingly enthronement festival reflected in some psalms. In this setting the son of man would reflect the messianic king figure.

The vision presents the son of man, not as coming down to earth from God, but being presented to God *with the clouds of heaven.* The clouds are not his companions but are his vehicle. He was *presented before* God. Literally, the Aramaic reads, "they brought him near before him." Since it was not important enough to the author's purpose to identify the ones who brought him near, it is not important to argue over whether it was the celestial attendants of the Ancient of Days or some of his own angelic company.

Verses 13 and 14 are metric in structure. The words of v. 14 are a series of royal descriptions. *Dominion and glory and kingdom* as well as *all peoples, nations, and languages* are parts of the royal language protocol as seen in 3:4; 4:22; 5:18–19. The *everlasting* dominion is seen also in 4:3,34 (cf. 6:26).

The interpretation of the vision is in 7:15–28. The main point is that *the saints of the Most High shall receive the kingdom* (vv. 18,22,27). *These four great beasts* represent four kings. There is a consistency of figures and interpretation in the book of Daniel. The four kingdoms of 2:39–40 are the same ones referred to in this chapter. The interest is definitely in the fourth beast. This would be the figure contemporary with the writer and the ones to whom he addressed his message.

The saints of the Most High (also 7:22,25,27) is an unusual expression. The term *saints* is also found in 7:21,22, but it is not the regular word used for "the pious ones." There is no definite article and thus they are only called "holy ones" and not "the" saints. Most High (*'elyonin*) is not a true Aramaic word but is a Hebrew word

(cf. Canaanite *'elyon*) with an Aramaic plural ending. The plural ending is explained as an intense plural of majesty. The distinctiveness of this phrase calls attention to the specialness of the people whom God has chosen as his kingdom of priests.

The strict Aramaic form (*the Most High*) appears in 7:25a. The term "saints of the Most High" was a distinctive expression current among the pious ones in the Maccabean period.

The two figures (son of man and saints of the Most High) are closely interrelated. *Dominion* was given to a son of man according to v. 14; in 7:27 it was given to the people of the saints of the Most High. *Glory* was also given to the son of man in v. 14; in 7:27 the *greatness of the kingdom* was given to the people of the saints of the Most High. The kingdom was given to the son of man in v. 14, but to the people of the saints in vv. 18,22,27. The dominion of the son of man is noted as everlasting in v. 14 and that of the people of the saints of the Most High will be universal (v. 27). The kingdom of the son of man shall be *one that shall not be destroyed* and the kingdom of the people *shall be an everlasting kingdom.* Some see the saints as angels or the heavenly hosts; others think they refer to the righteous remnant of the Israelite community.

Attention to the fourth beast reveals the eagerness of the author to get to the hope for his own time. The fourth beast (vv. 7,19) is described in the same terms except it includes *claws of bronze* (cf. 2:32,39,45). In this description iron and bronze are both parts of the fourth beast.

The little horn (vv. 8,20) is of urgent concern. This little horn *seemed* (lit., appeared) *greater* than the other horns. This may mean that he became larger in size (8:9). However, he is still referred to as the little horn (7:8; 8:9). Therefore, it must be a sarcastic reference to the pompous haughtiness of a self-exalted ruler who had cut down three rightful contenders for the throne.

**(3) Interpretation of Victory for the Saints
(7:21–28)**

21 As I looked, this horn made war with the
saints, and prevailed over them, 22 until the
Ancient of Days came, and judgment was given
for the saints of the Most High, and the time
came when the saints received the kingdom.
23 "Thus he said: 'As for the fourth beast,
  there shall be a fourth kingdom on earth,
    which shall be different from all the
      kingdoms,
  and it shall devour the whole earth,
    and trample it down, and break it to
      pieces.
24 As for the ten horns,
  out of this kingdom
    ten kings shall arise,
    and another shall arise after them;
  he shall be different from the former ones,
    and shall put down three kings.
25 He shall speak words against the Most High,
    and shall wear out the saints of the Most
      High,
    and shall think to change the times and
      the law;
  and they shall be given into his hand
    for a time, two times, and half a time.
26 But the court shall sit in judgment,
    and his dominion shall be taken away,
  to be consumed and destroyed to the end.
27 And the kingdom and the dominion
    and the greatness of the kingdoms under
      the whole heaven
  shall be given to the people of the saints
    of the Most High;
  their kingdom shall be an everlasting king-
      dom,
    and all dominions shall serve and obey
      them.'
28 "Here is the end of the matter. As for me,
Daniel, my thoughts greatly alarmed me, and
my color changed; but I kept the matter in my
mind."

"As I looked" in v. 9 introduced the
imminence of the judgment of one who
was the Ancient of Days. The same phrase
in v. 11 explains that the judgment on the
little horn was destruction accompanied by
the exaltation of "one like a son of man."
As I looked in v. 21 enlarges even further
on the judgment of the horn and the
triumph of the saints of the Most High.
Note the addition of *made war* and *prevailed over them*. However, the main focus
of this account is in the victory for the
saints. Verse 22 records that the judgment

was not made by the saints but for them.
Another interpretation of the vision is
found in vv. 23–27. The fourth beast is
the fourth kingdom (7:17–18). *It shall devour the whole earth* has caused problems
for many interpreters. It should be taken
as rhetorical exaggeration. Just as Nebuchadnezzar's decree to "all peoples . . .
in all the earth" (4:1) is understood to indicate a completeness to his vast empire,
this expression indicates the power of the
fourth beast. The figure of the ten horns
and three horns is the same as above.

Verse 25 enlarges upon the terrifying
figure of the little horn. *He shall speak
words against the Most High.* Speaking
against God means evil words or blasphemy. This has reference to the attempt
on the part of Antiochus Epiphanes to
establish himself as powerful as any god.
He had nothing but contempt for the God
of Israel. The word translated *Most High*
(v. 25a) is not the same word as in the
following line ("saints of the Most High")
or in vv. 18,22,27. In v. 25a it is a pure
singular Aramaic form with the meaning of
"highest." *Wear out,* such as a garment
(cf. Deut. 8:4; 29:5), has a kindred
Arabic root meaning afflict or put to a
test. This reference is to the terrible persecutions perpetrated by Antiochus Epiphanes on the Jews in Jerusalem.

He would *think* (intend with the expectancy that it would take place) *to
change* (the same word translated "different" in vv. 3,19,23,24 and thus make
different). *The times* which Antiochus
Epiphanes commanded to change were
the designated religious practices.

The law brings to mind the Torah or
Mosaic law (cf. 6:5; 1 Macc. 1:56–57).
Antiochus Epiphanes sought to change
practically every expression of Jewish religious practice (1 Macc. 1:41–50). This
reference *to change the times and the law*
may be reflected also in 1 Maccabees 1:49,
"so that they should forget the law and
change all the ordinances." Antiochus
Epiphanes forbade burnt offerings and
sacrifices, sabbaths and feasts, circumcision

and dietary laws. He commanded them to become abominable by everything unclean and profane. How long this harassment and suffering would continue was unknown. The precision of the expressions stops sharply here.

A *time, two times, and half a time* is vague. The same figure is also in Daniel 12:7 and in Revelation 12:14. Related expressions are found in 8:14; 9:27; 12:11,12 (cf. Rev. 11:2,3; 13:5).

A *time* (*'iddah;* found ten times in Daniel; the root idea is probably appointed or definite time) is not a chronologically accurate term. It may convey the general force of time as duration. The expression *time, two times* does not use the same word as in the previous line, i.e., *times and the law.* If this word means year, the compilation would be a year, two years, and half a year (*ca.* 1277 days). The use of figures is so striking that it merits our attention. Daniel 8:14 uses the temporal expression "two thousand and three hundred evenings and mornings," which could equal 1,150 days. Revelation 11:2 and 13:5 have 42 months, which would be about 1,260 days. Revelation 11:3 had 1,260 days. Daniel 7:25 and 12:7 have time, two times, and half a time which may be about 1,277 days. Daniel 12:11 has 1,290 days. Daniel 12:12 has 1,335 days. Note the general closeness of these numbers: 1,150; 1,260; 1,277; 1,290; and 1,335.

There is an inexactitude which must have been intended and/or understood both by the writer, the hearers, and the readers. Copyists, scribes, or redactors felt no need to adjust the figures to be precisely identical. This fact should cause every interpreter to examine his use of the numbers. The lack of precise definition could indicate that these are not predictions in regard to time but directly as to event. When one permits himself to be bound by temporal requirements in regard to events he may impose restrictions on the text which the text does not impose on itself.

The event is that the little horn will afflict the saints of the Most High for a limited period of time. Though the temporal designation is in itself a "chronologically indefinite expression" (Young, p. 161), the general agreement within all of these passages is amazingly approximate. The attempt of Antiochus Epiphanes to annihilate the religion of the Jews spanned around three and a half years. It actually began to take effect when Apollonius, one of Antiochus' commanders, marched against Jerusalem, June, 168 B.C. (1 Macc. 1:20,29), leading to the desolation of the Temple. The persecution by Antiochus ended with the rededication of the Temple, December, 165 (1 Macc. 4:52; *ca.* three and one half years).

Some interpreters see this period of persecution from an edict of Antiochus (1 Macc. 1:41 f.) being enforced in December, 168 B.C., until the rededication of the temple in December, 165. The focus is on the fact that God's people would be subjected to persecutions for a very limited period. *Court shall sit in judgment.* The condemnation of the little horn was absolute. He was to be defeated. Verse 27 is a description of the beginning of the predicted eschatological kingdom.

The identification of *the people of the saints of the Most High* is a difficult problem. In 7:14, to the "one like a son of man" was given "dominion and glory and kingdom"; also his dominion and kingdom were everlasting. In v. 27 *the kingdom and the dominion and the greatness* are given to the people of the saints.

If vv. 14 and 27 are taken literally, there would be a contradiction, a further development or a change in the identity of the recipient(s) of the kingdom. A more valid view would be based on the thought pattern of the Hebrew, namely a certain flexibility in expression. In the earlier chapters of Daniel there was a fluidity between the use of king and kingdom. The one like a son of man may be the king while the saints of the Most High would be the people of that same king. Hebrew parallelism uses the same thought in various figures.

The same phenomenon is involved in

v. 25. The "other horn" speaks words *against the Most High* and in the parallel expression wears out the *saints of the Most High.* This is synonymous parallelism. Likewise when 7:18 indicates that "the saints of the Most High" will receive the kingdom there is no contradiction with v. 27 which has the kingdom given to "the people of the saints of the Most High."

Their kingdom is literally "kingdom of him" (KJV, "whose kingdom"; JB, "His sovereignty"; NEB, "their kingly power"). The antecedent is "the people." All dominions shall serve and obey *them.* The theological impact of this vision is that judgment will be made on all evil powers. Even though such evil power can hold threatening authority or even persecution over the saints, God, the Ancient of Days or the Eternal One, will sit in judgment. The saints of the Most High should be as faithful in living by the righteous principles as God is in watching over his people. God will bring in the expected messianic kingdom. Hope and expectancy are the predominant themes in the vision.

Here is the end of the matter may be comparable to the end of the book. But the term *matter* probably refers only to the visions and the interpretation inasmuch as v. 28 is the last verse which is in Palestinian Aramaic language. Chapter 8 resumes the Hebrew which was found in 1:1—2:4a. The shift in language and the expression "end of the matter" indicate that the vision and its interpretation are finished. Compare the situation in Jeremiah 51:64 where the words of Jeremiah of that moment are finished. The vision and its interpretation may have been written down originally in a separate account and included with the following chapters at a later time. The clarity of detail as compared to the more general nature of successive events would indicate that the writer knew that Antiochus was on the throne. God would act in imminent judgment and would exalt the saints of the Most High to dominion and an everlasting kingdom.

He *kept the matter* in his heart. He was not satisfied completely with his understanding of the whole affair. This serves to heighten anticipation at the end of chapter 7 for the beginning of chapters 8—12.

III. The Little Horn and the End (8: 1–27)

Chapter 8 contains the first vision of the book which is preserved in Hebrew. Chapters 2—7 were in the conversational language (Aramaic) and chapters 8—12 are in the sacred and religious language (Hebrew).

This chapter is a remarkably similar doublet to chapter 7. There are various reasons for the inclusion of both records. (1) Chapter 7 was in Aramaic and chapter 8 in Hebrew—both records are valid and were authentically used in their own circles; (2) chapter 7 is more developed poetically, while chapter 8 is technically more specific; (3) chapter 7 preserves more of the imaginative apocalyptic nature, while chapter 8 is more historical and concrete; (4) chapter 8 may be a commentary on chapter 7. Chapters 7 and 8 precede the events of chapter 5. The order of the chapters may have been affected by the religious character of chapters 8—12.

This vision is dated two years after that of chapter 7, i.e., *in the third year of the reign of Belshazzar (ca.* 552 B.C.). The name Belshazzar is spelled *Bel'shatstsar* in the superscription in chapters 7 and 8 (the only two times it appears in these chapters). It had a different spelling throughout chapter 5.

1. Description of the Vision (8:1–14)

(1) Introduction (8:1–3)

¹ In the third year of the reign of King Belshazzar a vision appeared to me, Daniel, after that which appeared to me at the first. ² And I saw in the vision; and when I saw, I was in Susa the capital, which is in the province of Elam; and I saw in the vision, and I was at the river Ulai. ³ I raised my eyes and saw, and behold, a ram standing on the bank of the river. It had two horns; and both horns were high, but one was higher than the other, and the higher one came up last.

At the first refers to the vision contained in chapter 7. In the vision of chapter 7 the writer was in Babylon. In 8:1–2 he is pictured as in Susa, capital of the Persian Empire. The visionary character is clear in that *and I saw* occurs three times. The pattern, seen in Ezekiel 8, may be followed here in that the writer was in Susa in the spirit, i.e., in the vision, rather than bodily. The writer, who is clearly interested in the conflict with the little horn, is transported by vision into the ancient land of Medo-Persia.

The river (*'uval*, only use in OT) is similar to the word stream (*yuval*) of Jeremiah 17:8 (cf. Isa. 30:25; 44:4). The LXX, Vulgate, and Peshitta translate it as "gate" (an Aramaic word with Assyrian background) thus making this the "watergate of the Ulai." The Ulai was a huge artificial canal (classical Eulaeus) which ran near Susa.

He saw a *ram* with *two horns*. Medo-Persia is the kingdom (8:20). Both parts of the kingdom were powerful (*were high*) but the *last* was the more powerful. Persia was much greater than Media (*higher than the other*).

(2) Vision of the Ram (8:4)

4 I saw the ram charging westward and northward and southward; no beast could stand before him, and there was no one who could rescue from his power; he did as he pleased and magnified himself.

The grammatical form of *I saw* indicates that this is the start of the vision proper. The ram was a figure of power and dominion. The ram is seen continuously *charging*, i.e., thrusting or butting in three directions. The LXX adds "eastward." Persia was regarded as so powerful that no one could resist. The Hebrew text notes the direction from Persia toward the Holy Land. *Westward* from Susa would be Babylon. *Northward* would be the next step toward Palestine, i.e., Armenia and Lydia with the territory south of the Caspian sea. Then the Persians came *southward* through Palestine to Egypt.

The choice of the figure of a *ram* may have some connection with zodiacal symbolism. In a document from the Persian period Persia was the country under the sign of Aries the Ram. Greece with Syria was under the sign of Capricorn, represented on ancient monuments under the figure of a goat.

(3) The He-goat (8:5–8)

5 As I was considering, behold, a he-goat came from the west across the face of the whole earth, without touching the ground; and the goat had a conspicuous horn between his eyes. 6 He came to the ram with the two horns, which I had seen standing on the bank of the river, and he ran at him in his mighty wrath. 7 I saw him come close to the ram, and he was enraged against him and struck the ram and broke his two horns; and the ram had no power to stand before him, but he cast him down to the ground and trampled upon him; and there was no one who could rescue the ram from his power. 8 Then the he-goat magnified himself exceedingly; but when he was strong, the great horn was broken, and instead of it there came up four conspicuous horns toward the four winds of heaven.

While he was paying attention to the ram, the *he-goat* (lit., the buck of the goats) *came from the west.* The conquest of the he-goat was rapid, *without touching the ground.* There was one predominant general, *a conspicuous horn.* This horn conquered the ram with the two horns (Medo-Persia). The he-goat was Greece (8:21). The notable horn was Alexander the Great. The major portion of chapter 8, devoted to the he-goat and the little horn (vv. 5–26), focuses on the sweep of Hellenism through the biblical world. Alexander set out to liberate the Greeks from the Persian yoke and at the same time to spread Hellenistic culture far and wide. Many of those conquered by Alexander had no relish for the intrusion of Hellenism into their way of life and religion.

Alexander crossed the Hellespont in 334 B.C. He and his forces clashed with Darius III Codomannus and his forces in 333 at Issus. Alexander so demolished the Persian army that Darius fled, abandoning his wife, family, and baggage to the

Greek forces. Before Alexander ventured further into the Persian territory he turned south to take Egypt quickly. Egypt was glad to exchange the Persian rule for that of Greece and offered no resistance to Alexander in 332. On the way, the cities along the Mediterranean fell before him.

No clear reference is made to the military campaigns of the Greek forces in Palestine. The sweep of the Greek culture and thought is afforded attention. In 331 B.C. Alexander proceeded on his original military target by marching against Mesopotamia. He crushed the final Persian stumblingblock at Gaugamela and Arbela, southeast of Nineveh. Darius was captured in his flight and assassinated by one of his satraps. Persian resistance was completely obliterated, and Alexander marched triumphantly into Babylon, Susa, and Persepolis.

The he-goat magnified himself exceedingly shows the author's estimation. Alexander is pictured as arrogant or presumptuous. *When he was strong* he was broken in pieces. Alexander was only 32 or 33 years of age when he fell sick with a fever and died in Babylon (323 B.C.). His career marked the beginning of the Hellenistic period in the Eastern world. Changes in educational, cultural, linguistic, and religious patterns were involved.

Instead of the great horn *there came up four* horns. The Hebrew text does not indicate whether the four horns came up immediately or after some years. The death of Alexander gave rise to a struggle among his generals for power. This struggle settled, after the battle of Ipsus in Phrygia in 301 B.C., into four basic divisions. Two of these four horns are of particular importance to the study of the book of Daniel. Ptolemy I Soter, Alexander's governor in Egypt, took firm control of Egypt with the city of Alexandria as the capital. Seleucus I Nicator controlled Syria and Babylonia with two capitals, Antioch in Syria and Seleucia on the Tigris River. For one in Palestine, Ptolemy was the "king of the south" and Seleucus was the "king of

the north." Palestine and Phoenicia were coveted by both kings. At first, the Ptolemies were able to retain political power. After about 100 years changes began to take place.

The other two horns were: Cassander, who controlled Macedonia and Greece; Lysimachus, who controlled Thrace and Asia Minor. Among these four rulers dominion was exercised in every direction from Palestine (*toward the four winds*).

(4) The Little Horn (8:9–14)

9 Out of one of them came forth a little horn, which grew exceedingly great toward the south, toward the east, and toward the glorious land. 10 It grew great, even to the host of heaven; and some of the host of the stars it cast down to the ground, and trampled upon them. 11 It magnified itself, even up to the Prince of the host; and the continual burnt offering was taken away from him, and the place of his sanctuary was overthrown. 12 And the host was given over to it together with the continual burnt offering through transgression; and truth was cast down to the ground, and the horn acted and prospered. 13 Then I heard a holy one speaking; and another holy one said to the one that spoke, "For how long is the vision concerning the continual burnt offering, the transgression that makes desolate, and the giving over of the sanctuary and host to be trampled under foot?" 14 And he said to him, "For two thousand and three hundred evenings and mornings; then the sanctuary shall be restored to its rightful state."

Out of one of these four appears *a little horn.* The translation of little horn is very difficult (lit., a horn from little or insignificance). This little horn was Antiochus Epiphanes, the eighth ruler of the Seleucid line. The author rushes to the central point of his interest, i.e., the attempt to change the religion of the Jews into Hellenism. More of the activities of Antiochus are seen in chapter 11, but the focus here is upon the incursion of Antiochus into the worship of Yahweh. The military activities of Antiochus in chapter 8 are classed in three directions. He exercised his strength *toward the south,* in reference to his wars against Egypt (cf. 11:25; 1 Macc. 1:18). *Toward the east* recalls the campaign against Persia as far as Elymais. This direction must be from the viewpoint of one in Palestine since the wars would not be east of Susa (1 Macc. 3:31,37; 6:1–4). *Toward the glorious land* refers to Palestine (cf. 11:16,41), as a land flowing with milk and honey, a pleasant land.

There is general agreement as to the reference being made (vv. 10–12), but the details cannot be pressed. The *host of heaven* and the parallel expression the *host of the stars* seem to refer figuratively to the people of Israel. They represent the people of God, not any special group but the people of Israel as opposed to other nations.

If the previous expressions refer to Israel, *the Prince of the host* would refer to God. This would be the only place in the Old Testament where prince refers to God. Based on 11:36, the fact that the little horn exalted himself above any god makes the interpretation of the Prince as God very likely. This chapter is set in the framework of a vision.

The little horn *magnified himself* in five ways: (1) He succumbed to his megalomania and made himself equal to God. He acted insolently in the presence of the Prince of the host. (2) He took away from the Prince (God) the expressions of worship which his people offered continually. The *continual burnt offering* is, literally, continual. It came to mean the lamb being offered every morning and every evening. The author may have intended to project all the regular expressions which worshipers offered to their God. (3) He overthrew *the place of his sanctuary.* This does not refer to destruction but to the desecration of the Temple. Just as the little horn despised God, he also despised God's holy place. First Maccabees 1:39 and 3:45 indicate that the "sanctuary became desolate as a desert" and "was trampled down." (4) *The host was given over . . . through transgression.* Host was used (vv. 10–11, three times) in the sense of large group. The root word means to serve or wage war. In v. 12 *host* could be translated "an army." If this be the proper meaning here, one could read this as "an army was set

against the continual offering because of rebellion." This could refer to a detachment of armed forces which Antiochus used to suppress the religious rights of the Jews who rebelled against his decrees. It is not certain whether *transgression* refers to the rebellion against Antiochus or against some divine direction. Comparing v. 11 and the deeds of Antiochus, something was done to the altar to make it unclean (1 Macc. 4:44). A decree of Antiochus forbade (1 Macc. 1:45) burnt offerings and sacrifices. (5) *Truth was cast down to the ground. Truth* was the true religion of the Jews consisting mainly of fidelity to the observance of the law of Moses. Daniel 9:13 uses the "law of Moses" and truth together, and 10:21 speaks of "the book of truth." In 167 B.C. Antiochus caused "the books of the law" to be torn in shreds and to be burned. Anyone found in possession of a copy of the book of the covenant was condemned to death.

The horn acted and prospered. The decrees of the little horn were carried out. The hellenization attempt was so successful that "a man could neither keep the sabbath, nor observe the feasts of his fathers, nor so much as confess himself to be a Jew" (2 Macc. 6:6). There were many Jews who resisted vigorously the hellenization of Palestine (1 Macc. 1:62–64). Many, however, fell in line with the pagan policies of Antiochus.

One who lived in Jerusalem during the time of Antiochus would see through the veil of the vision. The intensity of the persecution and the uncertainty of the endurance of Antiochus' decrees troubled the Jews. They could withstand such actions temporarily. But there was no hope that the Ptolemies or the Persians could intervene. There was no sign that Antiochus was becoming weaker. In fact, he was making life more and more unbearable. Every external expression of their faith was denied them. Hope could only be quickened by a renewal of God's power or a revelation that God's intervention was imminent.

The author breaks the literary pattern by interposing an overheard conversation between two holy ones. *A holy one* (cf. 4:13,17) was a celestial being as God's messenger or angel. One asks the other unidentified one, *how long?* This question was a frequent one in apocalyptic literature (cf. also Isa. 6:11; Zech. 1:12; Hab. 1:2). The "holy one" asks concerning: (1) the *continual*, i.e., the evening and morning, burnt offerings; (2) the *transgression* (cf. v. 12*a*) *that makes desolate*, which refers to the portion of the vision which was so obscure in v. 12*a*; if these passages are directly related, the reference is to Antiochus' offering abominable sacrifices in the Temple (1 Macc. 1:54); (3) the trampling of *the sanctuary* and the people.

The answer was a message of real hope. Basic to this hope is that the holy place will be restored. The time is given *two thousand three hundred evenings and mornings*. The expression, evening and morning, is unusual. This unique expression may have arisen by the repeated reference to the *continual*, which referred to the evening sacrifices and morning sacrifices. This background may indicate that only 2300 more sacrifices would be prohibited. These sacrifices would cover 1150 days. This span of time would be less than the time mentioned in 7:25. There are several suggestions to account for this: (1) According to 8:12 desecration had already begun. The starting point of the two reckonings was different, though the end point was the same. It is impossible, at the present state of knowledge, to be dogmatic as to the events and time. It is very clear, however, that this is a prediction that the desecration and persecutions would end. (2) The Jewish language often resorts to round figures to indicate a short, moderate, or lengthy period. Verse 14 may indicate a relative period without attempting a specific number of 24-hour periods.

It has also been held that the time span is 2300 days. To fit the figure of 2300 days in the time of Antiochus the starting point would be at some unspecified point early in the political career of Antiochus, six years before his death.

2. Interpretation of the Vision (8:15-27)

(1) Appearance of Gabriel (8:15-17)

15 When I, Daniel, had seen the vision, I sought to understand it; and behold, there stood before me one having the appearance of a man. 16 And I heard a man's voice between the banks of the Ulai, and it called, "Gabriel, make this man understand the vision." 17 So he came near where I stood; and when he came, I was frightened and fell upon my face. But he said to me, "Understand, O son of man, that the vision is for the time of the end."

In the vision of chapter 7 Daniel approaches a celestial being to find the meaning. In chapter 8 one having the appearance of a man appeared to him. This is the only use of the Hebrew noun (*gaber*) in Daniel, and it is used to anticipate Gabriel. Angels regularly are pictured in the form of humanity when having dealings with men (cf. Gen. 32:24–32; Judg. 13; 6:11). The voice of a man (*'adham*) came from the Ulai river instructing Gabriel to reveal the vision to *this man. Gabriel* is known in 1 Enoch as one of the archangels. The book of Daniel is the only book in the Old Testament in which angels are named. This would indicate a late date for this chapter. Gabriel (8:16; 9:21) and Michael (10:13,21; 12:1) are the only two named. In non-Jewish writings, Gabriel is given preference. Michael was the patron saint of Israel.

O son of man refers to a human being and would be natural as used by a celestial being. This term is used in Psalms 8:4; 80:17; and Ezekiel. *The time of the end* does not refer to the end of all time. Verse 19 makes clear that it refers to the end of the time of persecution of the Jews and the desecration of the Temple.

(2) Identification of the Two Figures (8:18-22)

18 As he was speaking to me, I fell into a deep sleep with my face to the ground; but he touched me and set me on my feet. 19 He said, "Behold, I will make known to you what shall be at the latter end of the indignation; for it

pertains to the appointed time of the end. 20 As for the ram which you saw with the two horns, these are the kings of Media and Persia. 21 And the he-goat is the king of Greece; and the great horn between his eyes is the first king. 22 As for the horn that was broken, in place of which four others arose, four kingdoms shall arise from his nation, but not with his power.

The framework of the vision is retained in the figure of *deep sleep*. He was set on his feet as Ezekiel (2:2) was made to stand by the Spirit.

Great hope is provided for the Jews in the phrase *at the latter end of the indignation.* Indignation is used in the Old Testament of the wrath of Yahweh. It had been expressed against Israel because of her sins (cf. Isa. 5:25). The Jews had been in subjection to non-Yahweh worshiping nations for a long time. The end of this punishment is directly related to the *appointed time* of Antiochus' end. Double grounds for hope are provided in the knowledge that there would be a simultaneous end of God's wrath upon Israel and the persecution by Antiochus.

Chapters 2 and 7 had four great figures but chapter 8 has only three. Chapters 2 and 7 began with the destroyer of Jerusalem, Nebuchadnezzar. Chapter 8 does not include Babylon but includes the final three as in chapters 2 and 7. The first figure of chapter 8 was of the ram. The *ram* was *the kings of Media and Persia.*

The second figure is the *he-goat*, the *king of Greece.* This is not the modern European Greece, but rather the entire Greek Empire including Persia, Egypt, Syria, Palestine, and Asia Minor. *The great horn* of the he-goat was Alexander the Great. The four conspicuous winds of 8:8 are the *four kingdoms* which arose from the nation of Alexander.

(3) *Description of the Third Figure* (8: 23-25)

23 And at the latter end of their rule, when the transgressors have reached their full measure, a king of bold countenance, one who understands riddles, shall arise. 24 His power shall be great, and he shall cause fearful destruction, and shall succeed in what he does, and destroy mighty men and the people of the saints. 25 By his cunning he shall make deceit prosper under his hand, and in his own mind he shall magnify himself. Without warning he shall destroy many; and he shall even rise up against the Prince of princes; but, by no human hand, he shall be broken.

The main focus of this chapter is not in the four divisions. The author hastens by them to *the latter end of their rule.* The Hebrew text parallels this phrase with *when the transgressors have reached full measure.* From the death of Alexander to the little horn was around 148 years. The word *transgressors* may refer to the Jews who fell in line with the hellenizing powers or to the hellenizing protagonists themselves. There is good evidence that an early reading of transgressors was "transgressions." Based on the LXX, Theodotion, Peshitta, and Vulgate, it would read "when they had completed their transgressions," there arose another king.

The king of bold countenance was Antiochus IV Epiphanes (175–164 B.C.), a Seleucid. *Bold countenance* (cf. Deut. 28:50; Prov. 7:13) refers to the fierceness, impudence, and shameless insolence of Antiochus. *Riddles* may mean dark and obscure utterances (Num. 12:8; Psalm 49:4), an enigmatic saying (Judg. 14:12-18), or perplexing questions (1 Kings 10:1). Bevan interprets this as being "skilled in double dealing" (cf. 11:23).

His power shall be great. The Hebrew adds "and not with his power" as in 7:22 (as KJV). It was not his power but rather intrigues by which he came to power. Others hold that Antiochus ruled "not in the power of Yahweh." This expression may be a parallel with that of 7:22. The four kings did not possess the power of Alexander and neither did Antiochus.

He shall cause fearful destruction. His destruction is extraordinary, hard to understand. Antiochus reeked havoc on Jerusalem (1 Macc. 1:24,30–33) and the entire territory. *The people of the saints* refers to Israel (cf. 7:25,27) as opposed to the *mighty men* who were Antiochus' political opponents.

Generally the word *cunning* has a complimentary force, but intelligence can be misused as by Antiochus. He devised many arrogant schemes which were far beyond his ability. Two of these are mentioned. The first may refer to Antiochus' sending Apollonius to Jerusalem, who spoke deceitfully (1 Macc. 1:29–30) with peaceable words and suddenly attacked the city. The other scheme was to *rise up against the Prince of princes.* Antiochus exalted himself above God (cf. 11:36). Such affrontery could not go unpunished for it was the Prince of princes (God) who would break him (2 Macc. 9:5–12). *By no human hand* refers to God. Polybius (xxxi. 9) reported that Antiochus died suddenly of madness (in Persia, 164 B.C.) shortly after the rededication of the Temple. Madness has been interpreted as a divine blow. Second Maccabees 9:5–12 describes an unrelievable pain in his bowels suggesting a malady which (Josephus, *Antiq.* XIX.8.2) was considered specifically as divine punishment.

(4) Conclusion (8:26–27)

26 The vision of the evenings and the mornings which has been told is true; but seal up the vision, for it pertains to many days hence."
27 And I, Daniel, was overcome and lay sick for some days; then I rose and went about the king's business; but I was appalled by the vision and did not understand it.

Verses 14 and 26 chapter 8 go together. Some interpreters think they are interpolations. Daniel is told to *seal up the vision,* i.e., keep it secret. It was for *many days hence.* When Daniel *went about the king's business,* he would be in Babylon. By vision he had been in Susa. He did not *understand* the vision (cf. 12:9–10) even though the vision had been explained.

IV. Basis for Hope (9:1–27)

The visions of chapters 2, 7, and 8 indicate that the "fourth beast" will come to an end and the people of the saints will not be destroyed. Daniel is troubled by the vision (8:27). The final verse of chapter 8 forms a connecting link between the visions and the more refined explanation of chapters 9—12. It serves to accent the scriptural, theological, revelational, and historical facets which follow.

1. Scriptural Background (9:1–2)

1 In the first year of Darius the son of Ahasuerus, by birth a Mede, who became king over the realm of the Chaldeans—2 in the first year of his reign, I, Daniel, perceived in the books the number of years which, according to the word of the LORD to Jeremiah the prophet, must pass before the end of the desolations of Jerusalem, namely, seventy years.

The announcement of hope would attract interest, but it would not necessarily give birth to sustained joy or lasting hope. The unifying purpose of chapter 9 is to give substance to the hope which had been expressed previously.

The "historical" data refers to the Darius chapter (6 in Aramaic; 5:31—6:28 in English; for the discussion of Darius' identity see the comment on ch. 6).

Ahasuerus is a transliteration of the Hebrew name; the Greek form gives rise to the name Xerxes. Darius was the father (not the son) of Xerxes I, who reigned 486–465 B.C. No Xerxes known in secular records fathered a Darius who became a king.

The historical references continue the effect as produced in chapter 6. In a time long after the Dariuses or the Ahasueruses, the names give a certain aura of authenticity without the necessity of chronological precision. The repetition in v. 2 of *in the first year of his reign,* omitted by the LXX, indicates that v. 1 was included as an explanatory superscription. This first year of Darius (cf. 5:30–31) brought to mind the fall of Babylon. Since it was Nebuchadnezzar and the Babylonians who had conquered Israel (605, 597, 587 B.C.), the fall of Babylon would raise hopes that the fate of the captives could change. The thoughts of the people of Israel naturally revolved around the possibility of their release and their return to their land.

Daniel *perceived,* i.e., considered with attention to *the books.* The first source of substantiation to which he turned was Scripture. The high esteem with which the Jews held the sacred writings made them the most authoritative place.

The word of the Lord is a characteristic of the prophets to which he turned. *Lord* is Yahweh, the covenant name.

Desolations occurs in Daniel only here, but it is used in Isaiah 44—64 and often in Jeremiah and Ezekiel. In the remembering or searching which Daniel did concerning *the number of years,* he found the word of Yahweh in Jeremiah (25:11–12; 29:10).

Namely, seventy years ("namely" is not in the Hebrew text) comes from the Jeremianic references. The most common manner of interpreting this figure would be as a specific number. But this span of time when examined in the light of the facts of history presents insurmountable difficulties. The first possible foray which Nebuchadnezzar made against Israel was 605 B.C. The second destruction by his forces was in 597, generally known as the first deportation (2 Kings 24:10 f.). The third attack was when the Temple was destroyed and the elite of the city were taken into captivity in 587 (the second deportation). The fourth attack was 582 (the third deportation). Seventy years after each of these attacks would give the following dates: 535; 528; 517; and 512. None of these dates marks the end of their enslavement. The decree of Cyrus which permitted the return of the Jews was made in 538 B.C. These dates are close but are not 70 years.

The captivity of Jerusalem is referred to also in Jeremiah 25:11,12; 29:10; 2 Chronicles 36:21; Zechariah 1:12; 7:5. Isaiah 23:15 uses the term 70 years, "like the days of one king." When this statement is compared to Psalm 90:10, "the years of our life are threescore and ten," another meaning for 70 years emerges. Seventy years is a round figure for the length of one man's life or one generation. The references of Jeremiah, Chronicles, Zechariah, and Daniel concerning captivity may come under this meaning. It is impossible to say

precisely which meaning was intended by the author.

The author used the Scripture to give canonical authority to the hope which had been envisioned for his people.

2. Reward of Faith (9:3–19)

Within this section there is a liturgical prayer which appears to break suddenly the continuity of historical and visionary materials. The authority of Jeremiah in regard to hope and the 70 years was unmistakable. Consequently, the author continued the use of the Jeremianic passage. Jeremiah 29:10 is the real source of hope: "For thus says the Lord: When seventy years are completed for Babylon, I will . . . bring you back to this place." That passage continues, "Then you will call upon me and come and pray to me, and I will hear you." Following the promise of the 70 years Jeremiah listed the prayer of the people as a part of their hope. The prayer is not an interpolation but was suggested by the knowledge of chapter 29 of Jeremiah.

(1) Confession of Sins (9:3–10)

³ Then I turned my face to the Lord God, seeking him by prayer and supplications with fasting and sackcloth and ashes. ⁴ I prayed to the Lᴏʀᴅ my God and made confession, saying, "O Lord, the great and terrible God, who keepest covenant and steadfast love with those who love him and keep his commandments, ⁵ we have sinned and done wrong and acted wickedly and rebelled, turning aside from thy commandments and ordinances; ⁶ we have not listened to thy servants the prophets, who spoke in thy name to our kings, our princes, and our fathers, and to all the people of the land. ⁷ To thee, O Lord, belongs righteousness, but to us confusion of face, as at this day, to the men of Judah, to the inhabitants of Jerusalem, and to all Israel, those that are near and those that are far away, in all the lands to which thou hast driven them, because of the treachery which they have committed against thee. ⁸ To us, O Lord, belongs confusion of face, to our kings, to our princes, and to our fathers, because we have sinned against thee. ⁹ To the Lord our God belong mercy and forgiveness; because we have rebelled against him, ¹⁰ and have not obeyed the voice of the Lᴏʀᴅ our God by following his laws, which he set before us by his servants the prophets.

I turned my face is preparation for prayer. *To the Lord God* (v. 3) does not contain the covenant name Yahweh, but v. 4 does, *I prayed to* Yahweh *my God.* *Seeking* is found also in Jeremiah 29:13. These cultic acts are generally preparation for a revelation. In this context (cf. Neh. 9:1–3) they are customs preparatory to the confession of sins by the people.

The penitential prayer begins *O Lord.* This prayer shows remarkable similarities in form and terms with Nehemiah 1:5–10. The part of the prayer in 9:4 is the same as Nehemiah 1:5 (cf. Neh. 9:32), except that Nehemiah uses "Yahweh, the God of heaven" instead of *Lord.*

The great and terrible God (cf. Neh. 1:5; 9:32; Deut. 10:17) is powerful and one to be feared (worshiped) continuously. *Who keepest* means without interruption. *Covenant and steadfast love* (Neh. 1:5; 9:32; Deut. 7:9) are used in a technical sense as would be understood by Jews in their later history. Verse 4 is a liturgical profession that God had loyally kept his covenant with the people and had been reaching out to them with an unerring quality of faithfulness.

Verses 4–10 contain a confessional in the form of a contrast between God and the people. God was faithful and loyal (v. 4). The people had sinned against God. The confession of "sins" has been taken from 1 Kings 8:47. They had turned aside from God's *commandments and ordinances* (Neh. 1:6; 9:29; Deut. 7:11). The ordinances were judgments or legal decisions of God on moral and religious matters.

Thy servants the prophets is a reference from Jeremiah 29:19 and the prayer of Nehemiah (cf. Jer. 7:25; 26:5; 35:15; Ezra 9:11). The message had been given to the entire nation from king to commoner. *Fathers* refer to the leaders or elders of the family unit.

To thee, O Lord, belongs righteousness. In a prayer of penitence such a statement is a confession that God was right, i.e., legally vindicated as right (Neh. 9:33).

Contrasted to the righteousness of God is the shamefulness of the people. *Confusion of face* (cf. Jer. 7:19) is a disgrace which involved being the reproach of other men. They deserved the punishment which had been heaped upon them. *As at this day* is indicative that long after the Babylonian captivity the people of Judah and Israel were a reproach instead of a light. The expression *to the men of Judah, to the inhabitants of Jerusalem* is Jeremianic (cf. Jer. 4:4; 11:2,9; 17:25; 18:11; 32:32).

To the Lord *belong mercy and forgiveness* (v. 9; cf. Neh. 9:17; lit., mercies and forgivenesses). They were guilty and could only throw themselves on the mercy of God. God was merciful, but the people were rebellious. Verse 10 reflects Jeremiah 26:4–5. The prophets had taught them properly, but the people rebelled and obeyed not.

(2) Punishment Was Just (9:11–14)

11 All Israel has transgressed thy law and turned aside, refusing to obey thy voice. And the curse and oath which are written in the law of Moses the servant of God have been poured out upon us, because we have sinned against him. 12 He has confirmed his words, which he spoke against us and against our rulers who ruled us, by bringing upon us a great calamity; for under the whole heaven there has not been done the like of what has been done against Jerusalem. 13 As it is written in the law of Moses, all this calamity has come upon us, yet we have not entreated the favor of the LORD our God, turning from our iniquities and giving heed to thy truth. 14 Therefore the LORD has kept ready the calamity and has brought it upon us; for the LORD our God is righteous in all the works which he has done, and we have not obeyed his voice.

The authority for the rightness of the Babylonian captivity and its ensuing sufferings are established. The *curse and oath* which are written in the law of Moses are recorded in Leviticus 26:14–33 and Deuteronomy 28:15–68. *A great calamity* is an exaggeration under the stress of intense disaster. The background was probably the destruction of Jerusalem in 587 B.C. The indescribable sacrilege of Antiochus upon people and Temple would be both physical

and mental calamity. They had not entreated God's favor, turned from their
sins, or obeyed his truth. Therefore, God
kept ready (cf. Jer. 1:11,12; 5:6; 31:28)
the calamity.

(3) Supplication for Restoration of Jerusalem (9:15–19)

15 And now, O Lord our God, who didst bring
thy people out of the land of Egypt with a
mighty hand, and hast made thee a name, as
at this day, we have sinned, we have done
wickedly. 16 O Lord, according to all thy righteous acts, let thy anger and thy wrath turn
away from thy city Jerusalem, thy holy hill; because for our sins, and for the iniquities of our
fathers, Jerusalem and thy people have become
a byword among all who are round about us.
17 Now therefore, O our God, hearken to the
prayer of thy servant and to his supplications,
and for thy own sake, O Lord, cause thy face
to shine upon thy sanctuary, which is desolate.
18 O my God, incline thy ear and hear; open
thy eyes and behold our desolations, and the
city which is called by thy name; for we do not
present our supplications before thee on the
ground of our righteousness, but on the ground
of thy great mercy. 19 O Lord, hear; O Lord,
forgive; O Lord, give heed and act; delay not,
for thy own sake, O my God, because thy city
and thy people are called by thy name."

The prayer of confession was deep repentance. The calamity which had come
to Jerusalem was their fault. God's righteousness demanded the application of the
Mosaic curse and oath. The prayer is not
based on what the people deserve but is
based solely on the merciful nature of their
Lord God. He was the one who had freed
his people from the slavery and the dominance of Egypt *with a mighty hand* (cf.
Jer. 32:21).

A name refers to the great renown in
which God was held. *As at this day* (cf.
v. 7; Jer. 32:20) refers to the time of
Antiochus when the author remembers particularly that God had delivered his people
from Egypt. The miracle of the Egyptian
deliverance played a dominant part in the
prayer life of Israel. The name of God had
been besmirched by the sins of the people.
The verse arrangement puts unusual emphasis upon *we have sinned, we have done
wickedly.* God's city and people were a

reproach and disgrace. The Edomites
and Ammonites treated the Jews with such
disrespect that they sought to kill all the
Jews who lived in their territory during
the time of Antiochus (1 Macc. 5:1–8).
The city which should have been a *holy
hill* was treated as a hill of reproach. The
prayer is that God would turn his *anger*
from Jerusalem to cause his *face to shine
upon the sanctuary.* This is the negative
outlook contrasted with the positive hope.
The sanctuary was *desolate* (cf. "abomination that makes desolate," 8:13; 9:27;
11:31; 12:11).

The basis for prayer is *for thy own sake*
(vv. 17,19) and *by thy name* (vv. 18,19).
Their prayer was that God would hear, forgive, and act (v. 19). There was an urgency for they, who felt that they represented God, were about to be destroyed.

It has been argued that this prayer has
no unity and is out of place in this context.
Constant use of materials from Jeremiah
and Nehemiah shows that this literary form
of prayer was integral to their worship.
Furthermore, examination of the Jeremianic
references to "seventy years" shows how he
connected the need of prayer and seeking
God with the whole heart (Jer. 29:12–13).

3. Angelic Revelation (9:20–27)

20 While I was speaking and praying, con-
fessing my sin and the sin of my people Israel,
and presenting my supplication before the
Lord my God for the holy hill of my God;
21 while I was speaking in prayer, the man
Gabriel, whom I had seen in the vision at the
first, came to me in swift flight at the time of
the evening sacrifice. 22 He came and he said to
me, "O Daniel, I have now come out to give
you wisdom and understanding. 23 At the beginning of your supplications a word went
forth, and I have come to tell it to you, for you
are greatly beloved; therefore consider the
word and understand the vision.

24 "Seventy weeks of years are decreed concerning your people and your holy city, to
finish the transgression, to put an end to sin,
and to atone for iniquity, to bring in everlasting righteousness, to seal both vision and
prophet, and to anoint a most holy place.
25 Know therefore and understand that from
the going forth of the word to restore and
build Jerusalem to the coming of an anointed

one, a prince, there shall be seven weeks. Then for sixty-two weeks it shall be built again with squares and moat, but in a troubled time. 26 And after the sixty-two weeks, an anointed one shall be cut off, and shall have nothing; and the people of the prince who is to come shall destroy the city and the sanctuary. Its end shall come with a flood, and to the end there shall be war; desolations are decreed. 27 And he shall make a strong covenant with many for one week; and for half of the week he shall cause sacrifice and offering to cease; and upon the wing of abominations shall come one who makes desolate, until the decreed end is poured out on the desolator."

Gabriel is pictured in anthropomorphic terms. *He came . . . in swift flight* (lit., being wearied in faintness). This is a very difficult phrase. It would be peculiar to attribute weariness to an angel. It has been taken to refer to Daniel (8:27), who lay sick for some time and thus could have been described as faint. In this way, the two chapters and contents are more closely interrelated. Some versions take the word from *'uph* (to fly) and thus translate it "in swift flight." The setting is in visionary prayer. An anthropomorphic description of swiftness would be such as this.

The time of the evening sacrifice is intended to give the time and setting of the revelation. It puts it within the context of Daniel's worship. Revelations were regularly set within the framework of habitual worship (cf. Isa. 6). *He came* (v. 22) is literally "and he caused to understand" (cf. Theodotion, Vulgate). The LXX and Syriac are the texts followed by the RSV. It reads smoother in English "he came." If the context puts so much emphasis upon understanding then it would be in keeping with the force of the text to reiterate that his understanding of the vision was an inbreaking of angelic interpretation (wisdom). Angels did not appear on their own initiative. They are messengers and thus are sent by God.

Consider the word, in this Jeremianic context, could refer to the figure of 70 years and its accompanying truths as vv. 24–27 direct his attention to this figure. This interpretation would involve the decree

which basically pointed out that God's imminent intervention against the perverting persecution of Antiochus was near at hand.

Seventy weeks of years is literally "seventy sevens" or seven periods of seven. It is translated weeks or sevens of years. The entire passage is a reinterpretation of the 70 years of Jeremiah 25 and 29 as applied to the time of the suffering under Antiochus. The seven ("weeks of years") is a "week" in 10:2,3. It is a basic term used for feast of weeks. The form as in Daniel 9 and 10 is a late usage. Regularly, it refers to a unit of seven days. However, the festival calendar does not demonstrate a uniformity of calculation in different periods of history. Leviticus 25:8 provides one possible clue as to meaning: "and you shall count seven weeks of years, seven times seven years, so that the time of the seven weeks of years shall be to you forty-nine years" (cf. Lev. 23:15). The sabbatical year is the basis for Daniel's interpretation (2 Chron. 36:21) of the 70 years.

Chapter 9 looks at the suffering of the people and the *holy city* in terms of 70 weeks of years. It is used in this manner often in the book of Jubilees (*ca.* 109–105 b.c.), in the Mishnah, and in the Talmud. The point of emphasis here is not time but effective realization of God's will. There are six segments to the decree. The first three are negative: *to finish the transgression* (rebellion), *to put an end to sin* (missing the mark), *and to atone for iniquity* (errings or pervertings). The second three are positive: *to bring in everlasting righteousness* as distinguished from the sins of the people, *to seal* (ratify or affix by attesting) *both vision and prophet, and to anoint* (the root word same as Messiah) *a most holy place.*

Some interpreters propose that Daniel was attempting to correct the 70 years prophecy of Jermiah since the captivity was not exactly 70 years. But this is reading a purpose into this chapter which is not in keeping with the context. The 70-year principle was used in 9:1–2 as substantiation for the hope which the book had been proclaiming in the first seven chapters. Instead of correcting the prophecy he used the Jeremianic principle and prophecy to reapply it to his own time. This understanding of Scripture is basic in the use of the events of the past to apply them to our day. The Bible performs the function of a compass for all men in all times and in all situations rather than being a road map which predicts every bend or turn in a specific and preknown segment of space or time.

The unfolding by Gabriel begins at the point that the *word* was sent forth to *restore and build* Jerusalem. The theme of the supplication (9:15-19) was the restoration of Jerusalem and the sanctuary. The opening of the chapter was based on (1) the word of the Lord to Jeremiah the prophet (v. 2); (2) the end of the desolations of Jerusalem; and (3) 70 years. These same three elements are found in vv. 24-25. Thus the *going forth of the word* refers to the word of the Lord by Jeremiah. This entire chapter has a Jeremianic frame of reference. When does the author begin his calculations? It would be highly unlikely that Jeremiah would have made his prophecy concerning Jerusalem's restoration while Jerusalem was still standing. So the word did not appear until after the destruction of Jerusalem (587 B.C.). We do not have the date of this word from Jeremiah. With the year following Jerusalem's destruction as our tentative starting point (586) we calculate the first event as the coming of *an anointed one, a prince*. A week of years would be 7 years, and 7 weeks of this length would be 49 years. After 586 B.C., 49 years would be 539-537 B.C., which was the time of the fall of Babylon, the destroyer of Jerusalem. The king who took control of Babylon was Cyrus, who also made the decree permitting the Jews to return to Jerusalem. Isaiah 44:28 and 45:1 record Yahweh as referring to Cyrus as "my shepherd" or "his anointed" in regard to rebuilding Jerusalem and the Temple.

At the same time there appeared Zerub-babel, one of the returnees after the decree of Cyrus (Ezra 2:2; 3:8). He was the grandson of king Jehoiachin, of the Davidic lineage, and in the lineage of Jesus (Matt. 1:12-13; Luke 3:27). He was "governor of Judah" (Hag. 1:1; 2:2) and was called the servant of Yahweh (Hag. 2:23). Thus, he could be a prince and also an anointed one.

A colleague of Zerubbabel in the religious and civil government of Jerusalem was Joshua a high priest. Joshua is pictured as wearing a crown (Zech. 6:11). As a high priest he may have been anointed (cf. Lev. 4:3 ff.). Both Joshua and Zerubbabel were governing officials who were involved in the rebuilding of Jerusalem and the reestablishing of the holy place. If Jeremiah's word were dated around 570, the focus would be directly upon Joshua and/or Zerubbabel.

Some interpreters see the decree of Cyrus in 537 B.C. as the starting point of this 70 weeks. The decree in the first year of Cyrus after Babylon fell to him was indeed a turning point in the affairs of Jerusalem. The decree (Ezra 6:3,7,8) was "concerning the house of God at Jerusalem." It is not certain that the word to *restore and build* Jerusalem is the same one as the decree about the house of God by Cyrus. Isaiah 44:28 and 45:13 speak of Jerusalem being built under Cyrus. If this be the time, 49 years after 537 B.C. would be 488. There is no known personage or event to correspond to the coming of an anointed one.

On the other hand, other interpreters restructure the Hebrew text (vv. 25 ff.) so that there would not be both a 7-week period and a 62-week period but there would be only a 69-week period. They arrive generally at the time of the coming of Jesus the Messiah. They recall the word to restore Jerusalem in the "seventh year of Artaxerxes the king" (Ezra 7:7 f.), 458 B.C. Ezra 7:7-28 states that the decree gave permission for any who desired to go to Jerusalem to accompany Ezra and renew worship in the house of their God. The attraction of this date is that 69 weeks of years (483 years) after 458 would be A.D. 25–26, the beginning of Jesus' ministry. One half of a week of years would be three and a half years, the length of Jesus' ministry, thus around A.D. 29, the death of Jesus.

Objections to this theory are: (1) The starting point is selected to fit the interpreter's desired end point, overlooking the context's point of beginning. (2) No interpretation is made of the 7 weeks and 62 weeks. (3) Which Artaxerxes is intended? A slight variation of this view is taken from Nehemiah 2:1 f., noting the 20th year of king Artaxerxes or around 444 B.C. These figures would afford the end of 7 weeks of years in 395 and the end of 62 weeks in A.D. 39. No known events of these dates would shed light on this text.

No specific manner of calculation meets the exigencies of this text. The three basic target times toward which these interpretations have been suggested are: (1) the period of Antiochus Epiphanes; (2) the first coming, the life and death of Jesus; (3) the second coming of Jesus. A close examination of the text must be made for the meaning which is directly applicable.

The word to restore (v. 25) fits the Jeremianic flavor of the entire chapter. The general period seems to be about 587 B.C. The passing of *seven weeks* is the period of the Babylonian captivity when Jerusalem was in ruins (587–537). The coming of *an anointed one, a prince,* could refer to Joshua the high priest of whom Haggai and Zechariah wrote.

Then for sixty-two weeks may refer to the period from the time of the return(s) while the city was comparatively rebuilt or was in the process of being built. The time was longer than the Babylonian captivity. During this period of time it was built with *squares and moat.* "Squares" were the broad open places or plazas, i.e., the essential part of the city. This would afford ample surroundings whereby the life of the city could go on in some order.

"Moat" is a word used only here in the Old Testament and means trench. The trench was dug for defensive purposes (cf. an 8th cent. B.C. inscription; the Dead Sea Copper Scroll uses this word as conduit). There was a semblance of the natural city life with a central business and with defenses. It was a *troubled time.* The life of the returnees was not without great difficulties (cf. fourth chapter of Ezra).

After the sixty-two weeks sums up the period during which life in Jerusalem was basically under the control of the Jewish inhabitants with the possibility of worshiping in freedom. *An anointed one shall be cut off. Mashiah* is the Hebrew word for Messiah and means anointed one. Some interpreters would apply this to Jesus' crucifixion, but this interpretation overlooks the immediate historical situation and the contextual meaning. This anointed one is different from that in v. 25.

In v. 25 it was seen that the anointed one, a ruling one, may have been a priest. Leviticus 4:3,5,16; 6:15 read "the priest the anointed one." This reference could be to the cutting off the legitimate line of priests. Joshua, the brother of Onias III, took the Greek name Jason. He became the high priest in 175 B.C. by corruption (2 Macc. 4:7–15), displacing Onias. Later Menelaus became high priest by outbidding Jason by 300 talents of silver (2 Macc. 4:23–24). When payment was demanded Menelaus stole some of the vessels of the Temple and gave them to the king's captain. Onias being faithful to his priesthood exposed Menelaus' evil. Whereupon, about 170, Onias III was treacherously killed. His murder affected the Jews.

The meaning of *shall have nothing* is not clear. It is literally "there is not to him." Theodotion interprets it to mean that the anointed one was cut off "although there is nothing against him judicially" (cf. Porteous, "without trial"). Jeffery (p. 497) prefers the meaning of the RSV to indicate that with him the true priesthood came to an end. With the death of Onias III, a priest and anointed one, there was a radical change in the priest's office.

The people of the prince. People is a synonym for troops or army (cf. Josh. 8:1 f.; Judg. 7:1; 9:49; 1 Sam. 11:11; 2 Sam. 10:13; Ezek. 30:11).

Who was *the prince who is to come?* The word prince regularly refers to a ruler or leader, often the king. The anointed one had been cut off. In this reference the prince would refer to the king and not the priest. The king reigning in Palestine during the time of Onias, Jason, and Menelaus was Antiochus Epiphanes. The use of *desolations* points specifically to Antiochus.

Who is to come (lit., coming) probably indicates that the prince is coming against the city as an invader (cf. 1:1). It is possible to take this in a temporal sense, that the prince would come in the future. In this sense, the prince is said to be one of the Roman conquerors (Vespasian, Hadrian, Pompey, Herod Agrippa), Christ, or the antichrist. However, these identifications do not fit the context of the chapter or the book as directly as Antiochus. The truths of the text may also be applicable during the time of these, but the focus of the biblical text is on Antiochus.

Its end shall come with a flood. Whose end is meant? The end of the prince or the destruction are the two possibilities within the text. The destruction ("end") is the last thing mentioned before the pronoun. So the author viewed the final struggle as that between good and evil which would come as an overwhelming flood, i.e., divine wrath (cf. Nah. 1:8). The entire expression could be translated literally: "People of a prince shall destroy both the city and the sanctuary. His coming and his end with the flood. But until an end of warfare, desolations are being strictly enforced." The whole chapter has presented a basis for hope. One real ground for hope would be a knowledge of the imminent end of such a prince. Until the end of the warfare there will be desolations upon the faithful.

He, i.e., the prince, *shall make a strong covenant with many.* Literally, it reads

"and he made strong a covenant with many." It has been thought that this refers to the covenant that Antiochus made with many Jews (1 Macc. 1:52: "many of the people, . . . joined them"; 1:42: "many even from Israel gladly adopted his religion"). Many Jews violated their religious covenant with Yahweh and followed the religious practices of Antiochus. Objection has been raised since covenant is elsewhere in Daniel (11:22,28,30,32) only used of the religion of Israel. Some translate many as "majority." But the term many is so general it could be used relatively in the sense of "some." Another possible explanation is to translate the phrase as "a word shall make burdensome the covenant for many."

If the two sections of v. 27 are synonymous parallelism, both parts of the verse explain the same event. The meaning of the first segment refers to the removal of the proper observance of Jewish worship. *For half of the week* (ca. three and a half years) he stops (lit., causes to sabbath) *sacrifice and offering* or all kinds of sacrifice. Antiochus desecrated their altars beginning "on the 15th day of Chislev," December 15, 168 B.C. No sacrifices to Yahweh could be brought until after the 25th of Chislev, 165 B.C. For three years and ten days the faithful Jews were the objects of religious persecution.

Upon the wing has been interpreted as a wing of the Temple or as wing of the altar. If the *desolator* (*shomem*) is a play on the Syrian god Baal Shamem (Baal of heavens), as is probable, the wing could have some reference to the picture of this god as an eagle. Some winged image may have been set up in the place of the Jewish sacrifices. The literal rendering of the Hebrew would be "and upon the wing of abominations desolation."

Abominations shall come one who makes desolate is a free translation of only two Hebrew words (abominations desolating, *skikkutsim meshomem*). Abominations is used for idol (1 Kings 11:7; 2 Kings 23:13; 2 Chron. 15:8). Antiochus erected an image upon the altar in Jerusalem. He called it Zeus Olympius, a Greek version of the ancient Canaanite "god of heaven." This is an intentional variation of the hated idol as a "play on words" which carried both the idea of the object and their interpretation of the object. This idolatrous image of Zeus (it is said to look like Antiochus himself) upon the altar made the altar so appalling and desecrated that it would evoke horror to the hearts of any faithful worshipers of the God of Israel. Antiochus erected the blasphemous image and so was known as the desolator.

This desolation would continue until the desolator was punished. The *decreed end* is literally "and until a complete destruction and a strict decision." The two nouns combine to emphasize the inescapable fate which would be *poured out* on Antiochus. The word end is annihilation or consumption. *Poured out* is the same word as used in 9:11, "the curse and oath . . . poured out upon us."

The time context of the book has been a four-unit view. These images were kingdoms with which Israel was deeply involved. The end of the vile figure, i.e., Antiochus, was the climax of the fourth unit. The author's purpose in chapter 9 was to demonstrate the bases which his people had for hope and for the end of their desolation. This was done by the use of Scripture (Jeremiah), prayer of confession as evidence of a continuing faith, and a revelation of God's messenger Gabriel.

The "Great Parenthesis" theory of the interpretation of Daniel 9 suggests that the 69 weeks ended during the time of Jesus. The event which marked the gap (great parenthesis) is often seen as the triumphal entry of Jesus. The explanation by those who hold the gap theory is that v. 25 contains the 69 weeks; v. 26 is the era of the big gap; v. 27 has the 70th week but that it is still in the future and does not come consecutively with the 69th week's end.

Interpreters are very divided in their attempts to show the amount of this material which refers to a time future to the author. Others seek to show how much is still future to the 20th century A.D. Before one applies the material, he is obligated to establish the exegetical, historical, and theological meaning of the book of Daniel itself.

There is no question that the future is an important part of the prophecy of this chapter. It must be asked whether it is the immediate future as also laying down principles for the remote future, the immediate future climaxing in an end of that segment of history, or the immediate future climaxing in the final years of time.

It is a mistake for any theologian to force a complete millennial theory into the ninth chapter of Daniel and demand that this is what the author was trying to convey. In fact, one must seek to discover the area of messianic process which is involved here. How far along the messianic development toward the Messiah had the book of Daniel gone? The term anointed has been applied to many persons. In 9:25 the anointed one was noted as a prince. Whereas the anointed one in 9:26 is different. Does this book relate to the messianic view as seen in the Dead Sea Scrolls that the Jews expected two Messiahs, i.e., a king Messiah and also a priest Messiah? Many questions defy dogmatic answers!

V. *Vision of the End* (10:1—12:13)

1. *Prologue to the Vision* (10:1—11:1)

The final three chapters form another member of the parallelism of the whole book. There are various things which are common between this unit and chapters 7—9. One is the content upon which the three chapters major. Another is the form of a vision. Visions are found in all three chapters. All of these visions approach the same situation from different angles.

(1) *Superscription* (10:1)

¹ In the third year of Cyrus king of Persia a word was revealed to Daniel, who was named Belteshazzar. And the word was true, and it was a great conflict. And he understood the word and had understanding of the vision.

The superscription for the final three chapters dates the vision *in the third year of Cyrus.* In 1:21, it had been stated that "Daniel continued until the first year of King Cyrus." It would have been natural for the reader to have interpreted that Daniel died in the first year of Cyrus. The LXX has the time here in the first year of Cyrus, probably to bring this section into agreement with 1:21. The times of these returns are not known. Some interpreters think that the first group left immediately upon the issuance of the decree. But this is not known. The extent of preparations and enlistment for these returns is conjecture. Daniel was no doubt aged at this time. If he were 18 years old when he was taken to Babylon (*ca.* 605 B.C.), he would now be about 88 years old.

Cyrus king of Persia is not the ordinary manner of referring to the king during his lifetime. This identification in all historical records is made of Cyrus only once (immediately after Persia had been captured and so such identification was specific). It is the Hellenistic usage or later. *The word was true* relates to 8:26, "the vision . . . is true." Word and vision are two important elements which serve to carry out the parallelism of the previous chapter (cf. 9:23). *A great conflict* refers to the hard circumstances which must be endured prior to the consummation of that era.

(2) Background of the Vision (10:2— 11:1)

² In those days I, Daniel, was mourning for three weeks. ³ I ate no delicacies, no meat or wine entered my mouth, nor did I anoint myself at all, for the full three weeks. ⁴ On the twenty-fourth day of the first month, as I was standing on the bank of the great river, that is, the Tigris, ⁵ I lifted up my eyes and looked, and behold, a man clothed in linen, whose loins were girded with gold of Uphaz. ⁶ His body was like beryl, his face like the appearance of lightning, his eyes like flaming torches, his arms and legs like the gleam of burnished bronze, and the sound of his words like the noise of a multitude. ⁷ And I, Daniel, alone saw the vision, for the men who were with me did not see the vision, but a great trembling fell upon them, and they fled to hide them-

selves. ⁸ So I was left alone and saw this great vision, and no strength was left in me; my radiant appearance was fearfully changed, and I retained no strength. ⁹ Then I heard the sound of his words; and when I heard the sound of his words, I fell on my face in a deep sleep with my face to the ground.

¹⁰ And behold, a hand touched me and set me trembling on my hands and knees. ¹¹ And he said to me, "O Daniel, man greatly beloved, give heed to the words that I speak to you, and stand upright, for now I have been sent to you." While he was speaking this word to me, I stood up trembling. ¹² Then he said to me, "Fear not, Daniel, for from the first day that you set your mind to understand and humbled yourself before your God, your words have been heard, and I have come because of your words. ¹³ The prince of the kingdom of Persia withstood me twenty-one days; but Michael, one of the chief princes, came to help me, so I left him there with the prince of the kingdom of Persia ¹⁴ and came to make you understand what is to befall your people in the latter days. For the vision is for days yet to come."

¹⁵ When he had spoken to me according to these words, I turned my face toward the ground and was dumb. ¹⁶ And behold, one in the likeness of the sons of men touched my lips; then I opened my mouth and spoke. I said to him who stood before me, "O my lord, by reason of the vision pains have come upon me, and I retain no strength. ¹⁷ How can my lord's servant talk with my lord? For now no strength remains in me, and no breath is left in me."

¹⁸ Again one having the appearance of a man touched me and strengthened me. ¹⁹ And he said, "O man greatly beloved, fear not, peace be with you; be strong and of good courage." And when he spoke to me, I was strengthened and said, "Let my lord speak, for you have strengthened me." ²⁰ Then he said, "Do you know why I have come to you? But now I will return to fight against the prince of Persia; and when I am through with him, lo, the prince of Greece will come. ²¹ But I will tell you what is inscribed in the book of truth: there is none who contends by my side against these except Michael, your prince.

¹ And as for me, in the first year of Darius the Mede, I stood up to confirm and strengthen him.

Daniel *was mourning* (cf. 9:3) is another expression for fasting as is made clear by v. 3. *For three weeks* is literally "three sevens days." "Sevens" is the same word as translated weeks of years in 9:24–27. The word *days* is used to show the difference in the meaning of sevens from the previous use. Three full weeks is the effect of this expression (cf. 10:2,13). *No delicacies* (lit., bread of desirablenesses) is the opposite of bread of affliction (Deut. 16:3). This was not an absolute fast. *Meat or wine* were luxuries. Omission of anointing was a sign also of mourning. Only food of bare necessity was taken.

A great river is generally understood to be the Euphrates (Gen. 15:18; Josh. 1:4). *The Tigris* (*Hiddekel*) was over 50 miles away from Babylon. *Hiddekel* is found only here and in Genesis 2:14. Daniel was in Babylon which is on the Euphrates. The visionary character of the chapter also accounts for the scene being placed at this secondary river location. Some interpreters contend that the location on the *Hiddekel* indicates a gloss included by a writer in Palestine who did not know the Mesopotamian geography.

Daniel saw *a man.* The identity of this angelic being is not given. In 8:16 and 9:21 Gabriel was mentioned and was called a "man." Parallelism strongly suggests this identification. In apocalyptic terminology a man often indicates an angelic being. Some early Christian commentators see this man as the Messiah Jesus. *Clothed in linen* is a phrase found elsewhere (also 12:6,7) only in Ezekiel. Biblical usage of "linen" outside of Ezekiel and Daniel is singular, but in these two books it is plural. Linen was a garment worn by priests (cf. Rev. 15:6).

He was *girded with gold of Uphaz.* Uphaz is used (cf. Jer. 10:9) as a place. Since no place is known by that name attempts have been made at understanding the phrase. By conjecturing an "r" instead of the "z" one gets the "gold of Ophir" (Isa. 13:12; Job 28:16; Psalm 45:9). On the other hand, by reading *ketem uphaz* instead of *ketem 'uphaz* (cf. Cant. 5:11), the translation is "gold and fine gold."

Verse 6 reflects a knowledge of the first chapter of Ezekiel. His appearance was dazzling, extraordinary, sure to attract attention. His words were of a great sound to make his presence uniquely sensed. An unusual thing was that Daniel *alone saw the vision.* The men who were with him sensed something and fled.

The effect on Daniel was shattering. He lost all his strength and fell to the ground in a deep sleep (cf. 8:18). Only with the assurance that he was a *man greatly beloved* did he dare rise to face the angelic tutor. *From the first day* refers to the fact that Daniel had fasted for 21 days. An explanation of the 21 days' delay is given him. The angel was sent by God at the first, but he was hindered by *the prince of the kingdom of Persia.* This was not the king but a "patron saint." He withstood the celestial messenger. When Michael came to help him, the angel was able to go to Daniel with the explanation of the vision.

The message which Gabriel brought was of what was *to befall* the people of Israel *in the latter days* (10:14). The purpose of the vision is hope for downtrodden Israel. In the latter days refers to the last days of the fourth segment of the historical period. The immediate situation was the one to which the book addressed itself. The author was looking into the future.

The result of the presence of the celestial messenger and message was that Daniel turned his *face toward the ground,* i.e., he did not fall prostrate but in humble fear looked down, and *was dumb.* Verses 10:16—11:1 give the explanation which prepares for a proper understanding of chapters 11 and 12. One who had the likeness of sons of Adam *touched* his lips. The celestial touch gives Daniel the power of speech which surpassed that of mere humanity (cf. Isa. 6:7–9; Jer. 1:9). He explains his silence *by reason of the vision. Pains* (generally of childbirth; cf. Isa. 13:8; 21:3) are the writhing pangs of physical effects under distress. He retained *no strength* is an idiom which occurs only in 10:8; 11:6, and Chronicles.

The recovery of Daniel was gradual (10:10,16,18–19). This third step in his recovery explains the final step in his being able to understand the interpretation. Verses 20–21 are very difficult to interpret.

The question, *Do you know why . . . ?*
is to effect attention rather than to secure
information. The interpretation about to be
given is thus brought into focus. The scene
is still the angelic one of vv. 10 f. The time
sequence is very difficult in all ancient
Semitic writing due to the fact that there
was more interest in types of action than in
times of action. The verbs of the Old Testament are not past, present, future as in
modern Indo-Germanic languages. Translators have a very difficult task in making
a smooth English translation from a Semitic
text which uses perfect forms to indicate
actions viewed as finished (*do you know*
and *I have come*), imperfect to show unfinished actions (and now I should *return*
to fight), and participles to show action in
uninterrupted process in the time of the
context (*I am through*—lit., I going out;
and *will come*).

The book of truth (lit., a register or
writing of certainty) is by most interpreters
compared with the Tablets of Fate which
indicate an absolute determinism in the
form of prediction. The terminology "book
of truth" is unknown from any other source.
Such tablets and books are known in the
Talmud, the books of Jubilees and the
Testament of the Twelve Patriarchs.
Porteous (p. 156) says that the effect of
this reference was "to suggest that these
events were included within the divine
providential control of history and were
moving towards the divinely planned
climax." The word *truth* is the same used
in 8:26 and 10:1 concerning the vision.
Certainty is an inescapable conclusion of
the text.

The historical note (11:1) follows the
pattern in 7:1; 8:1; 9:1; 10:1 indicating
parallelism of each chapter of the second
half of the book. The LXX, Aquila, and
Theodotion have Cyrus instead of Darius.
Theodotion omits "the Mede." The LXX
has "the king." Many interpreters think that
this note has found its way into the text as
a superscription to fill out the form previously established. It is unusual for an
angel to date an action by the work of a

human heathen ruler. This date has reference to Gabriel's assisting Michael, not to
the vision of Daniel which was in the
third year of Cyrus. Ginsberg (p. 46)
translates this verse, "And I since the first
year of Darius the Mede have been standing as a strengthener and fortifier for him."

2. Interpretation of the Vision (11:2-45)

(1) Persia and Greece (11:2-4)

2 "And now I will show you the truth. Behold, three more kings shall arise in Persia;
and a fourth shall be far richer than all of
them; and when he has become strong through
his riches, he shall stir up all against the
kingdom of Greece. ³ Then a mighty king shall
arise, who shall rule with great dominion and
do according to his will. ⁴ And when he has
arisen, his kingdom shall be broken and divided toward the four winds of heaven, but not
to his posterity, nor according to the dominion
with which he ruled; for his kingdom shall be
plucked up and go to others besides these.

A close study of the events of this section in the light of known history shows a
detailed and amazingly accurate agreement
up to a certain point. The first section is
detailed and relatively clear from a standpoint of accurate information. The latter
section of the book then becomes general,
nonspecific, with a real contrast in style.

One of the great values of this section is
the value of faith in the time of crisis. The
author's faith points out something greater
than determinism or fatalism in historical
events. Here is a man with the free moral
choice available standing firm to his convictions under the heaviest persecution
known to mankind up to that time. He
does not surrender and lapse into immo-
bility. He reveals God's interest is not
merely in having all things come out at the
right spot at the end of all time. God is involved with mankind at every point of time
until the very end. Daniel is convinced concerning the final end, but he is living each
event in the reality of his belief that God
must be glorified in these very events.

The truth to which he referred is the
vision interpreted (cf. 10:1,21; 8:26). Persia and Greece are placed in their proper

perspective, i.e., only three verses. The same type of treatment was given in 2:39 and chapters 7—8.

Three more kings . . . and a fourth. Cyrus was the king (10:1) of Persia at the beginning of this vision. The kings to follow him were: Cambyses (530–522 B.C.), Pseudo-Smerdis, also called Gautama (522), Darius I (522–486), and Xerxes (486–465). However, the four Persian kings mentioned in the Bible (Ezra 4: 5–7) are Cyrus, Darius, Xerxes or Ahasuerus, and Artaxerxes. Since these are the four in the biblical records, they may be the four of 11:2. The three rulers of note following Cyrus would be more likely, namely, Cambyses, Darius I, and Xerxes. The question as to the total number is apparent. The fourth most naturally refers to the last of the three more and would refer to Xerxes. *Far richer than all of them* agrees with the reference in Herodotus (vii. 20–99) and Esther.

Against the kingdom of Greece is difficult in that "against" is not in the text. Some have read this "he shall stir up all" and have suggested "the kingdom of Greece" to be a gloss. Young holds that "the kingdom of Greece" is used in apposition. Theodotion makes it read "he shall rouse himself against all the kingdoms of Greece." A *mighty man* mentioned in the context of Greece would be Alexander the Great (336–323 B.C.). *Mighty* is used of warriors. Reference is to the blitzkrieg career of Alexander (cf. 8:5–8,21). *Great dominion* describes the vast outreach of his conquests (see above).

Toward the four winds of heaven are the same words found in 8:8 concerning the king of Greece. The four main divisions of the empire of Alexander were under Seleucus, Ptolemy, Lysimachus, and Cassander (see the comment on ch. 8). *But not to his posterity* refers to the fact that none of the four were descendants of Alexander. There were three possible heirs of Alexander: (1) Phillip Arrhidaeus, his mentally deficient brother, was removed in 317 B.C.; (2) Alexander, his son by his

wife Roxana, was murdered in 311; (3) Herakles, his illegitimate son by his mistress Barsine, daughter of Darius. None of them figured in the ruling of the kingdom.

To others besides these may have reference to the minor kingdoms in Armenia, Cappadocia, and elsewhere in addition to the four chief divisions. On the other hand, it may mean the four chief generals who controlled the main divisions of Alexander's empire besides the three rightful heirs.

(2) *Ptolemies and Seleucids* (11:5–20)

5 "Then the king of the south shall be strong, but one of his princes shall be stronger than he and his dominion shall be a great dominion. 6 After some years they shall make an alliance, and the daughter of the king of the south shall come to the king of the north to make peace; but she shall not retain the strength of her arm, and he and his offspring shall not endure; but she shall be given up, and her attendants, her child, and he who got possession of her. 7 "In those times a branch from her roots shall arise in his place; he shall come against the army and enter the fortress of the king of the north, and he shall deal with them and shall prevail. 8 He shall also carry off to Egypt their gods with their molten images and with their precious vessels of silver and of gold; and for some years he shall refrain from attacking the king of the north. 9 Then the latter shall come into the realm of the king of the south but shall return into his own land.

10 "His sons shall wage war and assemble a multitude of great forces, which shall come on and overflow and pass through, and again shall carry the war as far as his fortress. 11 Then the king of the south, moved with anger, shall come out and fight with the king of the north; and he shall raise a great multitude, but it shall be given into his hand. 12 And when the multitude is taken, his heart shall be exalted, and he shall cast down tens of thousands, but he shall not prevail. 13 For the king of the north shall again raise a mutitude, greater than the former; and after some years he shall come on with a great army and abundant supplies.

14 "In those times many shall rise against the king of the south; and the men of violence among your own people shall lift themselves up in order to fulfil the vision; but they shall fail. 15 Then the king of the north shall come and throw up siegeworks, and take a well-fortified city. And the forces of the south shall not stand, or even his picked troops, for there shall be no strength to stand. 16 But he who comes against him shall do according to his own will,

and none shall stand before him; and he shall stand in the glorious land, and all of it shall be in his power. ¹⁷ He shall set his face to come with the strength of his whole kingdom, and he shall bring terms of peace and perform them. He shall give him the daughter of women to destroy the kingdom; but it shall not stand or be to his advantage. ¹⁸ Afterward he shall turn his face to the coastlands, and shall take many of them; but a commander shall put an end to his insolence; indeed he shall turn his insolence back upon him. ¹⁹ Then he shall turn his face back toward the fortresses of his own land; but he shall stumble and fall, and shall not be found.

²⁰ "Then shall arise in his place one who shall send an exactor of tribute through the glory of the kingdom; but within a few days he shall be broken, neither in anger nor in battle.

In the same manner as in 8:8–9, time and kingdoms are passed over from the division of Alexander's empire to the struggle between two contenders i.e., the Ptolemies and Seleucids. The fact of the omission of Babylon, the brief mention of Persia, and the scant reference to Greece compared with the very detailed treatment of the history of these two kingdoms point up the contemporaneity of the author and the Seleucids.

The south (negeb) generally refers to territory immediately south of Palestine. But throughout this chapter the term king of the south refers to the Ptolemies who ruled over Egypt. The dynasties other than the Ptolemies and the Seleucids are omitted for they had very little concern with events in Palestine after 322 B.C.

The king of the south is Ptolemy I (Soter), son of Lagos, one of Alexander's ablest generals. He secured Egypt on the partition of the Greek Empire, ruled as satrap 322–306 B.C., and assumed the title of king and ruled 305–285.

One of his princes is Seleucus I (Nicator). As a companion of Alexander, he became satrap of Babylon, 321–316 B.C. When he fled from Babylon to escape from Antigonus in 316, he attached himself to Ptolemy in Egypt. Seleucus I (312–280) assumed the title king in 306. Gradually, he began to extend his outreach and control. After the battle of Ipsus (301)

Seleucus possessed practically all of Alexander's former kingdom with the exception of Palestine and Egypt. Seleucus made his capital at Antioch (300). His dominion became the most powerful of the successors of Alexander.

After some years covers the years between about 280 and 249 B.C. They shall make an alliance refers to a marriage alliance. Ptolemy II, king of the south (Philadelphus, 285–246 B.C.), gave his daughter Berenice in marriage to Antiochus II Theos, the king of the north, in the hope of ending the war between the two peoples. There was a large dowry given with a condition that Antiochus put away his wife Laodice and also that he cut off his sons, Seleucus and Antiochus, from succession to the Seleucid throne. Any son of Berenice was to succeed him to the throne.

The last half of v. 6 is a clear reference to the fact that this agreement did not endure. Ptolemy II died (246 B.C.), and Antiochus divorced Berenice and took back Laodice. Laodice distrusted her husband Antiochus II and had him poisoned in an attempt to restore her sons to succession to the throne. Soon Laodice sent forces to Antioch to murder the infant son of Berenice. In due time, Berenice was killed with many of her Egyptian attendants.

The text of v. 7 is uncertain. In those times is the last word of v. 6 of the Hebrew text. Verses 7–8 cover the kings Ptolemy III Euergetes, 246–221 B.C., and Seleucus II Callinicus, 247–226. A branch from her roots was Ptolemy III, brother of Berenice, who succeeded their father Ptolemy II. He, with a view of avenging the murder of his sister, marched in 246 against the army of the king of the north (Seleucus II). He overran most of Syria and Babylonia and seized the Seleucid port of Antioch. The fortress of the king of the north probably refers to Seleucia, the fortified city on the coast. Jerome quotes Porphyry to the effect that Ptolemy III returned to Egypt the statutes of the Egyptian gods which Cambyses had taken away. He brought much booty in the form of

2,500 precious vessels and 40,000 talents of silver. This earned him the title Euergetes (Well-doer). He dealt with the Seleucids according to his own will, even slaying Laodice, his sister's murderess.

He shall refrain from attacking the king of the north. He could have conquered the entire Seleucid Empire but an insurrection broke out in his own empire.

Verse 9 is the record of the attempt by Seleucus (*the latter*) to invade Egypt after he had regained his power in Asia (242 B.C.). This counterattack was so disastrous that Seleucus was able to return with only a small remnant of his army in 240.

His sons (v. 10) are the sons of the king of the north, Seleucus II. The eldest son, Seleucus III Ceraunus, succeeded to the throne in 226 B.C. and reigned until 223. He was murdered in a war in Asia Minor and was succeeded by his brother Antiochus III the Great, 223–187 B.C. The Seleucids gained the greatest extent during his reign. The LXX and the written Hebrew text have "his son" and thus refer to Antiochus III in this entire section. The traditionally pronounced Hebrew reads "his sons" because the two following verbs (*wage war* and *assemble*) are plural.

Verse 10 refers to the two campaigns of Antiochus III beginning in 219 B.C. against the armies of Ptolemy IV Philopator, 221–205. These campaigns were so successful that the Seleucid ruler Antiochus conquered a great part of the Ptolemy territory. *As far as his fortress* is either to Gaza or Raphia to which he advanced in 217.

The king of the south, (v. 11) i.e., Ptolemy IV, was angry about the intrusion from the north into his territory. His forces fought with the king of the north at Raphia in 217 B.C. Ptolemy IV conquered (*given into his hand*) *a great multitude* which Antiochus had raised. Ptolemy IV, an effeminate and dissolute character, did not follow up the opportunity to conquer the entire kingdom of the north. Antiochus had to surrender Coele-Syria.

After some years (v. 13, lit., at the end of the times years) mark the passing of about 12 years of virtual peace between the two empires. Verse 13 records the fact that Antiochus raised a greater army than previously. During this time, Ptolemy IV died (205 B.C.) and was succeeded by his five-year-old son, Ptolemy V, Epiphaneus (205–181).

Abundant supplies (lit., great campbaggage; cf. Gen. 14:11,12, "goods") are probably weapons and equipment for an army. Montgomery calls attention to a possible play on words between the word "supply" and the word "horses." He suggests that the author referred to the horse and baggage animals, especially the quantity of elephants which Antiochus had brought from his campaign in India.

The succession to the throne of Egypt by the infant Ptolemy V was probably the event which tipped the scales in favor of Antiochus the Great. He, Antiochus, made a league with Philip of Macedon to launch an attack *against the king of the south.* There were also *men of violence* working with Antiochus (lit., the sons of the violent ones of thy people). These men were Jews who attached themselves to Antiochus.

The meaning of *in order to fulfil the vision* is unclear. The most appropriate application would be that the people who sided with Antiochus against Ptolemy in the attempt to throw off the dreaded yoke thought that they were acting in such a way as to bring to pass some prophecy concerning the deliverance of their nation. But their efforts were doomed to fail. The entire v. 14 has been interpreted as a parenthetical expression since v. 15 connects directly with v. 13. The verse, however, echoes the part of chapter 10 which confessed the sins of the people as a reason for their calamity.

The king of the south sent his troops under a mercenary soldier, Scopas, about 200 B.C. to make war in Judea against Antiochus. Antiochus marched against them and drove him and 100,000 picked soldiers to take refuge in Sidon. Note in v. 15 that *the king of the north* (Ptolemy) *shall . . . throw up siegeworks* against

Sidon in 198. The *forces* of Ptolemy and even the 100,000 *picked troops* could not win. *No strength to stand* would have reference to the effects of famine which caused Scopas to surrender.

He who comes against him is Antiochus. Since the troops from the south had been conquered, there were *none* to stand in his way. The *glorious land* (cf. 8:9) was Palestine. After the battle of Paneas (the NT Caesarea-Philippi) and the siege of Sidon around 198 B.C., Antiochus took unquestionable control of Palestine. *All of it* follows the LXX reading (KJV, JPS, and JB read "all of it" as "destruction"). The RSV and the LXX give the preferred reading. From then on, Palestine is Seleucid.

Antiochus *set his face* (v. 17) with his entire force toward Egypt. He directed his forces against the coastal cities of Cilicia, Lycia, and Caria, which were under Ptolemy V. Antiochus did not attack Egypt, but he took Gaza by storm. *He shall bring terms of peace and perform them* is a free rendering of the text.

Antiochus and Ptolemy came to terms. The treaty was sealed by the betrothal of Antiochus' daughter Cleopatra to the young king Ptolemy V in 198–197 B.C. Cleopatra was called the *daughter of women.* This unusual description may mean "the essence of femininity" or some such complimentary expression. She became the first Cleopatra of Egyptian history when she went to Egypt in 194–193 to marry Ptolemy V. Antiochus, no doubt, thought that by this union he would obtain a strong hand over Egyptian affairs. However, Cleopatra demonstrated a strong loyalty to her new country.

Since he had been so victorious in his campaign to the south, Antiochus turned *his face to the coastlands.* By 196 B.C. most of Asia Minor was under his power, so he crossed the Hellespont and seized control of the Thracian Chersonese. The next few years were occupied in the consolidation of his holdings. During this time, Antiochus met the representatives of Rome, who told him to leave Asia Minor alone. Polybius

(xvii.34) records Antiochus' telling the Romans to stop interfering with Asia just as he was not to touch Italy.

The real breaking point was Greece. In 192 B.C. Antiochus invaded Greece and seized control of parts of Greece north of Corinth. In 191 he was stopped overwhelmingly by the Romans at Thermopylae. The Roman consul, Lucius Cornelius Scipio, was the *commander* who *put an end* (190) to Antiochus' insolence. Scipio earned the title "Asiaticus" by the crushing defeat of Antiochus' army of 80,000 men at Magnesia near Smyrna. This disaster both humiliated and ruined Antiochus as far as Europe and Asia Minor were concerned. Rome demanded that Antiochus pay a great indemnity. Antiochus had no alternative but to return to *the fortresses of his own land.* He had to resort to robbing his own territories. *He shall stumble and fall* refers to his ingominious end. In 187 he plundered a temple of Bel in the wilds of Luristan (Elam) and was slain.

In his place, i.e., Antiochus III, his son Seleucus IV Philopator arose (187–175 B.C.). *An exactor of tribute* probably referred to Heliodorus, the prime minister of Seleucus IV (2 Macc. 3:1–40). Seleucus IV was not classed as a great king since he was forced to spend his time raising funds for empty treasuries. He had to pay an annual tribute of 1,000 talents to the Romans for nine years. Some interpreters think that the *exactor of tribute* refers to the Roman officer who came each year to collect this sum.

The glory of the kingdom would refer to Jerusalem. *Within a few days* was the short lapse of time between the mission of Heliodorus and the death of Seleucus IV. Seleucus was assassinated by Heliodorus, *neither in anger,* which could mean "not in a fair face-to-face encounter," since it was by a secret conspiracy, *nor in battle.*

(3) Antiochus IV Epiphanes (11:21–45)

21 In his place shall arise a contemptible person to whom royal majesty has not been given; he shall come in without warning and obtain the

kingdom by flatteries. 22 Armies shall be utterly swept away before him and broken, and the prince of the covenant also. 23 And from the time that an alliance is made with him he shall act deceitfully; and he shall become strong with a small people. 24 Without warning he shall come into the richest parts of the province; and he shall do what neither his fathers nor his fathers' fathers have done, scattering among them plunder, spoil, and goods. He shall devise plans against strongholds, but only for a time. 25 And he shall stir up his power and his courage against the king of the south with a great army; and the king of the south shall wage war with an exceedingly great and mighty army; but he shall not stand, for plots shall be devised against him. 26 Even those who eat his rich food shall be his undoing; his army shall be swept away, and many shall fall down slain. 27 And as for the two kings, their minds shall be bent on mischief; they shall speak lies at the same table, but to no avail; for the end is yet to be at the time appointed. 28 And he shall return to his land with great substance, but his heart shall be set against the holy covenant. And he shall work his will, and return to his own land.

29 "At the time appointed he shall return and come into the south; but it shall not be this time as it was before. 30 For ships of Kittim shall come against him, and he shall be afraid and withdraw, and shall turn back and be enraged and take action against the holy covenant. He shall turn back and give heed to those who forsake the holy covenant. 31 Forces from him shall appear and profane the temple and fortress, and shall take away the continual burnt offering. And they shall set up the abomination that makes desolate. 32 He shall seduce with flattery those who violate the covenant; but the people who know their God shall stand firm and take action. 33 And those among the people who are wise shall make many understand, though they shall fall by sword and flame, by captivity and plunder, for some days. 34 When they fall, they shall receive a little help. And many shall join themselves to them with flattery; 35 and some of those who are wise shall fall, to refine and to cleanse them and to make them white, until the time of the end, for it is yet for the time appointed.

36 "And the king shall do according to his will; he shall exalt himself and magnify himself above every god, and shall speak astonishing things against the God of gods. He shall prosper till the indignation is accomplished; for what is determined shall be done. 37 He shall give no heed to the gods of his fathers, or to the one beloved by women; he shall not give heed to any other god, for he shall magnify himself above all. 38 He shall honor the god of

fortresses instead of these; a god whom his fathers did not know he shall honor with gold and silver, with precious stones and costly gifts. 39 He shall deal with the strongest fortresses by the help of a foreign god; those who acknowledge him he shall magnify with honor. He shall make them rulers over many and shall divide the land for a price.

40 "At the time of the end the king of the south shall attack him; but the king of the north shall rush upon him like a whirlwind, with chariots and horsemen, and with many ships; and he shall come into countries and shall overflow and pass through. 41 He shall come into the glorious land. And tens of thousands shall fall, but these shall be delivered out of his hand: Edom and Moab and the main part of the Ammonites. 42 He shall stretch out his hand against the countries, and the land of Egypt shall not escape. 43 He shall become ruler of the treasures of gold and of silver, and all the precious things of Egypt; and the Libyans and the Ethiopians shall follow in his train. 44 But tidings from the east and the north shall alarm him, and he shall go forth with great fury to exterminate and utterly destroy many. 45 And he shall pitch his palatial tents between the sea and the glorious holy mountain; yet he shall come to his end, with none to help him.

The remainder of this chapter details the exploits of Antiochus IV Epiphanes (175–164 B.C.). His accession and early years are seen in vv. 21–24. *In his place,* i.e., to succeed Seleucus IV, shall be *a contemptible person.* This is the Jewish characterization of Antiochus IV in derision of the title which he assumed for himself *Theos Epiphanes* (God Manifest). *Royal majesty* was not his. He was the younger son of Antiochus the Great and the brother of the king Seleucus IV. The throne rightfully belonged to Demetrius Soter, nephew of Antiochus IV.

From 189 B.C. Antiochus IV had been a hostage in Rome according to the treaty concluded with his father Antiochus III the Great, following the disastrous battle at Magnesia. In the 12th year of his exile in Rome, Seleucus IV requested that Antiochus IV be released. So Demetrius the son of Seleucus IV took Antiochus' place as a hostage. Antiochus IV came to Athens and played the part of a real Greek, where he was elected a chief magistrate.

When he heard that his brother had been killed by Heliodorus, Antiochus rushed to Antioch *without warning*. *By flatteries* is used of Antiochus (vv. 32,34). He secured control of the kingdom by treachery and intrigue. This may be such a reference, or it may be an estimation of his actions after he had come to power. Antiochus was one to understand riddles (8:23) and by his cunning word to make deceit prosper (8:25).

Antiochus' exploits relating to Syria and Palestine are contained in vv. 21–24. The *armies* (lit., the arms of the flood; cf. 9:26—"come with a flood") shall be broken before him. They were the forces and resources in Syria, including Heliodorus and other domestic enemies.

The prince of the covenant probably refers to Onias III, the high priest 198–175 B.C. (cf. 9:26). He was deposed by Antiochus (2 Macc. 4:7–9) in 175 B.C. Onias was murdered in 170 B.C. when he condemned Menelaus the high priest for robbing the Temple. Some interpret "the prince of the covenant" to mean "a confederate prince," i.e., Ptolemy VI Philometor, reflecting the early Egyptian exploits.

Without warning (also 8:25; 11:21) estimates the swiftness with which Antiochus strikes. *The richest parts of the province* probably reveals the estimate of an inhabitant of Israel. Ewald is even more specific in seeing this as Galilee. Antiochus is recorded as worse than any of his predecessors. Through intrigue and alliance with Jason, Menelaus, and his priests, Antiochus pillaged, dominated, and spoiled. He gave gifts and lived more lavishly than his predecessors (1 Macc. 3:30; Livy XLI.20).

He shall devise plans against strongholds (v. 24). The deeds of Antiochus against the Jews were horrible. He attempted to remove every vestige of the presence of the God of the Jews and to replace the Jewish culture with that of Greece. But God would not permit an interminable sacrilege. It was a great comfort for the faithful Jews to hear the historical record that such suffering could occur but *for a time*

(*only* is not in the Hebrew; cf. v. 35).

Verses 25–35 cover the ambitions which Antiochus showed toward Egypt. The first campaign of Antiochus against Egypt (169 B.C.) is sketched in vv. 25–28. The situation which made Antiochus' foray in Egypt possibly developed at the death of Cleopatra, his sister the queen Mother of Egypt, in 172. Her two sons, Philometor and Physcon, were both minors. However, Ptolemy VI Philometor was on the throne (181–146 B.C.). The running of the kingdom was actually in the hands of the eunuch Eulaeus and a Syrian Lenaeus. These two counselors are the ones identified as (v. 26) *those who eat his rich food*. They precipitated the offensive thrust against Antiochus by convincing Philometor that all he had to do to conquer Syria and Palestine was to take the field in battle. Antiochus heard of their move and started toward Egypt. He paid a call on Jerusalem and Jason. Philometor sent a messenger to Rome to complain about Antiochus. In 169 B.C. Antiochus captured Pelusium on the Egyptian border. He subdued most of Egypt but was not able to win any battles against Alexandria, where the Alexandrian nobles had set up Physcon as their king.

The two kings (v. 27) who speak lies *at the same table* are probably Antiochus and Philometor. Philometor was wined and dined by his uncle in an attempt to deceive him. Since an Oriental host is responsible for the welfare of his guest, the actions of Antiochus were treachery. Antiochus professed that he was acting only in the interest of his nephew. Philometor professed to believe it. In reality they were speaking lies at the same table. *But to no avail* reflects the fact that the scheme whereby Antiochus would restore Philometor to the throne and would reign through him would not work out.

The end . . . is a refrain which runs through this chapter. Antiochus shall not endure long (cf. vv. 24,35). The idea of hope and the future are very important to the faithful Jews who were seemingly powerless to overcome or withstand the destructive presence of the Seleucid tyrant.

A combination of circumstances caused Antiochus to return to Jerusalem. (1) Naturally, he was angered at being prohibited from taking all of Egypt. (2) The convoy of three envoys from Rome was approaching. They had been sent to stop the war. (3) Also a disturbance was being created in Jerusalem by Jason's attempt to retain the high priesthood. This attempt was precipitated partially by rumors that Antiochus had been killed in Egypt. When Antiochus returned to Jerusalem he slaughtered many Jews, plundered the Temple, and joined forces with the hellenizing Jews (1 Macc. 1:20–24; 2 Macc. 5: 11–21).

Even though he was not as successful in Egypt, as he wished, he returned with a very large cache of booty spoils of Egypt. He gained more at Jerusalem *against the holy covenant* on his way back to his capital Antioch.

The account of the second campaign against Egypt is in vv. 29–30. *At the appointed time* has the force of God making the designation. For the writer of Daniel all times are in the hand of God. As soon as Antiochus left Egyptian soil, the two sons of Cleopatra became reconciled, thus thwarting the effort of Antiochus to control most of Egypt. But Antiochus made another attempt to seize Egypt with the full expectation of taking even Alexandria. This attempt was not to be as successful as the former invasion had been (v. 29b).

Ships of Kittim is a difficult expression. Kittim refers to Cyprus (Gen. 10:4) or to peoples of the Mediterranean (Jer. 2:10; Ezek. 27:6). In the Dead Sea Scrolls the term is used in such a way as possibly to refer to the Romans. The LXX (cf. Vulgate) here has Romans. An emendation of the Hebrew text would read "envoys from the west" (cf. Num. 24:24). C. Popilius Laenas and his accompanying entourage probably arrived in a single ship from Rome. Since there were many in his official party the term envoys (a change of *tsiyim*

to *tsirim* as in Isa. 18:2) would be directly applicable. If C. Popilius Laenas' ship came to Egypt in the company of other ships, perchance from the direction of Cyprus, the reference would be clear. Popilius gave Antiochus a written message from the Roman authorities, who had held him as a hostage earlier, ordering him to stop his war against Philometor. Polybius and Livy give the record of Antiochus' hesitation in following these orders. Whereupon Popilius drew a circle around the haughty Antiochus with a vine-stick and ordered him to give his answer to Rome before he stepped outside. After a brief embarrassed silence, Antiochus capitulated to the Roman.

Antiochus withdrew from Egypt *enraged.* In such a state of mind on his way back to Antioch he took *action against* the holy covenant. *The holy covenant* was the covenant and its observances by the Jews who worshiped the true and living God. Antiochus allied himself to the faithless Jews. It cannot be determined definitely that Antiochus entered Jerusalem in person, but records are clear that his officers acted against Jerusalem and the worship of Yahweh under his orders. This has reference to the persecution (167 B.C.).

The acts of persecution upon Hebrew religion and people are recorded in vv. 31–35. Verse 31 pictures Antiochus' chief collector Apollonius with an army of 22,000. He entered Jerusalem, waited until the sabbath day in order to find the Jews "not at work," and set about plundering, burning, and taking slaves. There was erected a "desolating sacrilege" upon the altar of burnt offering. A command that the Jews stop their observance of religion was only one of the repressive measures. The forces of Antiochus set up a cult of their own on the very sites of previous Yahweh worship. The altar and statue of Zeus Olympius erected alongside were the *abomination* that made the holy place desolate. The Jews could not sacrifice there for now it was desolated and desecrated.

There were three groups who were involved with Antiochus' hellenizing attempts: (1) those who *violated the covenant* with their God and forsook their faith to succumb to the flattery of the Greek; (2) the people who continuously acknowledged their God—these remained firm in their resolve to follow their God with no regard for personal safety; (3) in addition to these two groups there was a great number of common folk who were placed in a distressing dilemma. Were they to retain the dangerous loyalty to the religious laws of their God or to obey the civil laws of the political ruler of the time?

Many references are found in 1 and 2 Maccabees to substantiate the fact that there were many godly men and women who acted wisely in reaffirming by word and deed their fidelity to the God of all ages even in the face of persecution, harassment, suffering, humiliation, or death. The godly (both teachers and ones taught) are the ones called *wise* (vv. 33,35; 12:3). They shall cause *many* to *understand* by their example. Understand is much more than mental assent. It is profound reliance upon that which their hearts believed. The four kinds of persecution are not the only kinds which were used: *sword* (1 Macc. 2:9), *flame* (1 Macc. 1:31,56), *captivity* (1 Macc. 3:41), and *plunder* (1 Macc. 1:22–23,31).

A *little help* (v. 34) evidently refers to the temporary and relatively minor success of the Maccabean revolt under Mattathias and his son Judas (1 Macc. 2:15–28, 42–48; 3:11–12,23–26; 4:12–15). This is the only specific reference to this revolt contained in the Old Testament canon. For our author, they were not as important as the wise and faithful martyrs. The first victory of Mattathias attracted the fancy of many who joined the resistance movement with doubtful motives in the notion that Mattathias would be the winner. Many of these joined the revolt *with flattery* or from impure motives.

Many of the godly suffered. There is a play on words between *wise* and *fall*. The sufferings would cause those who were not faithful by conviction as well as practice to desert the cause of righteousness. Only those who were pure (refined), purged, and spiritual would endure. *White* is the absence of darkness, dirt, and uncleanness. These same three words are used together in 12:10. The persecutions will be the testing-stone of all Jews. Those who were not pure would not persevere.

Until the time of the end is related to vv. 24,27,29; 8:17 (cf. v. 40; 12:4). These verses have been variously interpreted. Some writers see the time as related to the end of all time and thus must be applied to the end of the world. However, the time of the context involved primarily the end of the persecutions in the time of Antiochus Epiphanes. The *time appointed* was clearly future to the time of the writer.

A summary of the character of Antiochus is found in vv. 36–39. Such arrogance of a man toward a deity is seldom found elsewhere in all of history. Antiochus set himself up to be god and adopted for himself the title *Theos Epiphanes*, i.e., God manifest. In all his madness (*Epimanes*) he sought to replace Yahweh with himself. The Temple in Jerusalem was dedicated by the Hellenizers to Zeus Olympius, thus equating the God of the Hebrews with Zeus. Such affrontery could not go unchallenged or uncondemned.

Kings were closely related to deity, but few ever took themselves so seriously as god as did Antiochus. He was the first to assume the title *Theos* (God) on his coins. His early coins contained only the inscription "King Antiochus," but successive changes saw his claim of deity in the inscription "King Antiochus God Manifest." The earlier coins had the representation of Apollo, but the later ones a figure of Zeus.

It is not surprising that he did *according to his will*, for the same thing is said of Alexander (v. 3) and Antiochus the Great (v. 16; 8:4). But for a king to *exalt himself . . . above every god* is insanity. He spoke *against the God of gods* (i.e., Yahweh).

Verses 37–39 are an enlargement of v. 30. *The gods of his fathers* could refer to the attempts of the king to exalt himself above every god. Antiochus replaced Apollo, one of the ancestral gods, with Zeus. We do not possess historical information which specifies deeds to Antiochus against his ancestral gods. This very fact has been the proof used by some interpreters to show that the king here is not Antiochus. Various theories have been given speculation. For instance, Calvin thought of the Roman Empire here. The Pope of Rome and the papal system have been cited. Herod the Great was advanced by Mauro. The antichrist was the view of Jerome. The entire verse may mean merely that the king did not follow the worship as had his fathers. There may also be a stern rebuke to any Jew who deserted the God of all good things.

The one beloved by women probably referred to the god Tammuz-Adonis (cf. Ezek. 8:14), the Syrian deity of vegetation whose death was mourned by women beside the river Adonis near Beirut. This cult was also one of the Grecian cults which Antiochus ignored. Verse 37 tells of the gods which Antiochus did not follow. Verse 38 describes the god that he honored. The identity of *the god of fortresses* is uncertain. Theodotion and the Vulgate read "fortresses" as a proper name and merely transliterated it "Maozim," perhaps thinking of the Syrian 'Aziz. Grotius and others see it as Mars the god of war. Most interpreters see it as Jupiter Capitolinus with whom Antiochus joined Zeus Olympius. Antiochus built a great image and a magnificent temple in Antioch. The last half of v. 38 shows the extent to which the king went in his adorations of a god. Antiochus sent to Rome golden vessels weighing as much as 500 pounds to be placed in various temples.

Verse 39 refers to the king's attempt to win over followers to his cause. The first part of the verse is literally, "and he had done to fortifications of strongholds with a strange god." Initially this applies to the victory which the king won over the strongholds which were thrown up against him

or against those who mounted an attack on him. Then secondarily it could refer to the foreign garrisons, brought in by Antiochus, who would follow the Hellenistic cult and win other followers. The king would give honor and positions of authority to those who would desert their ancestral gods and become adherents of Zeus.

Through v. 35 the writer spoke with amazing accuracy, specific details, and precise chronology of historical events. Verses 36–39 refer mainly to characterization and evaluation. These are generalized and show less detail. Verses 40–45 turn forward and are future and predictive. These are less specific and more general. Events in history have not been found to accord with these verses in detail. The comparison of accuracy and specific references between vv. 2–39 and those of 11: 40—12:13 has led many interpreters to find vv. 2–39 as past and present with vv. 40 ff. as future. Within the literary form so well known in interbiblical times, the writer used the events of history to substantiate the message of importance for the future. Past and future are not separated but are rather "two sides of the same coin," i.e., God who has acted in the past will be acting so in the future.

The events leading up to the end of the fourth epoch are seen in the remainder of the book (11:40—12:13). Some writers see no predictions in the book at all. However, such a view fails to take full consideration of the literary forms, the historical verities, or the evident purpose of the context.

This section begins *at the time of the end*, a point of focus yet in the future to the writer. In the previous uses, it has been related to the end of the fourth segment of history as viewed by the author, i.e., the fourth beast or fourth kingdom.

The king of the south was Ptolemy VI Philometor, ruler of Egypt. The king who is attacked is the same as the king in vv. 15,29,36, who has been identified as Antiochus. *Attack* is literally "thrust at" or "butt" (cf. 8:4). This is pictured as an all-out attack with the use of *chariots* and *horsemen* and *ships* in a victorious campaign. The *countries* would be the lands between Ptolemy and Antiochus. The king of the north comes to *the glorious land* (v. 41), i.e., Palestine (cf. v. 16; 8:9) in a successful campaign as he goes to encounter the king of the south.

The mention of the escape of Edom, Moab, and the Ammonites is surprising in apocalyptic writing since the mention of countries by their common name is not customary. It is especially surprising to find Moab mentioned since Moab was not in existence as a nation in the time of Antiochus. They had been displaced by the Nabatean Arabs. Edom and Ammon are mentioned in 1 Maccabees 5:3,6 as taking up arms against Judah following the policies of Antiochus. The three nations are linked together in prophetic thought as traditional enemies of Judah. It is probably this factor that caused their inclusion here (perhaps as a scribal note). In this context, the reference may point to the hellenizing Jews (v. 39*b*) who would not be dealt with severely by Antiochus. Just as vv. 37–39 enlarged upon the theme of v. 36, vv. 41–45 are an enlargement upon the idea of v. 40. Verse 42 explains v. 40*b* as including the *land of Egypt* also among the countries. No Roman envoy will take Egypt from the king of the north. Even the *treasures* (v. 43; lit., hidden things) will come into his hands. The hidden caches, underground or in the temples, would be under Antiochus' control.

The *Libyans* who were west of Egypt and the *Ethiopians* who were south of Egypt represented the remotest parts of the Egyptian Empire. All of Egypt will come under Antiochus this time. *Tidings* (lit., something heard) is the same term as used of the cause for Sennacherib's hasty retreat from Palestine (Isa. 37:7). Just as Antiochus heard rumors of the Palestinian uprising during his second Egyptian campaign he rushed away from Egypt toward the north. *With great fury* characterizes the reaction of an egotistical despot at such a reversal.

The king shall set up his royal abode between the Mediterranean and Mount Zion (v. 45). Antiochus actually died in Persia (at Tabae) in 164 B.C., where he had been forced to go by the people of Elymais whose temple he had attempted to rob (1 Macc. 3:31–37; 6:1–16).

There is a determinism which runs through all of the book. The defeat of the terrifying Antiochus had been determined at the throne of God. This again is the message. Even though the king will have his way with no regard for people or gods, he shall be brought low. Verses 40–45 may be the concluding evaluation of the career of Antiochus. The conclusion of the whole life of Antiochus was *yet he shall come to his end, with none to help him.* He had gotten away with his megalomania and sacrilege only up to a point. Verses 40–45 show that the end of this tyrant was very imminent. The victories and glories from the outreaches of the south to the extremity of the east would not protect him from infamy and isolation. Prediction is very clear that the end (v. 45) of this king of the north was imminent in spite of the large armies (v. 40), the dispatching of tens of thousands of enemies (vv. 41,44), and the control of all of Egypt (vv. 42–43).

3. Climax of the Vision (12:1–4)

[1] "At that time shall arise Michael, the great prince who has charge of your people. And there shall be a time of trouble, such as never has been since there was a nation till that time; but at that time your people shall be delivered, every one whose name shall be found written in the book. [2] And many of those who sleep in the dust of the earth shall awake, some to everlasting life, and some to shame and everlasting contempt. [3] And those who are wise shall shine like the brightness of the firmament; and those who turn many to righteousness, like the stars for ever and ever. [4] But you, Daniel, shut up the words, and seal the book, until the time of the end. Many shall run to and fro, and knowledge shall increase."

The end of Israel's troubles and the logical conclusion concerning the justice of God are in vv. 12:1–3. This paragraph is a part of the larger section concerning the vision beginning with chapter 10 (see the superscription, 10:1). Thus, vv. 1–4 are the climax of the vision and relate vitally with 11:40–45. Note the recurrence of the reference to "the time of the end" (11:40), "to his end" (11:45), and "at that time" (12:1). Michael, the patron saint of Israel, shall arise at that time. This is a parallel to 10:21 and 8:17–18 f. The outcome of all nations is determined in heaven and at the bidding of God through his angels. If the reader sees Antiochus in the previous verses, he should see him here. If the end of all time is referred to in the previous occasions, the same would be here. It should be noted, however, that if the reference is to Antiochus, the principle of the actions of God in reference to the punishment of evil would be applicable in the same situation throughout all time, all ages. It is not "either-or" but only the question as to the initial point of the application of our author. Those who exclude the early times are equally as wrong as those who exclude the latest of time. Both are involved in the extent of the unifying truth of the book.

A *time of trouble* occurs also in Jeremiah 30:7 (cf. Judges 10:14; Isa. 33:2; Jer. 14:8; 15:11). It is characteristic of the last times (cf. 1 Macc. 9:27; Matt. 24:21; Mark 13:19; Rev. 16:18). This great tribulation was *such as never has been* (cf. Joel 2:2; Ex. 9:18,24). Twice in v. 1 is the phrase *at that time* referring to the consummation of the fourth age when Michael takes charge. *Your people* are the Jews, Daniel's people. *In the book* of life refers to all of the Jews who are still living at the time of the end of the tribulation. There will be an escape for those who have endured the persecutions of the evil king.

As to what will happen to those Jews who were slain during the Antiochus persecution, read vv. 2–3. At first glance, we should expect "all" instead of *many*. This has given some occasion for an argument over general versus limited resurrection. But this should more logically be withheld until after the idea of resurrection had become a well established tenet or doctrine. The writer has indeed broken the silence of the grave. The argument over the type of resurrection is not really germane to this text for the author's interest is in the future of the faithful and the apostate Jews. It is pressing the text too far to force the *many* to read "all." The central focus is on those who shall awake to *everlasting life* (v. 2), the *wise* (v. 3), and those who *turn many to* righteousness (v. 3).

The dust of the earth is the figure of the grave. *Sleep* is the image for death (cf. Jer. 51:39,57 and the NT), and *awake* is the image for life. Death was considered absolute for all men die. As the author considered God as just and the source of judgment, he understood that death, its manner and its cause, did not signify particular judgment on an individual. Death comes to righteous and unrighteous alike, some in ease and some in pain. The God of justice will bring judgment to all his people.

To the righteous and faithful there would be *everlasting life*. This is the only place in the Old Testament in which this term occurs, though it does appear many times in apocalyptic and Christian literature (1 Enoch 15:4; Psalms of Sol. 3:1), in the Targums and other Jewish writings. It is a life as enduring as the kingdom itself. Resurrection is unmistakable.

To the unrighteous and those who forsook Yahweh for Antiochus, the judgment and future would be *shame and everlasting contempt* (lit., to reproaches and to everlasting abhorrence). *Shame* is plural to indicate intensity. It is the same word as byword (9:16) and insolence (11:18).

Verses 1–3 are poetic in structure. Verse 3 is a parallel to v. 2. The emphasis on the positive side indicates the prime purpose of the writing. The wise (cf. 1:4,17; 9:22) are the faithful and the martyrs (11: 33,35). They shall *shine like the brightness of the firmament.* This is not a clear expression but is found often in interbiblical literature (cf. 1 Enoch 39:7; 104:2; Wis. Sol. 3:7). This verb *shine* occurs nowhere else in the Old Testament (the noun is in Ezek. 8:2 only). There is nothing higher or brighter in man's world than the brilliance of the sky with sun, moon, and stars. This reference suggests strongly that the "Baal of heaven" (*Baal shamem*) and the "abomination-desolation" (*shomem*) will be dashed into complete destruction. Those who were persecuted by them will be raised to shine in the exalted manner of the lights of God's heavens.

These messages of hope and judgment are to be *shut up*. In 8:26 Daniel is told to "seal up" the vision (same word as *shut up*). Seal up is also in 9:24 (in Aramaic only in 6:17). The words and the book are to be concealed and sealed. When a scroll was written a seal was affixed to it to keep the roll from being unrolled without breaking the seal. Prophecies were to be sealed up until the time of the prediction. The literary form of apocryphal books often calls for being concealed in some secret place until the proper time for its being revealed (cf. 2 Esdras 12:37; Assumption of Moses 1:17–18; 1 Enoch 1:2; 2 Enoch 33:9–11). It was the accepted and understood literary form to use the names or figures of revered ancients (Enoch, Testament of Job, The Testaments of the Twelve Patriarchs, Apocalypse of Moses, Ascension of Isaiah, Psalms of Solomon). The figure of a revered ancestor was assumed with no thought of fraud or deceit. The imposition of the idea of fraudulence, pious or otherwise, on such works is a failure to see literary art in its own setting.

The use of the figure and fact of Daniel in such literary setting of the second century B.C. would be in accord with the literature of that day. The command to conceal and seal the word and the book would give an explanation for these things not being known earlier. Porteous (p. 171) says that sealing was a customary part of attributing prophecy pseudonymously to some ancient hero.

The last sentence of v. 4 is very uncertain as to its meaning. The running *to and fro* (cf. Amos 8:12) is a frantic search for

some explanation. *And knowledge shall increase* should read "in order that knowledge may increase." Such search shall be vain until the book is opened. Many would be seeking answers, but only to those who receive the book concerning the time of the end will the meaning be clear.

4. The Epilogue (12:5–13)

⁵ Then I Daniel looked, and behold, two others stood, one on this bank of the stream and one on that bank of the stream. ⁶ And I said to the man clothed in linen, who was above the waters of the stream, "How long shall it be till the end of these wonders?" ⁷ The man clothed in linen, who was above the waters of the stream, raised his right hand and his left hand toward heaven; and I heard him swear by him who lives for ever that it would be for a time, two times, and half a time; and that when the shattering of the power of the holy people comes to an end all these things would be accomplished. ⁸ I heard, but I did not understand. Then I said, "O my lord, what shall be the issue of these things?" ⁹ He said, "Go your way, Daniel, for the words are shut up and sealed until the time of the end. ¹⁰ Many shall purify themselves, and make themselves white, and be refined; but the wicked shall do wickedly; and none of the wicked shall understand; but those who are wise shall understand. ¹¹ And from the time that the continual burnt offering is taken away, and the abomination that makes desolate is set up, there shall be a thousand two hundred and ninety days. ¹² Blessed is he who waits and comes to the thousand three hundred and thirty-five days. ¹³ But go your way till the end; and you shall rest, and shall stand in your allotted place at the end of the days."

The setting of the epilogue is the same as the vision of 10:4 f. The *man clothed in linen* (12:6,7; 10:5; Ezek. 9:2,3,11) is joined by two other celestial beings, one on each side of the stream. *And I said* follows the LXX text, while the Masoretic Text reads "and he said." The LXX text has Daniel asking the question, and the Masoretic Text has one of the two angels asking a question of the one with whom Daniel had conversed previously (10:2 f.). *Above the waters* would indicate a superiority over the other two.

How long is the same question in 8:13. *Wonders* is from the same root word as "fearful" (8:24) and "astonishing things" (11:36). The wonders refer to the extraordinary words and persecutions of Antiochus. The answer to "how long?" is in terms of *a time, two times, and half a time* (cf. the Aramaic 7:27; also 8:14; Rev. 12:14), i.e., three and a half "appointed times." The length of each set period is not certain. Interpreters generally have understood "time" in terms of a year and thus three and a half years (see comment on 7:25). The point of beginning the counting of days is not certain. The two general times for such starting point are when the daily sacrifice was stopped (Dec., 167 B.C.) and when Apollonius entered Jerusalem by treachery (168).

Another point of uncertainty was also whether the *end of these wonders* (v. 6) would take place at a cataclysmic blow or over a period of time. Would one count, in number of days, at the inception of the end or at the absolute conclusion? The three and a half years is taken to mean the reign of Antiochus, the antichrist of that day.

The remaining section of v. 7 is difficult. The Masoretic Text has a *shattering of the power of the holy people,* but the LXX apparently reversed the order of "shattering" and "power" to read "and when the power of the shatterer of the holy people will come to an end." The LXX understood the text to refer to Antiochus and the persecution of the Jews. The Masoretic Text would read that the strength of the holy people (probably the Jews or sometime seen as any elect) would be destroyed. Some see this as a dispersion of the Jews.

All these things would be accomplished does not say "shall have been" accomplished but will be in the process of coming to the end. The difficulty of the text and the uncertainty of many elements have led some interpreters to project this entire section in the far distant future referring to the antichrist's work at the end of the world. This will also be true, but the criterion of prophecy establishes that a prophet spoke to his own generation. The book of Daniel initially brings great hope to the Jews of the time of Antiochus. With this hope as the historical pattern and the acts of God in that crisis, we can see the same pattern in the far distant future.

The conclusion of this vision follows the same literary pattern as in 8:15–26. Daniel did not understand the vision (8:27) and so he asks *what shall be the issue of these things?* The word *issue* is translated "latter" in 8:19,23; 10:14. The Peshitta and the Vulgate have "what will be after these things?" It is strange that Daniel would ask for further information after such angelic vision if he is merely asking for more understanding. The LXX reads "what is the interpretation of these things?" But Daniel is actually asking what is to come after "these things would be accomplished" (11:7), i.e., after the destruction of the one who shattered the holy people. The mere destruction of the little horn, Antiochus, would not necessarily bring peace and prosperity to the Jews. Daniel asked for enlightenment concerning the fate of the faithful ones. In this sense he asks for more understanding.

The answer (vv. 8–13) comes in the form of a rehearsal of the vision followed by a blessing and promise. No additional vision or words would be given him. *Shut up* and *sealed* are from 12:4; 8:26; 9:24. *The time of the end* is also in 8:17; 11:35,40; 12:4. The threefold purity (*purify . . . make themselves white* and *refined*) are also in 11:35. *Those who are wise* are in 11:33,35. *Understand* is a recurring theme.

The taking away of the continual burnt offering and the erection of the *abomination that makes desolate* are two of the most devastating acts of Antiochus against Jewish worship. From that time there will be 1290 days; the time is thus extended. This number of days would be 43 months of 30 days each. Three and a half years would be 42 months. Charles makes note of the insertion of an intercalary month and thus declares three and a half years would be 1290 days exactly. So this figure is one month more which would be three and a half years accurately. Revelation 11:3; 12:6 have a figure of 1260 (3½ years). Since the first half of v. 11 refers to the perversion of the Temple and the abolishment of sacrifice, it would be logical that the 1290 days would refer to the time that the worship would be reestablished and the Temple rededicated to Yahweh (164 B.C.; 1 Macc. 4:52).

Another dating is introduced in v. 12, 1335 days, which adds 45 days to the last figure. This figure also appears in Ascension of Isaiah 4:12. What will occur at this time? Some interpreters say that the first date was to the death of Antiochus and that the second date pointed to the rededication of the Temple which, it was thought, would take place after Antiochus' death. Others suggest that the first date referred to the deliverance from persecution and the second date to the time that the reign of righteousness would be set up.

Verses 5–9 could easily have been from the viewpoint of Daniel upon the banks of the great river as a writer in the sixth century. But vv. 10–13 place him in the second century.

The book ends with the blessing (v. 12) and the promise (v. 13). Once again he is told *go your way* (cf. v. 9). No new vision or understanding will be divulged. *Rest* probably refers to the rest in the grave. But after his death *at the end of the days* he will stand.[20]

In the "eschaton" Daniel would receive his inheritance. What higher spiritual conclusion could there be to the book of hope?

20 The LXX adds Bel and the Dragon and the Story of Susanna at this point.